Less managing. More teaching. Greater learning.

 INSTRUCTORS...

Would you like your **students** to show up for class more **prepared**? *(Let's face it, class is much more fun if everyone is engaged and prepared...)*

Want ready-made application-level **interactive assignments**, student progress reporting, and auto-assignment grading? *(Less time grading means more time teaching...)*

Want an **instant view of student or class performance** relative to learning objectives? *(No more wondering if students understand...)*

Need to **collect data and generate reports** required for administration or accreditation? *(Say goodbye to manually tracking student learning outcomes...)*

Want to **record and post your lectures** for students to view online?

With **McGraw-Hill's *Connect*™ Plus Business,**

INSTRUCTORS GET:

- Interactive Applications – **book-specific interactive assignments** that require students to APPLY what they've learned.

- Simple **assignment management**, allowing you to spend more time teaching.

- **Auto-graded** assignments, quizzes, and tests.

- **Detailed Visual Reporting** where student and section results can be viewed and analyzed.

- Sophisticated **online testing** capability.

- A **filtering and reporting** function that allows you to easily assign and report on materials that are correlated to accreditation standards, learning outcomes, and Bloom's taxonomy.

- An easy-to-use **lecture capture** tool.

Want an online, searchable version of your textbook?

Wish your textbook could be available online while you're doing your assignments?

Connect™ Plus Business eBook

If you choose to use *Connect™ Plus Business*, you have an affordable and searchable online version of your book integrated with your other online tools.

Connect™ Plus Business eBook offers features like:

- Topic search
- Direct links from assignments
- Adjustable text size
- Jump to page number
- Print by section

Want to get more value from your textbook purchase?

Think learning business should be a bit more interesting?

Check out the STUDENT RESOURCES section under the Connect™ Library tab.

Here you'll find a wealth of resources designed to help you achieve your goals in the course. You'll find things like **quizzes, PowerPoints, and Internet activities** to help you study. Every student has different needs, so explore the STUDENT RESOURCES to find the materials best suited to you.

Business

A Changing World

8e

O.C. Ferrell
University of New Mexico

Geoffrey A. Hirt
DePaul University

Linda Ferrell
University of New Mexico

BUSINESS: A CHANGING WORLD
Published by McGraw-Hill/Irwin, a business unit of The McGraw-Hill Companies, Inc., 1221 Avenue of the Americas, New York, NY, 10020. Copyright © 2011, 2009, 2008, 2006, 2003, 2000, 1996, 1993 by The McGraw-Hill Companies, Inc. All rights reserved. No part of this publication may be reproduced or distributed in any form or by any means, or stored in a database or retrieval system, without the prior written consent of The McGraw-Hill Companies, Inc., including, but not limited to, in any network or other electronic storage or transmission, or broadcast for distance learning.

Some ancillaries, including electronic and print components, may not be available to customers outside the United States.

This book is printed on acid-free paper.

1 2 3 4 5 6 7 8 9 0 WVR/WVR 1 0 9 8 7 6 5 4 3 2 1 0

ISBN 978-0-07-351175-7
MHID 0-07-351175-7

Vice president and editor-in-chief: *Brent Gordon*
Editorial director: *Paul Ducham*
Publisher: *Doug Hughes*
Director of development: *Ann Torbert*
Editorial coordinator: *Jonathan Thornton*
Vice president and director of marketing: *Robin J. Zwettler*
Senior marketing manager: *Sarah Schuessler*
Vice president of editing, design, and production: *Sesha Bolisetty*
Lead project manager: *Christine A. Vaughan*
Senior buyer: *Michael R. McCormick*
Cover and interior designer: *JoAnne Schopler*
Senior photo research coordinator: *Keri Johnson*
Media project manager: *Ron Nelms*
Typeface: *10.5/12 Minon*
Compositor: *Laserwords Private Limited*
Printer: *Worldcolor*

Library of Congress Cataloging-in-Publication Data
Ferrell, O. C.
    Business : a changing world / O. C. Ferrell, Geoffrey Hirt, Linda Ferrell.—8th ed.
      p. cm.
    Includes index.
    ISBN-13: 978-0-07-351175-7 (alk. paper)
    ISBN-10: 0-07-351175-7 (alk. paper)
    1. Business. 2. Management—United States. I. Hirt, Geoffrey A. II. Ferrell, Linda. III. Title.
HF1008.F47 2011
  650—dc22

                           2010030320

www.mhhe.com

To James and George

To Linda Hirt

To Zoe Iutzi and Kenneth Nafziger

Welcome

Welcome to the eighth edition of *Business: A Changing World*. The new edition reflects major changes in the business environment, especially the economy and information technology. All of these changes are presented in concepts that entry-level students can understand. Our book contains all of the essentials that most students should learn in a semester. *Business: A Changing World* has, since its inception, been a concise presentation of the essential material needed to teach introduction to business. From our experience in teaching the course, we know that the most effective way to engage a student is by making business exciting, relevant, and up-to-date. Our teachable, from-the-ground-up approach involves a variety of media, application exercises, and subject matter, including up-to-date content supplements, boxed examples, video cases, PowerPoints, and testing materials that work for entry-level business students. We have worked hard to make sure that the content of this edition is as up-to-date as possible in order to best reflect today's dynamic world of business. We cover major changes in our economy related to sustainability, digital marketing, social networking, and the most recent financial crisis. The most recent recession has changed business strategies, and many firms have had to learn how to manage in a difficult environment.

The Eighth Edition

In the last three years, we have witnessed the most devastating financial crisis since the Great Depression. The eighth edition of *Business: A Changing World* reflects these events as they relate to foundational concepts in business. The recession challenged businesses to critically analyze the business environment. Unemployment among those 18 to 25 years old reached 25 percent in 2010. Therefore, to be successful, students need to know how foundational business concepts must be adapted to survive in a down economy and how to gain competitive advantages in an up economy. Our feedback indicated that you want these changes in the environment reflected in content, boxes, and cases, and we have responded.

We also responded to your feedback that it is time to have a chapter on digital marketing and social networking in business. The importance of social networking sites such as Facebook, Twitter, and LinkedIn, as well as many other social networking sites, is changing the face of business. Entrepreneurs and small businesses have to be able to increase sales and reduce costs by using social networking to communicate and develop relationships with customers. Many of these businesses are utilizing messages that say "Follow us on Twitter" or encourage visitors to tour their Facebook pages to learn about their products and share their opinions and experiences. Our new Chapter 13, Digital Marketing and Social Networking, provides an overview of how the Internet is changing and how business is efficiently developing improved customer relationships. While students may use Facebook or MySpace for their personal relationships, this chapter will explore and help them understand the relationship of this new technology to business applications.

While the title of our book remains *Business: A Changing World,* we could have changed the title to *Business: A Green World.* Throughout the book we recognize the importance of sustainability and "green" business. By using the philosophy *reduce, reuse, and recycle,* we believe every business can be more profitable and contribute to a better world through green initiatives. There is a new "Going Green" box in each chapter that covers these environmental changes. Our "Entrepreneurship in Action" boxes also discuss many innovations and opportunities to use green business for success.

To make introduction to business relevant and up-to-date, the book has to reflect our current economic and political environment. The very visible hand of the government creates a constantly shifting business environment, and we pay special attention to how changes in policies relating to financial and banking markets have affected the economic business cycle. Fluctuating prices in commodities, such as oil and agricultural products like corn, wheat, and soybeans, have changed consumer behavior. In a consumer-driven industry, American automobile companies are recovering from a decline in sales because they were not making the products that consumers wanted. While Toyota was ranked third globally in corporate reputation, it lost this advantage quickly in 2010 with many product recalls and a $16.4 million fine for hiding safety defects from customers. We address all of these issues in this text through the use of examples and embedded content in order to help students better appreciate the dynamic changes in the business world. Success in business comes from anticipating these changes and being prepared to deal with the business risks associated with change.

We have been careful to continue our coverage of global business, ethics and social responsibility, and information technology as it relates to the foundations important in an introduction to business course. Our co-author team has a diversity of expertise in these important areas. O.C. Ferrell and Linda Ferrell have been recognized as leaders in business ethics education, and their insights are reflected in every chapter and in the "Consider Ethics and Social Responsibility" boxes. In addition, they maintain a Web site, www.e-businessethics.com, that provides free resources such as PowerPoints and cases that can be used in the classroom. Geoff Hirt has a strong background in global business development, especially world financial markets and trade relationships.

The foundational areas of introduction to business, entrepreneurship, small business management, marketing, accounting, and finance have been completely revised. Examples have been provided to which students can easily relate. An understanding of core functional areas of business is presented so students get a holistic view of the world of business. Box examples related to "Responding to Business Challenges," "Think Globally," "Going Green," and "Consider Ethics and Social Responsibility" help provide real-world examples in these areas.

Our goal is to make sure that the content and teaching package for this book are of the highest quality possible. We wish to seize this opportunity to gain your trust, and we appreciate any feedback to help us continually improve these materials. We hope that the real beneficiary of all of our work will be well-informed students who appreciate the role of business in society and take advantage of the opportunity to play a significant role in improving our world. As students understand how our free enterprise system operates and how we fit into the global competitive environment, they will develop the foundation for creating their own success and improving our quality of life.

Created from the ground up,

The best-selling paperback text on the market, *Business: A Changing World* was built from the ground up—that is, developed and written expressly for faculty and students who value a brief, flexible, and affordable paperback with the most up-to-date coverage available.

Conversly, most brief Introduction to Business textbooks on the market today are simply "ground-down" versions of much longer hardcover books. None of these books is truly designed to meet the needs of students or instructors; they're afterthoughts, products chiefly designed to leverage existing content, not to help you teach your course.

With market-leading teaching support and fresh content and examples, *Business: A Changing World* offers just the right mix of currency, flexibility, and value that you need. It is the fastest-growing book—and the best value available—in the brief Introductory Business market.

What sets Ferrell/Hirt/Ferrell apart from the competition? An unrivaled mixture of current content, topical depth, and the best teaching support around:

The Freshest Topics and Examples

Because it isn't tied to the revision cycle of a larger book, *Business: A Changing World* inherits no outdated or irrelevant examples or coverage. Everything in the eighth edition reflects the very latest developments in the business world, from the growth of digital marketing and social networking, to the recovery from the financial crisis. In addition, ethics continues to be a key issue, and Ferrell et al. use "Consider Ethics and Social Responsibility" boxes to instill in students the importance of ethical conduct in business.

Just Enough of a Good Thing

It's easy for students taking their first steps into business to become overwhelmed. Longer books try to solve this problem by chopping out examples or topics to make ad hoc shorter editions. *Business: A Changing World* carefully builds just the right mix of coverage and applications to give your students a firm grounding in business principles. Where other books have you sprinting through the semester to get everything in, Ferrell et al. allows you the breathing space to explore topics and incorporate other activities that are important to you and your students.

Teaching Assistance That Makes a Difference

The first and often most serious hurdle in teaching is engaging your students' interest, making them understand how textbook material plays a very real role in real business activities. The instructor's material for *Business: A Changing World* is full of helpful resources that enable you to do this, including detailed teaching notes and additional material in the Instructor's Manual, even for role-playing exercises found on the Web site. Furthermore, the **Active Classroom Resource Manual** is loaded with additional projects, cases, and exercises. The Instructor's Manual contains a matrix to help you decide which exercise to use with which chapter.

There's much more to **Business: A Changing World,** and much more it can do for your course. To learn about Ferrell et al.'s great pedagogical features and top-notch ancillaries, keep reading.

not ground down

Getting a Handle on Business

Business: A Changing World's pedagogy helps your students get the most out of their reading, from handy outlines at the beginning of the chapter to a range of questions and exercises at the end of it.

Chapter Outlines

These provide a useful overview of all the topics covered in the chapter, giving students a sneak preview of what they'll be learning.

The Dynamics of Business and Economics

OBJECTIVES

After reading this chapter, you will be able to:

- Define basic concepts such as business, product, and profit.
- Identify the main participants and activities of business and explain why studying business is important.
- Define economics and compare the four types of economic systems.
- Describe the role of supply, demand, and competition in a free enterprise system.
- Specify why and how the health of the economy is measured.
- Trace the evolution of the American economy and discuss the role of the entrepreneur in the economy.

Chapter Objectives

These appear at the beginning of each chapter to provide goals for students to reach in their reading. The objectives are then used in the "Review Your Understanding," the summary at the end of each chapter, and help the students gauge whether they've learned and retained the material.

OBJECTIVES

After reading this chapter, you will be able to:

- Define basic concepts such as business, product, and profit.
- Identify the main participants and activities of business and explain why studying business is important.
- Define economics and compare the four types of economic systems.
- Describe the role of supply, demand, and competition in a free enterprise system.
- Specify why and how the health of the economy is measured.
- Trace the evolution of the American economy and discuss the role of the entrepreneur in the economy.
- Evaluate a small-business owner's situation and propose a course of action.

Chapter-Opening Vignette

These anecdotes neatly illustrate the real-world implications of the business issues students will encounter in their reading. At the end of the chapter, students are asked to "Revisit the World of Business" and apply what they've learned throughout the chapter.

There Are Plenty of Fish

Markus Frind has taken the phrase "there are plenty of fish in the sea" to a whole new level by turning people's search for love into a strong business. Frind is a computer programmer who spent years going from job to job during the dot-com bust. Because he disliked his work and was growing tired of being laid off, Frind decided to increase his skills by learning ASP.net (a Microsoft Web building tool). To challenge himself, he built an online dating site entitled Plenty of Fish.

Frind's goal was to have a steady income without having to work much. Aware of the intense competition out there, he knew that his site needed to stand out. So he offered matchmaking services on Plenty of Fish for free. The target market is people curious about online dating but unwilling to pay for the privilege. Without collecting fees from the target market, however, Frind had to figure out another way to make a living off his site. His solution was advertisements. Advertisements on Plenty of Fish include banner ads along with advertisements supplied from Google. Interestingly, Plenty of Fish also uses its competition to earn money. Frind sells ad space to other dating sites that assume that Frind's free users will eventually upgrade to their more sophisticated sites (many never have). Within his first year, Frind was earning more than $3,300 monthly. Until recently, Plenty of Fish was designed and run by Frind out of his apartment. His success is largely due to minimal costs and a tiny staff.

Today, Plenty of Fish handles about 1.6 Web pages monthly and is set to hit $10 million in revenues. Best of all, Frind achieved his goal: he works about 10 hours each week.[1]

"So You Want a Job In . . ."

These end-of-chapter features offer valuable advice on a wide spectrum of business career choices.

So You Want a Job in the Business World

When most people think of a career in business, they see themselves entering the door to large companies and multinationals that they read about in the news and that are discussed in class. In a national survey, students indicated they would like to work for Google, Walt Disney, Apple, and Ernst & Young. In fact, most jobs are not with large corporations, but are in small companies, nonprofit organizations, government and even self-employed individuals. There are 20 million individuals that the Small Business Administration says own their businesses and have no employees. In addition, there are nearly 5 million small businesses which employ 10 or fewer workers. With more than 75 percent of the economy based on services, there are jobs available in industries such as healthcare, finance, education, hospitality, entertainment and transportation. The world is changing quickly and large corporations replace the equivalent of their entire workforce every four years.

The fast pace of technology today means that you have to be prepared to take advantage of emerging job opportunities and markets. You must also become adaptive and recognize that business is becoming more global, with job opportunities around the world. If you may want to obtain such a job, you shouldn't miss a chance to spend some time overseas. As get you started on the path to thinking about job opportunities, consider all of the changes in business today that might affect your possible long-term track and that could bring you lots of success. You may want to stay completely out of large organizations and corporations and put yourself in a position for an entrepreneurial role as a self-employed contractor or small-business owner. However, there are many that feel that experience in larger businesses is helpful to your success later as an entrepreneur.

You're on the road to learning the key knowledge, skills and trends that you can use to be a star in business. Businesses impact on our society, especially in the area of sustainability and improvement of the environment is a growing challenge and opportunity. Green businesses and green jobs in the business world are provided to give you a glimpse at the possibilities. Along the way, we will introduce you to some specific careers and offer advice on developing your own job opportunities. Research indicates that you won't be that happy with your job unless you enjoy your work and feel that it has a purpose. Since you spend most of your waking hours every day at work, you need to seriously think about what is important to you in a job.[27]

Getting a Handle on Business

These features, scattered liberally throughout the book, use real and often familiar companies to highlight various issues of importance in business today.

Consider Ethics and Social Responsibility

Ethics in business continues to be a major public concern, and it is vital for students to understand that unethical conduct hurts investors, customers, and indeed the entire business world. These features highlight the importance of ethical conduct and show how businesses can serve a vital, positive function in their communities.

Going Green

Businesses are becoming more aware of how their operations and products affect the world and environment they operate in. These boxes highlight companies taking steps to minimize their "carbon footprint"—or the measure of the impact their processes have on the environment.

Responding to Business Challenges

These boxes illustrate how businesses overcome tough challenges and provide an excellent vehicle for stimulating class discussions.

Entrepreneurship in Action

Successful entrepreneurs and their endeavors are spotlighted.

End-of-Chapter Material

Whether your students discover it on their own or you make it an integral part of your classroom and homework assignments, the end-of-chapter material provides a great opportunity to reinforce and expand upon the chapter content.

Review Your Understanding

Explore some of the factors within the international trade environment that influence business.

International business is the buying, selling, and trading of goods and services across national boundaries. Importing is the purchase of products and raw materials from another nation; exporting is the sale of domestic goods and materials to another nation. A nation's balance of trade is the difference in value between its exports and imports; a negative balance of trade is a trade deficit. The difference between the flow of money into a country and the flow of money out of it is called the balance of payments. An absolute or comparative advantage in trade may determine what products a company from a particular nation will export.

resources and effort, ranging from importing/exporting to multinational corporations. Countertrade agreements occur at the import/export level and involve bartering products for other products instead of currency. At the next level, a trading company links buyers and sellers in different countries to foster trade. In licensing and franchising, one company agrees to allow a foreign company the use of its company name, products, patents, brands, trademarks, raw materials, and production processes, in exchange for a flat fee or royalty. Contract manufacturing occurs when a company hires a foreign company to produce a specified volume of the firm's product to specification; the final product carries the domestic firm's name. A joint venture is a partnership in which companies from

Review Your Understanding

Are your students sometimes unsure whether they've properly absorbed the chapter material? This feature resummarizes the chapter objectives, leaving students in no doubt of what they're expected to remember.

Revisit the World of Business

These exercises refer to the chapter opening vignettes (see page xi) and ask students to answer more in-depth questions using the knowledge they gained in their reading.

Revisit the World of Business

1. Why does the NCAA seek to regulate advertising and sponsorships at collegiate sporting events?

2. What is the ethical dilemma involved in a student being paid by marketers?

3. What were the ethical objections raised by stakeholders regarding the Budweiser college can campaign?

Build Your Skills
MAKING DECISIONS ABOUT ETHICAL ISSUES

Background
The merger of Lockheed and Martin Marietta created Lockheed Martin, the number-one company in the defense industry—an industry that includes such companies as McDonnell Douglas and Northrop Grumman.

You and the rest of the class are managers at Lockheed Martin Corporation, Orlando, Florida. You are getting ready to do the group exercise in an ethics training session. The training instructor announces you will be playing *Gray Matters: The Ethics Game*. You are told that *Gray Matters*, which was prepared for your company's employees, is also played at 41 universities, including Harvard University, and at 65 other companies. Although there are 55 scenarios in *Gray Matters,* you will have time during this session to complete only the four scenarios that your group draws from the stack of cards.[75]

Task
Form into groups of four to six managers and appoint a group leader who will lead a discussion of the case, obtain a consensus answer to the case, and be the one to report the group's answers to the instructor. You will have five minutes to reach each decision, after which time, the instructor will give the point values and rationale for each choice. Then you will have five minutes for the next case, etc., until all four cases have been completed. Keep track of your group's score for each case; the winning team will be the group scoring the most points.

Since this game is designed to reflect life, you may believe that some cases lack clarity or that some of your choices are not as precise as you would have liked. Also, some cases have only one solution, while others have more than one solution. Each choice is assessed points to reflect which answer is the most correct. **Your group's task is to select only one option in each case.**

Build Your Skills

These activities are designed to be carried out in teams, giving you a launching pad for a lively in-class discussion.

Solve the Dilemma

These boxes give students an opportunity to think creatively in solving a realistic business situation.

Solve the Dilemma

MRS. ACRES HOMEMADE PIES

Shelly Acres, whose grandmother gave her a family recipe for making pies, loved to cook, and she decided to start a business she called Mrs. Acres Homemade Pies. The company produces specialty pies and sells them in local supermarkets and select family restaurants. In each of the first six months, Shelly and three part-time employees sold 2,000 pies for $4.50 each, netting $1.50 profit per pie. The pies were quite successful and Shelly could not keep up with demand. The company's success results from a quality product and productive employees who are motivated by incentives and who enjoy being part of a successful new business.

To meet demand, Shelly expanded operations, borrowing money and increasing staff to four full-time employees. Production and sales increased to 8,000 pies per month, and profits soared to $12,000 per month. However, demand for Mrs. Acres Homemade Pies continues to accelerate beyond what Shelly can supply. She has several options: (1) maintain current production levels and raise prices; (2) expand the facility and staff while maintaining the current price; or (3) contract the production of the pies to a national restaurant chain, giving Shelly a percentage of profits with minimal involvement.

Discussion Questions

1. Explain and demonstrate the relationship between supply and demand for Mrs. Acres Homemade Pies.
2. What challenges does Shelly face as she considers the three options?
3. What would you do in Shelly's position?

Build Your Business Plan

BUSINESS ETHICS AND SOCIAL RESPONSIBILITY

Think about which industry you are considering competing in with your product/service. Is there any kind of questionable practices in the way the product has been traditionally sold? Produced? Advertised? Have there been any recent accusations regarding safety within the industry? What about any environmental concerns?

For example, if you are thinking of opening a lawn care business, you need to be thinking about what possible effects the chemicals you are using will have on the client and the environment. You have a responsibility to keep your customers safe and healthy. You also have the social responsibility to let the community know of any damaging effect you may be directly or indirectly responsible for.

Build Your Business Plan

Written by Therese Maskulka of Walsh University, and used in her own classroom, the end-of-chapter feature "Build Your Business Plan" and Appendix A, "Guidelines for the Development of the Business Plan" help students through the steps of the business plan relating to each chapter. Additional information and resources can be found in the Instructor's Manual.

See for Yourself Videocase

Stimulate your students with these engaging case videos, all of which are new to this edition.

See for Yourself Videocase

HAPPINESS, MONEY, AND DOING GOOD—ICONTACT FOUNDERS HAVE IT ALL!

iContact co-founders, Aaron Houghton (Board Chairman & Chief Innovation Officer) and Ryan Allis (CEO), met and launched the iContact business while still in college. Each already owned a technology-based business, and they pooled their knowledge of online marketing and software to create iContact, a simple way for businesses of all sizes to take their marketing online by utilizing email.

All entrepreneurs take risks when starting a new business, but Houghton and Allis knew that that there was a demand for their product. The partners benefited from basing their business venture online because they required little initial capital—a good thing, since they had almost none. As iContact expanded, however, Houghton and Allis used venture capital funding to facilitate quick growth. The company has doubled its sales each year since its founding and is now a multimillion dollar business.

iContact emphasizes how it handles human resources. The company believes in hiring skilled, motivated people and giving them the freedom to truly do their jobs. It also hires with an eye toward diversity, not only because of the ethical have also endowed one percent of ownership to a grant-making foundation, The Humanity Campaign, aimed at eradicating extreme poverty and hunger. Houghton and Allis are also concerned with their impact on the environment. One of the motivating factors behind their business is that companies switching to online email marketing often move away from paper-based systems. Eliminating the production of paper-based marketing materials helps protect environmental assets such as trees and reduces the waste produced through paper making.

Today, the company has 180 employees and works with prestigious clients such as AT&T, ReMax, and Viacom. iContact has been voted number one as an email marketing service provider and resource for web professionals by *Website* magazine. Both Houghton and Allis have also received individual awards and recognition for their work as young entrepreneurs. For them, however, the goal has never been to increase the bottom line but to meet a consumer need, to create jobs and empower employees, and to make enough money to make a positive difference in both the company's local community and communities around the globe. They have come a long way toward achieving their dreams.[27]

See for Yourself Videocase

Team Exercise

Team Exercise

Major economic systems including capitalism, socialism, and communism, as well as mixed economies, were discussed in this chapter. Assuming that you want an economic system that is best for the majority, not just a few members of society, defend one of the economic systems as the best system. Form groups and try to reach agreement on one economic system. Defend why you support the system that you advance.

Team Exercise

Encourage your students to develop their teamwork and critical thinking skills while addressing real-world global business challenges.

Instructor Supplements

Instructor's Resource CD-ROM MHID: 0077324870 ISBN: 9780077324872

Everything you need to get the most from your textbook, including:

Instructor's Manual

Includes learning objectives; lecture outlines; PowerPoint notes; supplemental lecture; answers to discussion questions and end-of-chapter exercises; notes for video cases; term paper and project topics; suggestions for guest speakers; and roles and options for implementing role playing exercises.

Test Bank

Assurance of Learning Ready: Educational institutions are often focused on the notion of assurance of learning, an important element of many accreditation standards. *Business: A Changing World* is designed specifically to support your assurance of learning initiatives with a simple, yet powerful, solution. We've aligned our Test Bank questions with Bloom's Taxonomy and AACSB guidelines, tagging each question according to its knowledge and skills areas.

Each test bank question for *Business: A Changing World* also maps to a specific chapter learning objective listed in the text. You can use our test bank software, EZ Test, to easily query for learning objectives that directly relate to the learning objectives for your course. You can use the reporting features of EZ Test to aggregate student results in a similar fashion, making the collection and presentation of assurance of learning data quick and easy.

AACSB Statement: McGraw-Hill Companies is a proud corporate member of AACSB International. Understanding the importance and value of AACSB accreditation, the authors of *Business: A Changing World* have sought to recognize the curricula guidelines detailed in the AACSB standards for business accreditation by connecting selected questions in the Test Bank to the general knowledge and skill guidelines found in the AACSB standards.

The statements contained in *Business: A Changing World* are provided only as a guide for the users of this text. The AACSB leaves content coverage and assessment clearly within the realm and control of individual schools, the mission of the school, and the faculty. The AACSB does also charge schools with the obligation of doing assessment against their own content and learning goals. While *Business: A Changing World* and the teaching package make no claim of any specific AACSB qualification or evaluation, we have, within *Business: A Changing World,* labeled selected questions according to the six general knowledge and skills areas. The labels or tags within *Business: A Changing World* are as indicated. There are, of course, many more within the Test Bank, the text, and the teaching package which may be used as a standard for your course.

EZ Test Online: McGraw-Hill's EZ Test Online is a flexible and easy-to-use electronic testing program. The program allows instructors to create tests from book specific items, accommodates a wide range of question types, and enables instructors to even add their own questions. Multiple versions of the test can be created, and any test can be exported for use with course management systems such as WebCT, BlackBoard, or any course management system. EZ Test Online is accessible to busy instructors virtually anywhere via the Web, and the program eliminates the need for them to install test software. Utilizing EZ Test Online also allows instructors to create and deliver multiple-choice or true/false quiz questions using iQuiz for iPod. For more information about EZ Test Online, please see the Web site at: **www.eztestonline.com.**

PowerPoint Presentations

Developed by Jennifer Jackson, University of New Mexico, the PowerPoints consist of two formats: a detailed presentation (with additional information, figures, and links) and an outline presentation (an outline of the chapter). Each chapter contains 20–30 slides. Additional figures and tables from the text may be found on the CD-ROM in the "Digital Image Library."

Online Learning Center (OLC) with Premium Content

www.mhhe.com/ferrell8e

Access everything you need to teach a great course through our convenient online resource. A secured Instructor Resource Center stores your essential course materials to save you prep time before class. The Instructor's Manual, PowerPoint™, and additional resources are now just a couple of clicks away.

Instructor Video DVD   MHID 0077324927 ISBN 9780077324926

End of Chapter Video These videos offer a stimulating mix of topical reinforcement and real-world insight to help students master the most challenging business topics with segments such as "Walt Disney Around the World" or "Rebuilding America's Trust in Business" or "Should Employees Use Facebook at Work?" The videos can be found on the Instructor DVD-Rom and as downloadable files within the Instructor portion of the Web site. Summaries and discussion questions for the students can be found at the end of each chapter of the text and quizzes found online.

A Guide for Introducing and Teaching Ethics in Introduction to Business   The guide will be available on the OLC (Instructor Resources); only a limited number remain in print.

Written by O.C. Ferrell and Linda Ferrell, this is your one-stop guide for integrating this important issue into all aspects of your course. It helps you to demonstrate how business ethics lead to business success and offers a wide range of business ethics resources, including university centers, government resources, and corporate ethics programs. It is located with the Instructor Resources on the Web Site.

Active Classroom Resource Guide   The guide will be available on the OLC (Instructor Resources); only a limited number remain in print.

An additional collection of team projects, cases, and exercises that instructors can choose from to be used in class or out, which can be found electronically with the Instructor Resources on the Web Site.

eBooks

eBooks, or digital textbooks, are exact replicas of the print version, and can offer substantial savings to your students off the cost of their textbook. *Business: A Changing World* offers:

CourseSmart eBook MHID 0077324935 ISBN 9780077324933

With the CourseSmart eTextbook version of this title, students can save up to 50 percent off the cost of a print book, reduce their impact on the environment, and access powerful Web tools for learning. Faculty can also review and compare the full text online without having to wait for a print desk copy. CourseSmart is an online eTextbook, which means users need to be connected to the Internet in order to access. Students can also print sections of the book for maximum portability.

Student Supplements

Online Learning Center (OLC) with Premium Content
www.mhhe.com/ferrell8e

More and more students are studying online. That's why we offer an Online Learning Center (OLC) that follows *Business: A Changing World* chapter by chapter. It doesn't require any building or maintenance on your part, and is ready to go the moment you and your students type in the URL.

As your students study, they can refer to the OLC Web site for such benefits as:

- Internet-based activities
- Self-grading quizzes
- Learning objectives
- Additional video and related video exercises

The site includes an **online running video case** highlighting entrepreneur Todd McFarlane, who parlayed his artistic ability (and a passion for sports) into a multimillion dollar business that straddles film and television production, toys, comic books, sports licensing and games. Students watch and learn as McFarlane explains how he leads his company across all functional areas of business, illustrating how firms deal with the problems and opportunities of today's business world. With one video case for each part of the textbook highlighting this fun and unique company, students and instructors are provided a complete context for discussing every aspect of introductory business.

Acknowledgments

The eighth edition of *Business: A Changing World* would not have been possible without the commitment, dedication, and patience of Jennifer Jackson, Jennifer Sawayda, Harper Baird, and Julie Oliver. Jennifer Jackson provided oversight for editing and developing text content, cases, boxes, and the supplements. Alexi Sherrill assisted in developing most of the boxes in this edition. Doug Hughes, Executive Editor, provided leadership and creativity in planning and implementing all aspects of the seventh edition. Christine Scheid, Senior Developmental Editor, did an outstanding job of coordinating all aspects of the development and production process, with the assistance of Jonathan Thornton. Christine Vaughan was the Project Manager. Greg Bates managed the technical aspects of the Online Learning Center. Others important in this edition include Sarah Schuessler (Marketing Manager) and JoAnne Schopler (Design).

Michael Hartline developed the Personal Career Plan in Appendix C. Vickie Bajtelsmit developed Appendix D on personal financial planning. Eric Sandberg of Interactive Learning assisted in developing the interactive exercises found on the OLC.

Many others have assisted us with their helpful comments, recommendations, and support throughout this and previous editions. We'd like to express our thanks to the reviewers who helped us shape the eighth edition:

Brenda Anthony
Tallahassee Community College

Vondra Armstrong
Pulaski Tech College

Gene Baker
University of North Florida

Lia Barone
Norwalk Community College

Ellen Benowitz
Mercer County Community College

Dennis Brode
Sinclair Community College

Margaret Clark
Cincinnati State Tech & Community College

Peter Dawson
Collin County Community College—Plano

Mike Drafke
College of DuPage

Donna Everett
Santa Rosa Junior College

Gil Feiertag
Columbus State Community College

Jackie Flom
University of Toledo

Kris Gossett
Ivy Tech Community College of Indiana

Peggy Hager
Winthrop University

Susan Kendall
Arapahoe Community College

Daniel Montez
South Texas College

Mark Nygren
Brigham Young University—Idaho

Velvet Landingham
Kent State University—Geauga

Kent Lutz
University of Cincinnati

Dyan Pease
Sacramento City College

Elaine Simmons
Guilford Technical Community College

Delores Reha
Fullerton College

Morgan Shepherd
University of Colorado

Kurt Stanberry
University of Houston Downtown

Scott Taylor
Moberly Area Community College

Evelyn Thrasher
University of Mass—Dartmouth

Kristin Trask
Butler Community College

Richard Williams
Santa Clara University

We extend special appreciation to the following people who reviewed previous editions:

Linda Anglin, Mankato State University
Phyllis Alderdice, Jefferson Community College
John Bajkowski, American Association of Individual Investors
James Bartlett, University of Illinois
Stephanie Bibb, Chicago State University
Barbara Boyington, Brookdale County College of Monmouth
Suzanne Bradford, Angelina College
Alka Bramhandkar, Ithaca College
Eric Brooks, Orange County Community College
Nicky Buenger, Texas A&M University
Anthony Buono, Bentley College
Tricia Burns, Boise State University
William Chittenden, Texas Tech University
Michael Cicero, Highline Community College
M. Lou Cisneros, Austin Community College
Debbie Collins, Anne Arundel Community College—Arnold
Karen Collins, Lehigh University
Katherine Conway, Borough of Manhattan Community College
Rex Cutshall, Vincennes University
Dana D'Angelo, Drexel University
Laurie Dahlin, Worcester State College
John DeNisco, Buffalo State College
Tom Diamante, Adelphi University
Joyce Domke, DePaul University
Michael Drafke, College of DuPage
John Eagan, Erie Community College/City Campus SUNY
Glenda Eckert, Oklahoma State University
Thomas Enerva, Lakeland Community College
Robert Ericksen, Craven Community College
Joe Farinella, DePaul University
James Ferrell, R. G. Taylor, P.C.
Art Fischer, Pittsburg State University
Toni Forcino, Montgomery College—Germantown
Jennifer Friestad, Anoka—Ramsey Community College
Chris Gilbert, Tacoma Community College/University of Washington
Ross Gittell, University of New Hampshire
Frank Godfrey, St. Augustine's College
Bob Grau, Cuyahoga Community College—Western Campus

Gary Grau, Northeast State Tech Community College
Jack K. Gray, Attorney-at-Law, Houston, Texas
Catherine Green, University of Memphis
Claudia Green, Pace University
Phil Greenwood, University of St. Thomas
David Gribbin, East Georgia College
Peggy Hager, Winthrop University
Michael Hartline, Florida State University
Neil Herndon, University of Missouri
James Hoffman, Borough of Manhattan Community College
Joseph Hrebenak, Community College of Allegheny County—Allegheny Campus
Stephen Huntley, Florida Community College
Rebecca Hurtz, State Farm Insurance Co.
Roger Hutt, Arizona State University—West
Verne Ingram, Red Rocks Community College
Scott Inks, Ball State University
Steven Jennings, Highland Community College
Carol Jones, Cuyahoga Community College—Eastern Campus
Gilbert "Joe" Joseph, University of Tampa
Norm Karl, Johnson County Community College
Janice Karlan, LaGuardia Community College
Eileen Kearney, Montgomery County Community College
Craig Kelley, California State University—Sacramento
Ina Midkiff Kennedy, Austin Community College
Arbrie King, Baton Rouge Community College
John Knappenberger, Mesa State College
Gail Knell, Cape Cod Community College
Anthony Koh, University of Toledo
Daniel LeClair, AACSB
Frank Lembo, North Virginia Community College
Richard Lewis, East Texas Baptist College
Corinn Linton, Valencia Community College
Corrine Livesay, Mississippi College
Thomas Lloyd, Westmoreland Community College
Terry Loe, Kennerow University
Scott Lyman, Winthrop University
Dorinda Lynn, Pensacola Junior College
Isabelle Maignan, ING
Larry Martin, Community College of Southern Nevada—West Charles

Therese Maskulka, Youngstown State University
Kristina Mazurak, Albertson College of Idaho
Debbie Thorne McAlister, Texas State University—San Marcos
John McDonough, Menlo College
Tom McInish, University of Memphis
Noel McDeon, Florida Community College
Mary Meredith, University of Louisiana at Lafayette
Michelle Meyer, Joliet Junior College
George Milne, University of Massachusetts—Amherst
Glynna Morse, Augusta College
Stephanie Narvell, Wilmington College—New Castle
Fred Nerone, International College of Naples
Laura Nicholson, Northern Oklahoma College
Stef Nicovich, University of New Hampshire
Michael Nugent, SUNY—Stony Brook University New York
Wes Payne, Southwest Tennessee Community College
Dyan Pease, Sacramento City College
Constantine G. Petrides, Borough of Manhattan Community College
John Pharr, Cedar Valley College
Shirley Polejewski, University of St. Thomas
Daniel Powroznik, Chesapeake College
Krista Price, Heald College
Larry Prober, Rider University
Stephen Pruitt, University of Missouri—Kansas City
Kathy Pullins, Columbus State Community College
Charles Quinn, Austin Community College
Victoria Rabb, College of the Desert
Tom Reading, Ivy Tech State College
Susan Roach, Georgia Southern University
Dave Robinson, University of California—Berkely
Marsha Rule, Florida Public Utilities Commission
Carol A. Rustad, Sylvan Learning

Martin St. John, Westmoreland Community College
Don Sandlin, East Los Angeles College
Nick Sarantakes, Austin Community College
Andy Saucedo, Dona Ana Community College—Las Cruces
Elise "Pookie" Sautter, New Mexico State University
Dana Schubert, Colorado Springs Zoo
Marianne Sebok, Community College of Southern Nevada—West Charles
Jeffery L. Seglin, Seglin Associates
Daniel Sherrell, University of Memphis
Nicholas Siropolis, Cuyahoga Community College
Robyn Smith, Pouder Valley Hospital
Cheryl Stansfield, North Hennepin Community College
Ron Stolle, Kent State University—Kent
Jeff Strom, Virginia Western Community College
Wayne Taylor, Trinity Valley Community College
Ray Tewell, American River College
Steve Tilley, Gainesville College
Jay Todes, Northlake College
Amy Thomas, Roger Williams University
Ted Valvoda, Lakeland Community College
Sue Vondram, Loyola University
Elizabeth Wark, Springfield College
Emma Watson, Arizona State University—West
Jerry E. Wheat, Indiana University Southeast
Frederik Williams, North Texas State University
Pat Wright, Texas A&M University
Timothy Wright, Lakeland Community College
Lawrence Yax, Pensacola Junior College—Warrington

O.C. Ferrell
Geoffrey Hirt
Linda Ferrell
—July 2010

Authors

O.C. Ferrell

O.C. Ferrell is Professor of Marketing, Bill Daniels Professor of Business Ethics, and Creative Enterprise Scholar in the Anderson School of Management at the University of New Mexico. He recently served as the Bill Daniels Distinguished Professor of Business Ethics at the University of Wyoming and the Chair of the Department of Marketing and the Ehrhardt, Keefe, Steiner, and Hottman P. C. Professor of Business Administration at Colorado State University. He also has held faculty positions at the University of Memphis, University of Tampa, Texas A&M University, Illinois State University, and Southern Illinois University, as well as visiting positions at Queen's University (Ontario, Canada), University of Michigan (Ann Arbor), University of Wisconsin (Madison), and University of Hannover (Germany). He has served as a faculty member for the Master's Degree Program in Marketing at Thammasat University (Bangkok, Thailand). Dr. Ferrell received his B.A. and M.B.A. from Florida State University and his Ph.D. from Louisiana State University. His teaching and research interests include business ethics, corporate citizenship, and marketing.

Dr. Ferrell is widely recognized as a leading teacher and scholar in business. His articles have appeared in leading journals and trade publications. In addition to *Business: A Changing World,* he has two other textbooks, *Marketing: Concepts and Strategies* and *Business Ethics: Ethical Decision Making and Cases,* that are market leaders in their respective areas. He also has co-authored other textbooks for marketing, management, business and society, and other business courses, as well as a trade book on business ethics. He chaired the American Marketing Association (AMA) ethics committee that developed its current code of ethics. He is past president of the Academic Council for the AMA. Currently he is vice president of publications for the Academy of Marketing Science and a distinguished Fellow.

Dr. Ferrell's major focus is teaching and preparing learning material for students. He has taught the introduction to business course using this textbook. This gives him the opportunity to develop, improve, and test the book and ancillary materials on a first-hand basis. He has traveled extensively to work with students and understands the needs of instructors of introductory business courses. He lives in Albuquerque, New Mexico, and enjoys skiing, golf, and international travel.

Geoffrey A. Hirt

Geoffrey A. Hirt is currently Professor of Finance at DePaul University and a Mesirow Financial Fellow. From 1987 to 1997 he was Chairman of the Finance Department at DePaul University. He teaches investments, corporate finance, and strategic planning. He developed and was director of DePaul's M.B.A. program in Hong Kong and has taught in Poland, Germany, Thailand, and Hong Kong. He received his Ph.D. in Finance from the University of Illinois at Champaign–Urbana, his M.B.A. from Miami University of Ohio, and his B.A. from Ohio-Wesleyan University.

Dr. Hirt has directed the Chartered Financial Analysts Study program for the Investment Analysts Society of Chicago since 1987.

Dr. Hirt has published several books, including *Foundations of Financial Management* published by McGraw-Hill/Irwin. Now in its fourteenth edition, this book is used at more than 600 colleges and universities worldwide. It has been used in more than 31 countries and has been translated into more than 10 different languages. Additionally, Dr. Hirt is well known for his text, *Fundamentals of Investment Management,* also published by McGraw-Hill/Irwin, and now in its tenth edition has a 2011 publication date. He plays tennis and golf, is a music lover, and enjoys traveling with his wife, Linda.

Linda Ferrell

Dr. Linda Ferrell is Associate Professor of Marketing, Bill Daniels Professor of Business Ethics, and Albert and Mary Jane Black Professor of Economic Development in the Anderson School of Management at the University of New Mexico. She completed her Ph.D. in Business Administration, with a concentration in management, at the University of Memphis. She has taught at the University of Tampa, Colorado State University, University of Northern Colorado, University of Memphis, and the University of Wyoming. She also team teaches a class at Thammasat University in Bangkok, Thailand, as well as an online Business Ethics Certificate course through the University of New Mexico.

Her work experience as an account executive for McDonald's and Pizza Hut's advertising agencies supports her teaching of advertising, marketing management, marketing ethics and marketing principles. She has published in the *Journal of Public Policy and Marketing, Journal of Business Research, Journal of Business Ethics, Journal of Marketing Education, Marketing Education Review, Journal of Teaching Business Ethics, Case Research Journal,* and is co-author of *Business Ethics: Ethical Decision Making and Cases* (8th edition) and *Business and Society* (4th edition). She is the ethics content expert for the AACSB Ethics Education Resource Center (**www.aacsb.edu/eerc**) and leads a Daniels Fund business ethics initiative at the University of New Mexico.

Dr. Ferrell is the Vice President of Programs for the Academy of Marketing Science and a past president for the Marketing Management Association. She is a member of the college advisory board for Cutco Vector. She frequently speaks to organizations on "Teaching Business Ethics," including the Direct Selling Education Foundation's training programs and AACSB International Conferences. She has served as an expert witness in cases related to advertising, business ethics, and consumer protection.

Brief Contents

Contents

part

1

Business in a Changing World

The Dynamics of Business and Economics

OBJECTIVES

After reading this chapter, you will be able to:

- Define basic concepts such as business, product, and profit.
- Identify the main participants and activities of business and explain why studying business is important.
- Define economics and compare the four types of economic systems.
- Describe the role of supply, demand, and competition in a free enterprise system.
- Specify why and how the health of the economy is measured.
- Trace the evolution of the American economy and discuss the role of the entrepreneur in the economy.
- Evaluate a small-business owner's situation and propose a course of action.

There Are Plenty of Fish

Markus Frind has taken the phrase "there are plenty of fish in the sea" to a whole new level by turning people's search for love into a strong business. Frind is a computer programmer who spent years going from job to job during the dot-com bust. Because he disliked his work and was growing tired of being laid off, Frind decided to increase his skills by learning ASP.net (a Microsoft Web building tool). To challenge himself, he built an online dating site entitled Plenty of Fish.

Frind's goal was to have a steady income without having to work much. Aware of the intense competition out there, he knew that his site needed to stand out. So he offered matchmaking services on Plenty of Fish for free. The target market is people curious about online dating but unwilling to pay for the privilege. Without collecting fees from the target market, however, Frind had to figure out another way to make a living off his site. His solution was advertisements. Advertisements on Plenty of Fish include banner ads along with advertisements supplied from Google. Interestingly, Plenty of Fish also uses its competition to earn money. Frind sells ad space to other dating sites that assume that Frind's free users will eventually upgrade to their more sophisticated sites (many never have). Within his first year, Frind was earning more than $3,300 monthly. Until recently, Plenty of Fish was designed and run by Frind out of his apartment. His success is largely due to minimal costs and a tiny staff.

Today, Plenty of Fish handles about 1.6 Web pages monthly and is set to hit $10 million in revenues. Best of all, Frind achieved his goal: he works about 10 hours each week.[1]

Introduction

Even though organizations like Plenty of Fish may not seem like your typical business, they still must adhere to the same business concepts as any other company. A solid understanding of business, therefore, is necessary for anyone who wants to start their own company or work in the business field. We begin our study of business in this chapter by examining the fundamentals of business and economics. First, we introduce the nature of business, including its goals, activities, and participants. Next, we describe the basics of economics and apply them to the United States's economy. Finally, we establish a framework for studying business in this text.

The Nature of Business

A **business** tries to earn a profit by providing products that satisfy people's needs. The outcome of its efforts are **products** that have both tangible and intangible characteristics that provide satisfaction and benefits. When you purchase a product, you are buying the benefits and satisfaction you think the product will provide. A Subway sandwich, for example, may be purchased to satisfy hunger, while a Ford Mustang may be purchased to satisfy the need for transportation and the desire to present a certain image.

Most people associate the word *product* with tangible goods—an automobile, computer, phone, coat, or some other tangible item. However, a product can also be a service, which results when people or machines provide or process something of value to customers. Dry cleaning, a checkup by a doctor, a performance by a basketball player—these are examples of services. Some services, such as Flickr, an online photo management and sharing application, do not charge a fee for use but obtain revenue from ads on their sites. A product can also be an idea. Consultants and attorneys, for example, generate ideas for solving problems.

The Goal of Business

The primary goal of all businesses is to earn a **profit,** the difference between what it costs to make and sell a product and what a customer pays for it. If a company spends $2.00 to manufacture, finance, promote, and distribute a product that it sells for $2.75, the business earns a profit of 75 cents on each product sold. Businesses have the right to keep and use their profits as they choose—within legal limits—because profit is the reward for the risks they take in providing products. Earning profits contributes to society by providing employment, which in turn provides money that is reinvested in the economy. Not all organizations are businesses, however. **Nonprofit organizations,** such as the Red Cross, Special Olympics, and other charities and social causes, do not have the fundamental purpose of earning profits, although they may provide goods or services.

To earn a profit, a person or organization needs management skills to plan, organize, and control the activities of the business and to find and develop employees so that it can make products consumers will buy. A business also needs marketing expertise to learn what products consumers need and want and to develop, manufacture, price, promote, and distribute those products. Additionally, a business needs financial resources and skills to fund, maintain, and expand its operations. Other challenges for businesspeople include abiding by laws and government regulations; acting in an ethical and socially responsible manner; and adapting to

business
individuals or organizations who try to earn a profit by providing products that satisfy people's needs

product
a good or service with tangible and intangible characteristics that provide satisfaction and benefits

profit
the difference between what it costs to make and sell a product and what a customer pays for it

nonprofit organizations
organizations that may provide goods or services but do not have the fundamental purpose of earning profits

economic, technological, and social changes. Even nonprofit organizations engage in management, marketing, and finance activities to help reach their goals.

To achieve and maintain profitability, businesses have found that they must produce quality products, operate efficiently, and be socially responsible and ethical in dealing with customers, employees, investors, government regulators, the community, and society. Because these groups have a stake in the success and outcomes of a business, they are sometimes called **stakeholders.** Many businesses, for example, are concerned about how the production and distribution of their products affect the environment. For example, new computers are being designed by Apple, HP, and Dell to reduce energy consumption. Concerns about landfills becoming high-tech graveyards plague many electronics firms. Best Buy offers recycling of electronics at all of its stores. The stores take cell phones, DVD players, and most other electronic products in their green program, regardless of where they were purchased. Although there is a $10 dollar charge for laptops, monitors, CRTs, and TVs, a $10 Best Buy gift card is provided to offset the cost. Other businesses are concerned about the quality of life in the communities in which they operate. For example, the Kansas City Chiefs have raised more than $20 million for charitable organizations over the past 10 years. Annually, the franchise gives away 2,000 autographed items, most of which are used in auctions to benefit community groups.[2] Others are concerned with promoting business careers among African American, Hispanic, and Native American students. The Diversity Pipeline Alliance is a network of national organizations that work toward preparing students and professionals of color for leadership and management in the 21st-century workforce. The Pipeline assists individuals in getting into the appropriate college, pursuing a career in business, or earning an advanced degree in business.[3] Still other companies such as The Home Depot have a long history of supporting natural disaster victims from Hurricane Katrina to relief efforts and earthquake recovery for Haiti.

TerraCycle, founded by two former Princeton students, is a U.S. firm dedicated to preserving the environment. The company's flagship product, TerraCycle Plant Food, is an organic, liquid plant food made from waste (worm excrement) and packaged in reused soda bottles.

stakeholders
groups that have a stake in the success and outcomes of a business

The People and Activities of Business

Figure 1.1 shows the people and activities involved in business. At the center of the figure are owners, employees, and customers; the outer circle includes the primary business activities—management, marketing, and finance. Owners have to put up resources— money or credit—to start a business. Employees are responsible for the work that goes

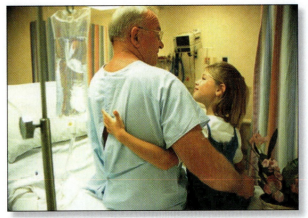

The goal of nonprofit organizations, including nonprofit hospitals and clinics, isn't to accumulate profits but to serve as many people as possible.

on within a business. Owners can manage the business themselves or hire employees to accomplish this task. The president of Procter & Gamble, Bob McDonald, does not own P&G, but is an employee who is responsible for managing all the other employees in a way that earns a profit for investors, who are the real owners. Finally, and most importantly, a business's major role is to satisfy the customers who buy its goods or services. Note also that people and forces beyond an organization's control—such as legal and regulatory forces, the economy, competition, technology, and ethical and social concerns—all have an impact on the daily operations of businesses. You will learn more about these participants in business activities throughout this book. Next, we will examine the major activities of business.

Management.   Notice that in Figure 1.1 management and employees are in the same segment of the circle. This is because management involves coordinating employees' actions to achieve the firm's goals, organizing people to work efficiently, and motivating them to achieve the business's goals. NASCAR has been a family-run business since its inception. Brian France, current chairman and chief executive officer (CEO), is following in the footsteps of his father and grandfather in providing leadership for the sport. NASCAR is now the second most popular spectator sport in the country, outperforming fan numbers and viewership for the IRL (It's Indy Racing League). NASCAR is also the second biggest television draw in sports, behind the NFL.[4] Management is also concerned with acquiring, developing, and

FIGURE I.I

Overview of the Business World

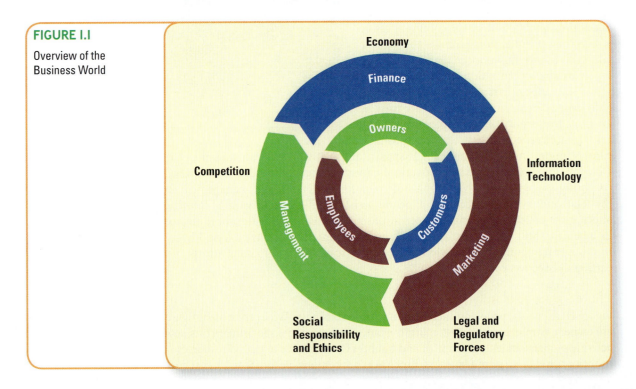

using resources (including people) effectively and efficiently. The most recent recession challenged NASCAR to be more efficient by reducing prices and using its resources more effectively.

Production and manufacturing is another element of management. In essence, managers plan, organize, staff, and control the tasks required to carry out the work of the company or nonprofit organization. We take a closer look at management activities in Parts 3 and 4 of this text.

Consider different management approaches by Samsung Electronics and Sony. Samsung believes it is important to manufacture its own TV sets. The firm believes that not manufacturing is to abandon the quality of your brand.

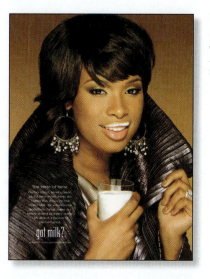

Did the "Got Milk?" campaign with celebrities such as Jennifer Hudson and their milk mustaches get you to drink more milk?

Sony is hiring others to build 40 percent of its TVs to reduce costs. In contrast, Samsung is the only TV maker that produces its own computer chips used in digital TVs. Samsung is managing manufacturing, design, and marketing to gain efficiencies.[5] Consequently, making decisions to ensure the business achieves its short- and long-term goals is a vital part of management.

Marketing.   Marketing and consumers are in the same segment of Figure 1.1 because the focus of all marketing activities is satisfying customers. Marketing includes all the activities designed to provide goods and services that satisfy consumers' needs and wants. Marketers gather information and conduct research to determine what customers want. Using information gathered from marketing research, marketers plan and develop products and make decisions about how much to charge for their products and when and where to make them available. In response to growing concerns over childhood obesity, Kellogg's has agreed to phase out advertising to children under the age of 12, unless those cereals are healthy (low calorie, low sugar and salt). In addition, Kellogg's will stop using cartoon and licensed characters such as Shrek to promote its products to children.[6] Other food producers have responded to consumer health concerns by modifying their products to make them healthier. Unilever, for example, announced that it was eliminating all hydrogenated oils, which contain trans-fats, from its soft-spread brands. I Can't Believe It's Not Butter will be one of several Unilever brands to have its hydrogenated oils replaced with palm and plant oils. Such a move reduces the risk of heart disease for consumers, while simultaneously allowing Unilever to market its brands as healthier.[7] Marketers use promotion—advertising, personal selling, sales promotion (coupons, games, sweepstakes, movie tie-ins), and publicity—to communicate the benefits and advantages of their products to consumers and increase sales. Nonprofit organizations also use promotion. For example, the National Fluid Milk Processor Promotion Board's "milk mustache" advertising campaign has featured Brooke Shields, Beyonce Knowles, Sheryl Crow, Elizabeth Hurley, Serena Williams, and even animated "celebrities" such as Garfield.[8] We will examine marketing activities in Part 5 of this text.

Finance.   Owners and finance are in the same part of Figure 1.1 because, although management and marketing have to deal with financial considerations, it is the primary responsibility of the owners to provide financial resources for the operation of the business. Moreover, the owners have the most to lose if the business fails to make a profit. Finance refers to all activities concerned with obtaining money and using it effectively. People who work as accountants, stockbrokers, investment advisors, or bankers are all part of the financial world. Owners sometimes have to borrow money to get started or attract additional owners who become partners or stockholders. Owners of small businesses in particular often rely on bank loans for funding. Part 6 of this text discusses financial management.

Why Study Business?

Studying business can help you develop skills and acquire knowledge to prepare for your future career, regardless of whether you plan to work for a multinational *Fortune* 500 firm, start your own business, work for a government agency, or manage or volunteer at a nonprofit organization. The field of business offers a variety of interesting and challenging career opportunities throughout the world, such as human resources management, information technology, finance, production and operations, wholesaling and retailing, and many more.

Studying business can also help you better understand the many business activities that are necessary to provide satisfying goods and services—and that these activities carry a price tag. For example, if you buy a new compact disk, about half of the price goes toward activities related to distribution and the retailer's expenses and profit margins. The production (pressing) of the CD represents about $1, or a small percentage of its price. Most businesses charge a reasonable price for their products to ensure that they cover their production costs, pay their employees, provide their owners with a return on their investment, and perhaps give something back to their local communities. Bill Daniels founded Cablevision, building his first cable TV system in Casper, Wyoming, in 1953, and is now considered "the father of cable television." Upon Daniels' passing in 2000, he had established a foundation that currently has funding of $1.4 billion and supports a diversity of causes from education to business ethics. During his career, Daniels created the Young American Bank, where children could create bank accounts and learn about financial responsibility, and this remains the world's only charter bank for young people. He created the Daniels College of Business through a donation of $20 million to the University of Denver. During his life, he affected many individuals and organizations, and his business success has allowed his legacy to be one of giving and impacting communities throughout the United States.[9] Thus, learning about business can help you become a well-informed consumer and member of society.

Business activities help generate the profits that are essential not only to individual businesses and local economies but also to the health of the global economy. Without profits, businesses find it difficult, if not impossible, to buy more raw materials, hire more employees, attract more capital, and create additional products that in turn make more profits and fuel the world economy. Understanding how our free-enterprise economic system allocates resources and provides incentives for industry and the workplace is important to everyone.

The Economic Foundations of Business

To continue our introduction to business, it is useful to explore the economic environment in which business is conducted. In this section, we examine economic systems, the free-enterprise system, the concepts of supply and demand, and the role of competition. These concepts play important roles in determining how businesses operate in a particular society.

Economics is the study of how resources are distributed for the production of goods and services within a social system. You are already familiar with the types of resources available. Land, forests, minerals, water, and other things that are not made by people are **natural resources. Human resources,** or labor, refers to the physical and mental abilities that people use to produce goods and services. **Financial resources,** or capital, are the funds used to acquire the natural and human resources needed to provide products. Because natural, human, and financial resources are used to produce goods and services, they are sometimes called *factors of production.* The firm can also have intangible resources such as a good reputation for quality products or being socially responsible. The goal is to turn the factors of production and intangible resources into a competitive advantage.

Economic Systems

An **economic system** describes how a particular society distributes its resources to produce goods and services. A central issue of economics is how to fulfill an unlimited demand for goods and services in a world with a limited supply of resources. Different economic systems attempt to resolve this central issue in numerous ways, as we shall see.

Although economic systems handle the distribution of resources in different ways, all economic systems must address three important issues:

1. What goods and services, and how much of each, will satisfy consumers' needs?
2. How will goods and services be produced, who will produce them, and with what resources will they be produced?
3. How are the goods and services to be distributed to consumers?

Communism, socialism, and capitalism, the basic economic systems found in the world today (Table 1.1), have fundamental differences in the way they address these issues. The factors of production in command economies are controlled by government planning. In many cases, the government owns or controls the production of goods and services. Communism and socialism are, therefore, considered command economies.

Communism.   Karl Marx (1818–1883) first described **communism** as a society in which the people, without regard to class, own all the nation's resources. In his ideal political-economic system, everyone contributes according to ability and receives benefits according to need. In a communist economy, the people (through the government) own and operate all businesses and factors of production. Central government planning determines what goods and services satisfy citizens' needs, how the goods and services are produced, and how they are distributed. However, no true communist economy exists today that satisfies Marx's ideal.

On paper, communism appears to be efficient and equitable, producing less of a gap between rich and poor. In practice, however, communist economies have been marked by low standards of living, critical shortages of consumer goods, high prices, and little freedom. Russia, Poland, Hungary, and other Eastern European nations have turned away from communism and toward economic systems governed by supply and demand rather than by central planning. However, their experiments with alternative economic systems have been fraught with difficulty

economics
the study of how resources are distributed for the production of goods and services within a social system

natural resources
land, forests, minerals, water, and other things that are not made by people

human resources
the physical and mental abilities that people use to produce goods and services; also called labor

financial resources
the funds used to acquire the natural and human resources needed to provide products; also called capital

economic system
a description of how a particular society distributes its resources to produce goods and services

communism
first described by Karl Marx as a society in which the people, without regard to class, own all the nation's resources

TABLE 1.1

Comparison of Communism, Socialism, and Capitalism

	Communism	Socialism	Capitalism
Business ownership	Most businesses are owned and operated by the government.	The government owns and operates major industries; individuals own small businesses.	Individuals own and operate all businesses.
Competition	None. The government owns and operates everything.	Restricted in major industries; encouraged in small business.	Encouraged by market forces and government regulations.
Profits	Excess income goes to the government.	Profits earned by small businesses may be reinvested in the business; profits from government-owned industries go to the government.	Individuals are free to keep profits and use them as they wish.
Product availability and price	Consumers have a limited choice of goods and services; prices are usually high.	Consumers have some choice of goods and services; prices are determined by supply and demand.	Consumers have a wide choice of goods and services; prices are determined by supply and demand.
Employment options	Little choice in choosing a career; most people work for government-owned industries or farms.	Some choice of careers; many people work in government jobs.	Unlimited choice of careers.

Source: "Gross Domestic Product or Expenditure, 1930–2002," *InfoPlease* (n.d.), www.infoplease.com/ipa/A0104575.html (accessed February 16, 2004).

and hardship. North Korea and Cuba continue to apply communist principles to their economies, but these countries are also enduring economic and political change. Countries such as Venezuela are trying to incorporate communist economic principles. Hugo Chavez, Venezuela's president, has developed a partnership with Cuba, but 85 percent of his citizens surveyed do not want their country to be like Cuba.[10] Consequently, communism is declining and its future as an economic system is uncertain. When Fidel Castro stepped down as president of Cuba, his younger brother Raul formally assumed the role and eliminated many of the bans, including allowing the purchase of electric appliances, microwaves, computers, and cell phones. The communist country appears more open to free enterprise now.[11] Similarly, China has become the first communist country to make strong economic gains by adopting capitalist approaches to business. Economic prosperity has advanced in China with the government claiming to ensure market openness, equality, and fairness.[12]

socialism
an economic system in which the government owns and operates basic industries but individuals own most businesses

Socialism.   **Socialism** is an economic system in which the government owns and operates basic industries—postal service, telephone, utilities, transportation, health care, banking, and some manufacturing—but individuals own most businesses. Central planning determines what basic goods and services are produced, how they are produced, and how they are distributed. Individuals and small businesses provide other goods and services based on consumer demand and the availability of resources. Citizens are dependent on the government for many goods and services.

Most socialist nations, such as Sweden, India, and Israel, are democratic and recognize basic individual freedoms. Citizens can vote for political offices, but central government planners usually make decisions about what is best for the nation. People are free to go into the occupation of their choice, but they often work in government-operated organizations. Socialists believe their system permits a higher standard of living than other economic systems, but the difference often applies to the nation as a whole rather than to its individual citizens. Socialist economies profess egalitarianism—equal distribution of income and social services. They believe their economies are more stable than those of other nations. Although this may be true, taxes and unemployment are generally higher in socialist countries. Perhaps as a result, many socialist countries have also experienced economic difficulties.

Capitalism.

Capitalism, or **free enterprise**, is an economic system in which individuals own and operate the majority of businesses that provide goods and services. Competition, supply, and demand determine which goods and services are produced, how they are produced, and how they are distributed. The United States, Canada, Japan, and Australia are examples of economic systems based on capitalism.

There are two forms of capitalism: pure capitalism and modified capitalism. In pure capitalism, also called a **free-market system,** all economic decisions are made without government intervention. This economic system was first described by Adam Smith in *The Wealth of Nations* (1776). Smith, often called the father of capitalism, believed that the "invisible hand of competition" best regulates the economy. He argued that competition should determine what goods and services people need. Smith's system is also called *laissez-faire* ("let it be") *capitalism* because the government does not interfere in business.

Modified capitalism differs from pure capitalism in that the government intervenes and regulates business to some extent. One of the ways in which the United States and Canadian governments regulate business is through laws. Laws such as the Federal Trade Commission Act, which created the Federal Trade Commission to enforce antitrust laws, illustrate the importance of the government's role in the economy. In the most recent recession, the government provided loans and took ownership positions in banks such as Citigroup, AIG (an insurance company), and General Motors. These actions were thought necessary to keep these firms from going out of business and creating a financial disaster for the economy.

Mixed Economies.

No country practices a pure form of communism, socialism, or capitalism, although most tend to favor one system over the others. Most nations operate as **mixed economies,** which have elements from more than one economic system. In socialist Sweden, most businesses are owned and operated by private individuals. In capitalist United States, the federal government owns and operates the postal service and the Tennessee Valley Authority, an electric utility. In Great Britain and Mexico, the governments are attempting to sell many state-run businesses to private individuals and companies. In once-communist Russia, Hungary, Poland, and other Eastern European nations, capitalist ideas have been implemented, including private ownership of businesses. Communist China allows citizens to invest in stocks and permits some private and foreign ownership of businesses.

capitalism, or free enterprise
an economic system in which individuals own and operate the majority of businesses that provide goods and services

free-market system
pure capitalism, in which all economic decisions are made without government intervention

mixed economies
economies made up of elements from more than one economic system

The Free-Enterprise System

Many economies—including those of the United States, Canada, and Japan—are based on free enterprise, and many communist and socialist countries, such as China and Russia, are applying more principles of free enterprise to their own economic systems. Free enterprise provides an opportunity for a business to succeed or fail on the basis of market demand. In a free-enterprise system, companies that can efficiently manufacture and sell products that consumers desire will probably succeed. Inefficient businesses and those that sell products that do not offer needed benefits will likely fail as consumers take their business to firms that have more competitive products.

A number of basic individual and business rights must exist for free enterprise to work. These rights are the goals of many countries that have recently embraced free enterprise.

1. Individuals must have the right to own property and to pass this property on to their heirs. This right motivates people to work hard and save to buy property.
2. Individuals and businesses must have the right to earn profits and to use the profits as they wish, within the constraints of their society's laws and values.
3. Individuals and businesses must have the right to make decisions that determine the way the business operates. Although there is government regulation, the philosophy in countries like the United States and Australia is to permit maximum freedom within a set of rules of fairness.
4. Individuals must have the right to choose what career to pursue, where to live, what goods and services to purchase, and more. Businesses must have the right to choose where to locate, what goods and services to produce, what resources to use in the production process, and so on.

The United States is not purely a capitalistic country. It owns and operates the U.S. Postal Service and provides is citizens with social programs, such as Social Security, Medicare, and free schooling for children.

Without these rights, businesses cannot function effectively because they are not motivated to succeed. Thus, these rights make possible the open exchange of goods and services. In the countries that favor free enterprise, such as the United States, citizens have the freedom to make many decisions about the employment they choose and create their own productivity systems. Many entrepreneurs are more productive in free-enterprise societies because personal and financial incentives are available that can aid in entrepreneurial success. For many entrepreneurs, their work becomes a part of their system of goals, values, and lifestyle. Consider Barbara Corcoran, who built one of New York's largest real estate companies. She is now a panelist on an ABC program, *Shark Tank,* which gives entrepreneurs a chance to receive funding to realize their dreams.

The Forces of Supply and Demand

In the United States and in other free-enterprise systems, the distribution of resources and products is determined by supply and demand. **Demand** is the number of goods and services that consumers are willing to buy at different prices at a specific time. From your own experience, you probably recognize that consumers are usually willing to buy more of an item as its price falls because they want to save money. Consider handmade rugs, for example. Consumers may be willing to buy six rugs at $350 each, four at $500 each, but only two at $650 each. The relationship between the price and the number of rugs consumers are willing to buy can be shown graphically, with a *demand curve* (see Figure 1.2).

Supply is the number of products that businesses are willing to sell at different prices at a specific time. In general, because the potential for profits is higher, businesses are willing to supply more of a good or service at higher prices. For example, a company that sells rugs may be willing to sell six at $650 each, four at $500 each, but just two at $350 each. The relationship between the price of rugs and the quantity the company is willing to supply can be shown graphically with a *supply curve* (see Figure 1.2).

In Figure 1.2, the supply and demand curves intersect at the point where supply and demand are equal. The price at which the number of products that businesses are willing to supply equals the amount of products that consumers are willing to buy at a specific point in time is the **equilibrium price.** In our rug example, the company is willing to supply four rugs at $500 each, and consumers are willing to buy four rugs at $500 each. Therefore, $500 is the equilibrium price for a rug at that point in time, and most rug companies will price their rugs at $500. As you might imagine, a business that charges more than $500 (or whatever the current equilibrium price is) for its rugs will not sell many and might not earn a profit. On the other hand, a business that charges less than $500 accepts a lower profit per rug than could be made at the equilibrium price.

If the cost of making rugs goes up, businesses will not offer as many at the old price. Changing the price alters the supply curve, and a new equilibrium price results. This is an ongoing process, with supply and demand constantly changing in

demand
the number of goods and services that consumers are willing to buy at different prices at a specific time

supply
the number of products—goods and services—that businesses are willing to sell at different prices at a specific time

equilibrium price
the price at which the number of products that businesses are willing to supply equals the amount of products that consumers are willing to buy at a specific point in time

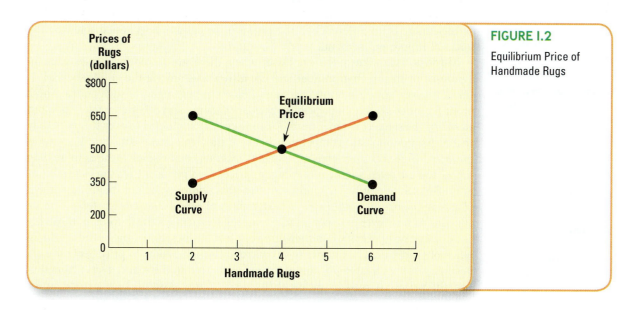

FIGURE 1.2

Equilibrium Price of Handmade Rugs

response to changes in economic conditions, availability of resources, and degree of competition. For example, the price of oil can change rapidly and has been between $35 and $145 a barrel over the last three years. Prices for goods and services vary according to these changes in supply and demand. This concept is the force that drives the distribution of resources (goods and services, labor, and money) in a free-enterprise economy.

Critics of supply and demand say the system does not distribute resources equally. The forces of supply and demand prevent sellers who have to sell at higher prices (because their costs are high) and buyers who cannot afford to buy goods at the equilibrium price from participating in the market. According to critics, the wealthy can afford to buy more than they need, but the poor are unable to buy enough of what they need to survive.

The Nature of Competition

competition
the rivalry among businesses for consumers' dollars

Competition, the rivalry among businesses for consumers' dollars, is another vital element in free enterprise. According to Adam Smith, competition fosters efficiency and low prices by forcing producers to offer the best products at the most reasonable price; those who fail to do so are not able to stay in business. Thus, competition should improve the quality of the goods and services available or reduce prices. For example, thanks to smart design and excellent timing, Apple dominates the market for downloadable music with its iTunes online service and iPod MP3 player. However, many companies have set their sights on capturing some of the firm's market share with new products of their own. Therefore, Apple must constantly seek to remain competitive by creating new innovations to maintain its market share—and sometimes capture market share from other companies. Its iPad device, released in 2010, is intended to combine the smart phone and the laptop into one product. The iPad also contains an interface that allows users to read books, which Apple hopes will capture some of the e-reader market dominated by Amazon's Kindle.[13]

Within a free-enterprise system, there are four types of competitive environments: pure competition, monopolistic competition, oligopoly, and monopoly.

pure competition
the market structure that exists when there are many small businesses selling one standardized product

Pure competition exists when there are many small businesses selling one standardized product, such as agricultural commodities like wheat, corn, and cotton. No one business sells enough of the product to influence the product's price. And, because there is no difference in the products, prices are determined solely by the forces of supply and demand.

monopolistic competition
the market structure that exists when there are fewer businesses than in a pure-competition environment and the differences among the goods they sell are small

Monopolistic competition exists when there are fewer businesses than in a pure-competition environment and the differences among the goods they sell is small. Aspirin, soft drinks, and vacuum cleaners are examples of such goods. These products differ slightly in packaging, warranty, name, and other characteristics, but all satisfy the same consumer need. Businesses have some power over the price they charge in monopolistic competition because they can make consumers aware of product differences through advertising. Consumers value some features more than others and are often willing to pay higher prices for a product with the features they want. For example, Advil, a nonprescription pain reliever, contains ibuprofen instead of aspirin. Consumers who cannot take aspirin or who believe ibuprofen is a more effective pain reliever may not mind paying a little extra for the ibuprofen in Advil.

oligopoly
the market structure that exists when there are very few businesses selling a product

An **oligopoly** exists when there are very few businesses selling a product. In an oligopoly, individual businesses have control over their products' price because each business supplies a large portion of the products sold in the marketplace. Nonetheless, the prices charged by different firms stay fairly close because a price cut or increase by one company will trigger a similar response from another company. In the airline industry, for example, when one airline cuts fares to boost sales, other airlines quickly follow with rate decreases to remain competitive. Oligopolies exist when it is expensive for new firms to enter the marketplace. Not just anyone can acquire enough financial capital to build an automobile production facility or purchase enough airplanes and related resources to build an airline.

When there is one business providing a product in a given market, a **monopoly** exists. Utility companies that supply electricity, natural gas, and water are monopolies. The government permits such monopolies because the cost of creating the good or supplying the service is so great that new producers cannot compete for sales. Government-granted monopolies are subject to government-regulated prices. Some monopolies exist because of technological developments that are protected by patent laws. Patent laws grant the developer of new technology a period of time (usually 17 years) during which no other producer can use the same technology without the agreement of the original developer. The United States granted the first patent in 1790, and the patent office received more than 485,000 patent applications in 2008.[15] This monopoly allows the developer to recover research, development, and production expenses and to earn a reasonable profit. An example of this type of monopoly is the dry-copier process developed by Xerox. Xerox's patents have expired, however, and many imitators have forced market prices to decline.

monopoly
the market structure that exists when there is only one business providing a product in a given market

Economic Cycles and Productivity

Expansion and Contraction. Economies are not stagnant; they expand and contract. **Economic expansion** occurs when an economy is growing and people are spending more money. Their purchases stimulate the production of goods

economic expansion
the situation that occurs when an economy is growing and people are spending more money; their purchases stimulate the production of goods and services, which in turn stimulates employment

inflation
a condition characterized by a continuing rise in prices

and services, which in turn stimulates employment. The standard of living rises because more people are employed and have money to spend. Rapid expansions of the economy, however, may result in **inflation,** a continuing rise in prices. Inflation can be harmful if individuals' incomes do not increase at the same pace as rising prices, reducing their buying power. Zimbabwe suffered from hyperinflation that became so bad that the inflation rate percentage was in the hundreds of millions. With the elimination of the Zimbabwean dollar and certain price controls in 2009, the inflation rate began to decrease, but not before the country's economy was virtually decimated.[16]

economic contraction
a slowdown of the economy characterized by a decline in spending and during which businesses cut back on production and lay off workers

Economic contraction occurs when spending declines. Businesses cut back on production and lay off workers, and the economy as a whole slows down. Contractions of the economy lead to **recession**—a decline in production, employment, and income. Recessions are often characterized by rising levels of **unemployment,** which is measured as the percentage of the population that wants to work but is unable to find jobs. Figure 1.3 shows the overall unemployment rate in the civilian labor force over the past 80 years. Rising unemployment levels tend to stifle demand for goods and services, which can have the effect of forcing prices downward, a condition known as *deflation*. The United States has experienced numerous recessions, the most recent ones occurring in 1990–1991, 2002–2003, and 2008–2009. The most recent recession (or economic slowdown) was caused by the collapse in housing prices and consumers' inability to stay current on their mortgage and credit card payments. This caused a crisis in the banking industry, with the government bailing out banks to keep them from failing. This in turn caused a slowdown in spending on consumer goods and a reduction in employment. Unemployment reached 10 percent of the labor force. Don't forget that personal consumption makes up almost 70 percent of gross domestic product, so consumer behavior is extremely

recession
a decline in production, employment, and income

unemployment
the condition in which a percentage of the population wants to work but is unable to find jobs

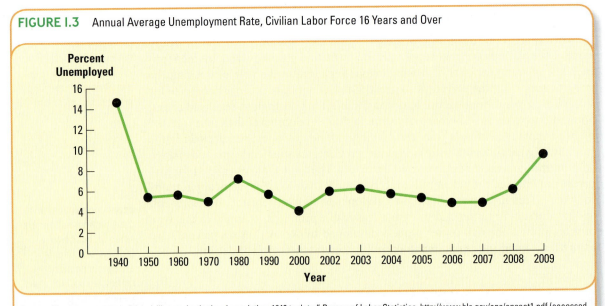

FIGURE 1.3   Annual Average Unemployment Rate, Civilian Labor Force 16 Years and Over

Source: "Employment status of the civilian noninstitutional population, 1940 to date," Bureau of Labor Statistics, http://www.bls.gov/cps/cpsaat1.pdf (accessed February 11, 2010); "Where can I find the unemployment rate for previous years?," Bureau of Labor Statistics, http://www.bls.gov/cps/prev_yrs.htm (accessed February 11, 2010).

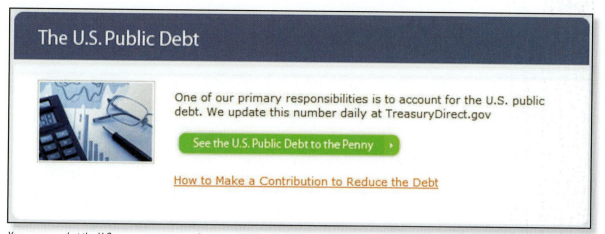

You can see what the U.S. government currently owes—down to the penny—by going to the Web site for the Bureau of the Public Debt, http://www.publicdebt.treas.gov/

important for economic activity. A severe recession may turn into a **depression,** in which unemployment is very high, consumer spending is low, and business output is sharply reduced, such as what occurred in the United States in the early 1930s. The most recent recession is often called the Great Recession because it was the longest and most severe economic decline since the Great Depression.

Economies expand and contract in response to changes in consumer, business, and government spending. War also can affect an economy, sometimes stimulating it (as in the United States during World Wars I and II) and sometimes stifling it (as during the Vietnam, Persian Gulf, and Iraq wars). Although fluctuations in the economy are inevitable and to a certain extent predictable, their effects—inflation and unemployment—disrupt lives and thus governments try to minimize them.

Measuring the Economy.   Countries measure the state of their economies to determine whether they are expanding or contracting and whether corrective action is necessary to minimize the fluctuations. One commonly used measure is **gross domestic product (GDP)**—the sum of all goods and services produced in a country during a year. GDP measures only those goods and services made within a country and therefore does not include profits from companies' overseas operations; it does include profits earned by foreign companies within the country being measured. However, it does not take into account the concept of GDP in relation to population (GDP per capita). Figure 1.4 shows the increase in GDP over several years, while Table 1.2 compares a number of economic statistics for a sampling of countries.

Another important indicator of a nation's economic health is the relationship between its spending and income (from taxes). When a nation spends more than it takes in from taxes, it has a **budget deficit.** In the 1990s, the U.S. government eliminated its long-standing budget deficit by balancing the money spent for social, defense, and other programs with the amount of money taken in from taxes.

In recent years, however, the budget deficit has reemerged and grown to record levels, partly due to defense spending in the aftermath of the terrorist attacks of September 11, 2001. Because Americans do not want their taxes increased, it is difficult for the federal government to bring in more revenue and reduce the deficit. Like consumers and businesses, when the government needs money, it borrows from the public, banks, and other institutions. The national debt (the amount of money

depression
a condition of the economy in which unemployment is very high, consumer spending is low, and business output is sharply reduced

gross domestic product (GDP)
the sum of all goods and services produced in a country during a year

budget deficit
the condition in which a nation spends more than it takes in from taxes

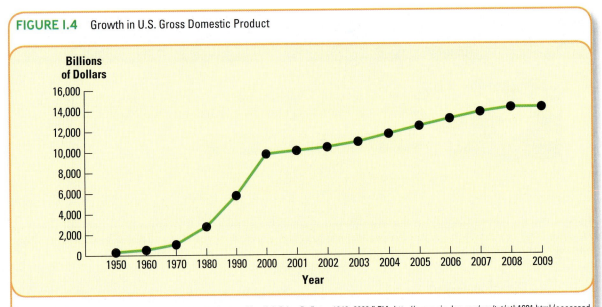

FIGURE I.4   Growth in U.S. Gross Domestic Product

Source: "Table D1. Population, U.S. Gross Domestic Product, and Implicit Price Deflator, 1949–2008," EIA, http://www.eia.doe.gov/aer/txt/ptb1601.html (accessed February 3, 2010).

TABLE I.2

A Comparative Analysis of a Sampling of Countries

Country	GDP (in billions of dollars)	GDP per capita	Unemployment Rate (%)	Inflation Rate (%)
Argentina	$558	$13,800	9.60	6.20
Australia	819	38,500	5.70	1.90
Brazil	2.24 (trillion)	10,200	7.40	4.20
Canada	1.287 (t)	38,400	8.50	0.20
China	8.767 (t)	6,500	4.30	−0.80
France	2.113 (t)	32,800	9.70	0.10
Germany	2.812 (t)	34,200	8.20	0.00
India	3.548 (t)	3,100	9.50	9.80
Israel	205.2	28,400	8.00	3.40
Japan	4.141 (t)	32,600	5.60	−1.30
Mexico	1.473 (t)	13,200	6.20	5.30
Russia	2.103 (t)	15,200	8.90	11.90
South Africa	488.6	10,000	24.00	7.20
United Kingdom	2.165 (t)	35,400	8.00	2.10
United States	14.25 (t)	46,400	9.40	−0.70

Source: CIA, "References: Guide to Country Comparisons—Economy," *The World Factbook,* https://www.cia.gov/library/publications/the-world-factbook/rankorder/rankorderguide.html (accessed February 22, 2010).

Unit of Measure	Description	TABLE I.3
Trade balance	The difference between our exports and our imports. If the balance is negative, as it has been since the mid-1980s, it is called a trade deficit and is generally viewed as unhealthy for our economy.	How Do We Evaluate Our Nation's Economy?
Consumer Price Index	Measures changes in prices of goods and services purchased for consumption by typical urban households.	
Per capita income	Indicates the income level of "average" Americans. Useful in determing how much "average" consumers spend and how much money Americans are earning.	
Unemployment rate	Indicates how many working age Americans are not working who otherwise want to work.*	
Inflation	Monitors price increases in consumer goods and services over specified periods of time. Used to determine if costs of goods and services are exceeding worker compensation over time.	
Worker productivity	The amount of goods and services produced for each hour worked.	

*Americans who do not work in a traditional sense, such as househusbands/housewives, are not counted as unemployed.

the nation owes its lenders) exceeded $12 trillion in 2009, due largely to increased spending by the government and an economic stimulus package to help stave off the worst effects of the Great Recession.[17] This figure is especially worrisome because, to reduce the debt to a manageable level, the government either has to increase its revenues (raise taxes) or reduce spending on social, defense, and legal programs, neither of which is politically popular. The national debt figure changes daily and can be seen at the Department of the Treasury, Bureau of the Public Debt, Web site. Table 1.3 describes some of the other ways we evaluate our nation's economy.

The American Economy

As we said previously, the United States is a mixed economy based on capitalism. The answers to the three basic economic issues are determined primarily by competition and the forces of supply and demand, although the federal government does intervene in economic decisions to a certain extent. To understand the current state of the American economy and its effect on business practices, it is helpful to examine its history and the roles of the entrepreneur and the government.

A Brief History of the American Economy

The Early Economy.   Before the colonization of North America, Native Americans lived as hunter/gatherers and farmers, with some trade among tribes. The colonists who came later operated primarily as an *agricultural economy*. People were self-sufficient and produced everything they needed at home, including food, clothing, and furniture. Abundant natural resources and a moderate climate nourished industries such as farming, fishing, shipping, and fur trading. A few manufactured goods and money for the colonies' burgeoning industries came from England and other countries.

As the nation expanded slowly toward the West, people found natural resources such as coal, copper, and iron ore and used them to produce goods such as horseshoes, farm implements, and kitchen utensils. Farm families who produced surplus

Going Green
Ethanol Faces a Bumpy Road

While green may be the new black for many consumers, the ethanol business has experienced a downward shift in popularity. Although most gas stations now carry gas containing up to 10 percent ethanol, many stakeholders are arguing against its future success.

The grocery industry is one such stakeholder, claiming that the increase in grocery prices is a result of corn-based ethanol. Indeed, corn prices have increased 50 percent since 2006 (the best year for ethanol). The ethanol business is most successful when corn prices are low and oil prices are high, two criteria that were not being met during the recent recession. Despite this problem, ethanol production is increasing beyond current demand, creating a surplus that drives down prices. When this happens, ethanol sells for a price below the equilibrium point.

One organization coming to ethanol's rescue is Growth Energy, an ethanol trade group run by former general and NATO (the North Atlantic Treaty Organization) commander Wesley Clark and Jeff Bronin of Poet Energy (the largest producer of ethanol). Growth Energy advocates increasing ethanol in gasoline from 10 to 15 percent, creating a gas blend called E15. This increase would help relieve excess supply. The group has applied to the Environmental Protection Agency for permission and the required waiver of the Clean Air Act. This possibility has concerned the automobile and boating industries, which fear that an increase may invalidate warranties on cars and boats designed to handle the old percentage. In response, Growth Energy claims it has conducted studies that prove the increase will not harm older engines and will create cleaner air. However, opposition to ethanol from various groups remains strong. The ethanol industry currently faces numerous challenges, from addressing stakeholder concerns that it is not green enough to increasing demand to eliminate the surplus.[18]

Discussion Questions:

1. Why has ethanol been promoted as a promising "green" fuel source?
2. What is the source of the backlash against ethanol? Do you think critics have valid concerns?
3. Why is there an excess supply of ethanol, and why is this bad for businesses?

goods sold or traded them for things they could not produce themselves, such as fine furniture and window glass. Some families also spent time turning raw materials into clothes and household goods. Because these goods were produced at home, this system was called the domestic system.

The Industrial Revolution. The 19th century and the Industrial Revolution brought the development of new technology and factories. The factory brought together all the resources needed to make a product—materials, machines, and workers. Work in factories became specialized as workers focused on one or two tasks. As work became more efficient, productivity increased, making more goods available at lower prices. Railroads brought major changes, allowing farmers to send their surplus crops and goods all over the nation for barter or for sale.

Factories began to spring up along the railways to manufacture farm equipment and a variety of other goods to be shipped by rail. Samuel Slater set up the first American textile factory after he memorized the plans for an English factory and emigrated to the United States. Eli Whitney revolutionized the cotton industry with his cotton gin. Francis Cabot Lowell's factory organized all the steps in manufacturing cotton cloth for maximum efficiency and productivity. John Deere's farm equipment increased farm production and reduced the number of farmers required to feed the young nation. Farmers began to move to cities to find jobs in factories and a higher standard of living. Henry Ford developed the assembly-line system to produce automobiles. Workers focused on one part of an automobile and then pushed it to the next stage until it rolled off the assembly line as a finished automobile. Ford's assembly line could manufacture many automobiles efficiently, and the price of his cars was $200, making them affordable to many Americans.

The Manufacturing and Marketing Economies. Industrialization brought increased prosperity, and the United States gradually became a *manufacturing economy*—one devoted to manufacturing goods and providing services rather than producing agricultural products. The assembly line was applied to more industries, increasing the variety of goods available to the consumer. Businesses became more concerned with the needs of the consumer and entered the *marketing economy*. Expensive goods such as cars and appliances could be purchased on a time-payment plan. Companies conducted research to find out what products consumers needed and wanted. Advertising made consumers aware of differences in products and prices.

Because these developments occurred in a free-enterprise system, consumers determined what goods and services were produced. They did this by purchasing the products they liked at prices they were willing to pay. The United States prospered, and American citizens had one of the highest standards of living in the world.

The Service and New Digital Economy. After World War II, with the increased standard of living, Americans had more money and more time. They began to pay others to perform services that made their lives easier. Beginning in the 1960s, more and more women entered the workforce. The profile of the family changed: Today there are more single-parent families and individuals living alone, and in two-parent families, both parents often work. One result of this trend is that time-pressed Americans are increasingly paying others to do tasks they used to do at home, like cooking, laundry, landscaping, and child care. These trends have gradually changed the United States to a *service economy*—one devoted to the production of services that make life easier for busy consumers. Service industries such as restaurants, banking, health care, child care, auto repair, leisure-related industries, and even education are growing rapidly and may account for as much as 80 percent of the U.S. economy. These trends continue with advanced technology contributing to new service products based on Internet-based e-business and digital media that provide smart phones, social networking, and a virtual world. Table 1.4 provides an overview of e-commerce in the United States. More about the Internet, business, and new online social media can be found in Chapter 13.

> **Did You Know?** Approximately 60 percent of adult women work.[19]

The Role of the Entrepreneur

An **entrepreneur** is an individual who risks his or her wealth, time, and effort to develop for profit an innovative product or way of doing something. Wolfgang Puck, although an Austrian by birth, is a true American entreprenuer. He moved to Los Angeles to be a chef and opened Spago, an Italian-style trattoria that served good food that attracted movie stars. When people found his pizza so good that they took home extras to place in their freezers, he decided to build his frozen pizza into a multi-million-dollar business. Today, he has 16 restuarants and Wolfgang Express bistros in 80 locations, mostly in airports.[20]

entrepreneur
an individual who risks his or her wealth, time, and effort to develop for profit an innovative product or way of doing something

The free-enterprise system provides the conditions necessary for entrepreneurs to succeed. In the past, entrepreneurs were often inventors who brought all the factors of production together to produce a new product. Thomas Edison, whose inventions include the record player and lightbulb, was an early American entrepreneur. Henry Ford was one of the first persons to develop mass assembly methods in the automobile industry. Other entrepreneurs, so-called captains of industry, invested in the country's growth. John D. Rockefeller built Standard Oil out of the fledgling oil industry, and Andrew Carnegie invested in railroads and founded the United States Steel Corporation. Andrew Mellon built the Aluminum Company of

Entrepreneurs like Bill Gates not only create jobs but sometimes change how the world works.

America and Gulf Oil. J. P. Morgan started financial institutions to fund the business activities of other entrepreneurs. Although these entrepreneurs were born in another century, their legacy to the American economy lives on in the companies they started, many of which still operate today. Milton Hershey began producing chocolate in 1894 in Lancaster, Pennsylvania. In 1900, the company was mass producing chocolate in many forms, lowering the cost of chocolate and making it more affordable to the masses, where it had once been a high-priced, luxury good. Early advertising touted chocolate as "a palatable confection and most nourishing food."

TABLE I.4

U.S. e-Commerce Overview

Internet users, worldwide	1.57 billion
Total e-commerce sales (excluding travel)	$145.6 billion
Total travel sales online	$105 billion
Internet advertising	$23.6 billion
Number of VOIP subscribers, U.S.	23.3 million
Active home Internet users in the U.S.	220.1 million
Number of high-speed Internet connections (U.S.)	145 million
Number of Web logs (worldwide)	133 million
Percent of U.S. adults online (daily)	72

Source: "E-Commerce and Internet Overview," Plunkett Research, Ltd., http://www.plunkettresearch.com/Industries/ECommerceInternet/ECommerceInternetStatistics/tabid/167/Default.aspx (accessed February 16, 2010).

Today, the Hershey Company employs more than 12,000 employees and sells almost $5 billion in chocolates and candies annually throughout the world.[21]

Entrepreneurs are constantly changing American business practices with new technology and innovative management techniques. Bill Gates, for example, built Microsoft, a software company whose products include Word and Windows, into a multibillion-dollar enterprise. Frederick Smith had an idea to deliver packages over-night, and now his FedEx Company plays an important role in getting documents and packages delivered all over the world for businesses and individuals. Entrepreneurs have been associated with such uniquely American concepts as Dell Computers, Ben & Jerry's, Levi's, Holiday Inns, McDonald's, Dr Pepper, and Walmart. Walmart, founded by entreprenuer Sam Walton, was the first retailer to reach $100 billion in sales in one year and now routinely passes that mark, with more than $405 billion in 2009.[22] Sam Walton's heirs own about 40 percent of the company.[23] We will examine the importance of entrepreneurship further in Chapter 5.

The Role of Government in the American Economy

The American economic system is best described as modified capitalism because the government regulates business to preserve competition and protect consumers and employees. Federal, state, and local governments intervene in the economy with laws and regulations designed to promote competition and to protect consumers, employees, and the environment. Many of these laws are discussed in Appendix A.

Additionally, government agencies such as the U.S. Department of Commerce measure the health of the economy (GDP, productivity, etc.) and, when necessary, take steps to minimize the disruptive effects of economic fluctuations and reduce unemployment. When the economy is contracting and unemployment is rising, the federal government through the Federal Reserve Board (see Chapter 14) tries to spur growth so that consumers will spend more money and businesses will hire more employees. To accomplish this, it may reduce interest rates or increase its own spending for goods and services. When the economy expands so fast that inflation results, the government may intervene to reduce inflation by slowing down economic growth. This can be accomplished by raising interest rates to discourage spending by businesses and consumers. Techniques used to control the economy are discussed in Chapter 14.

The Role of Ethics and Social Responsibility in Business

In the past few years, you may have read about a number of scandals at a number of well-known corporations, including Enron, Tyco, Arthur Andersen, Bear Stearns, AIG, and Lehman Brothers. In many cases, misconduct by individuals within these firms had an adverse effect on current and retired employees, investors, and others associated with these firms. In some cases, individuals went to jail for their actions. Top executives like Enron's Jeffrey Skilling and Tyco's Dennis Kozlowski received long prison sentences for their roles in corporate misconduct. These scandals undermined public confidence in corporate America and sparked a new debate about ethics in business. Business ethics generally refers to the standards and principles used by society to define appropriate and inappropriate conduct in the workplace. In many cases, these standards have been codified as laws prohibiting actions deemed unacceptable.

Society is increasingly demanding that businesspeople behave ethically and socially responsibly toward not only their customers but also their employees, investors, government regulators, communities, and the natural environment. "Intel helped establish a goal for PFCs (perfluorocompounds) that the entire industry could support," Intel President and CEO Paul Otellini told *CRO*. "It came together

Entrepreneurship in Action
NadaMoo! Challenges Traditional Ice Cream

Amy Ramm

Business: NadaMoo!

Founded: 2004

Success: Demand for NadaMoo! is rising exponentially, with more orders now coming in monthly than in its entire first two years in business.

Vegans, those who are lactose-intolerant, and dessert lovers alike can now all enjoy the same creamy frozen dessert. NadaMoo!, invented by natural foods chef Amy Ramm, is made without white sugar, dairy, or egg products. Ramm invented the first NadaMoo! recipe for her allergy-plagued

sister so she could enjoy dessert without consequences. It was first publically offered at Daily Juice in Austin, Texas. Soon after, Whole Foods began selling it in pints, and NadaMoo! obtained a distributor. What makes NadaMoo! tastier than some of its nondairy competition is coconut cream and agave nectar—giving it the smooth, creamy texture of ice cream. Although Ramm is pleased with NadaMoo!'s success, she prefers to keep the company small for now and become part of the communities in which NadaMoo! is marketed. NadaMoo! comes in five flavors and is sold in a growing number of locations throughout the western United States.[24]

before Kyoto and was the first worldwide, industry-wide goal to address climate change. We view our environmental strategies as integral to the way we do business. We strive to lead by example, and to be trusted stakeholders to governments worldwide."[25] Green business strategies create long-run relationships with all stakeholders by maintaining, supporting, and enhancing the natural environment.

One of the primary lessons of the scandals of the past 10 years has been that the reputation of business organizations depends not just on bottom-line profits but also on ethical conduct and concern for the welfare of others. Consider that in the aftermath of these scandals, the reputations of every U.S. company suffered regardless of their association with the scandals. However, there are signs that business ethics is improving. One respected survey reported well-implemented formal ethics and compliance programs dramatically increase reporting of observed misconduct and also help to decrease the rate of misconduct.[26] Although these results suggest that ethics is improving, the fact that employees continue to report observing misconduct and experiencing pressure to engage in unethical or illegal acts remains troubling and suggests that companies need to continue their efforts to raise ethical standards. In fact, beginning in 2007 and 2008, ethical questions surfaced about lending practices in the mortgage industry. Mortgage lenders had been making adjustable rate mortgage loans in previous years to people who were not necessarily good credit risks. The brokers earned fees for making the loans, and the fees were not contingent on the ability of the borrower to pay. It was later revealed that some mortgage lenders even knew that the borrowers were inflating their income to secure loans they could not afford. As interest rates rose and the monthly cost of the mortgage was adjusted upward, many borrowers were unable to make their monthly payments and so ended up defaulting on their loans and losing their homes. Many faulted the lenders for a lack of ethical behavior. The burst of this housing bubble helped contribute significantly to what many now refer to as the "Great Recession." We take a closer look at ethics and social responsibility in business in Chapter 2.

Can You Learn Business in a Classroom?

Obviously, the answer is yes, or there would be no purpose for this textbook! To be successful in business, you need knowledge, skills, experience, and good judgment. The topics covered in this chapter and throughout this book provide some of the knowledge you need to understand the world of business. The opening vignette at the beginning of each chapter, boxes, examples within each chapter, and the case at the end of each chapter describe experiences to help you develop good business judgment. The "Build Your Skills" exercise at the end of each chapter and the "Solve the Dilemma" box will help you develop skills that may be useful in your future career. However, good judgment is based on knowledge and experience plus personal insight and understanding. Therefore, you need more courses in business, along with some practical experience in the business world, to help you develop the special insight necessary to put your personal stamp on knowledge as you apply it. The challenge in business is in the area of judgment, and judgment does not develop from memorizing an introductory business textbook. If you are observant in your daily experiences as an employee, as a student, and as a consumer, you will improve your ability to make good business judgments.

Figure 1.5 is an overview of how the chapters in this book are linked together and how the chapters relate to the participants, the activities, and the environmental factors found in the business world. The topics presented in the chapters that follow are those that will give you the best opportunity to begin the process of understanding the world of business.

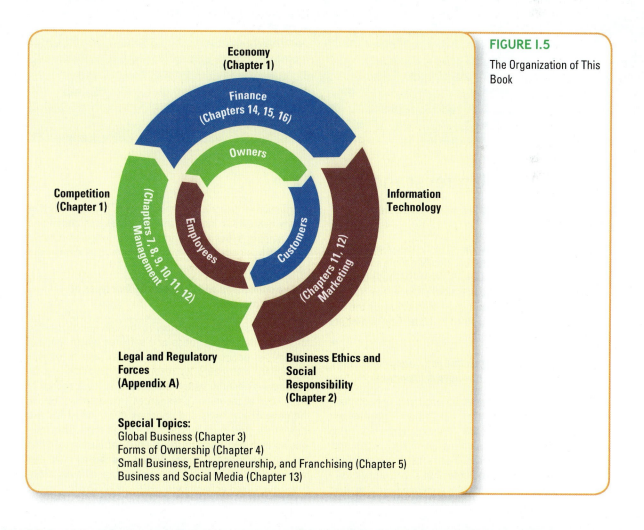

FIGURE I.5

The Organization of This Book

So You Want a Job in the Business World

When most people think of a career in business, they see themselves entering the door to large companies and multinationals that they read about in the news and that are discussed in class. In a national survey, students indicated they would like to work for Google, Walt Disney, Apple, and Ernst & Young. In fact, most jobs are not with large corporations, but are in small companies, nonprofit organizations, government and even self-employed individuals. There are 20 million individuals that the Small Business Administration says own their businesses and have no employees. In addition, there are nearly 5 million small businesses which employ 10 or fewer workers. With more than 75 percent of the economy based on services, there are jobs available in industries such as healthcare, finance, education, hospitality, entertainment and transportation. The world is changing quickly and large corporations replace the equivalent of their entire workforce every four years.

The fast pace of technology today means that you have to be prepared to take advantage of emerging job opportunities and markets. You must also become adaptive and recognize that business is becoming more global, with job opportunities around the world. If you may want to obtain such a job, you shouldn't miss a chance to spend some time overseas. As get you started on the path to thinking about job opportunities, consider all of the changes in business today that might affect your possible long-term track and that could bring you lots of success. You may want to stay completely out of large organizations and corporations and put yourself in a position for an entrepreneurial role as a self-employed contractor or small-business owner. However, there are many that feel that experience in larger businesses is helpful to your success later as an entrepreneur.

You're on the road to learning the key knowledge, skills and trends that you can use to be a star in business. Businesses impact on our society, especially in the area of sustainability and improvement of the environment is a growing challenge and opportunity. Green businesses and green jobs in the business world are provided to give you a glimpse at the possibilities. Along the way, we will introduce you to some specific careers and offer advice on developing your own job opportunities. Research indicates that you won't be that happy with your job unless you enjoy your work and feel that it has a purpose. Since you spend most of your waking hours every day at work, you need to seriously think about what is important to you in a job.[27]

Review Your Understanding

Define basic concepts such as business, product, and profit.

A business is an organization or individual that seeks a profit by providing products that satisfy people's needs. A product is a good, service, or idea that has both tangible and intangible characteristics that provide satisfaction and benefits. Profit, the basic goal of business, is the difference between what it costs to make and sell a product and what a customer pays for it.

Identify the main participants and activities of business and explain why studying business is important.

The three main participants in business are owners, employees, and customers, but others—government regulators, suppliers, social groups, etc.—are also important. Management involves planning, organizing, and controlling the tasks required to carry out the work of the company. Marketing refers to those activities—research, product development, promotion, pricing, and distribution—designed to provide goods and services that satisfy customers. Finance refers to activities concerned with funding a business and using its funds effectively. Studying business can help you prepare for a career and become a better consumer.

Define economics and compare the four types of economic systems.

Economics is the study of how resources are distributed for the production of goods and services within a social system; an economic system describes how a particular society distributes its resources. Communism is an economic system in which the people, without regard to class, own all the nation's resources. In a socialist system, the government owns and operates basic industries, but individuals own most businesses. Under capitalism, individuals own and operate the majority of businesses that provide goods and services. Mixed economies have elements from more than one economic system; most countries have mixed economies.

Describe the role of supply, demand, and competition in a free-enterprise system.

In a free-enterprise system, individuals own and operate the majority of businesses, and the distribution of resources is determined by competition, supply, and demand. Demand is the number of goods and services that consumers are willing to buy at different prices at a specific time. Supply is the number of goods or services that businesses are willing to sell at different prices at a specific time. The price at which the supply of a product equals demand at a specific point in time is the equilibrium price. Competition is the rivalry among businesses to convince consumers to buy goods or services. Four types of competitive environments are pure competition, monopolistic competition, oligopoly, and monopoly. These economic concepts determine how businesses may operate in a particular society and, often, how much they can charge for their products.

Specify why and how the health of the economy is measured.

A country measures the state of its economy to determine whether it is expanding or contracting and whether the country needs to take steps to minimize fluctuations. One commonly used measure is gross domestic product (GDP), the sum of all goods and services produced in a country during a year. A budget deficit occurs when a nation spends more than it takes in from taxes.

Trace the evolution of the American economy and discuss the role of the entrepreneur in the economy.

The American economy has evolved through several stages: the early economy, the Industrial Revolution, the manufacturing economy, the marketing economy, and the service and Internet-based economy of today. Entrepreneurs play an important role because they risk their time, wealth, and efforts to develop new goods, services, and ideas that fuel the growth of the American economy.

Evaluate a small-business owner's situation and propose a course of action.

"Solve the Dilemma" on page 29 presents a problem for the owner of the firm. Should you, as the owner, raise prices, expand operations, or form a venture with a larger company to deal with demand? You should be able to apply your newfound understanding of the relationship between supply and demand to assess the situation and reach a decision about how to proceed.

Revisit the World of Business

Revisit the World of Business Questions

1. How has Markus Frind achieved his goal in business?

2. Identify marketing, management, and finance activities at Plenty of Fish.

3. Go to the Plenty of Fish Web site (www.plentyoffish. com) and determine why this site is so successful.

Learn the Terms

budget deficit   17
business   4
capitalism, or free enterprise   11
communism   9
competition   14
demand   13
depression   17
economic contraction   16
economic expansion   15
economic system   9
economics   9

entrepreneur   21
equilibrium price   13
financial resources   9
free-market system   11
gross domestic product (GDP)   17
human resources   9
inflation   16
mixed economies   11
monopolistic competition   14
monopoly   15
natural resources   9

nonprofit organizations   4
oligopoly   14
product   4
profit   4
pure competition   14
recession   16
socialism   10
stakeholders   5
supply   13
unemployment   16

Check Your Progress

1. What is the fundamental goal of business? Do all organizations share this goal?

2. Name the forms a product may take and give some examples of each.

3. Who are the main participants of business? What are the main activities? What other factors have an impact on the conduct of business in the United States?

4. What are four types of economic systems? Can you provide an example of a country using each type?

5. Explain the terms *supply, demand, equilibrium price,* and *competition.* How do these forces interact in the American economy?

6. List the four types of competitive environments and provide an example of a product of each environment.

7. List and define the various measures governments may use to gauge the state of their economies. If unemployment is high, will the growth of GDP be great or small?

8. Why are fluctuations in the economy harmful?

9. How did the Industrial Revolution influence the growth of the American economy? Why do we apply the term *service economy* to the United States today?

10. Explain the federal government's role in the American economy.

Get Involved

1. Discuss the economic changes occurring in Russia and Eastern European countries, which once operated as communist economic systems. Why are these changes occurring? What do you think the result will be?

2. Why is it important for the government to measure the economy? What kinds of actions might it take to control the economy's growth?

3. Is the American economy currently expanding or contracting? Defend your answer with the latest statistics on GDP, inflation, unemployment, and so on. How is the federal government responding?

Build Your Skills

THE FORCES OF SUPPLY AND DEMAND

Background
WagWumps are a new children's toy with the potential to be a highly successful product. WagWumps are cute, furry, and their eyes glow in the dark. Each family set consists of a mother, a father, and two children. Wee-Toys' manufacturing costs are about $6 per set, with $3 representing marketing and distribution costs. The wholesale price of a WagWump family for a retailer is $15.75, and the toy carries a suggested retail price of $26.99.

Task
Assume you are a decision maker at a retailer, such as Target or Walmart, that must determine the price the stores in your district should charge customers for the WagWump family set. From the information provided, you know that the SRP (suggested retail price) is $26.99 per set and that your company can purchase the toy set from your wholesaler for $15.75 each. Based on the following assumptions, plot your company's supply curve on the graph provided in Figure 1.6 and label it "supply curve."

Quantity	Price
3,000	$16.99
5,000	21.99
7,000	26.99

Using the following assumptions, plot your customers' demand curve on Figure 1.6, and label it "demand curve."

Quantity	Price
10,000	$16.99
6,000	21.99
2,000	26.99

For this specific time, determine the point at which the quantity of toys your company is willing to supply equals the quantity of toys the customers in your sales district are willing to buy, and label that point "equilibrium price."

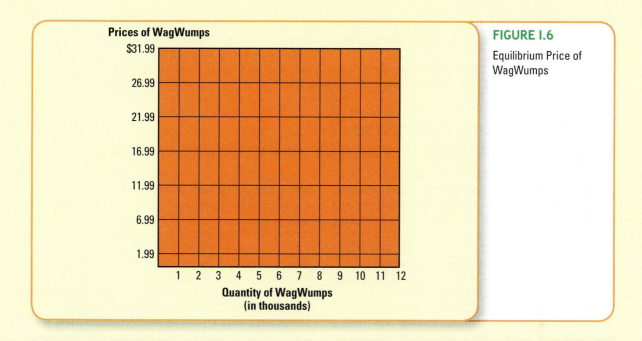

Prices of WagWumps

FIGURE I.6

Equilibrium Price of WagWumps

**Quantity of WagWumps
(in thousands)**

Solve the Dilemma

MRS. ACRES HOMEMADE PIES

Shelly Acres, whose grandmother gave her a family recipe for making pies, loved to cook, and she decided to start a business she called Mrs. Acres Homemade Pies. The company produces specialty pies and sells them in local supermarkets and select family restaurants. In each of the first six months, Shelly and three part-time employees sold 2,000 pies for $4.50 each, netting $1.50 profit per pie. The pies were quite successful and Shelly could not keep up with demand. The company's success results from a quality product and productive employees who are motivated by incentives and who enjoy being part of a successful new business.

To meet demand, Shelly expanded operations, borrowing money and increasing staff to four full-time employees. Production and sales increased to 8,000 pies per month,

and profits soared to $12,000 per month. However, demand for Mrs. Acres Homemade Pies continues to accelerate beyond what Shelly can supply. She has several options: (1) maintain current production levels and raise prices; (2) expand the facility and staff while maintaining the current price; or (3) contract the production of the pies to a national restaurant chain, giving Shelly a percentage of profits with minimal involvement.

Discussion Questions

1. Explain and demonstrate the relationship between supply and demand for Mrs. Acres Homemade Pies.

2. What challenges does Shelly face as she considers the three options?

3. What would you do in Shelly's position?

Build Your Business Plan

THE DYNAMICS OF BUSINESS AND ECONOMICS

Have you ever thought about owning your business? If you have, how did your idea come about? Is it your experience with this particular field? Or might it be an idea that evolved from your desires for a particular product or service not being offered in your community? For example, perhaps

you and your friends have yearned for a place to go have coffee, relax, and talk. Now is an opportunity to create the café bar you have been thinking of!

Whether you consider yourself a visionary or a practical thinker, think about your community. What needs are not being met? While it is tempting to suggest a new restaurant (maybe even one near campus), easier-to-implement business plans can range from a lawn care business or a designated driver business, to a placement service agency for teenagers.

Once you have an idea for a business plan, think about how profitable this idea might be. Is there sufficient demand for this business? How large is the market for this particular business? What about competitors? How many are there?

To learn about your industry you should do a thorough search of your initial ideas of a product/service on the Internet.

See for Yourself Videocase

HAPPINESS, MONEY, AND DOING GOOD—ICONTACT FOUNDERS HAVE IT ALL!

iContact co-founders, Aaron Houghton (Board Chairman & Chief Innovation Officer) and Ryan Allis (CEO), met and launched the iContact business while still in college. Each already owned a technology-based business, and they pooled their knowledge of online marketing and software to create iContact, a simple way for businesses of all sizes to take their marketing online by utilizing email.

All entrepreneurs take risks when starting a new business, but Houghton and Allis knew that that there was a demand for their product. The partners benefited from basing their business venture online because they required little initial capital—a good thing, since they had almost none. As iContact expanded, however, Houghton and Allis used venture capital funding to facilitate quick growth. The company has doubled its sales each year since its founding and is now a multimillion dollar business.

iContact emphasizes how it handles human resources. The company believes in hiring skilled, motivated people and giving them the freedom to truly do their jobs. It also hires with an eye toward diversity, not only because of the ethical implications but also because a diverse workforce provides diverse perspectives on the product. Because iContact works with many different businesses and does 20 percent of its business with clients outside the U.S., the company's customers are likely to be diverse as well. iContact, which is dedicated to charitable good works, matches employee donations up to $300 and allows employees roughly 2.5 paid days off each year to perform community service.

Houghton and Allis credit their success to the entrepreneurial freedom found in the United States and the instant worldwide access provided by the Internet. Thanks to the company's success, the iContact founders are able to give back to communities around the world. They donate one percent of payroll to local and global non-profits. They have also endowed one percent of ownership to a grant-making foundation, The Humanity Campaign, aimed at eradicating extreme poverty and hunger. Houghton and Allis are also concerned with their impact on the environment. One of the motivating factors behind their business is that companies switching to online email marketing often move away from paper-based systems. Eliminating the production of paper-based marketing materials helps protect environmental assets such as trees and reduces the waste produced through paper making.

Today, the company has 180 employees and works with prestigious clients such as AT&T, ReMax, and Viacom. iContact has been voted number one as an email marketing service provider and resource for web professionals by *Website* magazine. Both Houghton and Allis have also received individual awards and recognition for their work as young entrepreneurs. For them, however, the goal has never been to increase the bottom line but to meet a consumer need, to create jobs and empower employees, and to make enough money to make a positive difference in both the company's local community and communities around the globe. They have come a long way toward achieving their dreams.[27]

Discussion Questions

1. What are some of the risks that entrepreneurs take when starting a business? Why were Houghton and Allis confident that their business would succeed?

2. How does iContact handle human resources that sets it apart from other companies?

3. How does iContact engage in social responsibility? How does this help the company set itself apart from the competition?

Remember to check out our Online Learning Center at www.mhhe.com/ferrell8e.

Team Exercise

Major economic systems including capitalism, socialism, and communism, as well as mixed economies, were discussed in this chapter. Assuming that you want an economic system that is best for the majority, not just a few members of society, defend one of the economic systems as the best system. Form groups and try to reach agreement on one economic system. Defend why you support the system that you advance.

Appendix A

Guidelines for the Development of the Business Plan

These guidelines are for students to create a hypothetical business plan for a product/service/business of their choice. Students should assume to have $25,000 to start this new business in their community.

At the end of every chapter there will be a section entitled "Build Your Business Plan" to assist you in the development of the business plan.

Phase I: Development of the Business Proposal

You are encouraged to submit your idea for approval to your instructor as soon as possible. This will eliminate wasted effort on an idea that is not feasible in the instructor's view. Business plan proposals will be evaluated based on their thoroughness and your ability to provide support for the idea.

The business proposal consists of:

Business Description. This consists of an overview of the existing product/service or the product/service/business you will be starting (manufacturer, merchandiser, or service provider). This includes developing a mission (reason for existence; overall purpose of the firm) and a rationale for why you believe this business will be a success. What is your vision for this proposed product/business?

Brief Marketing Plan. (The marketing plan will be further developed as the plan evolves.) A description of your business/product/service is required. Identify the target market and develop a strategy for appealing to it. Justify your proposed location for this business. Describe how you will promote the new business and provide a rationale for your pricing strategy. Select a name for this business. The name should be catchy yet relate to the competencies of the business.

Competitive Analysis. Identify the competition as broadly as possible. Indicate why this business will be successful given the market.

Phase 2: Final Written Business Plan

Executive Summary. The executive summary appears first, but should be written last.

Business Description. This section requires fleshing out the body of the business plan including material from your revised preliminary proposal with more data, charts, and appendices. Include a description of the proposed form of organization, either a partnership or corporation, and the rationalization of the form chosen.

Industry and Market Analysis. An analysis of the industry including the growth rate of the industry and number of new entrants into this field is necessary. Identify uncontrollable variables within the industry. Determine an estimate of the proposed realistic size of the potential market. This will require interpretation of statistics from U.S. Census, as well as local sources such as the Chamber of Commerce.

Competitive Analysis. Include an exhaustive list of the primary and secondary competition, along with the competitive advantage of each.

Marketing Strategy. Target market specifics need to be developed.
Decisions on the marketing mix variables need to be made:

- Price (at the market, below market, above market).
- Promotion (sales associates, advertising budget, use of sales promotions, and publicity/goodwill).

- Distribution—Rationale of choice and level of distribution.
- Product/Service—A detailed rationale of the perceived differential advantage of your product/service offering.

Operational Issues.   How will you make or provide your product/service? Location rationale, facility type, leasing considerations and sources of suppliers need to be detailed. Software/hardware requirements necessary to maintain operations determined.

Human Resource Requirement. Number and description of personnel needed including realistic required education and skills.

Financial Projections. Statement of cash flows must be prepared for the first twelve months of the business. This must include start-up costs, opening expenses, estimation of cash inflows and outflows. A breakeven analysis should be included and an explanation of all financial assumptions.

Appendices

Phase 3: Oral Presentation

Specific separate guidelines on the oral presentation will be provided.

chapter 2

Business Ethics and Social Responsibility

OBJECTIVES

After reading this chapter, you will be able to:

- Define business ethics and social responsibility and examine their importance.

- Detect some of the ethical issues that may arise in business.

- Specify how businesses can promote ethical behavior.

- Explain the four dimensions of social responsibility.

- Debate an organization's social responsibilities to owners, employees, consumers, the environment, and the community.

- Evaluate the ethics of a business's decision.

The Ethics and Social Responsibility of Collegiate Sports Marketing

The National Collegiate Athletic Association (NCAA) is a governing body that creates rules meant to protect student-athletes and their colleges. For example, an enrolled student is not allowed to permit an agent to pursue professional engagements on the student's behalf. Students are also forbidden to accept money from agents or marketers. Additionally, advertisers/marketers are forbidden to pay to use student-athlete images, unless the usage is sanctioned by the NCAA. Students and colleges that break these rules face consequences from the NCAA.

Some college athletics departments have had trouble adhering to these guidelines. In 2006, University of Southern California (USC) football player Reggie Bush was accused of accepting cash and gifts from agents. Bush denied the charges. Former USC basketball coach Tim Floyd resigned after accusations surfaced that alleged Floyd had paid an individual to recruit basketball superstar O. J. Mayo. The NCAA responded by investigating the entire USC athletics program, and USC imposed sanctions on its basketball team.

College athletics also face a threat from outside companies looking to capitalize on their success. Some of these companies create ethical issues for underage students. For example, Anheuser-Busch was recently reprimanded for its Bud Light Fan Can campaign, which featured beer cans

continued

sporting the colors of 26 top teams. The Federal Trade Commission's alcohol attorney, Janet Evan, along with universities such as the University of Michigan and Boston College, argued that the promotion could encourage underage drinking among students. Anheuser-Busch countered that its cans were sold only to customers 21 and over. However, this argument was not enough to alleviate concerns, and Anheuser-Busch finally agreed to stop the program.

Determined to boost revenue, many college and professional sports teams are selling ad placements to the highest bidder, resulting in an overwhelming number of ads in most stadiums. The NCAA has become concerned about whether schools are too willing to compromise their integrity in exchange for marketing dollars. Certainly, colleges should be allowed to promote their teams, but where should the NCAA draw the line? Although it is challenging, and schools and individuals will hit road blocks along the way, behaving ethically and responsibly is the key to maintaining the integrity of schools, teams, and collegiate sports.[1]

Introduction

As the opening vignette illustrates, ethics in sports can be a challenge at most colleges. Any organization, including nonprofits, has to manage the ethical behavior of employees and participants in the overall operations of the organization. Wrongdoing by some businesses has focused public attention and government involvement on encouraging more acceptable business conduct. Any organizational decision may be judged as right or wrong, ethical or unethical, legal or illegal.

In this chapter, we take a look at the role of ethics and social responsibility in business decision making. First we define business ethics and examine why it is important to understand ethics' role in business. Next we explore a number of business ethics issues to help you learn to recognize such issues when they arise. Finally, we consider steps businesses can take to improve ethical behavior in their organizations. The second half of the chapter focuses on social responsibility. We survey some important responsibility issues and detail how companies have responded to them.

Business Ethics and Social Responsibility

business ethics
principles and standards that determine acceptable conduct in business

In this chapter, we define **business ethics** as the principles and standards that determine acceptable conduct in business organizations. The acceptability of behavior in business is determined by not only the organization but also stakeholders such as customers, competitors, government regulators, interest groups, and the public, as well as each individual's personal moral principles and values. The publicity and debate surrounding highly visible legal and ethical lapses at a number of well-known firms, including AIG, Countrywide Financial, and Fannie Mae, highlight the need for businesses to integrate ethics and responsibility into all business decisions. The most recent global financial crisis took a toll on consumer trust of financial services companies. Words used to describe these companies in a survey conducted by Lightspeed Research and Cohn & Wolfe were "greedy," "impersonal," "opportunistic," and "distant."[2] Most unethical activities within organizations are supported by an organizational culture that encourages employees to bend the rules.

Inflating earnings involves attempting to embellish or enhance a firm's profitability in a manner that is inconsistent with past practice, common regulatory guidelines, or industry practice. Many companies maintain a focus on making short-term profits and know that analysts and investors critique the company according to its ability to "make the numbers." PricewaterhouseCoopers (PWC) was forced to pay $97.5 million to settle a class-action lawsuit for involvement with AIG in overstating its earnings. This settlement is a small part of a larger case against both AIG and its former chief executive officer (CEO), Hank Greenberg. AIG's improper accounting for reinsurance and other dealings led to a restatement of earnings in the amount of $3.9 billion.[3]

Many consumers and social advocates believe that businesses should not only make a profit but also consider the social implications of their activities. We define **social responsibility** as a business's obligation to maximize its positive impact and minimize its negative impact on society. Although many people use the terms *social responsibility* and *ethics* interchangeably, they do not mean the same thing. Business ethics relates to an *individual's* or a *work group's* decisions that society evaluates as right or wrong, whereas social responsibility is a broader concept that concerns the impact of the *entire business's* activities on society. From an ethical perspective, for example, we may be concerned about a health care organization overcharging the government for Medicare services. From a social responsibility perspective, we might be concerned about the impact that this overcharging will have on the ability of the health care system to provide adequate services for all citizens. Even a company as well-known as Johnson & Johnson (J&J) is not immune from ethical misconduct accusations. The U.S. Justice Department charged the company with paying millions of dollars in kickbacks to a nursing home pharmacy company in order to boost sales of J&J drugs to nursing home patients. Under the kickback arrangement, the pharmacy company was accused of tripling its purchases of J&J drugs.[4]

The most basic ethical and social responsibility concerns have been codified by laws and regulations that encourage businesses to conform to society's standards, values, and attitudes. For example, after accounting scandals at a number of well-known firms in the early 2000s shook public confidence in the integrity of corporate America, the reputations of every U.S. company suffered regardless of their association with the scandals.[5] To help restore confidence in corporations and markets, Congress passed the Sarbanes-Oxley Act, which criminalized securities fraud and stiffened penalties for corporate fraud. At a minimum, managers are expected to obey all laws and regulations. Most legal issues arise as choices that society deems unethical, irresponsible, or otherwise unacceptable. However, all actions deemed unethical by society are not necessarily illegal, and both legal and ethical concerns change over time (see Table 2.1). Business law refers to the laws and regulations that govern the conduct of business. Many problems and conflicts in business can be avoided if owners, managers, and employees know more about business law and the legal system. Business ethics, social responsibility, and laws together act as a compliance system, requiring that businesses and employees act responsibly in society. In this chapter, we explore ethics and social responsibility; Appendix A addresses business law, including the Sarbanes-Oxley Act.

social responsibility
a business's obligation to maximize its positive impact and minimize its negative impact on society

TABLE 2.1   A Timeline of Ethical and Socially Responsible Concerns

1960s	1970s	1980s	1990s	2000s
• Environmental issues • Civil rights issues • Increased employee-employer tension • Honesty • Changing work ethic • Rising drug use	• Employee militancy • Human rights issues • Covering up rather than correcting issues • Discrimination • Harassment	• Bribes and illegal contracting practices • Influence peddling • Deceptive advertising • Financial fraud (e.g., savings and loan scandal) • Transparency issues	• Sweatshops and unsafe working conditions in third-world countries • Rising corporate liability for personal damages (e.g., cigarette companies) • Financial mismanagement and fraud • Formalizing business ethics	• Employee benefits • Privacy issues • Financial mismanagement • Intellectual property theft • Responsible consumption • The role of business in promoting sustainable development

Source: Adapted from "Business Ethics Timeline," Copyright © 2003, *Ethics Resource Center* (n.d.), www.ethics.org, updated 2010. Used with permission.

The Role of Ethics in Business

You have only to pick up *The Wall Street Journal* or *USA Today* to see examples of the growing concern about legal and ethical issues in business. For example, some of the recording industry's major labels are facing a large antitrust suit, which was reinstated by a federal appeals court in 2009 after first being filed in 2005. The suit claims that the record labels conspired to fix prices at an artificially high level for MP3 downloads. The record labels were allegedly able to do this because they controlled a majority of the industry.[6] Regardless of what an individual believes about a particular action, if society judges it to be unethical or wrong, whether correctly or not, that judgment directly affects the organization's ability to achieve its business goals.[7]

In 2009, Wall Street financier Bernie Madoff pleaded guilty to defrauding hundreds of investors out of more than $50 billion. How did he, and his employees, manage to deceive so many investors for so many years?

Well-publicized incidents of unethical and illegal activity—ranging from accounting fraud to using the Internet to steal another person's credit-card number, from deceptive advertising of food and diet products to unfair competitive practices in the computer software industry—strengthen the public's perceptions that ethical standards and the level of trust in business need to be raised. Author David Callahan has commented, "Americans who wouldn't so much as shoplift a pack of chewing gum are committing felonies at tax time, betraying the trust of their patients, misleading investors, ripping off their insurance companies, lying to their clients, and much more."[8] Often, such charges start as ethical conflicts but evolve into legal disputes when cooperative conflict resolution cannot be accomplished. Headline-grabbing scandals like those associated with executive compensation and benefits packages create ethical concerns. In the United States, Charles O. Prince III, former CEO of Citigroup; Stanley O'Neal, former CEO of Merrill Lynch; and Angelo Mozilo, founder and former CEO of Countrywide Financial, rejected suggestions that they reaped lavish compensation packages while engaging in highly risky subprime lending associated with an international financial crisis. While O'Neal was fired for Merrill Lynch's poor performance, he was given a $161 million severance package on top of the $70 million he earned during four years as CEO.[9]

However, it is important to understand that business ethics goes beyond legal issues. Ethical conduct builds trust among individuals and in business relationships, which validates and promotes confidence in business relationships. Establishing trust and confidence is much more difficult in organizations that have reputations for acting unethically. If you were to discover, for example, that a manager had misled you about company benefits when you were hired, your trust and confidence in that company would probably diminish. And if you learned that a colleague had lied to you about something, you probably would not trust or rely on that person in the future.

Ethical issues are not limited to for-profit organizations either. Ethical issues include all areas of organizational activities, including government. In government, several politicians and some high-ranking officials have been forced to resign in disgrace over ethical indiscretions. Illinois governor Rod Blagojevich was arrested on December 9, 2008, after wiretaps on Blagojevich's phone revealed strong evidence that he was attempting to sell former Illinois Senator Barack Obama's Senate seat after Obama was elected to the presidency. The Illinois Senate unanimously voted to impeach Blagojevich, who left his role as governor in disgrace. Blagojevich still maintains his innocence.[10] Even sports can be subject to ethical lapses as indicated in the opening feature in this chapter. At many universities, for example, coaches and athletic administrators have been put on administrative leave after allegations of improper recruiting practices came to light. After Tiger Woods's marital infidelity scandal broke, he was dropped by a number of major sponsors including Gatorade, AT&T, Gillette, and Tag Heuer. A match-fixing scandal in European soccer also exposed widespread unethical behavior. A betting syndicate was suspected of fixing matches in 17 different countries. A number of players came forward and admitted their role in the scandal, helping to shine a light on the unethical and illegal practice.[11] Thus, whether made in science, politics, sports, or business, most decisions are judged as right or wrong, ethical or unethical. Negative judgments can affect an organization's ability to build relationships with customers and suppliers, attract investors, and retain employees.[12]

Although we will not tell you in this chapter what you ought to do, others—your superiors, co-workers, and family—will make judgments about the ethics of your actions and decisions. Learning how to recognize and resolve ethical issues is an important step in evaluating ethical decisions in business.

Recognizing Ethical Issues in Business

Learning to recognize ethical issues is the most important step in understanding business ethics. An **ethical issue** is an identifiable problem, situation, or opportunity that requires a person to choose from among several actions that may be evaluated as right or wrong, ethical or unethical. In business, such a choice often involves weighing monetary profit against what a person considers appropriate

ethical issue
an identifiable problem, situation, or opportunity that requires a person to choose from among several actions that may be evaluated as right or wrong, ethical or unethical

Nobody likes a cheater, not even in the sports business. Although Mark McGwire broke baseball's home run record in 1998, he later admitted to taking steroids.

conduct. The best way to judge the ethics of a decision is to look at a situation from a customer's or competitor's viewpoint: Should liquid-diet manufacturers make unsubstantiated claims about their products? Should an engineer agree to divulge her former employer's trade secrets to ensure that she gets a better job with a competitor? Should a salesperson omit facts about a product's poor safety record in his presentation to a customer? Such questions require the decision maker to evaluate the ethics of his or her choice.

Many business issues may seem straightforward and easy to resolve on the surface, but are in reality very complex. A person often needs several years of experience in business to understand what is acceptable or ethical. For example, if you are a salesperson, when does offering a gift—such as season basketball tickets—to a customer become a bribe rather than just a sales practice? Clearly, there are no easy answers to such a question. But the size of the transaction, the history of personal relationships within the particular company, as well as many other factors may determine whether an action will be judged as right or wrong by others. Companies across the United States are starting to prevent access to Internet-video services at work. At issue is the theft of time by employees, who use online social networking sites for an hour on average each workday.[13] Another issue is the use of company resources to provide personal internet access.

Ethics is also related to the culture in which a business operates. In the United States, for example, it would be inappropriate for a businessperson to bring an elaborately wrapped gift to a prospective client on their first meeting—the gift could

Behaviors	2009	2007
Company resource abuse	23%	n/a
Abusive behavior	22	21%
Lying to employees	19	20
Email or Internet abuse	18	18
Conflicts of interest	16	22
Discrimination	14	12
Lying to outside stakeholders	12	14
Employee benefit violations	11	n/a
Health or safety violations	11	15
Employee privacy breach	10	n/a
Improper hiring practices	10	10
Falsifying time or expenses	10	n/a

TABLE 2.2

Percentage of U.S. Workforce Observing Specific Forms of Misconduct, 2007–2009

Source: Ethics Resource Center. *2009 National Business Ethics Survey: Business in the Recession*, *www.ethics.org*, p. 32.

be viewed as a bribe. In Japan, however, it is considered impolite *not* to bring a gift. Experience with the culture in which a business operates is critical to understanding what is ethical or unethical.

To help you understand ethical issues that perplex businesspeople today, we will take a brief look at some of them in this section. Ethical issues can be more complex now than in the past. The vast number of news-format investigative programs has increased consumer and employee awareness of organizational misconduct. In addition, the multitude of cable channels and Internet resources has improved the awareness of ethical problems among the general public. The National Business Ethics Survey found that workers witness many instances of ethical misconduct in their organizations (see Table 2.2).

One of the principal causes of unethical behavior in organizations is overly aggressive financial or business objectives. Many of these issues relate to decisions and concerns that managers have to deal with daily. It is not possible to discuss every issue, of course. However, a discussion of a few issues can help you begin to recognize the ethical problems with which businesspersons must deal. Many ethical issues in business can be categorized in the context of their relation with abusive and intimidating behavior, conflicts of interest, fairness and honesty, communications, misuse of company resources, and business associations.

Misuse of Company Resources.   Misuse of company resources has been identified by the Ethics Resource Center as the leading issue in observed misconduct in organizations (see Table 2.2). Other top issues are abusive behavior and lying to employees. Misconduct can range from firing workers for excessive use of e-mail at work to unauthorized use of equipment and computer systems to embezzling of company funds. In the retail area, internal employee theft is a much larger problem than consumer shoplifting. Time theft costs can be difficult to measure but are estimated to cost companies hundreds of billions of dollars annually. It is widely believed that the average employee "steals" 4.5 hours a week with late arrivals, leaving early, long lunch breaks, inappropriate sick days, excessive socializing, and engaging in personal activities such as online shopping and watching sports while on the job.

All of these activities add up to lost productivity and profits for the employer—and relate to ethical issues in the area of abusing company resources.

Because misuse of company resources is such a widespread problem, many companies, like Boeing, have implemented official policies delineating acceptable use of company resources. Boeing's policy states that use of company resources is acceptable when it does not result in "significant added costs, disruption of business processes, or any other disadvantage to the company."[14] The policy further states that use of company resources for noncompany purposes is only acceptable when an employee receives explicit permission to do so. This kind of policy is in line with that of many companies, particularly large ones that can easily lose millions of dollars and thousands of hours of productivity to these activities.

Abusive and Intimidating Behavior.

Abusive or intimidating behavior is the second most common ethical problem for employees. These concepts can mean anything from physical threats, false accusations, profanity, insults, yelling, harshness, and unreasonableness to ignoring someone or simply being annoying; and the meaning of these words can differ by person—you probably have some ideas of your own. Abusive behavior can be placed on a continuum from a minor distraction to a disruption of the workplace. For example, what one person may define as yelling might be another's definition of normal speech. Civility in our society is a concern, and the workplace is no exception. The productivity level of many organizations has been diminished by the time spent unraveling abusive relationships.

Abusive behavior is difficult to assess and manage because of diversity in culture and lifestyle. What does it mean to speak profanely? Is profanity only related to specific words or other such terms that are common in today's business world? If you are using words that are normal in your language but that others consider to be profanity, have you just insulted, abused, or disrespected them?

Within the concept of abusive behavior, intent should be a consideration. If the employee was trying to convey a compliment but the comment was considered abusive, then it was probably a mistake. The way a word is said (voice inflection) can be important. Add to this the fact that we now live in a multicultural environment—doing business and working with many different cultural groups—and the businessperson soon realizes the depth of the ethical and legal issues that may arise. There are problems of word meanings by age and within cultures. For example, an expression such as "Did you guys hook up last night?" can have various meanings, including some that could be considered offensive in a work environment.

Bullying is associated with a hostile workplace when a person or group is targeted and is threatened, harassed, belittled, verbally abused, or overly criticized. Bullying may create what some consider a hostile environment, a term generally

When Coby Brooks, the CEO of Hooters, went undercover in his own company on Undercover Boss, *he discovered on national television that one of his restaurant managers was acting abusively toward employees.*

	TABLE 2.3
1. Spreading rumors to damage others	**Actions Associated with Bullies**
2. Blocking others' communication in the workplace	
3. Flaunting status or authority to take advantage of others	
4. Discrediting others ideas and opinions	
5. Use of e-mails to demean others	
6. Failing to communicate or return communication	
7. Insults, yelling, and shouting	
8. Using terminology to discriminate by gender, race, or age	
9. Using eye or body language to hurt others or their reputation	
10. Taking credit for others' work or ideas	

Source: © O. C. Ferrell, 2010.

associated with sexual harassment. Although sexual harassment has legal recourse, bullying has little legal recourse at this time. Bullying is a widespread problem in the United States, and can cause psychological damage that can result in health endangering consequences to the target. A survey by the Workplace Bullying Institute found that "37% of U.S. workers have been bullied, that is, 54 million Americans."[15] Another 12 percent of workers have witnessed bullying. As Table 2.3 indicates, bullying can use a mix of verbal, nonverbal, and manipulative threatening expressions to damage workplace productivity. One may wonder why workers tolerate such activities. The problem is that 81 percent of workplace bullies are supervisors. A top officer at Boeing cited an employee survey indicating 26 percent had observed abusive or intimidating behavior by management.[16]

Conflict of Interest.   A conflict of interest, the most common ethical issue identified by employees, exists when a person must choose whether to advance his or her own personal interests or those of others. For example, a manager in a corporation is supposed to ensure that the company is profitable so that its stockholder-owners receive a return on their investment. In other words, the manager has a responsibility to investors. If she instead makes decisions that give her more power or money but do not help the company, then she has a conflict of interest—she is acting to benefit herself at the expense of her company and is not fulfilling her responsibilities as an employee. To avoid conflicts of interest, employees must be able to separate their personal financial interests from their business dealings. In the wake of the 2008 meltdown on Wall Street, stakeholders and legislators pushed for reform of the credit rating industry. Many cited rampant conflicts of interest between financial firms and the companies that rate them as part of the reason no one recognized the impending financial disaster. Conflict of interest has long been a serious problem in the financial industry because the financial companies pay the credit raters money in order to be rated. Because different rating companies exist, financial firms can also shop around for the best rating. There is no third-party mediator who oversees the financial industry and how firms are rated.[17]

As mentioned earlier, it is considered improper to give or accept **bribes**— payments, gifts, or special favors intended to influence the outcome of a decision. A bribe is a conflict of interest because it benefits an individual at the expense of an organization or society. Companies that do business overseas should be aware that bribes are a significant ethical issue and are, in fact, illegal in many countries. For example, U.S. federal agents exposed a bribery sting involving international

bribes
payments, gifts, or special favors intended to influence the outcome of a decision

Rank	Country	CPI Score[*]
1	New Zealand	9.4
2	Denmark	9.3
3	Singapore/Sweden	9.2
5	Switzerland	9.0
6	Finland/Netherlands	8.9
8	Australia/Canada/Iceland	8.7
11	Norway	8.6
12	Hong Kong/Luxembourg	8.2
14	Germany/Ireland	8.0
16	Austria	7.9
17	Japan/United Kingdom	7.7
19	United States	7.5
20	Barbados	7.4

TABLE 2.4

Least Corrupt Countries

[*]CPI score relates to perceptions of the degree of corruption as seen by businesspeople and country analysts, and ranges between 10 (highly transparent) and 0 (highly corrupt).

Source: "Corruption Perceptions Index 2009," Transparency International, http://www.transparency.org/policy_research/surveys_indices/cpi/2009/cpi_2009_table (accessed January 22, 2010).

arms dealers and foreign officials using a sting set-up at an arms-dealer gathering in Las Vegas. FBI agents posed as representatives of a senior government minister of an African nation to uncover the illegal bribes. Under the proposed deal, several arms companies would pay 20 percent "commissions" to the fake officials in order to gain business selling weapons. The deal that exposed the bribes was reported to have been worth $15 million in pistols, tear gas launchers, bulletproof vests, and other supplies. Among those arrested was an employee of Smith & Wesson and a former Secret Service agent. The sting took four years to orchestrate and was the FBI's largest foreign bribery case invoking the Foreign Corrupt Practices Act.[18] While bribery is an increasing issue in many countries, it is more prevalent in some countries than in others. Transparency International has developed a Corruption Perceptions Index (Table 2.4). Note that there are 18 countries perceived as less corrupt than the United States.[19]

Fairness and Honesty.   Fairness and honesty are at the heart of business ethics and relate to the general values of decision makers. At a minimum, business persons are expected to follow all applicable laws and regulations. But beyond obeying the law, they are expected not to harm customers, employees, clients, or competitors knowingly through deception, misrepresentation, coercion, or discrimination. Honesty and fairness can relate to how the employees use the resources of the organization. Most employees do not feel guilty about taking office supplies for personal use. Out of the 19 percent that reported taking office supplies, only 22 percent said they felt guilty or regretful about the theft. Although the majority of office supply thefts involve small things such as pencils or Post-it Notes, 8 percent of workers admitted to stealing more expensive equipment such as laptops, PDAs, and cell phones, a 5 percent increase from the year before.[20] Employees should be aware of policies on taking items and recognize how these decisions relate to ethical behavior. Figure 2.1 provides an overview of the most pilfered office supplies.

Many people felt like Toyota wasn't honest with consumers about its vehicles' accelerator problem—a problem that led to a massive recall of the company's automobiles in 2010 and a public-relations nightmare.

One aspect of fairness relates to competition. Although numerous laws have been passed to foster competition and make monopolistic practices illegal, companies sometimes gain control over markets by using questionable practices that harm competition. Bullying can also occur between companies that are intense competitors. Even respected companies such as Intel have been accused of monopolistic bullying. A competitor, Advanced Micro Devices (AMD), claimed in a lawsuit that 38 companies, including Dell and Sony, were strong-arming customers (such as Apple) into buying Intel chips rather than those marketed by AMD. In many cases,

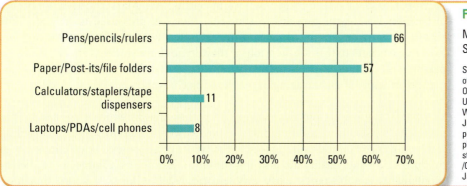

FIGURE 2.1

Most Popular Office Supplies Employees Pilfer

Source: "Nearly 20 Percent of U.S. Workers Have Taken Office Supplies for Personal Use, Despite Most Feeling It Is Wrong to Do So," *PR Newswire,* June 10, 2008, http://www2.prnewswire.com/cgi-bin/stories.pl?ACCT=104&STORY=/www/story/06-10-2008/0004829858&EDATE= (accessed January 22, 2010).

the alleged misconduct can have not only monetary and legal implications but can threaten reputation, investor confidence, and customer loyalty. A front-cover *Forbes* headline stated "Intel to ADM: Drop Dead." The intensely competitive atmosphere and Intel's ability to use its large size won it the high-profile Apple account, displacing IBM and Freescale. ADM claims it had no opportunity to bid because Intel had offered to deploy 600 Indian engineers to help Apple software run more smoothly on Intel chips.[21] Intel agreed to pay AMD $1.25 billion to settle the 2005 lawsuit. However, this did not represent the end of Intel's antitrust problems. Even the U.S. Federal Trade Commission has joined in on the antitrust accusations against Intel. The FTC alleged that Intel used illegal inducements and threats of retaliation to discourage computer makers from buying competitor AMD's chips.[22] These multiple allegations may amount to years of legal battles and billions in fines for the company, if found guilty of all charges.

Another aspect of fairness and honesty relates to disclosure of potential harm caused by product use. For example, many stakeholder groups have become increasingly concerned about the health effects of additives in food and manufactured products. The widespread use of plastic products have caused a number of stakeholder groups to raise questions about possible health problems associated with additives like Bisphenol A (BPA), which is suspected of causing health problems in infants and children. Many businesses, however, continue to include BPA in their products until research proves more conclusive on whether it is harmful.[23] While it is not mandatory to disclose whether a product contains BPA, some companies have turned a potential problem into a competitive advantage by labeling their BPA-free products to ease the fears of consumers.

Dishonesty has become a significant problem in the United States. A survey of nearly 25,000 high school students revealed that 64 percent of the students admitted to cheating on an exam at least once, 36 percent confessed to copying documents from the Internet, and 28 percent admitted to shoplifting.[24] If today's students are tomorrow's leaders, there is likely to be a correlation between acceptable behavior today and tomorrow. This adds to the argument that the leaders of today must be prepared for the ethical risks associated with this downward trend. According to a poll by Deloitte and Touche of teenagers aged 13 to 18, when asked if people who practice good business ethics are more successful than those who don't, 69 percent of teenagers agreed.[25] The same poll found only 12 percent of teens think business leaders today are ethical. On the other hand, another survey indicated that many students do not define copying answers from another students' paper or downloading music or content for classroom work as cheating.[26]

Even schoolteachers, who many expect to teach students ethical behavior, feel pressured to cheat. At a charter school in Springfield, Massachusetts, a number of teachers have come forward to state that they feel pressured to help students cheat. The growing emphasis on improving students' standardized test scores has led some teachers to fear for their jobs if they do not have students cheat in order to pass the tests. Other teachers at the school alleged that they were fired after accusing the principal of encouraging or overlooking cheating.[27]

Communications.   Communications is another area in which ethical concerns may arise. False and misleading advertising, as well as deceptive personal-selling tactics, anger consumers and can lead to the failure of a business. Truthfulness about product safety and quality are also important to consumers. Claims about dietary supplements can be particularly problematic. VMG Global, a sports nutrition

Consider Ethics and Social Responsibility
Bernard Madoff Pulls Off the Largest Ponzi Scheme Ever

In 2009, billionaire Bernie Madoff exchanged his $7 million penthouse for a prison cell. He pleaded guilty of operating a $65 billion fraudulent Ponzi scheme for decades. Madoff promised investors steady returns of 10 to 12 percent on their investments, no matter how the market was faring—earning him thousands of loyal investors. However, Madoff never invested the money. He used new clients' deposits to pay off older investors as well as to fund his family's lavish lifestyle. Ponzi schemes work well until money stops rolling in, but they always collapse when new funds dry up. Madoff's scam is unique in that it lasted nearly two decades.

Then the inevitable happened: new investors began dwindling. The situation quickly deteriorated with the worsening economic situation in late 2008. On December 11, 2009, Madoff admitted his guilt to his sons. The sons turned their father over to the authorities, but the damage was already catastrophic. Some investors, many of them retirees or charitable institutions, lost their entire investment.

Madoff's scam resulted in the loss of $65 billion, 16,000 claims for losses, and even a awsuit against the Securities and Exchange Commission (SEC). Many questioned why the SEC had not detected the scam despite numerous red flags. The organization had investigated Madoff many times over the years, but never uncovered any wrongdoing. As a result, some investors sued the SEC for negligence, the first time investors have sued a regulatory agency. No matter where the fault lies, officials agree that new safeguards will be necessary to prevent similar crimes in the future.[30]

Discussion Questions

1. Why did Bernard Madoff engage in such purposeful misconduct?
2. How would you describe how a Ponzi scheme works?
3. How can an individual avoid being a victim of a Ponzi scheme?

company, pleaded guilty to illegally putting steroids in two of its body-building supplements. For four years, the company knowingly spiked Tren Xtreme and Mass Xtreme, products that generated more than $5.6 million in revenue for the company. The company agreed to pay $500,000 in penalties and destroy all remaining inventory of the products.[28]

Some companies fail to provide enough information for consumers about differences or similarities between products. For example, driven by high prices for medicines, many consumers are turning to Canadian, Mexican, and overseas Internet sources for drugs to treat a variety of illnesses and conditions. However, research suggests that a significant percentage of these imported pharmaceuticals may not actually contain the labeled drug, and the counterfeit drugs could even be harmful to those who take them.[29]

Another important aspect of communications that may raise ethical concerns relates to product labeling. The U.S. Surgeon General currently requires cigarette manufacturers to indicate clearly on cigarette packaging that smoking cigarettes is harmful to the smoker's health. In Europe, at least 30 percent of the front side of product packaging and 40 percent of the back needs to be taken up by the warning. The use of descriptors such as "light" or "mild" has been banned.[31] However, labeling of other products raises ethical questions when it threatens basic rights, such as freedom of speech and expression. This is the heart of the controversy surrounding the movement to require warning labels on movies and videogames, rating their content, language, and appropriate audience age. Although people in the entertainment industry claim that such labeling violates their First Amendment right to freedom of expression, other consumers—particularly parents—believe that labeling is needed to protect children from harmful influences. Similarly, alcoholic beverage and cigarette manufacturers have argued that a total ban on cigarette and alcohol advertisements violates the First Amendment. Internet regulation, particularly that designed to protect children and the elderly, is on the forefront in consumer protection legislation. Because of the debate surrounding the acceptability of these business activities, they remain major ethical issues.

Business Relationships.   The behavior of businesspersons toward customers, suppliers, and others in their workplace may also generate ethical concerns. Ethical behavior within a business involves keeping company secrets, meeting obligations and responsibilities, and avoiding undue pressure that may force others to act unethically.

Managers in particular, because of the authority of their position, have the opportunity to influence employees' actions. For example, a manager might influence employees to use pirated computer software to save costs. The use of illegal software puts the employee and the company at legal risk, but employees may feel pressured to do so by their superior's authority. The National Business Ethics Survey found that employees who feel pressure to compromise ethical standards view top and middle managers as the greatest source of such pressure.[32]

It is the responsibility of managers to create a work environment that helps the organization achieve its objectives and fulfill its responsibilities. However, the methods that managers use to enforce these responsibilities should not compromise employee rights. Organizational pressures may encourage a person to engage in activities that he or she might otherwise view as unethical, such as invading others' privacy or stealing a competitor's secrets. The firm may provide only vague or lax supervision on ethical issues, creating the opportunity for misconduct. Managers who offer no ethical direction to employees create many opportunities for manipulation, dishonesty, and conflicts of interest.

plagiarism
the act of taking someone else's work and presenting it as your own without mentioning the source

Plagiarism—taking someone else's work and presenting it as your own without mentioning the source—is another ethical issue. As a student, you may be familiar with plagiarism in school; for example, copying someone else's term paper or quoting from a published work or Internet source without acknowledging it. In business, an ethical issue arises when an employee copies reports or takes the work or ideas of others and presents it as his or her own. A manager attempting to take credit for a subordinate's ideas is engaging in another type of plagiarism.

Making Decisions about Ethical Issues

Although we've presented a variety of ethical issues that may arise in business, it can be difficult to recognize specific ethical issues in practice. Whether a decision maker recognizes an issue as an ethical one often depends on the issue itself. Managers, for example, tend to be more concerned about issues that affect those close to them, as well as issues that have immediate rather than long-term consequences. Thus, the perceived importance of an ethical issue substantially affects choices. However, only a few issues receive scrutiny, and most receive no attention at all.[33]

Table 2.5 lists some questions you may want to ask yourself and others when trying to determine whether an action is ethical. Open discussion of ethical issues does not eliminate ethical problems, but it does promote both trust and learning in an organization.[34] When people feel that they cannot discuss what they are doing with their co-workers or superiors, there is a good chance that an ethical issue exists. Once a person has recognized an ethical issue and can openly discuss it with others, he or she has begun the process of resolving that issue.

Are there any potential legal restrictions or violations that could result from the action?
Does your company have a specific code of ethics or policy on the action?
Is this activity customary in your industry? Are there any industry trade groups that provide guidelines or codes of conduct that address this issue?
Would this activity be accepted by your co-workers? Will your decision or action withstand open discussion with co-workers and managers and survive untarnished?
How does this activity fit with your own beliefs and values?

TABLE 2.5
Questions to Consider in Determining Whether an Action Is Ethical

Improving Ethical Behavior in Business

Understanding how people make ethical choices and what prompts a person to act unethically may reverse the current trend toward unethical behavior in business. Ethical decisions in an organization are influenced by three key factors: individual moral standards, the influence of managers and co-workers, and the opportunity to engage in misconduct (Figure 2.2). While you have great control over your personal ethics outside the workplace, your co-workers and superiors exert significant control over your choices at work through authority and example. In fact, the activities and examples set by co-workers, along with rules and policies established by the firm, are critical in gaining consistent ethical compliance in an organization. If the company fails to provide good examples and direction for appropriate conduct, confusion and conflict will develop and result in the opportunity for misconduct. If your boss or co-workers leave work early, you may be tempted to do so as well. If you see co-workers engaged in personal activities such as shopping online or watching YouTube, then you may be more likely to do so also. In addition, having sound personal values contributes to an ethical workplace.

Because ethical issues often emerge from conflict, it is useful to examine the causes of ethical conflict. Business managers and employees often experience some tension between their own ethical beliefs and their obligations to the organizations in which they work. Many employees utilize different ethical standards at work than they do at home. This conflict increases when employees feel that their company is encouraging unethical conduct or exerting pressure on them to engage in it.

It is difficult for employees to determine what conduct is acceptable within a company if the firm does not have established ethics policies and standards. And without such policies and standards, employees may base decisions on how their peers and superiors behave. Professional **codes of ethics** are formalized rules and standards that describe what the company expects of its employees. Codes of ethics do not have to be so detailed that they take into account every situation, but they should provide guidelines and principles that can help employees achieve organizational objectives and address risks in an acceptable and ethical way. The development of a code of ethics should include not only a firm's executives and board of

codes of ethics formalized rules and standards that describe what a company expects of its employees

Individual Standards and Values + Managers' and Co-workers' Influence + Opportunity: Codes and Compliance Requirements = Ethical/Unethical Choices in Business

FIGURE 2.2
Three Factors That Influence Business Ethics

TABLE 2.6 Key Things to Consider in Developing a Code of Ethics	• Create a team to assist with the process of developing the code (include management and nonmanagement employees from across departments and functions).
	• Solicit input from employees from different departments, functions, and regions to compile a list of common questions and answers to include in the code document.
	• Make certain that the headings of the code sections can be easily understood by all employees.
	• Avoid referencing specific U.S. laws and regulations or those of specific countries, particularly for codes that will be distributed to employees in multiple regions.
	• Hold employee group meetings on a complete draft version (including graphics and pictures) of the text using language that everyone can understand.
	• Inform employees that they will receive a copy of the code during an introduction session.
	• Let all employees know that they will receive future ethics training which will, in part, cover the important information contained in the code document.

Source: Adapted from William Miller, "Implementing an Organizational Code of Ethics," *International Business Ethics Review* 7 (Winter 2004), pp. 1, 6–10.

directors, but also legal staff and employees from all areas of a firm.[35] Table 2.6 lists some key things to consider when developing a code of ethics.

Codes of ethics, policies on ethics, and ethics training programs advance ethical behavior because they prescribe which activities are acceptable and which are not, and they limit the opportunity for misconduct by providing punishments for violations of the rules and standards. Codes and policies on ethics encourage the creation of an ethical culture in the company. According to the National Business Ethics Survey (NBES), employees in organizations that have written codes of conduct and ethics training, ethics offices or hotlines, and systems for reporting are more likely to report misconduct when they observe it. The survey found that a company's ethical culture is the greatest determinant of future misconduct.[36] The enforcement of ethical codes and policies through rewards and punishments increases the acceptance of ethical standards by employees.

One of the most important components of an ethics program is a means through which employees can report observed misconduct anonymously. Although the risk of retaliation is still a major factor in whether an employee will report illegal conduct, the NBES found that whistleblowing has increased in the past few years. Approximately 63 percent of respondents said they reported misconduct when they observed it.[37] **Whistleblowing** occurs when an employee exposes an employer's wrongdoing to outsiders, such as the media or government regulatory agencies. However, more companies are establishing programs to encourage employees to report illegal or unethical practices internally so that they can take steps to remedy problems before they result in legal action or generate negative publicity. Unfortunately, whistleblowers are often treated negatively in organizations. The government seeks to discourage this practice by rewarding firms that encourage employees to report misconduct—with reduced fines and penalties when violations occur. Congress has also taken steps to close a legislative loophole in whistleblowing legislation that has led to the dismissal of many whistleblowers. The law, as it was originally written, did not apply to corporate subsidiaries. This resulted in the dismissal of many whistleblower complaints, who then faced the repercussions for their actions. Between 2002 when the law was passed and 2009, the government ruled in favor of whistleblowers in only 21 out of 1,455 complaints. An additional 996 cases were

whistleblowing

the act of an employee exposing an employer's wrongdoing to outsiders, such as the media or government regulatory agencies

dismissed because of the aforementioned technicality. The hope is that making it more difficult to fire or retaliate against whistleblowers will encourage more people to come forward with information regarding corporate misconduct.[38]

The current trend is to move away from legally based ethical initiatives in organizations to cultural- or integrity-based initiatives that make ethics a part of core organizational values. Organizations recognize that effective business ethics programs are good for business performance. Firms that develop higher levels of trust function more efficiently and effectively and avoid damaged company reputations and product images. Organizational ethics initiatives have been supportive of many positive and diverse organizational objectives, such as profit-

Sherron Watkins, Colleen Rowley, and Cynthia Cooper (left to right) jeopardized their careers by blowing the whistle on Enron, the FBI, and WorldCom, respectively. They later ended up on the cover of Time after being named the magazine's 2002 "Persons of the Year."

ability, hiring, employee satisfaction, and customer loyalty.[39] Conversely, lack of organizational ethics initiatives and the absence of workplace values such as honesty, trust, and integrity can have a negative impact on organizational objectives and employee retention. According to one report on employee loyalty and work practices, 79 percent of employees who questioned their bosses' integrity indicated that they felt uncommitted or were likely to quit soon.[40]

The Nature of Social Responsibility

There are four dimensions of social responsibility: economic, legal, ethical, and voluntary (including philanthropic) (Figure 2.3).[41] Earning profits is the economic foundation of the pyramid in Figure 2.3, and complying with the law is the next step. However a business whose *sole* objective is to maximize profits is not likely to consider its social responsibility, although its activities will probably be legal. (We looked at ethical responsibilities in the first half of this chapter.) Finally, voluntary responsibilities are additional activities that may not be required but which promote human welfare or goodwill. Legal and economic concerns have long been acknowledged in business, but voluntary and ethical issues are more recent concerns.

Corporate citizenship is the extent to which businesses meet the legal, ethical, economic, and voluntary responsibilities placed on them by their various stakeholders. It involves the activities and organizational processes adopted by businesses to meet their social responsibilities. A commitment to corporate citizenship by a firm indicates a strategic focus on fulfilling the social responsibilities expected of it by its stakeholders. Corporate citizenship involves action and measurement of the extent to which a firm embraces the corporate citizenship philosophy and then follows through by implementing citizenship and social responsibility initiatives. One of the major corporate citizenship issues is the focus on preserving the environment. Consumers, governments, and special interest groups such as The Nature Conservancy are concerned about greenhouse gases and CO_2 carbon emissions that are contributing to global warming. The majority of people agree that climate change

corporate citizenship
the extent to which businesses meet the legal, ethical, economic, and voluntary responsibilities placed on them by their stakeholders

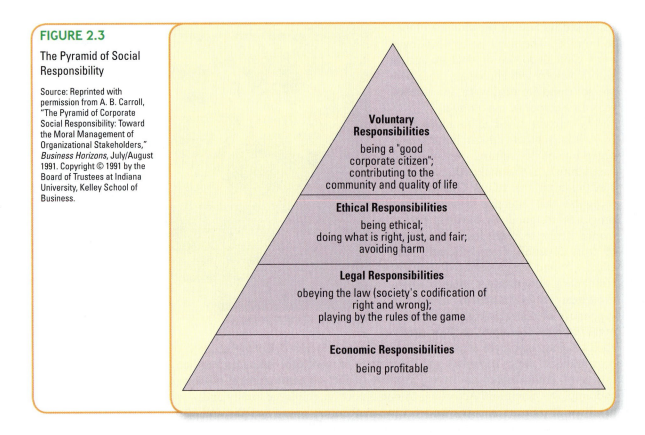

FIGURE 2.3

The Pyramid of Social Responsibility

Source: Reprinted with permission from A. B. Carroll, "The Pyramid of Corporate Social Responsibility: Toward the Moral Management of Organizational Stakeholders," *Business Horizons*, July/August 1991. Copyright © 1991 by the Board of Trustees at Indiana University, Kelley School of Business.

is a global emergency, but there is not agreement on how to solve the problem.[42] Another example of a corporate citizenship issue might be animal rights—an issue that is important to many stakeholders. As the organic and local foods movements grow and become more profitable, more and more stakeholders are calling for more humane practices in factory farms as well.[43] Large factory farms are where most Americans get their meat, but some businesses are looking at more animal-friendly options in response to public outcry.

Part of the answer to this crisis is alternative energy such as solar, wind, bio-fuels, and hydro applications. The American Solar Energy Society estimates that the number of "green" jobs could rise to 40 million by 2030.[44] The drive for alternative fuels such as ethanol from corn has added new issues such as food price increases and food shortages. More than 2 billion consumers earn less than $2 a day in wages. Sharply increased food costs has led to riots and government policies to restrict trade in basic commodities such as rice, corn, and soybeans.[45]

To respond to these developments, most companies are introducing eco-friendly products and marketing efforts. Even Walmart is taking advantage of the interest in the environment. The company is developing a new labeling system that shows consumers the carbon output of every product carried in Walmart's stores. Americans as consumers are generally concerned about the environment, but only 47 percent trust companies to tell them the truth in environmental marketing.[46] This is because most businesses are promoting themselves as green-conscious and concerned about the environment without actually making the necessary commitments to environmental health. Even employees feel their employers aren't doing enough to protect

1	Bristol Myers-Squibb	**TABLE 2.7**
2	General Mills, Inc.	Best Corporate Citizens
3	IBM Corp.	
4	Merck & Co., Inc.	
5	HP Co., LP	
6	Cisco Systems, Inc.	
7	Mattel, Inc.	
8	Abbott Laboratories	
9	Kimberly-Clark Corp.	
10	Entergy Corp.	
11	ExxonMobil Corp.	
12	Wisconsin Energy Corp.	
13	Intel Corp.	
14	Procter & Gamble Co.	
15	Hess Corp.	
16	Xerox Corp.	
17	3M Co.	
18	Avon Products, Inc.	
19	Baxter International Inc.	
20	Monsanto Co.	

Source: "CRO's 100 Best Corporate Citizens 2009." *CRO,* http://www.thecro.com/files/
CRO100BestCorporateCitizensList2009.pdf (accessed January 22, 2010).

the environment, with nearly 60 percent feeling that more needs to be to done to reduce, recycle, and support green policies.[47]

Corporate Responsibility Officer (CRO) magazine publishes an annual list of the 100 best American corporate citizens based on service to seven stakeholder groups: stockholders, local communities, minorities, employees, global stakeholders, customers, and the environment. Table 2.7 shows the top 20 from that list.

Although the concept of social responsibility is receiving more and more attention, it is still not universally accepted. Table 2.8 lists some of the arguments for and against social responsibility.

Social Responsibility Issues

As with ethics, managers consider social responsibility on a daily basis. Among the many social issues that managers must consider are their firms' relations with owners and stockholders, employees, consumers, the environment, and the community. For example, Indra Nooyi, CEO of PepsiCo, believes that companies must embrace "purpose," not just for financial results, but also for the imprint they leave on society. She goes on to say that stakeholders, including employees, consumers, and regulators, "will leave no doubt that performance without purpose is not a long-term sustainable formula."[48]

Social responsibility is a dynamic area with issues changing constantly in response to society's demands. There is much evidence that social responsibility is associated with improved business performance. Consumers are refusing to buy from businesses that receive publicity about misconduct. A number of studies have found a direct relationship between social responsibility and profitability, as well as a link that

TABLE 2.8	**For:**		
The Arguments For and Against Social Responsibility	1. Business helped to create many of the social problems that exist today, so it should play a significant role in solving them, especially in the areas of pollution reduction and cleanup.		
	2. Businesses should be more responsible because they have the financial and technical resources to help solve social problems.		
	3. As members of society, businesses should do their fair share to help others.		
	4. Socially responsible decision making by businesses can prevent increased government regulation.		
	5. Social responsibility is necessary to ensure economic survival: If businesses want educated and healthy employees, customers with money to spend, and suppliers with quality goods and services in years to come, they must take steps to help solve the social and environmental problems that exist today.		
	Against:		
	1. It sidetracks managers from the primary goal of business—earning profits. Every dollar donated to social causes or otherwise spent on society's problems is a dollar less for owners and investors.		
	2. Participation in social programs gives businesses greater power, perhaps at the expense of particular segments of society.		
	3. Some people question whether business has the expertise needed to assess and make decisions about social problems.		
	4. Many people believe that social problems are the responsibility of government agencies and officials, who can be held accountable by voters.		

exists between employee commitment and customer loyalty—two major concerns of any firm trying to increase profits.[49] This section highlights a few of the many social responsibility issues that managers face; as managers become aware of and work toward the solution of current social problems, new ones will certainly emerge.

Cosmetic-maker Estee Lauder donates all of the proceeds from its MAC's Viva Glam lipsticks to the MAC AIDS Fund. To get attention for the product line, the firm periodically names new lipstick colors after celebrities like Lady Gaga and signs them up to promote them. "We're not afraid to lend our name to talking about AIDS," says a company spokesperson. "We've been left with the responsibility of being loud about this."

Relations with Owners and Stockholders. Businesses must first be responsible to their owners, who are primarily concerned with earning a profit or a return on their investment in a company. In a small business, this responsibility is fairly easy to fulfill because the owner(s) personally manages the business or knows the managers well. In larger businesses, particularly corporations owned by thousands of stockholders, ensuring responsibility becomes a more difficult task.

A business's obligations to its owners and investors, as well as to the financial community at large, include maintaining proper accounting procedures, providing all relevant information to investors about the current and projected performance of the firm, and protecting the owners' rights and investments. In short, the business must maximize the owners' investment in the firm.

Entrepreneurship in Action
Not Your Typical Grocery Store

Stew Leonard's—a chain of grocery stores

Founded: 1969

Success: Stew Leonard's has been named as one of *Fortune* magazine's "100 Best Companies to Work For" for eight years running.

Stew Leonard's is not your typical grocery store. Dubbed "The Disneyland of Dairy Stores," Stew Leonard's features animatronics, a petting zoo, a milk-processing plant, and more. It all started when founder Stew Leonard was trying to save his family's Connecticut dairy farm, which started out delivering milk locally. Leonard opened his first dairy store in 1969, after delivery stopped being lucrative. Stew Leonard now has four grocery stores with annual sales of about $300 million. Customers love Stew Leonard's for its low prices, quality items, fun and friendly environment, and excellent customer service.

However, it has not always been smooth sailing. In 1993, Stew Leonard was convicted for tax evasion. He served 42 months in jail and repaid the Internal Revenue Service (IRS) . During his time in jail, he was asked (as part of his sentence) to advise troubled business owners in the area—which became a blessing that emerged from his mistake. Both Leonard and the company are now flourishing as one of *Fortune*'s "100 Best Companies to Work For" for eight years and are moving forward with the company motto of "the customer is always right."[51]

Employee Relations.   Another issue of importance to a business is its responsibilities to employees. Without employees, a business cannot carry out its goals. Employees expect businesses to provide a safe workplace, pay them adequately for their work, and keep them informed of what is happening in their company. They want employers to listen to their grievances and treat them fairly. In an effort to make Ford more competitive with foreign car companies, the United Auto Workers union agreed to allow the company to hire new workers at half the pay and with reduced benefits. This was a major concession on the part of the union, but was deemed a necessary step in keeping the company afloat. However, hiring new workers to do the same job as established ones for half the pay can result in dissatisfied employees and low morale.[50]

Congress has passed several laws regulating safety in the workplace, many of which are enforced by the Occupational Safety and Health Administration (OSHA). Labor unions have also made significant contributions to achieving safety in the workplace and improving wages and benefits. Most organizations now recognize that the safety and satisfaction of their employees are critical ingredients in their success, and many strive to go beyond what is legally expected of them. Healthy, satisfied employees also supply more than just labor to their employers. Employers are beginning to realize the importance of obtaining input from even the lowest-level employees to help the company reach its objectives.

A major social responsibility for business is providing equal opportunities for all employees regardless of their sex, age, race, religion, or nationality. Women and minorities have been slighted in the past in terms of education, employment, and advancement opportunities; additionally, many of their needs have not been addressed by business. For example, Outback Steakhouse agreed to pay nearly $1.9 million to settle a class-action lawsuit that alleged sexual discrimination against thousands of its female employees. The suit accused Outback of denying women the best job assignments, which prevented them from gaining the requisite experience to be eligible for upper-level management jobs.[52] Women, who continue to bear most child-rearing responsibilities, often experience conflict between those responsibilities and their duties as employees. Consequently, day care has become a major employment issue for women, and more companies are providing day care facilities as part of their effort to recruit and advance women in the workforce. In addition, companies are considering alternative scheduling such as flex-time and job sharing to accommodate employee concerns. Telecommuting has grown significantly over the past 5 to 10 years as well. Many Americans today believe business has a social obligation to provide special opportunities for women and minorities to improve their standing in society.

Consumer Relations.   A critical issue in business today is business's responsibility to customers, who look to business to provide them with satisfying, safe products and to respect their rights as consumers. The activities that independent individuals, groups, and organizations undertake to protect their rights as consumers are known as **consumerism**. To achieve their objectives, consumers and their advocates write letters to companies, lobby government agencies, make public service announcements, and boycott companies whose activities they deem irresponsible.

consumerism
the activities that independent individuals, groups, and organizations undertake to protect their rights as consumers

Many of the desires of those involved in the consumer movement have a foundation in John F. Kennedy's 1962 consumer bill of rights, which highlighted four rights. The *right to safety* means that a business must not knowingly sell anything that could result in personal injury or harm to consumers. Defective or dangerous products erode public confidence in the ability of business to serve society. They also result in expensive litigation that ultimately increases the cost of products for all consumers. The right to safety also means businesses must provide a safe place for consumers to shop. In recent years, many large retailers have been under increasing pressure to improve safety in their large stores. Walmart faced serious scrutiny after the death of a guard during an early morning Black Friday stampede at a store on Long Island in 2008. The company was faced with lawsuits, bad press, and negative allegations related to the incident. In response, it implemented new measures such as staying open 24 hours on Thanksgiving. The tragic occurrence led other companies, such as Best Buy, to improve their safety plans as well.[53]

New government regulations that took effect in 2010 give credit card holders additional rights, including protection against sudden hikes in their cards' interest rates.

The *right to be informed* gives consumers the freedom to review complete information about a product before they buy it. This means that detailed information about ingredients, risks, and instructions for use are to be printed on labels and packages. The *right to choose* ensures that consumers have access to a variety of products and services at competitive prices. The assurance of both satisfactory quality and service at a fair price is also a part of the consumer's right to choose. Some consumers are not being given this right. Many are being billed for products and services they never ordered. According to the Federal Trade Commission, complaints about unordered merchandise and services recently jumped 169 percent over a two-year period. The *right to be heard* assures consumers that their interests will receive full and sympathetic consideration when the government formulates policy. It also assures the fair treatment of consumers who voice complaints about a purchased product.

The role of the Federal Trade Commission's Bureau of Consumer Protection exists to protect consumers against unfair, deceptive, or fraudulent practices. The bureau, which enforces a variety of consumer protection laws, is divided into five divisions. The Division of Enforcement monitors legal compliance and investigates violations of laws, including unfulfilled holiday delivery promises by online shopping sites, employment opportunities fraud, scholarship scams, misleading advertising for health care products, and more.

Sustainability Issues.   Most people probably associate the term *environment* with nature, including wildlife, trees, oceans, and mountains. Until the 20th century, people generally thought of the environment solely in terms of how these resources could

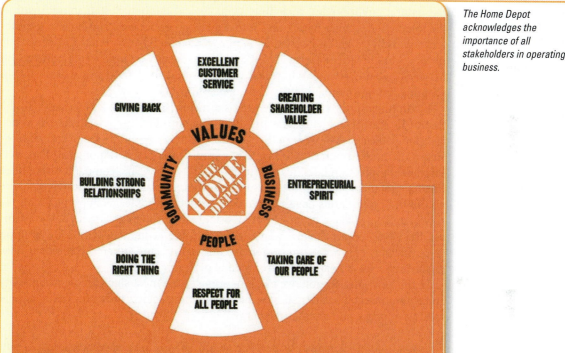

The Home Depot acknowledges the importance of all stakeholders in operating its business.

EXCELLENT CUSTOMER SERVICE
Along with our quality products, service, price and selection, we must go the extra mile to give customers knowledgeable advice about merchandise and to help them use those products to their maximum benefit.

CREATING SHAREHOLDER VALUE
The investors who provide the capital necessary to allow our Company to grow need and expect a return on their investment. We are committed to providing it.

ENTREPRENEURIAL SPIRIT
The Home Depot associates are encouraged to initiate creative and innovative ways of serving our customers and improving the business, as well as to adopt good ideas from others.

TAKING CARE OF OUR PEOPLE
The key to our success is treating people well. We do this by encouraging associates to speak up and take risks, by recognizing and rewarding good performance and by leading and developing people so they may grow.

RESPECT FOR ALL PEOPLE
In order to remain successful, our associates must work in an environment of mutual respect where each associate is regarded as part of The Home Depot team.

DOING THE RIGHT THING
We exercise good judgment by "doing the right thing" instead of just "doing things right." We strive to understand the impact of our decisions, and we accept responsibility for our actions.

BUILDING STRONG RELATIONSHIPS
Strong relationships are built on trust, honesty and integrity. We listen and respond to the needs of customers, associates, communities and vendors, treating them as partners.

GIVING BACK
An important part of the fabric of The Home Depot is in giving our time, talents, energy and resources to worthwhile causes in our communities and society.

be harnessed to satisfy their needs for food, shelter, transportation, and recreation. As the earth's population swelled throughout the 20th century, however, humans began to use more and more of these resources and, with technological advancements, to do so with ever-greater efficiency. Although these conditions have resulted in a much-improved standard of living, they come with a cost. Plant and animal species, along with wildlife habitats, are disappearing at an accelerated rate, while pollution has rendered the atmosphere of some cities a gloomy haze. How to deal with these issues has become a major concern for business and society in the 21st century.

Although the scope of the word *sustainability* is broad, in this book we discuss the term from a strategic business perspective. Thus, we define **sustainability** as conducting activities in such as way as to provide for the long-term well-being of the natural environment, including all biological entities. Sustainability involves the interaction among nature and individuals, organizations, and business strategies and includes the assessment and improvement of business strategies, economic sectors, work practices, technologies, and lifestyles, so that they maintain the health of the natural environment. In recent years, business has played a significant role in adapting, using, and maintaining the quality of sustainability.

Environmental protection emerged as a major issue in the 20th century in the face of increasing evidence that pollution, uncontrolled use of natural resources, and population growth were putting increasing pressure on the long-term sustainability of these resources. Governments around the globe responded with environmental protection laws during the 1970s. In recent years, companies have been increasingly incorporating these issues into their overall business strategies. Some nonprofit organizations have stepped forward to provide leadership in gaining the cooperation of diverse groups in responsible environmental activities. For example, the Coalition for Environmentally Responsible Economies (CERES)—a union of businesses, consumer groups, environmentalists, and other stakeholders—has established a set of goals for environmental performance.

In the following section, we examine some of the most significant sustainability and environmental health issues facing business and society today, including animal rights, pollution, and alternative energy.

Pollution.   Another major issue in the area of environmental responsibility is pollution. Water pollution results from dumping toxic chemicals and raw sewage into rivers and oceans, oil spills, and the burial of industrial waste in the ground where it may filter into underground water supplies. Fertilizers and insecticides used in farming and grounds maintenance also run off into water supplies with each rainfall. Water pollution problems are especially notable in heavily industrialized areas. Medical waste—such as used syringes, vials of blood, and HIV-contaminated materials—has turned up on beaches in New York, New Jersey, and Massachusetts, as well as other places. Society is demanding that water supplies be clean and healthful to reduce the potential danger from these substances.

Air pollution is usually the result of smoke and other pollutants emitted by manufacturing facilities, as well as carbon monoxide and hydrocarbons emitted by motor vehicles. In addition to the health risks posed by air pollution, when some chemical compounds emitted by manufacturing facilities react with air and rain, acid rain results. Acid rain has contributed to the deaths of many forests and lakes in North America as well as in Europe. Air pollution may also contribute to global warming; as carbon dioxide collects in the earth's atmosphere, it traps the sun's heat and prevents the earth's surface from cooling. It is indisputable that the

sustainability
conducting activities in a way that allows for the long-term well-bring of the natural environment, including all biological entities. Sustainability involves the assessment and improvement of business strategies, economic sectors, work practices, technologies and lifestyles so that they maintain the health of the natural environment.

> **Facts Related to Reducing Energy Consumption**
>
> - Keep your tires inflated at the recommended pressure. Not only is it safer, it can improve your gas mileage by more than 3 percent.
> - The next time you buy a refrigerator, choose an ENERGY STAR model. If everyone buying a new refrigerator chose an ENERGY STAR model, it could save 914 million kilowatt-hours of electricity and more than $101 million in energy bills each year.
> - Turn off your electronics when not in use. Stand-by power can account for up to 20 percent of energy use in the home.
> - Use ENERGY STAR CFL light bulbs. If every home in America replaced just one light bulb with a CFL bulb, it could save as much as 6 billion kilowatts a year. This would save consumers more than $600 million in energy costs per year and reduce greenhouse gases by the equivalent of almost 750,000 cars.
> - More than 50 percent of energy used in American homes is used for space heating and cooling. By properly sealing and insulating your attic, you can save up to 10 percent per year on your energy bills.
>
> Source: "Make Every Day Earth Day," U.S. Department of Energy, http://www.energy.gov/energytips.htm (accessed January 25, 2010).

global surface temperature has been increasing over the past 35 years. Worldwide passenger vehicle ownership has been growing due to rapid industrialization and consumer purchasing power in China, India, and other developing countries with large populations. The most important way to contain climate change is to control carbon emissions. The move to green buildings, higher-mileage cars, and other emissions reductions resulting from better efficiency have the potential to generate up to 50 percent of the reductions needed to keep warming at no more than 2°C above present temperatures—considered the "safe" level.[55] The 2007 U.S. Federal Energy bill raised average fuel economy (CAFE) standards to 35 mpg for cars by 2020, while Europe has the goal of a 40 mpg standard by the same deadline. Because buildings create half of U.S. greenhouse emissions, there is tremendous opportunity to develop conservation measures. For example, some utilities charge more for electricity in peak demand periods, which encourages behavioral changes that reduce consumption. On the positive side, there are more than 100 million bicycles produced annually worldwide, more than double the passenger vehicles produced.[56]

Land pollution is tied directly to water pollution because many of the chemicals and toxic wastes that are dumped on the land eventually work their way into the water supply. A study conducted by the Environmental Protection Agency found residues of prescription drugs, soaps, and other contaminants in virtually every waterway in the United States. Effects of these pollutants on humans and wildlife are uncertain, but there is some evidence to suggest that fish and other water-dwellers are starting to suffer serious effects.[57] Land pollution results from the dumping of residential and industrial waste, strip mining, forest fires, and poor forest conservation. In Brazil and other South American countries, rain forests are being destroyed—to make way for farms and ranches, at a cost of the extinction of the many animals and plants (some endangered species) that call the rain forest home. In the second half of 2007 alone, an area the size of Rhode Island was lost in the Brazilian Amazon—a rate that is speeding up as agriculture becomes a more attractive industry.[58] Large-scale deforestation also depletes the oxygen supply available to humans and other animals.

Related to the problem of land pollution is the larger issue of how to dispose of waste in an environmentally responsible manner. Americans use 100 billion

Going Green
Walmart Seeks to Define Green Products

Walmart, long criticized by socially and environmentally conscious consumers for its large size and wastefulness, is trying to position itself as a leader in going green. The company announced a plan to launch a green labeling program in its stores. These labels will essentially be a rating system that will inform consumers about the environmental impact of products. Walmart plans to require its suppliers to provide these statistics and will then translate this information into a rating system.

This is one of the largest socially conscious steps Walmart has ever taken, and it may force manufacturers and other retailers to attain a much higher level of eco-transparency. The move, which is logistically complex and will take years to fully implement, has pros and cons. On the one hand, this move could revolutionize the way products are sold due to Walmart's impact on the overall retail market. Walmart also hopes to attract a new demographic to its stores—younger shoppers and those concerned about a company's ethical, environmental, and socially responsible behavior. On the other hand, defining "green" is going to be a major challenge; without some unified set of guidelines, the labels may end up meaning nothing. Another concern is that labels only tell so much—how a consumer uses a product also impacts its "greenness."

Rivals of Walmart criticize this move, saying that Walmart is attempting to thwart soon-to-be established government regulations by setting the standards itself. Regardless, Walmart is undergoing a significant eco-overhaul and is continuing to move in an environmentally friendly direction.[54]

Discussion Questions:

1. What is Walmart doing to help improve its reputation as a green company?
2. Why is it considered ethical to take steps to improve sustainability?
3. What are some of the stakeholder concerns of Walmart's eco-labeling system?

plastic bags each year, which is between 10 and 20 percent of the total global usage (estimated at 500 billion to 1 trillion bags).[59] It takes 1,000 years for the bags to decompose. San Francisco has banned plastic bags; Ireland is now charging a nationwide tax of 15 cents on all supermarket shopping bags; and Australia and China are planning a similar program.[60] Whole Foods, the nation's leading natural and organic supermarket, ended its use of plastic bags on Earth Day 2008.[61] Whole Foods estimates that this move will keep 150 million new plastic grocery bags out of the environment each year.

Alternative Energy. With ongoing plans to reduce global carbon emissions, countries and companies alike are looking toward alternative energy sources. Traditional fossil fuels are problematic because of their emissions, but also because stores have been greatly depleted. Foreign fossil fuels are often imported from politically and economically unstable regions, often making it unsafe to conduct business there. The United States spent a high of $700 billion on foreign oil in 2007.[62] With global warming concerns and rising gas prices, the U.S. government has begun to recognize the need to look toward alternative forms of energy as a source of fuel and electricity. There have been many different ideas as to which form of alternative energy would best suit the United States' energy needs. These sources include wind power, solar power, nuclear power, biofuels, electric cars, and hydro and geothermal power. As of yet, no "best" form of alternative fuel has been selected to replace gasoline. However, the U.S. government has begun to recognize the need to reduce the nation's dependence on fossil fuels. It allocated billions of dollars toward renewable energy as part of President Obama's stimulus package.[63]

Response to Environmental Issues. Partly in response to federal legislation such as the National Environmental Policy Act of 1969 and partly due to consumer concerns, businesses are responding to environmental issues. Many small and large companies, including Walt Disney Company, Chevron, and Scott Paper, have created a new executive position—a vice president of environmental affairs—to help them achieve their business goals in an environmentally responsible manner. A survey indicated that 83.5 percent of *Fortune* 500 companies have a written environmental policy, 74.7 percent engage in recycling efforts, and 69.7 percent have made investments in waste-reduction efforts.[64] Some companies are finding that environmental consciousness can save them money. DuPont saved more than $3 billion through energy conservation by replacing natural gas with methane in its industrial boilers in many of its plants.[65]

Many firms are trying to eliminate wasteful practices, the emission of pollutants, and/or the use of harmful chemicals from their manufacturing processes. Other companies are seeking ways to improve their products. Utility providers, for example, are increasingly supplementing their services with alternative energy sources, including solar, wind, and geothermal power. Environmentalists are concerned that some companies are merely *greenwashing,* or "creating a positive association with environmental issues for an unsuitable product, service, or practice."

> **Did You Know?**   In one year, Americans generated 230 million tons of trash and recycled 23.5 percent of it.[66]

In many places, local utility customers can even elect to purchase electricity from green sources—primarily wind power—for a few extra dollars a month. Austin Energy of Austin, Texas, has an award-winning GreenChoice program that includes many small and large businesses among its customers.[67] Indeed, a growing number of businesses and consumers are choosing green power sources where available. New Belgium Brewing, the third-largest craft brewer in the United States, is the first all-wind-powered brewery in the country. Many businesses have turned to *recycling,* the reprocessing of materials—aluminum, paper, glass, and some plastic—for reuse. Such efforts to make products, packaging, and processes more environmentally friendly have been labeled "green" business or marketing by the public and media. New Belgium, for instance, started selling aluminum cans of its beers because aluminum is easily recyclable and creates less waste. Lumber products at The Home Depot may carry a seal from the Forest Stewardship Council to indicate that they were harvested from sustainable forests using environmentally friendly methods.[68] Likewise, most Chiquita bananas are certified through the Better Banana Project as having been grown with more environmentally and labor-friendly practices.[69]

It is important to recognize that, with current technology, environmental responsibility requires trade-offs. Society must weigh the huge costs of limiting or eliminating pollution against the health threat posed by the pollution. Environmental responsibility imposes costs on both business and the public. Although people certainly do not want oil fouling beautiful waterways and killing wildlife, they insist on low-cost, readily available gasoline and heating oil. People do not want to contribute to the growing garbage-disposal problem, but they often refuse to pay more for "green" products packaged in an environmentally friendly manner, to recycle as much of their own waste as possible, or to permit the building of additional waste-disposal facilities (the "not in my backyard," or NIMBY, syndrome). Managers must coordinate environmental goals with other social and economic ones.

Community Relations.   A final, yet very significant, issue for businesses concerns their responsibilities to the general welfare of the communities and societies in which they operate. Many businesses simply want to make their communities better places for everyone to live and work. The most common way that businesses exercise their community responsibility is through donations to local and national charitable organizations. Corporations contribute more than $14 billion each year to charitable causes.[70] For example, Safeway, the nation's fourth-largest grocer, has donated millions of dollars to organizations involved in medical research, such as Easter Seals and the Juvenile Diabetes Research Foundation International. The company's employees have also raised funds to support social causes of interest.[71] Avon's Breast Cancer Awareness Crusade has helped raise $300 million to fund community-based breast cancer education and early detection services. Avon, a marketer of women's cosmetics, is also known for employing a large number of women and promoting them to top management; the firm has more female top managers (86 percent) than any other *Fortune* 500 company.[72] Even small companies participate in philanthropy through donations and volunteer support of local causes and national charities, such as the Red Cross and the United Way.

After realizing that the current pool of prospective employees lacks many basic skills necessary to work, many companies have become concerned about the quality of education in the United States. Recognizing that today's students are tomorrow's employees and customers, firms such as Kroger, Campbell's Soup, Kodak, American Express, Apple Computer, Xerox, and Coca-Cola are donating money, equipment, and employee time to help improve schools in their communities and around the nation. They provide scholarship money, support for teachers, and computers for students, and they send employees out to tutor and motivate young students to stay in school and succeed. Target, for example, contributes significant resources to education, including direct donations of $100 million to schools as well as fund-raising and scholarship programs that assist teachers and students. Through the retailer's Take Charge of Education program, customers using a Target Guest Card can designate a specific school to which Target donates 1 percent of their total purchase price. This program is designed to make customers feel that their purchases are benefiting their community while increasing the use of Target Guest Cards.[73]

Many companies encourage their employees to volunteer for charitable organizations such as Habitat for Humanity.

Another tactic taken by some companies is to let consumers decide whether they want to contribute to socially responsible activities. What if Dell sold one notebook computer for $1,000 and the same computer for $1,150, with the understanding that the purchase of *this* computer would support the fight against AIDS around the world? Dell and Microsoft created products for the Product(Red) campaign, joining other large corporations such as The Gap, Apple, and Motorola in support of The Global Fund, an international organization fighting AIDS, tuberculosis, and malaria. The Product(Red) computer sold by Dell is significant to consumers and communicates their support to others.

Business is also beginning to take more responsibility for the hard-core unemployed. These are people who have never had a job or who have been unemployed for a long period of time. Some are mentally or physically handicapped; some are homeless. Organizations such as the National Alliance of Businessmen fund programs to train the hard-core unemployed so that they can find jobs and support themselves. In addition to fostering self-support, such opportunities enhance self-esteem and help people become productive members of society.

So You Want a Job in Business Ethics and Social Responsibility

In the words of Kermit the Frog, "It's not easy being green." It may not be easy, but green business opportunities abound. A popular catch phrase, "Green is the new black," indicates how fashionable green business is becoming. Consumers are more in tune with and concerned about green products, policies, and behaviors by companies than ever before. Companies are looking for new hires to help them see their business creatively and bring insights to all aspects of business operations. The American Solar Energy Society estimates that the number of green jobs could rise to 40 million in the United States by 2030. Green business strategies not only give a firm a commercial advantage in the marketplace, but help lead the way toward a greener world. The fight to reduce our carbon footprint in an attempt against climate change has opened up opportunities for renewable energy, recycling, conservation and increasing overall efficiency in the way resources are used. New businesses that focus on hydro, wind, and solar power are on the rise and will need talented business people to lead them. Carbon emissions' trading is gaining popularity as large corporations and individuals alike seek to lower their footprints. A job in this growing field could be similar to that of a stock trader or you could lead the search for carbon efficient companies in which to invest.

In the ethics arena, current trends in business governance strongly support the development of ethics and compliance departments to help guide organizational integrity. This alone is a billion-dollar business, and there are jobs in developing organizational ethics programs, developing company policies and training employees and management. An entry-level position might be as a communication specialist or trainer for programs in a business ethics department. Eventually there's an opportunity to become an ethics officer that would have typical responsibilities of meeting with employees, the Board of Directors, and top management to discuss and provide advice about ethics issues in the industry, developing and distributing a code of ethics, creating and maintaining an anonymous, confidential service to answer questions about ethical issues, taking actions on possible ethics code violations, and reviewing and modifying the code of ethics of the organization.

There are also opportunities to help with initiatives to help companies relate social responsibility to stakeholder interests and needs. These jobs could involve coordinating and implementing philanthropic programs that give back to others important to the organization or developing a community volunteering program for employees. In addition to the human relations function, most companies develop programs to assist employees and their families to improve their quality of life. Companies have found that the healthier and happier employees are the more productive they will be in the workforce.

Social responsibility, ethics, and sustainable business practices are not a trend, they are good for business and the bottom line. New industries are being created and old ones are adapting to the new market demands, opening up many varied job opportunities that will lead to not only a paycheck, but to the satisfaction of making the world a better place.[74]

Review Your Understanding

Define business ethics and social responsibility and examine their importance.

Business ethics refers to principles and standards that define acceptable business conduct. Acceptable business behavior is defined by customers, competitors, government regulators, interest groups, the public, and each individual's personal moral principles and values. Social responsibility is the obligation an organization assumes to maximize its positive impact and minimize its negative impact on society. Socially responsible businesses win the trust and respect of their employees, customers, and society and, in the long run, increase profits. Ethics is important in business because it builds trust and confidence in business relationships. Unethical actions may result in negative publicity, declining sales, and even legal action.

Detect some of the ethical issues that may arise in business.

An ethical issue is an identifiable problem, situation, or opportunity requiring a person or organization to choose from among several actions that must be evaluated as right or wrong. Ethical issues can be categorized in the context of their relation with conflicts of interest, fairness and honesty, communications, and business associations.

Specify how businesses can promote ethical behavior by employees.

Businesses can promote ethical behavior by employees by limiting their opportunity to engage in misconduct. Formal codes of ethics, ethical policies, and ethics training programs reduce the incidence of unethical behavior by informing employees what is expected of them and providing punishments for those who fail to comply.

Explain the four dimensions of social responsibility.

The four dimensions of social responsibility are economic (being profitable), legal (obeying the law), ethical (doing what is right, just, and fair), and voluntary (being a good corporate citizen).

Debate an organization's social responsibilities to owners, employees, consumers, the environment, and the community.

Businesses must maintain proper accounting procedures, provide all relevant information about the performance of the firm to investors, and protect the owners' rights and investments. In relations with employees, businesses are expected to provide a safe workplace, pay employees adequately for their work, and treat them fairly. Consumerism refers to the activities undertaken by independent individuals, groups, and organizations to protect their rights as consumers. Increasingly, society expects businesses to take greater responsibility for the environment, especially with regard to animal rights, as well as water, air, land, and noise pollution. Many businesses engage in activities to make the communities in which they operate better places for everyone to live and work.

Evaluate the ethics of a business's decision.

"Solve the Dilemma" on page 66 presents an ethical dilemma at Checkers Pizza. Using the material presented in this chapter, you should be able to analyze the ethical issues present in the dilemma, evaluate Barnard's plan, and develop a course of action for the firm.

Revisit the World of Business

1. Why does the NCAA seek to regulate advertising and sponsorships at collegiate sporting events?
2. What is the ethical dilemma involved in a student being paid by marketers?
3. What were the ethical objections raised by stakeholders regarding the Budweiser college can campaign?

Learn the Terms

bribes   43
business ethics   36
codes of ethics   49
consumerism   56
corporate citizenship   51
ethical issue   39
plagiarism   48
social responsibility   37
sustainability   58
whistleblowing   50

Check Your Progress

1. Define business ethics. Who determines whether a business activity is ethical? Is unethical conduct always illegal?
2. Distinguish between ethics and social responsibility.
3. Why has ethics become so important in business?
4. What is an ethical issue? What are some of the ethical issues named in your text? Why are they ethical issues?
5. What is a code of ethics? How can one reduce unethical behavior in business?
6. List and discuss the arguments for and against social responsibility by business (Table 2.8). Can you think of any additional arguments (for or against)?
7. What responsibilities does a business have toward its employees?

8. What responsibilities does business have with regard to the environment? What steps have been taken by some responsible businesses to minimize the negative impact of their activities on the environment?

9. What are a business's responsibilities toward the community in which it operates?

Get Involved

1. Discuss some recent examples of businesses engaging in unethical practices. Classify these practices as issues of conflict of interest, fairness and honesty, communications, or business relationships. Why do you think the businesses chose to behave unethically? What actions might the businesses have taken?

2. Discuss with your class some possible methods of improving ethical standards in business. Do you think that business should regulate its own activities or that the federal government should establish and enforce ethical standards? How do you think businesspeople feel?

3. Find some examples of socially responsible businesses in newspapers or business journals. Explain why you believe their actions are socially responsible. Why do you think the companies chose to act as they did?

Build Your Skills

MAKING DECISIONS ABOUT ETHICAL ISSUES

Background

The merger of Lockheed and Martin Marietta created Lockheed Martin, the number-one company in the defense industry—an industry that includes such companies as McDonnell Douglas and Northrop Grumman.

You and the rest of the class are managers at Lockheed Martin Corporation, Orlando, Florida. You are getting ready to do the group exercise in an ethics training session. The training instructor announces you will be playing *Gray Matters: The Ethics Game.* You are told that *Gray Matters,* which was prepared for your company's employees, is also played at 41 universities, including Harvard University, and at 65 other companies. Although there are 55 scenarios in *Gray Matters,* you will have time during this session to complete only the four scenarios that your group draws from the stack of cards.[75]

Task

Form into groups of four to six managers and appoint a group leader who will lead a discussion of the case, obtain a consensus answer to the case, and be the one to report the group's answers to the instructor. You will have five minutes to reach each decision, after which time, the instructor will give the point values and rationale for each choice. Then you will have five minutes for the next case, etc., until all four cases have been completed. Keep track of your group's score for each case; the winning team will be the group scoring the most points.

Since this game is designed to reflect life, you may believe that some cases lack clarity or that some of your choices are not as precise as you would have liked. Also, some cases have only one solution, while others have more than one solution. Each choice is assessed points to reflect which answer is the most correct. **Your group's task is to select only one option in each case.**

4

Mini-Case

For several months now, one of your colleagues has been slacking off, and you are getting stuck doing the work. You think it is unfair. What do you do?

Potential Answers

A. Recognize this as an opportunity for you to demonstrate how capable you are.
B. Go to your supervisor and complain about this unfair workload.
C. Discuss the problem with your colleague in an attempt to solve the problem without involving others.
D. Discuss the problem with the human resources department.

7

Mini-Case

You are aware that a fellow employee uses drugs on the job. Another friend encourages you to confront the person instead of informing the supervisor. What do you do?

Potential Answers

A. You speak to the alleged user and encourage him to get help.
B. You elect to tell your supervisor that you suspect an employee is using drugs on the job.
C. You confront the alleged user and tell him either to quit using drugs or you will "turn him in."
D. Report the matter to employee assistance.

36

Mini-Case

You work for a company that has implemented a policy of a smoke-free environment. You discover employees smoking in the restrooms of the building. You also smoke and don't like having to go outside to do it. What do you do?

Potential Answers

A. You ignore the situation.
B. You confront the employees and ask them to stop.
C. You join them, but only occasionally.
D. You contact your ethics or human resources representative and ask him or her to handle the situation

40

Mini-Case

Your co-worker is copying company-purchased software and taking it home. You know a certain program costs $400, and you have been saving for a while to buy it. What do you do?

Potential Answers

A. You figure you can copy it too since nothing has ever happened to your co-worker.
B. You tell your co-worker he can't legally do this.
C. You report the matter to the ethics office.
D. You mention this to your supervisor.

Solve the Dilemma

CUSTOMER PRIVACY

Checkers Pizza was one of the first to offer home delivery service, with overwhelming success. However, the major pizza chains soon followed suit, taking away Checkers's competitive edge. Jon Barnard, Checkers's founder and co-owner, needed a new gimmick to beat the competition. He decided to develop a computerized information database that would make Checkers the most efficient competitor and provide insight into consumer buying behavior at the same time. Under the system, telephone customers were asked their phone number; if they had

ordered from Checkers before, their address and previous order information came up on the computer screen.

After successfully testing the new system, Barnard put the computerized order network in place in all Checkers outlets. After three months of success, he decided to give an award to the family that ate the most Checkers pizza. Through the tracking system, the company identified the biggest customer, who had ordered a pizza every weekday for the past three months (63 pizzas). The company put together a program to surprise the family with an award, free-food certificates, and a news story announcing the award. As Barnard began to plan for the event, however, he began to think that maybe the family might not want all the attention and publicity.

Discussion Questions

1. What are some of the ethical issues in giving customers an award for consumption behavior without notifying them first?

2. Do you see this as a potential violation of privacy? Explain.

3. How would you handle the situation if you were Barnard?

Build Your Business Plan

BUSINESS ETHICS AND SOCIAL RESPONSIBILITY

Think about which industry you are considering competing in with your product/service. Is there any kind of questionable practices in the way the product has been traditionally sold? Produced? Advertised? Have there been any recent accusations regarding safety within the industry? What about any environmental concerns?

For example, if you are thinking of opening a lawn care business, you need to be thinking about what possible effects the chemicals you are using will have on the client and the environment. You have a responsibility to keep your customers safe and healthy. You also have the social responsibility to let the community know of any damaging effect you may be directly or indirectly responsible for.

See for Yourself Videocase

REBUILDING AMERICA'S TRUST IN BUSINESS

Corporate scandals, a growing awareness of environmental issues, and the most recent global recession have greatly altered the public's perspective of corporate America. Gone are the days in which consumers blindly trusted company publicity and rhetoric. The public's trust in business has been shattered, and many companies have a long way to go to earn it back.

The Arthur Page Society and the Business Roundtable Institute for Corporate Ethics are dedicated to corporate accountability and ethics. The organizations released a study addressing Americans' mistrust of business and how corporations can begin to win back the hearts and minds of consumers. The study, entitled The Dynamics of Public Trust in Business—Emerging Opportunities for Leaders, cites public trust of business as resting at a very low 15 percent. A major issue appears to be the imbalance of power. The public is angry over corporate bailouts and rising unemployment while corporate management still makes huge profits. For example, Wells Fargo CEO John Stumpf's 2009 pay increased dramatically to $21.3 million dollars. A recent *Bloomberg BusinessWeek* report indicates that CEO pay in 81 large companies fell by 8.6 percent in 2009; however, CEO cash compensation rose 8.3 percent. Although the growth in cash payout is, for some companies, a reflection of the fact that they did not award cash in 2008, it is, for

others, a loophole. Regardless, analysts believe this shift moves the focus away from the connection between pay company performance, potentially creating a greater disconnect between CEOs and their businesses. Behavior of this nature is only going to fuel public distrust.

Although the Arthur Page Society and the Business Roundtable see their report as a way to start a national dialogue, the report does offer a series of suggestions for businesses. First and foremost, the balance of power must be equalized. Companies must focus on creating mutual value and leaders must try to gain and retain trust. The study also suggests that corporations create quality products/services, sell products/services at fair prices, create and maintain positive employment practices, give investors a fair return, remain active in social responsibility, and create transparency.

Companies can use these suggestions to change their policies and behavior, but in order to be truly successful, companies must truly embrace these values. Perhaps the most important step companies can take is to align business interests with public interests. For example, it's no longer enough that businesses earn money for their shareholders; people want to know exactly how that money is being earned. Another example involves the growing public concern regarding how businesses impact the environment—investors want details on a business's impact and what that business is doing to be more sustainable.

As the public fights to make its desires known regarding business behavior, businesses that sincerely want to help the world are receiving some help. Maryland recently made "benefit corporations" legal. These corporations must make their values public, report yearly on their socially-beneficial behavior, and agree to third party audits of their social responsibility actions. Acquiring this designation requires the approval of more than half a company's shareholders. Vermont and California are looking into similar legislation. Companies may also establish themselves as B Corporations (over 30,000 companies hold this designation), which certifies their socially responsible focus. It is entirely possible for businesses to regain public trust, but it means a change in values for many businesses in today's corporate America.[76]

Discussion Questions:

1. What are some of the reasons cited in the Arthur Page Society and the Business Roundtable Institute for Corporate Ethics report for public distrust of corporations?

2. What are some of the recommendations made by the report? Can you think of any other recommendations to give companies on how to behave more ethically?

3. What are the benefits of being perceived as an ethical company? What are the downsides of having a reputation for ethical misconduct?

Remember to check out our Online Learning Center at www.mhhe.com/ferrell8e.

Team Exercise

Sam Walton, founder of Walmart, had an early strategy for growing his business related to pricing. The "Opening Price Point" strategy used by Walton involved offering the introductory product in a product line at the lowest point in the market. For example, a minimally equipped microwave oven would sell for less than anyone else in town could sell the same unit. The strategy was that if consumers saw a product, such as the microwave, and saw it as a good value, they would assume that all of the microwaves were good values. Walton also noted that most people don't buy the entry-level product; they want more features and capabilities and often trade up.

Form teams and assign the role of defending this strategy or casting this strategy as an unethical act. Present your thoughts on either side of the issue.

Appendix B

The Legal and Regulatory Environment

Business law refers to the rules and regulations that govern the conduct of business. Problems in this area come from the failure to keep promises, misunderstandings, disagreements about expectations, or, in some cases, attempts to take advantage of others. The regulatory environment offers a framework and enforcement system in order to provide a fair playing field for all businesses. The regulatory environment is created based on inputs from competitors, customers, employees, special interest groups, and the public's elected representatives. Lobbying by pressure groups who try to influence legislation often shapes the legal and regulatory environment.

Sources of Law

Laws are classified as either criminal or civil. *Criminal law* not only prohibits a specific kind of action, such as unfair competition or mail fraud, but also imposes a fine or imprisonment as punishment for violating the law. A violation of a criminal law is thus called a crime. *Civil law* defines all the laws not classified as criminal, and it specifies the rights and duties of individuals and organizations (including businesses). Violations of civil law may result in fines but not imprisonment. The primary difference between criminal and civil law is that criminal laws are enforced by the state or nation, whereas civil laws are enforced through the court system by individuals or organizations.

Criminal and civil laws are derived from four sources: the Constitution (constitutional law), precedents established by judges (common law), federal and state statutes (statutory law), and federal and state administrative agencies (administrative law). Federal administrative agencies established by Congress control and influence business by enforcing laws and regulations to encourage competition and protect consumers, workers, and the environment. The Supreme Court is the ultimate authority on legal

and regulatory decisions for appropriate conduct in business.

Courts and the Resolution of Disputes

The primary method of resolving conflicts and business disputes is through **lawsuits,** where one individual or organization takes another to court using civil laws. The legal system, therefore, provides a forum for businesspeople to resolve disputes based on our legal foundations. The courts may decide when harm or damage results from the actions of others.

Because lawsuits are so frequent in the world of business, it is important to understand more about the court system where such disputes are resolved. Both financial restitution and specific actions to undo

Marcia & Bill Baker found Heinz was underfilling their 20-oz. ketchup bottles by 1.5 oz. Heinz paid civil penalties and costs of $180,000 and had to overfill all ketchup bottles in California by 1/8 oz. for a year.

wrongdoing can result from going before a court to resolve a conflict. All decisions made in the courts are based on criminal and civil laws derived from the legal and regulatory system.

A businessperson may win a lawsuit in court and receive a judgment, or court order, requiring the loser of the suit to pay monetary damages. However, this does not guarantee the victor will be able to collect those damages. If the loser of the suit lacks the financial resources to pay the judgment—for example, if the loser is a bankrupt business—the winner of the suit may not be able to collect the award. Most business lawsuits involve a request for a sum of money, but some lawsuits request that a court specifically order a person or organization to do or to refrain from doing a certain act, such as slamming telephone customers.

The Court System

Jurisdiction is the legal power of a court, through a judge, to interpret and apply the law and make a binding decision in a particular case. In some instances, other courts will not enforce the decision of a prior court because it lacked jurisdiction. Federal courts are granted jurisdiction by the Constitution or by Congress. State legislatures and constitutions determine which state courts hear certain types of cases. Courts of general jurisdiction hear all types of cases; those of limited jurisdiction hear only specific types of cases. The Federal Bankruptcy Court, for example, hears only cases involving bankruptcy. There is some combination of limited and general jurisdiction courts in every state.

In a **trial court** (whether in a court of general or limited jurisdiction and whether in the state or the federal system), two tasks must be completed. First, the court (acting through the judge or a jury) must determine the facts of the case. In other words, if there is conflicting evidence, the judge or jury must decide who to believe. Second, the judge must decide which law or set of laws is pertinent to the case and must then apply those laws to resolve the dispute.

An **appellate court,** on the other hand, deals solely with appeals relating to the interpretation of law. Thus, when you hear about a case being appealed, it is not retried, but rather reevaluated. Appellate judges do not hear witnesses but instead base their decisions on a written transcript of the original trial. Moreover, appellate courts do not draw factual conclusions; the appellate judge is limited to deciding

whether the trial judge made a mistake in interpreting the law that probably affected the outcome of the trial. If the trial judge made no mistake (or if mistakes would not have changed the result of the trial), the appellate court will let the trial court's decision stand. If the appellate court finds a mistake, it usually sends the case back to the trial court so that the mistake can be corrected. Correction may involve the granting of a new trial. On occasion, appellate courts modify the verdict of the trial court without sending the case back to the trial court.

Alternative Dispute Resolution Methods

Although the main remedy for business disputes is a lawsuit, other dispute resolution methods are becoming popular. The schedules of state and federal trial courts are often crowded; long delays between the filing of a case and the trial date are common. Further, complex cases can become quite expensive to pursue. As a result, many businesspeople are turning to alternative methods of resolving business arguments: mediation and arbitration, the mini-trial, and litigation in a private court.

Mediation is a form of negotiation to resolve a dispute by bringing in one or more third-party mediators, usually chosen by the disputing parties, to help reach a settlement. The mediator suggests different ways to resolve a dispute between the parties. The mediator's resolution is nonbinding—that is, the parties do not have to accept the mediator's suggestions; they are strictly voluntary.

Arbitration involves submission of a dispute to one or more third-party arbitrators, usually chosen by the disputing parties, whose decision usually is final. Arbitration differs from mediation in that an arbitrator's decision must be followed, whereas a mediator merely offers suggestions and facilitates negotiations. Cases may be submitted to arbitration because a contract—such as a labor contract—requires it or because the parties agree to do so. Some consumers are barred from taking claims to court by agreements drafted by banks, brokers, health plans, and others. Instead, they are required to take complaints to mandatory arbitration. Arbitration can be an attractive alternative to a lawsuit because it is often cheaper and quicker, and the parties frequently can choose arbitrators who are knowledgeable about the particular area of business at issue.

A method of dispute resolution that may become increasingly important in settling complex disputes is the **mini-trial,** in which both parties agree to present a summarized version of their case to an independent third party. That person then advises them of his or her impression of the probable outcome if the case were to be tried. Representatives of both sides then attempt to negotiate a settlement based on the advisor's recommendations. For example, employees in a large corporation who believe they have muscular or skeletal stress injuries caused by the strain of repetitive motion in using a computer could agree to a mini-trial to address a dispute related to damages. Although the mini-trial itself does not resolve the dispute, it can help the parties resolve the case before

going to court. Because the mini-trial is not subject to formal court rules, it can save companies a great deal of money, allowing them to recognize the weaknesses in a particular case.

In some areas of the country, disputes can be submitted to a private nongovernmental court for resolution. In a sense, a **private court system** is similar to arbitration in that an independent third party resolves the case after hearing both sides of the story. Trials in private courts may be either informal or highly formal, depending on the people involved. Businesses typically agree to have their disputes decided in private courts to save time and money.

TABLE B.I   The Major Regulatory Agencies

Agency	Major Areas of Responsibility
Federal Trade Commission (FTC)	Enforces laws and guidelines regarding business practices; takes action to stop false and deceptive advertising and labeling.
Food and Drug Administration (FDA)	Enforces laws and regulations to prevent distribution of adulterated or misbranded foods, drugs, medical devices, cosmetics, veterinary products, and particularly hazardous consumer products.
Consumer Product Safety Commission (CPSC)	Ensures compliance with the Consumer Product Safety Act; protects the public from unreasonable risk of injury from any consumer product not covered by other regulatory agencies.
Interstate Commerce Commission (ICC)	Regulates franchises, rates, and finances of interstate rail, bus, truck, and water carriers.
Federal Communications Commission (FCC)	Regulates communication by wire, radio, and television in interstate and foreign commerce.
Environmental Protection Agency (EPA)	Develops and enforces environmental protection standards and conducts research into the adverse effects of pollution.
Federal Energy Regulatory Commission (FERC)	Regulates rates and sales of natural gas products, thereby affecting the supply and price of gas available to consumers; also regulates wholesale rates for electricity and gas, pipeline construction, and U.S. imports and exports of natural gas and electricity.
Equal Employment Opportunity Commission (EEOC)	Investigates and resolves discrimination in employment practices.
Federal Aviation Administration (FAA)	Oversees the policies and regulations of the airline industry.
Federal Highway Administration (FHA)	Regulates vehicle safety requirements.
Occupational Safety and Health Administration (OSHA)	Develops policy to promote worker safety and health and investigates infractions.
Securities and Exchange Commission (SEC)	Regulates corporate securities trading and develops protection from fraud and other abuses; provides an accounting oversight board.

Regulatory Administrative Agencies

Federal and state administrative agencies (listed in Table B.1) also have some judicial powers. Many administrative agencies, such as the Federal Trade Commission, decide disputes that involve their regulations. In such disputes, the resolution process is usually called a "hearing" rather than a trial. In these cases, an administrative law judge decides all issues.

Federal regulatory agencies influence many business activities and cover product liability, safety, and the regulation or deregulation of public utilities. Usually, these bodies have the power to enforce specific laws, such as the Federal Trade Commission Act, and have some discretion in establishing operating rules and regulations to guide certain types of industry practices. Because of this discretion and overlapping areas of responsibility, confusion or conflict regarding which agencies have jurisdiction over which activities is common.

Of all the federal regulatory units, the **Federal Trade Commission (FTC)** most influences business activities related to questionable practices that create disputes between businesses and their customers. Although the FTC regulates a variety of business practices, it allocates a large portion of resources to curbing false advertising, misleading pricing, and deceptive packaging and labeling. When it receives a complaint or otherwise has reason to believe that a firm is violating a law, the FTC issues a complaint stating that the business is in violation.

If a company continues the questionable practice, the FTC can issue a cease-and-desist order, which is an order for the business to stop doing whatever has caused the complaint. In such cases, the charged firm can appeal to the federal courts to have the order rescinded. However, the FTC can seek civil penalties in court—up to a maximum penalty of $10,000 a day for each infraction—if a cease-and-desist order is violated. In its battle against unfair pricing, the FTC has issued consent decrees alleging that corporate attempts to engage in price fixing or invitations to competitors to collude are violations even when the competitors in question refuse the invitations. The commission can also require companies to run corrective advertising in response to previous ads considered misleading.

The FTC also assists businesses in complying with laws. New marketing methods are evaluated every year. When general sets of guidelines are needed to improve business practices in a particular industry, the FTC sometimes encourages firms within that industry to establish a set of trade practices voluntarily. The FTC may even sponsor a conference bringing together industry leaders and consumers for the purpose of establishing acceptable trade practices.

Unlike the FTC, other regulatory units are limited to dealing with specific products, services, or business activities. The Food and Drug Administration (FDA) enforces regulations prohibiting the sale and distribution of adulterated, misbranded, or hazardous food and drug products. For example, the FDA outlawed the sale and distribution of most over-the-counter hair-loss remedies after research indicated that few of the products were effective in restoring hair growth.

The Environmental Protection Agency (EPA) develops and enforces environmental protection standards and conducts research into the adverse effects of pollution. The Consumer Product Safety Commission recalls about 300 products a year, ranging from small, inexpensive toys to major appliances. The Consumer Product Safety Commission's Web site provides details regarding current recalls.

The Consumer Product Safety commission has fallen under increasing scrutiny in the wake of a number of product safety scandals involving children's toys. The most notable of these issues was lead paint discovered in toys produced in China. Other problems have included the manufacture of toys that include small magnets that pose a choking hazard, and lead-tainted costume jewelry.[77]

Important Elements of Business Law

To avoid violating criminal and civil laws, as well as discouraging lawsuits from consumers, employees, suppliers, and others, businesspeople need to be familiar with laws that address business practices.

The Uniform Commercial Code

At one time, states had their own specific laws governing various business practices, and transacting business across state lines was difficult because of the variation in the laws from state to state. To simplify

Consider Ethics and Social Responsibility
Pfizer: Puffery or Deception?

Pfizer Inc. is a well-known drug company that produces a number of popular medications. Its blockbuster cholesterol-reducing product, Lipitor, has been proven to lower cholesterol. However, increased competition brought on by the introduction of a generic version of Merck & Co.'s Zocor cholesterol medication prompted Pfizer to rethink its advertising strategy. In order to promote this product, the company hired Robert Jarvik, inventor of a kind of artificial heart, to star in new ads for the drug. Although a doctor, Jarvik is not a practicing physician and this has called into question the validity and morality of the endorsement. The ads had been running since 2006 when the company abruptly pulled them in January 2008, in the wake of a federal investigation into the matter.

The accusations do not call into question the importance of Jarvik's accomplishments or the effectiveness of the medication. They do, however, question Jarvik's credentials, as he is not a practicing physician. They also question whether or not the ads sought to mislead consumers in a fraudulent way. One of the television advertisements shows Jarvik at a lake discussing the benefits of Lipitor. In the ad he states, "just because I'm a doctor doesn't mean I don't worry about my cholesterol," thereby potentially leading the audience to believe that he is a physician.

Exaggerated marketing claims are known as *puffery,* which is defined by the FTC as "exaggerations reasonably to be expected of a seller" where "truth or falsity cannot be precisely determined." Advertising moves beyond puffery into the realm of deceptive, or false, advertising if it gives consumers untrue or unrealistic ideas about the product being promoted. False advertising can range from straight out misrepresenting the product, advertising the maximum or best features rather than the basic or standards ones, or using fillers or oversized packaging to make the consumer think that he or she is buying more. Deceptive advertising can be considered fraud, which is illegal. The House Committee on Energy and Commerce probe has called into question the validity of the claims asserted by Jarvik in the ad, and is considering whether the ads should be considered deceptive, or merely puffery. This distinction can be difficult to determine. According to the Better Business Bureau's Code of Advertising, "subjective claims are not subject to test of their truth or accuracy," meaning there is no objective test of such claims. Some believe that the best approach for Pfizer would be to move towards advertising that utilizes scientific data over emotional appeals.[78]

Discussion Questions

1. If the information conveyed in the ads is truthful, should it matter that Dr. Jarvik is associated with development of an artificial heart but is not a practicing physician?

2. What advertising approaches do you think that Pfizer should take in the future in order to avoid the same kind of scrutiny and criticism engendered by the Jarvik Lipitor ads?

3. How might one determine when a company has crossed the line between puffery and outright deception?

commerce, every state—except Louisiana—has enacted the Uniform Commercial Code (Louisiana has enacted portions of the code). The **Uniform Commercial Code (UCC)** is a set of statutory laws covering several business law topics. Article II of the Uniform Commercial Code, which is discussed in the following paragraphs, has a significant impact on business.

Sales Agreements. Article II of the Uniform Commercial Code covers sales agreements for goods and services such as installation but does not cover the sale of stocks and bonds, personal services, or real estate. Among its many provisions, Article II stipulates that a sales agreement can be enforced even though it does not specify the selling price or the time or place of delivery. It also requires that a buyer pay a reasonable price for goods at the time of delivery if the buyer and seller have not reached an agreement on price. Specifically, Article II addresses the rights of buyers and sellers, transfers of ownership, warranties, and the legal placement of risk during manufacture and delivery.

Article II also deals with express and implied warranties. An **express warranty** stipulates the specific terms the seller will honor. Many automobile manufacturers, for example, provide three-year or 36,000-mile warranties on their vehicles, during which period they will fix any and all defects specified in the warranty. An **implied warranty** is imposed on the producer or seller by law, although it may not be a written document provided at the time of sale. Under Article II, a consumer may assume that the product for sale has a clear title (in other words, that it is not stolen) and that the product will both serve the purpose for which it was made and sold as well as function as advertised.

The Law of Torts and Fraud

A **tort** is a private or civil wrong other than breach of contract. For example, a tort can result if the driver of a Domino's Pizza delivery car loses control of the vehicle and damages property or injures a person. In the case of the delivery car accident, the injured persons might sue the driver and the owner of the company—Domino's in this case—for damages resulting from the accident.

Fraud is a purposeful unlawful act to deceive or manipulate in order to damage others. Thus, in some cases, a tort may also represent a violation of criminal law. Health care fraud has become a major issue in the courts.

An important aspect of tort law involves **product liability**—businesses' legal responsibility for any negligence in the design, production, sale, and consumption of products. Product liability laws have evolved from both common and statutory law. Some states have expanded the concept of product liability to include injuries by products whether or not the producer is proven negligent. Under this strict product liability, a consumer who files suit because of an injury has to prove only that the product was defective, that the defect caused the injury, and that the defect made the product unreasonably dangerous. For example, a carving knife is expected to be sharp and is not considered defective if you cut your finger using it. But an electric knife could be considered defective and unreasonably dangerous if it continued to operate after being switched off.

Reforming tort law, particularly in regard to product liability, has become a hot political issue as businesses look for relief from huge judgments in lawsuits. Although many lawsuits are warranted—few would disagree that a wrong has occurred when a patient dies because of negligence during a medical procedure or when a child is seriously injured by a defective toy, and that the families deserve some compensation—many suits are not. Because of multimillion-dollar judgments, companies are trying to minimize their liability, and sometimes they pass on the costs of the damage awards to their customers in the form of higher prices. Some states have passed laws limiting damage awards and some tort reform is occurring at the federal level. Table B.2 lists the state courts systems the U.S. Chamber of Commerce's Institute for Legal Reform has identified as being "friendliest" and "least friendly" to business in terms of juries' fairness, judges' competence and impartiality, and other factors.

TABLE B.2 State Court Systems' Reputations for Supporting Business

Most Friendly to Business	Least Friendly to Business
Delaware	Mississippi
Nebraska	West Virginia
Virginia	Alabama
Iowa	Louisiana
Idaho	California
Utah	Texas
New Hampshire	Illinois
Minnesota	Montana
Kansas	Arkansas
Wisconsin	Missouri

Source: U.S. Chamber of Commerce Institute for Legal Reform, in Martin Kasindorf, "Robin Hood Is Alive in Court, Say Those Seeking Lawsuit Limits," *USA Today,* March 8, 2004, p. 4A.

The Law of Contracts

Virtually every business transaction is carried out by means of a **contract,** a mutual agreement between two or more parties that can be enforced in a court if one party chooses not to comply with the terms of the contract. If you rent an apartment or house, for example, your lease is a contract. If you have borrowed money under a student loan program, you have a contractual agreement to repay the money. Many aspects of contract law are covered under the Uniform Commercial Code.

A "handshake deal" is in most cases as fully and completely binding as a written, signed contract agreement. Indeed, many oil-drilling and construction contractors have for years agreed to take on projects on the basis of such handshake deals. However, individual states require that some contracts be in writing to be enforceable. Most states require that at least some of the following contracts be in writing:

- Contracts involving the sale of land or an interest in land.
- Contracts to pay somebody else's debt.
- Contracts that cannot be fulfilled within one year.
- Contracts for the sale of goods that cost more than $500 (required by the Uniform Commercial Code).

Only those contracts that meet certain requirements—called *elements*—are enforceable by the courts. A person or business seeking to enforce a contract must show that it contains the following elements: voluntary agreement, consideration, contractual capacity of the parties, and legality.

For any agreement to be considered a legal contract, all persons involved must agree to be bound by the terms of the contract. *Voluntary agreement* typically comes about when one party makes an offer and the other accepts. If both the offer and the acceptance are freely, voluntarily, and knowingly made, the acceptance forms the basis for the contract. If, however, either the offer or the acceptance are the result of fraud or force, the individual or organization subject to the fraud or force can void, or invalidate, the resulting agreement or receive compensation for damages.

The second requirement for enforcement of a contract is that it must be supported by *consideration*— that is, money or something of value must be given in return for fulfilling a contract. As a general rule, a person cannot be forced to abide by the terms of a promise unless that person receives a consideration. The something-of-value could be money, goods, services, or even a promise to do or not to do something.

Contractual capacity is the legal ability to enter into a contract. As a general rule, a court cannot enforce a contract if either party to the agreement lacks contractual capacity. A person's contractual capacity may be limited or nonexistent if he or she is a minor (under the age of 18), mentally unstable, retarded, insane, or intoxicated.

Legality is the state or condition of being lawful. For an otherwise binding contract to be enforceable, both the purpose of and the consideration for the contract must be legal. A contract in which a bank loans money at a rate of interest prohibited by law, a practice known as usury, would be an illegal contract, for example. The fact that one of the parties may commit an illegal act while performing a contract does not render the contract itself illegal, however.

Breach of contract is the failure or refusal of a party to a contract to live up to his or her promises. In the case of an apartment lease, failure to pay rent would be considered breach of contract. The breaching party— the one who fails to comply—may be liable for monetary damages that he or she causes the other person.

The Law of Agency

An **agency** is a common business relationship created when one person acts on behalf of another and under that person's control. Two parties are involved

in an agency relationship: The **principal** is the one who wishes to have a specific task accomplished; the **agent** is the one who acts on behalf of the principal to accomplish the task. Authors, movie stars, and athletes often employ agents to help them obtain the best contract terms.

An agency relationship is created by the mutual agreement of the principal and the agent. It is usually not necessary that such an agreement be in writing, although putting it in writing is certainly advisable. An agency relationship continues as long as both the principal and the agent so desire. It can be terminated by mutual agreement, by fulfillment of the purpose of the agency, by the refusal of either party to continue in the relationship, or by the death of either the principal or the agent. In most cases, a principal grants authority to the agent through a formal *power of attorney*, which is a legal document authorizing a person to act as someone else's agent. The power of attorney can be used for any agency relationship, and its use is not limited to lawyers. For instance, in real estate transactions, often a lawyer or real estate agent is given power of attorney with the authority to purchase real estate for the buyer. Accounting firms often give employees agency relationships in making financial transactions.

Both officers and directors of corporations are fiduciaries, or people of trust, who use due care and loyalty as an agent in making decisions on behalf of the organization. This relationship creates a duty of care, also called duty of diligence, to make informed decisions. These agents of the corporation are not held responsible for negative outcomes if they are informed and diligent in their decisions. The duty of loyalty means that all decisions should be in the interests of the corporation and its stakeholders. Many people believe that executives at financial firms such as Countrywide Financial, Lehman Brothers, and Merrill Lynch failed to carry out their fiduciary duties. Lawsuits from shareholders called for the officers and directors to pay large sums of money from their own pockets.

The Law of Property

Property law is extremely broad in scope because it covers the ownership and transfer of all kinds of real, personal, and intellectual property. **Real property** consists of real estate and everything permanently attached to it; **personal property** basically is everything else. Personal property can be further subdivided into tangible and intangible property. *Tangible property* refers to items that have a physical existence, such as automobiles, business inventory, and clothing. *Intangible property* consists of rights and duties; its existence may be represented by a document or by some other tangible item. For example, accounts receivable, stock in a corporation, goodwill, and trademarks are all examples of intangible personal property. **Intellectual property** refers to property, such as musical works, artwork, books, and computer software, that is generated by a person's creative activities.

Copyrights, patents, and trademarks provide protection to the owners of property by giving them the exclusive right to use it. *Copyrights* protect the ownership rights on material (often intellectual property) such as books, music, videos, photos, and computer software. The creators of such works, or their heirs, generally have exclusive rights to the published or unpublished works for the creator's lifetime, plus 50 years. *Patents* give inventors exclusive rights to their invention for 17 years. The most intense competition for patents is in the pharmaceutical industry. Most patents take a minimum of 18 months to secure.

A *trademark* is a brand (name, mark, or symbol) that is registered with the U.S. Patent and Trademark Office and is thus legally protected from use by any other firm. Among the symbols that have been so protected are McDonald's golden arches and Coca-Cola's distinctive bottle shape. It is estimated that large multinational firms may have as many as 15,000 conflicts related to trademarks. Companies are diligent about protecting their trademarks both to avoid confusion in consumers' minds and because a term that becomes part of everyday language can no longer be trademarked. The names *aspirin* and *nylon,* for example, were once the exclusive property of their creators but became so widely used as product names (rather than brand names) that now anyone can use them.

As the trend toward globalization of trade continues, and more and more businesses trade across national boundaries, protecting property rights, particularly intellectual property such as computer software, has become an increasing challenge. While a company may be able to register as a trademark a brand name or symbol in its home country, it may not be able to secure that protection abroad. Some countries have copyright and patent laws that are less strict than those of the United States; some countries will not enforce U.S. laws. China, for example, has often been criticized for permitting U.S. goods to be counterfeited there. Such counterfeiting harms not only the sales of U.S. companies but also their reputations if the knockoffs are of poor quality. Thus, businesses engaging in foreign trade may have to take extra steps to protect their property because local laws may be insufficient to protect them.

The Law of Bankruptcy

Although few businesses and individuals intentionally fail to repay (or default on) their debts, sometimes they cannot fulfill their financial obligations. Individuals may charge goods and services beyond their ability to pay for them. Businesses may take on too much debt in order to finance growth or business events such as an increase in the cost of commodities can bankrupt a company. An option of last resort in these cases is bankruptcy, or legal insolvency. The recent financial crisis caused a number of well-known companies to declare bankruptcy, including Six Flags, Chrysler, Eddie Bauer, and Circuit City. While some of these companies managed to negotiate deals with their creditors or received a government bailout, the electronics retailer Circuit City had no such luck. The company was forced to liquidate all its U.S. stores.[79]

Individuals or companies may ask a bankruptcy court to declare them unable to pay their debts and thus release them from the obligation of repaying those debts. The debtor's assets may then be sold to pay off as much of the debt as possible. In the case of a personal bankruptcy, although the individual is released from repaying debts and can start over with a clean slate, obtaining credit after bankruptcy proceedings is very difficult. About 2 million households in the United States filed for bankruptcy in 2005, the most ever. However, a new, more restrictive law went into effect in late 2005, and fewer consumers are using bankruptcy to eliminate their debts. The law makes it harder for consumers to prove that they should be allowed to clear their debts for what is called a "fresh start" or Chapter 7 bankruptcy. Although the person or company in debt usually initiates bankruptcy proceedings, creditors may also initiate them. The subprime mortgage crisis of early 2008 caused a string of bankruptcies among individuals; and Chapter 7 and 11 bankruptcies among banks, and other businesses as well. Tougher bankruptcy laws and a slowing economy converged on the subprime crisis to create a situation where bankruptcy filings skyrocketed.

TABLE B.3   Types of Bankruptcy

Chapter 7	Requires that the business be dissolved and its assets liquidated, or sold, to pay off the debts. Individuals declaring Chapter 7 retain a limited amount of exempt assets, the amount of which may be determined by state or federal law, at the debtor's option. Although the type and value of exempt assets varies from state to state, most states' laws allow a bankrupt individual to keep an automobile, some household goods, clothing, furnishings, and at least some of the value of the debtor's residence. All nonexempt assets must be sold to pay debts
Chapter 11	Temporarily frees a business from its financial obligations while it reorganizes and works out a payment plan with its creditors. The indebted company continues to operate its business during bankruptcy proceedings. Often, the business sells off assets and less-profitable subsidiaries to raise cash to pay off its immediate obligations.
Chapter 13	Similar to Chapter 11 but limited to individuals. This proceeding allows an individual to establish a three- to five-year plan for repaying his or her debt. Under this plan, an individual ultimately may repay as little as 10 percent of his or her debt.

Table B.3 describes the various levels of bankruptcy protection a business or individual may seek.

Laws Affecting Business Practices

One of the government's many roles is to act as a watchdog to ensure that businesses behave in accordance with the wishes of society. Congress has enacted a number of laws that affect business practices; some of the most important of these are summarized in Table B.4. Many state legislatures have enacted similar laws governing business within specific states.

The **Sherman Antitrust Act,** passed in 1890 to prevent businesses from restraining trade and monopolizing markets, condemns "every contract, combination, or conspiracy in restraint of trade." For example, a request that a competitor agree to fix prices or divide markets would, if accepted, result in a violation of the Sherman Act. The search engine Google has faced increased attention from antitrust authorities. In 2009, antitrust authorities were investigating a settlement Google had reached with the Author's Guild and the Association of American Publishers. The $125 million settlement would give Google the ability to scan millions of books into what will be known as the Google Book Search service. The Department of Justice thought this settlement might give Google too much control, particularly over the distribution and pricing of certain books. It began investigating whether Google was breaking any antitrust laws. This was not the first time Google was investigated for antitrust violations. A year earlier, Google had been investigated for a partnership it was forming with Yahoo!. The deal allowed Google to sell and place advertisements on Yahoo!'s Web pages for a share in the revenue. Authorities felt this would give Google too much power that could enable it to gain monopolistic control over online advertising. Increased pressure caused Google and Yahoo! to delay the alliance.[80] The Sherman Antitrust Act, still highly relevant 100 years after its passage, is being copied throughout the world as the basis for regulating fair competition.

Because the provisions of the Sherman Antitrust Act are rather vague, courts have not always interpreted it as its creators intended. The Clayton Act was passed in 1914 to limit specific activities that can reduce competition. The **Clayton Act** prohibits price discrimination, tying and exclusive agreements, and the acquisition of stock in another corporation where the effect may be to substantially lessen competition or tend to create a monopoly. In addition, the Clayton Act prohibits members of one company's board of directors from holding seats on the boards of competing corporations. The act also exempts farm cooperatives and labor organizations from antitrust laws.

In spite of these laws regulating business practices, there are still many questions about the regulation of business. For instance, it is difficult to determine what constitutes an acceptable degree of competition and whether a monopoly is harmful to a particular market. Many mergers were permitted that resulted in less competition in the banking, publishing, and automobile industries. In some industries, such as

TABLE B.4   Major Federal Laws Affecting Business Practices

Act (Date Enacted)	Purpose
Sherman Antitrust Act (1890)	Prohibits contracts, combinations, or conspiracies to restrain trade; establishes as a misdemeanor monopolizing or attempting to monopolize
Clayton Act (1914)	Prohibits specific practices such as price discrimination, exclusive dealer arrangements, and stock acquisitions in which the effect may notably lessen competition or tend to create a monopoly.
Federal Trade Commission Act (1914)	Created the Federal Trade Commission; also gives the FTC investigatory powers to be used in preventing unfair methods of competition.
Robinson-Patman Act (1936)	Prohibits price discrimination that lessens competition among wholesalers or retailers; prohibits producers from giving disproportionate services of facilities to large buyers.
Wheeler-Lea Act (1938)	Prohibits unfair and deceptive acts and practices regardless of whether competition is injured; places advertising of foods and drugs under the jurisdiction of the FTC.
Lanham Act (1946)	Provides protections and regulation of brand names, brand marks, trade names, and trademarks.
Celler-Kefauver Act (1950)	Prohibits any corporation engaged in commerce from acquiring the whole or any part of the stock or other share of the capital assets of another corporation when the effect substantially lessens competition or tends to create a monopoly.
Fair Packaging and Labeling Act (1966)	Makes illegal the unfair or deceptive packaging or labeling of consumer products.
Magnuson-Moss Warranty (FTC) Act (1975)	Provides for minimum disclosure standards for written consumer product warranties; defines minimum consent standards for written warranties; allows the FTC to prescribe interpretive rules in policy statements regarding unfair or deceptive practices.
Consumer Goods Pricing Act (1975)	Prohibits the use of price maintenance agreements among manufacturers and resellers in interstate commerce.
Antitrust Improvements Act (1976)	Requires large corporations to inform federal regulators of prospective mergers or acquisitions so that they can be studied for any possible violations of the law.
Trademark Counterfeiting Act (1980)	Provides civil and criminal penalties against those who deal in counterfeit consumer goods or any counterfeit goods that can threaten health or safety.
Trademark Law Revision Act (1988)	Amends the Lanham Act to allow brands not yet introduced to be protected through registration with the Patent and Trademark Office.
Nutrition Labeling and Education Act (1990)	Prohibits exaggerated health claims and requires all processed foods to contain labels with nutritional information.
Telephone Consumer Protection Act (1991)	Establishes procedures to avoid unwanted telephone solicitations; prohibits marketers from using automated telephone dialing system or an artificial or prerecorded voice to certain telephone lines.
Federal Trademark Dilution Act (1995)	Provides trademark owners the right to protect trademarks and requires relinquishment of names that match or parallel existing trademarks.

continued

TABLE B.4   *continued*

Act (Date Enacted)	Purpose
Digital Millennium Copyright Act (1998)	Refined copyright laws to protect digital versions of copyrighted materials, including music and movies.
Children's Online Privacy Protection Act (2000)	Regulates the collection of personally identifiable information (name, address, e-mail address, hobbies, interests, or information collected through cookies) online from children under age 13.
Sarbanes-Oxley Act (2002)	Made securities fraud a criminal offense; stiffened penalties for corporate fraud; created an accounting oversight board; and instituted numerous other provisions designed to increase corporate transparency and compliance.
Do Not Call Implementation Act (2003)	Directs FCC and FTC to coordinate so their rules are consistent regarding telemarketing call practices, including the Do Not Call Registry.

utilities, it is not cost effective to have too many competitors. For this reason, the government permits utility monopolies, although recently, the telephone, electricity, and communications industries have been deregulated. Furthermore, the antitrust laws are often rather vague and require interpretation, which may vary from judge to judge and court to court. Thus, what one judge defines as a monopoly or trust today may be permitted by another judge a few years from now. Businesspeople need to understand what the law says on these issues and try to conduct their affairs within the bounds of these laws.

The Internet: Legal and Regulatory Issues

Our use and dependence on the Internet is increasingly creating a potential legal problem for businesses. With this growing use come questions of maintaining an acceptable level of privacy for consumers and proper competitive use of the medium. Some might consider that tracking individuals who visit or "hit" their Web site by attaching a "cookie" (identifying you as a Web site visitor for potential recontact and tracking your movement throughout the site) is an improper use of the Internet for business purposes. Others may find such practices acceptable and similar to the practices of non-Internet retailers who copy information from checks or ask customers for their name, address, or phone number before they will process a transaction. There are few specific laws that regulate business on the Internet,

but the standards for acceptable behavior that are reflected in the basic laws and regulations designed for traditional businesses can be applied to business on the Internet as well. One law aimed specifically at advertising on the internet is the CAN-SPAM Act of 2004. The law restricts unsolicited email advertisements by requiring the consent of the recipient. Furthermore, the CAN-SPAM Act follows the "opt-out" model wherein recipients can elect to not receive further emails from a sender simply by clicking on a link.[81]

The central focus for future legislation of business conducted on the Internet is the protection of personal privacy. The present basis of personal privacy protection is the U.S. Constitution, various Supreme

Whether you like it or not, Google, like Yahoo! and AOL, tracks people's Web browsing patterns. By tracking the sites you visit, the companies' advertisers can aim ads targeted closer to your interests.

Court rulings, and laws such as the 1971 Fair Credit Reporting Act, the 1978 Right to Financial Privacy Act, and the 1974 Privacy Act, which deals with the release of government records. With few regulations on the use of information by businesses, companies legally buy and sell information on customers to gain competitive advantage. Sometimes existing laws are not enough to protect people, and the ease with which information on customers can be obtained becomes a problem. For example, identity theft has increased due to the proliferation of the use of the internet. In 2009, it was estimated that data and security breaches cost organizations more than $6 million on average each time they occurred. Some of the more common security breaches (and most disturbing) occur at universities, banks, and insurance companies. Another concern is companies that use information from online consumers without the person's knowledge or permission.[82] It has been suggested that the treatment of personal data as property will ensure privacy rights by recognizing that customers have a right to control the use of their personal data.

Internet use is different from traditional interaction with businesses in that it is readily accessible, and most online businesses are able to develop databases of information on customers. Congress has restricted the development of databases on children using the Internet. The Children's Online Privacy Protection Act of 2000 prohibits Web sites and Internet providers from seeking personal information from children under age 13 without parental consent.

The Internet has also created a copyright dilemma for some organizations that have found that the Web addresses of other online firms either match or are very similar to their company trademark. "Cybersquatters" attempt to sell back the registration of these matching sites to the trademark owner. Companies such as Taco Bell, MTC, and KFC have paid thousands of dollars to gain control of domain names that match or parallel company trademarks. The Federal Trademark Dilution Act of 1995 helps companies address this conflict. The act provides trademark owners the right to protect trademarks, prevents the use of trademark-protected entities, and requires the relinquishment of names that match or closely parallel company trademarks. The reduction of geographic barriers, speed of response, and memory capability of the Internet will continue to create new challenges for the legal and regulatory environment in the future.

Legal Pressure for Responsible Business Conduct

To ensure greater compliance with society's desires, both federal and state governments are moving toward increased organizational accountability for misconduct. Before 1991, laws mainly punished those employees directly responsible for an offense. Under new guidelines established by the Federal Sentencing Guidelines for Organizations (FSGO), however, both the responsible employees and the firms that employ them are held accountable for violations of federal law. Thus, the government now places responsibility for controlling and preventing misconduct squarely on the shoulders of top management. The main objectives of the federal guidelines are to train employees, self-monitor and supervise employee conduct, deter unethical acts, and punish those organizational members who engage in illegal acts.

A 2004 amendment to the FSGO requires that a business's governing authority be well informed about its ethics program with respect to content, implementation, and effectiveness. This places the responsibility squarely on the shoulders of the firm's leadership, usually the board of directors. The board must ensure that there is a high-ranking manager accountable for the day-to-day operational oversight of the ethics program. The board must provide for adequate authority, resources, and access to the board or an appropriate subcommittee of the board. The board must ensure that there are confidential mechanisms available so that the organization's employees and agents may report or seek guidance about potential or actual misconduct without fear of retaliation. Finally, the board is required to oversee the discovery of risks and to design, implement, and modify approaches to deal with those risks.

If an organization's culture and policies reward or provide opportunities to engage in misconduct through lack of managerial concern or failure to comply with the seven minimum requirements of the FSGO (provided in Table B.5), then the organization may incur not only penalties but also the loss of customer trust, public confidence, and other intangible assets. For this reason, organizations cannot succeed solely through a legalistic approach to compliance with the sentencing guidelines; top management must cultivate high ethical standards that will serve

TABLE B.5   Seven Steps to Compliance

1. Develop standards and procedures to reduce the propensity for criminal conduct.
2. Designate a high-level compliance manager or ethics officer to oversee the compliance program.
3. Avoid delegating authority to people known to have a propensity to engage in misconduct.
4. Communicate standards and procedures to employees, other agents, and independent contractors through training programs and publications.
5. Establish systems to monitor and audit misconduct and to allow employees and agents to report criminal activity.
6. Enforce standards and punishments consistently across all employees in the organization.
7. Respond immediately to misconduct and take reasonable steps to prevent further criminal conduct.

Source: United States Sentencing Commission, *Federal Sentencing Guidelines for Organizations,* 1991.

as barriers to illegal conduct. The organization must want to be a good citizen and recognize the importance of compliance to successful workplace activities and relationships.

The federal guidelines also require businesses to develop programs that can detect—and that will deter employees from engaging in—misconduct. To be considered effective, such compliance programs must include disclosure of any wrongdoing, cooperation with the government, and acceptance of responsibility for the misconduct. Codes of ethics, employee ethics training, hotlines (direct 800 phone numbers), compliance directors, newsletters, brochures, and other communication methods are

TABLE B.6   Major Provisions of the Sarbanes-Oxley Act

1. Requires the establishment of a Public Company Accounting Oversight Board in charge of regulations administered by the Securities and Exchange Commission.
2. Requires CEOs and CFOs to certify that their companies' financial statements are true and without misleading statements.
3. Requires that corporate boards of directors' audit committees consist of independent members who have no material interests in the company.
4. Prohibits corporations from making or offering loans to officers and board members.
5. Requires codes of ethics for senior financial officers; code must be registered with the SEC.
6. Prohibits accounting firms from providing both auditing and consulting services to the same client without the approval of the client firm's audit committee.
7. Requires company attorneys to report wrongdoing to top managers and, if necessary, to the board of directors; if managers and directors fail to respond to reports of wrongdoing, the attorney should stop representing the company.
8. Mandates "whistleblower protection" for persons who disclose wrongdoing to authorities.
9. Requires financial securities analysts to certify that their recommendations are based on objective reports.
10. Requires mutual fund managers to disclose how they vote shareholder proxies, giving investors information about how their shares influence decisions.
11. Establishes a 10-year penalty for mail/wire fraud.
12. Prohibits the two senior auditors from working on a corporation's account for more than five years; other auditors are prohibited from working on an account for more than seven years. In other words, accounting firms must rotate individual auditors from one account to another from time to time.

Source: O. C. Ferrell, John Fraedrich, and Linda Ferrell, *Business Ethics: Ethical Decision Making and Cases,* 8th ed. (Mason, OH: South-Western Cengage Learning, 2011), pp. 108–109.

typical components of a compliance program. The ethics component, discussed in Chapter 2, acts as a buffer, keeping firms away from the thin line that separates unethical and illegal conduct.

Despite the existing legislation, a number of ethics scandals in the early 2000s led Congress to pass—almost unanimously—the **Sarbanes-Oxley Act,** which criminalized securities fraud and strengthened penalties for corporate fraud. It also created an accounting oversight board that requires corporations to establish codes of ethics for financial reporting and to develop greater transparency in financial reports to investors and other interested parties. Additionally, the law requires top corporate executives to sign off on their firms' financial reports, and they risk fines and jail sentences if they misrepresent their companies' financial position. Table B.6 summarizes the major provisions of the Sarbanes-Oxley Act.

The Sarbanes Oxley Act has created a number of concerns and is considered burdensome and expensive to corporations. Large corporations report spending more than $4 million each year to comply with the Act according to Financial Executives International. The Act has caused more than 500 public companies a year to report problems in their accounting systems. Additionally, Sarbanes-Oxley failed to prevent and detect the widespread misconduct of financial institutions that led to the financial crisis. This means that the overwhelming majority of businesses are in compliance with the law.

On the other hand, there are many benefits, including greater accountability of top managers and boards of directors, that improve investor confidence and protect employees, especially their retirement plans. It is believed that the law has more benefits than drawbacks—with the greatest benefit being that boards of directors and top managers are better informed. Some companies such as Cisco and Pitney Bowes report improved efficiency and cost savings from better financial information.

chapter 3

Business in a Borderless World

OBJECTIVES

After reading this chapter, you will be able to:

- Explore some of the factors within the international trade environment that influence business.

- Investigate some of the economic, legal-political, social, cultural, and technological barriers to international business.

- Specify some of the agreements, alliances, and organizations that may encourage trade across international boundaries.

- Summarize the different levels of organizational involvement in international trade.

- Contrast two basic strategies used in international business.

- Assess the opportunities and problems facing a small business considering expanding into international markets.

Nokia Wins with Global Strategy

Think "cool, trendy cell phone maker," and companies like Apple or BlackBerry producer Research in Motion (RIM) may come to mind. Yet in terms of global market share, Apple and RIM hold about 0.9 and 1.9 percent, respectively. Conversely, their less trend-setting competitor Nokia holds a whopping 38.6 percent of the market. The reason has to do with the different target markets of the companies. Apple and RIM cater to a more elite, smaller portion of the market. For instance, the iPhone ranges from $99 to $299 while the BlackBerry Storm costs about $279.99. Many people around the world cannot afford such high-priced products. Nokia, however, caters to a much broader set of consumers. Its phones range widely in price from $10 to $700, which allows Nokia to reach many more customers in emerging economies and elsewhere.

Nokia boasts more than 1 billion customers in more than 150 countries. The secret to its success is its understanding of global marketing. Nokia extensively researches both its current and potential customers, taking into account their cultures and needs. It then creates programs to meet those needs. For example, its program Life Tools allows customers in India to spend $1.30 per month to receive information on daily crop prices or weather updates—coveted information for consumers whose livelihood depends on farming. Nokia funds 10 research labs throughout the world to help it learn more about its global consumers.

As a result, Nokia has become an expert on efficiency, cost management, and top-notch distribution. Apple and RIM may be responsible for changing the cell phone experience for higher-end smart phone users, but Nokia is responsible for allowing people in hard-to-reach areas throughout the world to access cellular service.[1]

Introduction

Consumers around the world can drink Coca-Cola and Pepsi; eat at McDonald's and Pizza Hut; see movies from Mexico, England, France, Australia, and China; and watch CNN and MTV on Samsung and Panasonic televisions. It may surprise you that the Japanese firm Komatsu sells earth-moving equipment to China that is manufactured in Peoria, Illinois.[2] The products you consume today are just as likely to have been made in China, Korea, or Germany as in the United States. Likewise, consumers in other countries buy Western electrical equipment, clothing, rock music, cosmetics, and toiletries, as well as computers, robots, and earth-moving equipment.

international business
the buying, selling, and trading of goods and services across national boundaries

Many U.S. firms are finding that international markets provide tremendous opportunities for growth. Accessing these markets can promote innovation, while intensifying global competition spurs companies to market better and less expensive products. Today, the 6.8 billion people that inhabit the earth comprise one tremendous marketplace.

In this chapter, we explore business in this exciting global marketplace. First, we'll look at the nature of international business, including barriers and promoters of trade across international boundaries. Next, we consider the levels of organizational involvement in international business. Finally, we briefly discuss strategies for trading across national borders.

The Role of International Business

International business refers to the buying, selling, and trading of goods and services across national boundaries. Falling political barriers and new technology are making it possible for more and more companies to sell their products overseas as well as at home. And, as differences among nations continue to narrow, the trend toward the globalization of business is becoming increasingly important. Starbucks, for example, serves 20 million customers a week at more than 16,000 coffee shops, 5,500 of which are outside the United States, in 50 countries.[4] The Internet provides many companies easier entry to access global markets than opening bricks-and-mortar stores.[5] Amazon.com, an online retailer, has distribution centers from Nevada

Laws and regulations in other countries can trip up companies trying to expand internationally. The insurer Zurich has set up programs for companies to take the headaches out of going global.

to Germany that fill millions of orders a day and ship them to customers in every corner of the world. In China, Procter & Gamble has developed bargain-priced versions of Tide, Crest, and Oil of Olay, and it regularly relies on groups that live in the countryside for consumer information.[6] Indeed, most of the world's population and two-thirds of its total purchasing power are outside the United States.

When McDonald's sells a Big Mac in Moscow, Sony sells a stereo in Detroit, or a small Swiss medical supply company sells a shipment of orthopedic devices to a hospital in Monterrey, Mexico, the sale affects the economies of the countries involved. The U.S. market, with around 300 million consumers, makes up only a small part of the 6.8 billion people elsewhere in the world to whom global companies must consider marketing. Global marketing requires balancing your global brand with the needs of local consumers.[7] To begin our study of international business, we must first consider some economic issues: why nations trade, exporting and importing, and the balance of trade.

Why Nations Trade

Nations and businesses engage in international trade to obtain raw materials and goods that are otherwise unavailable to them or are available elsewhere at a lower price than that at which they themselves can produce. A nation, or individuals and organizations from a nation, sell surplus materials and goods to acquire funds to buy the goods, services, and ideas its people need. Poland and Hungary, for example, want to trade with Western nations so that they can acquire new technology and techniques to revitalize their formerly communist economies. Which goods and services a nation sells depends on what resources it has available.

Some nations have a monopoly on the production of a particular resource or product. Such a monopoly, or **absolute advantage,** exists when a country is the only source of an item, the only producer of an item, or the most efficient producer of an item. Because South Africa has the largest deposits of diamonds in the world, one company, De Beers Consolidated Mines Ltd. controls a major portion of the world's diamond trade and uses its control to maintain high prices for gem-quality diamonds. The United States, until recently, held an absolute advantage in oil-drilling equipment. But an absolute advantage not based on the availability of natural resources rarely lasts, and Japan and Russia are now challenging the United States in the production of oil-drilling equipment.

Most international trade is based on **comparative advantage,** which occurs when a country specializes in products that it can supply more efficiently or at a lower cost than it can produce other items. The United States has a comparative advantage in producing agricultural commodities such as corn and wheat. Until recently, the United States had a comparative advantage in manufacturing automobiles, heavy machinery, airplanes, and weapons; other countries now hold the comparative advantage for many of these products. Other countries, particularly India and Ireland, are also gaining a comparative advantage over the United States in the provision of some services, such as call-center operations, engineering, and software programming. As a result, U.S. companies are increasingly **outsourcing,** or transferring manufacturing and other tasks to countries where labor and supplies are less expensive. Outsourcing has become a controversial practice in the United States because many jobs have moved overseas where those tasks can be accomplished for lower costs. For example, India is a popular choice for call centers for U.S. firms. As call centers are the first job choice for millions of young Indians, employers are getting choosier about the people they hire, and it is difficult to train

absolute advantage
a monopoly that exists when a country is the only source of an item, the only producer of an item, or the most efficient producer of an item

comparative advantage
the basis of most international trade, when a country specializes in products that it can supply more efficiently or at a lower cost than it can produce other items

outsourcing
the transferring of manufacturing or other tasks—such as data processing—to countries where labor and supplies are less expensive

Indians to speak the kind of colloquial English, French, Spanish, German, or Dutch that customers want. This can be frustrating for customers when they have trouble understanding the customer service representative, resulting in increased customer dissatisfaction with the service.

Trade between Countries

To obtain needed goods and services and the funds to pay for them, nations trade by exporting and importing. **Exporting** is the sale of goods and services to foreign markets. The United States exported more than $1.5 trillion in goods and services in 2009.[8] In China, General Motors is targeting wealthier customers with the Cadillac, middle management with the Buick Excelle, office workers with the Chevrolet Spark, and rural consumers with the Wuling minivan.[9] U.S. companies that view China as both a growth market for exports and a market for lower cost labor for imports and can strategically integrate these into their operations enjoy significantly higher profits than companies who only focus on one of these opportunities.[10] U.S. businesses export many goods and services, particularly agricultural, entertainment (movies, television shows, etc.), and technological products. **Importing** is the purchase of goods and services from foreign sources. Many of the goods you buy in the United States are likely to be imports or to have some imported components. Sometimes, you may not even realize they are imports. The United States imported more than $1.9 trillion in goods and services in 2009.[11]

Balance of Trade

You have probably read or heard about the fact that the United States has a trade deficit, but what is a trade deficit? A nation's **balance of trade** is the difference in value between its exports and imports. Because the United States (and some other nations as well) imports more products than it exports, it has a negative balance of trade, or **trade deficit.** In 2009, the United States had a trade deficit of around $380 billion, which was nearly half of what it was in 2008. Total U.S. imports exceeded $1.9 trillion in 2009, about 27 percent more than the $1.5 trillion in exports (see Table 3.1).[12] The trade deficit fluctuates according to such factors as the health of the United States and other economies, productivity, perceived quality, and exchange rates. In 2009 the United States had a $226.8 billion trade deficit with China.[13] As Figure 3.1 indicates, U.S. exports to China have been rapidly increasing but not fast enough to offset the imports from China. Trade deficits are harmful because they can mean the failure of businesses, the loss of jobs, and a lowered standard of living.

exporting
the sale of goods and services to foreign markets

importing
the purchase of goods and services from foreign sources

balance of trade
the difference in value between a nation's exports and its imports

trade deficit
a nation's negative balance of trade, which exists when that country imports more products than it exports

TABLE 3.1   U.S. Trade Deficit, 1980–2009 (in billions of dollars)

	1980	1990	2000	2005	2006	2007	2008	2009
Exports	$333	$576	$1,133	$1,300	$1,455.7	$1,621.8	$1,826.6	$1,553.1
Imports	326	632	1,532	2,026	2,204.2	2,333.4	2,522.5	1,933.7
Trade surplus/ deficit	7	57	399	726	758.5	711.6	695.9	380.7

Sources: Department of Commerce and Robert E. Scott and David Ratner, "Trade Picture," The Economic Policy Institute, February 10, 2006, http://www.epinet.org/content.cfm/webfeatures_econindicators_tradepich20060210 (accessed June 5, 2006); "2006 Annual Trade Highlights, Dollar Change from Prior Year," U.S. Census Bureau, Foreign Trade Statistics, http://www.census.gov/foreign-trade/statistics/highlights/annual.html (accessed April 4, 2008); "2009 Annual Trade Highlights, Dollar Change from Prior Year," U.S. Census Bureau, Foreign Trade Statistics, http://www.census.gov/foreign-trade/statistics/highlights/annual.html (accessed February 17, 2010).

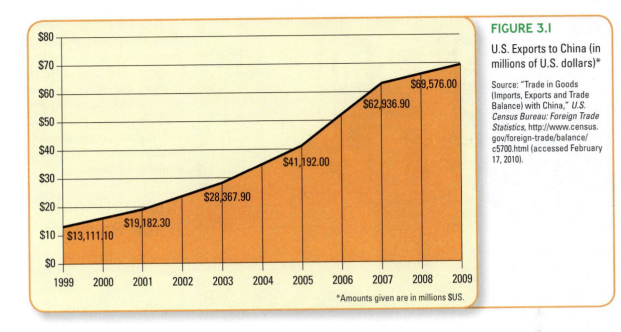

FIGURE 3.1

U.S. Exports to China (in millions of U.S. dollars)*

Source: "Trade in Goods (Imports, Exports and Trade Balance) with China," *U.S. Census Bureau: Foreign Trade Statistics,* http://www.census.gov/foreign-trade/balance/c5700.html (accessed February 17, 2010).

Of course, when a nation exports more goods than it imports, it has a favorable balance of trade, or trade surplus. Until about 1970, the United States had a trade surplus due to an abundance of natural resources and the relative efficiency of its manufacturing systems. Table 3.2 shows the top 10 countries with which the United States has a trade deficit and a trade surplus.

The difference between the flow of money into and out of a country is called its **balance of payments.** A country's balance of trade, foreign investments, foreign aid, loans, military expenditures, and money spent by tourists comprise its balance of payments. As you might expect, a country with a trade surplus generally has a favorable balance of payments because it is receiving more money from trade with foreign countries than it is paying out. When a country has a trade deficit,

balance of payments
the difference between the flow of money into and out of a country

Trade Deficit	Trade Surplus
1. China	Hong Kong
2. Mexico	Netherlands
3. Japan	Australia
4. Canada	United Arab Emirates
5. Federal Republic of Germany	Singapore
6. Nigeria	Brazil
7. Venezuela	Panama
8. Ireland	Turkey
9. Italy	Chile
10. Algeria	Qatar

TABLE 3.2

Top 10 Countries with Which the United States Has Trade Deficits/Surpluses

Sources: "Top Ten Countries with Which the U.S. Has a Trade Deficit," December 2009, http://www.census.gov/foreign-trade/top/dst/current/deficit.html (accessed February 17, 2010); "Top Ten Countries with Which the U.S. Has a Trade Surplus," December 2009, http://www.census.gov/foreign-trade/top/dst/current/surplus.html (accessed February 17, 2010).

Works in over 200 countries, like Egypt.

The best coverage of any carrier worldwide.   For more information click att.com/wirelessinternational

The infrastructure of countries—their transportation, communication, and other systems—differ around the world. AT&T has used the opportunity to make inroads with consumers who don't want their cell phones to stop working when they go abroad.

more money flows out of the country than into it. If more money flows out of the country than into it from tourism and other sources, the country may experience declining production and higher unemployment, because there is less money available for spending.

International Trade Barriers

Completely free trade seldom exists. When a company decides to do business outside its own country, it will encounter a number of barriers to international trade. Any firm considering international business must research the other country's economic, legal, political, social, cultural, and technological background. Such research will help the company choose an appropriate level of involvement and operating strategies, as we will see later in this chapter.

Economic Barriers

When looking at doing business in another country, managers must consider a number of basic economic factors, such as economic development, infrastructure, and exchange rates.

Economic Development.   When considering doing business abroad, U.S. business people need to recognize that they cannot take for granted that other countries offer the same things as are found in *industrialized nations*—economically advanced countries such as the United States, Japan, Great Britain, and Canada. Many countries in Africa, Asia, and South America, for example, are in general poorer and less economically advanced than those in North America and Europe; they are often called *less-developed countries* (LDCs). LDCs are characterized by low per-capita income (income generated by the nation's production of goods and services divided by the population), which means that consumers are less likely to purchase nonessential products. Nonetheless, LDCs represent a potentially huge and profitable market for many businesses because they may be buying technology to improve their infrastructures, and much of the population may desire consumer products. For example, pharmaceutical companies offer infant vaccines in LDCs at a fraction of what they cost in developed countries. While the companies make less in profit on these drugs, they build their reputation as good corporate citizens and help many people have better lives. As emerging economies such as China and India have begun to prosper, more citizens are demanding health care. With China now the third-largest vaccine market in the world, pharmaceutical manufacturers like Novartis are partnering with Chinese companies to offer medicines at affordable prices and increase their share in this lucrative industry.[14]

A country's level of development is determined in part by its **infrastructure,** the physical facilities that support its economic activities, such as railroads, highways, ports, airfields, utilities and power plants, schools, hospitals, communication systems, and commercial distribution systems. When doing business in LDCs, for example, a business may need to compensate for rudimentary distribution and communication systems, or even a lack of technology.

Exchange Rates.   The ratio at which one nation's currency can be exchanged for another nation's currency is the **exchange rate.** Exchange rates vary daily and can be found in newspapers and through many sites on the Internet. Familiarity with exchange rates is important because they affect the cost of imports and exports. When the value of the U.S. dollar declines relative to other currencies, such as the euro, the price of imports becomes relatively expensive for U.S. consumers. On the other hand, U.S. exports become relatively cheap for international markets—in this example, the European Union.

Occasionally, a government may intentionally alter the value of its currency through fiscal policy. Devaluation decreases the value of currency in relation to other currencies. If the U.S. government were to devalue the dollar, it would lower the cost of American goods abroad and make trips to the United States less expensive for foreign tourists. Thus, devaluation encourages the sale of domestic goods and tourism. Mexico has repeatedly devalued the peso for this reason. Revaluation, which increases the value of a currency in relation to other currencies, occurs rarely.

Ethical, Legal, and Political Barriers

A company that decides to enter the international marketplace must contend with potentially complex relationships among the different laws of its own nation, international laws, and the laws of the nation with which it will be trading; various trade restrictions imposed on international trade; changing political climates; and different ethical values. Legal and ethical requirements for successful business are increasing globally. Japan's Finance Minister Shoichi Nakagawa resigned after he appeared drunk at a press conference related to a G7 meeting in Rome. During his briefing with reporters, Nakagawa slurred his words and often appeared to be nodding off. Although he blamed his behavior on too much cold medication, the public outcry began almost immediately. Nakagawa decided that resigning would be "better for the country." Such a blow was particularly hard for Japan's government, as it occurred during the midst of a worldwide recession.[15]

Laws and Regulations.   The United States has a number of laws and regulations that govern the activities of U.S. firms engaged in international trade. For example, the Webb-Pomerene Export Trade Act of 1918 exempts American firms from antitrust laws if those firms are acting together to enter international trade. This law allows selected U.S. firms to form monopolies to compete with foreign monopolistic organizations, although they are not allowed to limit free trade and competition within the United States or to use unfair methods of competition in international trade. The United States also has a variety of friendship, commerce, and navigation treaties with other nations. These treaties allow business to be transacted between citizens of the specified countries. For example, Belgium is a gateway to European markets and has lowered its taxes to give U.S. companies greater reason to locate their European operations there. For example, Belgium has the lowest patent income tax

infrastructure
the physical facilities that support a country's economic activities, such as railroads, highways, ports, airfields, utilities and power plants, schools, hospitals, communication systems, and commercial distribution systems

exchange rate
the ratio at which one nation's currency can be exchanged for another nation's currency

Responding to Business Challenges
Walmart Opens in India, in Spite of Protests

For Walmart, the chance of penetrating India was too large an opportunity to pass up. However, laws forbid foreign companies from competing directly with Indian retailers. Walmart found a solution by forming a joint venture with Bharti Enterprises, based outside of New Delhi. It opened its first store in 2009, with a major difference from Walmart stores in other countries: it cannot sell directly to consumers.

The result is a Walmart that does not resemble its North American counterparts. Instead of selling directly to consumers, this Walmart sells to other vendors and organizations. India's Walmart even sports a new name—Best Price Modern Wholesale. This has required Walmart to revamp its approach, particularly in the wake of protests regarding Walmart's entry into India. The Indian people were concerned for the small merchants making up much of India's economy. Therefore, Best Price Modern Wholesale offers free memberships to small merchants and organizations. According to Walmart representatives, the goal is to provide products for small merchants rather than compete with them. Because Best Price Modern Wholesale is styled in such a way, it operates using a multinational strategy—adapting products to the Indian market—over a global strategy.

Walmart currently operates in 15 international markets with a goal toward rapid expansion. It announced its plans to open 40 cash-and-carry stores in India, hoping to secure a large share of the retail market. With global grocery giants Tesco (Great Britain) and Carrefour (France) hot on its heels, Walmart has a lot riding on success in India.[17]

Discussion Questions
1. What barrier to entry did Walmart encounter in India, and what did the corporation do to overcome that hurdle?
2. How is Walmart in India different from Walmart in other countries?
3. What is Walmart's international strategy? What are its major international competitors?

The salt-and pepper shaker on the right, manufactured by Shantou Lian Plastic Products of Guangdong, China, was a winner of a "Plagiarius Award." The dubious honor is given to the "best" product knockoffs by the organization Aktion Plagiarius in an effort to shame their makers. (The salt-and-pepper set on the left, made by WMF, a German company, is the original product.)

and has 0 percent withholding tax on corporate dividends and interest from a U.S. company. This prevents a company from paying both U.S. and Belgian tax, or double taxation.[16]

Once outside U.S. borders, businesspeople are likely to find that the laws of other nations differ from those of the United States. Many of the legal rights that Americans take for granted do not exist in other countries, and a firm doing business abroad must understand and obey the laws of the host country. Many countries forbid foreigners from owning real property outright; others have strict laws limiting the amount of local currency that can be taken out of the country and the amount of foreign currency that can be brought in.

For example, the African country of Zambia recently banned U.S. currency in domestic transactions. It has also prohibited short-term loans of its local currency (the kwatcha) to nonresidents. The country is hoping to boost the value of the kwatcha and mitigate losses after the downturn in the Zambian economy.[18]

Some countries have copyright and patent laws that are less strict than those of the United States, and some countries fail to honor U.S. laws. Because copying is a tradition in China and Vietnam and laws protecting copyrights and intellectual property are weak and minimally enforced, those countries are flooded with counterfeit videos, movies, CDs, computer software, furniture, and clothing. Companies are angry because the counterfeits harm not only their sales, but also their reputations if the knockoffs are of poor quality. Such counterfeiting is not limited to China or Vietnam. It is estimated that nearly half of all software installed on personal computers worldwide is illegally pirated or copied, amounting to more than $50 billion in global revenue losses annually.[19] In countries where these activities occur, laws against them may not be sufficiently enforced, if counterfeiting is deemed illegal. Thus, businesses engaging in foreign trade may have to take extra steps to protect their products because local laws may be insufficient to do so.

Tariffs and Trade Restrictions.

Tariffs and other trade restrictions are part of a country's legal structure but may be established or removed for political reasons. An **import tariff** is a tax levied by a nation on goods imported into the country. A *fixed tariff* is a specific amount of money levied on each unit of a product brought into the country, while an *ad valorem tariff* is based on the value of the item. Most countries allow citizens traveling abroad to bring home a certain amount of merchandise without paying an import tariff. A U.S. citizen may bring $200 worth of merchandise into the United States duty free. After that, U.S. citizens must pay an ad valorem tariff based on the cost of the item and the country of origin. Thus, identical items purchased in different countries might have different tariffs.

import tariff
a tax levied by a nation on goods imported into the country

Countries sometimes levy tariffs for political reasons, as when they impose sanctions against other countries to protest their actions. However, import tariffs are more commonly imposed to protect domestic products by raising the price of imported ones. Such protective tariffs have become controversial, as Americans become increasingly concerned over the U.S. trade deficit. Protective tariffs allow more expensive domestic goods to compete with foreign ones. For example, the United States has lost a significant number of steelworks over the past few decades to foreign competition in places such as China. Other markets can produce steel more cheaply than the United States. Many people and special interest groups in the United States, such as unions, would like to see tariffs placed on Chinese steel, which is significantly less expensive, in order to protect remaining U.S. steel production. The United States has also imposed tariffs on imported sugar for almost two centuries. The European Union levies tariffs on many products, including some seafood imports.

Critics of protective tariffs argue that their use inhibits free trade and competition. Supporters of protective tariffs say they insulate domestic industries, particularly new ones, against well-established foreign competitors. Once an industry matures, however, its advocates may be reluctant to let go of the tariff that protected it. Tariffs also help when, because of low labor costs and other advantages, foreign competitors can afford to sell their products at prices lower than those charged by domestic companies. Some Americans argue that tariffs should be used to keep domestic wages high and unemployment low.

Exchange controls restrict the amount of currency that can be bought or sold. Some countries control their foreign trade by forcing businesspeople to buy and sell foreign products through a central bank. If John Deere, for example, receives payments for its tractors in a foreign currency, it may be required to sell the currency to that nation's central bank. When foreign currency is in short supply, as it is in many less-developed countries, the government uses foreign currency to purchase necessities and capital goods and produces other products locally, thus limiting its need for foreign imports.

exchange controls
regulations that restrict the amount of currency that can be bought or sold

quota
a restriction on the number of units of a particular product that can be imported into a country

embargo
a prohibition on trade in a particular product

dumping
the act of a country or business selling products at less than what it costs to produce them

A **quota** limits the number of units of a particular product that can be imported into a country. A quota may be established by voluntary agreement or by government decree. The United States imposes quotas on certain goods, such as garments produced in Vietnam and China. Quotas are designed to protect the industries and jobs of the country imposing the quota.

An **embargo** prohibits trade in a particular product. Embargoes are generally directed at specific goods or countries and may be established for political, economic, health, or religious reasons. While the United States maintains a trade embargo with Cuba, European hotel chains are engaged in a building boom on the Caribbean island, where tourism is the number-one industry. U.S. hotel chains are eager to build in Cuba but have no opportunity until the embargo is lifted. Even U.S. tourists are forbidden by the U.S. government to vacation in Cuba, although the push to lift the government embargo is growing stronger all the time. If permitted, cruise ships would likely be the first type of U.S. tourism to reach the island since the early 1960s. It may be surprising to know that U.S. farmers export hundreds of millions of dollars worth of commodities to Cuba each year, based on a 2000 law that provided permission for some trade to the embargoed country.[20] Health embargoes prevent the importing of various pharmaceuticals, animals, plants, and agricultural products. Muslim nations forbid the importation of alcoholic beverages on religious grounds.

One common reason for setting quotas or tariffs is to prohibit **dumping,** which occurs when a country or business sells products at less than what it costs to produce them. President Obama, for example, restricted tire imports from China after union workers accused the country of dumping its products into the U.S. markets, which in turn affected domestic tire makers. China retaliated by threatening its own investigations into whether the United States is dumping auto and chicken parts on the Chinese market.[21] A company may dump its products for several reasons. Dumping permits quick entry into a market. Sometimes dumping occurs when the domestic market for a firm's product is too small to support an efficient level of production. In other cases, technologically obsolete products that are no longer salable in the

Dumping can spark trade wars. After the Obama administration imposed stiff tariffs on Chinese-made tires it alleged were being dumped on the market, China retaliated by slapping tariffs on U.S. chicken products exported to China.

country of origin are dumped overseas. Dumping is relatively difficult to prove, but even the suspicion of dumping can lead to the imposition of quotas or tariffs.

Political Barriers.   Unlike legal issues, political considerations are seldom written down and often change rapidly. Nations that have been subject to economic sanctions for political reasons in recent years include Cuba, Iran, Syria, and North Korea. While these were dramatic events, political considerations affect international business daily as governments enact tariffs, embargoes, or other types of trade restrictions in response to political events.

Businesses engaged in international trade must consider the relative instability of countries such as Iraq, Haiti, and Venezuela. Political unrest in countries such as Pakistan, Somalia, and the Democratic Republic of the Congo may create a hostile or even dangerous environment for foreign businesses. Natural disasters, like the Haitian or Chilean earthquakes in 2010, can cripple a country's government, making the region even more unstable. Finally, a sudden change in power can result in a regime that is hostile to foreign investment. Some businesses have been forced out of a country altogether, as when Hugo Chávez conducted a socialist revolution in Venezuela to force out or take over American oil companies. Whether they like it or not, companies are often involved directly or indirectly in international politics.

Political concerns may lead a group of nations to form a **cartel**, a group of firms or nations that agrees to act as a monopoly and not compete with each other, to generate a competitive advantage in world markets. Probably the most famous cartel is OPEC, the Organization of Petroleum Exporting Countries, founded in the 1960s to increase the price of petroleum throughout the world and to maintain high prices. By working to ensure stable oil prices, OPEC hopes to enhance the economies of its member nations.

cartel
a group of firms or nations that agrees to act as a monopoly and not compete with each other, in order to generate a competitive advantage in world markets

Social and Cultural Barriers

Most businesspeople engaged in international trade underestimate the importance of social and cultural differences; but these differences can derail an important transaction. For example, when Big Boy opened a restaurant in Bangkok, it quickly became popular with European and American tourists, but the local Thais refused to eat there. Instead, they placed gifts of rice and incense at the feet of the Big Boy statue (a chubby boy holding a hamburger) because it reminded them of Buddha. In Japan, customers tiptoed around a logo painted on the floor at the entrance to an Athlete's Foot store because in Japan it is considered taboo to step on a crest.[23] And in Russia, consumers found the American-style energetic happiness of McDonald's employees insincere and offensive when the company opened its first stores there.[24] Unfortunately, cultural norms are rarely written down, and what is written down may well be inaccurate.

Cultural differences include differences in spoken and written language. Although it is certainly possible to translate words from one language to another, the true meaning is sometimes misinterpreted or lost. Consider some translations that went awry in foreign markets:

- Scandinavian vacuum manufacturer Electrolux used the following in an American campaign: "Nothing sucks like an Electrolux."
- The Coca-Cola name in China was first read as "Ke-kou-ke-la," meaning "bite the wax tadpole."
- In Italy, a campaign for Schweppes Tonic Water translated the name into Schweppes Toilet Water.[25]

Entrepreneurship in Action
EcoMom Empowers Moms to Make a Difference

Kimberly Danek Pinkson

Business: EcoMom.com: EcoMom Inc. and EcoMom Alliance

Founded: 2006

Success: EcoMom Alliance boasts more than 11,000 members worldwide, including celebrity moms such as Robin Wright Penn and Nicole Ritchie.

Kimberly Danek Pinkson desires a world where people can once again connect with nature and children can look forward to a sustainable future. Believing that women, particularly mothers, could make this goal a reality, Pinkson created EcoMom Inc. It combines a nonprofit organization that supports global sustainability and female empowerment with a sustainable online market and social networking site. With thousands of members across the world, EcoMom Inc. allows moms to access eco-friendly advice and feel empowered to make positive changes in the environment. In addition to an online forum, EcoMom leaders connect with members through parties, circles, and other outreach programs. Together, the organization is expanding its global outreach, with one program focused on helping women in the Congo deal with violence. Pinkson's goal is to create positive change toward a more sustainable future one EcoMom at time.[22]

Translators cannot just translate slogans, advertising campaigns, and Web site language; they must know the cultural differences that could affect a company's success.

Differences in body language and personal space also affect international trade. Body language is nonverbal, usually unconscious communication through gestures, posture, and facial expression. Personal space is the distance at which one person feels comfortable talking to another. Americans tend to stand a moderate distance away from the person with whom they are speaking. Arab businessmen tend to stand face-to-face with the object of their conversation. Additionally, gestures vary from culture to culture, and gestures considered acceptable in American society—pointing, for example—may be considered rude in others. Table 3.3 shows some of the behaviors considered rude or unacceptable in other countries. Such cultural differences may generate uncomfortable feelings or misunderstandings when business people of different countries negotiate with each other.

Family roles also influence marketing activities. Many countries do not allow children to be used in advertising, for example. Advertising that features people in nontraditional social roles may or may not be successful either. One airline featured

TABLE 3.3 Cultural Behavioral Differences	Region	Gestures Viewed as Rude or Unacceptable
	Japan, Hong Kong, Middle East	Summoning with the index finger
	Middle and Far East	Pointing with index finger
	Thailand, Japan, France	Sitting with soles of shoes showing
	Brazil, Germany	Forming a circle with fingers (e.g., the "O.K." sign in the United States)
	Japan	Winking means "I love you"
	Buddhist countries	Patting someone on the head

Source: Adapted from Judie Haynes, "Communicating with Gestures," *EverythingESL* (n.d.), http://www.everythingesl.net/inservices/body_language.php (accessed March 8, 2010).

advertisements with beautiful hostesses serving champagne on a flight. The ad does not seem unusual in Western markets, but there was a major backlash in the Middle East. Saudi Arabia even considered restricting the airline from flights in that country. Not only is alcohol usage forbidden among Muslims, unveiled women are not allowed to interact with men—especially without their husbands around. Some in Saudi Arabia saw the airline as being insensitive to their religious beliefs and customs.[26]

The people of other nations quite often have a different perception of time as well. Americans value promptness; a business meeting scheduled for a specific time seldom starts more than a few minutes late. In Mexico and Spain, however, it is not unusual for a meeting to be delayed half an hour or more. Such a late start might produce resentment in an American negotiating in Spain for the first time.

Companies engaged in foreign trade must observe the national and religious holidays and local customs of the host country. In many Islamic countries, for example, workers expect to take a break at certain times of the day to observe religious rites. Companies also must monitor their advertising to guard against offending customers. In Thailand and many other countries, public displays of affection between the sexes are unacceptable in advertising messages; in many Middle Eastern nations, it is unacceptable to show the soles of one's feet.[27] In Russia, smiling is considered appropriate only in private settings, not in business.

With the exception of the United States, most nations use the metric system. This lack of uniformity creates problems for both buyers and sellers in the international marketplace. American sellers, for instance, must package goods destined for foreign markets in liters or meters, and Japanese sellers must convert to the English system if they plan to sell a product in the United States. Tools also must be calibrated in the correct system if they are to function correctly. Hyundai and Honda service technicians need metric tools to make repairs on those cars.

The literature dealing with international business is filled with accounts of sometimes humorous but often costly mistakes that occurred because of a lack of understanding of the social and cultural differences between buyers and sellers. Such problems cannot always be avoided, but they can be minimized through research on the cultural and social differences of the host country.

Technological Barriers

Many countries lack the technological infrastructure found in the United States, and some marketers are viewing such barriers as opportunities. For instance, marketers are targeting many countries such as India and China and some African countries where there are few private phone lines. Citizens of these countries are turning instead to wireless communication through cell phones. Technological advances are creating additional global marketing opportunities. Along with opportunities, changing technologies also create new challenges and competition. The U.S. market share of the personal computer market is dropping as new competitors emerge to challenge U.S. PC makers. Apple has dropped to fifth place in the United States, while Acer, a PC company based in Taiwan, overtook Dell to become the second-largest PC vendor. With the exception of U.S. company Hewlett-Packard, the main PC makers to experience double-digit growth in 2009 included Acer, Toshiba, and Lenovo—all companies from Asia.[28]

Trade Agreements, Alliances, and Organizations

Although these economic, political, legal, and sociocultural issues may seem like daunting barriers to international trade, there are also organizations and agreements—such as the General Agreement on Tariffs and Trade, the World Bank, and the International Monetary Fund—that foster international trade and can help companies get involved in and succeed in global markets. Various regional trade agreements, such as the North American Free Trade Agreement and the European Union, also promote trade among member nations by eliminating tariffs and trade restrictions. In this section, we'll look briefly at these agreements and organizations.

General Agreement on Tariffs and Trade (GATT) a trade agreement, originally signed by 23 nations in 1947, that provided a forum for tariff negotiations and a place where international trade problems could be discussed and resolved

General Agreement on Tariffs and Trade

During the Great Depression of the 1930s, nations established so many protective tariffs covering so many products that international trade became virtually impossible. By the end of World War II, there was considerable international momentum to liberalize trade and minimize the effects of tariffs. The **General Agreement on Tariffs and Trade (GATT),** originally signed by 23 nations in 1947, provided a forum for tariff negotiations and a place where international trade problems could be discussed and resolved. More than 100 nations abided by its rules. GATT sponsored rounds of negotiations aimed at reducing trade restrictions. The most recent

Trade and economic growth around the world exploded after the passage of GATT.

round, the Uruguay Round (1988–1994), further reduced trade barriers for most products and provided new rules to prevent dumping.

The **World Trade Organization (WTO),** an international organization dealing with the rules of trade between nations, was created in 1995 by the Uruguay Round. Key to the World Trade Organization are the WTO agreements, which are the legal ground rules for international commerce. The agreements were negotiated and signed by most of the world's trading nations and ratified by their parliaments. The goal is to help producers of goods and services and exporters and importers conduct their business. In addition to administering the WTO trade agreements, the WTO presents a forum for trade negotiations, monitors national trade policies, provides technical assistance and training for developing countries, and cooperates with other international organizations. Based in Geneva, Switzerland, the WTO has also adopted a leadership role in negotiating trade disputes among nations.[29] For example, the WTO investigated allegations that Airbus, a division of European Aeronautic Defence and Space, had engaged in anticompetitive practices to beat out Boeing on a bid to replace the U.S. Air Force's aerial tankers. The WTO eventually ruled that the European Union had provided Airbus with illegal subsidies, leading the Air Force to resume the bidding process.[30]

World Trade Organization (WTO)
international organization dealing with the rules of trade between nations

The North American Free Trade Agreement

The **North American Free Trade Agreement (NAFTA),** which went into effect on January 1, 1994, effectively merged Canada, the United States, and Mexico into one market of nearly 440 million consumers. NAFTA virtually eliminated all tariffs on goods produced and traded among Canada, Mexico, and the United States to create a free trade area. The estimated annual output for this trade alliance is more than $14 trillion. NAFTA makes it easier for U.S. businesses to invest in Mexico and Canada; provides protection for intellectual property (of special interest to high-technology and entertainment industries); expands trade by requiring equal treatment of U.S. firms in both countries; and simplifies country-of-origin rules, hindering Japan's use of Mexico as a staging ground for further penetration into U.S. markets.

North American Free Trade Agreement (NAFTA)
agreement that eliminates most tariffs and trade restrictions on agricultural and manufactured products to encourage trade among Canada, the United States, and Mexico

Canada's 33.4 million consumers are relatively affluent, with a per-capita GDP of $38,400.[31] Trade between the United States and Canada totals approximately $430 billion. About 80 percent of Canada's exports go to the United States, including gold, oil, and uranium.[32] In fact, Canada is the single largest trading partner of the United States.[33]

With a per-capita GDP of $13,200, Mexico's 111 million consumers are less affluent than Canadian consumers. However, trade with the United States and Mexico has tripled since NAFTA was initiated. Trade between the United States and Mexico totals approximately $305 billion.[34] More than 30 million Americans cite their heritage as Mexican, making them the most populous Hispanic group in the country. They have a median household income of just under $38,000, making them a large and desirable market for businesses.[35] These individuals often have close ties to relatives in Mexico and assist in Mexican–U.S. economic development and trade. Mexico is on a course of a market economy, rule of law, respect for human rights, and responsible public policies. There is also a commitment to the environment and sustainable human development. Many U.S. companies have taken advantage of Mexico's low labor costs and proximity to the United States to set up production facilities, sometimes called *maquiladoras.* Mexico is also attracting major technological industries, including electronics, software, and aerospace. Mexicali, for example, has attracted such companies as Skyworks Solutions, a maker of cell phone and PDA semiconductors; Gulfstream, a maker of executive jets; and Honeywell, which recently opened a $40 million center in the city. Engineering in Mexicali is booming, with the enrollment of the engineering department at Mexicali's Universidad Autonoma de Baja California doubling within the last five years. Other companies that have an interest in Mexico include Eurocopter, which will be investing $550 million for the manufacturing of helicopters in the city of Queretaro, and Lenovo, which has a plant in Monterrey.[36] With the maquiladoras and the influx of foreign technological industries, Mexico became the world's 12th-largest economy.[37]

However, there is great disparity within Mexico. The country's southern states cannot seem to catch up with the more affluent northern states on almost any socioeconomic indicator. For example, 47 percent of rural Mexicans in the south are considered extremely poor, compared with just 12 percent in the north. The disparities are growing, as can be seen comparing the south to the northern industrial capital of Monterrey, which is beginning to seem like south Texas.[38]

Mexico's membership in NAFTA links the United States and Canada with other Latin American countries, providing additional opportunities to integrate trade among all the nations in the Western Hemisphere. Indeed, efforts to create a free trade agreement among the 34 nations of North and South America was expected to be completed by 2005. Like NAFTA, the *Free Trade Area of the Americas (FTAA)* will progressively eliminate trade barriers and create the world's largest free trade zone with 800 million people.[39] However, opposition and demonstrations have hampered efforts to move forward with the proposed plan. Although the deadline was missed and it is not in place yet, there is still a chance for the FTAA to become a reality. However, the worldwide economic recession will likely delay the final agreement. The recession was the topic of focus for the Fifth Summit of the Americas in 2009, when leaders of North America, South America, Central America, and the Caribbean nations got together to make decisions on issues concerning the Americas.[40]

Despite its benefits, NAFTA has been controversial, and disputes continue to arise over the implementation of the trade agreement. Archer Daniels Midland, for example, filed a claim against the Mexican government for losses resulting from a tax on soft drinks containing high-fructose corn syrup, which the company believes violates the provisions of NAFTA.[41] While many Americans feared the agreement would erase jobs in the United States, Mexicans have been disappointed that the agreement failed to create more jobs. Moreover, Mexico's rising standard of living has increased the cost of doing business there; many hundreds of *maquiladoras* have closed their doors and transferred work to China and other nations where labor costs are cheaper. Indeed, China has become the United States's second-largest importer.[42] On the other hand, high transportation costs, intellectual property theft, quality failures, and the difficulty management often incurs in controlling a business so far away and under a communist regime are now causing some manufacturers to reconsider opting for Mexican factories over China, even going so far as to relocate from China back to Mexico.[43]

Although NAFTA has been controversial, it has become a positive factor for U.S. firms wishing to engage in international marketing. Because licensing requirements have been relaxed under the pact, smaller businesses that previously could not afford to invest in Mexico and Canada will be able to do business in those markets without having to locate there. NAFTA's long phase-in period provides ample time for adjustment by those firms affected by reduced tariffs on imports. Furthermore, increased competition should lead to a more efficient market, and the long-term prospects of including most countries in the Western Hemisphere in the alliance promise additional opportunities for U.S. marketers.

The European Union

The **European Union (EU),** also called the *European Community* or *Common Market,* was established in 1958 to promote trade among its members, which initially included Belgium, France, Italy, West Germany, Luxembourg, and the Netherlands. East and West Germany united in 1991, and by 1995 the United Kingdom, Spain, Denmark, Greece, Portugal, Ireland, Austria, Finland, and Sweden had joined as well. The Czech Republic, Estonia, Hungary, Latvia, Lithuania, Poland, Slovakia, and Slovenia joined in 2004. In 2007, Bulgaria and Romania also became members, and Cyprus and Malta joined in 2008, which brought total membership to 27. Croatia, the Former Yugoslav Republic of Macedonia, and Turkey are candidate countries that hope to join the European Union in the near future.[44] Until 1993 each nation functioned as a separate market, but at that time the members officially unified into one of the largest single world markets, which today has 491.5 million consumers with a GDP of $14.52 trillion.[45]

To facilitate free trade among members, the EU is working toward standardization of business regulations and requirements, import duties, and value-added taxes; the elimination of customs checks; and the creation of a standardized currency for use by all members. Many European nations (Austria, Belgium, Finland, France, Germany, Greece, Ireland, Italy, Luxembourg, the Netherlands, Portugal, Spain, and Slovenia) link their exchange rates together to a common currency, the *euro;* however, several EU members have rejected use of the euro in their countries. Although the common currency requires many marketers to modify their pricing strategies and will subject them to increased competition, the use of a single currency frees companies that sell goods among European countries from the nuisance of dealing with complex exchange rates.[46] The long-term goals are to eliminate all trade barriers within the EU, improve the economic efficiency of the EU nations, and stimulate economic growth, thus making the union's economy more competitive in global markets, particularly against Japan and other Pacific Rim nations, and North America. However, several disputes and debates still divide the member nations, and many barriers to completely free trade remain. Consequently, it may take many years before the EU is truly one deregulated market.

The EU has enacted some of the world's strictest laws concerning antitrust issues, which have had unexpected consequences for some non-European firms. For example, the EU fined Intel 1.06 billion euros ($1.45 billion) for anticompetitive practices. Between 2002 and 2007, Intel was accused of paying manufacturers and retailers to purchase chips from Intel instead of from its competitor Advanced Micro Devices. The commission alleges that Intel offered computer makers like Acer and Dell hidden rebates for only using its chips. Intel plans to appeal the verdict.[47]

Asia-Pacific Economic Cooperation

The **Asia-Pacific Economic Cooperation (APEC),** established in 1989, promotes open trade and economic and technical cooperation among member nations, which initially included Australia, Brunei Darussalam, Canada, Indonesia, Japan, Korea, Malaysia, New Zealand, the Philippines, Singapore, Thailand, and the United States. Since then the alliance has grown to include China, Hong Kong, Chinese Taipei, Mexico, Papua New Guinea, Chile, Peru, Russia, and Vietnam. The 21-member alliance represents approximately 41 percent of the world's

European Union (EU) a union of European nations established in 1958 to promote trade among its members; one of the largest single markets today

Asia-Pacific Economic Cooperation (APEC) an international trade alliance that promotes open trade and economic and technical cooperation among member nations

population, 44 percent of world trade, and 54 percent of world GDP. APEC differs from other international trade alliances in its commitment to facilitating business and its practice of allowing the business/private sector to participate in a wide range of APEC activities.[48]

Companies of the APEC have become increasingly competitive and sophisticated in global business in the last three decades. The Japanese and South Koreans in particular have made tremendous inroads on world markets for automobiles, motorcycles, watches, cameras, and audio and video equipment. Products from Samsung, Sony, Sanyo, Toyota, Daewoo, Mitsubishi, Suzuki, and Toshiba are sold all over the world and have set standards of quality by which other products are often judged. The People's Republic of China, a country of 1.3 billion people, has launched a program of economic reform to stimulate its economy by privatizing many industries, restructuring its banking system, and increasing public spending on infrastructure (including railways and telecommunications).[49] As a result, China has become a manufacturing powerhouse, with an estimated economic growth rate of 8 to 10 percent a year.[50] China's export market has consistently outpaced its import growth in recent years. China ranks behind the United States as the world's largest importer and exporter, and China's GDP is the world's second-largest economy, behind the United States. As it becomes a major driver of economic growth, China overtook the United States as the country with the largest number of Internet users in 2008. On the negative side, China became the world's largest emitter of greenhouse gases in 2008. China mainly uses coal-fired power plants; in fact, it builds a new one every 10 days, so it has become the world's largest emitter of carbon dioxide. As companies transfer their manufacturing to China, they increase their CO_2 emissions because China emits 22 percent more than the global average of carbon per kilowatt-hour.[51] On the other hand, as you will see later in the chapter, China has also begun a quest to become a world leader in green initiatives and renewable energy. This is an increasingly important quest as the country becomes more polluted.

Less visible Pacific Rim regions, such as Thailand, Singapore, Taiwan, Vietnam, and Hong Kong, have also become major manufacturing and financial centers. Vietnam, with one of the world's most open economies, has bypassed its communist government with private firms moving ahead despite bureaucracy, corruption, and poor infrastructure. In a country of 85 million barely able to feed themselves, Vietnamese firms now compete internationally with an agricultural miracle, making the country one of the world's main providers of farm produce. Intel recently opened a $1 billion factory near Hanoi.[52]

World Bank

World Bank
an organization established by the industrialized nations in 1946 to loan money to underdeveloped and developing countries; formally known as the International Bank for Reconstruction and Development

The **World Bank,** more formally known as the International Bank for Reconstruction and Development, was established by the industrialized nations, including the United States, in 1946 to loan money to underdeveloped and developing countries.

It loans its own funds or borrows funds from member countries to finance projects ranging from road and factory construction to the building of medical and educational facilities. The World Bank and other multilateral development banks (banks with international support that provide loans to developing countries) are the largest source of advice and assistance for developing nations. The International Development Association and the International Finance Corporation are associated with the World Bank and provide loans to private businesses and member countries.

International Monetary Fund

The **International Monetary Fund (IMF)** was established in 1947 to promote trade among member nations by eliminating trade barriers and fostering financial cooperation. It also makes short-term loans to member countries that have balance-of-payment deficits and provides foreign currencies to member nations. The International Monetary Fund tries to avoid financial crises and panics by alerting the international community about countries that will not be able to repay their debts. The IMF's Internet site provides additional information about the organization, including news releases, frequently asked questions, and members.

The IMF is the closest thing the world has to an international central bank. If countries get into financial trouble, they can borrow from the World Bank. However, the global economic crisis created many challenges for the IMF as it was forced to double its financial assistance to emerging economies. The IMF has lent funds to many struggling nations such as Belarus, Iceland, Hungary, Latvia, Pakistan, Poland, Romania, Serbia, Sri Lanka, and Ukraine.[53] The usefulness of the IMF for developed countries is limited because these countries use private markets as a major source of capital.[54]

International Monetary Fund (IMF) organization established in 1947 to promote trade among member nations by eliminating trade barriers and fostering financial cooperation

Getting Involved in International Business

Businesses may get involved in international trade at many levels—from a small Kenyan firm that occasionally exports African crafts to a huge multinational corporation such as Shell Oil that sells products around the globe. The degree of commitment of resources and effort required increases according to the level at which a business involves itself in international trade. This section examines exporting and importing, trading companies, licensing and franchising, contract manufacturing, joint ventures, direct investment, and multinational corporations.

Exporting and Importing

Many companies first get involved in international trade when they import goods from other countries for resale in their own businesses. For example, a grocery store chain may import bananas from Honduras and coffee from Colombia. A business may get involved in exporting when it is called upon to supply a foreign company with a particular product. Such exporting enables enterprises of all sizes to participate in international business. Exporting to other countries becomes a necessity for established countries that seek to grow continually. Products often have higher sales growth potential in foreign countries than they have in the parent country. For example, Heinz exports its ketchup to other countries, including Mexico, Africa, and the Middle East, because there exists much greater potential for growth. Retail sales of packaged food have risen 32 percent in Asian-Pacific countries and 27 percent in Africa, while only rising a mere 4 percent in Europe and declining 1 percent in North America. Mexico in particular has become a crucial part of Heinz's growth strategy because Mexicans consume more ketchup than all but eight other nations.[55] Table 3.4 shows the number of U.S. exporters and the export value by company size, while Figure 3.2 shows some of the world's largest exporting countries.

Exporting sometimes takes place through **countertrade agreements,** which involve bartering products for other products instead of for currency. Such arrangements are fairly common in international trade, especially between Western companies and eastern European nations. An estimated 40 percent or more of all international trade agreements contain countertrade provisions.

countertrade agreements foreign trade agreements that involve bartering products for other products instead of for currency

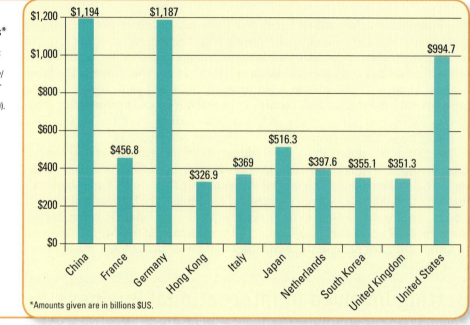

Source: "Country Comparison: Exports," *CIA—The World Factbook,* https://www.cia.gov/library/publications/the-world-factbook/rankorder/2078rank.html (accessed March 8, 2010).

FIGURE 3.2

Top Exporting Countries*

*Amounts given are in billions $US.

Although a company may export its wares overseas directly or import directly from their manufacturer, many choose to deal with an intermediary, commonly called an *export agent*. Export agents seldom produce goods themselves; instead, they usually handle international transactions for other firms. Export agents either purchase products outright or take them on consignment. If they purchase them outright, they generally mark up the price they have paid and attempt to sell the product in the international marketplace. They are also responsible for storage and transportation.

An advantage of trading through an agent instead of directly is that the company does not have to deal with foreign currencies or the red tape (paying tariffs and handling paperwork) of international business. A major disadvantage is that, because the export agent must make a profit, either the price of the product must be increased or the domestic company must provide a larger discount than it would in a domestic transaction.

TABLE 3.4

U.S. Exporters and Value by Company Size

	Number of Exporters	Percentage	Value (millions of dollars)	Percentage
Unknown	85,229	32	74,891	7.3
Small (<100 employees)	156,404	58.7	141,404	13.7
Medium (100–499 employees)	17,748	6.7	95,389	9.2
Large (>500 employees)	7,076	2.7	719,322	69.8

Source: "A Profile of U.S. Exporting Companies, 2006–2007," *U.S. Census Bureau News,* April 9, 2009, http://www.census.gov/foreign-trade/Press-Release/edb/2007/edbrel.pdf (accessed February 17, 2010).

Trading Companies

A **trading company** buys goods in one country and sells them to buyers in another country. Trading companies handle all activities required to move products from one country to another, including consulting, marketing research, advertising, insurance, product research and design, warehousing, and foreign exchange services to companies interested in selling their products in foreign markets. Trading companies are similar to export agents, but their role in international trade is larger. By linking sellers and buyers of goods in different countries, trading companies promote international trade. The best known U.S. trading company is Sears World Trade, which specializes in consumer goods, light industrial items, and processed foods.

Licensing and Franchising

Licensing is a trade arrangement in which one company—the *licensor*—allows another company—the *licensee*—to use its company name, products, patents, brands, trademarks, raw materials, and/or production processes in exchange for a fee or royalty. The Coca-Cola Company and PepsiCo frequently use licensing as a means to market their soft drinks, apparel, and other merchandise in other countries. Licensing is an attractive alternative to direct investment when the political stability of a foreign country is in doubt or when resources are unavailable for direct investment. Licensing is especially advantageous for small manufacturers wanting to launch a well-known brand internationally. Yoplait is a French yogurt that is licensed for production in the United States.

Franchising is a form of licensing in which a company—the *franchiser*—agrees to provide a *franchisee* the name, logo, methods of operation, advertising, products, and other elements associated with the franchiser's business, in return for a financial commitment and the agreement to conduct business in accordance with the franchiser's standard of operations. Wendy's, McDonald's, Pizza Hut, and Holiday Inn are well-known franchisers with international visibility. Table 3.5 lists the top 10 global franchises.

Licensing and franchising enable a company to enter the international marketplace without spending large sums of money abroad or hiring or transferring personnel to handle overseas affairs. They also minimize problems associated with shipping costs, tariffs, and trade restrictions. And, they allow the firm to establish

trading company
a firm that buys goods in one country and sells them to buyers in another country

licensing
a trade agreement in which one company—the licensor—allows another company—the licensee—to use its company name, products, patents, brands, trademarks, raw materials, and/or production processes in exchange for a fee or royalty

franchising
a form of licensing in which a company—the franchiser—agrees to provide a franchisee a name, logo, methods of operation, advertising, products, and other elements associated with a franchiser's business, in return for a financial commitment and the agreement to conduct business in accordance with the franchiser's standard of operations

1. McDonald's	United States	**TABLE 3.5**
2. Subway	United States	Top 10 Global Franchises Rankings
3. 7 Eleven	United States	
4. InterContinental Hotels Group	United Kingdom	
5. Pizza Hut	United States	
6. KFC	United States	
7. Burger King	United States	
8. A&W Restaurants	United States	
9. Ace Hardware Corporation	United States	
10. Naturhouse	Spain	

Source: "Top 100 Global Franchises—Ranking," *Franchise Direct,* http://www.franchisedirect.com/top100globalfranchises/rankings/ (accessed February 17, 2010).

goodwill for its products in a foreign market, which will help the company if it decides to produce or market its products directly in the foreign country at some future date. However, if the licensee (or franchisee) does not maintain high standards of quality, the product's image may be hurt; therefore, it is important for the licensor to monitor its products overseas and to enforce its quality standards.

Contract Manufacturing

Contract manufacturing occurs when a company hires a foreign company to produce a specified volume of the firm's product to specification; the final product carries the domestic firm's name. Spalding, for example, relies on contract manufacturing for its sports equipment; Reebok uses Korean contract manufacturers to manufacture many of its athletic shoes.

Outsourcing

Earlier, we defined outsourcing as transferring manufacturing or other tasks (such as information technology operations) to companies in countries where labor and supplies are less expensive. Many U.S. firms have outsourced tasks to India, Ireland, Mexico, and the Philippines, where there are many well-educated workers and significantly lower labor costs. Experts estimate that 80 percent of *Fortune* 500 companies have some relationship with an offshore company.[56]

Although outsourcing has become politically controversial in recent years amid concerns over jobs lost to overseas workers, foreign companies transfer tasks and jobs to U.S. companies—sometimes called *insourcing*—far more often than U.S. companies outsource tasks and jobs abroad.[57] However, some firms are bringing their outsourced jobs back after concerns that foreign workers were not adding enough value. For example, some of the bigger banks are now choosing to set up offshore operations themselves rather than outsource. This has to do with increased regulations in foreign countries, concerns over data security, and a recent fraud at the Indian outsourcer Satyam amounting to more than $1 billion.[58]

Domino's Pizza has expanded around the world via franchising. In Asia, the chain's stores serve up pizzas with toppings such as squid, sweet mayonnaise, and duck gizzards.

Offshoring

Offshoring is the relocation of a business process by a company, or a subsidiary, to another country. Offshoring is different than outsourcing: the company retains control of the process because it is not subcontracting to a different company. Companies may choose to offshore for a number of reasons, ranging from lower wages, skilled labor, or taking advantage of time zone differences in order to offer services around the clock. Some banks have chosen not to outsource because of concerns about data security in other countries. These institutions may instead engage in offshoring, which allows a company more control over international operations because the offshore office is an extension of the company. Barclays Bank, for instance, has an international offshore banking unit called Barclays Wealth International. This branch helps the company better serve wealthy clients with international banking needs.[59]

Joint Ventures and Alliances

Many countries, particularly LDCs, do not permit direct investment by foreign companies or individuals. Or, a company may lack sufficient resources or expertise to operate in another country. In such cases, a company that wants to do business in another country may set up a **joint venture** by finding a local partner (occasionally, the host nation itself) to share the costs and operation of the business. The French hypermarket chain Carrefour, for example, has a joint venture with Majid al Futtaim (MAF), a group of companies that has become a highly successful Middle Eastern business. The venture between Carrefour and MAF resulted in the expansion of MAF-Carrefour hypermarkets in the United Arab Emirates, Qatar, Oman, Saudi Arabia, and Egypt. The partnership has allowed Carrefour to become one of the most popular retailers in Egypt.[60]

joint venture
the sharing of the costs and operation of a business between a foreign company and a local partner

In some industries, such as automobiles and computers, strategic alliances are becoming the predominant means of competing. A **strategic alliance** is a partnership formed to create competitive advantage on a worldwide basis. In such industries, international competition is so fierce and the costs of competing on a global basis are so high that few firms have the resources to go it alone, so they collaborate with other companies. An example of such an alliance is New United Motor Manufacturing Inc. (NUMMI), formed by Toyota and General Motors in 1984 to make automobiles for both firms. This alliance joined the quality engineering of Japanese cars with the marketing expertise and market access of General Motors. Today, NUMMI manufactures the popular Toyota Tacoma compact pick-up truck as well as the Toyota Corolla and the Pontiac Vibe.[61]

strategic alliance
a partnership formed to create competitive advantage on a worldwide basis

Direct Investment

Companies that want more control and are willing to invest considerable resources in international business may consider **direct investment,** the ownership of overseas facilities. Direct investment may involve the development and operation of new facilities—such as when Starbucks opens a new coffee shop in Japan—or

direct investment
the ownership of overseas facilities

Apparently "things don't always go better with Coke." When Coke attempted to extend its reach into China by purchasing the country's biggest juice maker, the Chinese government blocked the deal. It also blocked the sale of GM's Hummer to a Chinese company that wanted to purchase the brand.

	Company	Revenue (in millions)
	TABLE 3.6 Top 10 Largest Corporations	

Company	Revenue (in millions)
1. Royal Dutch Shell	$458,361
2. Exxon Mobil	442,851
3. Walmart Stores	405,607
4. BP	367,053
5. Chevron	263,159
6. Total	234,674.1
7. ConocoPhillips	230,764
8. ING Group	226,577
9. Sinopec	207,814.5
10. Toyota Motor	204,352.3

TABLE 3.6
Top 10 Largest Corporations

Source: "Global 500: *Fortune*'s Annual Ranking of the World's Largest Corporations," *CNNMoney*, http://money.cnn.com/ magazines/fortune/global500/2009/index.html (accessed February 17, 2010).

the purchase of all or Fpart of an existing operation in a foreign country. India's Tata Motors purchased Jaguar and Land Rover from Ford Motor Company. Tata, a maker of cars and trucks, is attempting to broaden its global presence, including manufacturing these vehicles in the United Kingdom.[62]

multinational corporation (MNC)
a corporation that operates on a worldwide scale, without significant ties to any one nation or region

The highest level of international business involvement is the **multinational corporation (MNC),** a corporation, such as IBM or ExxonMobil, that operates on a worldwide scale, without significant ties to any one nation or region. Table 3.6 lists the 10 largest multinational corporations. MNCs are more than simple corporations. They often have greater assets than some of the countries in which they do business. Nestlé, with headquarters in Switzerland, operates more than 300 plants around the world and receives revenues from Europe; North, Central, and South America; Africa; and Asia. The Royal Dutch/Shell Group, one of the world's major oil producers, is another MNC. Its main offices are located in The Hague and London. Other MNCs include BASF, British Petroleum, Matsushita, Mitsubishi, Siemens, Texaco, Toyota, and Unilever. Many MNCs have been targeted by antiglobalization activists at global business forums, and some protests have turned violent. The activists contend that MNCs increase the gap between rich and poor nations, misuse and misallocate scarce resources, exploit the labor markets in LDCs, and harm their natural environments.[63]

International Business Strategies

Planning in a global economy requires businesspeople to understand the economic, legal, political, and sociocultural realities of the countries in which they will operate. These factors will affect the strategy a business chooses to use outside its own borders.

Developing Strategies

multinational strategy
a plan, used by international companies, that involves customizing products, promotion, and distribution according to cultural, technological, regional, and national differences

Companies doing business internationally have traditionally used a **multinational strategy,** customizing their products, promotion, and distribution according to cultural, technological, regional, and national differences. To succeed in India, for example, McDonald's had to adapt its products to respect religious customs. McDonald's India does not serve beef or pork products and also has vegetarian dishes for its largely vegetarian consumer base. Many soap and detergent manufacturers have

Going Green
China Fights Back Against Pollution

As the largest producer of greenhouse gases, China has become associated with high pollution and environmental damage. However, China's government seems ready to make up for lost time with several ambitious green policies. To assist with this endeavor, China recently established the Ministry of Environmental Protection with a goal to clean up China's air and water and to establish the country as an alternative energy powerhouse.

In a short amount of time, China has implemented a wide variety of environmental initiatives. For example, the country currently has tighter fuel efficiency standards at 43 miles per gallon (mpg) than the United States' 2020 goal of 35 mpg. CEOs of companies caught dumping waste in China now must pay hefty fines. Chinese banks are instructed to refuse loans to highly polluting industries or to recall loans for companies that are found to be violating the country's environmental standards. China has also embarked on a wide-scale renewable energy program. The country's goal is to have 15 percent of China's energy needs supplied by renewable energy sources by 2015.

China's green initiatives have not gone unchallenged. In addition to internal opposition, the United Nations is accusing China of accepting carbon credit funding for alternative energy programs that it would have implemented with or without the funding. This goes against the carbon credit sales aspect of the Kyoto Protocol, which is designed to assist countries otherwise unable to create alternative energy resources. Despite these criticisms, China has achieved some environmental successes. For instance, the city of Dalian, once packed with chemical plants and polluting factories, is now filled with green technology and other environmentally conscious companies. Although China's pollution problems will be hard to overcome, the country is actively taking on the challenge.[64]

Discussion Questions

1. What steps has China taken to reduce its pollution output? Do you think these measures will help or hurt businesses?
2. What are some of the criticisms levied against China regarding its environmental initiatives?
3. Do you think that China will ultimately be successful in reducing pollution and improving its environmental record? Why or why not?

adapted their products to local water conditions, washing equipment, and washing habits. For customers in some less-developed countries, Colgate-Palmolive Co. has developed an inexpensive, plastic, hand-powered washing machine for use in households that have no electricity. Even when products are standardized, advertising often has to be modified to adapt to language and cultural differences. Also, celebrities used in advertising in the United States may be unfamiliar to foreign consumers and thus would not be effective in advertising products in other countries.

More and more companies are moving from this customization strategy to a **global strategy (globalization),** which involves standardizing products (and, as much as possible, their promotion and distribution) for the whole world, as if it were a single entity. Examples of globalized products are American clothing, movies, music, and cosmetics. As it has become a global brand, Starbucks has standardized its products and stores. Starbucks was ranked as the world's most engaged brand in terms of online activities, even surpassing Coca-Cola, which is another global brand. Starbucks communicates with fans around the world via Facebook, Twitter, YouTube, and its company Web site.

Before moving outside their own borders, companies must conduct environmental analyses to evaluate the potential of and problems associated with various markets and to determine what strategy is best for doing business in those markets. Failure to do so may result in losses and even negative publicity. Some companies rely on local managers to gain greater insights and faster response to changes within a country. Astute businesspeople today "think globally, act locally." That is, while constantly being aware of the total picture, they adjust their firms' strategies to conform to local needs and tastes.

global strategy (globalization) a strategy that involves standardizing products (and, as much as possible, their promotion and distribution) for the whole world, as if it were a single entity

Managing the Challenges of Global Business

As we've pointed out in this chapter, many past political barriers to trade have fallen or been minimized, expanding and opening new market opportunities. Managers who can meet the challenges of creating and implementing effective and sensitive business strategies for the global marketplace can help lead their companies to success. For example, the Commercial Service is the global business solutions unit of the U.S. Department of Commerce that offers U.S. firms wide and deep practical knowledge of international markets and industries, a unique global network, inventive use of information technology, and a focus on small and mid-sized businesses. Another example is the benchmarking of best international practices that benefits U.S. firms, which is conducted by the network of CIBERs (Centers for International Business Education and Research) at leading business schools in the United States. These 30 CIBERs are funded by the U.S. government to help U.S. firms become more competitive globally. A major element of the assistance that these governmental organizations can provide firms (especially for small and medium-sized firms) is knowledge of the internationalization process.[65] Small businesses, too, can succeed in foreign markets when their managers have carefully studied those markets and prepared and implemented appropriate strategies. Being globally aware is therefore an important quality for today's managers and will become a critical attribute for managers of the 21st century.

So You Want a Job in Global Business

Have you always dreamt of traveling the world? Whether backpacking your way through Central America or sipping espressos at five-star European restaurants is your style, the increasing globalization of business might just give you your chance to see what the world has to offer. Most new jobs will have at least some global component, even if located within the United States, so being globally aware and keeping an open mind to different cultures is vital in today's business world. Think about the 1.3 billion consumers in China that have already purchased 500 million mobile phones. In the future, some of the largest markets will be in Asia.

Many jobs discussed in chapters throughout this book tend to have strong international components. For example, product management and distribution management are discussed as marketing careers in Chapter 12. As more and more companies sell products around the globe, their function, design, packaging, and promotions need to be culturally relevant to many different people in many different places. Products very often cross multiple borders before reaching the final consumer, both in their distribution and through the supply chain to produce the products.

Jobs exist in export and import management, product and pricing management, distribution and transportation, and advertising. Many "born global" companies such as Google operate virtually and consider all countries their market. Many companies sell their products through eBay and other internet sites and never leave the U.S. Today communication and transportation facilitates selling and buying products worldwide with delivery in a few days. You may have sold or purchased a product on eBay outside the U.S. without thinking about how easy and accessible international markets are to business. If you have, welcome to the world of global business.

To be successful you must have an idea not only of differing regulations from country to country, but of different language, ethics, and communication styles and varying needs and wants of international markets. From a regulatory side, you may need to be aware of laws related to intellectual property, copyrights, antitrust, advertising, and pricing in every country. Translating is never only about translating the language. Perhaps even more important is ensuring that your message gets through. Whether on a product label or in advertising or promotional materials, the use of images and words varies widely across the globe.

Review Your Understanding

Explore some of the factors within the international trade environment that influence business.

International business is the buying, selling, and trading of goods and services across national boundaries. Importing is the purchase of products and raw materials from another nation; exporting is the sale of domestic goods and materials to another nation. A nation's balance of trade is the difference in value between its exports and imports; a negative balance of trade is a trade deficit. The difference between the flow of money into a country and the flow of money out of it is called the balance of payments. An absolute or comparative advantage in trade may determine what products a company from a particular nation will export.

Investigate some of the economic, legal-political, social, cultural, and technological barriers to international business.

Companies engaged in international trade must consider the effects of economic, legal, political, social, and cultural differences between nations. Economic barriers are a country's level of development (infrastructure) and exchange rates. Wide-ranging legal and political barriers include differing laws (and enforcement), tariffs, exchange controls, quotas, embargoes, political instability, and war. Ambiguous cultural and social barriers involve differences in spoken and body language, time, holidays and other observances, and customs.

Specify some of the agreements, alliances, and organizations that may encourage trade across international boundaries.

Among the most important promoters of international business are the General Agreement on Tariffs and Trade, the World Trade Organization, the North American Free Trade Agreement, the European Union, the Asia-Pacific Economic Cooperation, the World Bank, and the International Monetary Fund.

Summarize the different levels of organizational involvement in international trade.

A company may be involved in international trade at several levels, each requiring a greater commitment of resources and effort, ranging from importing/exporting to multinational corporations. Countertrade agreements occur at the import/export level and involve bartering products for other products instead of currency. At the next level, a trading company links buyers and sellers in different countries to foster trade. In licensing and franchising, one company agrees to allow a foreign company the use of its company name, products, patents, brands, trademarks, raw materials, and production processes, in exchange for a flat fee or royalty. Contract manufacturing occurs when a company hires a foreign company to produce a specified volume of the firm's product to specification; the final product carries the domestic firm's name. A joint venture is a partnership in which companies from different countries agree to share the costs and operation of the business. The purchase of overseas production and marketing facilities is direct investment. Outsourcing, a form of direct investment, involves transferring manufacturing to countries where labor and supplies are cheap. A multinational corporation is one that operates on a worldwide scale, without significant ties to any one nation or region.

Contrast two basic strategies used in international business.

Companies typically use one of two basic strategies in international business. A multinational strategy customizes products, promotion, and distribution according to cultural, technological, regional, and national differences. A global strategy (globalization) standardizes products (and, as much as possible, their promotion and distribution) for the whole world, as if it were a single entity.

Assess the opportunities and problems facing a small business considering expanding into international markets.

"Solve the Dilemma" on page 114 presents a small business considering expansion into international markets. Based on the material provided in the chapter, analyze the business's position, evaluating specific markets, anticipating problems, and exploring methods of international involvement.

Revisit the World of Business

1. How has Nokia created a competitive advantage?
2. Why does Nokia offer such a wide range of products at such a wide range of prices?
3. Are there any disadvantages to Nokia's strategy?

Learn the Terms

absolute advantage   87
Asia-Pacific Economic Cooperation (APEC)   101
balance of payments   89
balance of trade   88
cartel   95
comparative advantage   87
contract manufacturing   106
countertrade agreements   103
direct investment   107
dumping   94
embargo   94
European Union (EU)   101
exchange controls   93

exchange rate   91
exporting   88
franchising   105
General Agreement on Tariffs and Trade (GATT)   98
global strategy (globalization)   109
import tariff   93
importing   88
infrastructure   91
international business   86
International Monetary Fund (IMF)   103
joint venture   107
licensing   105

multinational corporation (MNC)   108
multinational strategy   108
North American Free Trade Agreement (NAFTA)   99
offshoring   106
outsourcing   87
quota   94
strategic alliance   107
trade deficit   88
trading company   105
World Bank   102
World Trade Organization (WTO)   99

Check Your Progress

1. Distinguish between an absolute advantage and a comparative advantage. Cite an example of a country that has an absolute advantage and one with a comparative advantage.
2. What effect does devaluation have on a nation's currency? Can you think of a country that has devaluated or revaluated its currency? What have been the results?
3. What effect does a country's economic development have on international business?
4. How do political issues affect international business?
5. What is an import tariff? A quota? Dumping? How might a country use import tariffs and quotas to control its balance of trade and payments? Why can dumping result in the imposition of tariffs and quotas?

6. How do social and cultural differences create barriers to international trade? Can you think of any additional social or cultural barriers (other than those mentioned in this chapter) that might inhibit international business?
7. Explain how a countertrade agreement can be considered a trade promoter. How does the World Trade Organization encourage trade?
8. At what levels might a firm get involved in international business? What level requires the least commitment of resources? What level requires the most?
9. Compare and contrast licensing, franchising, contract manufacturing, and outsourcing.
10. Compare multinational and global strategies. Which is best? Under what circumstances might each be used?

Get Involved

1. If the United States were to impose additional tariffs on cars imported from Japan, what would happen to the price of Japanese cars sold in the United States? What would happen to the price of American cars? What action might Japan take to continue to compete in the U.S. automobile market?
2. Although NAFTA has been controversial, it has been a positive factor for U.S. firms desiring to engage in international business. What industries and specific companies have the greatest potential for opening stores in Canada and Mexico? What opportunities

exist for small businesses that cannot afford direct investment in Mexico and Canada?
3. Identify a local company that is active in international trade. What is its level of international business involvement and why? Analyze the threats and opportunities it faces in foreign markets, as well as its strengths and weaknesses in meeting those challenges. Based on your analysis, make some recommendations for the business's future involvement in international trade. (Your instructor may ask you to share your report with the class.)

Build Your Skills

GLOBAL AWARENESS

Background
As American businesspeople travel the globe, they encounter and must quickly adapt to a variety of cultural norms quite different from the United States. When encountering individuals from other parts of the world, the best attitude to adopt is "Here is my way. Now what is yours?" The more you see that you are part of a complex world and that your culture is different from, not better than, others, the better you will communicate and the more effective you will be in a variety of situations. It takes time, energy, understanding, and tolerance to learn about and appreciate other cultures. Naturally you're more comfortable doing things the way you've always done them. Remember, however, that this fact will also be true of the people from other cultures with whom you are doing business.

Task
You will "travel the globe" by answering questions related to some of the cultural norms that are found in other countries. Form groups of four to six class members and determine the answers to the following questions. Your instructor has the answer key, which will allow you to determine your group's Global Awareness IQ, which is based on a maximum score of 100 points (10 points per question).

Match the country with the cultural descriptor provided.

A. Saudi Arabia

B. Japan

C. Great Britain

D. Germany

E. Venezuela

_____ **1.** When people in this country table a motion, they want to discuss it. In America, "to table a motion" means to put off discussion.

_____ **2.** In this country, special forms of speech called *keigo* convey status among speakers. When talking with a person in this country, one should know the person's rank. People from this country will not initiate a conversation without a formal introduction.

_____ **3.** People from this country pride themselves on enhancing their image by keeping others waiting.

_____ **4.** When writing a business letter, people in this country like to provide a great deal of background information and detail before presenting their main points.

_____ **5.** For a man to inquire about another man's wife (even a general question about how she is doing) is considered very offensive in this country.

Match the country with the cultural descriptor provided.

F. China

G. Greece

H. Korea

I. India

J. Mexico

_____ **6.** When in this country, you are expected to negotiate the price on goods you wish to purchase.

_____ **7.** While North Americans want to decide the main points at a business meeting and leave the details for later, people in this country need to have all details decided before the meeting ends, to avoid suspicion and distrust.

_____ **8.** Children in this country learn from a very early age to look down respectfully when talking to those of higher status.

_____ **9.** In this country the husband is the ruler of the household, and the custom is to keep the women hidden.

_____ **10.** Many businesspeople from the United States experience frustration because yes does not always mean the same thing in other cultures. For example, the word *yes* in this country means, "OK, I want to respect you and not offend you." It does not necessarily show agreement.

Solve the Dilemma

GLOBAL EXPANSION OR BUSINESS AS USUAL?

Audiotech Electronics, founded in 1959 by a father and son, currently operates a 35,000-square-foot factory with 75 employees. The company produces control consoles for television and radio stations and recording studios. It is involved in every facet of production—designing the systems, installing the circuits in its computer boards, and even manufacturing and painting the metal cases housing the consoles. The company's products are used by all the major broadcast and cable networks. The firm's newest products allow television correspondents to simultaneously hear and communicate with their counterparts in different geographic locations. Audiotech has been very successful meeting its customers' needs efficiently.

Audiotech sales have historically been strong in the United States, but recently growth is stagnating. Even though Audiotech is a small, family-owned firm, it believes it should evaluate and consider global expansion.

Discussion Questions

1. What are the key issues that need to be considered in determining global expansion?
2. What are some of the unique problems that a small business might face in global expansion that larger firms would not?
3. Should Audiotech consider a joint venture? Should it hire a sales force of people native to the countries it enters?

Build Your Business Plan

BUSINESS IN A BORDERLESS WORLD

Think about the product/service you are contemplating for your business plan. If it is an already established product or service, try to find out if the product is currently being sold internationally. If not, can you identify opportunities to do so in the future? What countries do you think would respond most favorably to your product? What problems would you encounter if you attempted to export your product to those countries?

If you are thinking of creating a new product or service for your business plan, think about the possibility of eventually marketing that product in another country. What countries or areas of the world do you think would be most responsive to your product?

Are there countries that the U.S. has trade agreements or alliances with which would make your entry into the market easier? What would be the economic, social, cultural, and technological barriers you would have to recognize before entering the prospective country (ies)? Think about the specific cultural differences that would have to be taken into consideration before entering the prospective country.

See for Yourself Videocase

WALT DISNEY AROUND THE GLOBE

Mickey Mouse has been a beloved American icon since the 1930s. The success of his and other Disney characters helped to build Disney theme parks; first in Anaheim, California in 1955 and then in Orlando, Florida 16 years later. For decades, tourists from all over the globe traveled in droves to California or Florida to experience the "happiest place on earth." What could be more natural for Disney than to introduce Mickey around the globe with international parks? Disneyland first opened on the international front in Tokyo, Japan, in 1983. Ten years later, Disney brought the magic to Paris, France. Finally, in 2005, Disneyland opened its gates in Hong Kong, China.

Global expansion is tricky for any business. There are many challenges to overcome, such as economic, legal, political, social, and cultural barriers. While Mickey may be recognized and loved around the world, this does not mean that duplicating American parks in other countries would be a success. Perhaps the greatest challenge for Disney when entering new international markets has been how to handle cultural differences.

Euro Disney (later renamed Disneyland Resort Paris) opened near Paris, France, in 1992 to fanfare and problems. Many well-known French citizens and labor unions vocally opposed the park as they felt that it was wrong to allow a symbol of American culture to become a focal point in France. Attendance for the first three years was well below expectations, causing grave financial difficulties. Finally, in 1995, the park experienced a turnaround. Financial restructuring helped the park achieve profitability. New attractions, lower admission prices, renaming the park Disneyland Paris, and a marketing campaign increased attendance. The park, now the number one tourist attraction in Europe with 15 million visitors per year, continues to expand in anticipation of future growth.

Having learned from its experience in France, The Walt Disney Company entered its venture in Hong Kong with an eye to embracing and honoring local culture. The company had learned to be sensitive to cultural variations in events, trends, and cuisine. The parks must embrace local culture while staying true to the Disney message. To this end, Disney hired a feng shui consultant to assist with the layout of the Hong Kong park. The fourth floor was eliminated at all hotels because of the cultural belief that the number four is bad luck. One of the Hong Kong Disneyland ballrooms measures 888 square meters, since eight signifies wealth in Chinese culture. Even with this attention to detail, Hong Kong Disneyland's first years have been rough, with attendance far below projections and protestors raising cultural and social objections. A major complaint among guests has been that the park is small. Over the next decade, the company plans to invest half a billion dollars in expansion efforts, which will begin with Toy Story Land (set to open 2011/2012) and carry on to Grizzly Trail (a Frontier Land-like area set to open in 2012/2013) and Mystic Point (2013/2014).[66]

While some locals continue to protest Disney's presence, there are benefits to allowing a global company like Disney to enter foreign markets. Disney theme parks attract both local and global tourists, which can be a major stimulus to the local economy. For example, Hong Kong expects that Hong Kong Disneyland will bring over 50,000 jobs to the city between 2005 and 2025. Experts predict that the park will bring $19 billion (U.S.) to the local economy during the park's first 40 years. It is likely that, with expansion and further refinement, Hong Kong Disneyland will be a success in the long run. Problems in France and Hong Kong have not deterred The Walt Disney Company from further global expansion. Hopefully the company has learned that it must pay close attention to cultural and social variances in global markets in order to succeed.

Discussion Questions

1. What led The Walt Disney Company to believe that its theme parks would be successful internationally?

2. What stumbling blocks did Disney encounter at their France and Hong Kong theme parks?

3. What are some of the factors complicating international expansion of a brand like Disney? What can a multinational corporation do to mitigate these issues?

Remember to check out our Online Learning Center at www.mhhe.com/ferrell8e.

Team Exercise

Visit Transparency International's Country Corruption Index Web site: http://www.transparency.org/news_room/in_focus/2008/cpi2008/cpi_2008_table. Form groups and select two countries. Research some of the economic, ethical, legal, regulatory, and political barriers that would have an impact on international trade. Be sure to pair a fairly ethical country with a fairly unethical country (i.e., Sweden with Myanmar, Ireland with Haiti, etc). Report your findings.

part

2

Starting and Growing a Business

Options for Organizing Business

OBJECTIVES

After reading this chapter, you will be able to:

- Define and examine the advantages and disadvantages of the sole proprietorship form of organization.
- Identify two types of partnership, and evaluate the advantages and disadvantages of the partnership form of organization.
- Describe the corporate form of organization, and cite the advantages and disadvantages of corporations.
- Define and debate the advantages and disadvantages of mergers, acquisitions, and leveraged buyouts.
- Propose an appropriate organizational form for a startup business.

KIVA
loans that change lives

Microlending Helps Small Entrepreneurs Start Businesses

Sending food and money to disadvantaged communities meets immediate needs, but ending long-term poverty is much more difficult. Kiva.org is one business that seeks to tackle this problem head on. Founded by Stanford graduates with an interest in business and technology, Kiva was first designed to lend money to impoverished Ugandan entrepreneurs. It soon expanded its reach to include other developing countries. Kiva is a microfinance business, which means it provides small loans—as little as $25 for equipment, for example—to individuals to start their own businesses.

Kiva partners with microfinance institutions worldwide. These field partners approve entrepreneurs and send their profiles to Kiva. The entrepreneurs' profiles are then posted on Kiva's Web site, and people who want to lend to an entrepreneur send their donations through the site. Kiva's field partners distribute the loans and work with the entrepreneurs and collect repayments. Kiva.org does not earn returns on investments for lenders, but it does charge interest rates of between 23 and 48 percent. These interest rates cover loan costs, transaction costs, defaults, and inflation rates—and are much lower than rates charged by informal lenders or predatory lenders who typically supply loans to those who do not qualify for bank loans.

Kiva and about 575,000 lenders have succeeded in providing loans to over a quarter million entrepreneurs since 2005. In October 2009, the company reached $100 million in worldwide loans—up $60 million in one year. Kiva has established a five-year plan, aiming to reach $1 billion in global loans, help 2 million entrepreneurs, and achieve organizational sustainability. Kiva.org

continued

Introduction

The legal form of ownership taken by a business is seldom of great concern to you as a customer. When you eat at a restaurant, you probably don't care whether the restaurant is owned by one person (a sole proprietorship), has two or more owners who share the business (a partnership), or is an entity owned by many stockholders (a corporation); all you want is good food. If you buy a foreign car, you probably don't care whether the company that made it has laws governing its form of organization that are different from those for businesses in the United States. You are buying the car because it is well made, fits your price range, or appeals to your sense of style. Nonetheless, a business's legal form of ownership affects how it operates, how much tax it pays, and how much control its owners have.

This chapter examines three primary forms of business ownership—sole proprietorship, partnership, and corporation—and weighs the advantages and disadvantages of each. These forms are the most often used whether the business is a traditional bricks and mortar company, an online-only one, or a combination of both. We also take a look at S corporations, limited liability companies, and cooperatives and discuss some trends in business ownership. You may wish to refer to Table 4.1 to compare the various forms of business ownership mentioned in the chapter.

Sole Proprietorships

sole proprietorships
businesses owned and operated by one individual; the most common form of business organization in the United States

Sole proprietorships, businesses owned and operated by one individual, are the most common form of business organization in the United States. Common examples include many restaurants, hair salons, flower shops, dog kennels, and

TABLE 4.1 Various Forms of Business Ownership

Structure	Ownership	Taxation	Liability	Use
Sole Proprietorship	1 owner	Individual income taxed	Unlimited	Owned by a single individual and is the easiest way to conduct business.
Partnership	2 or more owners	Individual owners' income taxed	Somewhat limited	Easy way for two individuals to conduct business
Corporation	Any number of shareholders	Corporate and shareholder taxed	Limited	A legal entity with shareholders or stockholders
S Corporation	Up to 75 shareholders	Taxed as a partnership	Limited	A legal entity with tax advantages for restricted number of shareholders
Limited Liability Company	Unlimited number of shareholders	Taxed as a partnership	Limited	Avoid personal lawsuits

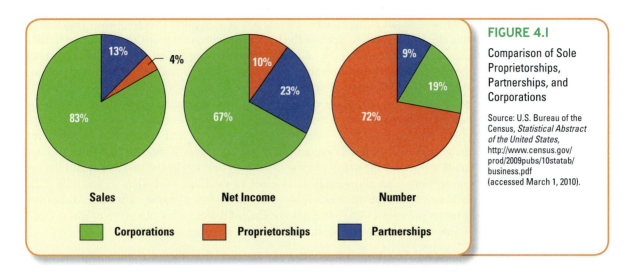

FIGURE 4.1

Comparison of Sole
Proprietorships,
Partnerships, and
Corporations

Source: U.S. Bureau of the
Census, *Statistical Abstract
of the United States,*
http://www.census.gov/
prod/2009pubs/10statab/
business.pdf
(accessed March 1, 2010).

independent grocery stores. Many sole proprietors focus on services—small retail
stores, financial counseling, appliance repair, child care, and the like—rather than
on the manufacture of goods, which often requires large sums of money not available
to most small businesses. As you can see in Figure 4.1, proprietorships far outnumber
corporations, but they net far fewer sales and less income.

Sole proprietorships are typically small businesses employing fewer than 50 people.
(We'll look at small businesses in greater detail in Chapter 5.) There are 15 to 20
million sole proprietorships in the United States, constituting three-fourths of all
businesses in the United States. It is interesting to note that men are twice as likely as
women to start their own business.[2]

Advantages of Sole Proprietorships

Sole proprietorships are generally managed by their owners. Because of this
simple management structure, the owner/
manager can make decisions quickly. This
is just one of many advantages of the sole
proprietorship form of business.

Ease and Cost of Formation.   Form-
ing a sole proprietorship is relatively easy
and inexpensive. In some states, creating a sole proprietorship involves merely
announcing the new business in the local
newspaper. Other proprietorships, such
as barber shops and restaurants, may
require state and local licenses and permits because of the nature of the business.
The cost of these permits may run from
$25 to $100. No lawyer is needed to create
such enterprises, and the owner can usually take care of the required paperwork
without outside assistance.

*Many "olderpreneurs" (older
people who start their own
businesses) formed sole
proprietorships after being
laid off in the latest economic
downturn.*

Of course, an entrepreneur starting a new sole proprietorship must find a suitable site from which to operate the business. Some sole proprietors look no farther than their garage or a spare bedroom when seeking a workshop or office. Among the more famous businesses that sprang to life in their founders' homes are Google, Walt Disney, Dell, eBay, Hewlett-Packard, Apple Computer, and Mattel.[3] Computers, personal copiers, scanners, and other high-tech gadgets have been a boon for home-based businesses, permitting them to interact quickly with customers, suppliers, and others. Many independent salespersons and contractors can perform their work using a notebook computer as they travel. E-mail and cell phones have made it possible for many proprietorships to develop in the services area. Internet connections also allow small businesses to establish Web sites to promote their products and even to make low-cost long-distance phone calls with voice-over Internet protocol (VOIP) technology. One of the most famous services using VOIP is Skype, which allows people to make free calls over the Internet.

Secrecy.   Sole proprietorships make possible the greatest degree of secrecy. The proprietor, unlike the owners of a partnership or corporation, does not have to discuss publicly his or her operating plans, minimizing the possibility that competitors can obtain trade secrets. Financial reports need not be disclosed, as do the financial reports of publicly owned corporations.

Distribution and Use of Profits.   All profits from a sole proprietorship belong exclusively to the owner. He or she does not have to share them with any partners or stockholders. The owner decides how to use the funds—for expansion of the business, or salary increases, for travel to purchase additional inventory, or to find new customers.

Flexibility and Control of the Business.   The sole proprietor has complete control over the business and can make decisions on the spot without anyone else's approval. This control allows the owner to respond quickly to competitive business conditions or to changes in the economy.

Government Regulation.   Sole proprietorships have the most freedom from government regulation. Many government regulations—federal, state, and local—apply only to businesses that have a certain number of employees, and securities laws apply only to corporations that issue stock. Nonetheless, sole proprietors must ensure that they follow all laws that do apply to their business.

Taxation.   Profits from sole proprietorships are considered personal income and are taxed at individual tax rates. The owner, therefore, pays one income tax that includes the business and individual income. Another tax benefit is that a sole proprietor is allowed to establish a tax-exempt retirement account or a tax-exempt profit-sharing account. Such accounts are exempt from current income tax, but payments taken after retirement are taxed when they are received.

Closing the Business.   A sole proprietorship can be dissolved easily. No approval of co-owners or partners is necessary. The only legal condition is that all loans must be paid off.

Disadvantages of Sole Proprietorships

What may be seen as an advantage by one person may turn out to be a disadvantage to another. For profitable businesses managed by capable owners, many of the following factors do not cause problems. On the other hand, proprietors starting out

Entrepreneurship in Action
Ukrainian Immigrant Becomes Subway Success

Lyudmila Khononov

Business: Subway Franchisee

Founded: Khononov opened her first franchise in 2001.

Success: Lyudmila Khononov has successfully run four Subway franchises and was named Franchisee of the Year.

Lyudmila Khononov was used to risk. She and her family had to start over after moving to the United States from Ukraine 30 years ago. So when it came to running a business, Khononov took on the challenge. She and her husband started off with a diner in Queens, New York, but eventually decided to move in a different direction. With the help of a bank, family, and friends, they opened their first Subway franchise in 2001. For Khononov, the Subway method made running a business easier, with companywide national marketing, pre-prepared food, and a proven formula. However, it was her entrepreneurial spirit that led to the 4 franchises she now owns, with 2 more in construction and plans for a total of 10 within a year. Khononov's achievements earned her Franchisee of the Year, thanks to her skills in adding stores, building sales, increasing profits, and receiving positive store evaluations.[4]

with little management experience and little money are likely to encounter many of the disadvantages.

Unlimited Liability. The sole proprietor has unlimited liability in meeting the debts of the business. In other words, if the business cannot pay its creditors, the owner may be forced to use personal, nonbusiness holdings such as a car or a home to pay off the debts. There are only a few states in which houses and homesteads cannot be taken by creditors, even if the proprietor declares bankruptcy. The more wealth an individual has, the greater is the disadvantage of unlimited liability.

Limited Sources of Funds. Among the relatively few sources of money available to the sole proprietorship are banks, friends, family, the Small Business Administration, or his or her own funds. The owner's personal financial condition determines his or her credit standing. Additionally, sole proprietorships may have to pay higher interest rates on funds borrowed from banks than do large corporations because they are considered greater risks. Often, the only way a sole proprietor can borrow for business purposes is to pledge a car, a house, other real estate, or other personal assets to guarantee the loan. If the business fails, the owner may lose the personal assets as well as the business. Publicly owned corporations, in contrast, can not only obtain funds from commercial banks but can sell stocks and bonds to the public to raise money. If a public company goes out of business, the owners do not lose personal assets.

Limited Skills. The sole proprietor must be able to perform many functions and possess skills in diverse fields such as management, marketing, finance, accounting, bookkeeping, and personnel management. Business owners can rely on specialized professionals for advice and services, such as accountants and attorneys. Musicians, for example, can turn to agents for assistance in navigating through the complex maze of the recording business. One startup firm specializing in this type of assistance for online musicians and bands is the Digital Artists Agency, whose clients include David Lombardi, Chris LeDoux, and Academy Award–winner Tim McGovern. The DAA researches, markets, and cultivates online music talent in exchange for a commission on online sales of music, tickets, and merchandise.[5] In the end, however, it is up to the business owner to make the final decision in all areas of the business.

Lack of Continuity.   The life expectancy of a sole proprietorship is directly linked to that of the owner and his or her ability to work. The serious illness of the owner could result in failure of the business if competent help cannot be found.

It is difficult to arrange for the sale of a proprietorship and at the same time assure customers that the business will continue to meet their needs. For instance, how does one sell a veterinary practice? A veterinarian's major asset is patients. If the vet dies suddenly, the equipment can be sold, but the patients will not necessarily remain loyal to the office. On the other hand, a veterinarian who wants to retire could take in a younger partner and sell the practice to the partner over time. One advantage to the partnership is that some of the customers are likely to stay with the business, even if ownership changes.

Lack of Qualified Employees.   It is usually difficult for a small sole proprietorship to match the wages and benefits offered by a large competing corporation because the proprietorship's profits may not be as high. In addition, there is little room for advancement within a sole proprietorship, so the owner may have difficulty attracting and retaining qualified employees. On the other hand, the trend of large corporations downsizing and outsourcing tasks has created renewed opportunities for small businesses to acquire well-trained employees.

Taxation.   Although we listed taxation as an advantage for sole proprietorships, it can also be a disadvantage, depending on the proprietor's income. Under current tax rates, sole proprietors pay a higher marginal tax rate than do small corporations on income of less than $75,000. The tax effect often determines whether a sole proprietor chooses to incorporate his or her business.

Partnerships

One way to minimize the disadvantages of a sole proprietorship and maximize its advantages is to have more than one owner. Most states have a model law governing partnerships based on the Uniform Partnership Act. This law defines a **partnership** as "an association of two or more persons who carry on as co-owners of a business for profit." Partnerships are the least used form of business. (see Figure 4.1). They are typically larger than sole proprietorships but smaller than corporations.

Partnerships can be a fruitful form of business, as long as you follow some basic keys to success, which are outlined in Table 4.3.

Types of Partnership

There are two basic types of partnership: general partnership and limited partnership. A **general partnership** involves a complete sharing in the management of a business. In a general partnership, each partner has unlimited liability for the debts of the business. For example, Cirque du Soleil grew from a group of Quebec street performers, who acted as partners, into a half-billion-dollar global company. Cirque du Soleil, however, ended its 16-year run as a partnership in the year 2000. Guy Laliberte bought out the other principle partner, Daniel Gauthier. Laliberte maintains a controlling share of the company, and Dubai's state-run private equity firm, Istithmar World, picked up a 20 percent stake in Cirque du Soleil for more global expansion of permanent show venues.[6] Professionals such as lawyers, accountants, and architects often join together in general partnerships.

partnership
a form of business organization defined by the Uniform Partnership Act as "an association of two or more persons who carry on as co-owners of a business for profit"

general partnership
a partnership that involves a complete sharing in both the management and the liability of the business

1. Name, purpose, location	**TABLE 4.2**
2. Duration of the agreement	Issues and Provisions in Articles of Partnership
3. Authority and responsibility of each partner	
4. Character of partners (i.e., general or limited, active or silent)	
5. Amount of contribution from each partner	
6. Division of profits or losses	
7. Salaries of each partner	
8. How much each partner is allowed to withdraw	
9. Death of partner	
10. Sale of partnership interest	
11. Arbitration of disputes	
12. Required and prohibited actions	
13. Absence and disability	
14. Restrictive covenants	
15. Buying and selling agreements	

Source: Adapted from "Partnership Agreement Sample," State of New Jersey, http://www.state.nj.us/njbusiness/starting/basics/partnership_agreement_sample.shtml (accessed March 15, 2010).

1. Keep profit sharing and ownership at 50/50, or you have an employer/employee relationship.	**TABLE 4.3**
2. Partners should have different skill sets to complement one another.	Keys to Success in Business Partnerships
3. Honesty is critical.	
4. Must maintain face-to-face communication in addition to phone and e-mail.	
5. Maintain transparency, sharing more information over time.	
6. Be aware of funding constraints, and do not put yourself in a situation where neither you nor your partner can secure additional financial support.	
7. To be successful, you need experience.	
8. Whereas family should be a priority, be careful to minimize the number of associated problems.	
9. Do not become too infatuated with "the idea" as opposed to implementation.	
10. Couple optimism with realism in sales and growth expectations and planning.	

Source: Abstracted from J. Watananbe, "14 Reasons Why 80% of New Business Partnerships Would Fail Within Their First 5 Years of Existence," http://ezinearticles.com/?14-Reasons-Why-80-Percent-Of-New-Business-Partnerships-Would-Fail-Within-Their-First-5-Years-Of-Exis&id=472498 (accessed March 16, 2010).

A **limited partnership** has at least one general partner, who assumes unlimited liability, and at least one limited partner, whose liability is limited to his or her investment in the business. Limited partnerships exist for risky investment projects where the chance of loss is great. The general partners accept the risk of loss; the limited partners' losses are limited to their initial investment. Limited partners do not participate in the management of the business but share in the profits in accordance with the terms of a partnership agreement. Usually the general partner receives a larger share of the profits after the limited partners have received their initial investment back. Popular examples are oil-drilling partnerships and real estate partnerships.

limited partnership
a business organization that has at least one general partner, who assumes unlimited liability, and at least one limited partner, whose liability is limited to his or her investment in the business

Articles of Partnership

Articles of partnership are legal documents that set forth the basic agreement between partners. Most states require articles of partnership, but even if they are not required, it makes good sense for partners to draw them up. Articles of partnership usually list the money or assets that each partner has contributed (called *partnership capital*), state each partner's individual management role or duty, specify how the profits and losses of the partnership will be divided among the partners, and describe how a partner may leave the partnership as well as any other restrictions that might apply to the agreement. Table 4.2 lists some of the issues and provisions that should be included in articles of partnership.

Advantages of Partnerships

Law firms, accounting firms, and investment firms with several hundred partners have partnership agreements that are quite complicated in comparison with the partnership agreement among two or three people owning a computer repair shop. The advantages must be compared with those offered by other forms of business organization, and not all apply to every partnership.

Ease of Organization.
Starting a partnership requires little more than drawing up articles of partnership. No legal charters have to be granted, but the name of the business should be registered with the state.

Friends since junior high. Ben Cohen and Jerry Greenfield began Ben & Jerry's Homemade Ice Cream as a partnership in 1977. The pair took a correspondence course in ice-cream making before founding the company in a renovated Vermont gas station.

Availability of Capital and Credit.
When a business has several partners, it has the benefit of a combination of talents and skills and pooled financial resources. Partnerships tend to be larger than sole proprietorships and therefore have greater earning power and better credit ratings. Because many limited partnerships have been formed for tax purposes rather than for economic profits, the combined income of all U.S. partnerships is quite low, as shown in Figure 4.1. Nevertheless, the professional partnerships of many lawyers, accountants, and investment banking firms make quite large profits. Goldman Sachs, a large New York investment banking partnership, earns several hundred million dollars in an average year.

Combined Knowledge and Skills.
Partners in the most successful partnerships acknowledge each other's talents and avoid confusion and conflict by specializing in a particular area of expertise such as marketing, production, accounting, or service. The diversity of skills in a partnership makes it possible for the business to be run by a management team of specialists instead of by a generalist sole proprietor. Additionally, by splitting up the work, partners can often tackle projects that would have been much more difficult for a sole proprietor. For example, one surprising trend is the growth of organic farm

partnerships among young people. Young people who are interested in organic farming often find the work too difficult for just one person, so they are partnering up to share the responsibilities.[7] Service-oriented partnerships in fields such as law, financial planning, and accounting may attract customers because clients may think that the service offered by a diverse team is of higher quality than that provided by one person. Larger law firms, for example, often have individual partners who specialize in certain areas of the law—such as family, bankruptcy, corporate, entertainment, and criminal law.

Decision Making.   Small partnerships can react more quickly to changes in the business environment than can large partnerships and corporations. Such fast reactions are possible because the partners are involved in day-to-day operations and can make decisions quickly after consultation. Large partnerships with hundreds of partners in many states are not common. In those that do exist, decision making is likely to be slow.

Regulatory Controls.   Like a sole proprietorship, a partnership has fewer regulatory controls affecting its activities than does a corporation. A partnership does not have to file public financial statements with government agencies or send out quarterly financial statements to several thousand owners, as do corporations such as Apple and Ford Motor Co. A partnership does, however, have to abide by all laws relevant to the industry or profession in which it operates as well as state and federal laws relating to hiring and firing, food handling, and so on, just as the sole proprietorship does.

Disadvantages of Partnerships

Partnerships have many advantages compared to sole proprietorships and corporations, but they also have some disadvantages. Limited partners have no voice in the management of the partnership, and they may bear most of the risk of the business while the general partner reaps a larger share of the benefits. There may be a change in the goals and objectives of one partner but not the other, particularly when the partners are multinational organizations. This can cause friction, giving rise to an enterprise that fails to satisfy both parties or even forcing an end to the partnership. Many partnership disputes wind up in court or require outside mediation. A partnership can be jeopardized when two business partners cannot resolve disputes. In *Saunders v. Firtel* (Firtel held a 51 percent stake and Saunders 49 percent in Adco Medical Supplies Inc.), Saunders was not only a partner, but a paid employee. When the two entered into an unresolvable dispute, Firtel fired Saunders and did not pay wages. Saunders sued under Connecticut law, which states that "when any employer fails to pay an employee's wages . . . the employee may recover, in civil action, twice the full amount of such wages." Saunders won the case because the trial court found the failure to pay wages was willful.[8] In some cases, the ultimate solution may be dissolving the partnership. Major disadvantages of partnerships include the following.

Unlimited Liability.   In general partnerships, the general partners have unlimited liability for the debts incurred by the business, just as the sole proprietor has unlimited liability for his or her business. Such unlimited liability can be a distinct disadvantage to one partner if his or her personal financial resources are greater than those of the others. A potential partner should check to make sure that all partners have comparable resources to help the business in time of trouble. This disadvantage is eliminated for limited partners, who can lose only their initial investment.

Going Green
E-Bikes Offer Exercise and Environmental Consciousness

You surely have heard of electric cars, but what about electric bikes? The bicycle industry found a way to compete with cars and motorcycles through superior environmental friendliness, with the introduction of bikes that allow riders to reduce their carbon footprint and travel without breaking a sweat. Electric bikes (e-bikes) are equipped with a motor and battery. With each pedal stroke, the motor provides additional power, allowing riders to pedal without expending as much energy as with conventional bicycles. Typical e-bikes generally go a maximum of 25 mph and cost between $500 and $3,000.

E-bikes are common in bicycle-focused cultures in Asia and Europe, but they are also making inroads in America. Americans bought 170,000 e-bikes in 2008, around 200,000 in 2009, and growth is expected to continue to increase. Best Buy even introduced e-bikes in some of its stores. Schwinn has come out with the motto "Save the world without killing your knees" to advertise its line of e-bikes, playing off the e-bike's environmental friendliness and ease of use. Schwinn offers the high-end Tailwind, with batteries that charge in under 30 minutes.

Other companies are focusing on e-bikes specifically. One such company is Ultra Motor Company Limited, a private corporation and developer of light electric vehicles. Its product, the A2B Metro, can go for 20 miles. This 100 percent electric vehicle resembles a mix of scooter and bicycle. Unlike motorcycles, this e-bike's motor is quiet, allowing for peaceful commutes. The e-bike could very well be the answer for urban commuters. Its zero carbon emissions make it a good deal for those who care about the environment, have a hard time finding parking, or who simply want to get more exercise.[9]

Discussion Questions
1. Ultra Motor Company Limited is a private corporation. What are the advantages of being private and not being traded on a stock exchange?
2. Schwinn is a division of a public corporation—publicly traded company Dorel Industries. What advantages are there in being part of a public corporation?
3. What could be a disadvantage of operating an electric bike firm as a sole proprietorship?

Business Responsibility.   All partners are responsible for the business actions of all others. Partners may have the ability to commit the partnership to a contract without approval of the other partners. A bad decision by one partner may put the other partners' personal resources in jeopardy. Personal problems such as a divorce can eliminate a significant portion of one partner's financial resources and weaken the financial structure of the whole partnership.

Life of the Partnership.   A partnership is terminated when a partner dies or withdraws. In a two-person partnership, if one partner withdraws, the firm's liabilities would be paid off and the assets divided between the partners. Obviously, the partner who wishes to continue in the business would be at a serious disadvantage. The business could be disrupted, financing would be reduced, and the management skills of the departing partner would be lost. The remaining partner would have to find another or reorganize the business as a sole proprietorship. In very large partnerships such as those found in law firms and investment banks, the continuation of the partnership may be provided for in the articles of partnership. The provision may simply state the terms for a new partnership agreement among the remaining partners. In such cases, the disadvantage to the other partners is minimal.

Selling a partnership interest has the same effect as the death or withdrawal of a partner. It is difficult to place a value on a partner's share of the partnership. No public value is placed on the partnership, as there is on publicly owned corporations. What is a law firm worth? What is the local hardware store worth? Coming up with a fair value that all partners can agree to is not easy. Selling a partnership interest is easier if the articles of partnership specify a method of valuation. Even if there is not a procedure for selling one partner's interest, the old partnership must still be dissolved and a new one created. In contrast, in the corporate form of business, the departure of owners has little effect on the financial resources of the business, and the loss of managers does not cause long-term changes in the structure of the organization.

Distribution of Profits.   Profits earned by the partnership are distributed to the partners in the proportions specified in the articles of partnership. This may be a disadvantage if the division of the profits does not reflect the work each partner puts into the business. You may have encountered this disadvantage while working on a student group project: You may have felt that you did most of the work and that the other students in the group received grades based on your efforts. Even the perception of an unfair profit-sharing agreement may cause tension between the partners, and unhappy partners can have a negative effect on the profitability of the business.

Limited Sources of Funds.   As with a sole proprietorship, the sources of funds available to a partnership are limited. Because no public value is placed on the business (such as the current trading price of a corporation's stock), potential partners do not know what one partnership share is worth. Moreover, because partnership shares cannot be bought and sold easily in public markets, potential owners may not want to tie up their money in assets that cannot be readily sold on short notice. Accumulating enough funds to operate a national business, especially a business requiring intensive investments in facilities and equipment, can be difficult. Partnerships also may have to pay higher interest rates on funds borrowed from banks than do large corporations because partnerships may be considered greater risks.

Taxation of Partnerships

Partnerships are quasi-taxable organizations. This means that partnerships do not pay taxes when submitting the partnership tax return to the Internal Revenue Service. The tax return simply provides information about the profitability of the organization and the distribution of profits among the partners. Partners must report their share of profits on their individual tax returns and pay taxes at the income tax rate for individuals.

Corporations

When you think of a business, you probably think of a huge corporation such as General Electric, Procter & Gamble, or Sony because a large portion of your consumer dollars go to such corporations. A **corporation** is a legal entity, created by the state, whose assets and liabilities are separate from its owners. As a legal entity, a corporation has many of the rights, duties, and powers of a person, such as the right to receive, own, and transfer property. Corporations can enter into contracts with individuals or with other legal entities, and they can sue and be sued in court.

corporation
a legal entity, created by the state, whose assets and liabilities are separate from its owners

Corporations account for the majority of all U.S. sales and income. Thus, most of the dollars you spend as a consumer probably go to incorporated businesses (see Figure 4.1). Most corporations are not mega-companies like General Mills or Ford Motor Co.; even small businesses can incorporate. As we shall see later in the chapter, many smaller firms elect to incorporate as "S Corporations," which operate under slightly different rules and have greater flexibility than do traditional "C Corporations" like General Mills.

stock
shares of a corporation that may be bought or sold

dividends
profits of a corporation that are distributed in the form of cash payments to stockholders

Corporations are typically owned by many individuals and organizations who own shares of the business, called **stock** (thus, corporate owners are often called *shareholders* or *stockholders*). Stockholders can buy, sell, give or receive as gifts, or inherit their shares of stock. As owners, the stockholders are entitled to all profits that are left after all the corporation's other obligations have been paid. These profits may be distributed in the form of cash payments called **dividends.** For example, if a corporation earns $100 million after expenses and taxes and decides to pay the owners $40 million in dividends, the stockholders receive 40 percent of the profits in cash dividends. However, not all after-tax profits are paid to stockholders in dividends. Some corporations may retain profits to expand the business.

Creating a Corporation

A corporation is created, or incorporated, under the laws of the state in which it incorporates. The individuals creating the corporation are known as *incorporators.* Each state has a specific procedure, sometimes called *chartering the corporation,* for incorporating a business. Most states require a minimum of three incorporators; thus, many small businesses can be and are incorporated. Another requirement is that the new corporation's name cannot be similar to that of another business. In most states, a corporation's name must end in "company," "corporation," "incorporated," or "limited" to show that the owners have limited liability. (In this text, however, the word *company* means any organization engaged in a commercial enterprise and can refer to a sole proprietorship, a partnership, or a corporation.)

The incorporators must file legal documents generally referred to as *articles of incorporation* with the appropriate state office (often the secretary of state). The articles of incorporation contain basic information about the business. The following 10 items are found in the Model Business Corporation Act, issued by the American Bar Association, which is followed by most states:

1. Name and address of the corporation.
2. Objectives of the corporation.
3. Classes of stock (common, preferred, voting, nonvoting) and the number of shares for each class of stock to be issued.
4. Expected life of the corporation (corporations are usually created to last forever).
5. Financial capital required at the time of incorporation.
6. Provisions for transferring shares of stock between owners.
7. Provisions for the regulation of internal corporate affairs.
8. Address of the business office registered with the state of incorporation.
9. Names and addresses of the initial board of directors.
10. Names and addresses of the incorporators.

corporate charter
a legal document that the state issues to a company based on information the company provides in the articles of incorporation

Based on the information in the articles of incorporation, the state issues a **corporate charter** to the company. After securing this charter, the owners hold an organizational meeting at which they establish the corporation's bylaws and elect a board of directors. The bylaws might set up committees of the board of directors and describe the rules and procedures for their operation.

Types of Corporations

If the corporation does business in the state in which it is chartered, it is known as a *domestic corporation.* In other states where the corporation does business, it is known as a *foreign corporation.* If a corporation does business outside the nation in which it incorporated, it is called an *alien corporation.* A corporation may be privately or publicly owned.

A **private corporation** is owned by just one or a few people who are closely involved in managing the business. These people, often a family, own all the corporation's stock, and no stock is sold to the public. Many corporations are quite large, yet remain private, including Cargill, a farm products business. It is the nation's largest private corporation with annual revenues of well over $100 billion. Founded at the end of the Civil War, descendents of the original founder have owned equity in the company for more than 140 years.[10] The sixth-largest privately held company in the United States is Mars, founded by Forrest Mars Sr. who spent time in Switzerland learning to create chocolate confectionaries. Mars recently grew significantly through the acquisition of the Wm. Wrigley Jr. Company. Founded in Tacoma, Washington, in 1911, Mars is now the world's leading confectionary company and a leader in pet care products with Pedigree and Whiskas.[11]

The snack and food company Mars is privately owned by the Mars family. Forrest Mars Sr. founded the firm after creating the recipe for M&Ms, which were first sold in the United States in 1941.

The business was successful early on because it paid employees three times the normal wage for the time. The company remains successful to this day, largely because of its established brands, such as M&Ms, and healthy snack lines for kids, like Generation Max.[12] Other well-known privately held companies include Chrysler, Publix Supermarkets, Dollar General, and MGM Entertainment. Privately owned corporations are not required to disclose financial information publicly, but they must, of course, pay taxes.

A **public corporation** is one whose stock anyone may buy, sell, or trade. Table 4.4 lists the largest U.S. corporations by revenues. Despite their high revenues, Conoco Phillips, Ford Motors, General Motors, and Valero Energy all had negative profits in 2009.[13] Thousands of smaller public corporations in the United States have sales under $10 million. In large public corporations such as AT&T, the stockholders are often far removed from the management of the company. In other public corporations, the managers are often the founders and the major shareholders. NASCAR, for example, was founded by William France in 1948, and ever since then his descendents have manned the helm as CEO. Grandson Brian France currently fills the post.[14] *Forbes* Global 2000 companies generate around $32 trillion in revenues, $1.6 trillion in profits, and $125 trillion in assets. They are worth $20 trillion in market value. The United States still has the majority of the Global 2000 companies, but other nations are catching up. The rankings of the Global 2000 span across 62 countries.[15] Publicly owned corporations must disclose financial information to the public under specific laws that regulate the trade of stocks and other securities.

private corporation
a corporation owned by just one or a few people who are closely involved in managing the business

public corporation
a corporation whose stock anyone may buy, sell, or trade

TABLE 4.4

The Largest U.S. Corporations, Arranged by Revenues

Rank	Company	Revenues (in millions of $)
1.	Walmart	$378,799.0
2.	ExxonMobil	372,824.0
3.	Chevron	210,783.0
4.	General Motors	182,347.0
5.	Conoco Phillips	178,558.0
6.	General Electric	176,656.0
7.	Ford Motor	172,468.0
8.	Citigroup	159,229.0
9.	Bank of America Corp.	119,190.0
10.	AT&T	118,928.0
11.	Berkshire Hathaway	118,245.0
12.	JPMorgan Chase & Co.	116,353.0
13.	American International Group	110,064.0
14.	Hewlett-Packard	104,286.0
15.	International Business Machines (IBM)	98,786.0
16.	Valero Energy	96,758.0
17.	Verizon Communications	93,775.0
18.	McKeeson	93,574.0
19.	Cardinal Health	88,363.9
20.	Goldman Sachs Group	87,968.0

Source: "*Fortune* 500: *Fortune*'s Annual Ranking of America's Largest Corporations," *Fortune,* http://money.cnn.com/magazines/fortune/fortune500/2009/full_list/ (accessed March 1, 2010).

initial public offering (IPO)

selling a corporation's stock on public markets for the first time

A private corporation that needs more money to expand or to take advantage of opportunities may have to obtain financing by "going public" through an **initial public offering (IPO),** that is, becoming a public corporation by selling stock so that it can be traded in public markets. For example, the applications software maker SolarWinds Inc., headquartered in Austin, Texas, had an initial public offering of about $12.50 a share in May 2009. Originally, the stock price range was set at $9.50 to $11.50 a share, but underwriters eventually gave it a higher value. The shares generated a 67 percent return by December. SolarWinds Inc.'s IPO was one of the first major successes for venture capitalists after a long slump.[16]

Also, privately owned firms are occasionally forced to go public with stock offerings when a major owner dies and the heirs have large estate taxes to pay. The tax payment may only be possible with the proceeds of the sale of stock. This happened to the brewer Adolph Coors Inc. After Adolph Coors died, the business went public and his family sold shares of stock to the public in order to pay the estate taxes.

On the other hand, public corporations can be "taken private" when one or a few individuals (perhaps the management of the firm) purchase all the firm's stock so that it can no longer be sold publicly. Taking a corporation private may be desirable when new owners want to exert more control over the firm or they want to avoid the necessity of public disclosure of future activities for competitive reasons. For example, RCN Corporation, a broadband provider, was purchased by a private equity group, Abry Partners LLC, for about $535 million in cash. Abry's goal with the purchase is to expand its companies offering broadband and cable service in

Google founders Larry Page and Sergey Brin were able to raise a whopping $1.66 billion via an initial public offering of the company's stock in 2004. The IPO is one of the largest in stock market history.

New York, Boston, and Philadelphia.[17] Taking a corporation private is also one technique for avoiding a takeover by another corporation.

Quasi-public corporations and nonprofit are two types of public corporations. **Quasi-public corporations** are owned and operated by the federal, state, or local government. The focus of these entities is to provide a service to citizens, such as mail delivery, rather than earning a profit. Indeed, many quasi-public corporations operate at a loss. Examples of quasi-public corporations include the National Aeronautics and Space Administration (NASA) and the U.S. Postal Service.

Like quasi-public corporations, **nonprofit corporations** focus on providing a service rather than earning a profit, but they are not owned by a government entity. Organizations such as the Sesame Workshop, the Elks Clubs, the American Lung Association, the American Red Cross, museums, and private schools provide services without a profit motive. To fund their operations and services, nonprofit organizations solicit donations from individuals and companies and grants from the government and other charitable foundations.

Elements of a Corporation

The Board of Directors.   A **board of directors,** elected by the stockholders to oversee the general operation of the corporation, sets the long-range objectives of the corporation. It is the board's responsibility to ensure that the objectives are achieved on schedule. Board members are legally liable for the mismanagement of the firm

quasi-public corporations
corporations owned and operated by the federal, state, or local government

nonprofit corporations
corporations that focus on providing a service rather than earning a profit but are not owned by a government entity

board of directors
a group of individuals, elected by the stockholders to oversee the general operation of the corporation, who set the corporation's long-range objectives

The sharp rise of CEO's pay in the United States has called into question how independent firms' board members are, given the fact that many of them are CEOs themselves.

or for any misuse of funds. An important duty of the board of directors is to hire corporate officers, such as the president and the chief executive officer (CEO), who are responsible to the directors for the management and daily operations of the firm. The role and expectations of the board of directors took on greater significance after the accounting scandals of the early 2000s and the passage of the Sarbanes-Oxley Act.[18] As a result, most corporations have restructured how they compensate board directors for their time and expertise.

Directors can be employees of the company *(inside directors)* or people unaffiliated with the company *(outside directors)*. Inside directors are usually the officers responsible for running the company. Outside directors are often top executives from other companies, lawyers, bankers, even professors. Directors today are increasingly chosen for their expertise, competence, and ability to bring diverse perspectives to strategic discussions. Outside directors are also thought to bring more independence to the monitoring function because they are not bound by past allegiances, friendships, a current role in the company, or some other issue that may create a conflict of interest. Many of the corporate scandals uncovered in recent years might have been prevented if each of the companies' boards of directors had been better qualified, more knowledgeable, and more independent.

There is a growing shortage of available and qualified board members. Boards are increasingly telling their own CEOs that they should be focused on serving their company, not serving on outside boards. Because of this, the average CEO sits on less than one outside board. This represents a decline from a decade ago when the average was two. Because many CEOs are turning down outside positions, many companies have taken steps to ensure that boards have experienced directors. They have increased the mandatory retirement age to 72 or older, and some have raised it to 75 or even older. Minimizing the amount of overlap between directors sitting on different boards helps to limit conflicts of interest and provides for independence in decision making.

Stock Ownership.

preferred stock
a special type of stock whose owners, though not generally having a say in running the company, have a claim to profits before other stockholders do

common stock
stock whose owners have voting rights in the corporation, yet do not receive preferential treatment regarding dividends

Corporations issue two types of stock: preferred and common. Owners of **preferred stock** are a special class of owners because, although they generally do not have any say in running the company, they have a claim to profits before any other stockholders do. Other stockholders do not receive any dividends unless the preferred stockholders have already been paid. Dividend payments on preferred stock are usually a fixed percentage of the initial issuing price (set by the board of directors). For example, if a share of preferred stock originally cost $100 and the dividend rate was stated at 7.5 percent, the dividend payment will be $7.50 per share per year. Dividends are usually paid quarterly. Most preferred stock carries a cumulative claim to dividends. This means that if the company does not pay preferred-stock dividends in one year because of losses, the dividends accumulate to the next year. Such dividends unpaid from previous years must also be paid to preferred stockholders before other stockholders can receive any dividends.

Although owners of **common stock** do not get such preferential treatment with regard to dividends, they do get some say in the operation of the corporation. Their ownership gives them the right to vote for members of the board of directors and on other important issues. Common stock dividends may vary according to the profitability of the business, and some corporations do not issue dividends at all, but instead plow their profits back into the company to fund expansion.

Common stockholders are the voting owners of a corporation. They are usually entitled to one vote per share of common stock. During an annual stockholders' meeting, common stockholders elect a board of directors. Some boards find it easier than others to attract high profile individuals. For example, the board of Procter & Gamble consists of Ernesto Zedillo, former president of Mexico; Kenneth I. Chenault, CEO of the American Express Company; Rajat Gupta, former managing director at McKinsey; as well as the CEO of Archer Daniels Midland; the CEO of Boeing; a former CEO of Verizon; and a director of eBay.[19] Because they can choose the board of directors, common stockholders have some say in how the company will operate. Common stockholders may vote by *proxy,* which is a written authorization by which stockholders assign their voting privilege to someone else, who then votes for his or her choice at the stockholders' meeting. It is a normal practice for management to request proxy statements from shareholders who are not planning to attend the annual meeting. Most owners do not attend annual meetings of the very large companies, such as Westinghouse or Boeing, unless they live in the city where the meeting is held.

Common stockholders have another advantage over preferred shareholders. In most states, when the corporation decides to sell new shares of common stock in the marketplace, common stockholders have the first right, called a *preemptive right,* to purchase new shares of the stock from the corporation. A preemptive right is often included in the articles of incorporation. This right is important because it allows stockholders to purchase new shares to maintain their original positions. For example, if a stockholder owns 10 percent of a corporation that decides to issue new shares, that stockholder has the right to buy enough of the new shares to retain the 10 percent ownership.

Advantages of Corporations

Because a corporation is a separate legal entity, it has some very specific advantages over other forms of ownership. The biggest advantage may be the limited liability of the owners.

Limited Liability.   Because the corporation's assets (money and resources) and liabilities (debts and other obligations) are separate from its owners', in most cases the stockholders are not held responsible for the firm's debts if it fails. Their liability or potential loss is limited to the amount of their original investment. Although a creditor can sue a corporation for not paying its debts, even forcing the corporation into bankruptcy, it cannot make the stockholders pay the corporation's debts out of their personal assets. Occasionally, the owners of a private corporation may pledge personal assets to secure a loan for the corporation; this would be most unusual for a public corporation.

Ease of Transfer of Ownership.   Stockholders can sell or trade shares of stock to other people without causing the termination of the corporation, and they can do this without the prior approval of other shareholders. The transfer of ownership (unless it is a majority position) does not affect the daily or long-term operations of the corporation.

Perpetual Life.   A corporation usually is chartered to last forever unless its articles of incorporation stipulate otherwise. The existence of the corporation is unaffected by the death or withdrawal of any of its stockholders. It survives until the owners sell it or liquidate its assets. However, in some cases, bankruptcy ends a corporation's life. Bankruptcies occur when companies are unable to compete and earn profits. Eventually, uncompetitive businesses must close or seek protection from creditors in bankruptcy court while the business tries to reorganize.

External Sources of Funds.   Of all the forms of business organization, the public corporation finds it easiest to raise money. When a corporation needs to raise more money, it can sell more stock shares or issue bonds (corporate "IOUs," which pledge to repay debt), attracting funds from anywhere in the United States and even overseas. The larger a corporation becomes, the more sources of financing are available to it. We take a closer look at some of these in Chapter 15.

Expansion Potential.   Because large public corporations can find long-term financing readily, they can easily expand into national and international markets. And, as a legal entity, a corporation can enter into contracts without as much difficulty as a partnership.

Disadvantages of Corporations
Corporations have some distinct disadvantages resulting from tax laws and government regulation.

Double Taxation.   As a legal entity, the corporation must pay taxes on its income just like you do. When after-tax corporate profits are paid out as dividends to the stockholders, the dividends are taxed a second time as part of the individual owner's income. This process creates double taxation for the stockholders of dividend paying corporations. Double taxation does not occur with the other forms of business organization.

Following a run-up in gas prices in 2008, ExxonMobil reported to shareholders and the SEC that it had earned $45 billion—more than any other publicly traded company in the world.

Forming a Corporation.   The formation of a corporation can be costly. A charter must be obtained, and this usually requires the services of an attorney and payment of legal fees. Filing fees ranging from $25 to $150 must be paid to the state that awards the corporate charter, and certain states require that an annual fee be paid to maintain the charter. Today, a number of Internet services such as LegalZoom.com and Business.com make it easier, quicker, and less costly to form a corporation. However, in making it easier for people to form businesses without expert consultation, these services have increased the risk that people will not choose the kind of organizational form that is right for them. Sometimes, one form works better than another. The business's founders may fail to take into account disadvantages, such as double taxation with corporations.

Disclosure of Information.   Corporations must make information available to
their owners, usually through an annual report to
shareholders. The annual report contains financial
information about the firm's profits, sales, facilities
and equipment, and debts, as well as descriptions of
the company's operations, products, and plans for the
future. Public corporations must also file reports with
the Securities and Exchange Commission (SEC), the government regulatory agency
that regulates securities such as stocks and bonds. The larger the firm, the more data
the SEC requires. Because all reports filed with the SEC are available to the public,
competitors can access them. Additionally, complying with securities laws takes time.

> **Did You Know?**   The first corporation with
> a net income of more than $1 billion in one year
> was General Motors, with a net income in 1955 of
> $1,189,477,082.[20]

Employee–Owner Separation.   Many employees are not stockholders of the
company for which they work. This separation of owners and employees may cause
employees to feel that their work benefits only the owners. Employees without an
ownership stake do not always see how they fit into the corporate picture and may
not understand the importance of profits to the health of the organization. If managers are part owners but other employees are not, management–labor relations
take on a different, sometimes difficult, aspect from those in partnerships and sole
proprietorships. However, this situation is changing as more corporations establish
employee stock ownership plans (ESOPs), which give shares of the company's stock
to its employees. Such plans build a partnership between employee and employer
and can boost productivity because they motivate employees to work harder so that
they can earn dividends from their hard work as well as from their regular wages.

Other Types of Ownership

In this section we take a brief look at joint ventures, S corporations, limited liability
companies, and cooperatives—businesses formed for special purposes.

Joint Ventures

A **joint venture** is a partnership established for a specific project or for a limited
time. The partners in a joint venture may be individuals or organizations, as in the
case of the international joint ventures discussed in Chapter 3. Control of a joint
venture may be shared equally, or one partner may control decision making. Joint
ventures are especially popular in situations that call for large investments, such as
extraction of natural resources and the development of new products. Dow Jones,
owner of *The Wall Street Journal,* recently formed a joint venture with financial
company SBI Holdings in Tokyo to begin an online Japanese version of the *WSJ* site.
Dow Jones has a 60 percent stake in the venture. Each company hopes to benefit
from the venture, with Dow Jones hoping to increase Web ad sales and SBI Holdings
wanting to expand its number of holdings.[21]

joint venture
a partnership established
for a specific project or for
a limited time

S Corporations

An **S corporation** is a form of business ownership that is taxed as though it were a
partnership. Net profits or losses of the corporation pass to the owners, thus eliminating double taxation. The benefit of limited liability is retained. Formally known as
Subchapter S Corporations, they have become a popular form of business ownership
for entrepreneurs and represent almost half of all corporate filings.[22] Accounting Systems, a Fort Collins, Colorado, accounting software firm, elected to incorporate as an

S corporation
corporation taxed as
though it were a partner-
ship with restrictions on
shareholders

S corporation to gain credibility, tax advantages, and limited liability. Advantages of S corporations include the simple method of taxation, the limited liability of shareholders, perpetual life, and the ability to shift income and appreciation to others. Disadvantages include restrictions on the number (75) and types (individuals, estates, and certain trusts) of shareholders and the difficulty of formation and operation.

Limited Liability Companies

limited liability company (LLC)
form of ownership that provides limited liability and taxation like a partnership but places fewer restrictions on members

A **limited liability company (LLC)** is a form of business ownership that provides limited liability, as in a corporation, but is taxed like a partnership. Although relatively new in the United States, LLCs have existed for many years abroad. Professionals such as lawyers, doctors, and engineers often use the LLC form of ownership. Many consider the LLC a blend of the best characteristics of corporations, partnerships, and sole proprietorships. One of the major reasons for the LLC form of ownership is to protect the members' personal assets in case of lawsuits. LLCs are flexible, simple to run, and do not require the members to hold meetings, keep minutes, or make resolutions, all of which are necessary in corporations. For example, Segway, which markets the Segway Human Transporter, is a limited liability company.

Cooperatives

cooperative or co-op
an organization composed of individuals or small businesses that have banded together to reap the benefits of belonging to a larger organization

Another form of organization in business is the **cooperative or co-op,** an organization composed of individuals or small businesses that have banded together to reap the benefits of belonging to a larger organization. Oglethorpe Power Corp., for example, is a power cooperative based in the suburbs of Atlanta;[23] Ocean Spray is a cooperative of cranberry farmers. A co-op is set up not to make money as an entity but so that its members can become more profitable or save money. Co-ops are generally expected to operate without profit or to create only enough profit to maintain the co-op organization.

Many cooperatives exist in small farming communities. The co-op stores and markets grain; orders large quantities of fertilizer, seed, and other supplies at discounted prices; and reduces costs and increases efficiency with good management. A co-op can purchase supplies in large quantities and pass the savings on to its members. It also can help distribute the products of its members more efficiently than each could on an individual basis. A cooperative can advertise its members' products and thus generate demand. Ace Hardware, a cooperative of independent hardware store owners, allows its members to share in the savings that result from buying supplies in large quantities; it also provides advertising, which individual members might not be able to afford on their own.

A credit union is an example of a cooperative. The owners are not outside shareholders but people who deposit money in the credit union. They essentially pool their money together and loan it to one another.

Trends in Business Ownership: Mergers and Acquisitions

Companies large and small achieve growth and improve profitability by expanding their operations, often by developing and selling new products or selling current products to new groups of customers in different geographic areas. Such growth,

Consider Ethics and Social Responsibility
Birkenstock Values Comfort, Employees, and Sustainability

Birkenstocks have long had the reputation of being hippie shoes, but they have been made in Germany since 1897. Nearly 70 years later, a woman named Margot Fraser discovered them while on a trip. Wearing the sandals helped alleviate the foot pain she had experienced for years. She liked them so much she wanted to sell them in the United States. She contacted the German manufacturer and requested permission to market the shoes in the United States. Receiving permission was easy, but distributing the shoes was anything but. After being rejected by numerous shoe store owners, Fraser finally found a niche for her Birks at health food stores.

With the help of friends, Fraser officially opened Birkenstock U.S.A. as a limited partnership in 1969. In the early 1970s, shoe store owners finally began seeing the value of a shoe specifically designed for comfort and quality. Soon Birkenstocks were being sold in more than 200 stores in the United States. Throughout the 1970s and 1980s, Birks grew in popularity, with Birkenstock U.S.A. doubling sales annually.

The company's success has had its ups and downs as fashions change, but it has always enjoyed a strong following.

Fraser began an employee pension plan, but when she could not fund it one year, she started giving her employees shares of stock. By the mid-1990s, employees owned 10 percent of the company. These employee stock ownership plans culminated in a 100 percent employee-owned company once Fraser retired. Birkenstocks are produced with little waste and use packaging made from 90 percent recycled paper. A combination of high quality, hard work, and social responsibility has turned this old type of shoe into a modern success story.[24]

Discussion Questions

1. What competitive advantage allowed Birkenstock to be a success?
2. What does Birkenstock offer in lieu of a traditional pension plan? Would you like this option or not?
3. What is unique about the way Birkenstock U.S.A. is organized?

---

when carefully planned and controlled, is usually beneficial to the firm and ultimately helps it reach its goal of enhanced profitability. But companies also grow by merging with or purchasing other companies.

A **merger** occurs when two companies (usually corporations) combine to form a new company. An **acquisition** occurs when one company purchases another, generally by buying most of its stock. The acquired company may become a subsidiary of the buyer, or its operations and assets may be merged with those of the buyer. The government sometimes scrutinizes mergers and acquisitions in an attempt to protect customers from monopolistic practices. For example, the decision to authorize Whole Foods' acquisition of Wild Oats was carefully analyzed, as was the merger of Sirius and XM Satellite Radio. In 2010, Novartis announced its plans to take over Alcon, an eye care company owned by Nestlé, for $50 billion. This was the largest merger in Swiss history. By acquiring Alcon, Novartis hopes to tap into the high-growth eye care market, which is expected to have a global growth of 7 percent annually.[25] Acquisitions sometimes involve the purchase of a division or some other part of a company rather than the entire company. The late 1990s saw a merger and acquisition frenzy, which is slowing in the 21st century (see Table 4.5).

When firms that make and sell similar products to the same customers merge, it is known as a *horizontal merger*, as when Martin Marietta and Lockheed, both defense contractors, merged to form Lockheed Martin. Horizontal mergers, however, reduce the number of corporations competing within an industry, and for this reason they are usually reviewed carefully by federal regulators before the merger is allowed to proceed.

When companies operating at different but related levels of an industry merge, it is known as a *vertical merger*. In many instances, a vertical merger results when one corporation merges with one of its customers or suppliers. For example, if

merger
the combination of two companies (usually corporations) to form a new company

acquisition
the purchase of one company by another, usually by buying its stock

TABLE 4.5

Major Mergers and Acquisitions Worldwide 2000–2010

Rank	Year	Acquirer*	Target	Transaction Value (in millions of U.S. dollars)
1.	2000	America Online Inc. (AOL) *(Merger)*	Time Warner	$164,747
2.	2000	Glaxo Wellcome Plc.	SmithKline Beecham Plc.	75,961
3.	2004	Royal Dutch Petroleum Co.	Shell Transport & Trading Co.	74,559
4.	2006	AT&T Inc.	BellSouth Corporation	72,671
5.	2001	Comcast Corporation	AT&T Broadband & Internet Svcs.	72,041
6.	2002	Pfizer Inc.	Pharmacia Corporation	59,515
7.	2004	JPMorgan Chase & Co.	Bank One Corporation	58,761
8.	2010	Kraft	Cadbury	19,500
9.	2008	Bank of America	Countrywide	4,000
10.	2008	JPMorgan Chase & Co.	Bear Stearns Companies Inc.	1,100

*Unless noted, deal was an acquisition.

Sources: Institute of Mergers, Acquisitions and Alliances Research, *Thomson Financial,* http://www.imaa-institute.org/en/publications+mergers+acquisitions+m&a.php#Reports (accessed March 16, 2010); David Mildenberg, "Bank of America to Acquire Countrywide for $4 Billion (Correct)," *Bloomberg.com,* January 14, 2008, http://www.bloomberg.com/apps/news?pid=20601103&sid=ay8OUcTZ01RM&refer=us (accessed March 16, 2010); Guy Beaudin, "Kraft Acquires Cadbury," *BusinessWeek,* January 3, 2010, http://www.businessweek.com/managing/content/feb2010/ca2010028_928488.htm (accessed March 1, 2010); "JPMorgan Chase Completes Bear Stearns Acquisition," JPMorganChase News Release, May 31, 2008, http://www.bearstearns.com/includes/pdfs/PressRelease_BSC_31May08.pdf (accessed March 1, 2010).

Burger King were to purchase a large Idaho potato farm—to ensure a ready supply of potatoes for its french fries—a vertical merger would result.

A *conglomerate merger* results when two firms in unrelated industries merge. For example, the purchase of Sterling Drug, a pharmaceutical firm, by Eastman Kodak, best-known for its films and cameras, represents a conglomerate merger because the two companies are of different industries.

When a company (or an individual), sometimes called a *corporate raider,* wants to acquire or take over another company, it first offers to buy some or all of the other company's stock at a premium over its current price in a *tender offer.* Most such offers are "friendly," with both groups agreeing to the proposed deal, but some are "hostile," when the second company does not want to be taken over. CKE Restaurants, which operates Carl's Jr. and Hardees fast-food restaurants, adopted a "poison pill" plan to discourage any attempted hostile takeovers. CKE's poison pill is designed to make a hostile takeover more difficult and/or more expensive. The poison pill plan involved giving stockholders the opportunity to receive preferred stock rights in the event of an attempt to buy a minimum of 15 percent of the company's shares.[26]

To head off a hostile takeover attempt, a threatened company's managers may use one or more of several techniques. They may ask stockholders not to sell to the raider; file a lawsuit in an effort to abort the takeover; institute a *poison pill* (in which the firm allows stockholders to buy more shares of stock at prices lower than the current market value) or *shark repellant* (in which management requires a large majority of stockholders to approve the takeover); or seek a *white knight* (a more acceptable

After the banking crisis hit in 2008, many big banks used mergers and acquisitions to try to stay afloat. Others, such as the investment banking firm Lehman Brothers, simply folded.

firm that is willing to acquire the threatened company). In some cases, management may take the company private or even take on more debt so that the heavy debt obligation will "scare off" the raider.

In a **leveraged buyout (LBO),** a group of investors borrows money from banks and other institutions to acquire a company (or a division of one), using the assets of the purchased company to guarantee repayment of the loan. In some LBOs, as much as 95 percent of the buyout price is paid with borrowed money, which eventually must be repaid.

Because of the explosion of mergers, acquisitions, and leveraged buyouts in the 1980s and 1990s, financial journalists coined the term *merger mania.* Many companies joined the merger mania simply to enhance their own operations by consolidating them with the operations of other firms. Mergers and acquisitions enabled these companies to gain a larger market share in their industries, acquire valuable assets, such as new products or plants and equipment, and lower their costs. Mergers also represent a means of making profits quickly, as was the case during the 1980s when many companies' stock was undervalued. Quite simply, such companies represent a bargain to other companies that can afford to buy them. Additionally, deregulation of some industries has permitted consolidation of firms within those industries for the first time, as is the case in the banking and airline industries.

Some people view mergers and acquisitions favorably, pointing out that they boost corporations' stock prices and market value, to the benefit of their stockholders. In

leveraged buyout (LBO)
a purchase in which a group of investors borrows money from banks and other institutions to acquire a company (or a division of one), using the assets of the purchased company to guarantee repayment of the loan

many instances, mergers enhance a company's ability to meet foreign competition in an increasingly global marketplace. And, companies that are victims of hostile takeovers generally streamline their operations, reduce unnecessary staff, cut costs, and otherwise become more efficient with their operations, which benefits their stockholders whether or not the takeover succeeds.

Critics, however, argue that mergers hurt companies because they force managers to focus their efforts on avoiding takeovers rather than managing effectively and profitably. Some companies have taken on a heavy debt burden to stave off a takeover, later to be forced into bankruptcy when economic downturns left them unable to handle the debt. Mergers and acquisitions also can damage employee morale and productivity, as well as the quality of the companies' products.

Many mergers have been beneficial for all involved; others have had damaging effects for the companies, their employees, and customers. No one can say if mergers will continue to slow, but many experts say the utilities, telecommunications, financial services, natural resources, computer hardware and software, gaming, managed health care, and technology industries are likely targets.

So You'd Like to Start a Business

If you have a good idea and want to turn it into a business, you are not alone. Small businesses are popping up all over the United States, and the concept of entrepreneurship is hot. Entrepreneurs seek opportunities and creative ways to make profits. Business emerges in a number of different organizational forms, each with its own advantages and disadvantages. Sole proprietorships are the most common form of business organization in the U.S. They tend to be small businesses and can take pretty much any form—anything from a hair salon to a scuba shop, from an organic produce provider to a financial advisor. Proprietorships are everywhere serving consumers' wants and needs. Proprietorships have a big advantage in that they tend to be simple to manage—decisions get made quickly when the owner and the manager are the same person and they are fairly simple and inexpensive to set up. Rules vary by state, but at most all you will need is a license from the state.

Many people have been part of a partnership at some point in their life. Group work in school is an example of a partnership. If you ever worked as a DJ on the weekend with your friend and split the profits, then you have experienced a partnership. Partnerships can be either general or limited. General partners have unlimited liability and share completely in the management, debts and profits of the business. Limited partners, on the other hand, consist of at least one general partner and one or more limited partners who do not participate in the management of the company but share in the profits. This form of partnership is used more often in risky investments where the limited partner stands only to lose his or her initial investment. Real estate

limited partnerships are an example of how investors can minimize their financial exposure, given the poor performance of the real estate market in recent years. Although it has its advantages, partnership is the least utilized form of business. Part of the reason is that all partners are responsible for the actions and decisions of all other partners, whether or not all of the partners were involved. Usually, partners will have to write up an Articles of Partnership that outlines respective responsibilities in the business. Even in states where it is not required, it is a good idea to draw up this document as a way to cement each partner's role and hopefully minimize conflict. Unlike a corporation, proprietorships and partnerships both expire upon the death of one or more of those involved.

Corporations tend to be larger businesses, but do not need to be. A corporation can consist of nothing more than a small group of family members. In order to become a corporation you will have to file in the state under which you wish to incorporate. Each state has its own procedure for incorporation, meaning there are no general guidelines to follow. You can make your corporation private or public, meaning the company issues stocks and shareholders are the owners. While incorporating is a popular form of organization because it gives the company an unlimited lifespan and limited liability (meaning that if your business fails you cannot lose personal funds to make up for losses), there is a downside. You will be taxed as a corporation and as an individual resulting in double taxation. No matter what form of organization suits your business idea best, there is a world of options out there for you if you want to be or experiment with being an entrepreneur.

Review Your Understanding

Define and examine the advantages and disadvantages of the sole proprietorship form of organization.

Sole proprietorships—businesses owned and managed by one person—are the most common form of organization. Their major advantages are the following: (1) They are easy and inexpensive to form, (2) they allow a high level of secrecy, (3) all profits belong to the owner, (4) the owner has complete control over the business, (5) government regulation is minimal, (6) taxes are paid only once, and (7) the business can be closed easily. The disadvantages include: (1) The owner may have to use personal assets to borrow money, (2) sources of external funds are difficult to find, (3) the owner must have many diverse skills, (4) the survival of the business is tied to the life of the owner and his or her ability to work, (5) qualified employees are hard to find, and (6) wealthy sole proprietors pay a higher tax than they would under the corporate form of business.

Identify two types of partnership, and evaluate the advantages and disadvantages of the partnership form of organization.

A partnership is a business formed by several individuals; a partnership may be general or limited. Partnerships offer the following advantages: (1) They are easy to organize, (2) they may have higher credit ratings because the partners possibly have more combined wealth, (3) partners can specialize, (4) partnerships can make decisions faster than larger businesses, and (5) government regulations are few. Partnerships also have several disadvantages: (1) General partners have unlimited liability for the debts of the partnership, (2) partners are responsible for each others' decisions, (3) the death or termination of one partner requires a new partnership agreement to be drawn up, (4) it is difficult to sell a partnership interest at a fair price, (5) the distribution of profits may not correctly reflect the amount of work done by each partner, and (6) partnerships cannot find external sources of funds as easily as can large corporations.

Describe the corporate form of organization, and cite the advantages and disadvantages of corporations.

A corporation is a legal entity created by the state, whose assets and liabilities are separate from those of its owners. Corporations are chartered by a state through articles of incorporation. They have a board of directors made up of corporate officers or people from outside the company. Corporations, whether private or public, are owned by stockholders. Common stockholders have the right to elect the board of directors. Preferred stockholders do not have a vote but get preferential dividend treatment over common stockholders.

Advantages of the corporate form of business include: (1) The owners have limited liability, (2) ownership (stock) can be easily transferred, (3) corporations usually last forever, (4) raising money is easier than for other forms of business, and (5) expansion into new businesses is simpler because of the ability of the company to enter into contracts. Corporations also have disadvantages: (1) The company is taxed on its income, and owners pay a second tax on any profits received as dividends; (2) forming a corporation can be expensive; (3) keeping trade secrets is difficult because so much information must be made available to the public and to government agencies; and (4) owners and managers are not always the same and can have different goals.

Define and debate the advantages and disadvantages of mergers, acquisitions, and leveraged buyouts.

A merger occurs when two companies (usually corporations) combine to form a new company. An acquisition occurs when one company buys most of another company's stock. In a leveraged buyout, a group of investors borrows money to acquire a company, using the assets of the purchased company to guarantee the loan. They can help merging firms to gain a larger market share in their industries, acquire valuable assets such as new products or plants and equipment, and lower their costs. Consequently, they can benefit stockholders by improving the companies' market value and stock prices. However, they also can hurt companies if they force managers to focus on avoiding takeovers at the expense of productivity and profits. They may lead a company to take on too much debt and can harm employee morale and productivity.

Propose an appropriate organizational form for a startup business.

After reading the facts in "Solve the Dilemma" on page 146 and considering the advantages and disadvantages of the various forms of business organization described in this chapter, you should be able to suggest an appropriate form for the start-up nursery.

Revisit the World of Business

1. Kiva.org has been very successful at extending microlending to entrepreneurs in need. What about Kiva.org has helped to make it so successful?

2. What is unique about the way Kiva.org is organized that sets it apart from more traditional businesses?

3. Do you think the Kiva.org model of giving loans would work for larger loans, or even for other kinds of businesses?

Learn the Terms

acquisition   139
articles of partnership   126
board of directors   133
common stock   134
cooperative (or co-op)   138
corporate charter   130
corporation   129
dividends   130

general partnership   124
initial public offering (IPO)   132
joint venture   137
leveraged buyout (LBO)   141
limited liability company (LLC)   138
limited partnership   125
merger   139
nonprofit corporations   133

partnership   124
preferred stock   134
private corporation   131
public corporation   131
quasi-public corporations   133
S corporation   137
sole proprietorships   120
stock   130

Check Your Progress

1. Name five advantages of a sole proprietorship.

2. List two different types of partnerships and describe each.

3. Differentiate among the different types of corporations. Can you supply an example of each type?

4. Would you rather own preferred stock or common stock? Why?

5. Contrast how profits are distributed in sole proprietorships, partnerships, and corporations.

6. Which form of business organization has the least government regulation? Which has the most?

7. Compare the liability of the owners of partnerships, sole proprietorships, and corporations.

8. Why would secrecy in operating a business be important to an owner? What form of organization would be most appropriate for a business requiring great secrecy?

9. Which form of business requires the most specialization of skills? Which requires the least? Why?

10. The most common example of a cooperative is a farm co-op. Explain the reasons for this and the benefits that result for members of cooperatives.

Get Involved

1. Select a publicly owned corporation and bring to class a list of its subsidiaries. These data should be available in the firm's corporate annual report, *Standard & Poor's Corporate Records*, or *Moody Corporate Manuals*. Ask your librarian for help in finding these resources.

2. Select a publicly owned corporation and make a list of its outside directors. Information of this nature can be found in several places in your library: the company's annual report, its list of corporate directors, and various financial sources. If possible, include each director's title and the name of the company that employs him or her on a full-time basis.

Build Your Skills

SELECTING A FORM OF BUSINESS

Background:
Ali Bush sees an opportunity to start her own Web site development business. Ali has just graduated from the University of Mississippi with a master's degree in computer science. Although she has many job opportunities outside the Oxford area, she wishes to remain there to care for her aging parents. She already has most of the computer equipment necessary to start the business, but she needs additional software. She is considering the purchase of a server to maintain Web sites for small businesses. Ali feels she has the ability to take this start-up firm and create a long-term career opportunity for herself and others. She knows she can hire Ole Miss students to work on a part-time basis to support her business. For now, as she starts the business, she can work out of the extra bedroom of her apartment. As the business grows, she'll hire the additional full- and/or part-time help needed and reassess the location of the business.

Task:

1. Using what you've learned in this chapter, decide which form of business ownership is most appropriate for Ali. Use the tables provided to assist you in evaluating the advantages and disadvantages of each decision

Sole Proprietorships	
Advantages	Disadvantages
•	•
•	•
•	•
•	•
•	•
•	•
•	•

Corporation	
Advantages	Disadvantages
•	•
•	•
•	•
•	•
•	•
•	•
•	•

Limited Liability Company	
Advantages	Disadvantages
•	•
•	•
•	•
•	•
•	•
•	•
•	•

Solve the Dilemma

TO INCORPORATE OR NOT TO INCORPORATE

Thomas O'Grady and Bryan Rossisky have decided to start a small business buying flowers, shrubs, and trees whole-sale and reselling them to the general public. They plan to contribute $5,000 each in startup capital and lease a 2.5-acre tract of land with a small, portable sales office.

Thomas and Bryan are trying to decide what form of organization would be appropriate. Bryan thinks they should create a corporation because they would have limited liability and the image of a large organization. Thomas thinks a partnership would be easier to start and would allow them to rely on the combination of their talents and financial resources. In addition, there might be fewer reports and regulatory controls to cope with.

Discussion Questions

1. What are some of the advantages and disadvantages of Thomas and Bryan forming a corporation?

2. What are the advantages and disadvantages of their forming a partnership?

3. Which organizational form do you think would be best for Thomas and Bryan's company and why?

Build Your Business Plan

OPTIONS FOR ORGANIZING BUSINESS

Your team needs to think about how you should organize yourselves that would be most efficient and effective for your business plan. The benefits of having partners include having others to share responsibilities with and to toss ideas off of each other. As your business evolves you will have to decide whether one or two members will manage the business while the other members are silent partners. Or perhaps you will all decide on working in the business to keep costs down, at least initially. However you decide on team member involvement in the business, it is imperative to have a written agreement so that all team members understand what their responsibilities are and what will happen if the partnership dissolves.

It is not too soon for you and your partners to start thinking about how you might want to find additional funding for your business. Later on in the development of your business plan you might want to show your business plan to family members. Together you and your partners will want to develop a list of potential investors in your business.

See for Yourself Videocase

NEW BELGIUM BREWING

New Belgium Brewing is an employee-owned business that not only produces great beers, but also stresses employee satisfaction and empowerment. At New Belgium, a synergy of brand and values naturally evolved into the firm's ethical culture in the form of core values and beliefs. Back in early 1991, before they signed any business paperwork, Jeff Lebesch and Kim Jordan (Lebesch's wife) took a hike into Rocky Mountain National Park. Armed with a pen and a notebook, they took their first stab at what the fledgling company's core purpose would be. Before New Beligum even became a business Lebesch and Jordan formulated the business' core values, to which the company has remained true for two decades. Ask any New Belgium employee and he or she can list for you many of these shared values. For New Belgium, branding strategies are as rooted in their company values as in other business practices.

Having fun and allowing their employees to have fun has always been an important goal of the company. In keeping with its fun and eco-friendly attitude, New Belgium gifts all employees with "cruiser bikes" after one year of employment. Employees are encouraged to ride to work, rather than drive. Members of the sales force receive Toyota Prius hybrids. Recognizing employees' value to the business' success, New Belgium has a generous benefits package. In addition to the usual paid health and dental insurance and retirement plans, employees get a free lunch every other week as well as a free massage once a year. They can also bring their children and dogs to work.

Other perks include yoga classes, free beer after hours, and a climbing wall. Employees who stay with the company for five years earn an all-expenses paid trip to Belgium to "study beer culture."

Perhaps most importantly, New Belgium has an Employee Stock Ownership Plan. After one year, employees are granted stock ownership. This also allows employees to vote in company decisions. Currently, New Belgium's 348 employees own about 32 percent of the company stock. A transparent open-book policy reinforces this mentality and ensures that all employees feel more involved in day-to-day operations. Employees can access all the company's financial information and receive education on how to read the information.

The decentralized structure of the company also allows employees at all levels to make decisions, often without seeking approval from managers. Team members are all held mutually accountable for decisions and the company's success. Even the philanthropy committee is composed of employees across the business. The group collectively decides where philanthropy money should be spent.

From the very beginning, New Belgium has been concerned with the environment. While the company tries to continue to decrease its carbon footprint, it also encourages employees to help improve the natural environment. Employees can even bring in difficult-to-recycle items from home, such as batteries. Employees took an active role in the company's green efforts by voting to run the brewery on wind power.

According to employee Dave Kemp, New Belgium's commitment to its employees along with its environmental and social dedication give it a competitive advantage. New Belgium's most important asset is its image. Defining itself as more than just a beer company, it also sees itself as a caring, employee-centered organization concerned for all stakeholders.

Discussion Questions

1. What is unique about New Belgium's organizational structure that creates a high level of employee commitment and satisfaction?

2. Do you think New Belgium would have such a high degree of control over business decisions if it were a publicly traded company? Do you think New Belgium's owners should consider an initial public offering (IPO) if the company continues to expand rapidly?

3. What gives New Belgium a competitive advantage over other craft brewers? Do you think its organizational structure plays a role?

Remember to check out our Online Learning Center at www.mhhe.com /ferrell8e

Team Exercise

Form groups and find examples of mergers and acquisitions. Mergers can be broken down into traditional mergers, horizontal mergers, and conglomerate mergers. When companies are found, note how long the merger or acquisition took, if there were any requirements by the government before approval of the merger or acquisition, and if any failed mergers or acquisitions were found that did not achieve government approval. Report your findings to the class, and explain what the companies hoped to gain from the merger or acquisition.

chapter 5

Small Business, Entrepreneurship, and Franchising

OBJECTIVES

After reading this chapter, you will be able to:

- Define *entrepreneurship* and *small business*.

- Investigate the importance of small business in the U.S. economy and why certain fields attract small business.

- Specify the advantages of small-business ownership.

- Summarize the disadvantages of small-business ownership, and analyze why many small businesses fail.

- Describe how you go about starting a small business and what resources are needed.

- Evaluate the demographic, technological, and economic trends that are affecting the future of small business.

- Explain why many large businesses are trying to "think small."

- Assess two entrepreneurs' plans for starting a small business.

Aquacopia: Funding a Fish Startup

You have probably heard about venture capital firms funding tech start-ups, but have you heard of venture capital for aquaculture (the farming of aquatic life under controlled conditions)? Founded by David Tze and Jared Polis, Aquacopia invests in early-stage aquaculture entrepreneurs, including seafood farms, farming technologies, and related firms. In return for its investments, Aquacopia receives 2.5 percent of assets and 20 percent of capital gains. According to Tze, funding aquaculture is a smart investment because the world's oceans cannot produce enough fish to meet the growing demand. The United Nations' Food and Agriculture Organization estimates that 75 percent of the world's natural fisheries are being fished at a rate at or beyond their limits. Today, fish farms supply 43 percent of the world's fish. Tze and Polis decided to create an investment firm so they could invest in several different and promising aquaculture technologies.

The companies funded by Aquacopia are innovative. For example, Open Blue Sea Farms raises cobia, a species of mild white fish, in large open-water wire mesh globes called Aqua Pods, which were designed by Ocean Farm Technologies (another Aquacopia-backed company). Open Blue Sea Farms' founder, 29-year-old Brian O'Hanlon, plans to transport 30,000 baby cobia each month from Miami to Panama City and eventually to the Aqua Pods via airplane and boat. O'Hanlon's revenues are expected to reach $20 million by 2013.

Also under Aquacopia's wing is Oberon FMR, a fish meal replacement (FMR) company. Oberon FMR is revolutionizing the fish feed industry by using bacteria from wastewater (currently acquired from New Belgium Brewing in

continued

Colorado), thereby using another company's waste and creating a low cost option for fish feed. Other Aquacopia companies include Snapperfarm (an open-sea cobia farm in Puerto Rico) and Litchfield Farms Organic & Natural (a seafood distributor).[1]

Introduction

Although many business students go to work for large corporations upon graduation, others may choose to start their own business or to find employment opportunities in small organizations with 500 or fewer employees. Small businesses employ more than half of all private-sector employees.[2] Each small business represents the vision of its owners to succeed through providing new or better products. Small businesses are the heart of the U.S. economic and social system because they offer opportunities and demonstrate the freedom of people to make their own destinies. Today, the entrepreneurial spirit is growing around the world, from Russia and China to Germany, Brazil, and Mexico.

This chapter surveys the world of entrepreneurship and small business. First we define entrepreneurship and small business and examine the role of small business in the American economy. Then we explore the advantages and disadvantages of small-business ownership and analyze why small businesses succeed or fail. Next, we discuss how an entrepreneur goes about starting a business and the challenges facing small businesses today. Finally, we look at entrepreneurship in larger organizations.

The Nature of Entrepreneurship and Small Business

enterpreneurship
the process of creating and managing a business to achieve desired objectives

In Chapter 1, we defined an entrepreneur as a person who risks his or her wealth, time, and effort to develop for profit an innovative product or way of doing something. **Entrepreneurship** is the process of creating and managing a business to achieve desired objectives. Many large businesses you may recognize (Levi Strauss and Co., Procter & Gamble, McDonald's, Dell Computers, Microsoft, and Google) all began as small businesses based on the visions of their founders. Some entrepreneurs who start small businesses have the ability to see emerging trends; in response, they create a company to provide a product that serves customer needs. For example, rather than inventing a major new technology, an innovative company may take advantage of technology to create new markets, such as Amazon.com. Or they may offer a familiar product that has been improved or placed in a unique retail environment, such as Starbucks and its coffee shops. A company may innovate by focusing on a particular market segment and delivering a combination of features that consumers in that segment could not find anywhere else. For example, Patagonia, a company that uses many organic materials in its clothing, has pledged 1 percent of sales to the preservation and restoration of the natural environment. Customers can return their worn-out Capilene® Performance Baselayers for recycling.[3]

Of course, smaller businesses do not have to evolve into such highly visible companies to be successful, but those entrepreneurial efforts that result in rapidly growing businesses gain visibility along with success. Entrepreneurs who have achieved success, like Michael Dell, Bill Gates (Microsoft), and Larry Page and Sergey Brin (Google), are some of the most well known.

The entrepreneurship movement is accelerating, and many new, smaller businesses are emerging. Technology once available only to the largest firms can now be obtained by a small business. Web sites, podcasts, online videos, social networks, cellular phones, and even overnight delivery services enable small businesses to be more competitive with today's giant corporations. Small businesses can also form alliances with other companies to produce and sell products in domestic and global markets.

What Is a Small Business?

This question is difficult to answer because smallness is relative. In this book, we will define a **small business** as any independently owned and operated business that is not dominant in its competitive area and does not employ more than 500 people. A local Mexican restaurant may be the most patronized Mexican restaurant in your community, but because it does not dominate the restaurant industry as a whole, the restaurant can be considered a small business. This definition is similar to the one used by the **Small Business Administration (SBA),** an independent agency of the federal government that offers managerial and financial assistance to small businesses. On its Web site, the SBA outlines the first steps in starting a small business and offers a wealth of information to current and potential small-business owners.

small business
any independently owned and operated business that is not dominant in its competitive area and does not employ more than 500 people

Small Business Administration (SBA)
an independent agency of the federal government that offers managerial and financial assistance to small businesses

The Role of Small Business in the American Economy

No matter how you define a small business, one fact is clear: They are vital to the American economy. As you can see in Table 5.1, more than 99 percent of all U.S. firms are classified as small businesses, and they employ 50 percent of private workers. Small firms are also important as exporters, representing 97 percent of U.S. exporters of goods and contributing 29 percent of the value of exported goods.[4] In addition, small businesses are largely responsible for fueling job creation and innovation. Small businesses also provide opportunities for minorities and women to succeed in business. Women-owned businesses are responsible for more than 23 million American jobs and contribute almost $3 trillion to the national economy. Women own more than 8 million businesses nationwide, with great success in the professional services, retail, communication, and administrative industries.[5] Minority-owned businesses have been growing faster than other classifiable firms as well, representing 17.6 percent of all small businesses. The number of minority-owned businesses is increasing at a rate of 30 percent, even higher than for women-owned firms. Hispanics own the most small businesses (7 percent) followed by African Americans (5.3 percent) Asian (4.9 percent), American Indian and Native Alaskan (0.9 percent), and Native Hawaiian and other Pacific Islander (0.1 percent).[6] For example, Sacred Power is a Native American–owned power and telecommunications company that generates solar, thermal, and wind energy. As a small business, Sacred Power produces and sells alternative energy to larger power companies for distribution to consumers around the Southwest.

Job Creation.   The energy, creativity, and innovative abilities of small-business owners have resulted in jobs for many people. In fact, in the last 15 years, 64 percent of net new jobs annually were created by small businesses.[7] Table 5.2 indicates that 99.7 percent of all businesses employ fewer than 500 people, and businesses employing 19 or fewer people account for 89 percent of all businesses.[8]

Many small businesses today are being started because of encouragement from larger ones. Many new jobs are also created by big-company/small-company alliances.

TABLE 5.1	
Small Business Facts	Small firms represent 99.7 percent of all employer firms.
	Small firms have generated 64 percent of net new jobs over the past 15 years.
	Small firms hire 40 percent of high-tech workers (such as scientists, engineers, and computer programmers).
	Small firms produce 13 times more patents per employee than large patenting firms.
	Seven out of 10 new-employer firms last at least two years, and about half survive five years.
	Commercial banks and other depository institutions are the largest lenders of debt capital to small businesses.

Source: "FAQs," U.S. Small Business Administration, http://web.sba.gov/faqs/faqindex.cfm?areaID=24 (accessed March 9, 2010).

Whether through formal joint ventures, supplier relationships, or product or marketing cooperative projects, the rewards of collaborative relationships are creating many jobs for small-business owners and their employees. In India, many small information technology (IT) firms provide IT services to global markets. Because of lower costs, international companies often can find Indian businesses to provide their information processing solutions.[9]

Innovation.   Perhaps one of the most significant strengths of small businesses is their ability to innovate and to bring significant benefits to customers. Small firms produce 55 percent of all innovations. Among the important 20th-century innovations by U.S. small firms are the airplane, the audio tape recorder, fiber-optic examining equipment, the heart valve, the optical scanner, the pacemaker, the personal computer, soft contact lenses, and the zipper. Not all innovations are based on new technology. Consider Oprah Winfrey's success. She developed her own brand image and media production company. She went from having nothing to amassing a fortune of $2.3 billion as one of the most recognizable figures in global media. After 26 years on her CBS talk show, she created the Oprah Winfrey Network. Oprah has refused to take her company public in order to maintain maximum control, and she protects her brand and media products by refusing to let retailers or other businesses use her name.[10]

The innovation of successful firms take many forms. Small businessman Ray Kroc found a new way to sell hamburgers and turned his ideas into one of the most successful fast-food franchises in the world—McDonald's. Small businesses have become an integral part of our lives. James Dyson's name is synonymous with high-quality vacuum cleaners. Today, his $1 billion company produces a bag-less vacuum cleaner that commands 25 percent of the U.S. market. However, it took a lot of work to achieve such success. Dyson developed 5,127 prototypes before he got the design and function right. He recently created a successful hand dryer and is working to develop other

Most of America's new jobs aren't created by big corporations. They are created by small businesses such as Rush Trucking. Rush Trucking was founded in Detroit in the 1980s by Andra Rush after she interned with a transportation company and decided she could do the job better.

Firm Size	Number of Firms	Percentage of All Firms
0–19 employees	5,150,316	89.3
20–99 employees	515,056	8.9
100–499 employees	84,829	1.5
500 or more employees	16,926	0.3

TABLE 5.2

Number of Firms by Employment Size

Source: U.S. Census Bureau, "Statistics about Business Size (including small businesses) from the U.S. Census Bureau," http://www.census.gov/epcd/www/smallbus.html#EMpSize (accessed March 9, 2010).

innovative appliances. Similarly, Bikram Choudhury's name is associated with yoga. Bikram Yoga uses a sequence of 26 signature poses, and the business has expanded to training courses, books, CDs, clothing, and numerous franchises. Choudhury is credited with popularizing yoga in the United States and with turning "his particular brand of yoga into the McDonald's of a $3 billion industry."[11] Entrepreneurs provide fresh ideas and usually have greater flexibility to change than do large companies.

Industries That Attract Small Business

Small businesses are found in nearly every industry, but retailing and wholesaling, services, manufacturing, and high technology are especially attractive to entrepreneurs. These fields are relatively easy to enter and require low initial financing. Small-business owners in these industries also find it easier to focus on specific groups of consumers; new firms in these industries, initially suffer less from heavy competition, than do established firms.

Retailing and Wholesaling.   Retailers acquire goods from producers or wholesalers and sell them to consumers. Main streets and shopping strips and malls are generally lined with independent music stores, sporting-goods shops, dry cleaners, boutiques, drugstores, restaurants, caterers, service stations, and hardware stores that sell directly to consumers. Retailing attracts entrepreneurs because gaining experience and exposure in retailing is relatively easy. Additionally, an entrepreneur opening a new retail store does not have to spend the large sums of money for the equipment and distribution systems that a manufacturing business requires. All that a new retailer needs is a lease on store space, merchandise, money to sustain the business, knowledge about prospective customers' needs and desires, and basic management and marketing skills. Some small retailers are also taking their businesses online. For example, Susan Brown invented a donut-shaped pillow with an opening in one side called the "Boppy." The product is sold online and in Babies R Us and Pottery Barn Kids stores. Although approached by Walmart, Brown declined the offer in a desire to keep a more upscale feel. The Boppy has annual sales around $50 million and was provided startup capital through a microloan of $25,000 from the Colorado Enterprise Fund (a nonprofit, community-development institution).[12] The Boppy was voted the number-one baby product by *American Baby* magazine a record seven times since the award was created in 1998. It remains the industry leader among baby feeding and support pillows.[13]

K. R. Sridhar, who founded Bloom Energy, just might change the world with a new, innovative "power plant in a box" device. The device produces clean energy wirelessly transmitted to your home. Major companies are now experimenting with it.

Wholesalers supply products to industrial, retail, and institutional users for resale or for use in making other products. Wholesaling activities range from planning and negotiating for supplies, promoting, and distributing (warehousing and transporting) to providing management and merchandising assistance to clients. Wholesalers are extremely important for many products, especially consumer goods, because of the marketing activities they perform. Although it is true that wholesalers themselves can be eliminated, their functions must be passed on to some other organization such as the producer, or another intermediary, often a small business. Frequently, small businesses are closer to the final customers and know what it takes to keep them satisfied. Some smaller businesses start out manufacturing, but find their real niche as a supplier or distributor of larger firms' products.

Services.   The service sector includes businesses that do not actually produce tangible goods. The service sector accounts for 80 percent of U.S. jobs, excluding farmworkers.[14] Real-estate, insurance and personnel agencies, barbershops, banks, television and computer repair shops, copy centers, dry cleaners, and accounting firms are all service businesses. Services also attract individuals—such as beauticians, morticians, jewelers, doctors, and veterinarians—whose skills are not usually required by large firms. Many of these service providers are also retailers because they provide their services to ultimate consumers.

Geek Squad employees vow to "fix any PC problem anytime, anywhere." The Geek Squad began as a one-man service firm in Minnesota in 1994. Founder Robert Stephens initially traveled by bicycle to and from service calls.

Manufacturing.   Manufacturing goods can provide unique opportunities for small businesses. Started in 1988, the Malcolm Baldrige Award recognizes achievements in quality and performance in businesses of all sizes. It is designed to spur competitive business practices in American industry. In 2009, Midway USA, a shooting and gun supply business in Missouri, won the award in the small-business category. Midway USA is a family-owned employer of around 240 people. It does most of its sales over the Internet. Part of the reason Midway won this award was its high level of commitment to quality and customer satisfaction, as well as its strong financial performance in 2008–2009 as demands for guns and supplies rose across the United States.[15] Small businesses sometimes have an advantage over large firms because they can customize products to meet specific customer needs and wants. Such products include custom artwork, jewelry, clothing, and furniture.

High Technology.   *High technology* is a broad term used to describe businesses that depend heavily on advanced scientific and engineering knowledge. People who were able to innovate or identify new markets in the fields of computers, biotechnology, genetic engineering, robotics, and other markets have become today's high-tech giants. Mark Zuckerberg, the 24-year-old CEO of Facebook (a social networking Web site), for instance, has created a company that is one of the fastest growing dot-coms in history.

Did You Know?   Small businesses hire 40 percent of high-tech workers in the United States?[16]

Facebook has more than 400 million active users, and half of all active users log on to the site on any given day. The average Facebook user spends almost an hour each day

Intuitive	Persistent	**TABLE 5.3**
Creative	Innovative	10 Successful Traits of
Productive	Frugal	Young Entrepreneurs
Patient	Friendly	
Charismatic	Fearless	

Source: Yan Susanto, "10 Successful Traits of Young Entrepreneurs," *Retire @ 21,* April 10, 2009, http://www.retireat21. com/blog/10-successful-traits-of-young-entrepreneurs (accessed March 9, 2010).

on the site.[17] In general, high-technology businesses require greater capital and have higher initial startup costs than do other small businesses. Many of the biggest, nonetheless, started out in garages, basements, kitchens, and dorm rooms.

Advantages of Small-Business Ownership

There are many advantages to establishing and running a small business. These can be categorized into personal advantages and business advantages. Table 5.3 lists some of the traits that can help entrepreneurs succeed.

Independence

Independence is probably one of the leading reasons that entrepreneurs choose to go into business for themselves. Being a small-business owner means being your own boss. Many people start their own businesses because they believe they will do better for themselves than they could do by remaining with their current employer or by changing jobs. They may feel stuck on the corporate ladder and that no business would take them seriously enough to fund their ideas. Sometimes people who venture forth to start their own small business are those who simply cannot work for someone else. Such people may say that they just do not fit the "corporate mold."

More often, small-business owners just want the freedom to choose whom they work with, the flexibility to pick where and when to work, and the option of working in a family setting. The availability of the computer, copy machine, business telephone, and fax machine has permitted many people to work at home. Only a few years ago, most of them would have needed the support that an office provides.

Costs

As already mentioned, small businesses often require less money to start and maintain than do large ones. Obviously, a firm with just 25 people in a small factory spends less money on wages and salaries, rent, utilities, and other expenses than does a firm employing tens of thousands of people in several large facilities. Rather than maintain the expense of keeping separate departments for accounting, advertising, and legal counseling, small businesses often hire other firms (sometimes small businesses themselves) to supply these services as they are needed. Additionally, small-business owners can sometimes rely on friends and family members to help them save money by volunteering to work on a difficult project.

Flexibility

With small size comes the flexibility to adapt to changing market demands. Small businesses usually have only one layer of management—the owners. Decisions therefore can be made and executed quickly. In larger firms, decisions about even

Entrepreneurship in Action

Cistercian Monks Take Advantage of Their Hardworking Culture to Become Entrepreneurs

Business: LaserMonks

Founded: 2002

Success: Last year, the company sold more than $4 million in products.

When Father Bernard McCoy needed a toner cartridge for his monastery's printer, he was dismayed by the huge mark-ups on printing supplies. Father McCoy decided his monastic order would run an ink and toner business that worked directly with manufacturers and eliminated mark-ups. The scenario seemed perfect—customers would purchase ink and toner at lower prices and support the monks' good works. However, the business was struggling when Father McCoy received an inquiry from Sarah Caniglia and Cindy Griffith. The two women wanted to sell their ink and toner business and thought the abbey was a great candidate. After finalizing an agreement, the women offered to visit the monastery and assist the monks with the business. A brief visit turned into a vocation, and the two women now run LaserMonks. Today, LaserMonks is highly successful, even helping other monasteries sell other goods online.[18]

routine matters can take weeks because they must pass through multiple levels of management before action is authorized. When McDonald's introduces a new product, for example, it must first research what consumers want, then develop the product and test it before introducing it nationwide—a process that sometimes takes years. An independent snack shop, however, can develop and introduce a new product (perhaps to meet a customer's request) in a much shorter time.

Focus

Small firms can focus their efforts on a precisely defined market niche—that is, a specific group of customers. Many large corporations must compete in the mass market or for large market segments. Smaller firms can develop products for particular groups of customers or to satisfy a need that other companies have not addressed. For example, Fatheadz, based in Indianapolis, Indiana focuses on producing sunglasses for people with big heads. To be an official "fathead" you need a ball cap size of at least 7⅝ and a head circumference above the ear of at least 23.5 inches. The idea arose when Rico Elmore was walking down the Las Vegas strip with his brother and realized that he had lost his sunglasses. He went to a nearby sunglass shop, and out of 300 pairs of glasses, he could not find one that fit. He decided to start a company addressing this need, and Fatheadz now distributes its designs in Walmart optical stores throughout the country.[19] By targeting small niches or product needs, small businesses can sometimes avoid competition from larger firms, helping them to grow into stronger companies.

Reputation

Small firms, because of their capacity to focus on narrow niches, can develop enviable reputations for quality and service. A good example of a small business with a formidable reputation is W. Atlee Burpee and Co., which has the country's premier bulb and seed catalog. Burpee has an unqualified returns policy (complete satisfaction or your money back) that demonstrates a strong commitment to customer satisfaction.

Disadvantages of Small-Business Ownership

The rewards associated with running a small business are so enticing that it's no wonder many people dream of it. However, as with any undertaking, small-business ownership has its disadvantages.

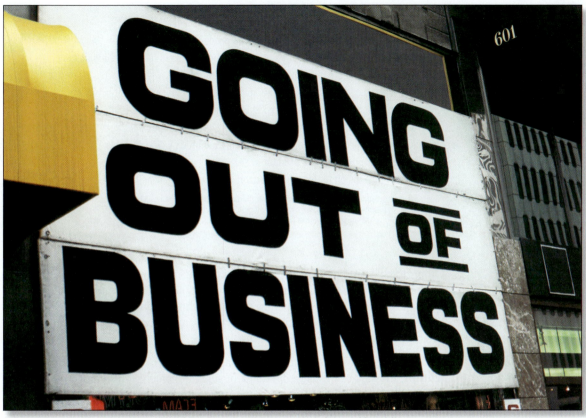

Entrepreneurs experience a great deal of independence but also a great deal of stress. Many fail.

High Stress Level

A small business is likely to provide a living for its owner, but not much more (although there are exceptions as some examples in this chapter have shown). There are ongoing worries about competition, employee problems, new equipment, expanding inventory, rent increases, or changing market demand. In addition to other stresses, small-business owners tend to be victims of physical and psychological stress. The small-business person is often the owner, manager, sales force, shipping and receiving clerk, bookkeeper, and custodian. Having to multitask can result in long hours for most small-business owners. Many creative persons fail, not because of their business concepts, but rather because of difficulties in managing their business.

High Failure Rate

Despite the importance of small businesses to our economy, there is no guarantee of success. Half of all new employer firms fail within the first five years.[20] Restaurants are a case in point. Look around your own neighborhood, and you can probably spot the locations of several restaurants that are no longer in business.

Small businesses fail for many reasons (see Table 5.4). A poor business concept—such as insecticides for garbage cans (research found that consumers are not concerned with insects in their garbage)—will produce disaster nearly every time. Expanding a hobby into a business may work if a genuine market niche exists, but all too often people start such a business without identifying a real need for the goods or services.

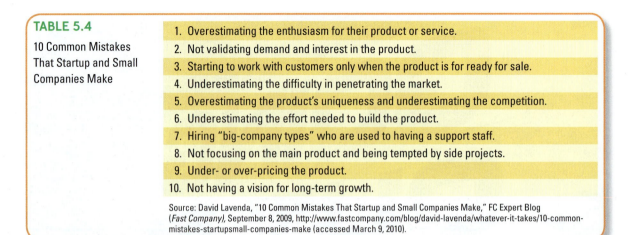

TABLE 5.4

10 Common Mistakes That Startup and Small Companies Make

1. Overestimating the enthusiasm for their product or service.
2. Not validating demand and interest in the product.
3. Starting to work with customers only when the product is for ready for sale.
4. Underestimating the difficulty in penetrating the market.
5. Overestimating the product's uniqueness and underestimating the competition.
6. Underestimating the effort needed to build the product.
7. Hiring "big-company types" who are used to having a support staff.
8. Not focusing on the main product and being tempted by side projects.
9. Under- or over-pricing the product.
10. Not having a vision for long-term growth.

Source: David Lavenda, "10 Common Mistakes That Startup and Small Companies Make," FC Expert Blog (*Fast Company*), September 8, 2009, http://www.fastcompany.com/blog/david-lavenda/whatever-it-takes/10-common-mistakes-startupsmall-companies-make (accessed March 9, 2010).

Other notable causes of small-business failure include the burdens imposed by government regulation, insufficient funds to withstand slow sales, and vulnerability to competition from larger companies. However, three major causes of small-business failure deserve a close look: undercapitalization, managerial inexperience or incompetence, and inability to cope with growth.

undercapitalization
the lack of funds to operate a business normally

Undercapitalization.   The shortest path to failure in business is **undercapitalization,** the lack of funds to operate a business normally. Too many entrepreneurs think that all they need is enough money to get started, that the business can survive on cash generated from sales soon thereafter. But almost all businesses suffer from seasonal variations in sales, which make cash tight, and few businesses make money from the start. Many small rural operations cannot obtain financing within their own communities because small rural banks often lack the necessary financing expertise or assets sizable enough to counter the risks involved with small-business loans. Without sufficient funds, the best small-business idea in the world will fail.

Managerial Inexperience or Incompetence.   Poor management is the cause of many business failures. Just because an entrepreneur has a brilliant vision for a small business does not mean he or she has the knowledge or experience to manage a growing business effectively. A person who is good at creating great product ideas and marketing them may lack the skills and experience to make good management decisions in hiring, negotiating, finance, and control. Moreover, entrepreneurs may neglect those areas of management they know little about or find tedious, at the expense of the business's success.

Inability to Cope with Growth.   Sometimes, the very factors that are advantages for a small business turn into serious disadvantages when the time comes to grow. Growth often requires the owner to give up a certain amount of direct authority, and it is frequently hard for someone who has called all the shots to give up control. It has often been said that the greatest impediment to the success of a business is the entrepreneur. Similarly, growth requires specialized management skills in areas such as credit analysis and promotion—skills that the founder may lack or not have time to apply. The founders of many small businesses, including those of Gateway and Dell Computers, found that they needed to bring in more experienced managers to help manage their companies through growing pains.

Poorly managed growth probably affects a company's reputation more than anything else, at least initially. And products that do not arrive on time or goods that are poorly made can quickly reverse a success. The principle immediate threats to small and mid-sized businesses include rising inflation, collapse of the dollar's value, energy and other supply shortages, excessive household and/or corporate debt, and the growing federal deficit.

Starting a Small Business

We've told you how important small businesses are, and why they succeed and fail, but *how do you go about* starting your own business in the first place? To start any business, large or small, you must have some kind of general idea. Sam Walton, founder of Walmart stores, had a vision of a discount retailing enterprise that spawned the world's largest retailing empire and changed the way companies look at business. Next, you need to devise a strategy to guide planning and development in the business. Finally, you must make decisions about form of ownership, the financial resources needed, and whether to acquire an existing business, start a new one, or buy a franchise.

The Business Plan

A key element of business success is a **business plan**—a precise statement of the rationale for the business and a step-by-step explanation of how it will achieve its goals. The business plan should include an explanation of the business, an analysis of the competition, estimates of income and expenses, and other information. It should also establish a strategy for acquiring sufficient funds to keep the business going. Many financial institutions decide whether to loan a small business money

business plan
a precise statement of the rationale for a business and a step-by-step explanation of how it will achieve its goals

based on its business plan. A good business plan should act as a guide and reference document—not a shackle that limits the business's flexibility and decision making ability. The business plan must be revised periodically to ensure that the firm's goals and strategies adapt to changes in the environment. Business plans allow companies to assess market potential, determine price and manufacturing requirements, identify optimal distribution channels, and refine product selection. Ben and Matthew Freund, who grew up on their father's dairy farm in Connecticut, developed an innovative way to deal with their abundance of cow manure. They created a digestion and dehydration process to eliminate the odor and to form the product into CowPots, which can be buried in the ground to fertilize plants. CowPots will last for months above ground but begin to degrade when planted. Business plans allow for companies such as Ben and Matthew's to assess market potential, determine price, manufacturing possibilities and requirements, identify optimal distribution channels, and brand the products. The U.S. Department of Agriculture's Cooperative State Research, Education, and Extension Service funded this project.[22] The Small Business Administration Web site provides an overview of a plan for small businesses to use to gain financing. Appendix A presents a comprehensive business plan.

Forms of Business Ownership

After developing a business plan, the entrepreneur has to decide on an appropriate legal form of business ownership—whether it is best to operate as a sole proprietorship, partnership, or corporation—and to examine the many factors that affect that decision, which we explored in Chapter 4.

Financial Resources

The old adage "it takes money to make money" holds especially true in developing a business enterprise. To make money from a small business, the owner must first provide or obtain money (capital) to get started and to keep it running smoothly. Even a small retail store will probably need at least $50,000 in initial financing to rent space, purchase or lease necessary equipment and furnishings, buy the initial inventory, and provide working capital. Often, the small-business owner has to put up a significant percentage of the necessary capital. Few new business owners have a large amount of their own capital and must look to other sources for additional financing.

Equity Financing.   The most important source of funds for any new business is the owner. Many owners include among their personal resources ownership of a home, the accumulated value in a life-insurance policy, or a savings account. A new business owner may sell or borrow against the value of such assets to obtain funds to operate a business. Additionally, the owner may bring useful personal assets—such as a computer, desks and other furniture, a car or truck—as part of his or her ownership interest in the firm. Such financing is referred to as *equity financing* because the owner uses real personal assets rather than borrowing funds from outside sources to get started in a new business. The owner can also provide working capital by reinvesting profits into the business or simply by not drawing a full salary.

Small businesses can also obtain equity financing by finding investors for their operations. They may sell stock in the business to family members, friends, employees, or other investors. In 2003, Petra Cooper was the 41-year-old president of McGraw-Hill Ryerson Publishing in Toronto when she decided to make a dramatic career change. After researching small-business opportunities, she decided to start a creamery, Fifth Town Artisan Cheese. Before quitting McGraw-Hill, she took two years of vacation time to study cheese making and constructed a model, energy-efficient dairy on 20 acres in Prince Edward Island, Canada. Cooper exceeded her initial $500,000 budget, but found an investor and obtained a bridge loan from a bank. By the end of her first year, Cooper already had $1 million in revenues and nearly broke even on the investment.[23] **Venture capitalists** are persons or organizations that agree to provide some funds for a new business in exchange for an ownership interest or stock. Venture capitalists hope to purchase the stock of a small business at a low price and then sell the stock for a profit after the business has grown successful. The renewable energy industry has recently become a popular investment option among venture capitalists, who have invested over $20 billion in "cleantech," or renewable energy technology, since 2005.[24] Although these forms of equity financing have helped many small businesses, they require that the small-business owner share the profits of the business—and sometimes control, as well—with the investors.

venture capitalists
persons or organizations that agree to provide some funds for a new business in exchange for an ownership interest or stock

Debt Financing.   New businesses sometimes borrow more than half of their financial resources. Banks are the main suppliers of external financing to small businesses. On the federal level, the Small Business Administration offers financial assistance to qualifying businesses. More detail on the SBA's loan programs can be found at the SBA Web site. They can also look to family and friends as sources for long-term loans or other assets, such as computers or an automobile, that are exchanged for an ownership interest in a business. In such cases, the business owner can usually structure a favorable repayment schedule and sometimes negotiate an interest rate below current bank rates. If the business goes bad, however, the emotional losses for all concerned may greatly exceed the money involved. Anyone lending a friend or family member money for a venture should state the agreement clearly in writing before any money changes hands.

The amount a bank or other institution is willing to loan depends on its assessment of the venture's likelihood of success and of the entrepreneur's ability to repay the loan. The bank will often require the entrepreneur to put up *collateral,* a financial interest in the property or fixtures of the business, to guarantee payment of the debt. Additionally, the small-business owner may have to provide personal property as collateral, such as his or her home, in which case the loan is called a *mortgage.* If the small business fails to repay the loan, the lending institution may eventually claim and sell the collateral or mortgage to recover its loss.

Banks and other financial institutions can also grant a small business a *line of credit*—an agreement by which a financial institution promises to lend a business a predetermined sum on demand. A line of credit permits an entrepreneur to take quick advantage of opportunities that require a bank loan. Small businesses may obtain funding from their suppliers in the form of a *trade credit*—that is, suppliers allow the business to take possession of the needed goods and services and pay for them at a later date or in installments. Occasionally, small businesses engage in *bartering*—trading their own products for the goods and services offered by other businesses. For example,

Franson Nwaeze and Paula Merrell wanted to open a restaurant, but most lenders were skeptical about their lack of restaurant experience and money. When the husband-and-wife team learned that banks were much more willing to loan them money to buy a gas station, they purchased a Conoco station sin Watauga, Texas, and opened up a successful restaurant in one-half of it. The business's motto is "fill'er-up outside, fill'er-up inside."

1-800-Got-Junk will haul away what your garbage man won't. The company has more than 300 franchises, most of which are in the United States and Canada.

an accountant may offer accounting services to an office supply firm in exchange for computer paper and disks.

Additionally, some community groups sponsor loan funds to encourage the development of particular types of businesses. State and local agencies may guarantee loans, especially to minority business people or for development in certain areas.

Approaches to Starting a Small Business

Starting from Scratch versus Buying an Existing Business. Although entrepreneurs often start new small businesses from scratch much the way we have discussed in this section, they may elect instead to buy an existing business. This has the advantage of providing a built-in network of customers, suppliers, and distributors and reducing some of the guesswork inherent in starting a new business from scratch. However, an entrepreneur who buys an existing business also takes on any problems the business already has.

Franchising.   Many small-business owners find entry into the business world through franchising. A license to sell another's products or to use another's name in business, or both, is a **franchise.** The company that sells a franchise is the **franchiser.** Dunkin' Donuts, McDonald's, and Jiffy Lube are well-known franchisers with national visibility. The purchaser of a franchise is called a **franchisee.**

The franchisee acquires the rights to a name, logo, methods of operation, national advertising, products, and other elements associated with the franchiser's business in return for a financial commitment and the agreement to conduct business in accordance with the franchiser's standard of operations. The initial fee to join a franchise varies greatly. In addition, franchisees buy equipment, pay for training, and obtain a mortgage or lease. The franchisee also pays the franchiser a monthly or annual fee based on a percentage of sales or profits. In return, the franchisee often receives building specifications and designs, site recommendations, management and accounting support, and perhaps most importantly, immediate name recognition. Visit the Web site of the International Franchise Association to learn more on this topic.

The practice of franchising first began in the United States in the 19th century when Singer used it to sell sewing machines. The method of goods distribution soon became commonplace in the automobile, gasoline, soft drink, and hotel industries. The concept of franchising grew especially rapidly during the 1960s, when it expanded to diverse industries. Table 5.5 shows the 10 fastest growing franchises and the top 10 new franchises.

The entrepreneur will find that franchising has both advantages and disadvantages. Franchising allows a franchisee the opportunity to set up a small business relatively quickly, and because of its association with an established brand, a franchise outlet

franchise
a license to sell another's products or to use another's name in business, or both

franchiser
the company that sells a franchise

franchisee
the purchaser of a franchise

often reaches the breakeven point faster than an independent business would. Franchisees commonly report the following advantages:

- Management training and support.
- Brand-name appeal.
- Standardized quality of goods and services.
- National advertising programs.
- Financial assistance.
- Proven products and business formats.
- Centralized buying power.
- Site selection and territorial protection.
- Greater chance for success.[25]

However, the franchisee must sacrifice some freedom to the franchiser. Some shortcomings experienced by franchisees include:

- Franchise fees and profit sharing with the franchiser.
- Strict adherence to standardized operations.
- Restrictions on purchasing.
- Limited product line.
- Possible market saturation.
- Less freedom in business decisions.[26]

Strict uniformity is the rule rather than the exception. Entrepreneurs who want to be their own bosses are often frustrated with a franchise.

Help for Small-Business Managers

Because of the crucial role that small business and entrepreneurs play in the U.S. economy, a number of organizations offer programs to improve the small-business owner's ability to compete. These include entrepreneurial training programs and programs sponsored by the Small Business Administration. Such programs provide small-business owners with invaluable assistance in managing their businesses, often at little or no cost to the owner.

Top 10 Fastest-Growing Franchises	Top 10 New Franchises
Jan-Pro Franchising International Inc.	Stratus Building Solutions
Subway	Senior Helpers
Stratus Building Solutions	Mr. Sandless
Dunkin' Donuts	HealthSource Chiropractic and Progressive Rehab
Anago Cleaning Systems	Oreck Clean Home Center
McDonald's	Guard-A-Kid
CleanNet USA Inc.	Fresh Coat
Bonus Building Care	Murphey Business & Financial Corp.
Liberty Tax Service	Oxi Fresh Franchising Co.
Vanguard Cleaning Systems	The Senior's Choice Inc.

TABLE 5.5

Fastest Growing and Hottest New Franchises

Sources: "2010 Fastest-Growing Franchises," *Entrepreneur,* http://www.entrepreneur.com/franzone/fastestgrowing (accessed March 9, 2010); "2010 Top New Franchises," *Entrepreneur,* http://www.entrepreneur.com/franchises/topnew (accessed March 9, 2010).

Entrepreneurs can learn critical marketing, management, and finance skills in seminars and college courses. In addition, knowledge, experience, and judgment are necessary for success in a new business. While knowledge can be communicated and some experiences can be simulated in the classroom, good judgment must be developed by the entrepreneur. Local chambers of commerce and the U.S. Department of Commerce offer information and assistance helpful in operating a small business. National publications such as *Inc.* and *Entrepreneur* share statistics, advice, tips, and success/failure stories. Additionally, many urban areas—including Chicago, Illinois; Jacksonville, Florida; Portland, Oregon; St. Louis, Missouri; and Nashville, Tennessee—have weekly business journal/newspapers that provide stories on local businesses as well as on business techniques that a manager or small business can use.

The Small Business Administration offers many types of management assistance to small businesses, including counseling for firms in difficulty, consulting on improving operations, and training for owner/managers and their employees. Among its many programs, the SBA funds Small Business Development Centers (SBDCs). These are business clinics, usually located on college campuses, that provide counseling at no charge and training at only a nominal charge. SBDCs are often the SBA's principal means of providing direct management assistance.

The Service Corps of Retired Executives (SCORE) and the Active Corps of Executives (ACE) are volunteer agencies funded by the SBA to provide advice for owners of small firms. Both are staffed by experienced managers whose talents and experience the small firms could not ordinarily afford. SCORE has 10,500 volunteers at nearly 400 locations in the United States and has served more than 8.5 million small businesses.[28] The SBA also has organized Small Business Institutes (SBIs) on almost 500 university and college campuses in the United States. Seniors, graduate students, and faculty at each SBI provide on-site management counseling.

Finally, the small-business owner can obtain advice from other small-business owners, suppliers, and even customers. A customer may approach a small business it frequents with a request for a new product, for example, or a supplier may offer suggestions for improving a manufacturing process. Networking—building relationships and sharing information with colleagues—is vital for any businessperson, whether you work for a huge corporation or run your own small business. Communicating with other business owners is a great way to find ideas for dealing with employees and government regulation, improving processes, or solving problems. New technology is making it easier to network. For example, some states are establishing social networking sites for the use of their businesses to network and share ideas.

The Future for Small Business[29]

Although small businesses are crucial to the economy, their size and limited resources can make them more vulnerable to turbulence and change in the marketplace than large businesses. Next, we take a brief look at the demographic, technological, and economic trends that will have the most impact on small business in the future.

Demographic Trends

America's baby boom started in 1946 and ended in 1964. Many boomers are past 50, and in the next few years, millions more will pass that mark. The baby boomer generation represents 26.1 percent of Americans and includes about 78 million people.[30] This segment of the population is wealthy, but many small businesses do not actively pursue it. Some exceptions, however, include Gold Violin, which sells designer canes and other products online and through a catalog, and LifeSpring, which delivers nutritional meals and snacks directly to the customer. Industries such as travel, financial planning, and health care will continue to grow as boomers age. Many experts believe that the boomer demographic is the market of the future.

The Latino population is the biggest and fastest growing minority segment in the United States—and a lucrative market for businesses looking for ways to meet the segment's many needs.

Another market with huge potential for small business is the echo boomers, also called millennials or Generation Y. Millennials number around 75 million and possess a number of unique characteristics. Born between 1977 and 1994, this cohort is not solely concerned about money. Those that fall into this group are also concerned with advancement, recognition, and improved capabilities. They need direct, timely feedback and frequent encouragement and recognition. Millennials do well when training sessions combine entertainment with learning. Working remotely is more acceptable to this group than previous generations, and virtual communication may become as important as face-to-face meetings.[31]

Yet another trend is the growing number of immigrants living in the United States, who now represent about one-eighth, or 12 percent of the population. If this trend continues, by 2050 nearly one in five Americans will be classified as immigrants. The Latino population, the nation's largest minority group, is expected to triple in size by 2050.[32]

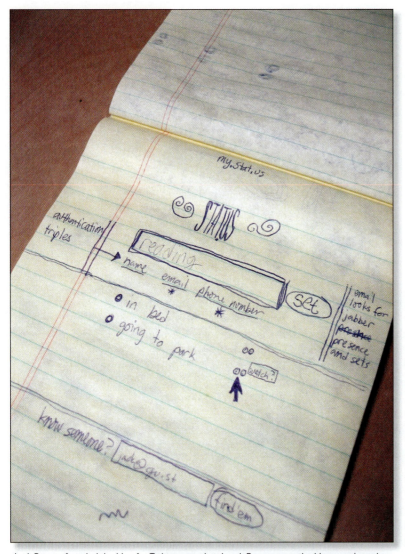

Jack Dorsey founded the idea for Twitter on a sketchpad. Dorsey says the idea was based on how dispatched vehicles, such as cabs, communicate with one another. Via radio, they are constantly squawking to each other about where they are and what they are doing.

This vast group provides still another greatly untapped market for small businesses. Retailers who specialize in ethnic products, and service providers who offer bi- or multilingual employees, will find a large amount of business potential in this market. Table 5.6 ranks top cities in the United States for small businesses and startups.

Technological and Economic Trends

Advances in technology have opened up many new markets to small businesses. Undoubtedly, the Internet will continue to provide new opportunities for small businesses. Arianna Huffington launched the popular *Huffington Post*, a news and blogging Web site, in 2005. The site has an editorial staff of 53 and has broken a number of important news stories. Partly because of its accessible format and the way it agglomerates news stories from many sites, HuffPo attracts more than 8 million views a month.[33]

Technological advances and an increase in service exports have created new opportunities for small companies to expand their operations abroad. Changes in communications and technology can allow small companies to customize their services quickly for international customers. Also, free trade agreements and trade alliances are helping to create an environment in which small businesses have fewer regulatory and legal barriers.

In recent years, economic turbulence has provided both opportunities and threats for small businesses. As large information technology companies such as Cisco, Oracle, and Sun Microsystems had to recover from an economic slowdown and an oversupply of Internet infrastructure products, some smaller firms found new niche markets. Smaller companies can react quickly to change and can stay close to their customers. While well-funded dot-coms were failing, many small businesses were learning how to use the Internet to promote themselves and sell products online. For example, arts and crafts dealers and makers of specialty products found they could sell their wares on existing Web sites, such as eBay. Service providers related to tourism, real estate, and construction also found they could reach customers through their own or existing Web sites.

1	Oklahoma City, OK	
2	Pittsburgh, PA	
3	Raleigh, NC	
4	Houston, TX	
5	Hartford, CT	
6	Washington, DC	
7	Charlotte, NC	
8	Austin, TX	
9	New York City, NY	
10	Baltimore, MD	

TABLE 5.6

Top Cities to Launch a Small Business

Source: "Best Places to Launch," *CNN Money,* http://money.cnn.com/smallbusiness/best_places_launch/2009/full_list/index.html (accessed March 16, 2010).

Deregulation of the energy market and interest in alternative fuels and in fuel conservation have spawned many small businesses. Southwest Windpower Inc. manufactures and markets small wind turbines for producing electric power for homes, sailboats, and telecommunications. Solar Attic Inc. has developed a process to recover heat from home attics to use in heating water or swimming pools. As entrepreneurs begin to realize that worldwide energy markets are valued in the hundreds of billions of dollars, the number of innovative companies entering this market will increase. In addition, many small businesses have the desire and employee commitment to purchase such environmentally friendly products. New Belgium Brewing Company received the U.S. Environmental Protection Agency and Department of Energy Award for leadership in conservation for making a 10-year commitment to purchase wind energy. The company's employees unanimously agreed to cover the increased costs of wind-generated electricity from the employee profit-sharing program.

The future for small business remains promising. The opportunities to apply creativity and entrepreneurship to serve customers are unlimited. While large organizations such as Walmart, which has more than 2.1 million employees, typically must adapt to change slowly, a small business can adapt immediately to customer and community needs and changing trends. This flexibility provides small businesses with a definite advantage over large companies.

Making Big Businesses Act "Small"

The continuing success and competitiveness of small businesses through rapidly changing conditions in the business world have led many large corporations to take a closer look at what makes their smaller rivals tick. More and more firms are emulating small businesses in an effort to improve their own bottom line. Beginning in the 1980s and continuing through the present, the buzzword in business has been to *downsize* or *right-size* to reduce management layers, corporate staff, and work tasks in order to make the firm more flexible, resourceful, and innovative. Many well-known U.S. companies, including IBM, Ford, Apple Computer, General Electric, Xerox, and 3M, have downsized to improve their competitiveness, as have German, British, and Japanese firms. Other firms have sought to make their businesses "smaller" by making their operating units function more like independent small businesses, each responsible for its profits, losses, and resources. Of course, some large corporations, such as Southwest Airlines, have acted like small businesses from their inception, with great success.

Trying to capitalize on small-business success in introducing innovative new products, more and more companies are attempting to instill a spirit of entrepreneurship into even the largest firms. In major corporations, **intrapreneurs,** like entrepreneurs, take responsibility for, or "champion," the development of innovations of any kind *within* the larger organization.[34] Often, they use company resources and time to develop a new product for the company.

intrapreneurs
individuals in large firms who take responsibility for the development of innovations within the organizations

So You Want to be an Entrepreneur or Small-Business Owner

In times when jobs are scarce, many people turn to entrepreneurship as a way to find employment. As long as there are unfulfilled needs from consumers, there will be a demand for entrepreneurs and small businesses. Entrepreneurs and small-business owners have been, and will continue to be, a vital part of the U.S. economy, whether in retailing, wholesaling, manufacturing, technology, or services. Creating a business around your idea has a lot of advantages. For many people, independence is the biggest advantage of forming their own small business, especially for those who do not work well in a corporate setting and like to call their own shots. Smaller businesses are also cheaper to start up than large ones in terms of salaries, infrastructure, and equipment. Smallness also provides a lot of flexibility to change with the times. If consumers suddenly start demanding new and different products or services, a small business is more likely to deliver quickly.

Starting your own business is not easy, especially in slow economic times. Even in a good economy, taking an idea and turning it into a business has a very high failure rate. The possibility of failure can increase even more when money is tight. Reduced revenues and expensive materials can hurt a small business more than a large one because small businesses have fewer resources. When people are feeling the pinch from rising food and fuel prices, they tend to cut back on other expenditures—which could potentially harm your small business. The increased cost of materials will also affect your bottom line. However, several techniques can help your company survive:

- Set clear payment schedules for all clients. Small businesses tend to be worse about collecting payments than large ones, especially if the clients are acquaintances. However, you need to keep cash flowing into the company in order to keep business going.

- Take the time to learn about tax breaks. A lot of people do not realize all of the deductions they can claim on items such as equipment and health insurance.

- Focus on your current customers, and don't spend a lot of time looking for new ones. It is far less expensive for a company to keep its existing customers happy.

- Although entrepreneurs and small-business owners are more likely to be friends with their customers, do not let this be a temptation to give things away for free. Make it clear to your customers what the basic price is for what you are selling and charge for extra features, extra services, etc.

- Make sure the office has the conveniences employees need—like a good coffee maker and other drinks and snacks. This will not only make your employees happy, but it will also help maintain productivity up by keeping employees closer to their desks.

- Use your actions to set an example. If money is tight, show your commitment to cutting costs and making the business work by doing simple things like taking the bus to work or bringing a sack lunch every day.

- Don't forget to increase productivity in addition to cutting costs. Try not to focus so much attention on cost cutting that you don't try to increase sales.

In unsure economic times, these measures should help new entrepreneurs and small-business owners sustain their businesses. Learning how to run a business on a shoestring is a great opportunity to cut the fat and to establish lean, efficient operations.[35]

Review Your Understanding

***Define* entrepreneurship *and* small business.**

An entrepreneur is a person who creates a business or product and manages his or her resources and takes risks to gain a profit; entrepreneurship is the process of creating and managing a business to achieve desired objectives. A small business is one that is not dominant in its competitive area and does not employ more than 500 people.

Investigate the importance of small business in the U.S. economy and why certain fields attract small business.

Small businesses are vital to the American economy because they provide products, jobs, innovation, and opportunities. Retailing, wholesaling, services, manufacturing, and high technology attract small businesses because these industries are relatively easy to enter, require relatively low initial financing, and may experience less heavy competition.

Specify the advantages of small-business ownership.

Small-business ownership offers some personal advantages, including independence, freedom of choice, and the option of working at home. Business advantages include flexibility, the ability to focus on a few key customers, and the chance to develop a reputation for quality and service.

Summarize the disadvantages of small-business ownership, and analyze why many small businesses fail.

Small businesses have many disadvantages for their owners such as expense, physical and psychological stress, and a high failure rate. Small businesses fail for many reasons: undercapitalization, management inexperience or incompetence, neglect, disproportionate burdens imposed by government regulation, and vulnerability to competition from larger companies.

Describe how you go about starting a small business and what resources are needed.

First, you must have an idea for developing a small business. Next, you need to devise a business plan to guide planning and development of the business. Then you must decide what form of business ownership to use: sole proprietorship, partnership, or corporation. Small-business owners are expected to provide some of the funds required to start their businesses, but funds also can be obtained from friends and family, financial institutions, other businesses in the form of trade credit, investors (venture capitalists), state and local organizations, and the Small Business Administration. In addition to loans, the Small Business Administration and other organizations offer counseling, consulting, and training services. Finally, you must decide whether to start a new business from scratch, buy an existing one, or buy a franchise operation.

Evaluate the demographic, technological, and economic trends that are affecting the future of small business.

Changing demographic trends that represent areas of opportunity for small businesses include more elderly people as baby boomers age, a large group in the 11 to 28 age range known as echo boomers, millennials, or Generation Y, and an increasing number of immigrants to the United States. Technological advances and an increase in service exports have created new opportunities for small companies to expand their operations abroad, while trade agreements and alliances have created an environment in which small business has fewer regulatory and legal barriers. Economic turbulence presents both opportunities and threats to the survival of small businesses.

Explain why many large businesses are trying to "think small."

More large companies are copying small businesses in an effort to make their firms more flexible, resourceful, and innovative, and generally to improve their bottom line. This effort often involves downsizing (reducing management layers, laying off employees, and reducing work tasks) and intrapreneurship, where an employee takes responsibility for (champions) developing innovations of any kind within the larger organization.

Assess two entrepreneurs' plans for starting a small business.

Based on the facts given in "Solve the Dilemma" on page 171 and the material presented in this chapter, you should be able to assess the feasibility and potential success of Gray and McVay's idea for starting a small business.

Revisit the World of Business

1. What is aquaculture? Why do Tze and Polis think it is such a promising area for starting a business?

2. What is unique about Aquacopia's business model?

3. Do you think Aquacopia has a sustainable business idea? Why or why not?

Learn the Terms

Check Your Progress

1. Why are small businesses so important to the U.S. economy?

2. Which fields tend to attract entrepreneurs the most? Why?

3. What are the advantages of starting a small business? The disadvantages?

4. What are the principal reasons for the high failure rate among small businesses?

5. What decisions must an entrepreneur make when starting a small business?

6. What types of financing do small entrepreneurs typically use? What are some of the pros and cons of each?

7. List the types of management and financial assistance that the Small Business Administration offers.

8. Describe the franchising relationship.

9. What demographic, technological, and economic trends are influencing the future of small business?

10. Why do large corporations want to become more like small businesses?

Get Involved

1. Interview a local small-business owner. Why did he or she start the business? What factors have led to the business's success? What problems has the owner experienced? What advice would he or she offer a potential entrepreneur?

2. Using business journals, find an example of a company that is trying to emulate the factors that make small businesses flexible and more responsive.

Describe and evaluate the company's activities. Have they been successful? Why or why not?

3. Using the business plan outline in Appendix B, create a business plan for a business idea that you have. (A man named Fred Smith once did a similar project for a business class at Yale. His paper became the basis for the business he later founded: Federal Express!)

Build Your Skills

CREATIVITY

Background:
The entrepreneurial success stories in this chapter are about people who used their creative abilities to develop innovative products or ways of doing something that became the basis of a new business. Of course, being creative is not just for entrepreneurs or inventors; creativity is an important tool to help you find the optimal solutions to the problems you face on a daily basis. Employees rely heavily on their creativity skills to help them solve daily workplace problems.

According to brain experts, the right-brain hemisphere is the source of creative thinking; and the creative part of the brain can "atrophy" from lack of use. Let's see how much "exercise" you're giving your right-brain hemisphere.

Task:

1. Take the following self-test to check your Creativity Quotient.[36]

2. Write the appropriate number in the box next to each statement according to whether the statement describes your behavior always (3), sometimes (2), once in a while (1), or never (0).

	Always 3	Sometimes 2	Once in a While 1	Never 0
1. I am a curious person who is interested in other people's opinions.				
2. I look for opportunities to solve problems.				
3. I respond to changes in my life creatively by using them to redefine my goals and revising plans to reach them.				
4. I am willing to develop and experiment with ideas of my own.				
5. I rely on my hunches and insights.				
6. I can reduce complex decisions to a few simple questions by seeing the "big picture."				
7. I am good at promoting and gathering support for my ideas.				
8. I think further ahead than most people I associate with by thinking long term and sharing my vision with others.				
9. I dig out research and information to support my ideas.				
10. I am supportive of the creative ideas from my peers and subordinates and welcome "better ideas" from others.				
11. I read books and magazine articles to stay on the "cutting edge" in my areas of interest. I am fascinated by the future.				
12. I believe I am creative and have faith in my good ideas.				
Subtotal for each column				
Grand Total				

3. Check your score using the following scale:

30–36   High creativity. You are giving your right-brain hemisphere a regular workout.

20–29   Average creativity. You could use your creativity capacity more regularly to ensure against "creativity atrophy."

10–19   Low creativity. You could benefit by reviewing the questions you answered "never" in the above assessment and selecting one or two of the behaviors that you could start practicing.

0–9   Undiscovered creativity. You have yet to uncover your creative potential.

Solve the Dilemma

The Small-Business Challenge

Jack Gray and his best friend, Bruce McVay, decided to start their own small business. Jack had developed recipes for fat-free and low-fat cookies and muffins in an effort to satisfy his personal health needs. Bruce had extensive experience in managing food-service establishments. They knew that a startup company needs a quality product, adequate funds, a written business plan, some outside financial support, and a good promotion program. Jack and Bruce felt they had all of this and more and were ready to embark on their new low-fat cookie/muffin store. Each had $35,000 to invest and with their homes and other resources they had borrowing power of an additional $125,000.

However, they still have many decisions to make, including what form or organization to use, how to market their product, and how to determine exactly what products to sell—whether just cookies and muffins or additional products.

Discussion Questions

1. Evaluate the idea of a low-fat cookie and muffin retail store.

2. Are there any concerns in connection with starting a small business that Jack and Bruce have not considered?

3. What advice would you give Jack and Bruce as they start up their business?

Build Your Business Plan

SMALL BUSINESS, ENTREPRENEURSHIP, AND FRANCHISING

Now you can get started writing your business plan! Refer to Guidelines for the Development of the Business Plan following Chapter 1, which provides you with an outline for your business plan. As you are developing your business plan keep in mind that potential investors might be reviewing it. Or you might have plans to go to your local Small Business Development Center for an SBA loan.

At this point in the process you should think about collecting information from a variety of (free) resources.

For example, if you are developing a business plan for a local business, product or service you might want to check out any of the following sources for demographic information: your local Chamber of Commerce, Economic Development Office, Census Bureau, or City Planning Office.

Go on the Internet and see if there have been any recent studies done or articles on your specific type of business, especially in your area. Remember, you always want to explore any secondary data before trying to conduct your own research.

See for Yourself Videocase

SONIC IS A SUCCESSFUL FRANCHISE THAT OFFERS AN OLD-FASHIONED DRIVE-IN EXPERIENCE

For those who are nostalgic for the classic drive-in diner experience, the Sonic fast-food chain helps fill that need. Sonic offers customers a dose of nostalgia with its 1950s-style curbside speakers and carhop service. As the United States' largest drive-in fast food chain, Sonic offers a unique and diverse menu selection that helps set it apart from a highly competitive fast-food franchise market. Founder Troy Smith launched the first Sonic Drive-In (known then as Top Hat Drive-In) in Shawnee, Oklahoma, in 1953 as a sole proprietorship. He later added a partner, Charlie Pappe, and eventually turned the business into a franchise. Today, Sonic is a publicly traded company and ranks #22 on *Entrepreneur* magazine's "Franchise 500" list and #13 on the magazine's "Fastest Growing Franchise" list.

Franchising is an appealing option for entrepreneurs looking to begin businesses without creating them from scratch. In the case of Sonic, when a franchisee purchases a franchise, he or she is getting a business that already has a national reputation and a national advertising campaign. The company also offers its franchisees tremendous support and training. As a pioneer, Troy Smith was required to innovate; as a Sonic franchisee, one steps into an already proven system. That being said, successfully running a franchise is not easy. Cody Barnett, owner of 22 Sonic franchises, says the franchisee's job is to ensure that each customer has the best experience possible, thereby making repeat visits more likely. To accomplish this, a franchisee must build his or her locations, purchase equipment, hire excellent employees, make certain the products live up to Sonic's reputation, maintain a

clean, inviting facility, and much more. In order to run 22 franchises, Barnett runs his locations as limited partnerships, ensuring that a managing partner is on site at each location to keep day-to-day operations running smoothly.

Some of Sonic's success may be attributed to its stringent requirements for selecting franchisees. Although franchisees must have excellent financial credentials and prior restaurant/entrepreneurial experience, the most important factor is that each franchisee fit into the Sonic culture. Sonic offers two types of franchises. The traditional franchise, which includes the full restaurant set up, requires an initial investment of between $710,000 and $3 million. Franchisees are required to pay four to five percent in royalty fees and just under six percent in advertising fees. Sonic also offers the non-traditional franchise. A Sonic in a travel plaza, a mall food court, or a college campus are all examples of the non-traditional model. Because these set-ups do not include the drive-in and carhop features, initial investment is less—somewhere between $107,000 and more than half a million. Royalty and advertising fees still apply.

For entrepreneurs looking for limited risk, franchises like Sonic are great options. The advantages are abundant, as discussed above. There is a high failure rate among small businesses. Entering into a successful franchise significantly cuts down on the risk of failure, although a franchisee does have to watch for market saturation, poor location choice, and other determining factors. However, there are also disadvantages; chiefly, franchisees are often required to follow a strict model set by the franchiser For instance, in addition to prior restaurant experience, Sonic requires its franchisees to be financially and operationally able to open two or more drive-ins. These types of requirements may make it difficult for entrepreneurs who want to set their own terms. However, with Sonic's successful business model and brand equity, there is no shortage of individuals who would like to operate a Sonic franchise.

Discussion Questions

1. What is Sonic's competitive advantage over other fast food franchises?

2. What are the pros of becoming a Sonic franchisee?
3. What are the cons of buying into the Sonic franchise?

Remember to check out our Online Learning Center at www.mhhe.com/ferrell8e.

Team Exercise

Explore successful global franchises. Go to the companies' Web sites and find the requirements for applying for three franchises. The chapter provides examples of successful franchises. What do the companies provide, and what is expected to be provided by the franchiser? Compare and contrast each group's findings for the franchises researched. For example, at Subway, the franchisee is responsible for the initial franchise fee, finding locations, leasehold improvements and equipment, hiring employees and operating restaurants, and paying an 8 percent royalty to the company and a fee into the advertising fund. The company provides access to formulas and operational systems, store design and equipment ordering guidance, a training program, an operations manual, a representative on-site during opening, periodic evaluations and ongoing support, and informative publications.

Managing for Quality and Competitiveness

The Nature of Management

OBJECTIVES

After reading this chapter, you will be able to:

- Define *management,* and explain its role in the achievement of organizational objectives.

- Describe the major functions of management.

- Distinguish among three levels of management and the concerns of managers at each level.

- Specify the skills managers need in order to be successful.

- Summarize the systematic approach to decision making used by many business managers.

- Recommend a new strategy to revive a struggling business.

Ursula Burns: From Intern to CEO

In 2009, Ursula Burns became the first black female CEO of a *Fortune* 500 corporation when she took over the top position at Xerox. Burns credits her rise from intern to CEO to hard work. While she admits that Xerox's support of diversity probably helped her at the beginning of her career, Burns's straightforward style and work ethic helped her rise to the top. She says, "My perspective comes in part from being a New York black lady, in part from being an engineer. I know I'm smart and have opinions worth being heard."

Raised in poverty by a single mother who worked hard so that her children could attend private school, Burns learned the value of hard work and a good education at an early age. Burns excelled in math and earned degrees in engineering at Brooklyn's Polytechnic Institute and Columbia University. She first went to work at Xerox as an intern in 1980 and never left the company. Burns was quickly promoted, finally becoming president in 2007. Thanks to her no-nonsense management style, Burns helped Xerox find success by improving efficiency and customer service.

According to her peers, Burns has all the skills necessary to successfully lead Xerox as the company's top manager: technical expertise and conceptual, analytical, and human relations skills. Her abilities to make tough decisions, explore options, and handle the consequences appear impressive, and Burns will need these skills in coming years. During the economic recession of 2008–2009, Xerox faced losses as customers purchased less and product prices fell. A growing concern for the environment is also affecting Xerox. As people and businesses strive to become more sustainable, they use less paper and move from copies to e-mail to share information. However, Burns has a strong history of innovation. If anyone can find a new direction for Xerox in a changing global economy, Burns may just be the one to make it happen.[1]

Introduction

For any organization—small or large, for profit or nonprofit—to achieve its objectives, it must have equipment and raw materials to turn into products to market, employees to make and sell the products, and financial resources to purchase additional goods and services, pay employees, and generally operate the business. To accomplish this, it must also have one or more managers to plan, organize, staff, direct, and control the work that goes on.

This chapter introduces the field of management. It examines and surveys the various functions, levels, and areas of management in business. The skills that managers need for success and the steps that lead to effective decision making are also discussed.

The Importance of Management

Management is a process designed to achieve an organization's objectives by using its resources effectively and efficiently in a changing environment. *Effectively* means having the intended result; *efficiently* means accomplishing the objectives with a minimum of resources. **Managers** make decisions about the use of the organization's resources and are concerned with planning, organizing, staffing, directing, and controlling the organization's activities so as to reach its objectives. The decision to introduce new products in order to reach objectives is often a key management duty. After several years of decline in the automobile industry, Ford management brought the Ford Fiesta from Europe. The car provides good driving dynamics, European styling, a low price and up to 38 mpg. The car fits well with Ford's existing product mix in the United States.[2] Management is universal. It takes place not only in business, but also in government, the military, labor unions, hospitals, schools, and religious groups—any organization requiring the coordination of resources.

management
a process designed to achieve an organization's objectives by using its resources effectively and efficiently in a changing environment

managers
those individuals in organizations who make decisions about the use of resources and who are concerned with planning, organizing, staffing, directing, and controlling the organization's activities to reach its objectives

Sergio Marchionne, the CEO of Fiat, saved the company from near bankruptcy and put it on the road to multimillion-dollar profits and the purchase of Chrysler. Can Marchionne save Chrysler, too? Time will tell.

Every organization must acquire resources (people, raw materials and equipment, money, and information) to effectively pursue its objectives and coordinate their use to turn out a final good or service. Employees are one of the most important resources in helping a business attain its objectives. Successful companies recruit, train, compensate, and provide benefits (such as shares of stock and health insurance) to foster employee loyalty. Acquiring suppliers is another important part of managing resources and in ensuring that products are made available to customers. As firms reach global markets, companies such as Walmart, Union Pacific, and Cargill enlist hundreds of diverse suppliers that provide goods and services to support operations. A good supplier maximizes efficiencies and provides creative solutions to help the company reduce expenses and reach its objectives. Finally, the manager needs adequate financial resources to pay for essential activities: Primary funding comes from owners and shareholders, as well as banks and other financial institutions. All these resources and activities must be coordinated and controlled if the company is to earn a profit. Organizations must also have adequate supplies of resources of all types, and managers must carefully coordinate their use if they are to achieve the organization's objectives.

Management Functions

To harmonize the use of resources so that the business can develop, produce, and sell products, managers engage in a series of activities: planning, organizing, staffing, directing, and controlling (Figure 6.1). Although this book discusses each of the five functions separately, they are interrelated; managers may perform two or more of them at the same time.

Planning

Planning, the process of determining the organization's objectives and deciding how to accomplish them, is the first function of management. Planning is a crucial activity, for it designs the map that lays the groundwork for the other functions. It involves forecasting events and determining the best course of action from a set of options or choices. The plan itself specifies what should be done, by whom, where, when, and how. For example, General Electric implemented a plan to improve its reputation for sustainability and to reduce costs resulting from inefficiencies. Its planning resulted in a program called "Ecomagination," which addresses sustainability through calling attention to GE's solar energy programs, hybrid locomotives, fuel cell development, lower-emissions aircraft, and development of lighter and stronger materials, among many other projects. Ecomagination is part of GE's specific plans to produce products with an emphasis on clean technology and renewable energy.[3] All businesses—from the smallest restaurant to the largest multinational corporation—need to develop plans for achieving success. But before an organization can plan a course of action, it must first determine what it wants to achieve.

Mission.   A **mission,** or mission statement, is a declaration of an organization's fundamental purpose and basic philosophy. It seeks to answer the question: "What business are we in?" Good mission statements are clear and concise statements

planning
the process of determining the organization's objectives and deciding how to accomplish them; the first function of management

mission
the statement of an organization's fundamental purpose and basic philosophy

FIGURE 6.1

The Functions of Management

Managers

Planning	Organizing	Staffing	Directing	Controlling
activities to achieve the organization's objectives	resources and activities to achieve the organization's objectives	the organization with qualified people	employees' activities toward achievement of objectives	the organization's activities to keep it on course

Entrepreneurship in Action
MobileJets Provides a Luxury Travel Experience

Rich Mann

Business: MobileJets

Founded: 2009

Success: This concept has yet to be tested, but early predictions are positive. Keep watching!

Texas-based entrepreneur Rich Mann offers executives (and others) a unique travel opportunity through MobileJets. Mann has converted Mercedes-Benz vans into private-jet-like accommodations. Each boasts satellite TVs, reclining/rotating seats, WiFi, a galley kitchen, a bathroom, and a staff consisting of a driver and a concierge. MobileJets are being offered four ways: charter, land cruise, frequent user, and for purchase. Costs for the first two options are $250 hourly, $1,725 for 8 hours, or $2,400 for 12 hours. Although prices may seem steep to the average Joe, Mann's argument is this: rather than flying on short trips and losing productive time, executives can safely travel and work or play at the same time. MobileJets are also available on your schedule—no waiting for flights or dealing with cancellations/postponements.[4]

that explain the organization's reason for existence. A well-developed mission statement, no matter what the industry or size of business, will answer five basic questions:

1. Who are we?
2. Who are our customers?
3. What is out operating philosophy (basic beliefs, values, ethics, etc)?
4. What are our core competencies and competitive advantages?
5. What are our responsibilities with respect to being a good steward of environmental, financial, and human resources?

A mission statement that delivers a clear answer to these questions provides the foundation for the development of a strong organizational culture, a good marketing plan, and a coherent business strategy. The tea company Celestial Seasonings states that its mission is to provide "the highest quality, most environmentally responsible product possible" and to "be an active participant in making the world a better place."[5]

Goals.   A goal is the result that a firm wishes to achieve. A company almost always has multiple goals, which illustrates the complex nature of business. A goal has three key components: an attribute sought, such as profits, customer satisfaction, or product quality; a target to be achieved, such as the volume of sales or extent of management training to be achieved; and a time frame, which is the time period in which the goal is to be achieved. Walmart, for example, under its former CEO Lee Scott, set goals of improving its reputation as an environmentally friendly company. Some of its goals involve reducing greenhouse gas emissions, increasing the fuel efficiency of its fleet, and requiring its suppliers to use less packaging. To be successful, company goals should be specific. Walmart plans to improve the fuel efficiency of its truck fleet by 25 percent within a specified time frame. It also has systems in place to measure its progress toward these goals. To be successful at achieving goals, it is necessary to know what is to be achieved, how much, when, and how succeeding at a goal is to be determined.

Objectives.   Objectives, the ends or results desired by an organization, derive from the organization's mission. A business's objectives may be elaborate or simple.

Common objectives relate to profit, competitive advantage, efficiency, and growth. The principal difference between goals and objectives is that objectives are generally stated in such a way that they are measurable. Organizations with profit as an objective want to have money and assets left over after paying off business expenses. Objectives regarding competitive advantage are generally stated in terms of percentage of sales increase and market share, with the goal of increasing those figures. Efficiency objectives involved making the best use of the organization's resources. Dalhousie University has developed energy calculators for small and medium-sized businesses to help them become more aware of their energy usage and to reduce their energy expenditure. Growth objectives relate to an organization's ability to adapt and to get new products to the marketplace

A firm's top managers are responsible for developing its strategic plans. However, they rely on information and advice of other employees to develop those plans.

in a timely fashion. Other organizational objectives include service and social responsibility goals. Capital One, Deloitte LLP, Eli Lilly and Company, Pinnacol Assurance, and salesforce.com received the 2009 Corporate Engagement Award of Excellence from Points of Light Institute for their commitment to employee volunteerism, which helps the community, improves stakeholder relations, and motivates employees.[6] Objectives provide direction for all managerial decisions; additionally, they establish criteria by which performance can be evaluated.

Plans.   There are three general types of plans for meeting objectives—strategic, tactical, and operational. A firm's highest managers develop its **strategic plans,** which establish the long-range objectives and overall strategy or course of action by which the firm fulfills its mission. Strategic plans generally cover periods ranging from 2 to 10 years or even longer. They include plans to add products, purchase companies, sell unprofitable segments of the business, issue stock, and move into international markets. Faced with stiff competition, rising costs, and slowing sales, some companies are closing U.S. plants and moving production to factories abroad. For example, Converse Inc. (sneaker maker), Lionel LLC (producer of model trains), and Zebco (fishing reel manufacturer) all stopped U.S. production in favor of Asian factories. Strategic plans must take into account the organization's capabilities and resources, the changing business environment, and organizational objectives. Plans should be market-driven, matching customers' desire for value with operational capabilities, processes, and human resources.[7]

strategic plans
those plans that establish the long-range objectives and overall strategy or course of action by which a firm fulfills its mission

   Tactical plans are short range and designed to implement the activities and objectives specified in the strategic plan. These plans, which usually cover a period of one year or less, help keep the organization on the course established in the strategic plan. Because tactical plans allow the organization to react to changes in the environment while continuing to focus on the company's overall strategy, management must periodically review and update them. Declining performance or failure to meet objectives set out in tactical plans may be one reason for revising them. Jordan Zimmerman, of Zimmerman Advertising, utilizes tactical planning to address and adapt to his customers' needs. Each morning he goes over his clients' sales numbers from the previous day and adjusts his short-term plans based on current client problems and opportunities. Zimmerman is constantly adjusting

tactical plans
short-range plans designed to implement the activities and objectives specified in the strategic plan

Firms need to develop contingency plans—sometimes quickly. To prevent folding, the investment banking firm Merrill Lynch hastily arranged to sell itself to Bank of America in 2008. The move saved Merrill, but Bank of America's stock price plummeted because investors feared it had paid too much for Merrill.

and reassessing his advertising plans in order to successfully respond to market dynamics.[8] When public concern emerged over Americans' high level of plastic bag consumption, which stands at more than 110 billion bags a year, the grocery chain Whole Foods stopped offering plastic bags altogether. Walmart and Kroger also began to offer reusable canvas and nylon bags in response to this problem.[9] A fast-paced and ever-changing market requires companies to develop short-run or tactical plans to deal with stakeholder concerns.

A retailing organization with a five-year strategic plan to invest $5 billion in 500 new retail stores may develop five tactical plans (each covering one year) specifying how much to spend to set up each new store, where to locate, and when to open each new store. Tactical plans are designed to execute the overall strategic plan. Because of their short-term nature, they are easier to adjust or abandon if changes in the environment or the company's performance so warrant.

Operational plans are very short term and specify what actions specific individuals, work groups, or departments need to accomplish in order to achieve the tactical plan and ultimately the strategic plan. They may apply to just one month, week, or even day. For example, a work group may be assigned a weekly production quota to ensure there are sufficient products available to elevate market share (tactical goal) and ultimately help the firm be number one in its product category (strategic goal). Returning to our retail store example, operational plans may specify the schedule for

operational plans
very short-term plans that specify what actions individuals, work groups, or departments need to accomplish in order to achieve the tactical plan and ultimately the strategic plan

opening one new store, hiring and training new employees, obtaining merchandise, and opening for actual business.

Another element of planning is **crisis management or contingency planning,** which deals with potential disasters such as product tampering, oil spills, fire, earthquake, computer viruses, or even a reputation crisis due to unethical or illegal conduct by one or more employees. Investment bank Bear Stearns found itself on the brink of collapse in 2008. Its problems were largely due to the credit crisis and subprime lending disasters. Within minutes, Bear Stearns lost half of its market value. The bank's financial condition deteriorated to the point of failure within 24 hours, which could have brought down the U.S. stock market. To save the company and to prevent widespread financial panic, another bank, JPMorgan Chase, joined with the U.S. Federal Reserve to provide loans and to create a merger between Bear Stearns and JPMorgan Chase. Businesses that have contingency plans tend to respond more effectively when problems occur than do businesses who lack such planning, hopefully avoiding a Bear Stearns–level disaster.

Many companies, including Ashland Oil, H. J. Heinz, and Johnson & Johnson, have crisis management teams to deal specifically with problems, permitting other managers to continue to focus on their regular duties. Some companies even hold periodic disaster drills to ensure that their employees know how to respond when a crisis does occur. Crisis management plans generally cover maintaining business operations throughout a crisis and communicating with the public, employees, and officials about the nature of and the company's response to the problem. Communication is especially important to minimize panic and damaging rumors; it also demonstrates that the company is aware of the problem and plans to respond. Despite more than 2,000 customer complaints about unintended acceleration in Toyota vehicles that began in 2002, the company did not issue recalls for faulty accelerator pedals until early 2010. Toyota's failure to communicate with its customers and provide accurate information led to decreased sales and damage to the company's image.[10] Incidents such as this highlight the importance of tactical planning for crises and the need to respond publicly and quickly when a disaster occurs.

Organizing

Rarely are individuals in an organization able to achieve common goals without some form of structure. **Organizing** is the structuring of resources and activities to accomplish objectives in an efficient and effective manner. Managers organize by reviewing plans and determining what activities are necessary to implement them; then, they divide the work into small units and assign it to specific individuals, groups, or departments. As companies reorganize for greater efficiency, more often than not, they are organizing work into teams to handle core processes such as new product development instead of organizing around traditional departments such as marketing and production.

Organizing is important for several reasons. It helps create synergy, whereby the effect of a whole system equals more than that of its parts. It also establishes lines of authority, improves communication, helps avoid duplication of resources, and can improve competitiveness by speeding up decision making. When media company Thompson, a business information giant, purchased Reuters Group, a news agency and financial data group, a new organizational structure was needed in order to merge core services for customers. The new organization resulted in

crisis management or contingency planning an element in planning that deals with potential disasters such as product tampering, oil spills, fire, earthquake, computer virus, or airplane crash

organizing the structuring of resources and activities to accomplish objectives in an efficient and effective manner

four customer divisions: financial data and trading, legal and tax, scientific and health care, and media.[11] Because organizing is so important, we'll take a closer look at it in Chapter 7.

Staffing

staffing
the hiring of people to carry out the work of the organization

downsizing
the elimination of a significant number of employees from an organization

Once managers have determined what work is to be done and how it is to be organized, they must ensure that the organization has enough employees with appropriate skills to do the work. Hiring people to carry out the work of the organization is known as **staffing.** Beyond recruiting people for positions within the firm, managers must determine what skills are needed for specific jobs, how to motivate and train employees, how much to pay, what benefits to provide, and how to prepare employees for higher-level jobs in the firm at a later date. These elements of staffing will be explored in detail in Chapters 9 and 10.

Another aspect of staffing is **downsizing,** the elimination of significant numbers of employees from an organization, which has been a pervasive and much-talked-about trend. Staffing can be outsourced to companies that focus on hiring and managing employees. The Bartech Group bills and manages $1 billion for customers such as General Motors and Verizon.[12] Many firms downsize by outsourcing production, sales, and technical positions to companies in other countries with lower labor costs. Downsizing has helped numerous firms reduce costs quickly and become more profitable (or become profitable after lengthy losses) in a short period of time. Whether it is called downsizing, rightsizing, trimming the fat, or the new reality in business, the implications of downsizing have been dramatic. During the economic recession of 2009, many companies laid off workers to cut costs, and the nationwide unemployment rate climbed above 10 percent.[13]

Downsizing and outsourcing, however, have painful consequences. Obviously, the biggest casualty is those who lose their jobs, along with their incomes, insurance, and pensions. Some find new jobs quickly; others do not. Another victim is the morale of the remaining employees at downsized firms. Those left behind often feel insecure, angry, and sad, and their productivity may decline as a result, the opposite of the effect sought. Managers can expect that 70 to 80 percent of those surviving a downsize will take a "wait-and-see" attitude and will require active leadership. Ten to 15 percent will be openly hostile or try to sabotage change in order to return to the way things were before. The remaining 10 to 15 percent will be the leaders who will try proactively to help make the situation work.[14]

Downsizing workers and outsourcing their jobs isn't a popular move by companies. But it can help a firm rapidly reduce its costs and stay in business.

After a downsizing situation, an effective manager will promote optimism and positive thinking and minimize criticism and fault-finding. Management should also build teamwork and encourage positive group discussions. Honest communication is important during a time of change and will lead to trust. Truthfulness about what has happened and also about future expectations is essential.

Directing

Once the organization has been staffed, management must direct the employees. **Directing** is motivating and leading employees to achieve organizational objectives. Good directing involves telling employees what to do and when to do it through the implementation of deadlines, and then encouraging them to do their work. For example, as a sales manager you would need to learn how to motivate salespersons; provide leadership; teach sales teams to be responsive to customer needs; manage organizational issues; as well as evaluate sales results. Finally, directing also involves determining and administering appropriate rewards and recognition. All managers are involved in directing, but it is especially important for lower-level managers who interact daily with the employees operating the organization. For example, an assembly-line supervisor for Frito-Lay must ensure that her workers know how to use their equipment properly and have the resources needed to carry out their jobs, and she must motivate her workers to achieve their expected output of packaged snacks.

directing
motivating and leading employees to achieve organizational objectives

Managers may motivate employees by providing incentives—such as the promise of a raise or promotion—for them to do a good job. But most workers want more than money from their jobs: They need to know that their employer values their ideas and input. Smart managers, therefore, ask workers to contribute ideas for reducing costs, making equipment more efficient, improving customer service, or even developing new products. This participation makes workers feel important, and the company benefits. Recognition and appreciation are often the best motivators. Employees who understand more about their effect on the financial success of the company may be induced to work harder for that success, and managers who understand the needs and desires of workers can encourage their employees to work harder and more productively. The motivation of employees is discussed in detail in Chapter 9.

Controlling

Planning, organizing, staffing, and directing are all important to the success of an organization, whether its objective is earning a profit or something else. But what happens when a firm fails to reach its goals despite a strong planning effort? **Controlling** is the process of evaluating and correcting activities to keep the organization on course. Control involves five activities: (1) measuring performance, (2) comparing present performance with standards or objectives, (3) identifying deviations from the standards, (4) investigating the causes of deviations, and (5) taking corrective action when necessary.

controlling
the process of evaluating and correcting activities to keep the organization on course

Controlling and planning are closely linked. Planning establishes goals and standards. By monitoring performance and comparing it with standards, managers can determine whether performance is on target. When performance is substandard, management must determine why and take appropriate actions to get the firm back on course. In short, the control function helps managers assess the success of their plans. When the outcomes of plans do not meet expectations, the control process facilitates revision of the plans. Control can take many forms such as visual inspections, testing, and statistical modeling processes. The basic idea is to ensure that operations meet requirements and are satisfactory to reach objectives.

The control process also helps managers deal with problems arising outside the firm. For example, if a firm is the subject of negative publicity, management should use the control process to determine why and to guide the firm's response.

Types of Management

All managers—whether the sole proprietor of a small video store or the hundreds of managers of a large company such as Paramount Pictures—perform the five functions just discussed. In the case of the video store, the owner handles all the functions, but in a large company with more than one manager, responsibilities must be divided and delegated. This division of responsibility is generally achieved by establishing levels of management and areas of specialization—finance, marketing, and so on.

Levels of Management

top managers
the president and other top executives of a business, such as the chief executive officer (CEO), chief financial officer (CFO), and chief operations officer (COO), who have overall responsibility for the organization

As we have hinted, many organizations have multiple levels of management—top management, middle management, and first-line, or supervisory management. These levels form a pyramid, as shown in Figure 6.2. As the pyramid shape implies, there are generally more middle managers than top managers, and still more first-line managers. Very small organizations may have only one manager (typically, the owner), who assumes the responsibilities of all three levels. Large businesses have many managers at each level to coordinate the use of the organization's resources. Managers at all three levels perform all five management functions, but the amount of time they spend on each function varies, as we shall see (Figure 6.3).

Top Management.   In businesses, **top managers** include the president and other top executives, such as the chief executive officer (CEO), chief financial officer (CFO), and chief operations officer (COO), who have overall responsibility for the organization. For example, Steve Jobs, CEO of Apple, manages every aspect of the company, from finance and advertising to product design and corporate strategy. Under Jobs's

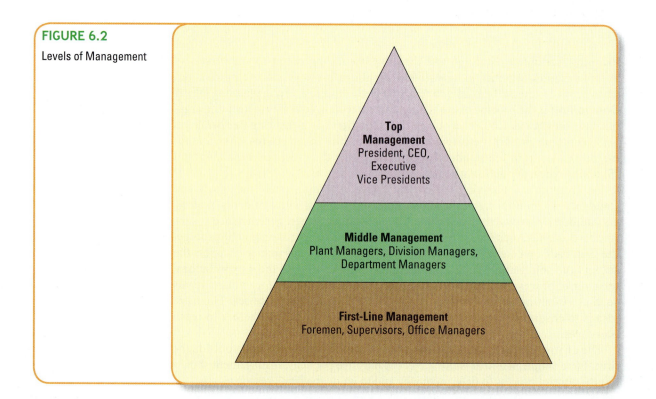

FIGURE 6.2

Levels of Management

Top Management
President, CEO, Executive Vice Presidents

Middle Management
Plant Managers, Division Managers, Department Managers

First-Line Management
Foremen, Supervisors, Office Managers

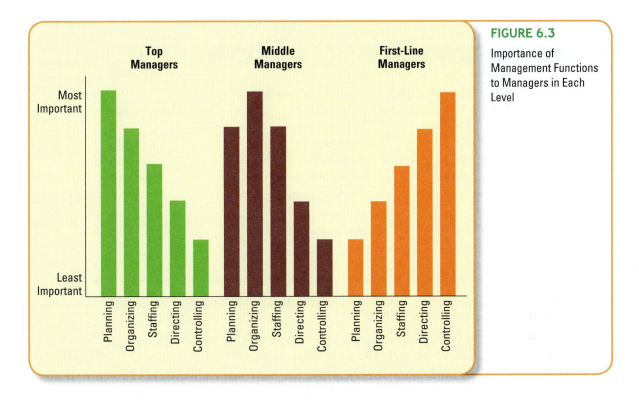

FIGURE 6.3

Importance of Management Functions to Managers in Each Level

direction, Apple revolutionized the computing, music, and telecommunications industries, releasing the iMac, the Mac OS X operating system, iTunes music software, the iPod, and the iPhone. In one decade as CEO, Jobs generated $150 billion for Apple's shareholders.[15] In public corporations, even chief executive officers have a boss—the firm's board of directors. With technological advances accelerating and privacy concerns increasing, some companies are adding a new top management position—chief privacy officer (CPO). The position of privacy officer has grown so widespread that the International Association of Privacy Professional boasts 6,700 members in 52 countries.[16] In government, top management refers to the president, a governor, or a mayor or city manager; in education, a chancellor of a university or a county superintendent of education.

Top-level managers spend most of their time planning. They make the organization's strategic decisions, decisions that focus on an overall scheme or key idea for using resources to take advantage of opportunities. They decide whether to add products, acquire companies, sell unprofitable business segments, and move into foreign markets. Top managers also represent their company to the public and to government regulators.

> **Did You Know?**   Only 3 percent of *Fortune* 500 CEOs are women.[17]

Given the importance and range of top management's decisions, top managers generally have many years of varied experience and command top salaries. In addition to salaries, top managers' compensation packages typically include bonuses, long-term incentive awards, stock, and stock options. Table 6.1 lists the 10 highest paid CEOs including bonuses, stock options and other compensation. Top management may also get perks and special treatment that is criticized by stakeholders.

TABLE 6.1   The 10 Highest Paid CEOs

Rank	CEO	Company	Total Compensation[a] ($ in millions)
1.	Lawrence J. Ellison	Oracle	$556.98
2.	Ray R. Irani	Occidental Petroleum	222.64
3.	John B. Hess	Hess	154.58
4.	Michael D. Watford	Ultra Petroleum	116.93
5.	Mark G. Papa	EOG Resources	90.47
6.	William R. Berkley	WR Berkley	87.45[b]
7.	Matthew K. Rose	Burlington Santa Fe	68.62
8.	Paul J. Evanson	Allegheny Energy	67.26
9.	Hugh Grant	Monsanto	64.60
10.	Robert W. Lane	Deer & Co	61.30

[a]compensation includes salary and bonuses, other compensation, and stock gains.

[b]Prior-year data.

Source: Scott DeCarlo and Brian Zajac, "CEO Compensation," *Forbes,* April 22, 2009, http://www.forbes.com/lists/2009/12/best-boss-09_CEO-Compensation_Rank .html (accessed March 4, 2010).

Compensation committees are increasingly working with boards of directors and CEOs to attempt to keep pay in line with performance in order to benefit stockholders and key stakeholders. The majority of major companies cite their concern about attracting capable leadership for the CEO and other top executive positions in their organizations. Sixty-seven percent are concerned about their ability to attract and retain the most competent leadership. Many companies are attempting to curb high CEO pay by connecting compensation and job performance. James P. Gorman, CEO of Morgan Stanley, received a compensation package based on a variety of stocks and options. The total package could be worth almost $9 million. Many of the units are tied to his performance, such as meeting financial and corporate goals and remaining at Morgan Stanley for the length of his contract.[18] Successful management translates into happy stockholders who are willing to compensate their top executives fairly and in line with performance.

Workforce diversity is an important issue in today's corporations. Effective managers at enlightened corporations have found that diversity is good for workers and for the bottom line. Putting together different kinds of people to solve problems often results in better solutions. Betsy Holden, CEO of Kraft Foods, said, "When we look at the composition of teams within our company, we have found that those with a variety of perspectives are simply the most creative."[19] A diverse workforce is better at making decisions regarding issues related to consumer diversity. W. Garrison Jackson runs a multicultural public relations and advertising agency that helps corporate America reach black, Hispanic, Asian, and other minority consumers. These fastgrowing demographic groups are key target markets for many companies including Colgate-Palmolive, General Mills, and IBM.[20] Managers from companies devoted to workforce diversity devised five rules that make diversity recruiting work (see Table 6.2). Diversity is explored in greater detail in Chapter 10.

Middle Management.   Rather than making strategic decisions about the whole organization, **middle managers** are responsible for tactical planning that will implement the general guidelines established by top management. Thus, their responsibility is more narrowly focused than that of top managers. Middle managers

middle managers
those members of an organization responsible for the tactical planning that implements the general guidelines established by top management

Rule	Action	
1. Get everyone involved.	Educate all employees on the tangible benefits of diversity recruiting to garner support and enthusiasm for those initiatives.	**TABLE 6.2** Five Rules of Successful Diversity Recruiting
2. Showcase your diversity.	Prospective employees are not likely to become excited about joining your company just because you say that your company is diversity-friendly; they need to see it.	
3. Work with diversity groups within your community.	By supporting community-based diversity organizations, your company will generate the priceless word-of-mouth publicity that will lead qualified diversity candidates to your company.	
4. Spend money.	If you are serious about diversity recruiting, you will need to spend some money getting your message out to the right places.	
5. Sell, sell, sell—and measure your return on investment.	Employers need to sell their company to prospective diversity employees and present them with a convincing case as to why their company is a good fit for the diversity candidate.	

Source: Adapted from Juan Rodriguez, "The Five Rules of Successful Diversity Recruiting," *Diversityjobs.com,* http://www.diversityjobs.com/Rules-of-Successful-Diversity-Recruiting (accessed February 25, 2010).

are involved in the specific operations of the organization and spend more time organizing than other managers. In business, plant managers, division managers, and department managers make up middle management. The product manager for laundry detergent at a consumer products manufacturer, the department chairperson in a university, and the head of a state public health department are all middle managers. The ranks of middle managers have been shrinking as more and more companies downsize to be more productive.

First-Line Management.   Most people get their first managerial experience as **first-line managers,** those who supervise workers and the daily operations of the organization. They are responsible for implementing the plans established by middle management and directing workers' daily performance on the job. They spend most of their time directing and controlling. Common titles for first-line managers are foreman, supervisor, and office manager.

first-line managers
those who supervise both workers and the daily operations of an organization

Areas of Management
At each level, there are managers who specialize in the basic functional areas of business: finance, production and operations, human resources (personnel), marketing, and administration.

Financial Management.   **Financial managers** focus on obtaining the money needed for the successful operation of the organization and using that money in accordance with organizational goals. Among the responsibilities of financial managers are projecting income and expenses over a specified period, determining short- and long-term financing needs and finding sources of financing to fill those needs, identifying and selecting appropriate ways to invest extra funds, monitoring the flow of financial resources, and protecting the financial resources of the organization. A financial manager at Ford, for example, may be asked to analyze the costs and revenues of a car model to determine its contribution to Ford's profitability.

financial managers
those who focus on obtaining needed funds for the successful operation of an organization and using those funds to further organizational goals

All organizations must have adequate financial resources to acquire the physical and human resources that are necessary to create goods and services. Consequently, financial resource management is of the utmost importance.

Production and Operations Management.
Production and operations managers develop and administer the activities involved in transforming resources into goods, services, and ideas ready for the marketplace. Production and operations managers are typically involved in planning and designing production facilities, purchasing raw materials and supplies, managing inventory, scheduling processes to meet demand, and ensuring that products meet quality standards. Because no business can exist without the production of goods and services, production and operations managers are vital to an organization's success. Production can be a complicated process because companies, no matter what the size, must balance different considerations such as cost, performance, extra features, and styling. For example, the Tesla Roadster Sport is faster than the Porsche Boxter Spyder, but it does not handle as well. Both companies face the challenges inherent in producing products that balance high performance and maintaining quality standards in order to gain competitive advantage from their designs, production, and operations excellence. An additional challenge to small companies is to do all these things while remaining profitable.[21]

production and operations managers
those who develop and administer the activities involved in transforming resources into goods, services, and ideas ready for the marketplace

Human Resources Management.
Human resources managers handle the staffing function and deal with employees in a formalized manner. Once known as personnel managers, they determine an organization's human resource needs; recruit and hire new employees; develop and administer employee benefits, training, and performance appraisal programs; and deal with government regulations concerning employment practices. For example, some companies recognize that their employees' health affects their costs. Therefore, more progressive companies provide health care facilities and outside health club memberships, encourage proper nutrition, and discourage smoking in an effort to improve employee health and lower the costs of providing health care benefits.

human resources managers
those who handle the staffing function and deal with employees in a formalized manner

Marketing Management.
Marketing managers are responsible for planning, pricing, and promoting products and making them available to customers through distribution. The marketing manager who oversees Sony televisions, for example, must make decisions regarding a new television's size, features, name, price, and packaging, as well as plan what type of stores to distribute the television through and the advertising campaign that will introduce the new television to consumers. General Motors must determine a way to make the vehicles that consumers want to buy while still turning a profit.[22] This will require top management to get rank-and-file employees to understand and support a fleet of green, eco-friendly cars, including the Volt, a plug-in hybrid launched in 2010.[23] Within the realm of marketing, there are several areas of specialization: product development and management, pricing, promotion, and distribution. Specific jobs are found in areas such as marketing research, advertising, personal selling, retailing, telemarketing, and Internet marketing.

marketing managers
those who are responsible for planning, pricing, and promoting products and making them available to customers

Information Technology (IT) Management.

Information technology (IT) managers are responsible for implementing, maintaining, and controlling technology applications in business, such as computer networks. Google, the world's largest online search engine, employs more than 10,000 employees, many of whom are IT managers. Google searches for IT managers and employees who are enthusiastic about their field and Google's products. To keep their engineers motivated, Google allows them to spend up to 20 percent of their time working on personal projects.[24] One major task in IT management is securing computer systems from unauthorized users while making the system easy to use for employees, suppliers, and others who have legitimate reason to access the system. Another crucial task is protecting the systems' data, even during a disaster such as a fire. IT managers are also responsible for teaching and helping employees use technology resources efficiently through training and support. At many companies, some aspects of IT management are outsourced to third-party firms that can perform this function expertly and efficiently.

Administrative Management.

Administrative managers are not specialists; rather they manage an entire business or a major segment of a business. Such managers coordinate the activities of specialized managers, which would include

information technology (IT) managers
those who are responsible for implementing, maintaining, and controlling technology applications in business, such as computer networks

administrative managers
those who manage an entire business or a major segment of a business; they are not specialists but coordinate the activities of specialized managers

TABLE 6.3   Managerial Roles

Type of Role	Specific Role	Examples of Role Activities
Decisional	Entrepreneur	Commit organizational resources to develop innovative goods and services; decide to expand internationally to obtain new customers for the organization's products.
	Disturbance handler	Move quickly to take corrective action to deal with unexpected problems facing the organization from the external environment, such as a crisis like an oil spill, or from the internal environment, such as producing faulty goods or services.
	Resource allocator	Allocate organizational resources among different functions and departments of the organization; set budgets and salaries of middle and first-level managers.
	Negotiator	Work with suppliers, distributors, and labor unions to reach agreements about the quality and price of input, technical, and human resources; work with other organizations to establish agreements to pool resources to work on joint projects.
Informational	Monitor	Evaluate the performance of managers in different functions and take corrective action to improve their performance; watch for changes occurring in the external and internal environment that may affect the organization in the future.
	Disseminator	Inform employees about changes taking place in the external and internal environment that will affect them and the organization; communicate to employees the organization's vision and purpose.
	Spokesperson	Launch a national advertising campaign to promote new goods and services; give a speech to inform the local community about the organization's future intentions.
Interpersonal	Figurehead	Outline future organizational goals to employees at company meetings; open a new corporate headquarters building; state the organization's ethical guidelines and the principles of behavior employees are to follow in their dealings with customers and suppliers.
	Leader	Provide an example for employees to follow; give direct commands and orders to subordinates; make decisions concerning the use of human and technical resources; mobilize employee support for specific organizational goals.
	Liaison	Coordinate the work of managers in different departments; establish alliances between different organizations to share resources to produce new goods and services.

Source: Gareth R. Jones and Jennifer M. George, *Essentials of Contemporary Management* (Burr Ridge, IL: McGraw-Hill/Irwin, 2007, 3rd Edition), p. 14.

marketing managers, production managers, and financial managers. Because of the broad nature of their responsibilities, administrative managers are often called general managers. However, this does not mean that administrative managers lack expertise in any particular area. Many top executives have risen through the ranks of financial management, production and operations management, or marketing management; but most top managers are actually administrative managers, employing skills in all areas of management.

Skills Needed by Managers

Managers are typically evaluated using the metrics of how effective and efficient they are. Managing effectively and efficiently requires certain skills—leadership, technical expertise, conceptual skills, analytical skills, and human relations skills. Table 6.3 describes some of the roles managers may fulfill.

Leadership

leadership
the ability to influence employees to work toward organizational goals

Leadership is the ability to influence employees to work toward organizational goals. Strong leaders manage and pay attention to the culture of their organizations and the needs of their customers. Table 6.4 offers some tips for successful leadership while Table 6.5 lists the world's 10 most admired companies and their CEOs. The

TABLE 6.4

Seven Tips for Successful Leadership

- Build effective and responsive interpersonal relationships.
- Communicate effectively—in person, print, e-mail, etc.
- Build the team and enable employees to collaborate effectively.
- Understand the financial aspects of the business.
- Know how to create an environment in which people experience positive morale and recognition.
- Lead by example.
- Help people grow and develop.

Source: Susan M. Heathfield, "Seven Tips About Successful Management," *About.com*, http://humanresources.about.com/cs/managementissues/qt/mgmtsuccess.htm (accessed February 25, 2010)

TABLE 6.5

America's Most Admired Companies and Their CEOs

Company	Chief Executive Officer
Apple	Steve Jobs
Google	Eric Schmidt
Berkshire Hathaway	Warren Buffett
Johnson & Johnson	William Weldon
Amazon.com	Jeff Bezos
Procter & Gamble	Alan Lafley
Toyota Motor	Akio Toyoda
Goldman Sachs	Lloyd Blankfein
Walmart	Mike Duke
Coca-Cola	Muhtar Kent

Source: Adapted from "America's Most Admired Companies 2010," *Fortune*, http://money.cnn.com/magazines/fortune/mostadmired/2010/index.html (accessed March 4, 2010).

Going Green

It Isn't Easy Being Green at Nike

Sustainable products are usually great for business, but Nike discovered going green doesn't always work. In 2005, the company launched "Considered," a line of eco-friendly shoes made from hemp. Quickly nicknamed "Air Hobbits," the line flopped. Nike customers wanted high-tech shoes to make them perform well, not to save the planet. However, the company still wanted to be more sustainable, so Nike is going green on the sly.

In 1993, Nike launched the Reuse-A-Shoe Program, which aimed to reduce the company's environmental footprint and decrease the waste Nike sent to landfills. Old shoes, along with excess materials from manufacturing, are recycled into "Nike Grind," a material used to create sports surfaces such as basketball courts and running tracks. The Reuse-A-Shoe Program is now linked to the National Recycling Coalition and has collected more than 20 million shoes.

Nike also has a corporate vision of eventually creating zero waste and providing products that can be continuously reused. Today, the company uses recycled and renewable materials as well as materials that reduce toxic output, such as organic cotton. Nike also uses environmentally friendly production techniques to produce its shoes. The Air Jordan is made using a faster, more efficient sewing machine that saves energy. The soles of Air Jordans are made from ground-up sneakers, and the manufacturing process prevents the use of excess plastic. The best part? The new Air Jordans sell so well that Nike now has a line of eco-friendly basketball, football, soccer, tennis, and running shoes.[25]

Discussion Questions

1. Why did the "Considered" line fail?
2. Shoes and textiles are notoriously polluting industries. What has Nike done to improve its reputation as an environmentally friendly company?
3. What decisions have Nike managers made to improve the reputation of the company and increase sales?

list is compiled annually for *Fortune* magazine by executives and analysts who grade companies according to nine attributes, including quality of management.

Managers often can be classified into three types based on their leadership style. *Autocratic leaders* make all the decisions and then tell employees what must be done and how to do it. They generally use their authority and economic rewards to get employees to comply with their directions. *Democratic leaders* involve their employees in decisions. The manager presents a situation and encourages his or her subordinates to express opinions and contribute ideas. The manager then considers the employees' points of view and makes the decision. *Free-rein leaders* let their employees work without much interference. The manager sets performance standards and allows employees to find their own ways to meet them. For this style to be effective, employees must know what the standards are, and they must be motivated to attain them. The free-rein style of leadership can be a powerful motivator because it demonstrates a great deal of trust and confidence in the employee.

The effectiveness of the autocratic, democratic, and free-rein styles depends on several factors. One consideration is the type of employees. An autocratic style of leadership is generally best for stimulating unskilled, unmotivated employees; highly skilled, trained, and motivated employees may respond better to democratic or free-rein leadership styles. Employees who have been involved in decision making generally require less supervision than those not similarly involved. Other considerations are the manager's abilities and the situation itself. When a situation requires quick decisions, an autocratic style of leadership may be best because the manager does not have to consider input from a lot of people. If a special task force must be set up to solve a quality-control problem, a normally democratic manager may give free rein to the task force. Many managers, however, are unable to use more than one style of leadership. Some are incapable allowing their subordinates to participate in decision making, let alone make any decisions. Thus, what leadership style is "best" depends on specific circumstances, and effective managers will strive to adapt their leadership style as circumstances warrant. Many organizations offer programs to develop goal leadership skills. When plans fail, very often leaders are held responsible for what goes wrong. For example, banking giant Citigroup's CFO Charles Prince resigned after the subprime credit meltdown forced Citigroup to write down billions of dollars. While at Citigroup, Prince had focused on improving ethics. He also supported a corporate creed that leaders should "accept accountability for our failures."[26]

Technical Expertise

technical expertise
the specialized knowledge and training needed to perform jobs that are related to particular areas of management

Managers need **technical expertise,** the specialized knowledge and training required to perform jobs related to their area of management. Accounting managers need to be able to perform accounting jobs, and production managers need to be able to perform production jobs. Although a production manager may not actually perform a job, he or she needs technical expertise to train employees, answer questions, provide guidance, and solve problems. Technical skills are most needed by first-line managers and least critical to top-level managers.

Today, most organizations rely on computers to perform routine data processing, simplify complex calculations, organize and maintain vast amounts of information to communicate, and help managers make sound decisions. For this reason, most managers have found computer expertise to be an essential skill in doing their jobs well.

Conceptual Skills

conceptual skills
the ability to think in abstract terms and to see how parts fit together to form the whole

Conceptual skills, the ability to think in abstract terms, and to see how parts fit together to form the whole, are needed by all managers, but particularly top-level managers. Top management must be able to evaluate continually where the company will be in the future. Conceptual skills also involve the ability to think creatively. Recent scientific research has revealed that creative thinking, which is behind the development of many innovative products and ideas, including fiber optics and compact disks, can be learned. As a result, IBM, AT&T, GE, Hewlett-Packard, Intel, and other top U.S. firms hire creative consultants to teach their managers how to think creatively.

Analytical Skills

analytical skills
the ability to identify relevant issues, recognize their importance, understand the relationships between them, and perceive the underlying causes of a situation

Analytical skills refer to the ability to identify relevant issues and recognize their importance, understand the relationships between them, and perceive the underlying causes of a situation. When managers have identified critical factors and causes, they can take appropriate action. All managers need to think logically, but this skill is probably most important to the success of top-level managers. To be analytical, it is necessary to think about a broad range of issues and to weigh different options before taking action. Because analytical skills are so important, questions that require analytical skills are often a part of job interviews. Questions such as "Tell me how you would resolve a problem at work if you had access to a large amount of data?" may be part of the interview process. The answer would require the interviewee to try to explain how to sort data to find relevant facts that could resolve the issue. Analytical thinking is required in complex or difficult situations where the solution is often not clear. Resolving ethical issues often requires analytical skills.

Human Relations Skills

human relations skills
the ability to deal with people, both inside and outside the organization

People skills, or **human relations skills,** are the ability to deal with people, both inside and outside the organization. Those who can relate to others, communicate

Flight attendant David Holmes became a YouTube sensation by rapping passenger instructions on Southwest Airlines flights. Southwest Airlines' managers and employees are well known for their excellent human relations skills and making the workplace fun.

well with others, understand the needs of others, and show a true appreciation for others are generally more successful than managers who lack such skills. People skills are especially important in hospitals, airline companies, banks, and other organizations that provide services. For example, at Southwest Airlines, every new employee attends "You, Southwest and Success," a day-long class designed to teach employees about the airline and its reputation for impeccable customer service. All employees in management positions at Southwest take mandatory leadership classes that address skills related to listening, staying in touch with employees, and handling change without compromising values.

Where Do Managers Come From?

Good managers are not born; they are made. An organization acquires managers in three ways: promoting employees from within, hiring managers from other organizations, and hiring managers straight out of universities.

Promoting people within the organization into management positions tends to increase motivation by showing employees that those who work hard and are competent can advance in the company. Internal promotion also provides managers who are already familiar with the company's goals and problems. Procter & Gamble prefers to promote managers from within, which creates managers who are familiar with the company's products and policies and builds company loyalty. Promoting from within, however,

General Electric's excellent managerial training programs are renowned around the world. The company knows good managers aren't born. They are made.

can lead to problems: It may limit innovation. The new manager may continue the practices and policies of previous managers. Thus it is vital for companies—even companies committed to promotion from within—to hire outside people from time to time to bring fresh ideas to the table.

Finding managers with the skills, knowledge, and experience required to run an organization or department can be difficult. Specialized executive employment agencies—sometimes called headhunters, recruiting managers, or executive search firms—can help locate candidates from other companies. The downside is that even though outside people can bring fresh ideas to a company, hiring them may cause resentment among existing employees as well as involve greater expense in relocating an individual to another city or state.

Schools and universities provide a large pool of potential managers, and entry-level applicants can be screened for their developmental potential. People with specialized management skills such as those with an MBA (master's of business administration) degree may be good candidates. Business students in the 21st century must remain flexible during their job searches. Before applying for a job, graduates should understand the company, the people, and the company's core values to ascertain whether they would be a good fit. Students may not have the exact skills for which the company is searching, but if they fit well with the culture, they can be trained. On-the-job training and socialization can help new recruits achieve success in their position and can help them reach their objectives. Finding employees who are trainable and a good fit with corporate culture means that organizations have a workforce staffed with potential future managers. Businesses that are recovering from the most recent economic recession should be willing to embrace new ideas and new employees willing to undergo change.

Decision Making

Managers make many different kinds of decisions, such as the hours in a workday, which employees to hire, what products to introduce, and what price to charge for a product. Decision making is important in all management functions and at all levels, whether the decisions are on a strategic, tactical, or operational level. A systematic approach using the following six steps usually leads to more effective decision making: (1) recognizing and defining the decision situation, (2) developing options to resolve the situation, (3) analyzing the options, (4) selecting the best option, (5) implementing the decision, and (6) monitoring the consequences of the decision (Figure 6.4).

FIGURE 6.4

Steps in the Decision-Making Process

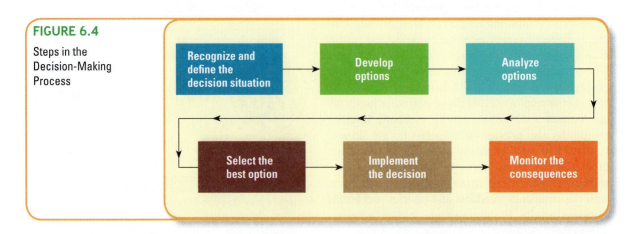

Consider Ethics and Social Responsibility
Countrywide's Subprime Loans

Countrywide Financial was the largest provider of home loans in the country before becoming involved in the subprime mortgage scandal. At first, Countrywide's offering of subprime loans looked like a good way to help lower-income individuals achieve the American dream of owning a house. Yet due to the decisions of reckless company officials, Countrywide is now thought to be a major instigator of the 2008–2009 financial crisis.

Much of its culpability stems from risky and deceptive business practices. Numerous "liar loans" have been traced back to the company. Liar loans were created when consumers overstated their income on home loan applications, some by at least 50 percent. They were a major factor in the chain reaction leading to the financial crisis, and experts estimate that losses from such loans could total about $100 billion. Many believe the company knowingly issued these liar loans in exchange for quick profits. Countrywide officials, including CEO Angelo Mozilo, also sold hundreds of millions of dollars in stock and stock options, possibly due to insider information.

Mozilo himself is accused of taking $10 million more than what was disclosed in reports, which, if true, would make the company guilty of inaccurate financial reporting. These unethical actions make it more likely that company officials knew Countrywide was engaging in dishonest mortgage practices. As a result of its major losses, the company started to flounder. In 2008, Bank of America agreed to purchase it for $4 billion, a fraction of what the company was worth. Bank of America announced that it would not retain the Countrywide name or logo.[26]

Discussion Questions
1. Which management functions did Countrywide fail to implement properly (planning, organizing, staffing, directing, or controlling)?
2. How could top management better manage risks so as to prevent a Countrywide-type scandal?
3. What went wrong with decision making at Countrywide?

Recognizing and Defining the Decision Situation

The first step in decision making is recognizing and defining the situation. The situation may be negative—for example, huge losses on a particular product—or positive—for example, an opportunity to increase sales.

Situations calling for small-scale decisions often occur without warning. Situations requiring large-scale decisions, however, generally occur after some warning signs. Effective managers pay attention to such signals. Declining profits, small-scale losses in previous years, inventory buildup, and retailers' unwillingness to stock a product are signals that may foreshadow huge losses to come. If managers pay attention to such signals, problems can be contained.

Once a situation has been recognized, management must define it. Losses reveal a problem—for example, a failing product. One manager may define the situation as a product quality problem; another may define it as a change in consumer preference. These two viewpoints may lead to vastly different solutions. The first manager, for example, may seek new sources of raw materials of better quality. The second manager may believe that the product has reached the end of its lifespan and decide to discontinue it. This example emphasizes the importance of carefully defining the problem rather than jumping to conclusions.

Developing Options

Once the decision situation has been recognized and defined, the next step is to develop a list of possible courses of action. The best lists include both standard and creative plans. As a general rule, more time and expertise are devoted to the development stage of decision making when the decision is of major importance. When the decision is of lesser importance, less time and expertise will be spent on this stage. Options may be developed individually, by teams, or through analysis of similar situations in comparable organizations. Creativity is a very important part of selecting the most viable option. Creativity depends on new and useful ideas, regardless of where they originate or the method used to create them. The best option can range from a required solution to an identified problem a to a volunteered solution, to an observed problem by an outside work group member.[27]

Analyzing Options

After developing a list of possible courses of action, management should analyze the practicality and appropriateness of each option. An option may be deemed impractical because of a lack of financial resources, legal restrictions, ethical and social responsibility considerations, authority constraints, technological constraints, economic limitations, or simply a lack of information and expertise. For example, a small computer manufacturer may recognize an opportunity to introduce a new type of computer but lack the financial resources to do so. Other options may be more practical for the computer company: It may consider selling its technology to another computer company that has adequate resources, or it may allow itself to be purchased by a larger company that can introduce the new technology.

When assessing appropriateness, the decision maker should consider whether the proposed option adequately addresses the situation. When analyzing the consequences of an option, managers should consider its impact on the situation and on the organization as a whole. For example, when considering a price cut to boost sales, management must think about the consequences of the action on the organization's cash flow and consumers' reaction to the price change.

Selecting the Best Option

When all courses of action have been analyzed, management must select the best one. Selection is often a subjective procedure because many situations do not lend themselves to quantitative analysis. Of course, it is not always necessary to select only one option and reject all others; it may be possible to select and use a combination of several options. William Wrigley Jr. made a decision to sell his firm to Mars for $23 billion. The firm was founded by his great-grandfather in 1891, but hard times forced Wrigley to take what was considered to be the best option. This option was to create the Mars-Wrigley firm, currently the world's largest confectionary company with a distribution network in 180 countries.[28] A different set of choices would have been available to the company had it been able to purchase Hershey for $12 billion a few years earlier.

Implementing the Decision

To deal with the situation at hand, the selected option or options must be put into action. Implementation can be fairly simple or very complex, depending on the nature of the decision. Effective implementation of a decision to abandon a product, close a plant, purchase a new business, or something similar requires planning. For example, when a product is dropped, managers must decide how to handle distributors and customers and what to do with the idle production facility. Additionally, they should anticipate resistance from people within the organization (people tend to resist change because they fear the unknown). Finally, management should be ready to deal with the unexpected consequences. No matter how well planned implementation is, unforseen problems will arise. Management must be ready to address these situations when they occur.

Monitoring the Consequences

After managers have implemented the decision, they must determine whether it has accomplished the desired result. Without proper monitoring, the consequences of decisions may not be known quickly enough to make efficient changes. If the desired result is achieved, management can reasonably conclude that it made a good choice. If the desired result is not achieved, further analysis is warranted. Was the decision simply wrong, or did the situation change? Should some other option have been implemented?

If the desired result is not achieved, management may discover that the situation was incorrectly defined from the beginning. That may require starting the decision-making process all over again. Finally, management may determine that the decision was good even though the desired results have not yet shown up, or it may determine a flaw in the decision's implementation. In the latter case, management would not change the decision but would change the way in which it is implemented.

The Reality of Management

Management is not a cut-and-dried process. There is no mathematical formula for managing an organization and achieving organizational goals, although many managers passionately wish for one! Managers plan, organize, staff, direct, and control, but management expert John P. Kotter says even these functions can be boiled down to two basic activities:

1. Figuring out what to do despite uncertainty, great diversity, and an enormous amount of potentially relevant information, and
2. Getting things done through a large and diverse set of people despite having little direct control over most of them.[29]

Managers spend as much as 75 percent of their time working with others—not only with subordinates but with bosses, people outside their hierarchy at work, and people outside the organization itself. In these interactions they discuss anything and everything remotely connected with their business.

Managers spend a lot of time establishing and updating an agenda of goals and plans for carrying out their responsibilities. An **agenda** contains both specific and vague items, covering short-term goals and long-term objectives. Like a calendar, an agenda helps the manager figure out what must be done and how to get it done to meet the objectives set by the organization. Technology tools such as smart phones can help managers manage their agendas, contacts, and time.

Managers also spend a lot of time **networking**—building relationships and sharing information with colleagues who can help them achieve the items on their agendas. Managers spend much of their time communicating with a variety of people and participating in activities that on the surface do not seem to have much to do with the goals of their organization. Nevertheless, these activities are crucial to getting the job done. Networks are not limited to immediate subordinates and bosses; they include other people in the company as well as customers, suppliers, and friends. These contacts provide managers with information and advice on diverse topics. Managers ask, persuade, and even intimidate members of their network in order to get information and to get things done. Networking helps managers carry

agenda
a calender, containing both specific and vague items, that covers short-term goals and long-term objectives

networking
the building of relationships and sharing of information with colleagues who can help managers achieve the items on their agendas

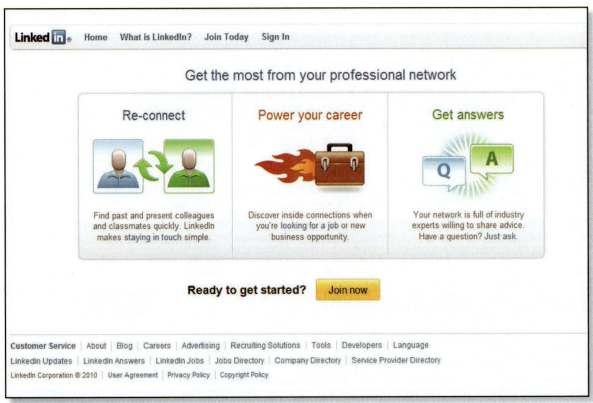

Web sites like LinkedIn are helping managers and employees network with one another to achieve their professional.goals.

out their responsibilities. Andrea Nierenberg, independent business consultant and founder of Nierenberg Group Inc., has been called a "networking success story" by *The Wall Street Journal.* She writes three notes a day: one to a client, one to a friend, and one to a prospective client. She maintains a database of 3,000 contacts. However, she believes that it isn't how many people you know, but how many you have helped and who know you well enough to recommend you that really count. Opportunity can knock almost anywhere with such extensive networking. Grateful for numerous referrals to her friends, Nierenberg's dentist introduced her to a Wall Street executive who happened to be in the dentist's office at the same time as Nierenberg. She followed up on the meeting and later landed four consulting projects at the executive's firm.[30] Her clients include Citigroup, Time Inc., TIAA-CREF, Food Network, Coach, and Tiffany.[31]

Finally, managers spend a great deal of time confronting the complex and difficult challenges of the business world today. Some of these challenges relate to rapidly changing technology (especially in production and information processing), increased scrutiny of individual and corporate ethics and social responsibility, the changing nature of the workforce, new laws and regulations, increased global competition and more challenging foreign markets, declining educational standards (which may limit the skills and knowledge of the future labor and customer pool), and time itself—that is, making the best use of it. But such diverse issues cannot simply be plugged into a computer program that supplies correct, easy-to-apply solutions. It is only through creativity and imagination that managers can make effective decisions that benefit their organizations.

So You Want to Be a Manager
What Kind of Manager Do You Want to Be?

Managers are needed in a wide variety of organizations. Experts suggest that employment will increase by millions of jobs by 2016. But the requirements for the jobs become more demanding with every passing year— with the speed of technology and communication increasing by the day, and the stress of global commerce increasing pressures to perform. However, if you like a challenge and if you have the right kind of personality, management remains a viable field. Even as companies are forced to restructure, management remains a vital role in business. In fact, the Bureau of Labor Statistics predicts that management positions in public relations, marketing and advertising are set to increase around 12% overall between 2006 and 2016. Financial managers will be in even more demand, with jobs increasing 13% in the same time period. Computer and IT managers will continue to be in strong demand, with the number of jobs increasing 16% between 2006 and 2016.[32]

Salaries for managerial positions remain strong overall. While pay can vary significantly depending on your level of experience, the firm where you work, and the region of the country where you live, below is a list of the nationwide average incomes for a variety of different managers:

Chief Executives: $151,370
Computer and Information Systems Managers: $113, 880
Financial Managers: $106,200
Marketing Managers: $113,400
Human Resource Managers: $99,810
Operations Managers: $103,780
Medical/ Health Services Managers: $84,980
Administrative Managers: $76,370
Sales Managers: $106,790[33]

In short, if you want to be a manager, there are opportunities in almost every field. There may be fewer middle management positions available in firms, but managers remain a vital part of most industries and will continue to be long into the future—especially as navigating global business becomes ever more complex.

Review Your Understanding

Define management, and explain its role in the achievement of organizational objectives.

Management is a process designed to achieve an organization's objectives by using its resources effectively and efficiently in a changing environment. Managers make decisions about the use of the organization's resources and are concerned with planning, organizing, staffing, directing, and controlling the organization's activities so as to reach its objectives.

Describe the major functions of management.

Planning is the process of determining the organization's objectives and deciding how to accomplish them. Organizing is the structuring of resources and activities to accomplish those objectives efficiently and effectively. Staffing obtains people with the necessary skills to carry out the work of the company. Directing is motivating and leading employees to achieve organizational objectives. Controlling is the process of evaluating and correcting activities to keep the organization on course.

Distinguish among three levels of management and the concerns of managers at each level.

Top management is responsible for the whole organization and focuses primarily on strategic planning. Middle management develops plans for specific operating areas and carries out the general guidelines set by top management. First-line, or supervisory, management supervises the workers and day-to-day operations. Managers can also be categorized as to their area of responsibility: finance, production and operations, human resources, marketing, or administration.

Specify the skills managers need in order to be successful.

To be successful, managers need leadership skills (the ability to influence employees to work toward organizational goals), technical expertise (the specialized knowledge and training needed to perform a job), conceptual skills (the ability to think in abstract terms and see how parts fit together to form the whole), analytical skills (the ability to identify relevant issues and recognize their importance, understand the relationships between issues, and perceive the underlying causes of a situation), and human relations (people) skills.

Summarize the systematic approach to decision making used by many business managers.

A systematic approach to decision making follows these steps: recognizing and defining the situation, developing options, analyzing options, selecting the best option, implementing the decision, and monitoring the consequences.

Recommend a new strategy to revive a struggling business.

Using the decision-making process described in this chapter, analyze the struggling company's problems described in "Solve the Dilemma" on page 204 and formulate a strategy to turn the company around and aim it toward future success.

Revisit the World of Business

1. What characteristics have helped Ursula Burns become such a great success?
2. What are some of the challenges to continued growth and success that Xerox faces?
3. If you were Ursula Burns, what decisions would you make to help Xerox remain a leader in its industry?

Learn the Terms

administrative managers   191
agenda   199
analytical skills   194
conceptual skills   194
controlling   185
crisis management or contingency planning   183
directing   185
downsizing   184
financial managers   189
first-line managers   189
human relations skills   194
human resources managers   190
information technology (IT) managers   191
leadership   192
management   178
managers   178
marketing managers   190
middle managers   188
mission   179
networking   199
operational plans   182
organizing   183
planning   179
production and operations managers   190
staffing   184
strategic plans   181
tactical plans   181
technical expertise   194
top managers   186

Check Your Progress

1. Why is management so important, and what is its purpose?
2. Explain why the American Heart Association would need management, even though its goal is not profit related.
3. Why must a company have financial resources before it can use human and physical resources?
4. Name the five functions of management, and briefly describe each function.
5. Identify the three levels of management. What is the focus of managers at each level?
6. In what areas can managers specialize? From what area do top managers typically come?
7. What skills do managers need? Give examples of how managers use these skills to do their jobs.
8. What are three styles of leadership? Describe situations in which each style would be appropriate.
9. Explain the steps in the decision-making process.
10. What is the mathematical formula for perfect management? What do managers spend most of their time doing?

Get Involved

1. Give examples of the activities that each of the following managers might be involved in if he or she worked for the Coca-Cola Company:

   Financial manager
   Production and operations manager
   Personnel manager
   Marketing manager
   Administrative manager
   Information technology manager
   Foreman

2. Interview a small sample of managers, attempting to include representatives from all three levels and all areas of management. Discuss their daily activities and relate these activities to the management functions of planning, organizing, staffing, directing, and controlling. What skills do the managers say they need to carry out their tasks?

3. You are a manager of a firm that manufactures conventional ovens. Over the past several years, sales of many of your products have declined; this year, your losses may be quite large. Using the steps of the decision-making process, briefly describe how you arrive at a strategy for correcting the situation.

Build Your Skills

FUNCTIONS OF MANAGEMENT

Background:
Although the text describes each of the five management functions separately, you learned that these five functions are interrelated, and managers sometimes perform two or more of them at the same time. Here you will broaden your perspective of how these functions occur simultaneously in management activities.

Task:

1. Imagine that you are the manager in each scenario described in the table below and you have to decide which management function(s) to use in each.

2. Mark your answers using the following codes:

Codes	Management Functions
P	Planning
O	Organizing
S	Staffing
D	Directing
C	Controlling

No.	Scenario	Answer(s)
1	Your group's work is centered around a project that is due in two months. Although everyone is working on the project, you have observed your employees involved in what you believe is excessive socializing and other time-filling behaviors. You decide to meet with the group to have them help you break down the project into smaller subprojects with mini-deadlines. You believe this will help keep the group members focused on the project and that the quality of the finished project will then reflect the true capabilities of your group.	
2	Your first impression of the new group you'll be managing is not too great. You tell your friend at dinner after your first day on the job: "Looks like I got a baby sitting job instead of a management job."	
3	You call a meeting of your work group and begin it by letting them know that a major procedure used by the work group for the past two years is being significantly revamped, and your department will have to phase in the change during the next six weeks. You proceed by explaining to them the reasoning your boss gave you for this change. You then say, "Let's take the next 5 to 10 minutes to let you voice your reactions to this change." After 10 minutes elapse with the majority of comments being critical of the change, you say: "I appreciate each of you sharing your reactions; and I, too, recognize that *all* change creates problems. The way I see it, however, is that we can spend the remaining 45 minutes of our meeting focusing on why we don't want the change and why we don't think it's necessary; or we can work together to come up with viable solutions to solve the problems that implementing this change will most likely	

	create." After about five more minutes of comments being exchanged, the consensus of the group is that the remainder of the meeting needs to be focused on how to deal with the potential problems the group anticipates having to deal with as the new procedure is implemented.	
4	You are preparing for the annual budget allocation meetings to be held in the plant manager's office next week. You are determined to present a strong case to support your department getting money for some high-tech equipment that will help your employees do their jobs better. You will stand firm against any suggestions of budget cuts in your area.	
5	Early in your career you learned an important lesson about employee selection. One of the nurses on your floor unexpectedly quit. The other nurses were putting pressure on you to fill the position quickly because they were overworked even before the nurse left, and then things were really bad. After a hasty recruitment effort, you made a decision based on insufficient information. You ended up regretting your quick decision during the three months of problems that followed until you finally had to discharge the new hire. Since then, you have never let anybody pressure you into making a quick hiring decision.	

Solve the Dilemma

MAKING INFINITY COMPUTERS COMPETITIVE

Infinity Computers Inc. produces notebook computers, which it sells through direct mail catalog companies under the Infinity name and in some retail computer stores under their private brand names. Infinity's products are not significantly different from competitors', nor do they have extra product-enhancing features, although they are very price competitive. The strength of the company has been its CEO and president, George Anderson, and a highly motivated, loyal workforce. The firm's weakness is having too many employees and too great a reliance on one product. The firm switched to computers with the Intel Core i5 processors after it saw a decline in its netbook computers sales.

Recognizing that the strategies that initially made the firm successful are no longer working effectively, Anderson wants to reorganize the company to make it more responsive and competitive and to cut costs. The threat of new technological developments and current competitive conditions could eliminate Infinity.

Discussion Questions

1. Evaluate Infinity's current situation and analyze its strengths and weaknesses.

2. Evaluate the opportunities for Infinity, including using its current strategy, and propose alternative strategies.

3. Suggest a plan for Infinity to compete successfully over the next 10 years.

Build Your Business Plan

THE NATURE OF MANAGEMENT

The first thing you need to be thinking about is "What is the mission of your business? What is the shared vision your team members have for this business? How do you know if there is demand for this particular business? Remember, you need to think about the customer's *ability and willingness* to try this particular product.

Think about the various processes or stages of your business in the creation and selling of your product, or service.

What functions need to be performed for these processes to be completed? These functions might include buying, receiving, selling, customer service and/or merchandising.

Operationally, if you are opening up a retail establishment, how do you plan to provide your customers with superior customer service? What hours will your customers expect you to be open? At this point in time, how many employees are you thinking you will need to run your business? Do you (or one of your partners) need to be there all the time to supervise?

See for Yourself Videocase

FAILURE ACTS AS LEARNING TOOL FOR SAVVY ENTREPRENEURS

By its very nature, entrepreneurship is steeped in risk. Even the most innovative ideas can sometimes fail if the public does not catch on. Given this, anyone considering him or herself to be an entrepreneur is a risk-taker by nature. However, the degree of risk involved is sometimes altered by outside forces. Such is the case in the aftermath of the recent global recession. Entrepreneurs are now operating in a far riskier universe than they were prior to 2008. What this means, essentially, is that it is possible to see a higher failure rate these days. Most of us tend to take failure as a negative, but in the business world it can be the opposite.

Silicon Valley, best known for its heyday during the tech bubble and for housing companies such as Apple and Adobe, has a culture that believes strongly in failure as a learning tool. In fact, in some cases, it's almost a requirement. Intel co-founder Gordon Moore agrees. In the eyes of these companies, successfully making it through failure can be an attribute. Not all risks pay off; therefore, it is critical to learn from and gain strength from those ventures that fail.

According to Paul Ofman, a psychologist and managing director of RHR International (a business consultancy), in order to learn and grow, entrepreneurs must be willing to analyze what they could have done differently. For example, how did leadership, personal traits, and decision making impact the result? A savvy entrepreneur can also look back to recognize what may have been warning signs, thereby making those signs easier to spot and perhaps avoid the same mistakes the next time around. By successfully learning from mistakes, savvy entrepreneurs could apply these lessons to their next venture—and possibly succeed.

This was the case of entrepreneur Marc Pincus. Pincus, who now runs Zynga Inc. (home to popular social media games Farmville and Mafia Wars among others), views his first company, tribe.net, as an educational failure. Founded in 2003, tribe.net was among the early forays into social networking. Its software was sold to Cisco four years later. With this site, Pincus admitted that he jumped in head first without a clear plan. Although the site grew, it grew linearly rather than in a viral sense, which we now know to be the success behind sites such as Facebook. Pincus mistook a lot of users for committed users. The problem was these users were not sharing the site with their friends, which in turn failed to create a network effect. This left the site with no retention. Rather than moving forward with innovation, Pincus merely let the site continue on its original path. The company was liquidated in 2006.

However, Pincus did not stop there. Having learned from the venture, he solidified his business model at Zynga, his new company, before fully committing. The company conducts continuous testing and now discontinues work quickly on any products that do not catch on. This allows the company to innovate constantly to find those concepts that stick and yield committed users. Today, more than 120 million people are involved with Zynga's games, revenue is set to pass $450 million, and an initial public offering is being considered.

Another excellent example of learning from failure comes from one of today's hottest companies, Apple. In 1997, Apple's stock was trading for $3 a share thanks to a string of bad decisions and products that didn't take off. Today, Apple's stock trades for just under $250 a share. This company has not learned merely by failing once but by succeeding and failing many times over. Now, with the iPhone, the iTouch, the iPod, and the iPad, Apple is on a roll. Its sales have grown almost 50 percent and its profits by 90 percent thanks to its current success.

It would seem, given such examples, that entrepreneurs should approach failure rationally and intelligently, with an eye toward reflection. Failing does not have to be the kiss of death to an entrepreneurial career, but could instead act as a learning opportunity for future success.[34]

Discussion Questions

1. Why can risk taking as an entrepreneur sometimes be a positive thing?

2. Why is failure not always a negative in the business world? Name a positive outcome from a business failure.

3. Given the high failure rate of start-ups, would you be willing to start a new business?

Remember to check out our Online Learning Center at www.mhhe.com/ferrell8e

Team Exercise

Form groups and assign the responsibility of locating examples of crisis management implementation for companies dealing with natural disasters (explosions, fires, earthquakes, etc), technology disasters (viruses, plane crashes, compromised customer data, etc), or ethical or legal disasters. How did these companies communicate with key stakeholders? What measures did the company take provide support to those involved in the crisis? Report your findings to the class.

chapter 7

Organization, Teamwork, and Communication

OBJECTIVES

After reading this chapter, you will be able to:

- Define *organizational structure,* and relate how organizational structures develop.

- Describe how specialization and departmentalization help an organization achieve its goals.

- Distinguish between groups and teams, and identify the types of groups that exist in organizations.

- Determine how organizations assign responsibility for tasks and delegate authority.

- Compare and contrast some common forms of organizational structure.

- Describe how communication occurs in organizations.

- Analyze a business's use of teams.

Yahoo! Focuses on Organization and Teamwork

Immediately after assuming the position of CEO of Yahoo! in 2009, Carol Bartz has been working to improve the fortunes of the Internet giant. The company had undergone a takeover attempt by Microsoft and a proxy fight with activist investor Carl Icahn the year before. Long before Bartz's arrival, Yahoo!'s sales had been falling. Bartz was selected as CEO in part for her successful track record with companies such as Sun Microsystems and Autodesk. She is known as a tough, matter-of-fact boss who believes in focusing on the customer above all else. When Bartz took the helm, her first order of business was restructuring the company and downsizing to help restore Yahoo!'s profitability. She trimmed jobs, did away with segments of the company hampering growth, and met with employees to receive feedback and listen to complaints and ideas. Over a number of years, Yahoo! had splintered into many small groups that were often at odds with each other; Bartz worked to reassemble Yahoo! and make it work as a unit again. Upper-level managers cite Bartz's willingness to include everyone in the rebuilding of Yahoo! as a true positive, saying that Yahoo! is now working more as a whole to achieve success.

To narrow Yahoo!'s focus, Bartz entered into a deal with Microsoft in which Microsoft received Yahoo!'s Web crawling technology. In exchange, Yahoo! received a portion of the search ad revenue for 10 years and has retained its ability to innovate around search results on its network. Yahoo! Will also serve as the exclusive sales force for the combined search ad market. This decision made some investors and stakeholders nervous, but Bartz stands by her decision, saying that Yahoo!'s future is in ad sales. Her focus is to

continued

ENTER THE WORLD OF BUSINESS

improve Yahoo!'s functions and tailor them to users, so that consumers view Yahoo! as the center of their online lives.

Despite nearly doubling the stock price and restoring growth by the first quarter of 2010, Bartz tries to be self-aware and has criticized her performance as CEO, saying she was a little slow to get moving and that she struggled with getting the various aspects of Yahoo! back on track. After spending some time cleaning house and breaking down walls between Yahoo!'s many compartments, Bartz says the company is ready to grow and move forward. She now focuses on making wise acquisitions and on bolstering relevant content and services for consumers and advertisers, again going back to that focus on the customer—making Yahoo! relevant to its advertisers and 600 million users in different parts of the globe. Analysts speak positively about Yahoo!'s path and see revenue growth for the future. It seems that Bartz's focus on customers and a cohesive team are set to work, but only time will tell.[1]

Introduction

An organization's structure determines how well it makes decisions and responds to problems, and it influences employees' attitudes toward their work. A suitable structure can minimize a business's costs and maximize its efficiency. Even companies that operate within the same industry may utilize different organizational structures. For example, in the medical device industry, 3M is organized by line of business (health care products, office products, security tools), whereas Medtronic has similar business groups, but it also has top-level, functional units that focus on legal issues, strategy, and human resources operating above each of the lines of business.[2]

Because a business's structure can so profoundly affect its success, this chapter will examine organizational structure in detail. First, we discuss how an organization's culture affects its operations. Then we consider the development of structure, including how tasks and responsibilities are organized through specialization and departmentalization. Next, we explore some of the forms organizational structure may take. Finally, we consider communications within business.

Organizational Culture

organizational culture
a firm's shared values, beliefs, traditions, philosophies, rules, and role models for behavior

One of the most important aspects of organizing a business is determining its **organizational culture,** a firm's shared values, beliefs, traditions, philosophies, rules, and role models for behavior. Also called corporate culture, an organizational culture exists in every organization, regardless of size, organizational type, product, or profit objective. Sometimes behaviors, programs, and policies enhance and support the organizational culture. For example, when unemployment hit 10 percent, Pfizer implemented a program whereby customers who had lost their jobs and did not have prescription coverage could get 70 of its brand name drugs (Lipitor, Celebrex, Zoloft, Lyrica, etc.) for free for one year. According to Pfizer CEO Jeffrey Kindler, "We did it because we thought it was the right thing to do. But, it

Business Challenges
ATA Engineering Embraces Teamwork

How often do you see genuine and effective teamwork in your day-to-day life? At least in the workplace, the call for teamwork often remains unheard. Not so at ATA Engineering Inc., a San Diego–based provider of analysis and test-driven design solutions for structural, mechanical, electromechanical, and aerospace products.

When managers from a larger engineering firm formed ATA Engineering in 2000, they wanted to create a decentralized organization with few organizational layers—in other words, a flat, equalized business culture. In 2004, the company went further, making ATA entirely employee-owned via a stock ownership plan. Thanks to this flat structure and transparent culture, large and small decisions alike are made through employee consensus. All employees are also granted a high level of trust, making it possible for them to make decisions and lead projects without first receiving approval from those higher up. At times, senior employees find themselves working under lower-level employees, but that's the way they like it. The entire company is dedicated to the outcome of a project, rather than to catering to egos and titles. Salary and compensation are part of the culture as well. All employees receive the same percentage of their salaries as an annual bonus. There is no separate executive bonus system. The many facets of ATA's culture create a system that eliminates the resentment and frustration common to the organizational systems of other companies.

ATA Engineering has been recognized as one of the Most Innovative Companies by the National Center for Employee Ownership, and the Beyster Institute at the University of California–San Diego awarded the company the Innovations in Employee Ownership Award. The company has also been named one of San Diego's 100 fastest growing companies and one of *The Wall Street Journal*'s Top Small Workplaces. ATA Engineering is dedicated to creating a working environment in which every employee matters and feels valued.[3]

Discussion Questions

1. How does organizational structure affect the day-to-day operations and the work environment at ATA Engineering?
2. ATA Engineering does not have an executive bonus system, which eliminates frustrations over pay among lower-ranking employees. Do you think this system might affect the quality of talent the company is able to attract for upper management positions?
3. If ATA Engineering continues to be successful and to grow, do you think its organizational structure and corporate culture will be affected?

was motivational for our employees and got a great response from customers. In the long run it will help our business."[4] A firm's culture may be expressed formally through its mission statement, codes of ethics, memos, manuals, and ceremonies, but it is more commonly expressed informally. Examples of informal expressions of culture include dress codes (or the lack thereof), work habits, extracurricular activities, and stories. Employees often learn the accepted standards through discussions with co-workers.

TOMS Shoes' organizational culture is determined by the founder's desire to provide as many shoes as possible to children in developing countries (where shoeless children walk for miles to get water, food, and medical care). Blake Mycoskie gives hundreds of thousands of shoes to children around the world each year, creating a strong organizational culture of giving back and corporate social responsibility. His company operates with a program that for every shoe purchased, a shoe will be donated to children in need.[5] Disneyland/DisneyWorld and McDonald's have organizational cultures focused on cleanliness, value, and service. At Matsushita, employees sing a company song every morning that translates, "As individuals we will work to improve life and contribute to human progress." The company's president, Kunio Nakamura, also believes the highest paid employee should earn no more than 10 times the lowest paid employee. The effort to hire younger employees and more women is also affecting the Japanese firm's culture.[6] When such values and philosophies are shared by all members of an organization, they will be expressed in its relationships with stakeholders.

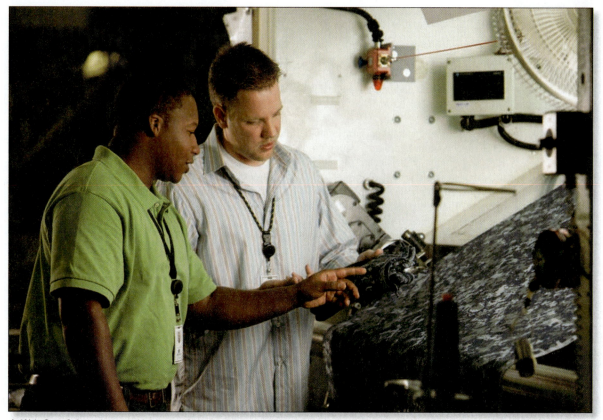

At W. L. Gore & Associates—which makes Gore-Tex fabric, surgical, aerospace, and other products—there are no bosses. Employees are hired as "associates" and assigned to "sponsors" in the functional groups in which they work. The structure has helped create a culture of innovation within the company.

However, organizational cultures that lack such positive values may result in employees who are unproductive and indifferent and have poor attitudes, which will be reflected externally to customers. Unethical cultures may have contributed to the misconduct at a number of well-known companies, such as Enron or Countrywide Financial. To increase profits, employees at Countrywide Financial encouraged clients to apply for large loans that were much higher than they could afford. To ensure that they qualified for the loans, Countrywide employees allowed clients to lie about their income and their financial stability. Many of the people who received these so-called liar loans were forced to default on the loans when they could not pay. Countrywide is blamed for a large portion of the housing market instability that began in 2007 because it was one of the largest lenders in the United States.[7]

Organizational culture helps ensure that all members of a company share values and suggests rules for how to behave and deal with problems within the organization. Table 7.1 confirms that executives in this study believe that corporate culture has a significant impact on organizational performance and the ability to retain good employees. The key to success in any organization is satisfying stakeholders, especially customers. Establishing a positive organizational culture sets the tone for all other decisions, including building an efficient organizational structure.

Culture has a strong or very strong impact on an organization's performance	82%
My corporate culture has a strong impact on the ability to retain top talent	68
My organization's culture drives sales and increases revenue	61
My organization's culture creates a sense of belonging	57
My organization's culture lowers turnover	53

TABLE 7.1

Impact of Corporate Culture on Business Performance

Source: "Ten Most Admired Corporate Cultures," February 10, 2010, http://cthrc.ca/en/member_area/member_news/ten_most_admired_corporate_cultures.aspx (accessed March 1, 2010).

Developing Organizational Structure

Structure is the arrangement or relationship of positions within an organization. Rarely is an organization, or any group of individuals working together, able to achieve common objectives without some form of structure, whether that structure is explicitly defined or only implied. A professional baseball team such as the Colorado Rockies is a business organization with an explicit formal structure that guides the team's activities so that it can increase game attendance, win games, and sell souvenirs such as T-shirts. But even an informal group playing softball for fun has an organization that specifies who will pitch, catch, bat, coach, and so on. Governments and nonprofit organizations also have formal organizational structures to facilitate the achievement of their objectives. Getting people to work together efficiently and coordinating the skills of diverse individuals require careful planning. Developing appropriate organizational structures is therefore a major challenge for managers in both large and small organizations.

An organization's structure develops when managers assign work tasks and activities to specific individuals or work groups and coordinate the diverse activities required to reach the firm's objectives. When Macy's, for example, has a sale, the store manager must work with the advertising department to make the public aware of the sale, with department managers to ensure that extra salespeople are scheduled to handle the increased customer traffic, and with merchandise buyers to ensure that enough sale merchandise is available to meet expected consumer demand. All the people occupying these positions must work together to achieve the store's objectives.

The best way to begin to understand how organizational structure develops is to consider the evolution of a new business such as a clothing store. At first, the business is a sole proprietorship in which the owner does everything—buys, prices, and displays the merchandise; does the accounting and tax records; and assists customers. As the business grows, the owner hires a salesperson and perhaps a merchandise buyer to help run the store. As the business continues to grow, the owner hires more salespeople. The growth and success of the business now require the owner to be away from the store frequently, meeting with suppliers, engaging in public relations, and attending trade shows. Thus, the owner must designate someone to manage the salespeople and maintain the accounting, payroll, and tax functions. If the owner decides to expand by opening more stores, still more managers will be needed. Figure 7.1 shows these stages of growth with three **organizational charts** (visual displays of organizational structure, chain of command, and other relationships).

Growth requires organizing—the structuring of human, physical, and financial resources to achieve objectives in an effective and efficient manner. Growth

structure
the arrangement or relationship of positions within an organization

organizational chart
a visual display of the organizational structure, lines of authority (chain of command), staff relationships, permanent committee arrangements, and lines of communication

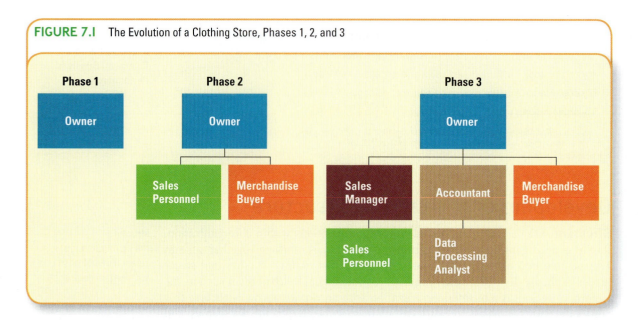

FIGURE 7.I   The Evolution of a Clothing Store, Phases 1, 2, and 3

necessitates hiring people who have specialized skills. With more people and greater specialization, the organization needs to develop a formal structure to function efficiently. Imagine the organizational changes that Nathan's Famous hot dogs underwent from 1916 when they operated a single Coney Island hot dog shop to a company that now operates an international chain of fast-food restaurants as well as selling food products through supermarkets. With just over 200 employees, the company sells more than 380 million hot dogs a year and generates nearly $50 million in revenue.[8] As we shall see, structuring an organization requires that management assign work tasks to specific individuals and departments and assign responsibility for the achievement of specific organizational objectives.

Assigning Tasks

For a business to earn profits from the sale of its products, its managers must first determine what activities are required to achieve its objectives. At Celestial Seasonings, for example, employees must purchase herbs from suppliers, dry the herbs and place them in tea bags, package and label the tea, and then ship the packages to grocery stores around the country. Other necessary activities include negotiating with supermarkets and other retailers for display space, developing new products, planning advertising, managing finances, and managing employees. All these activities must be coordinated, assigned to work groups, and controlled. Two important aspects of assigning these work activities are specialization and departmentalization.

Specialization

specialization
the division of labor into small, specific tasks and the assignment of employees to do a single task

After identifying all activities that must be accomplished, managers then break these activities down into specific tasks that can be handled by individual employees. This division of labor into small, specific tasks and the assignment of employees to do a single task is called **specialization.**

The rationale for specialization is efficiency. People can perform more efficiently if they master just one task rather than all tasks. In *The Wealth of Nations,*

18th-century economist Adam Smith discussed specialization, using the manufacture of straight pins as an example. Individually, workers could produce 20 pins a day when each employee produced complete pins. Thus, 10 employees working independently of each other could produce 200 pins a day. However, when one worker drew the wire, another straightened it, a third cut it, and a fourth ground the point, 10 workers could produce 48,000 pins per day.[9] To save money and achieve the benefits of specialization, some companies outsource and hire temporary workers to provide key skills. Many highly skilled, diverse, experienced workers are available through temp agencies.

Specialization means workers do not waste time shifting from one job to another, and training is easier. However, efficiency is not the only motivation for specialization. Specialization also occurs when the activities that must be performed within an organization are too numerous for one person to handle. Recall the example of the clothing store. When the business was young and small, the owner could do everything; but when the business grew, the owner needed help waiting on customers, keeping the books, and managing other business activities.

Henry Ford, the founder of Ford Motor Company, revolutionized manufacturing by creating assembly lines like this one to specialize the tasks his workers performed.

Overspecialization can have negative consequences. Employees may become bored and dissatisfied with their jobs, and the result of their unhappiness is likely to be poor quality work, more injuries, and high employee turnover. This is why some manufacturing firms allow job rotation so that employees do not become dissatisfied and leave. Although some degree of specialization is necessary for efficiency, because of differences in skills, abilities, and interests, all people are not equally suited for all jobs. We examine some strategies to overcome these issues in Chapter 9.

Departmentalization

After assigning specialized tasks to individuals, managers next organize workers doing similar jobs into groups to make them easier to manage. **Departmentalization** is the grouping of jobs into working units usually called departments, units, groups, or divisions. As we shall see, departments are commonly organized by function, product, geographic region, or customer (Figure 7.2). Most companies use more than one departmentalization plan to enhance productivity. For instance, many consumer goods manufacturers have departments for specific product lines (beverages, frozen dinners, canned goods, and so on) as well as departments dealing with legal, purchasing, finance, human resources, and other business functions. For smaller companies, accounting can be set up online, almost as an automated department. Accounting software can handle electronic transfers so you never have to worry about a late bill. Many city governments also have departments for specific services (e.g., police, fire, waste disposal) as well as departments for legal, human resources, and other business functions. Figure 7.3 depicts the organizational chart for the city of Corpus Christi, Texas, showing these departments.

departmentalization
the grouping of jobs into working units usually called departments, units, groups, or divisions

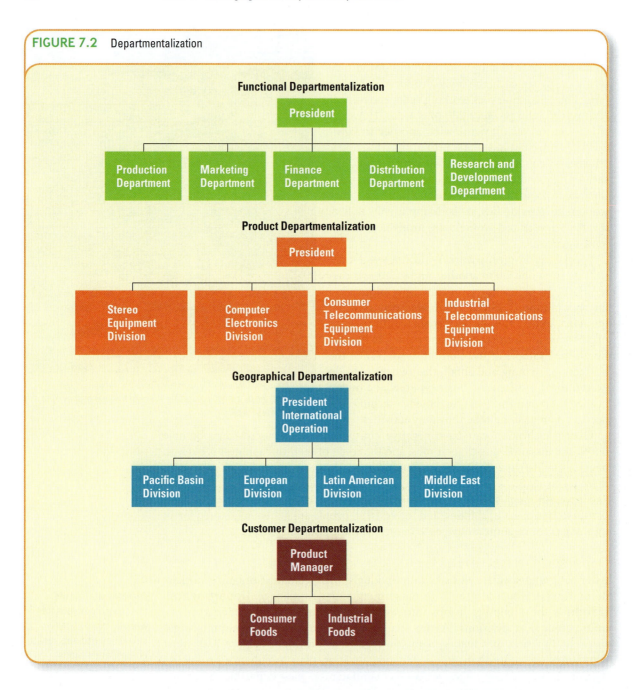

FIGURE 7.2   Departmentalization

Functional Departmentalization

President

- Production Department
- Marketing Department
- Finance Department
- Distribution Department
- Research and Development Department

Product Departmentalization

President

- Stereo Equipment Division
- Computer Electronics Division
- Consumer Telecommunications Equipment Division
- Industrial Telecommunications Equipment Division

Geographical Departmentalization

President International Operation

- Pacific Basin Division
- European Division
- Latin American Division
- Middle East Division

Customer Departmentalization

Product Manager

- Consumer Foods
- Industrial Foods

functional departmentalization the grouping of jobs that perform similar functional activities, such as finance, manufacturing, marketing, and human resources

Functional Departmentalization.   **Functional departmentalization** groups jobs that perform similar functional activities, such as finance, manufacturing, marketing, and human resources. Each of these functions is managed by an expert in the work done by the department—an engineer supervises the production department; a financial executive supervises the finance department. This approach is common in small organizations. A weakness of functional departmentalization is that, because it tends to emphasize departmental units rather than the organization as a whole, decision making that involves more than one department may be

FIGURE 7.3   An Organizational Chart for the City of Corpus Christi

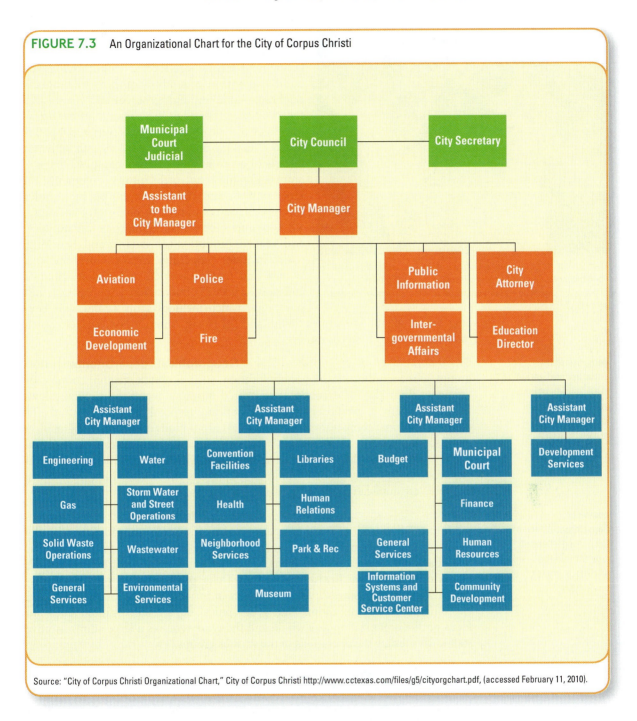

Source: "City of Corpus Christi Organizational Chart," City of Corpus Christi http://www.cctexas.com/files/g5/cityorgchart.pdf, (accessed February 11, 2010).

slow, and it requires greater coordination. Thus, as business grow, they tend to adopt other approaches to organizing jobs.

Product Departmentalization.   **Product departmentalization,** as you might guess, organizes jobs around the products of the firm. Procter & Gamble has global units, such as laundry and cleaning products, paper products, and health care products. Each division develops and implements its own product plans, monitors the

product departmentalization
the organization of jobs in relation to the products of the firm

Product departmentalization is common in the companies that produce your textbooks. Teams of editors specialize, depending on the types of books they work on—business, social science, hard science, and so forth.

results, and takes corrective action as necessary. Functional activities—production, finance, marketing, and others—are located within each product division. Consequently, organizing by products duplicates functions and resources and emphasizes the product rather than achievement of the organization's overall objectives. However, it simplifies decision making and helps coordinate all activities related to a product or product group. Campbell's Soup Company is organized into four segments: (1) U.S. Soup, Sauces and Beverages, which includes Campbell's soups, Swanson broth, Prego pasta sauce, V8 juice and juice drinks, Campbell's tomato juice, and related products; (2) Baking and Snacking, which includes Pepperidge Farm cookies, crackers, bakery, and frozen products and Arnott's biscuits and salty snacks; (3) International Soup, Sauces and Beverages, which includes soup, sauces, and beverages sold outside the United States, and (4) North America Foodservice, which includes prepared food operations.[10]

geographical departmentalization
the grouping of jobs according to geographic location, such as state, region, country, or continent

Geographical Departmentalization.   Geographical departmentalization
groups jobs according to geographic location, such as a state, region, country, or continent. FritoLay, for example, is organized into four regional divisions, allowing the company to get closer to its customers and respond more quickly and efficiently to regional competitors. Multinational corporations often use a geographical approach because of vast differences between different regions. Coca-Cola, General Motors, and Caterpillar are organized by region. However, organizing by region requires a large administrative staff and control system to coordinate operations, and tasks are duplicated among the different regions.

customer departmentalization
the arrangement of jobs around the needs of various types of customers

Customer Departmentalization.   Customer departmentalization arranges
jobs around the needs of various types of customers. Banks, for example, typically have separate departments for commercial banking activities and for consumer or retail banking. This permits the bank to address the unique requirements of each group. Airlines, such as British Airways and Delta, provide prices and services customized for either business/frequent travelers or infrequent/vacationing customers. Customer departmentalization, like geographical departmentalization, does not focus on the organization as a whole and therefore requires a large administrative staff to coordinate the operations of the various groups.

Assigning Responsibility

After all workers and work groups have been assigned their tasks, they must be given the responsibility to carry them out. Management must determine to what extent it will delegate responsibility throughout the organization and how many employees will report to each manager.

delegation of authority
giving employees not only tasks, but also the power to make commitments, use resources, and take whatever actions are necessary to carry out those tasks

Delegation of Authority
Delegation of authority means not only giving tasks to employees but also empowering them to make commitments, use resources, and take whatever actions

are necessary to carry out those tasks. Let's say a marketing manager at Nestlé has assigned an employee to design a new package that is less wasteful (more environmentally responsible) than the current package for one of the company's frozen dinner lines. To carry out the assignment, the employee needs access to information and the authority to make certain decisions on packaging materials, costs, and so on. Without the authority to carry out the assigned task, the employee would have to get the approval of others for every decision and every request for materials.

As a business grows, so do the number and complexity of decisions that must be made; no one manager can handle them all. Hotels such as Westin Hotels and Resorts and the Ritz-Carlton give authority to service providers, including front desk personnel, to make service decisions such as moving a guest to another room or providing a discount to guests who experience a problem at the hotel. Delegation of authority frees a manager to concentrate on larger issues, such as planning or dealing with problems and opportunities.

Delegation also gives a **responsibility,** or obligation, to employees to carry out assigned tasks satisfactorily and holds them accountable for the proper execution of their assigned work. The principle of **accountability** means that employees who accept an assignment and the authority to carry it out are answerable to a superior for the outcome. Returning to the Nestlé example, if the packaging design prepared by the employee is unacceptable or late, the employee must accept the blame. If the new design is innovative, attractive, and cost-efficient, as well as environmentally responsible, or is completed ahead of schedule, the employee will accept the credit.

The process of delegating authority establishes a pattern of relationships and accountability between a superior and his or her subordinates. The president of a firm delegates responsibility for all marketing activities to the vice president of marketing. The vice president accepts this responsibility and has the authority to obtain all relevant information, make certain decisions, and delegate any or all activities to his or her subordinates. The vice president, in turn, delegates all advertising activities to the advertising manager, all sales activities to the sales manager, and so on. These managers then delegate specific tasks to their subordinates. However, the act of delegating authority to a subordinate does not relieve the superior of accountability for the delegated job. Even though the vice president of marketing delegates work to subordinates, he or she is still ultimately accountable to the president for all marketing activities.

responsibility
the obligation, placed on employees through delegation, to perform assigned tasks satisfactorily and be held accountable for the proper execution of work

accountability
the principle that employees who accept an assignment and the authority to carry it out are answerable to a superior for the outcome

Degree of Centralization

The extent to which authority is delegated throughout an organization determines its degree of centralization.

Centralized Organizations.

In a **centralized organization,** authority is concentrated at the top, and very little decision-making authority is delegated to lower levels. Although decision-making authority in centralized organizations rests with top levels of management, a vast amount of responsibility for carrying out daily and routine procedures is delegated to even the lowest levels of the organization. Many government organizations, including the U.S. Army, the Postal Service, and the IRS, are centralized.

Businesses tend to be more centralized when the decisions to be made are risky and when low-level managers are not highly skilled in decision making. In the banking industry, for example, authority to make routine car loans is given to all

centralized organization
a structure in which authority is concentrated at the top, and very little decision-making authority is delegated to lower levels

loan managers, while the authority to make high-risk loans, such as for a large residential development, may be restricted to upper-level loan officers.

Overcentralization can cause serious problems for a company, in part because it may take longer for the organization as a whole to implement decisions and to respond to changes and problems on a regional scale. McDonald's, for example, was one of the last chains to introduce a chicken sandwich because of the amount of research, development, test marketing, and layers of approval the product had to go through.

decentralized organization
an organization in which decision-making authority is delegated as far down the chain of command as possible

Decentralized Organizations.

A **decentralized organization** is one in which decision-making authority is delegated as far down the chain of command as possible. Decentralization is characteristic of organizations that operate in complex, unpredictable environments. Businesses that face intense competition often decentralize to improve responsiveness and enhance creativity. Lower-level managers who interact with the external environment often develop a good understanding of it and thus are able to react quickly to changes.

Delegating authority to lower levels of managers may increase the organization's productivity. Decentralization requires that lower-level managers have strong decision-making skills. In recent years the trend has been toward more decentralized organizations, and some of the largest and most successful companies, including GE, IBM, Google, Nike, and JCPenney, have decentralized decision-making authority. McDonald's, realizing most of its growth outside the United States, is becoming increasingly decentralized and "glo-cal," varying products in specific markets to better meet consumer demands. This change in organizational structure for McDonald's is fostering greater innovation and local market success. McDonald's, which was long known for the homogeneity of its products, has embraced local cuisine on a limited scale. In Italy, McDonald's introduced the McItaly, a burger made with only Italian products. The burger is designed with the red and green Italian flag in mind; customers can choose from artichoke spread and Asiago cheese or onion, lettuce, and pancetta.[12] Diversity and decentralization seem to be McDonald's keys to being better, not just bigger. Nonprofit organizations benefit from decentralization as well.

Span of Management

How many subordinates should a manager manage? There is no simple answer. Experts generally agree, however, that top managers should not directly supervise more than four to eight people, while lower-level managers who supervise routine tasks are capable of managing a much larger number of subordinates. For example, the manager of the finance department may supervise 25 employees, whereas the vice president of finance may supervise only five managers. **Span of management** refers to the number of subordinates who report to a particular manager. A *wide span of management* exists when a manager directly supervises a very large number of employees. A *narrow span of management* exists when a manager directly supervises only a few subordinates (Figure 7.4). At Whole Foods, the best employees are recruited and placed in small teams in one of eight departments. Employees are empowered to discount, give away, and sample products, as well as to assist in creating a respectful workplace where goals are achieved, individual employees succeed, and customers are core in business decisions. This approach allows Whole Foods to offer unique and "local market" experiences in each of its stores. This level of customization is in contrast to more centralized national supermarket chains such as Kroger, Safeway, and Publix.[13]

span of management
the number of subordinates who report to a particular manager

Should the span of management be wide or narrow? To answer this question, several factors need to be considered. A narrow span of management is appropriate when superiors and subordinates are not in close proximity, the manager has many responsibilities in addition to the supervision, the interaction between superiors and subordinates is frequent, and problems are common. However, when superiors and subordinates are located close to one another, the manager has few responsibilities other than supervision, the level of interaction between superiors and subordinates is low, few problems arise, subordinates are highly competent, and a set of specific operating procedures governs the activities of managers and their subordinates, a wide span of management will be more appropriate. Narrow spans of management are typical in centralized organizations, while wide spans of management are more common in decentralized firms.

Organizational Layers

Complementing the concept of span of management is **organizational layers,** the levels of management in an organization.

organizational layers
the levels of management in an organization

A company with many layers of managers is considered tall; in a tall organization, the span of management is narrow (see Figure 7.4). Because each manager supervises only a few subordinates, many layers of management are necessary to carry out the operations of the business. McDonald's, for example, has a tall organization with many layers, including store managers, district managers, regional managers,

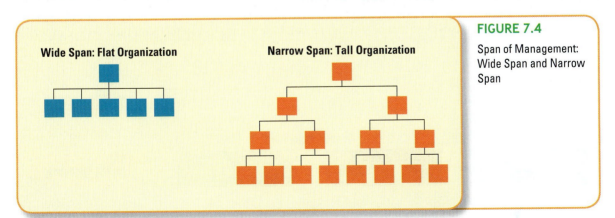

FIGURE 7.4

Span of Management: Wide Span and Narrow Span

and functional managers (finance, marketing, and so on), as well as a chief executive officer and many vice presidents. Because there are more managers in tall organizations than in flat organizations, administrative costs are usually higher. Communication is slower because information must pass through many layers.

Organizations with few layers are flat and have wide spans of management. When managers supervise a large number of employees, fewer management layers are needed to conduct the organization's activities. Managers in flat organizations typically perform more administrative duties than managers in tall organizations because there are fewer of them. They also spend more time supervising and working with subordinates.

Many of the companies that have decentralized also flattened their structures and widened their spans of management, often by eliminating layers of middle management. Many corporations, including Avon, AT&T, and Ford Motor Company, did so to reduce costs, speed decision making, and boost overall productivity.

Forms of Organizational Structure

Along with assigning tasks and the responsibility for carrying them out, managers must consider how to structure their authority relationships—that is, what structure the organization itself will have and how it will appear on the organizational chart. Common forms of organization include line structure, line-and-staff structure, multidivisional structure, and matrix structure.

Line Structure

line structure
the simplest organizational structure in which direct lines of authority extend from the top manager to the lowest level of the organization

The simplest organizational structure, **line structure,** has direct lines of authority that extend from the top manager to employees at the lowest level of the organization. For example, a convenience store employee may report to an assistant manager, who reports to the store manager, who reports to a regional manager, or, in an independent store, directly to the owner (Figure 7.5). This structure has a clear chain of command, which enables managers to make decisions quickly. A mid-level manager facing a decision must consult only one person, his or her immediate supervisor. However, this structure requires that managers possess a wide range of knowledge and skills. They are responsible for a variety of activities and must be knowledgeable about them all. Line structures are most common in small businesses.

Line-and-Staff Structure

line-and-staff structure
a structure having a traditional line relationship between superiors and subordinates and also specialized managers—called staff managers—who are available to assist line managers

The **line-and-staff structure** has a traditional line relationship between superiors and subordinates, and specialized managers—called staff managers—are available to assist line managers (Figure 7.6). Line managers can focus on their area of expertise

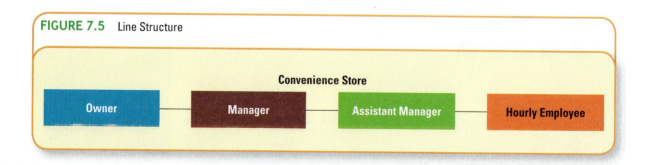

FIGURE 7.5   Line Structure

Convenience Store

Owner — Manager — Assistant Manager — Hourly Employee

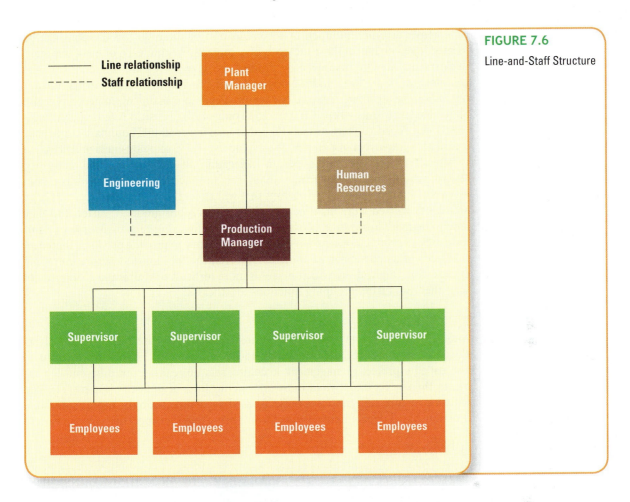

FIGURE 7.6

Line-and-Staff Structure

in the operation of the business, while staff managers provide advice and support to line departments on specialized matters such as finance, engineering, human resources, and the law. In the city of Corpus Christi (refer back for Figure 7.3), for example, assistant city managers are line managers who oversee groups of related departments. However, the city attorney, police chief, and fire chief are effectively staff managers who report directly to the city manager (the city equivalent of a business chief executive officer). Staff managers do not have direct authority over line managers or over the line manager's subordinates, but they do have direct authority over subordinates in their own departments. However, line-and-staff organizations may experience problems with overstaffing and ambiguous lines of communication. Additionally, employees may become frustrated because they lack the authority to carry out certain decisions.

Multidivisional Structure

As companies grow and diversify, traditional line structures become difficult to coordinate, making communication difficult and decision making slow. When the weaknesses of the structure—the "turf wars," miscommunication, and working at cross-purposes—exceed the benefits, growing firms tend to restructure, often into the divisionalized form. A **multidivisional structure** organizes departments into larger groups called divisions. Just as departments might be formed on the basis of

multidivisional structure
a structure that organizes departments into larger groups called divisions

geography, customer, product, or a combination of these, so too divisions can be formed based on any of these methods of organizing. Within each of these divisions, departments may be organized by product, geographic region, function, or some combination of all three. Indra Nooyi, CEO of PepsiCo, rearranged the company's organizational structure. Prior to her tenure, PepsiCo was organized geographically. She created new units—PepsiCo Americas Foods (PAF), PepsiCo Americas Beverages (PAB), and PepsiCo International (PI)—that span international boundaries and make it easier for employees in different geographic regions to share business practices.[14]

Multidivisional structures permit delegation of decision-making authority, allowing divisional and department managers to specialize. They allow those closest to the action to make the decisions that will affect them. Delegation of authority and divisionalized work also mean that better decisions are made faster, and they tend to be more innovative. Most importantly, by focusing each division on a common region, product, or customer, each is more likely to provide products that meet the needs of its particular customers. However, the divisional structure inevitably creates work duplication, which makes it more difficult to realize the economies of scale that result from grouping functions together.

matrix structure
a structure that sets up teams from different departments, thereby creating two or more intersecting lines of authority; also called a project-management structure

Matrix Structure

Another structure that attempts to address issues that arise with growth, diversification, productivity, and competitiveness, is the matrix. A **matrix structure,** also called a project management structure, sets up teams from different departments, thereby creating two or more intersecting lines of authority (Figure 7.7). The matrix structure superimposes project-based departments on the more traditional, function-based departments. Project teams bring together specialists from a variety

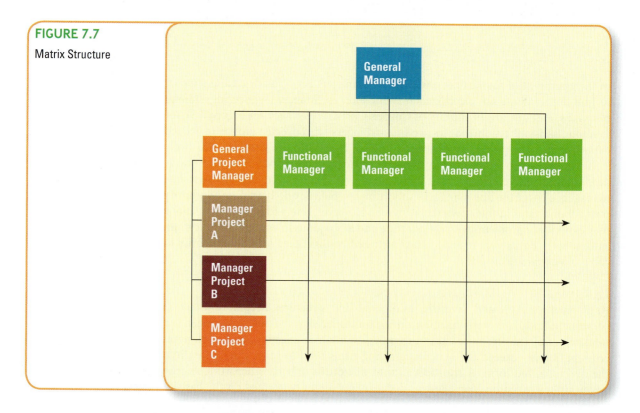

FIGURE 7.7

Matrix Structure

of areas to work together on a single project, such as developing a new fighter jet. In this arrangement, employees are responsible to two managers—functional managers and project managers. Matrix structures are usually temporary: Team members typically go back to their functional or line department after a project is finished. However, more firms are becoming permanent matrix structures, creating and dissolving project teams as needed to meet customer needs. The aerospace industry was one of the first to apply the matrix structure, but today it is used by universities and schools, accounting firms, banks, and organizations in other industries.

Matrix structures provide flexibility, enhanced cooperation, and creativity, and they enable the company to respond quickly to changes in the environment by giving special attention to specific projects or problems. However, they are generally expensive and quite complex, and employees may be confused as to whose authority has priority—the project manager's or the immediate supervisor's.

The Role of Groups and Teams in Organizations

Regardless of how they are organized, most of the essential work of business occurs in individual work groups and teams, so we'll take a closer look at them now. Although some experts do not make a distinction between groups and teams, in recent years there has been a gradual shift toward an emphasis on teams and managing them to enhance individual and organizational success. Some experts now believe that highest productivity results only when groups become teams.[15]

Traditionally, a **group** has been defined as two or more individuals who communicate with one another, share a common identity, and have a common goal. A **team** is a small group whose members have complementary skills; have a common purpose, goals, and approach; and hold themselves mutually accountable.[16] All teams are groups, but not all groups are teams. Table 7.2 points out some important differences between them. Work groups emphasize individual work products, individual accountability, and even individual leadership. Salespeople

group
two or more individuals who communicate with one another, share a common identity, and have a common goal

team
a small group whose members have complementary skills; have a common purpose, goals, and approach; and hold themselves mutually accountable

Working Group	Team
Has strong, clearly focused leader	Has shared leadership roles
Has individual accountability	Has individual and group accountability
Has the same purpose as the broader organizational mission	Has a specific purpose that the team itself delivers
Creates individual work products	Creates collective work products
Runs efficient meetings	Encourages open-ended discussion and active problem-solving meetings
Measures its effectiveness indirectly by its effects on others (e.g., financial performance of the business)	Measures performance directly by assessing collective work products
Discusses, decides, and delegates	Discusses, decides, and does real work together

TABLE 7.2

Differences between Groups and Teams

Source: Robert Gatewood, Robert Taylor, and O. C. Ferrell, *Management: Comprehension Analysis and Application,* 1995, p. 427. Copyright © 1995 Richard D. Irwin, a Times Mirror Higher Education Group, Inc., company. Reproduced with permission of the McGraw-Hill Companies.

working independently for the same company could be a work group. In contrast, work teams share leadership roles, have both individual and mutual accountability, and create collective work products. In other words, a work group's performance depends on what its members do as individuals, while a team's performance is based on creating a knowledge center and a competency to work together to accomplish a goal. When CEO Joe Albanese had to leave his CEO position at Commodore Builders for active duty in the Army, his team rebalanced his workload and continued its projects. Albanese had established teams that focused on collaboration. A core team was prepared to lead the company in his absence. Albanese simply unplugged himself, leaving the team to perform his duties, including day-to-day leadership.[17]

The type of groups an organization establishes depends on the tasks it needs to accomplish and the situation it faces. Some specific kinds of groups and teams include committees, task forces, project teams, product-development teams, quality-assurance teams, and self-directed work teams. All of these can be *virtual teams*—employees in different locations who rely on e-mail, audio conferencing, fax, Internet, videoconferencing, or other technological tools to accomplish their goals. With more than 84 percent of American employees working in a different location than their supervisors, virtual teams are becoming a part of everyday business.[18]

Committees

committee
a permanent, formal group that performs a specific task

A **committee** is usually a permanent, formal group that does some specific task. For example, many firms have a compensation or finance committee to examine the effectiveness of these areas of operation as well as the need for possible changes. Ethics committees are formed to develop and revise codes of ethics, suggest methods for implementing ethical standards, and review specific issues and concerns.

Task Forces

task force
a temporary group of employees responsible for bringing about a particular change

A **task force** is a temporary group of employees responsible for bringing about a particular change. They typically come from across all departments and levels of an organization. Task force membership is usually based on expertise rather than organizational position. Occasionally, a task force may be formed from individuals outside a company. When Toyota experienced a major ethics and legal crisis, the president, Akio Toyoda, formed and led a Global Quality Task Force to conduct quality improvements throughout the worldwide operations of the company. With massive recalls looming, the company focused on (1) improving the quality inspection process, (2) enhancing customer research, (3) establishing an automotive center of quality excellence, (4) utilizing external industry experts, (5) increasing the frequency of communication with regional authorities, and (6) improving regional autonomy.[19]

Teams

Teams are becoming far more common in the U.S. workplace as businesses strive to enhance productivity and global competitiveness. In general, teams have the benefit of being able to pool members' knowledge and skills and make greater use of them than can individuals working alone. Team building is becoming increasingly popular in organizations, with around half of executives indicating their companies had team-building training. Teams require harmony, cooperation, synchronized effort, and flexibility to maximize their contribution.[20] Teams can also create more solutions to problems than can individuals. Furthermore, team participation enhances employee acceptance of, understanding of, and commitment to team goals. Teams motivate workers by providing internal rewards in the form of an enhanced sense of accomplishment for employees as they achieve more, and external rewards in the form of praise and certain perks. Consequently, they can help get workers more involved. They can help companies be more innovative, and they can boost productivity and cut costs.

According to psychologist Ivan Steiner, team productivity peaks at about five team members. People become less motivated and group coordination becomes more difficult after this size. Jeff Bezos, Amazon.com CEO, says that he has a "two-pizza rule": If a team cannot be fed by two pizzas, it is too large. Keep teams small enough where everyone gets a piece of the action.[21]

Project Teams.   **Project teams** are similar to task forces, but normally they run their operation and have total control of a specific work project. Like task forces, their membership is likely to cut across the firm's hierarchy and be composed of people from different functional areas. They are almost always temporary, although a large project, such as designing and building a new airplane at Boeing Corporation, may last for years.

Product-development teams are a special type of project team formed to devise, design, and implement a new product. Sometimes product-development teams exist within a functional area—research and development—but now they more frequently include people from numerous functional areas and may even include customers to help ensure that the end product meets the customers' needs. Washington State University's School of Food Science has several student product development teams. Students develop innovative new food products and present them annually at the Institute of Food Technologists Student Association competition. WSU student projects include Tu Mazi, a mango-flavored probiotic milk powder created for consumers in developing nations, and Erupt-a-Cake, a ready-to-bake dessert featuring gummy dinosaurs.[22]

Quality-Assurance Teams.   **Quality-assurance teams,** sometimes called **quality circles,** are fairly small groups of workers brought together from throughout the organization to solve specific quality, productivity, or service problems. Although the *quality circle* term is not as popular as it once was, the concern about quality is stronger than ever. The use of teams to address quality issues will no doubt continue to increase throughout the business world.

Self-directed Work Teams.   A **self-directed work team (SDWT)** is a group of employees responsible for an entire work process or segment that delivers a product to an internal or external customer.[23] SDWTs permit the flexibility to change rapidly to meet the competition or respond to customer needs. The defining characteristic of an SDWT is the extent to which it is empowered or given authority to make and implement work decisions. Thus, SDWTs are designed to give employees a feeling of "ownership" of a whole job. With shared team responsibility for work outcomes, team members often have broader job assignments and cross-train to master other jobs, thus permitting greater team flexibility.

project teams
groups similar to task forces which normally run their operation and have total control of a specific work project

product-development teams
a specific type of project team formed to devise, design, and implement a new product

quality-assurance teams (or quality circles)
small groups of workers brought together from throughout the organization to solve specific quality, productivity, or service problems

self-directed work team (SDWT)
a group of employees responsible for an entire work process or segment that delivers a product to an internal or external customer

The software company My SQL has a worldwide workforce but no offices. Employees work virtually in self-directed work teams.

Communicating in Organizations

Communication within an organization can flow in a variety of directions and from a number of sources, each using both oral and written forms of communication.

The success of communication systems within the organization has a tremendous effect on the overall success of the firm. Communication mistakes can lower productivity and morale.

Alternatives to face-to face communications—such as meetings—are growing thanks to technology such as voice-mail, e-mail, and online newsletters. Many companies use internal networks called intranets to share information with employees. Intranets increase communication across different departments and levels of management and help with the flow of everyday business activities. Companies can even integrate aspects of social media into their intranets, allowing employees to post comments and pictures, participate in polls, and create group calendars. However, increased access to the Internet at work has also created many problems, including employee abuse of company mail and Internet access.[25]

Formal Communication

Formal channels of communication are intentionally defined and designed by the organization. They represent the flow of communication within the formal organizational structure, as shown on organizational charts. Traditionally, formal communication patterns were classified as vertical and horizontal, but with the increased use of teams and matrix structures, formal communication may occur in a number of patterns (Figure 7.8).

Upward communication flows from lower to higher levels of the organization and includes information such as progress reports, suggestions for improvement,

Online sites such as wikis are allowing employee teams to share information and work collaboratively on documents. The most well-known wiki is the online encyclopedia Wikipedia.

Going Green

The Rainforest Alliance Uses Teamwork and Organization to Become a Success

When you envision nonprofit organizations, you may imagine bare-bones operations, little money flowing through the organization, and poor working conditions for employees more dedicated to a cause than to their careers. The Rainforest Alliance, a highly recognized nonprofit organization that promotes biodiversity and sustainability, defies this stereotype. In fact, the company works hard to ensure a positive workplace. With 35,000 members and supporters and an annual budget of more than $30 million, the Rainforest Alliance has been fighting globally for the environment and communities since 1987 by working to change business practices and consumer behavior. An organization such the Rainforest Alliance requires dedicated employees; therefore, the company promotes a motivational, encouraging work environment.

The Rainforest Alliance has grown rapidly in the past five years and now employs more than 250 employees worldwide. Thanks in part to expansion, Rainforest is a decentralized organization, delegating authority by encouraging employees at all ranks to take charge of projects. These individuals are promoted as a result of their efforts. This allows employees to follow their own interests within the organization, which builds morale. The company also offers U.S. employees opportunities to work in foreign offices, which provides the chance to travel along with the learning experience. For individuals looking to aid the environment and support small growers, a nonprofit such as the Rainforest Alliance that is dedicated to encouraging its employees is a great place to work.[26]

Discussion Questions

1. How does the Rainforest Alliance balance employee welfare with pursuing its mission as a nonprofit?
2. How does its decentralized structure affect the responsibilities that employees take on?
3. Do you think it is important to believe in the mission of the organization in order to be a satisfied employee of the Rainforest Alliance?

---

inquiries, and grievances. *Downward communication* refers to the traditional flow of information from upper organizational levels to lower levels. This type of communication typically involves directions, the assignment of tasks and responsibilities, performance feedback, and certain details about the organization's strategies and goals. Speeches, policy and procedures manuals, employee handbooks,

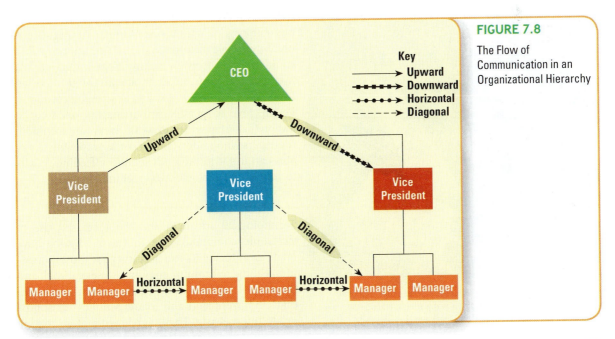

FIGURE 7.8

The Flow of Communication in an Organizational Hierarchy

company leaflets, telecommunications, and job descriptions are examples of downward communication.

Horizontal communication involves the exchange of information among colleagues and peers on the same organizational level, such as across or within departments. Horizontal information informs, supports, and coordinates activities both within the department and with other departments. At times, the business will formally require horizontal communication among particular organizational members, as is the case with task forces or project teams.

With more and more companies downsizing and increasing the use of selfmanaged work teams, many workers are being required to communicate with others in different departments and on different levels to solve problems and coordinate work. When these individuals from different units and organizational levels communicate, it is *diagonal communication.* One benefit of companies doing more with fewer employees is that productivity (output per work hour) increased by 9.5 percent late in 2009. Increased productivity allows companies to increase wages and leads to increased standards of living.[27]

Informal Communication Channels

Along with the formal channels of communication shown on an organizational chart, all firms communicate informally as well. Communication between friends, for instance, cuts across department, division, and even management-subordinate boundaries. Such friendships and other nonwork social relationships comprise the *informal organization* of a firm, and their impact can be great.

grapevine
an informal channel of communication, separate from management's formal, official communication channels

The most significant informal communication occurs through the **grapevine,** an informal channel of communication, separate from management's formal, official communication channels. Grapevines exist in all organizations. Information passed along the grapevine may relate to the job or organization, or it may be gossip and rumors unrelated to either. The accuracy of grapevine information has been of great concern to managers.

Many companies monitor their workers' Internet usage and other communications with special software. Are they spending hours on Facebook? YouTube? What kind of e-mails are they sending?

Additionally, managers can turn the grapevine to their advantage. Using it as a "sounding device" for possible new policies is one example. Managers can obtain valuable information from the grapevine that could improve decision making. Some organizations use the grapevine to their advantage by floating ideas, soliciting feedback, and reacting accordingly. People love to gossip, and managers need to be aware that grapevines exist in every organization. Managers who understand how the grapevine works also can use it to their advantage by feeding it facts to squelch rumors and incorrect information.

Monitoring Communications

Technological advances and the increased use of electronic communication in the workplace have made monitoring its use necessary for most companies. Failing to monitor employee's use of e-mail and the Internet can be costly. Many companies require that employees sign and follow a policy on appropriate Internet use. These agreements often require that employees will use corporate computers only for work-related activities. Additionally, several companies use software programs to monitor employee computer usage.[28] Instituting practices that show respect for employee privacy but do not abdicate employer responsibility are increasingly necessary in today's workplace. Several Web sites provide model policies and detailed guidelines for conducting electronic monitoring, including the Model Electronic Privacy Act on the American Civil Liberties Union site.

So You Want a Job in Managing Organizational Culture, Teamwork and Communication

Jobs dealing with organizational culture and structure are usually at the top of the organization. If you want to be a CEO or high level manager you will help shape these areas of business. On the other hand, if you are an entrepreneur or small business person you will need to make decisions about assigning tasks, departmentalization and assigning responsibility. Even managers in small organizations have to make decisions about decentralization, span of management and forms of organizational structure. While these decisions may be part of your job, there are usually no job titles dealing with these specific areas. Specific jobs that attempt to improve organizational culture could include ethics and compliance positions as well as those who are in charge of communicating memos, manuals and policies that help establish the culture. These positions will be in communications, human resources and positions that assist top organizational managers.

Teams are becoming more common in the workplace and it is possible to become a member of a product development group or quality assurance team. There are also human resource positions that encourage teamwork through training activities. The area of corporate communications provides lots of opportunities for specific jobs that facilitate communication systems. Thanks to technology, there are job positions to help disseminate information through online newsletters, intranets or internal computer networks to share information to increase collaboration. In addition to the many advances using electronic communications, there are technology concerns that create new job opportunities. Monitoring workplace communications such as the use of e-mail and the Internet have created new industries. There have to be internal controls in the organization to make sure that the organization does not engage in any copyright infringement. If this is an area of interest, there are specific jobs that provide an opportunity to use your technological skills to assist in maintaining appropriate standards in communicating and using technology.

If you go to work for a large company with many divisions, you can expect a number of positions dealing with the tasks discussed here. If you go to work for a small company you will probably engage in most of these tasks as a part of your position. Organizational flexibility requires individual flexibility and those employees willing to take on new domains and challenges will be the employees who survive and prosper in the future.

Review Your Understanding

Define organizational structure, and relate how organizational structures develop.

Structure is the arrangement or relationship of positions within an organization; it develops when managers assign work activities to work groups and specific individuals and coordinate the diverse activities required to attain organizational objectives. Organizational structure evolves to accommodate growth, which requires people with specialized skills.

Describe how specialization and departmentalization help an organization achieve its goals.

Structuring an organization requires that management assign work tasks to specific individuals and groups. Under specialization, managers break labor into small, specialized tasks and assign employees to do a single task, fostering efficiency. Departmentalization is the grouping of jobs into working units (departments, units, groups, or divisions). Businesses may departmentalize by function, product, geographic region, or customer, or they may combine two or more of these.

Distinguish between groups and teams, and identify the types of groups that exist in organizations.

A group is two or more persons who communicate, share a common identity, and have a common goal. A team is a small group whose members have complementary skills, a common purpose, goals, and approach; and who hold themselves mutually accountable. The major distinction is that individual performance is most important in groups, while collective work group performance counts most in teams. Special kinds of groups include task forces, committees, project teams, product-development teams, quality-assurance teams, and self-directed work teams.

Determine how organizations assign responsibility for tasks and delegate authority.

Delegation of authority means assigning tasks to employees and giving them the power to make commitments, use resources, and take whatever actions are necessary to accomplish the tasks. It lays responsibility on employees to carry out assigned tasks satisfactorily and holds them accountable to a superior for the proper execution of their assigned work. The extent to which authority is delegated throughout an organization determines its degree of centralization. Span of management refers to the number of subordinates who report to a particular manager. A wide span of management occurs in flat organizations; a narrow one exists in tall organizations.

Compare and contrast some common forms of organizational structure.

Line structures have direct lines of authority that extend from the top manager to employees at the lowest level of the organization. The line-and-staff structure has a traditional line relationship between superiors and subordinates, and specialized staff managers are available to assist line managers. A multidivisional structure gathers departments into larger groups called divisions. A matrix, or project-management, structure sets up teams from different departments, thereby creating two or more intersecting lines of authority.

Describe how communication occurs in organizations.

Communication occurs both formally and informally in organizations. Formal communication may be downward, upward, horizontal, and even diagonal. Informal communication takes place through friendships and the grapevine.

Analyze a business's use of teams.

"Solve the Dilemma" on page 232 introduces a firm attempting to restructure to a team environment. Based on the material presented in this chapter, you should be able to evaluate the firm's efforts and make recommendations for resolving the problems that have developed.

Revisit the World of Business

1. Why was Yahoo! struggling as a company before Bartz took over as CEO?
2. What has Bartz done during her first years as CEO to help get the company back on track?
3. How has organizational restructuring helped Yahoo! return to the path of profitability?

Learn the Terms

accountability   217
centralized organization   217
committee   224
customer departmentalization   216
decentralized organization   218
delegation of authority   216
departmentalization   213
functional departmentalization   214
geographical departmentalization   216
grapevine   228
group   223
line-and-staff structure   220
line structure   220
matrix structure   222
multidivisional structure   221
organizational chart   211
organizational culture   208
organizational layers   219
product departmentalization   215
product-development teams   225
project teams   225
quality-assurance teams (or quality circles)   225
responsibility   217
self-directed work team (SDWT)   225
span of management   219
specialization   212
structure   211
task force   224
team   223

Check Your Progress

1. Identify four types of departmentalization and give an example of each type.

2. Explain the difference between groups and teams.

3. What are self-managed work teams and what tasks might they perform that traditionally are performed by managers?

4. Explain how delegating authority, responsibility, and accountability are related.

5. Distinguish between centralization and decentralization. Under what circumstances is each appropriate?

6. Define span of management. Why do some organizations have narrow spans and others wide spans?

7. Discuss the different forms of organizational structure. What are the primary advantages and disadvantages of each form?

8. Discuss the role of the grapevine within organizations. How can managers use it to further the goals of the firm?

9. How have technological advances made electronic oversight a necessity in many companies?

10. Discuss how an organization's culture might influence its ability to achieve its objectives. Do you think that managers can "manage" the organization's culture?

Get Involved

1. Explain, using a specific example (perhaps your own future business), how an organizational structure might evolve. How would you handle the issues of specialization, delegation of authority, and centralization? Which structure would you use? Explain your answers.

2. Interview the department chairperson in charge of one of the academic departments in your college or university. Using Table 7.2 as a guideline, explore whether the professors function more like a group or a team. Contrast what you find here with what you see on your school's basketball, football, or baseball team.

Build Your Skills

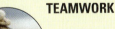

TEAMWORK

Background:
Think about all the different kinds of groups and teams you have been a member of or been involved with. Here's a checklist to help you remember them—with "Other" spaces to fill in ones not listed. Check all that apply.

School Groups/Teams
- ☐ Sports teams
- ☐ Cheerleading squads
- ☐ Musical groups
- ☐ Hobby clubs
- ☐ Foreign language clubs
- ☐ Study groups
- ☐ Other _____

Community Groups/Teams
- ☐ Fund-raising groups
- ☐ Religious groups
- ☐ Sports teams
- ☐ Political groups
- ☐ Boy/Girl Scout Troops
- ☐ Volunteer organizations
- ☐ Other _____

Employment Groups/Teams
- ☐ Problem-solving teams
- ☐ Work committees
- ☐ Project teams
- ☐ Labor union groups
- ☐ Work crews
- ☐ Other _____

Task

1. Of those you checked, circle those that you would categorize as a "really great team."

2. Examine the following table[29] and circle those characteristics from columns two and three that were represented in your "really great" team experiences.

Indicator	Good Team Experience	Not-So-Good Team Experience
Members arrive on time?	Members are prompt because they know others will be.	Members drift in sporadically, and some leave early.
Members prepared?	Members are prepared and know what to expect.	Members are unclear what the agenda is.
Meeting organized?	Members follow a planned agenda.	The agenda is tossed aside, and freewheeling discussion ensues.
Members contribute equally?	Members give each other a chance to speak; quiet members are encouraged.	Some members always dominate the discussion; some are reluctant to speak their minds.
Discussions help members make decisions?	Members learn from others' points of view, new facts are discussed, creative ideas evolve, and alternatives emerge.	Members reinforce their belief in their own points of view, or their decisions were made long before the meeting.

Indicator	Good Team Experience	Not-So-Good Team Experience
Any disagreement?	Members follow a conflict-resolution process established as part of the team's policies.	Conflict turns to argument, angry words, emotion, blaming.
More cooperation or more conflict?	Cooperation is clearly an important ingredient.	Conflict flares openly, as well as simmering below the surface.
Commitment to decisions?	Members reach consensus before leaving.	Compromise is the best outcome possible; some members don't care about the result.
Member feelings after team decision?	Members are satisfied and are valued for their ideas.	Members are glad it's over, not sure of results or outcome.
Members support decision afterward?	Members are committed to implementation.	Some members second-guess or undermine the team's decision.

3. What can you take with you from your positive team experiences and apply to a work-related group or team situation in which you might be involved?

_____
_____
_____

Solve the Dilemma

QUEST STAR IN TRANSITION

Quest Star (QS), which manufactures quality stereo loudspeakers, wants to improve its ability to compete against Japanese firms. Accordingly, the company has launched a comprehensive quality-improvement program for its Iowa plant. The QS Intracommunication Leadership Initiative (ILI) has flattened the layers of management. The program uses teams and peer pressure to accomplish the plant's goals instead of multiple management layers with their limited opportunities for communication. Under the initiative, employees make all decisions within the boundaries of their responsibilities, and they elect team representatives to coordinate with other teams. Teams are also assigned tasks ranging from establishing policies to evaluating on-the-job safety.

However, employees who are not self-motivated team players are having difficulty getting used to their peers' authority within this system. Upper-level managers face stress and frustration because they must train workers to supervise themselves.

Discussion Questions

1. What techniques or skills should an employee have to assume a leadership role within a work group?

2. If each work group has a team representative, what problems will be faced in supervising these representatives?

3. Evaluate the pros and cons of the system developed by QS.

Build Your Business Plan

ORGANIZATION, TEAMWORK, AND COMMUNICATION

Developing a business plan as a team is a deliberate move of your instructor to encourage you to familiarize yourself with the concept of teamwork. You need to realize that you are going to spend a large part of your professional life working with others. At this point in time you are working on the business plan for a grade, but after graduation you will be "teaming" with co-workers and the successfulness of your endeavor may determine whether or not you get a raise or a bonus. It is important that you be comfortable as soon as possible with working with others and holding them accountable for their contributions.

Some people are natural "leaders" and leaders often feel that if team members are not doing their work, they take it upon themselves to "do it all." This is not leadership, but rather micro-managing.

Leadership means holding members accountable for their responsibilities. Your instructor may provide ideas on how this could be implemented, possibly by utilizing peer reviews. Remember you are not doing a team member a favor by doing their work for them.

If you are a "follower" (someone who takes directions well) rather than a leader, try to get into a team where others are hard workers and you will rise to their level. There is nothing wrong with being a follower; not everyone can be a leader!

See for Yourself Videocase

ROWE HELPS ORGANIZATIONS IMPROVE PRODUCTIVITY WHILE INCREASING EMPLOYEE SATISFACTION

Given the choice, what employee wouldn't prefer to work on his or her own schedule and at the location of his or her choice? Although the majority of businesses still adhere to the traditional work week spent in a cubicle, a handful have branched out and adopted something called ROWE—Results Only Work Environment. Under ROWE, salaried employees are required to put in the hours it takes to complete their tasks, while hourly employees must work set hours. However, employees under a ROWE system get to choose when and where they work.

Best Buy implemented ROWE after struggling to retain employees. The company conducted a survey to gain some insight and found that employees felt micromanaged by supervisors to the point where they wanted to quit. The company had been functioning as a centralized organization and managers decided it needed to move toward a more decentralized structure. With the help of the survey, Jody Thompson and Cali Ressler discovered that employee productivity improved with increased flexibility. However, telecommuting and flextime simply were not sufficient. These benefits, often distributed to only a segment of employees, created friction with those employees denied the benefit. Thompson and Ressler suggested the ROWE concept and the company agreed to test it out. Initially, upper level management was skeptical. However, it quickly became clear that work was getting done faster and better. Productivity quickly improved by one third and skeptics became converts. Suddenly, the company was able to retain its top performing employees. Today, ROWE is a key recruiting tool for Best Buy, which ranked 37 on Fortune's "World's Most Admired Companies" 2010 list.

You might wonder why ROWE works so well. Employees in traditional work settings often waste many hours in meetings, talking to colleagues, or merely looking busy while daydreaming of vacation. Through ROWE, employees are judged only on their productivity. Working at home or in another chosen environment allows employees to focus free from distraction. Being given the opportunity to work from Cancun, the Rocky Mountains, or the Egyptian Pyramids removes the desire to always be somewhere else, which can be a major distraction. In the case of ROWE, freedom creates a sense of loyalty and dedication to the company. This lowers turnover, which saves a company a great deal of money.

ROWE founders Thompson and Ressler now run CultureRx—a consulting firm assisting companies and implementing and managing ROWE. Other companies using similar models are IBM, AT&T, and Sun Microsystems. The model works particularly well for technology companies in which many employees require only their laptops to accomplish work goals. Teams are able to teleconference via phone or computer programs such as Skype when necessary. Companies can realize significant savings by doing away with office space. Although it may not be a good fit for all companies, ROWE provides businesses with many benefits and creates happy employees—a combination bound to positively impact the bottom line.[30]

Discussion Questions

1. What about Best Buy's organizational culture was driving employees to quit?

2. How did ROWE help solve Best Buy's problems while increasing productivity and loyalty?

3. What other companies might benefit from implementing a ROWE system?

Remember to check out our Online Learning Center at www.mhhe.com/ferrell8e.

Team Exercise

Assign the responsibility of providing the organizational structure for a company one of your team members has worked for. Was your organization centralized or decentralized in terms of decision making? Would you consider the span of control to be wide or narrow? Were there any types of teams, committees, or task forces utilized in the organization? Report your work to the class.

chapter 8

Managing Service and Manufacturing Operations

OBJECTIVES

After reading this chapter, you will be able to:

- Define operations management, and differentiate between operations and manufacturing.

- Explain how operations management differs in manufacturing and service firms.

- Describe the elements involved in planning and designing an operations system.

- Specify some techniques managers may use to manage the logistics of transforming inputs into finished products.

- Assess the importance of quality in operations management.

- Evaluate a business's dilemma and propose a solution.

Toyota: Once Renowned for Excellence, Experiences Growing Pains

For decades, Toyota set the standard for quality and reliability. Known worldwide for their commitment to quality production, Toyota created the "Toyota Way," a manufacturing philosophy that emphasized continuous progress and reduced waste. Among the important principles of the Toyota Way are long-term planning, working to find and solve problems, and creating a corporate culture that encourages improvement. Thanks to the success of the Toyota Way, Toyota became the top automobile manufacturer in the world in 2008.

However, Toyota's success was cut short by a desire to grow rapidly at the expense of quality. In 2009 and 2010, Toyota issued a series of recalls on several of their popular models because of safety problems with accelerators, brakes, and power steering. The recalls affected more than 8 million vehicles across five continents. Following the announcement of the recalls, Toyota engineers and mechanics began to search for solutions to the problems and started the process of repairing millions of cars. The company also temporarily suspended production in the United States while they researched the causes of the problems. Many critics accused the company of acting too slowly to recall the defective cars and trying to push the problem under the rug. Because of the negative press, Toyota sales declined significantly. Toyota president Akio Toyoda admitted, "We so aggressively pursued numbers that we were unable to keep up with training staff to oversee quality." Toyoda also recognized that Toyota was slow to act on reports of problems provided by consumers.

continued

ENTER THE WORLD OF BUSINESS

In addition to repairing its vehicles, Toyota had to repair its reputation. Shortly after the recalls, Toyota established a global quality committee and promised to appoint chief quality officers for each of its regions. Toyota is also designing new safety systems and inspection processes for its vehicles. All future models will include a new brake-override system designed to activate the brakes in the event that both the brake and accelerator pedals are pushed down. Additionally, Toyota will have a third party test its electronic acceleration system. Ultimately, it will take more than committees, promises, and programs to rebuild Toyota. To regain its reputation and eventually innovate, Toyota will have to return to the Toyota Way.[1]

Introduction

All organizations create products—goods, services, or ideas—for customers. Thus, organizations as diverse as Toyota, Campbell Soup, UPS, and a public hospital share a number of similarities relating to how they transform resources into the products we consume. Most hospitals use similar admission procedures, while online social media companies, like Facebook and Twitter, use their technology and operating systems to create social networking opportunities and sell advertising. Such similarities are to be expected. But even organizations in unrelated industries take similar steps in creating goods or services. The check-in procedures of hotels and commercial airlines are comparable, for example. The way Subway assembles a sandwich and the way GMC assembles a truck are similar (both use automation and an assembly line). These similarities are the result of operations management, the focus of this chapter.

Here, we discuss the role of production or operations management in acquiring and managing the resources necessary to create goods and services. Production and operations management involves planning and designing the processes that will transform those resources into finished products, managing the movement of those resources through the transformation process, and ensuring that the products are of the quality expected by customers.

The Nature of Operations Management

operations management (OM)
the development and administration of the activities involved in transforming resources into goods and services

Operations management (OM), the development and administration of the activities involved in transforming resources into goods and services, is of critical importance. Operations managers oversee the transformation process and the planning and designing of operations systems, managing logistics, quality, and productivity. Quality and productivity have become fundamental aspects of operations management because a company that cannot make products of the quality desired by consumers, using resources efficiently and effectively, will not be able to remain in business. OM is the "core" of most organizations because it is responsible for the creation of the organization's goods or services.

Historically, operations management has been called "production" or "manufacturing" primarily because of the view that it was limited to the manufacture of physical goods. Its focus was on methods and techniques required to operate a factory efficiently. The change from "production" to "operations" recognizes the increasing importance of organizations that provide services and ideas. Additionally, the term *operations* represents an interest in viewing the operations function as a whole rather than simply as an analysis of inputs and outputs.

Today, OM includes a wide range of organizational activities and situations outside of manufacturing, such as health care, food service, banking, entertainment, education, transportation, and charity. Thus, we use the terms **manufacturing** and **production** interchangeably to represent the activities and processes used in making *tangible* products, whereas we use the broader term **operations** to describe those processes used in the making of *both tangible and intangible products.* Manufacturing provides tangible products such as Hewlett-Packard's latest printer, and operations provides intangibles such as a stay at Wyndham Hotels and Resorts.

The Transformation Process

At the heart of operations management is the transformation process through which **inputs** (resources such as labor, money, materials, and energy) are converted into **outputs** (goods, services, and ideas). The transformation process combines inputs in predetermined ways using different equipment, administrative procedures, and technology to create a product (Figure 8.1). To ensure that this process generates quality products efficiently, operations managers control the process by taking measurements (feedback) at various points in the transformation process and comparing them to previously established standards. If there is any deviation between the actual and desired outputs, the manager may take some sort of corrective action. All adjustments made to create a satisfying product are a part of the transformation process.

Transformation may take place through one or more processes. In a business that manufactures oak furniture, for example, inputs pass through several processes before being turned into the final outputs—furniture that has been designed to meet the desires of customers (Figure 8.2). The furniture maker must first strip the oak trees of their bark and saw them into appropriate sizes—one step in the transformation process. Next, the firm dries the strips of oak lumber, a second form of transformation. Third, the dried wood is routed into its appropriate shape and made

manufacturing
the activities and processes used in making tangible products; also called production

production
the activities and processes used in making tangible products; also called manufacturing

operations
the activities and processes used in making both tangible and intangible products

inputs
the resources—such as labor, money, materials, and energy—that are converted into outputs

outputs
the goods, services, and ideas that result from the conversion of inputs

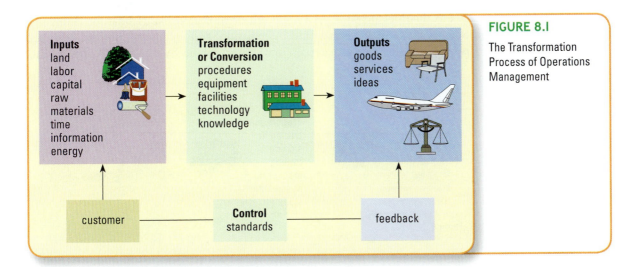

FIGURE 8.1

The Transformation Process of Operations Management

RESPONDING TO BUSINESS CHALLENGES
Domino's Goes Online to Improve Service and Customer Satisfaction

In 2009, Domino's Pizza launched a new online feature called Build Your Own Pizza, which allows customers to submit their order via dominos.com. As customers customize the size, crust, sauce, and toppings for their pizza, their selections appear on an image of a pizza. When customers are finished, they can review their orders, see the final price, and pay for their food. In addition to ordering online, customers can track their pizzas as the pies enter the oven and leave stores.

The build-your-own-pizza feature is part of a new sales system for Domino's. The completely redesigned system also includes a new phone and onsite ordering system. Domino's also maintains profiles on millions of customers. Each profile contains information on a customer's order history so employees can suggest additional items tailored to each individual.

Domino's competitors, Pizza Hut and Papa John's, also have online ordering systems, but neither system features an image of the pizza or order tracking. However, Pizza Hut has an iPhone application that allows customers to drag and drop toppings, while Papa John's accepts orders through text messaging.

Domino's new ordering system has helped the company improve customer service. The system created more consistency across Domino's independent franchises and increased order accuracy. In one year, online orders increased from 15 to 20 percent of total orders. The new system has also increased revenue and customer loyalty.[2]

Discussion Questions
1. What has Domino's done to regain market share?
2. Do you think the build-your-own pizza feature on Domino's website helps to give the company a competitive advantage?
3. How does the new ordering system help to improve customer service?

smooth. Fourth, workers assemble and treat the wood pieces, then stain or varnish the piece of assembled furniture. Finally, the completed piece of furniture is stored until it can be shipped to customers at the appropriate time. Of course, many businesses choose to eliminate some of these stages by purchasing already processed materials—lumber, for example—or outsourcing some tasks to third-party firms with greater expertise.

Operations Management in Service Businesses

Different types of transformation processes take place in organizations that provide services, such as airlines, colleges, and most nonprofit organizations. An airline transforms inputs such as employees, time, money, and equipment through processes such as booking flights, flying airplanes, maintaining equipment, and training crews. The output of these processes is flying passengers and/or packages to their destinations. In a nonprofit organization like Habitat for Humanity, inputs such as money, materials, information, and volunteer time and labor are used to transform raw materials into homes for needy families. In this setting,

FIGURE 8.2

Inputs, Outputs, and Transformation Processes in the Manufacture of Oak Furniture

Inputs
oak trees
labor
information/
knowledge
stain or varnish
router/saw
warehouse space/
time

Transformation
cutting or
sawing
routing
measuring
assembling
staining/varnishing
storing

Outputs
oak furniture

transformation processes include fund-raising and promoting the cause in order to gain new volunteers and donations of supplies, as well as pouring concrete, raising walls, and setting roofs. Transformation processes occur in all organizations, regardless of what they produce or their objectives. For most organizations, the ultimate objective is for the produced outputs to be worth more than the combined costs of the inputs.

Unlike tangible goods, services are effectively actions or performances that must be directed toward the consumers who use them. Thus, there is a significant customer-contact component to most services. Examples of high-contact services include health care, real estate, tax preparation, and food service. At the Inn at Little Washington in Washington, Virginia, for example, food servers are critical to delivering the perfect dining experience expected by the most discriminating diners.

The staff at the world-renowned Inn at Little Washington in the Shenandoah Valley take operations management to new heights in terms of how well they attend to patrons. Eating at the restaurant has been likened to "a performance in which the guest is always the star."

Wait staff are expected not only to be courteous, but also to demonstrate a detailed knowledge of the restaurant's offerings, and even to assess the mood of guests in order to respond to diners appropriately.[3] Low-contact services, such as online auction services like eBay, often have a strong high-tech component.

Regardless of the level of customer contact, service businesses strive to provide a standardized process, and technology offers an interface that creates an automatic and structured response. The ideal service provider will be high-tech and high-touch. JetBlue, for example, strives to maintain an excellent Web site; friendly, helpful customer contact; and satellite TV service at every seat on each plane. Thus, service organizations must build their operations around good execution, which comes from hiring and training excellent employees, developing flexible systems, customizing services, and maintaining adjustable capacity to deal with fluctuating demand.[4]

Another challenge related to service operations is that the output is generally intangible and even perishable. Few services can be saved, stored, resold, or returned.[5] A seat on an airline or a table in a restaurant, for example, cannot be sold or used at a later date. Because of the perishability of services, it is can be extremely difficult for service providers to accurately estimate the demand in order to match the right supply of a service. If an airline overestimates demand, for example, it will still have to fly each plane even with empty seats. The flight costs the same regardless of whether it is 50 percent full or 100 percent full, but the former will result in much higher costs per passenger. If the airline underestimates demand, the result can be long lines of annoyed customers or even the necessity of bumping some customers off of an overbooked flight.

Businesses that manufacture tangible goods and those that provide services or ideas are similar yet different. For example, both types of organizations must make design and operating decisions. Most goods are manufactured prior to purchase, but most services are performed after purchase. Flight attendants at Southwest Airlines, hotel service personnel, and even the New Orleans Saints football team engage in performances that are a part of the total product. Though manufacturers and service providers often perform similar activities, they also differ in several respects. We can classify these differences in five basic ways.

Nature and Consumption of Output.

First, manufacturers and service providers differ in the nature and consumption of their output. For example, the term *manufacturer* implies a firm that makes tangible products. A service provider, on the other hand, produces more intangible outputs such as U.S. Postal Service delivery of priority mail or a business stay in a Hyatt hotel. As mentioned earlier, the very nature of the service provider's product requires a higher degree of customer contact. Moreover, the actual performance of the service typically occurs at the point of consumption. At the Hyatt, the business traveler may evaluate in-room communications and the restaurant. Automakers, on the other hand, can separate the production of a car from its actual use. Manufacturing, then, can occur in an isolated environment, away from the customer. On the other hand, service providers, because of their need for customer contact, are often more limited than manufacturers in selecting work methods, assigning jobs, scheduling work, and exercising control over operations. At FedEx, the Quality Improvement Process (QIP) includes sayings such as "Do it right the first time," and "Make the first time you do it the only time anyone has to do it." The quality of the service experience is often controlled by a service contact employee. However, some hospitals are studying the manufacturing processes and quality control mechanisms applied in the automotive industry in an effort to improve their service quality. By analyzing work processes to find unnecessary steps to eliminate and using teams to identify and address problems as soon as they occur, these hospitals are slashing patient waiting times, decreasing inventories of wheelchairs, readying operating rooms sooner, and generally moving patients through their hospital visit more quickly, with fewer errors, and at a lower cost.[6]

Uniformity of Inputs.

A second way to classify differences between manufacturers and service providers has to do with the uniformity of inputs. Manufacturers typically have more control over the amount of variability of the resources they use than do service providers. For example, each customer calling Fidelity Investments is likely to require different services due to differing needs, whereas many of the tasks required to manufacture a Ford Focus are the same across each unit of output. Consequently, the products of service organizations tend to be more "customized" than those of their manufacturing counterparts. Consider, for example, a haircut versus a bottle of shampoo. The haircut is much more likely to incorporate your specific desires (customization) than is the bottle of shampoo.

Manufacturers produce more standardized products than service organizations. Even at different McDonald's restaurants, in which the products are carefully standardized, your service experience with the food and service can be very different.

Uniformity of Output.

Manufacturers and service providers also differ in the uniformity of their output, the final product. Because of the human element inherent in providing services, each service tends to be performed differently. Not all grocery checkers, for example, wait on customers in the same way. If a barber or stylist performs 15 haircuts in a day, it is unlikely that any two of them will be exactly the same. Consequently, human and technological elements associated with a service can result in a different day-to-day or even hour-to-hour performance of that service. The service experience can even vary at McDonald's or Burger King despite the fact that the two chains employ very similar procedures and processes. Moreover, no two customers are exactly alike in their perception of the service experience. Health care offers another excellent example of this challenge. Every diagnosis, treatment, and surgery varies because every individual is different. In manufacturing, the high degree of automation available allows manufacturers to generate uniform outputs and, thus, the operations are more effective and efficient. For example, we would expect every Movado or Rolex watch to maintain very high standards of quality and performance.

Labor Required.   A fourth point of difference is the amount of labor required to produce an output. Service providers are generally more labor-intensive (require more labor) because of the high level of customer contact, perishability of the output (must be consumed immediately), and high degree of variation of inputs and outputs (customization). For example, Adecco provides temporary support personnel. Each temporary worker's performance determines Adecco's product quality. A manufacturer, on the other hand, is likely to be more capital-intensive because of the machinery and technology used in the mass production of highly similar goods. For instance, it would take a considerable investment for Nokia to make a digital phone that has a battery with longer life.

Measurement of Productivity.   The final distinction between service providers and manufacturers involves the measurement of productivity for each output produced. For manufacturers, measuring productivity is fairly straightforward because of the tangibility of the output and its high degree of uniformity. For the service provider, variations in demand (for example, higher demand for air travel in some seasons than in others), variations in service requirements from job to job, and the intangibility of the product make productivity measurement more difficult. Consider, for example, how much easier it is to measure the productivity of employees involved in the production of Intel computer processors as opposed to serving the needs of Prudential Securities' clients.

It is convenient and simple to think of organizations as being either manufacturers or service providers as in the preceding discussion. In reality, however, most organizations are a combination of the two, with both tangible and intangible qualities embodied in what they produce. For example, Porsche provides customer services such as toll-free hotlines and warranty protection, while banks may sell checks and other tangible products that complement their primarily intangible product offering. Thus, we consider "products" to include both tangible physical goods as well as intangible service offerings. It is the level of tangibility of its principal product that tends to classify a company as either a manufacturer or a service provider. From an OM standpoint, this level of tangibility greatly influences the nature of the company's operational processes and procedures.

Planning and Designing Operations Systems

Before a company can produce any product, it must first decide what it will produce and for what group of customers. It must then determine what processes it will use to make these products as well as the facilities it needs to produce them. These decisions comprise operations planning. Although planning was once the sole realm of the production and operations department, today's successful companies involve all departments within an organization, particularly marketing and research and development, in these decisions.

Planning the Product

Before making any product, a company first must determine what consumers want and then design a product to satisfy that want. Most companies use marketing research (discussed in Chapter 11) to determine the kinds of goods and services to provide and the features they must possess. Twitter and Facebook provide new opportunities for businesses to discover what consumers want, then design the product accordingly. Cordarounds.com, a clothing company based in San Francisco, found that many people in California bike to work. Based on information gathered on Twitter, the company developed a line of bike-ready clothing lined with reflective material. When bike commuters roll up their pant legs to ride home, the reflective material helps them stay safe even when they are riding home after dark. Cordarounds also uses Google's AdWords, another digital media source, to advertise affordably. Cordarounds began as a small company and is growing rapidly as more people become concerned about the environment and choose biking over driving.[7] Marketing research can also help gauge the demand for a product and how much consumers are willing to pay for it. But when a market's environment changes, firms have to be flexible.

Developing a product can be a lengthy, expensive process. For example, in the automobile industry, developing the new technology for night vision, bumper-mounted sonar systems that make parking easier, and a satellite service that locates and analyzes car problems has been a lengthy, expensive process. Most companies work to reduce development time and costs. For example, through Web collaboration, faucet manufacturer Moen reduced the time required to take an idea to a finished product in stores to just 16 months, a drop of 33 percent.[8] Once management has developed an idea for a product that customers will buy, it must then plan how to produce the product.

Within a company, the engineering or research and development department is charged with turning a product idea into a workable design that can be produced economically. In smaller companies, a single individual (perhaps the owner) may be solely responsible for this crucial activity. Regardless of who is responsible for product design, planning does not stop with a blueprint for a product or a description of a service; it must also work out efficient production of the product to ensure that enough is available to satisfy consumer demand. How does a lawn mower company transform steel, aluminum, and other materials into a mower design that satisfies consumer and environmental requirements? Operations managers must plan for the types and quantities of materials needed to produce the product, the skills and quantity of people needed to make the product, and the actual processes through which the inputs must pass in their transformation to outputs.

Designing the Operations Processes

Before a firm can begin production, it must first determine the appropriate method of transforming resources into the desired product. Often, consumers' specific needs and desires dictate a process. Customer needs, for example, require that all 3/4-inch bolts have the same basic thread size, function, and quality; if they did not, engineers and builders could not rely on 3/4-inch bolts in their construction projects. A bolt manufacturer, then, will likely use a standardized process so that every 3/4-inch bolt produced is like every other one. On the other hand, a bridge often must be customized so that it is appropriate for the site and expected load; furthermore, the bridge must be constructed on site rather than in a factory. Typically, products are designed to be manufactured by one of three processes: standardization, modular design, or customization.

Standardization.   Most firms that manufacture products in large quantities for many customers have found that they can make them cheaper and faster by standardizing designs. **Standardization** is making identical, interchangeable components or even complete products. With standardization, a customer may not get exactly what he or she wants, but the product generally costs less than a custom-designed product. Television sets, ballpoint pens, and tortilla chips are standardized products; most are manufactured on an assembly line. Standardization speeds up production and quality control and reduces production costs. And, as in the example of the 34-inch bolts, standardization provides consistency so that customers who need certain products to function uniformly all the time will get a product that meets their expectations. As a result of its entry into the World Trade Organization, China promoted the standardization of agricultural production across the country, resulting in increased agricultural production.

standardization
the making of identical interchangeable components or products

Modular Design.   **Modular design** involves building an item in self-contained units, or modules, that can be combined or interchanged to create different products. Personal computers, for example, are generally composed of a number of components—CPU case, motherboard, chips, hard drives, graphics card, etc.—that can be installed in different configurations to meet the customer's needs. Because many modular components are produced as integrated units, the failure of any portion of a modular component usually means replacing the entire component. Modular design allows products to be repaired quickly, thus reducing the cost of labor, but the component itself is expensive, raising the cost of repair materials. Many automobile manufacturers use modular design in the production process. Manufactured homes are built on a modular design and often cost about one-fourth the cost of a conventionally built house.

modular design
the creation of an item in self-contained units, or modules, that can be combined or interchanged to create different products

Customization.   **Customization** is making products to meet a particular customer's needs or wants. Products produced in this way are generally unique. Such products include repair services, photocopy services, custom artwork, jewelry, and

customization
making products to meet a particular customer's needs or wants

Clayton Homes, a manufactured-home company, has begun building eco-friendly modular "ihomes" like the one shown here. Homebuyers can choose the components they want in the home and have them configured how they like.

Entrepreneurship in Action
In a Downturn, Restaurants Have to Stand Out from a Crowd

J. H. Whitney

Business: Ignite Restaurant Group

Founded: 2006

Success: Ignite had $126.8 million in sales in 2008.

Is there such a thing as a recession-proof restaurant? Ignite Restaurant Group, formerly known as JCS Holdings, believes it has what it takes to survive and profit. In its founding year, Ignite purchased the majority of the Joe's Crab Shack locations, and in 2009 it launched Brick House Tavern & Tap. The company is convinced that it has two ideal restaurant formulas for surviving economic downturns. The first, Joe's Crab Shack, is an established and well-loved family dining spot. Ignite tweaked the menu to offer Steampots, which are not usually available in casual dining restaurants. Although Steampots cost more, they are popular with diners. The second restaurant, Brick House Tavern & Tap, offers a unique dining experience. Although customers span all demographics, Brick House caters to the bachelor—serving its beer in beer bongs, hiring an all-female wait staff who wear short shorts and are encouraged to socialize with customers, and boasting a frat house/bachelor pad style. In a sense, Ignite has taken the Hooters formula and boosted it up a notch. Both restaurants have fared well, and Ignite believes its success is due to its unique spins on tried and true formulas.[9]

furniture, as well as large-scale products such as bridges, ships, and computer software. Custom designs are used in communications and service products. A Web-based design service, myemma.com, creates a custom template using a company's logo and colors to create a unique page for a Web site. It also provides tools for interacting with customers and tracking deliveries.[10] Although there may be similarities among ships, for example, builders generally design and build each ship to meet the needs of the customer who will use it. Delta Marine Industries custom-builds each luxury yacht to the customer's exact specifications and preferences for things like helicopter garages, golf courses, and swimming pools. Mass customization relates to making products that meet the needs or wants of a large number of individual customers. The customer can select the model, size, color, style, or design of the product. Dell can customize a computer with the exact configuration that fits a customer's needs. Services such as fitness programs and travel packages can also be custom designed for a large number of individual customers. For both goods and services, customers get to make choices and have options to determine the final product.

Planning Capacity

Planning the operational processes for the organization involves two important areas: capacity planning and facilities planning. The term **capacity** basically refers to the maximum load that an organizational unit can carry or operate. The unit of measurement may be a worker or machine, a department, a branch, or even an entire plant. Maximum capacity can be stated in terms of the inputs or outputs provided. For example, an electric plant might state plant capacity in terms of the maximum number of kilowatt-hours that can be produced without causing a power outage, while a restaurant might state capacity in terms of the maximum number of customers who can be effectively—comfortably and courteously—served at any one particular time.

Efficiently planning the organization's capacity needs is an important process for the operations manager. Capacity levels that fall short can result in unmet demand, and consequently, lost customers. On the other hand, when there is more capacity

capacity
the maximum load that an organizational unit can carry or operate

Zhu Zhu Pet Hamsters were a smash hit when they first hit the market. The problem? The maker initially lacked the production capacity to make as many of them as demanded.

available than needed, operating costs are driven up needlessly due to unused and often expensive resources. To avoid such situations, organizations must accurately forecast demand and then plan capacity based on these forecasts. Another reason for the importance of efficient capacity planning has to do with long-term commitment of resources. Often, once a capacity decision—such as factory size—has been implemented, it is very difficult to change the decision without incurring substantial costs. Large utilities companies have come to real-ize that although change can be expensive, not adjusting to future demand and stakeholder desires will be more expensive in the long run. For this reason, utilities companies like PNM in New Mexico have made a commitment to including more renewable energy in their supply mix, complying with ISO 14001 emissions guide-lines for power plants, and taking a pro-cap-and-trade stance.[12]

> **Did You Know?**   Hershey's has the production capacity to make more than 80 million chocolate kisses per day.[11]

Planning Facilities

Once a company knows what process it will use to create its products, it then can design and build an appropriate facility in which to make them. Many products are manufactured in factories, but others are produced in stores, at home, or where the product ultimately will be used. Companies must decide where to locate their operations facilities, what layout is best for producing their particular product, and even what technology to apply to the transformation process.

Many firms are developing both a traditional organization for customer contact as well as a virtual organization. Charles Schwab Corporation, a securities broker-age and investment company, maintains traditional offices and has developed com-plete telephone and Internet services for customers. Through its Web site, investors can obtain personal investment information and trade securities over the Internet without leaving their home or office.

Facility Location. Where to locate a firm's facilities is a significant question because, once the decision has been made and implemented, the firm must live with it due to the high costs involved. When a company decides to relocate or open a facility at a new location, it must pay careful attention to factors such as proximity to market, availability of raw materials, availability of transportation, availability of power, climatic influences, availability of labor, community characteristics (quality of life), and taxes and inducements. Inducements and tax reductions have become an increasingly important criterion in recent years. To increase production and to provide incentives for small startups, many states are offering tax inducements for solar companies. State governments are willing to forego some tax revenue in exchange for job growth, getting in on a burgeoning industry as well as the good publicity generated by the company. In a very solar-friendly state like Colorado, companies may get tax reductions for starting production, and consumers receive additional rebates for installing solar systems in their homes and businesses.[13] Because it is such a large corporation, many communities induce Walmart to locate there through offering millions of dollars in free roads, land, sewers, and tax abatements from local governments as incentives to locate new stores or distribution centers in certain areas.[14] The facility-location decision is complex because it involves the evaluation of many factors, some of which cannot be measured with precision. Because of the long-term impact of the decision, however, it is one that cannot be taken lightly.

Facility Layout. Arranging the physical layout of a facility is a complex, highly technical task. Some industrial architects specialize in the design and layout of certain types of businesses. There are three basic layouts: fixed-position, process, and product.

A company using a **fixed-position layout** brings all resources required to create the product to a central location. The product—perhaps an office building, house, hydroelectric plant, or bridge—does not move. A company using a fixed-position layout may be called a **project organization** because it is typically involved in large, complex projects such as construction or exploration. Project organizations generally make a unique product, rely on highly skilled labor, produce very few units, and have high production costs per unit.

Firms that use a **process layout** organize the transformation process into departments that group related processes. A metal fabrication plant, for example, may have a cutting department, a drilling department, and a polishing department. A hospital may have an X-ray unit, an obstetrics unit, and so on. These types of organizations are sometimes called **intermittent organizations,** which deal with products of a lesser magnitude than do project organizations, and their products are not necessarily unique but possess a significant number of differences. Doctors, makers of custom-made cabinets, commercial printers, and advertising agencies are intermittent organizations because they tend to create products to customers' specifications and produce relatively few units of each product. Because of the low level of output, the cost per unit of product is generally high.

The **product layout** requires that production be broken down into relatively simple tasks assigned to workers, who are usually positioned along an assembly line. Workers remain in one location, and the product moves from one worker to another. Each person in turn performs his or her required tasks or activities. Companies that use assembly lines are usually known as **continuous manufacturing organizations,** so named because once they are set up, they run continuously,

---

fixed-position layout
a layout that brings all resources required to create the product to a central location

project organization
a company using a fixed-position layout because it is typically involved in large, complex projects such as construction or exploration

process layout
a layout that organizes the transformation process into departments that group related processes

intermittent organizations
organizations that deal with products of a lesser magnitude than do project organizations; their products are not necessarily unique but possess a significant number of differences

product layout
a layout requiring that production be broken down into relatively simple tasks assigned to workers, who are usually positioned along an assembly line

continuous manufacturing organizations
companies that use continuously running assembly lines, creating products with many similar characteristics

creating products with many similar characteristics. Examples of products produced on assembly lines are automobiles, television sets, vacuum cleaners, toothpaste, and meals from a cafeteria. Continuous manufacturing organizations using a product layout are characterized by the standardized product they produce, the large number of units produced, and the relatively low unit cost of production.

Many companies actually use a combination of layout designs. For example, an automobile manufacturer may rely on an assembly line (product layout) but may also use a process layout to manufacture parts.

Technology.   Every industry has a basic, underlying technology that dictates the nature of its transformation process. The steel industry continually tries to improve steelmaking techniques. The health care industry performs research into medical technologies and pharmaceuticals to improve the quality of health care service. Two developments that have strongly influenced the operations of many businesses are computers and robotics.

Computers have been used for decades and on a relatively large scale since IBM introduced its 650 series in the late 1950s. The operations function makes great use of computers in all phases of the transformation process. **Computer-assisted design (CAD),** for example, helps engineers design components, products, and processes on the computer instead of on paper. **Computer-assisted manufacturing (CAM)** goes a step further, employing specialized computer systems to actually guide and control the transformation processes. Such systems can monitor the transformation process, gathering information about the equipment used to produce the products and about the product itself as it goes from one stage of the transformation process to the next. The computer provides information to an operator who may, if necessary, take corrective action. In some highly automated systems, the computer itself can take corrective action. At Dell's OptiPlex Plant, electronic instructions are sent to double-decker conveyor belts that speed computer components to assembly stations. Two-member teams are told by computers which PC or server to build, with initial assembly taking only three to four minutes. Then more electronic commands move the products (more than 20,000 machines on a typical day) to a finishing area to be customized, boxed, and sent to waiting delivery trucks.

Using **flexible manufacturing,** computers can direct machinery to adapt to different versions of similar operations. For example, with instructions from a computer, one machine can be programmed to carry out its function for several different versions of an engine without shutting down the production line for refitting.

Robots are also becoming increasingly useful in the transformation process. These "steel-collar" workers have become particularly important in industries such as nuclear power, hazardous-waste disposal, ocean research, and space construction and maintenance, in which human lives would otherwise be at risk. Robots are used in numerous applications by companies around the world. Many assembly operations—cars, television sets, telephones, stereo equipment, and numerous other products—depend on industrial robots. The Robotic Industries Association estimates that about 194,000 robots are now at work in U.S. factories, making the United States one of the two largest the users of robotics, second only to Japan.[15] Researchers continue to make more sophisticated robots, and some speculate that in the future robots will not be limited to space programs and production and operations, but will also be able to engage in farming, laboratory research, and even household activities. Moreover, robotics are increasingly being used in the medical field. There are an estimated 1 million robots being used in manufacturing around

computer-assisted design (CAD)
the design of components, products, and processes on computers instead of on paper

computer-assisted manufacturing (CAM)
manufacturing that employs specialized computer systems to actually guide and control the transformation processes

flexible manufacturing
the direction of machinery by computers to adapt to different versions of similar operations

Autodesk Inc.'s computer-aided design (CAD) software helps architects and engineers design, draft, and model buildings and products, including custom guitars like this one.

the world, most of them in high-tech industries. They now help doctors perform an estimated 86 percent of prostate cancer surgeries in the United States.[16].

When all these technologies—CAD/CAM, flexible manufacturing, robotics, computer systems, and more—are integrated, the result is **computer-integrated manufacturing (CIM),** a complete system that designs products, manages machines and materials, and controls the operations function. Companies adopt CIM to boost productivity and quality and reduce costs. Such technology, and computers in particular, will continue to make strong inroads into operations on two fronts—one dealing with the technology involved in manufacturing and one dealing with the administrative functions and processes used by operations managers. The operations

computer-integrated manufacturing (CIM) a complete system that designs products, manages machines and materials, and controls the operations function

manager must be willing to work with computers and other forms of technology and to develop a high degree of computer literacy.

Sustainability and Manufacturing

Manufacturing and operations systems are moving quickly to establish environmental sustainability and minimize negative impact on the natural environment. Sustainability deals with reducing the consumption of resources and the long-term well-being of the planet, including natural entities and the interactions of individuals, organizations, and businesses. Sustainability issues are becoming increasingly important to stakeholders and consumers, as they pertain to the future health of the planet. Some sustainability issues include pollution of the land, air, and water, climate change, waste management, deforestation, urban sprawl, protection of biodiversity, and genetically modified foods.

For example, Walmart is working to make its stores and products more environmentally friendly. Walmart has created a series of broad environmental goals, striving to eventually create zero waste, to run entirely on renewable energy, and to sell sustainable products. The company works with suppliers to reduce cardboard and plastic packaging. Walmart already increased the efficiency of its truck fleet by 38 percent and intends to double its efficiency by October 2015. Walmart is also changing its lighting and other electrical use for maximum efficiency. All of these initiatives relate to making operations greener, contributing to environmental sustainability, providing savings, and being a role model for other businesses.[17]

While Walmart illustrates green initiatives in operations, New Belgium Brewing illustrates green initiatives in operations and manufacturing. New Belgium was the first brewery to adopt 100 percent wind-powered electricity, reducing carbon emissions by 1,800 metric tons a year. They use a steam condenser to capture hot water to be reused for boiling the next batch of barley and hops, then the steam is redirected to heat the floor tiles and de-ice the loading docks in cold Colorado weather. Used barley and hops are given to local farmers to feed cattle. New Belgium gives employees a bicycle after one year of employment to ride to work, further reducing carbon emissions. The company is moving to aluminum cans because they can be recycled an infinite number of times and recycling one can saves enough electricity to run a television for three hours or save a half gallon of gasoline. The company has won an award from the Environmental Protection Agency and is a role model for other businesses.

The outdoor clothing company Patagonia is always looking for a greener way to design, produce, and recycle its products. The company's mission statement: Build the best product, cause no unnecessary harm, and use business to inspire and implement solutions to the environmental crisis.

Walmart and New Belgium Brewing demonstrate that reducing waste, recycling, conserving, and using renewable energy not only protect the environment, but can also gain the support of stakeholders. Green operations and manufacturing can improve a firm's reputation and customer and employee loyalty that leads to improved profits.

Much of the movement to green manufacturing and operations is the belief that global warming and climate change must decline. The McKinsey Global Institute (MGI) says that just by investing in existing technologies, the world's energy use could be reduced by 50 percent by the year 2020. Just creating green buildings and higher mileage cars could yield $900 billion savings per year by 2020.[18] Companies like General Motors are adapting to stakeholder demands for greater sustainability by producing smaller and more fuel-efficient cars. For example, the Chevy Volt can run for up to 40 miles on one overnight charge before switching to a gas-powered generator. The volt is also a Flex-Fuel vehicle, which means that it can use either traditional gasoline or E85 ethanol, which some people believe is better for the environment.[19] Green products produced through green operations and manufacturing are our future. A report authored by the Center for American Progress cites ways that cities and local governments can play a role. For example, Los Angeles plans to save the city utility costs by retrofitting hundreds of city buildings while creating a green careers training program for low-income residents. Newark, New Jersey, and Richmond, California, also have green jobs training programs. Albuquerque, New Mexico, was the first city to sign on to a pledge to build a green economy as part of its efforts to create green jobs to stimulate the city's economy.[20] Government initiatives provide space for businesses to innovate their green operations and manufacturing.

Managing the Supply Chain

supply chain management
connecting and integrating all parties or members of the distribution system in order to satisfy customers

A major function of operations is **supply chain management,** which refers to connecting and integrating all parties or members of the distribution system in order to satisfy customers.[21] Also called logistics, supply chain management includes all the activities involved in obtaining and managing raw materials and component parts, managing finished products, packaging them, and getting them to customers. Sunny Delight had to quickly recreate its supply chain after spinning off from Procter & Gamble. This means it had to develop ordering, shipping, and billing, as well as warehouse management systems and transportation, so it could focus on growing and managing the Sunny Delight brand.[22] The supply chain integrates firms such as raw material suppliers, manufacturers, retailers, and ultimate consumers into a seamless flow of information and products.[23] Some aspects of logistics (warehousing, packaging, distributing) are so closely linked with marketing that we will discuss them in Chapter 12. In this section, we look at purchasing, managing inventory, outsourcing, and scheduling, which are vital tasks in the transformation of raw materials into finished goods. To illustrate logistics, consider a hypothetical small business—we'll call it Rushing Water Canoes Inc.—that manufactures aluminum canoes, which it sells primarily to sporting goods stores and river-rafting expeditions. Our company also makes paddles and helmets, but the focus of the following discussion is the manufacture of the company's quality canoes as they proceed through the logistics process.

Purchasing

purchasing
the buying of all the materials needed by the organization; also called procurement

Purchasing, also known as procurement, is the buying of all the materials needed by the organization. The purchasing department aims to obtain items of the desired quality in the right quantities at the lowest possible cost. Rushing Water Canoes, for example, must procure not only aluminum and other raw materials, and various canoe parts and components, but also machines and equipment, manufacturing supplies (oil, electricity, and so on), and office supplies in order to make its canoes. People in the purchasing department locate and evaluate suppliers of these items. They must constantly be on the lookout for new materials or parts that will do a better job or cost less than those currently being used. The purchasing function can be quite complex and is one area made much easier and more efficient by technological advances.

Not all companies purchase all the materials needed to create their products. Oftentimes, they can make some components more economically and efficiently than can an outside supplier. Coors, for example, manufactures its own cans at a subsidiary plant. On the other hand, firms sometimes find that it is uneconomical to make or purchase an item, and instead arrange to lease it from another organization. Some airlines, for example, lease airplanes rather than buy them. Whether to purchase, make, or lease a needed item generally depends on cost, as well as on product availability and supplier reliability.

Managing Inventory

Once the items needed to create a product have been procured, some provision has to be made for storing them until they are needed. Every raw material, component, completed or partially completed product, and piece of equipment a firm uses—its **inventory**—must be accounted for, or controlled. There are three basic types of inventory. *Finished-goods inventory* includes those products that are ready for sale,

FAC Food Service Logistics helps manage the supply chain and inventory of food companies in the United States so their products—chicken included—arrive on time and unspoiled.

such as a fully assembled automobile ready to ship to a dealer. *Work-in-process inventory* consists of those products that are partly completed or are in some stage of the transformation process. At McDonald's, a cooking hamburger represents work-in-process inventory because it must go through several more stages before it can be sold to a customer. *Raw materials inventory* includes all the materials that have been purchased to be used as inputs for making other products. Nuts and bolts are raw materials for an automobile manufacturer, while hamburger patties, vegetables, and buns are raw materials for the fast-food restaurant. Our fictional Rushing Water Canoes has an inventory of materials for making canoes, paddles, and helmets, as well as its inventory of finished products for sale to consumers.

inventory
all raw materials, components, completed or partially completed products, and pieces of equipment a firm uses

inventory control
the process of determining how many supplies and goods are needed and keeping track of quantities on hand, where each item is, and who is responsible for it

Inventory control is the process of determining how many supplies and goods are needed and keeping track of quantities on hand, where each item is, and who is responsible for it.

Operations management must be closely coordinated with inventory control. The production of televisions, for example, cannot be planned without some knowledge of the availability of all the necessary materials—the chassis, picture tubes, color guns, and so forth. Also, each item held in inventory—any type of inventory—carries with it a cost. For example, storing fully assembled televisions in a warehouse to sell to a dealer at a future date requires not only the use of space, but also the purchase of insurance to cover any losses that might occur due to fire or other unforeseen events.

Inventory managers spend a great deal of time trying to determine the proper inventory level for each item. The answer to the question of how many units to hold in inventory depends on variables such as the usage rate of the item, the cost of maintaining the item in inventory, future costs of inventory and other procedures associated with ordering or making the item, and the cost of the item itself. For example, the price of copper has fluctuated between $1.50 and $4 a pound during the 2000s. Between February 2009 and February 2010, copper prices more than doubled. Firms using copper wiring for construction, copper pipes for plumbing, and other industries requiring copper have to analyze the trade-offs between inventory costs and expected changes in the price of copper. Several approaches may be

Walmart tracks its sales minute-by-minute. Following the 9/11 terrorist attacks on America in 2001, the company realized American flags were flying off the shelves. It quickly ordered as many as possible from suppliers, leaving none for competitors like Target, which monitored its inventory only daily.

used to determine how many units of a given item should be procured at one time and when that procurement should take place.

The Economic Order Quantity Model.   To control the number of items maintained in inventory, managers need to determine how much of any given item they should order. One popular approach is the **economic order quantity (EOQ) model,** which identifies the optimum number of items to order to minimize the costs of managing (ordering, storing, and using) them.

Just-in-Time Inventory Management.   An increasingly popular technique is **just-in-time (JIT) inventory management,** which eliminates waste by using smaller quantities of materials that arrive "just in time" for use in the transformation process and therefore require less storage space and other inventory management expense. JIT minimizes inventory by providing an almost continuous flow of items from suppliers to the production facility. Many U.S. companies, including Hewlett-Packard, IBM, and Harley Davidson, have adopted JIT to reduce costs and boost efficiency.

Let's say that Rushing Water Canoes uses 20 units of aluminum from a supplier per day. Traditionally, its inventory manager might order enough for one month at a time: 440 units per order (20 units per day times 22 workdays per month). The expense of such a large inventory could be considerable because of the cost of insurance coverage, recordkeeping, rented storage space, and so on. The just-in-time approach would reduce these costs because aluminum would be purchased in smaller quantities, perhaps in lot sizes of 20, which the supplier would deliver once a day. Of course, for such an approach to be effective, the supplier must be extremely reliable and relatively close to the production facility.

Material-requirements Planning.   Another inventory management technique is **material-requirements planning (MRP),** a planning system that schedules the precise quantity of materials needed to make the product. The basic components of MRP are a master production schedule, a bill of materials, and an inventory status file. At Rushing Water Canoes, for example, the inventory-control manager will look at the production schedule to determine how many canoes the company plans to make. He or she will then prepare a bill of materials—a list of all the materials needed to make that quantity of canoes. Next, the manager will determine the quantity of these items that RWC already holds in inventory (to avoid ordering excess materials) and then develop a schedule for ordering and accepting delivery of the right quantity of materials to satisfy the firm's needs. Because of the large number of parts and materials that go into a typical production process, MRP must be done on a computer. It can be, and often is, used in conjunction with just-in-time inventory management.

Outsourcing

Increasingly, outsourcing has become a component of supply chain management in operations. As we mentioned in Chapter 3, outsourcing refers to the contracting of manufacturing or other tasks to independent companies, often overseas. Many companies elect to outsource some aspects of their operations to companies that can provide these products more efficiently, at a lower cost, and with greater customer satisfaction. Globalization has put pressure on supply chain managers to improve speed and balance resources against competitive pressures. Companies outsourcing

economic order quantity (EOQ) model
a model that identifies the optimum number of items to order to minimize the costs of managing (ordering, storing, and using) them

just-in-time (JIT) inventory management
a technique using smaller quantities of materials that arrive "just in time" for use in the transformation process and therefore require less storage space and other inventory management expense

material-requirements planning (MRP)
a planning system that schedules the precise quantity of materials needed to make the product

TABLE 8.1   The World's Top Five Outsourcing Providers

Company	Services[*]
Accenture	Human resource management; information and communication technology management; financial management
IBM	Customer relationship management; human resource management; information technology; strategic consulting
Sodexo	Real estate and asset management; facility services; service vouchers and cards
Tata Consultancy Services	Information technology management; strategic consulting
Wipro Technologies	Information technology management; business and process solutions

Source: "The 2009 Global Outsourcing 100," The International Association of Outsourcing Professionals™, http://www.outsourcingprofessional.org/content/23/152/1197 (accessed February 16, 2010).

[*]The services section was provided by the authors.

to China, in particular, face heavy regulation, high transportation costs, inadequate facilities, and unpredictable supply chain execution. Therefore, suppliers need to provide useful, timely, and accurate information about every aspect of the quality requirements, schedules, and solutions to dealing with problems. For example, Chinese suppliers took responsibility for the lead paint on children's toys crisis in the United States, but it was an overall management and supply chain system failure that permitted these toxic toys to be sold in U.S. stores.[24]

Many high-tech firms have outsourced the production of chips, computers, and telecom equipment to Asian companies. The hourly labor costs in countries such as China, India, and Vietnam are far less than in the United States, Europe, or even Mexico. These developing countries have improved their manufacturing capabilities, infrastructure, and technical and business skills, making them more attractive regions for global sourcing. On the other hand, the cost of outsourcing halfway around the world must be considered in decisions. While information technology is often outsourced today, transportation, human resources, services, and even marketing functions can be outsourced. Our hypothetical Rushing Water Canoes might contract with a local janitorial service to clean its offices and with a local accountant to handle routine bookkeeping and tax-preparation functions.

Outsourcing, once used primarily as a cost-cutting tactic, has increasingly been linked with the development of competitive advantage through improved product quality, speeding up the time it takes products to get to the customer, and overall supply-chain efficiencies. Table 8.1 provides the world's top five outsourcing providers that assist mainly in information technology. Outsourcing allows companies to free up time and resources to focus on what they do best and to create better opportunities to focus on customer satisfaction. Many executives view outsourcing as an innovative way to boost productivity and remain competitive against low-wage offshore factories. However, outsourcing may create conflict with labor and negative public opinion when it results in U.S. workers being replaced by lower-cost workers in other countries.

Routing and Scheduling

routing
the sequence of operations through which the product must pass

After all materials have been procured and their use determined, managers must then consider the **routing,** or sequence of operations through which the product must pass. For example, before employees at Rushing Water Canoes can form aluminum sheets into a canoe, the aluminum must be cut to size. Likewise, the canoe's flotation material must be installed before workers can secure the wood seats. The sequence depends on the product specifications developed by the engineering department of the company.

Once management knows the routing, the actual work can be scheduled. **Scheduling** assigns the tasks to be done to departments or even specific machines, workers, or teams. At Rushing Water, cutting aluminum for the company's canoes might be scheduled to be done by the "cutting and finishing" department on machines designed especially for that purpose.

Many approaches to scheduling have been developed, ranging from simple trial and error to highly sophisticated computer programs. One popular method is the *Program Evaluation and Review Technique (PERT),* which identifies all the major activities or events required to complete a project, arranges them in a sequence or path, determines the critical path, and estimates the time required for each event. Producing a McDonald's Big Mac, for example, involves removing meat, cheese, sauce, and vegetables from the refrigerator; grilling the hamburger patties; assembling the ingredients; placing the completed Big Mac in its package; and serving it to the customer (Figure 8.3). The cheese, pickles, onions, and sauce cannot be put on before the hamburger patty is completely grilled and placed on the bun. The path that requires the longest time from start to finish is called the *critical path* because it determines the minimum amount of time in which the process can be completed. If any of the activities on the critical path for production of the Big Mac fall behind schedule, the sandwich will not be completed on time, causing customers to wait longer than they usually would.

scheduling
the assignment of required tasks to departments or even specific machines, workers, or teams

Managing Quality

Quality, like cost and efficiency, is a critical element of operations management, for defective products can quickly ruin a firm. Quality reflects the degree to which a good or service meets the demands and requirements of customers. Customers

FIGURE 8.3   A Hypothetical PERT Diagram for a McDonald's Big Mac

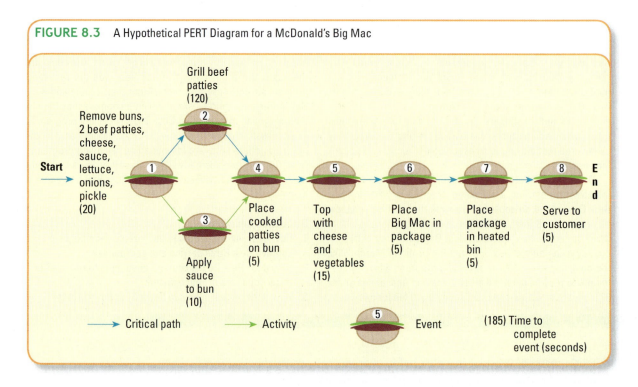

are increasingly dissatisfied with the quality of service provided by many airlines. Figure 8.4 provides an overview of the types of complaints reported to the Aviation Consumer Protection Division. Determining quality can be difficult because it depends on customers' perceptions of how well the product meets or exceeds their expectations. For example, customer satisfaction on airlines can vary wildly depending on individual customers' perspectives. However, the airline industry is notorious for its unsatisfied customers. Flight delays are a common complaint from airline

FIGURE 8.4

Types and Percentages of Air Travel Complaints

Source: Office of Aviation Enforcement and Proceedings, "Air Travel Consumer Reports for 2009," June 2009; Aviation *Consumer Protection Division,* http://airconsumer.ost.dot.gov/reports/atc.htm (accessed February 18, 2010).

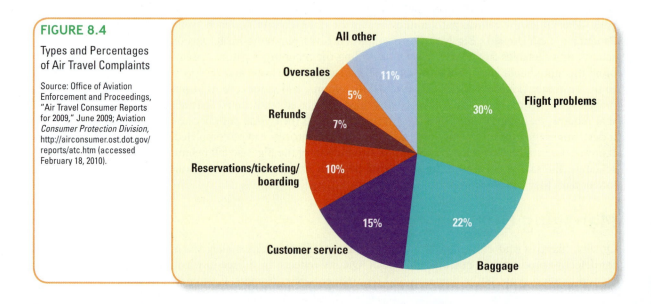

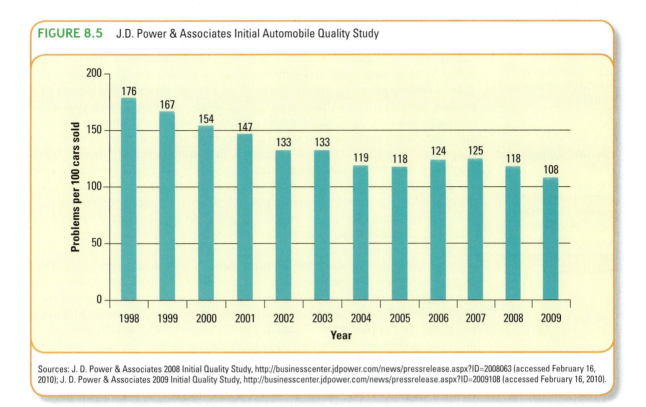

FIGURE 8.5   J.D. Power & Associates Initial Automobile Quality Study

Sources: J. D. Power & Associates 2008 Initial Quality Study, http://businesscenter.jdpower.com/news/pressrelease.aspx?ID=2008063 (accessed February 16, 2010); J. D. Power & Associates 2009 Initial Quality Study, http://businesscenter.jdpower.com/news/pressrelease.aspx?ID=2009108 (accessed February 16, 2010).

passengers; 20 percent of all flights arrive more than 15 minutes late. However, most passengers do not select an airline based on how often flights arrive on time.[26]

The fuel economy of an automobile or its reliability (defined in terms of frequency of repairs) can be measured with some degree of precision. Although automakers rely on their own measures of vehicle quality, they also look to independent sources such as the J. D. Power & Associates annual initial quality survey for confirmation of their quality assessment as well as consumer perceptions of quality for the industry, as indicated in Figure 8.5.

It is especially difficult to measure quality characteristics when the product is a service. A company has to decide exactly which quality characteristics it considers important and then define those characteristics in terms that can be measured. The inseparability of production and consumption and the level of customer contact influence the selection of characteristics of the service that are most important. Employees in high-contact services such as hairstyling, education, legal services, and even the barista at Starbucks are an important part of the product.

The Malcolm Baldrige National Quality Award is given each year to companies that meet rigorous standards of quality. The Baldrige criteria are (1) leadership, (2) information and analysis, (3) strategic planning, (4) human resource development and management, (5) process management, (6) business results, and (7) customer focus and satisfaction. The criteria have become a worldwide framework for driving business improvement. Five companies won the award in 2009, representing four different categories: Honeywell Federal Manufacturing & Technology (manufacturing), MidwayUSA (small business), AtlantiCare (health care), Heartland Health (health care), and VA Cooperative Studies Program Clinical Research Pharmacy Coordinating Center (nonprofit).[27]

Quality is so important that we need to examine it in the context of operations management. **Quality control** refers to the processes an organization uses to maintain its established quality standards. Best Buy's Geek Squad helps reduce returns of PCs by 40 percent when they deliver and set up a computer. This demonstrates that measuring perceived quality relates to more than just technical defects of a product, but also to other characteristics.[28] Quality has become a major concern in many organizations, particularly in light of intense foreign competition and increasingly demanding customers. To regain a competitive edge, a number of firms have adopted a total quality management approach. **Total quality management (TQM)** is a philosophy that uniform commitment to quality in all areas of the organization will promote a culture that meets customers' perceptions of quality. It involves coordinating efforts to improve customer satisfaction, increase employee participation and empowerment, form and strengthen supplier partnerships, and foster an organizational culture of continuous quality improvement. TQM requires continuous quality improvement and employee empowerment.

Continuous improvement of an organization's goods and services is built around the notion that quality is free; by contrast, *not* having high-quality goods and services can be very expensive, especially in terms of dissatisfied customers.[29] A primary tool of the continuous improvement process is *benchmarking,* the measuring and evaluating of the quality of the organization's goods, services, or processes as compared with the quality produced by the best-performing companies in the industry.[30] Benchmarking lets the organization know where it stands competitively in its industry, thus giving it a goal to aim for over time. Now that online digital media are becoming more important in businesses, companies such as Compuware Gomez offer benchmarking tools so companies can monitor and compare the success of their Web sites. Such tools allow companies to track traffic to the site versus competitors' sites. Studies have shown a direct link between Web site performance and online sales, meaning this type of benchmarking is important.[31]

Companies employing total quality management (TQM) programs know that quality control should be incorporated throughout the transformation process, from the initial plans to develop a specific product through the product and production-facility design processes to the actual manufacture of the product. In other words, they view quality control as an element of the product itself, rather than as simply a function of the operations process. When a company makes the product correctly from the outset, it eliminates the need to rework defective products, expedites the transformation process itself, and allows employees to make better use of their time and materials. One method through which many companies have tried to improve quality is **statistical process control,** a system in which management collects and analyzes information about the production process to pinpoint quality problems in the production system.

International Organization for Standardization (ISO)

Regardless whether a company has a TQM program for quality control, it must first determine what standard of quality it desires and then assess whether its products meet that standard. Product specifications and quality standards must be set so the company can create a product that will compete in the marketplace. Rushing Water Canoes, for example, may specify that each of its canoes has aluminum walls of a specified uniform thickness, that the front and back be reinforced with a specified level of steel, and that each contain a specified amount of flotation material for safety. Production facilities must be designed that can produce products with the desired specifications.

Quality standards can be incorporated into service businesses as well. A hamburger chain, for example, may establish standards relating to how long it takes to cook an order and serve it to customers, how many fries are in each order, how thick the burgers are, or how many customer complaints might be acceptable. Once the desired quality characteristics, specifications, and standards have been stated in measurable terms, the next step is inspection.

The International Organization for Standardization (ISO) has created a series of quality management standards—**ISO 9000**—designed to ensure the customer's quality standards are met. The standards provide a framework for documenting how a certified business keeps records, trains employees, tests products, and fixes defects. To obtain ISO 9000 certification, an independent auditor must verify that a business's factory, laboratory, or office meets the quality standards spelled out by the International Organization for Standardization. The certification process can require significant investment, but for many companies, the process is essential to being able to compete. Thousands of U.S. firms have been certified, and many more are working to meet the standards. Certification has become a virtual necessity for doing business in Europe in some high-technology businesses. ISO 9002 certification was established for service providers. **ISO 14000** is a comprehensive set of environmental standards that encourages a cleaner and safer world. ISO 14000 is a valuable standard because currently considerable variation exists between the regulations in different nations, and even regions within a nation. These variations make it difficult for organizations committed to sustainability to find acceptable global solutions to problems. The goal of the ISO 14000 standards is to promote a more uniform approach to environmental management and to help companies attain and measure improvements in their environmental performance.

The ISO 9000 standards are international standards that relate to quality management. ISO 14000 standards relate to environmental management—managing businesses to minimize harmful effects to the environment.

ISO 9000
a series of quality assurance standards designed by the International Organization for Standardization (ISO) to ensure consistent product quality under many conditions

ISO 14000
a comprehensive set of environmental standards that encourages companies to conduct business in a cleaner, safer, and less wasteful way. ISO 14000 provides a uniform set of standards globally.

Inspection

Inspection reveals whether a product meets quality standards. Some product characteristics may be discerned by fairly simple inspection techniques—weighing the contents of cereal boxes or measuring the time it takes for a customer to receive his or her hamburger. As part of the ongoing quality assurance program at Hershey Foods, all wrapped Hershey Kisses are checked, and all imperfectly wrapped kisses are rejected. Other inspection techniques are more elaborate. Automobile manufacturers use automated machines to open and close car doors to test the durability of latches and hinges. The food-processing and pharmaceutical industries use various chemical tests to determine the quality of their output. Rushing Water Canoes might use a special device that can precisely measure the thickness of each canoe wall to ensure that it meets the company's specifications.

Organizations normally inspect purchased items, work-in-process, and finished items. The inspection of purchased items and finished items takes place after the fact; the inspection of work-in-process is preventive. In other words, the purpose of inspection of purchased items and finished items is to determine what the quality level is. For items that are being worked on—an automobile moving down the assembly line or a canoe being assembled—the purpose of the inspection is to find defects before the product is completed so that necessary corrections can be made.

Sampling

An important question relating to inspection is how many items should be inspected. Should all canoes produced by Rushing Water be inspected or just some of them? Whether to inspect 100 percent of the output or only part of it is related to the cost of the inspection process, the destructiveness of the inspection process (some tests last until the product fails), and the potential cost of product flaws in terms of human lives and safety.

Some inspection procedures are quite expensive, use elaborate testing equipment, destroy products, and/or require a significant number of hours to complete. In such cases, it is usually desirable to test only a sample of the output. If the sample passes inspection, the inspector may assume that all the items in the lot from which the sample was drawn would also pass inspection. By using principles of statistical inference, management can employ sampling techniques that assure a relatively high probability of reaching the right conclusion—that is, rejecting a lot that does not meet standards and accepting a lot that does. Nevertheless, there will always be a risk of making an incorrect conclusion—accepting a population that *does not* meet standards (because the sample was satisfactory) or rejecting a population that *does* meet standards (because the sample contained too many defective items).

Sampling is likely to be used when inspection tests are destructive. Determining the life expectancy of lightbulbs by turning them on and recording how long they last would be foolish: There is no market for burned-out lightbulbs. Instead, a generalization based on the quality of a sample would be applied to the entire population of lightbulbs from which the sample was drawn. However, human life and safety often depend on the proper functioning of specific items, such as the navigational systems installed in commercial airliners. For such items, even though the inspection process is costly, the potential cost of flawed systems—in human lives and safety—is too great not to inspect 100 percent of the output.

So You Want a Job in Operations Management

While you might not have been familiar with terms such as supply chain or logistics or total quality management before taking this course, careers abound in the operations management field. You will find these careers in a wide variety of organizations—manufacturers, retailers, transportation companies, third-party logistics firms, government agencies, and service firms. Approximately $1.3 trillion is spent on transportation, inventory, and related logistics activities, and logistics alone accounts for more than 9.5 percent of U.S. gross domestic product.[32] Closely managing how a company's inputs and outputs flow from raw materials to the end consumer is vital to a firm's success. Successful companies also need to ensure that quality is measured and actively managed at each step.

Supply chain managers have a tremendous impact on the success of an organization. These managers are engaged in every facet of the business process, including planning, purchasing, production, transportation, storage and distribution, customer service, and more. Their performance helps organizations control expenses, boost sales, and maximize profits.

Warehouse managers are a vital part of manufacturing operations. A typical warehouse manager's duties include overseeing and recording deliveries and pickups, maintaining inventory records and the product tracking system, and adjusting inventory levels to reflect receipts and disbursements. Warehouse managers also have to keep in mind customer service and employee issues. Warehouse managers can earn up to $60,000 in some cases.

Operations management is also required in service businesses. With more than 80 percent of the U.S. economy in services, jobs exist for services operations. Many service contact operations require standardized processes that often use technology to provide an interface that provides an automatic quality performance. Consider jobs in health care, the travel industry, fast food, and entertainment. Think of any job or task that is a part of the final product in these industries. Even an online retailer such as Amazon.com has a transformation process that includes information technology and human activities that facilitate a transaction. These services have a standardized process and can be evaluated based on their level of achieved service quality.

Total quality management is becoming a key attribute for companies to ensure that quality pervades all aspects of the organization. Quality assurance managers may make salaries in the $55,000 to $65,000 range. These managers monitor and advise on how a company's quality management system is performing and publish data and reports regarding company performance in both manufacturing and service industries.

Review Your Understanding

Define operations management, and differentiate between operations and manufacturing.

Operations management (OM) is the development and administration of the activities involved in transforming resources into goods and services. Operations managers oversee the transformation process and the planning and designing of operations systems, managing logistics, quality, and productivity. The terms *manufacturing* and *production* are used interchangeably to describe the activities and processes used in making tangible products, whereas *operations* is a broader term used to describe the process of making both tangible and intangible products.

Explain how operations management differs in manufacturing and service firms.

Manufacturers and service firms both transform inputs into outputs, but service providers differ from manufacturers in several ways: They have greater customer contact because the service typically occurs at the point of consumption; their inputs and outputs are more variable than manufacturers', largely because of the human element; service providers are generally more labor intensive; and their productivity measurement is more complex.

Describe the elements involved in planning and designing an operations system.

Operations planning relates to decisions about what product(s) to make, for whom, and what processes and facilities are needed to produce them. OM is often joined by marketing and research and development in these decisions. Common facility layouts include fixed-position layouts, process layouts, or product layouts. Where to locate operations facilities is a crucial decision that depends on proximity to the market, availability of raw materials, availability of transportation, availability of power, climatic influences, availability of labor, and community characteristics. Technology is also vital to operations, particularly computer-assisted design, computer-assisted manufacturing, flexible manufacturing, robotics, and computer-integrated manufacturing.

Specify some techniques managers may use to manage the logistics of transforming inputs into finished products.

Logistics, or supply chain management, includes all the activities involved in obtaining and managing raw materials and component parts, managing finished products, packaging them, and getting them to customers. The organization must first make or purchase (procure) all the materials it needs. Next, it must control its inventory by determining how many supplies and goods it needs and keeping track of every raw material, component, completed or partially completed product, and piece of equipment, how many of each are on hand, where they are, and who has responsibility for them. Common approaches to inventory control include the economic order quantity (EOQ) model, the just-in-time (JIT) inventory concept, and material-requirements planning (MRP). Logistics also includes routing and scheduling processes and activities to complete products.

Assess the importance of quality in operations management.

Quality is a critical element of OM because low-quality products can hurt people and harm the business. Quality control refers to the processes an organization uses to maintain its established quality standards. To control quality, a company must establish what standard of quality it desires and then determine whether its products meet that standard through inspection.

Evaluate a business's dilemma and propose a solution.

Based on this chapter and the facts presented in "Solve the Dilemma" on page 266, you should be able to evaluate the business's problem and propose one or more solutions for resolving it.

Revisit the World of Business

1. What is the "Toyota Way?"

2. What changed at Toyota that led to its large product recalls?

3. What is Toyota doing to restore its reputation and to get back on track?

Learn the Terms

capacity   246

computer-assisted design (CAD)   249

computer-assisted manufacturing (CAM)   249

computer-integrated manufacturing (CIM)   250

continuous manufacturing organizations   248

customization   245

economic order quantity (EOQ) model   255

fixed-position layout   248

flexible manufacturing   249

inputs   239

intermittent organizations   248

inventory   253

inventory control   254

ISO 9000   261

ISO 14000   261

just-in-time (JIT) inventory management   255

manufacturing   239

material-requirements planning (MRP)   255

modular design   245

operations   239

operations management (OM)   238

outputs   239

process layout   248

product layout   248

production   239

project organization   248

purchasing   252

quality control   260

routing   256

scheduling   257

standardization   245

statistical process control   260

supply chain management   252

total quality management (TQM)   260

Check Your Progress

1. What is operations management?
2. Differentiate among the terms *operations, production,* and *manufacturing.*
3. Compare and contrast a manufacturer versus a service provider in terms of operations management.
4. Who is involved in planning products?
5. In what industry would the fixed-position layout be most efficient? The process layout? The product layout? Use real examples.

6. What criteria do businesses use when deciding where to locate a plant?
7. What is flexible manufacturing? How can it help firms improve quality?
8. Define supply chain management and summarize the activities it involves.
9. Describe some of the methods a firm may use to control inventory.
10. When might a firm decide to inspect a sample of its products rather than test every product for quality?

Get Involved

1. Compare and contrast OM at McDonald's with that of Honda of America. Compare and contrast OM at McDonald's with that of a bank in your neighborhood.
2. Find a real company that uses JIT, either in your local community or in a business journal. Why did the company decide to use JIT? What have been the advantages and disadvantages of using JIT for that particular company? What has been the overall effect on the quality of the company's products or services? What has been the overall effect on the company's bottom line?
3. Interview someone from your local Chamber of Commerce and ask him or her what incentives the community offers to encourage organizations to locate there. (See if these incentives relate to the criteria firms use to make location decisions.)

Build Your Skills

REDUCING CYCLE TIME

Background:
An important goal of production and operations management is reducing cycle time—the time it takes to complete a task or process. The goal in cycle time reduction is to reduce costs and/or increase customer service.[33] Many experts believe that the rate of change in our society is so fast that a firm must master speed and connectivity.[34] Connectivity refers to a seamless integration of customers, suppliers, employees, and organizational, production, and operations management. The use of the Internet and other telecommunications systems helps many organizations connect and reduce cycle time.

Task:
Break up into pairs throughout the class. Select two businesses (local restaurants, retail stores, etc.) that both of you frequent, are employed by, and/or are fairly well acquainted with. For the first business, one of you will role-play the "manager" and the other will role-play the

"customer." Reverse roles for the second business you have selected. As managers at your respective businesses, you are to prepare a list of five questions you will ask the customer during the role-play. The questions you prepare should be designed to get the customer's viewpoint on how good the cycle time is at your business. If one of the responses leads to a problem area, you may need to ask a follow-up question to determine the nature of the dissatisfaction. Prepare one main question and a follow-up, if necessary, for each of the five dimensions of cycle time:

1. **Speed**—the delivery of goods and services in the minimum time; efficient communications; the elimination of wasted time.
2. **Connectivity**—all operations and systems in the business appear connected with the customer.
3. **Interactive relationships**—a continual dialog exists between operations units, service providers, and customers that permits the exchange of feedback on concerns or needs.

4. **Customization**—each product is tailored to the needs of the customer.

5. **Responsiveness**—the willingness to make adjustments and be flexible to help customers and to provide prompt service when a problem develops.

Begin the two role-plays. When it is your turn to be the manager, listen carefully when your partner answers your prepared questions. You need to elicit information on how to improve the cycle time at your business. You will achieve this by identifying the problem areas (weaknesses) that need attention.

After completing both role-play situations, fill out the form below for the role-play where you were the manager. You may not have gathered enough information to fill in all the boxes. For example, for some categories, the customer may have had only good things to say; for others, the comments may all be negative. Be prepared to share the information you gain with the rest of the class.

I role-played the manager at (business). After listening carefully to the customer's responses to my five questions, I determined the following strengths and weaknesses as they relate to the cycle time at my business:

Dimension	Strength	Weakness
Speed		
Connectivity		
Interactive relationships		
Customization		
Responsiveness		

Solve the Dilemma

PLANNING FOR PIZZA

McKing Corporation operates fast-food restaurants in 50 states, selling hamburgers, roast beef and chicken sandwiches, french fries, and salads. The company wants to diversify into the growing pizza business. Six months of tests revealed that the ideal pizza to sell was a 16-inch pie in three varieties: cheese, pepperoni, and deluxe (multiple toppings). Research found the size and toppings acceptable to families as well as to individuals (single buyers could freeze the leftovers), and the price was acceptable for a fast-food restaurant ($7.99 for cheese, $8.49 for pepperoni, and $9.99 for deluxe).

Marketing and human resources personnel prepared training manuals for employees, advertising materials, and the rationale to present to the restaurant managers (many stores are franchised). Store managers, franchisees, and employees are excited about the new plan. There is just one problem: The drive-through windows in current restaurants are too small for a 16-inch pizza to pass through. The largest size the present windows can accommodate is a 12-inch pie. The managers and franchisees are concerned that if this aspect of operations has been overlooked perhaps the product is not ready to be launched. Maybe there are other problems yet to be uncovered.

Discussion Question

1. What mistake did McKing make in approaching the introduction of pizza?

2. How could this product introduction have been coordinated to avoid the problems that were encountered?

3. If you were an executive at McKing, how would you proceed with the introduction of pizza into the restaurants?

Build Your Business Plan

MANAGING SERVICE AND MANUFACTURING OPERATIONS

For your business you need to determine if you are providing raw materials that will be used in further production, or you are a reseller of goods and services, known as a retailer. If you are the former, you need to determine what processes you go through in making your product.

The text provides ideas of breaking the process into inputs, transformation processes and outputs. If you are a provider of a service or a link in the supply chain, you need to know exactly what your customer expectations are. Services are intangible so it is all the more important to better understand what exactly the customer is looking for in resolving a problem or filling a need.

See for Yourself Videocase

CRAFT BEERS TAKE OFF

Europeans have long favored craft beer, but Americans are just now jumping on the bandwagon. Americans are increasingly drawn to the local, quirky, and more personal feel of craft brews. Nielsen (the rating company) reveals that American beer drinkers' tastes are changing. Now, more beer drinkers than ever before prefer more robust beer flavors—the kind of beer produced by many craft breweries.

The Brewers Association defines craft beer as "small, independent, and traditional." Small breweries produce under two million barrels a year. Independent means that less than 25 percent of brewery ownership belongs to an outside party(s). According to craftbeer.com, there are more than 1,500 U.S. breweries, and over 90 percent of these meet the Brewers Association's criteria for craft brewery. However, these craft breweries represent less than ten percent of overall U.S. beer sales.

Because of their growing popularity, some major brands are getting into the craft beer market through acquiring smaller breweries or developing beers that taste more like craft brews. For example, Anheuser-Busch produces the organic Stone Mill Pale Ale and Molson-Coors produces Blue Moon. Some craft breweries have become so popular that they no longer fit the Brewers Association's definition. One such example is Samuel Adams. The company now brews over two million barrels, but still adheres to all other craft brewery guidelines.

Most craft breweries remain small, however. Scott Vaccaro founded Captain Lawrence Brewery in his hometown of Pleasantville, New York. Vaccaro discovered his passion for beer making at an early age and began brewing it in his parent's kitchen. After attending the University of California, Davis to receive a Fermentation Science degree, he worked for Sierra Nevada for six years. He then traveled through Europe sampling beers. In the end, he decided that his ultimate dream was to bring all that he had learned back to his hometown. He created a brewery where employees and customers would feel at home, and would want to explore and learn about beer. He now produces a handful of unique brews, some of which have won awards.

Many craft breweries produce loyal, happy employees who have opportunities to engage in numerous facets of the business. They can often be friendly places where hard work and dedication are both intrinsically and extrinsically rewarded. New Belgium Brewery, cited in Chapters 4 and 11, is an excellent example. Its employees actually share ownership in the company and are given bicycles and trips to Belgium, among other perks. Many craft breweries focus on sustainable, environmentally friendly practices, drawing employees with emotional connections to more than just paychecks. In addition, for most craft beer enthusiasts, exploring the nuances of various brews is a joyful experience; many employees are aware they have a hand in creating these positive experiences and they care about quality and innovation. Brewing beer is an ancient activity with a bright future ahead of it.

Discussion Questions

1. What kind of operations process do you think most craft brewers use (standardized, modular, customized)?

2. How do craft brewers maintain quality control?

3. Sustainability is a common goal in the craft brewing market. Why do you think manufacturing sustainability is such a popular goal in craft brewing?

Remember to check out our Online Learning Center at www.mhhe.com/ferrell8e.

Team Exercise

Form groups and assign the responsibility of finding companies that outsource their production to other countries. What are the key advantages of this outsourcing decision? Do you see any drawbacks or weaknesses in this approach? Why would a company not outsource when such a tactic can be undertaken to cut manufacturing cost? Report your findings to the class.

part 4

Creating the Human Resource Advantage

Motivating the Workforce

OBJECTIVES

After reading this chapter, you will be able to:

- Define human relations, and determine why its study is important.

- Summarize early studies that laid the groundwork for understanding employee motivation.

- Compare and contrast the human-relations theories of Abraham Maslow and Frederick Herzberg.

- Investigate various theories of motivation, including theories X, Y, and Z; equity theory; and expectancy theory.

- Describe some of the strategies that managers use to motivate employees.

- Critique a business's program for motivating its sales force.

J.A. Frate Motivates Its Drivers

J.A. Frate, a trucking company located in Crystal Lake, Illinois, is working to improve the public image of the trucking industry. Trucking became part of the America service sector in the early 1900s as a supplement to freight train transportation and continued to expand throughout the 20th century. Today the trucking industry is alive and well, but driver turnover is extremely high. Truckers often face low pay and long work hours in addition to the obstacles they face on the road. J.A. Frate, founded and run by R. Douglas Jennings, focuses on treating its drivers well.

At J.A. Frate, excellent drivers are recognized for their experience and their performance. The company only hires experienced drivers and requires that they dress and act professionally. The average J.A. Frate driver's employment lifetime is 7.3 years, a long time in the industry; however, many drivers have been with J.A. Frate for more than 20 years. The company uses a point system to identify high-achieving drivers for awards such as Drivers of the Month. Additionally, the company recognizes one driver as Driver of the Year, with the winner receiving prizes such as a new truck tractor containing $4,000 worth of extras. J.A. Frate employees also know their opinions and suggestions matter to the company. Each quarter, the employees who offer the top three suggestions are awarded financial prizes.

In tough times, J.A. Frate works with its employees to create the best possible outcome. When the company had to lay off drivers for the first time in 2001, the board of directors and the remaining employees agreed on a 10 percent pay cut. J.A. Frate rehired all laid-off employees and returned employees to their regular wages within six months and reimbursed all lost wages in 2006. In an industry of less than stellar reputation and full of disgruntled employees, J.A. Frate stands out as a positive influence.[1]

Introduction

Businesses like J.A. Frate teach some important lessons about how to interact with and motivate employees to do their best. Because employees do the actual work of the business and influence whether the firm achieves its objectives, most top managers agree that employees are an organization's most valuable resource. To achieve organizational objectives, employees must have the motivation, ability (appropriate knowledge and skills), and tools (proper training and equipment) to perform their jobs. Chapter 10 covers topics related to managing human resources, such as those listed earlier. This chapter focuses on how to motivate employees.

We examine employees' needs and motivation, managers' views of workers, and several strategies for motivating employees. Managers who understand the needs of their employees can help them reach higher levels of productivity and thus contribute to the achievement of organizational goals.

Nature of Human Relations

human relations
the study of the behavior of individuals and groups in organizational settings

What motivates employees to perform on the job is the focus of **human relations,** the study of the behavior of individuals and groups in organizational settings. In business, human relations involves motivating employees to achieve organizational objectives efficiently and effectively. The field of human relations has become increasingly important over the years as businesses strive to understand how to boost workplace morale, maximize employees' productivity and creativity, and motivate their ever more diverse employees to be more effective.

motivation
an inner drive that directs a person's behavior toward goals

Motivation is an inner drive that directs a person's behavior toward goals. A goal is the satisfaction of some need, and a need is the difference between a desired state and an actual state. Both needs and goals can be motivating. Motivation explains why people behave as they do; similarly, a lack of motivation explains, at times, why people avoid doing what they should do. Motivating employees to do the wrong things or for the wrong reasons can be problematic, however. Encouraging employees to take excessive risks through high compensation, for example, is not a good idea and can lead to ethical misconduct disasters for a corporation. The most recent financial crisis resulted from firms allowing or encouraging excessive risk taking in order to achieve financial rewards. A person who recognizes or feels a need is motivated to take action to satisfy the need and achieve a goal (Figure 9.1). Consider a person who takes a job as a salesperson. If his or her performance is far below other salespeople's, he or she will likely recognize a need to increase sales. To satisfy that need and achieve success, the person may try to acquire new insights from successful salespeople or obtain additional training to improve sales skills. In addition, a sales manager might try different means to motivate the salesperson to work harder and to improve his or her skills. Human relations is concerned with the needs of employees, their goals and how they try to achieve them, and the impact of those needs and goals on job performance.

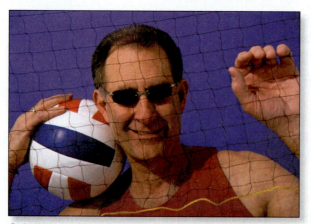

On its Web site, Google advertises the "benefits beyond the basics" to attract and retain top-notch employees. At the company's Mountain View, California, headquarters, employees can see an onsite doctor and get their oil changed, cars washed, bikes repaired, and dry cleaning done. The company also offers onsite massage therapy, a gym and volleyball court, hair styling, and fitness classes.

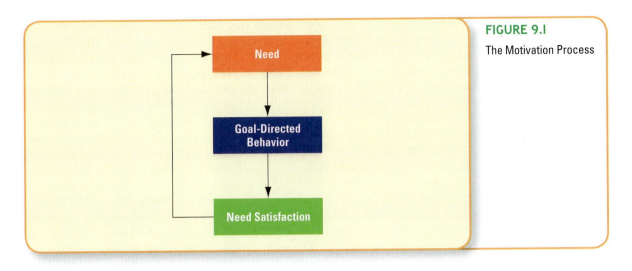

FIGURE 9.1
The Motivation Process

Effectively motivating employees helps keep them engaged in their work. Engagement involves emotional involvement and commitment. Being engaged results in carrying out the expectations and obligations of employment. Many employees are actively engaged in their jobs, while others are not. Some employees do the minimum amount of work required to get by, and some employees are completely disengaged. Motivating employees to stay engaged is a key responsibility of management. For example, to test if his onsite production managers were fully engaged in their jobs, former Van Halen frontman David Lee Roth placed a line in the band's rider asking for a bowl of M&Ms with the brown ones removed. It was a means for the band to test local stage production crews' attention to detail. Because their shows were highly technical, Lee Roth would demand a complete recheck of everything if he found brown M&Ms in the bowl.[2]

One prominent aspect of human relations is **morale**—an employee's attitude toward his or her job, employer, and colleagues. High morale contributes to high levels of productivity, high returns to stakeholders, and employee loyalty. Conversely, low morale may cause high rates of absenteeism and turnover (when employees quit or are fired and must be replaced by new employees). Google recognizes the value of happy, committed employees and strives to engage in practices that will minimize turnover. Employees have the opportunity to have a massage every other week; onsite laundry service; free all-you-can-eat gourmet meals and snacks; and the "20% a week" rule, which allows engineers to work on whatever project they want for one day each week.[3]

Employees are motivated by their perceptions of extrinsic and intrinsic rewards. An **intrinsic reward** is the personal satisfaction and enjoyment that you feel from attaining a goal. For example, in this class you may feel personal enjoyment in learning how business works and aspire to have a career in business or to operate your own business one day. **Extrinsic rewards** are benefits and/or recognition that you receive from someone else. In this class, your grade is extrinsic recognition of your efforts and success in the class. In business, praise and recognition, pay increases, and bonuses are extrinsic rewards. If you believe that your job provides an opportunity to contribute to society or the environment, then that aspect would represent an intrinsic reward. Both intrinsic and extrinsic rewards contribute to motivation that stimulates employees to do their best in contributing to business goals.

morale
an employee's attitude toward his or her job, employer, and colleagues

intrinsic rewards
the personal satisfaction and enjoyment feel after attaining a goal

extrinsic rewards
benefits and/or recognition received from someone else

Respect, involvement, appreciation, adequate compensation, promotions, a pleasant work environment, and a positive organizational culture are all morale boosters. Table 9.1 lists some ways to retain good employees. Nike seeks to provide a comprehensive compensation and benefits package, which includes traditional elements such as medical, dental, vision, life and disability insurance, paid holidays and time off as well as sabbaticals, and team as well as individual compensation plans. More comprehensive benefits include employee discounts on Nike products, health care and family care reimbursement accounts, scholarships for children of employees, employee assistance plans, work/life balance resources and referrals, adoption assistance, tuition assistance, group legal plan, group long-term care plan, and matching gift programs. At the Beaverton, Oregon, world headquarters, Nike employees may take advantage of onsite day care and fitness centers, onsite cafés and restaurants, an onsite hair and nail salon, discounted annual TriMet transit passes ($25 annual fee versus $600), and several other work/life resources.[5] Many companies offer a diverse array of benefits designed to improve the quality of employees' lives and increase their morale and satisfaction. Some of the "best companies to work for" offer onsite day care, concierge services (e.g., dry cleaning, shoe repair, prescription renewal), domestic partner benefits to same-sex couples, and fully paid sabbaticals. Table 9.2 offers suggestions as to how leaders can motivate employees on a daily basis.

> **Did You Know?**   Absenteeism can cost a company as much as 36 percent of payroll.[4]

Historical Perspectives on Employee Motivation

Throughout the 20th century, researchers have conducted numerous studies to try to identify ways to motivate workers and increase productivity. From these studies have come theories that have been applied to workers with varying degrees of success. A brief discussion of two of these theories—the classical theory of motivation

TABLE 9.1 Top 10 Ways to Retain Great Employees	
	1. Satisfied employees know clearly what is expected from them every day at work.
	2. The quality of the supervision an employee receives is critical to employee retention.
	3. The ability of the employee to speak his or her mind freely within the organization is another key factor in employee retention.
	4. Talent and skill utilization is another environmental factor your key employees seek in your workplace.
	5. The perception of fairness and equitable treatment is important in employee retention.
	6. Employees must have the tools, time, and training necessary to do their jobs well—or they will move to an employer who provides them.
	7. The best employees, those employees you want to retain, seek frequent opportunities to learn and grow in their careers, knowledge, and skill.
	8. Take time to meet with new employees to learn about their talents, abilities, and skills. Meet with each employee periodically.
	9. No matter the circumstances, never, never, ever threaten an employee's job or income.
	10. Staff members must feel rewarded, recognized, and appreciated.

Source: Susan M. Heathfield, "Top Ten Ways to Retain Your Great Employees," About.com, http://humanresources.about.com/od/retention/a/more_retention.htm (accessed February 18, 2010).

TABLE 9.2

You Can Make Their Day: Tips for the Leader about Employee Motivation

1. Use simple, powerful words.

2. Make sure people know what you expect.

3. Provide regular feedback.

4. People need positive and not so positive consequences.

5. It's about discipline, not magic.

6. Continue learning and trying out new ideas for employee motivation.

7. Make time for people.

8. Focus on the development of people.

9. Share the goals and the context: communicate.

Source: Susan M. Heathfield, "You Can Make Their Day: Ten Tips for the Leader About Employee Motivation," About.com, http://humanresources.about.com/od/motivationsucces3/a/lead_motivation.htm (accessed February 18, 2010).

and the Hawthorne studies—provides a background for understanding the present state of human relations.

Classical Theory of Motivation

The birth of the study of human relations can be traced to time and motion studies conducted at the turn of the century by Frederick W. Taylor and Frank and Lillian Gilbreth. Their studies analyzed how workers perform specific work tasks in an effort to improve the employees' productivity. These efforts led to the application of scientific principles to management.

According to the **classical theory of motivation,** money is the sole motivator for workers. Taylor suggested that workers who were paid more would produce more, an idea that would benefit both companies and workers. To improve productivity, Taylor thought that managers should break down each job into its component tasks (specialization), determine the best way to perform each task, and specify the output to be achieved by a worker performing the task. Taylor also believed that incentives would motivate employees to be more productive. Thus, he suggested that managers link workers' pay directly to their output. He developed the piecerate system, under which employees were paid a certain amount for each unit they produced; those who exceeded their quota were paid a higher rate per unit for all the units they produced.

classical theory of motivation
theory suggesting that money is the sole motivator for workers

We can still see Taylor's ideas in practice today in the use of financial incentives for productivity. Moreover, companies are increasingly striving to relate pay to performance at both the hourly and managerial level. Incentive planners choose an individual incentive to motivate and reward their employees. In contrast, team incentives are used to generate partnership and working together to accomplish organizational goals. Boeing develops sales teams for most of its products, including commercial airplanes. The team dedicated to each product shares in the sales incentive program.

More and more corporations are tying pay to performance in order to motivate—even up to the CEO level. The topic of executive pay has become

Larry Ellison, the CEO of Oracle Corporation, a software maker, often tops the list of best paid CEOs. Ellison's base pay is just $1, but he earns hundreds of millions of dollars annually in the form of stock.

Going Green
Lundberg Family Farms Cares about the Earth and ITS Employees

Lundberg Family Farms, whose rice products are available nationwide, is one of the original organic farming pioneers in the United States. Albert and Francis Lundberg founded the company in 1937. After seeing soil destruction in the Dust Bowl of the Midwest, the Lundbergs moved west, vowing to protect the soil, wildlife, air, and water. True to their word, Lundberg (now run by the third generation) excels in organic and eco-friendly farming. The company has won the Organic Trade Association's Organic Leadership Award and the EPA's Green Power Partnership Award. In addition to its organic practices, the company is powered by only renewable energy sources, including solar power and renewable energy credits. In fact, the company is a founding member of the Green e-Marketplace program—a certification and verification agency for renewable energy credits.

In addition to the environment, Lundberg also cares about its employees. The company does a great deal to support them, offering several incentives and programs including annual bonuses, profit sharing, tuition reimbursement, "Above and Beyond" prizes each month for those who exceed their normal duties, an employee garden, a wellness program, and rewards for children of employees who achieve good grades in school. Employees of Lundberg are very loyal to the company; of Lundberg's 180 employees, 22 have worked for Lundberg for more than 20 years and 60 have been with the company for more than 10 years. For those passionate about farming, the environment, or simply being treated well as an employee, Lundberg Family Farms is a great place to be.[6]

Discussion Questions
1. How does Lundberg Family Farms support and motivate its employees?
2. How has Lundberg Family Farms developed a competitive advantage over other farms?
3. Do you think caring about its employees has paid dividends for Lundberg, or is it an excessive expense?

controversial in recent years, and many corporate boards of directors have taken steps to link executive compensation more closely to corporate performance. Despite these changes, many top executives still receive large compensation packages. Aubrey K. McClendon, chairman and CEO of Chesapeake Energy, is the highest paid executive, with a total compensation of $112.5 million.[7]

Like most managers of the early 20th century, Taylor believed that satisfactory pay and job security would motivate employees to work hard. However, later studies showed that other factors are also important in motivating workers.

The Hawthorne Studies

Elton Mayo and a team of researchers from Harvard University wanted to determine what physical conditions in the workplace—such as light and noise levels—would stimulate employees to be most productive. From 1924 to 1932, they studied a group of workers at the Hawthorne Works Plant of the Western Electric Company and measured their productivity under various physical conditions.

What the researchers discovered was quite unexpected and very puzzling: Productivity increased regardless of the physical conditions. This phenomenon has been labeled the Hawthorne effect. When questioned about their behavior, the employees expressed satisfaction because their co-workers in the experiments were friendly and, more importantly, because their supervisors had asked for their help and cooperation in the study. In other words, they were responding to the attention they received, not the changing physical work conditions. The researchers concluded that social and psychological factors could significantly affect productivity and morale. Medtronic, often called the "Microsoft of the medical-device industry," has a built-in psychological factor that influences employee morale. The company makes life-saving medical devices, such as pacemakers, neurostimulators, and stents. New hires at Medtronic receive medallions inscribed with a portion of the firm's mission statement, "alleviate pain, restore health, and extend life." There is

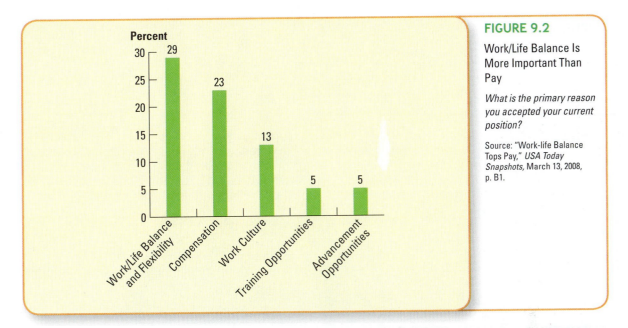

FIGURE 9.2

Work/Life Balance Is More Important Than Pay

What is the primary reason you accepted your current position?

Source: "Work-life Balance Tops Pay," *USA Today Snapshots,* March 13, 2008, p. B1.

an annual party where people whose bodies function thanks to Medtronic devices give testimonials. Obviously, Medtronic employees feel a sense of satisfaction in their jobs. Figure 9.2 indicates that work/life balance is important to many employees.

The Hawthorne experiments marked the beginning of a concern for human relations in the workplace. They revealed that human factors do influence workers' behavior and that managers who understand the needs, beliefs, and expectations of people have the greatest success in motivating their workers.

Theories of Employee Motivation

Working conditions are important. However, the Hawthorne studies, which were carried out at the electric company shown here beginning in the 1920s, found that the workers became more productive because of the attention they received—regardless of their working conditions.

The research of Taylor, Mayo, and many others has led to the development of a number of theories that attempt to describe what motivates employees to perform. In this section, we will discuss some of the most important of these theories. The successful implementation of ideas based on these theories will vary, of course, depending on the company, its management, and its employees. It should be noted, too, that what worked in the past may no longer work today. Good managers must have the ability to adapt their ideas to an ever-changing, diverse group of employees.

Maslow's Hierarchy of Needs

Psychologist Abraham Maslow theorized that people have five basic needs: physiological, security, social, esteem, and self-actualization. **Maslow's hierarchy** arranges these needs into the order in which people strive to satisfy them (Figure 9.3).

Maslow's hierarchy a theory that arranges the five basic needs of people—physiological, security, social, esteem, and self-actualization—into the order in which people strive to satisfy them

FIGURE 9.3

Maslow's Hierarchy
of Needs

Source: Adapted from Abraham
H. Maslow, "A Theory of Human
Motivation," *Psychology
Review* 50 (1943), pp. 370–396.
American Psychology
Association.

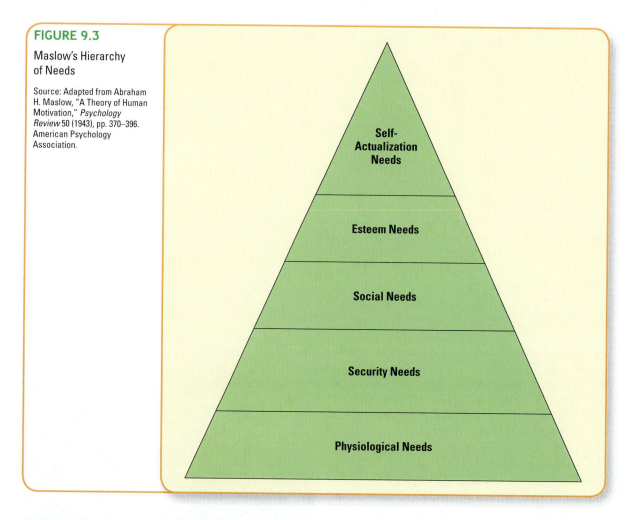

- Self-Actualization Needs
- Esteem Needs
- Social Needs
- Security Needs
- Physiological Needs

physiological needs
the most basic human
needs to be satisfied—
water, food, shelter, and
clothing

security needs
the need to protect
oneself from physical and
economic harm

social needs
the need for love,
companionship, and
friendship—the desire for
acceptance by others

esteem needs
the need for respect—
both self-respect and
respect from others

Physiological needs, the most basic and first needs to be satisfied, are the essentials for living—water, food, shelter, and clothing. According to Maslow, humans devote all their efforts to satisfying physiological needs until they are met. Only when these needs are met can people focus their attention on satisfying the next level of needs—security.

Security needs relate to protecting yourself from physical and economic harm. Actions that may be taken to achieve security include reporting a dangerous workplace condition to management, maintaining safety equipment, and purchasing insurance with income protection in the event you become unable to work. Once security needs have been satisfied, people may strive for social goals.

Social needs are the need for love, companionship, and friendship—the desire for acceptance by others. To fulfill social needs, a person may try many things: making friends with a co-worker, joining a group, volunteering at a hospital, throwing a party. Once their social needs have been satisfied, people attempt to satisfy their need for esteem.

Esteem needs relate to respect—both self-respect and respect from others. One aspect of esteem needs is competition—the need to feel that you can do something better than anyone else. Competition often motivates people to increase their productivity. Esteem needs are not as easily satisfied as the needs at lower levels in

Maslow's hierarchy because they do not always provide tangible evidence of success. However, these needs can be realized through rewards and increased involvement in organizational activities. Until esteem needs are met, people focus their attention on achieving respect. When they feel they have achieved some measure of respect, self-actualization becomes the major goal of life.

Self-actualization needs, at the top of Maslow's hierarchy, mean being the best you can be. Self-actualization involves maximizing your potential. A self-actualized person feels that she or he is living life to its fullest in every way. For Stephen King, self-actualization might mean being praised as the best fiction writer in the world; for actress Halle Berry, it might mean winning an Oscar.

Maslow's theory maintains that the more basic needs at the bottom of the hierarchy must be satisfied before higher-level goals can be pursued. Thus, people who are hungry and homeless are not concerned with obtaining respect from their colleagues. Only when physiological, security, and social needs have been more or less satisfied do people seek esteem. Maslow's theory also suggests that if a low-level need is suddenly reactivated, the individual will try to satisfy that need rather than higher-level needs. Many laid off workers probably shift their focus from high-level esteem needs to the need for security. When U.S. unemployment reached 10 percent in 2009 and the job market appeared increasingly insecure, many employees, particularly those in manufacturing, banking and finance, felt they had to shift their focus back to security needs. Managers should learn from Maslow's hierarchy that employees will be motivated to contribute to organizational goals only if they are able to first satisfy their physiological, security, and social needs through their work.

Herzberg's Two-Factor Theory

In the 1950s psychologist Frederick Herzberg proposed a theory of motivation that focuses on the job and on the environment where work is done. Herzberg studied various factors relating to the job and their relation to employee motivation and concluded that they can be divided into hygiene factors and motivational factors (Table 9.3).

Hygiene factors, which relate to the work setting and not to the content of the work, include adequate wages, comfortable and safe working conditions, fair company policies, and job security. These factors do not necessarily motivate employees to excel, but their absence may be a potential source of dissatisfaction and high turnover. Employee safety and comfort are clearly hygiene factors.

Many people feel that a good salary is one of the most important job factors, even more important than job security and the chance to use one's mind and abilities. Salary and security, two of the hygiene factors identified by Herzberg, make it possible for employees to satisfy the physiological and security needs identified by Maslow. However, the presence of hygiene factors is unlikely to motivate employees to work harder.

Motivational factors, which relate to the content of the work itself, include achievement, recognition, involvement, responsibility, and advancement. The absence of motivational factors may not result in dissatisfaction, but their presence is likely to motivate employees to excel. Many companies are beginning to employ methods to give employees more

self-actualization needs
the need to be the best one can be; at the top of Maslow's hierarchy

hygiene factors
aspects of Herzberg's theory of motivation that focus on the work setting and not the content of the work; these aspects include adequate wages, comfortable and safe working conditions, fair company policies, and job security

motivational factors
aspects of Herzberg's theory of motivation that focus on the content of the work itself; these aspects include achievement, recognition, involvement, responsibility, and advancement

If you have watched the Discovery Channel's *Dirty Jobs* series, you know that hygiene factors such as the quality of the work environment and safe conditions are important to employees.

TABLE 9.3
Herzberg's Hygiene and Motivational Factors

Hygiene Factors	Motivational Factors
Company policies	Achievement
Supervision	Recognition
Working conditions	Work itself
Relationships with peers, supervisors, and subordinates	Responsibility
Salary	Advancement
Security	Personal growth

responsibility and control and to involve them more in their work, which serves to motivate them to higher levels of productivity and quality. L.L. Bean employees have tremendous latitude to satisfy customer's needs. One employee drove 500 miles from Maine to New York to deliver a canoe to a customer who was leaving on a trip. L.L. Bean is one of the top 25 companies on *Business Week's* list of "Customer Service Champs." Besides empowering employees, the company has strict service training, answering every call within 20 seconds.[8]

Herzberg's motivational factors and Maslow's esteem and self-actualization needs are similar. Workers' low-level needs (physiological and security) have largely been satisfied by minimum-wage laws and occupational-safety standards set by various government agencies and are therefore not motivators. Consequently, to improve productivity, management should focus on satisfying workers' higher-level needs (motivational factors) by providing opportunities for achievement, involvement, and advancement and by recognizing good performance.

McGregor's Theory X and Theory Y

In *The Human Side of Enterprise,* Douglas McGregor related Maslow's ideas about personal needs to management. McGregor contrasted two views of management—the traditional view, which he called Theory X, and a humanistic view, which he called Theory Y.

Theory X
McGregor's traditional view of management whereby it is assumed that workers generally dislike work and must be forced to do their jobs

According to McGregor, managers adopting **Theory X** assume that workers generally dislike work and must be forced to do their jobs. They believe that the following statements are true of workers:

1. The average person naturally dislikes work and will avoid it when possible.
2. Most workers must be coerced, controlled, directed, or threatened with punishment to get them to work toward the achievement of organizational objectives.
3. The average worker prefers to be directed and to avoid responsibility, has relatively little ambition, and wants security.[9]

Theory Y
McGregor's humanistic view of management whereby it is assumed that workers like to work and that under proper conditions employees will seek out responsibility in an attempt to satisfy their social, esteem, and self-actualization needs

Managers who subscribe to the Theory X view maintain tight control over workers, provide almost constant supervision, try to motivate through fear, and make decisions in an autocratic fashion, eliciting little or no input from their subordinates. The Theory X style of management focuses on physiological and security needs and virtually ignores the higher needs discussed by Maslow.

The Theory X view of management does not take into account people's needs for companionship, esteem, and personal growth, whereas Theory Y, the contrasting view of management, does. Managers subscribing to the **Theory Y** view assume

Responding to Business Challenges
Sony Makes Changes to Motivate Managers

For 20 years, Sony was a key innovator in consumer electronics, creating the Walkman, the first portable music player, and the PlayStation. Today, however, the electronics giant has been suffering thanks to competition with Apple (portable music players), Microsoft, and Nintendo (gaming consoles). After the company posted more than $1 billion in losses, Chairman, CEO, and President Howard Stringer decided to make major changes at the company. Blaming Sony's traditional Japanese management style, Stringer declared that it was time to shake things up. He is searching for new ways motivate managers and employees to achieve organizational objectives.

After becoming president of Sony in early 2009, Stringer reorganized the company into two main groups. To run these groups, he promoted four Japanese executives known as "the four musketeers." Stringer also consolidated the company's large electronics division in order to streamline operations and maximize the productivity of workers.

Ultimately, Stringer's changes must yield profits over the long term in order for Sony to survive. In addition, the company must figure out how to rise to the levels of its competitors such as Apple and Microsoft at the same time that it figures out how to deal with new and smaller but more focused competitors. Fortunately, a new focus on human resources should help motivate employees at Sony to create a Web-to-TV platform similar to its successful PlayStation Network (an online PlayStation subscription service that connects gamers to each other). Given that it sells 15 million TVs each year, Sony hopes it's on to the next big thing.[10]

Discussion Questions

1. What happened to Sony to make it lose its competitive edge?
2. How does the company motivate its employees?
3. Do you think that the changes Sony has made will help it to regain a competitive advantage?

that workers like to work and that under proper conditions employees will seek out responsibility in an attempt to satisfy their social, esteem, and self-actualization needs. McGregor describes the assumptions behind Theory Y in the following way:

1. The expenditure of physical and mental effort in work is as natural as play or rest.
2. People will exercise self-direction and self-control to achieve objectives to which they are committed.
3. People will commit to objectives when they realize that the achievement of those goals will bring them personal reward.
4. The average person will accept and seek responsibility.
5. Imagination, ingenuity, and creativity can help solve organizational problems, but most organizations do not make adequate use of these characteristics in their employees.
6. Organizations today do not make full use of workers' intellectual potential.[11]

Obviously, managers subscribing to the Theory Y philosophy have a management style very different from managers subscribing to the Theory X philosophy. Theory Y managers maintain less control and supervision, do not use fear as the primary motivator, and are more democratic in decision making, allowing subordinates to participate in the process. Theory Y managers address the high-level needs in Maslow's hierarchy as well as physiological and security needs. Today, Theory Y enjoys widespread support and may have displaced Theory X.

Theory Z

Theory Z is a management philosophy that stresses employee participation in all aspects of company decision making. It was first described by William Ouchi in his book *Theory Z—How American Business Can Meet the Japanese Challenge.* Theory Z

Theory Z
a management philosophy that stresses employee participation in all aspects of company decision making

incorporates many elements associated with the Japanese approach to management, such as trust and intimacy, but Japanese ideas have been adapted for use in the United States. In a Theory Z organization, managers and workers share responsibilities; the management style is participative; and employment is long term and often lifelong. Japan has faced a significant period of slowing economic progress and competition from China and other Asian nations. This has led to experts questioning Theory Z, particularly at firms such as Sony and Toyota. Theory Z results in employees feeling organizational ownership. Research has found that such feelings of ownership may produce positive attitudinal and behavioral effects for employees.[12] In a Theory Y organization, managers focus on assumptions about the nature of the worker. The two theories can be seen as complementary. Table 9.4 compares the traditional American management style, the Japanese management style, and Theory Z (the modified Japanese management style).

Variations on Theory Z

Theory Z has been adapted and modified for use in a number of U.S. companies. One adaptation involves workers in decisions through quality circles. Quality circles (also called quality-assurance teams) are small, usually having five to eight members who discuss ways to reduce waste, eliminate problems, and improve quality, communication, and work satisfaction. Such quality teams are a common technique for harnessing the knowledge and creativity of hourly employees to solve problems in companies. As Theory Z has questioned the use of quality circles, their prevalence has declined. Quality circles have been replaced with quality methods.

Quality circles are often modified and operate under names such as *participative management, employee involvement,* or *self-directed work teams.* Regardless of the term used to describe such programs, they strive to give employees more control over their jobs while making them more responsible for the outcome of their

TABLE 9.4   Comparison of American, Japanese, and Theory Z Management Styles

	American	Japanese	Theory Z
Duration of employment	Relatively short term; workers subject to layoffs when business slows	Lifelong; no layoffs	Long term; layoffs rare
Rate of promotion	Rapid	Slow	Slow
Amount of specialization	Considerable; worker develops expertise in one area only	Minimal; worker develops expertise in all aspects of the organization	Moderate; worker learns all aspects of the organization
Decision making	Individual	Consensual; input from all concerned parties is considered	Consensual; emphasis on quality
Responsibility	Assigned to the individual	Shared by the group	Assigned to the individual
Control	Explicit and formal	Less explicit and less formal	Informal but with explicit performance measures
Concern for workers	Focus is on work only	Focus extends to worker's whole life	Focus includes worker's life and family

Source: Adapted from William Ouchi, *Theory Z—How American Business Can Meet the Japanese Challenge,* p. 58. © 1981 by Addison-Wesley Publishing Company, Inc. Reprinted by permission of Perseus Books Publishers, a member of Perseus Books, L.L.C.

efforts. Such programs often organize employees into work teams of 5 to 15 members who are responsible for producing an entire product item. Team members are cross-trained and can therefore move from job to job within the team. Each team essentially manages itself and is responsible for its quality, scheduling, ordering and use of materials, and problem solving. Many firms have successfully employed work teams to boost morale, productivity, quality, and competitiveness.

Equity Theory

According to **equity theory,** how much people are willing to contribute to an organization depends on their assessment of the fairness, or equity, of the rewards they will receive in exchange. In a fair situation, a person receives rewards proportional to the contribution he or she makes to the organization. However, in practice, equity is a subjective notion. Each worker regularly develops a personal input-output ratio by taking stock of his or her contribution (inputs) to the organization in time, effort, skills, and experience and assessing the rewards (outputs) offered by the organization in pay, benefits, recognition, and promotions. The worker compares his or her ratio to the input-output ratio of some other person—a "comparison other," who may be a co-worker, a friend working in another organization, or an "average" of several people working in the organization. If the two ratios are close, the individual will feel that he or she is being treated equitably.

Let's say you have a high-school education and earn $25,000 a year. When you compare your input-output ratio with that of a co-worker who has a college degree and makes $35,000 a year, you will probably feel that you are being paid fairly. However, if you perceive that your personal input-output ratio is lower than that of your college-educated co-worker, you may feel that you are being treated unfairly and be motivated to seek change. But, if you learn that co-worker who makes $35,000 has only a high-school diploma, you may feel cheated by your employer. To achieve equity, you could try to increase your outputs by asking for a raise or promotion. You could also try to have your co-worker's inputs increased or his or her outputs decreased. Failing to achieve equity, you may be motivated to look for a job at a different company.

Because almost all the issues involved in equity theory are subjective, they can be problematic. Author David Callahan has argued that feelings of inequity may underlie some unethical or illegal behavior in business. For example, due to employee theft and shoplifting, Walmart experiences billions in inventory losses every year. Some employees may take company resources to restore what they perceive to be equity. Theft of company resources is the number one ethical issue, based on a survey by the Ethics Resource Center.[13] Callahan believes that employees who do not feel they are being treated equitably may be motivated to equalize the situation by lying, cheating, or otherwise "improving" their pay, perhaps by stealing.[14] Managers should try to avoid equity problems by ensuring that rewards are distributed on the basis of performance and that all employees clearly understand the basis for their pay and benefits.

Expectancy Theory

Psychologist Victor Vroom described **expectancy theory,** which states that motivation depends not only on how much a person wants something but also on the person's perception of how likely he or she is to get it. A person who wants something and has reason to be optimistic will be strongly motivated. For example, say you really want a promotion. And, let's say because you have taken some night

equity theory
an assumption that how much people are willing to contribute to an organization depends on their assessment of the fairness, or equity, of the rewards they will receive in exchange

expectancy theory
the assumption that motivation depends not only on how much a person wants something but also on how likely he or she is to get it

Your motivation depends not only on how much you want something, but how likely you believe you are to get it.

classes to improve your skills, and moreover, have just made a large, significant sale, you feel confident that you are qualified and able to handle the new position. Therefore, you are motivated to try to get the promotion. In contrast, if you do not believe you are likely to get what you want, you may not be motivated to try to get it, even though you really want it.

Strategies for Motivating Employees

Based on the various theories that attempt to explain what motivates employees, businesses have developed several strategies for motivating their employees and boosting morale and productivity. Some of these techniques include behavior modification and job design, as well as the already described employee involvement programs and work teams.

Behavior Modification

behavior modification
changing behavior and encouraging appropriate actions by relating the consequences of behavior to the behavior itself

Behavior modification involves changing behavior and encouraging appropriate actions by relating the consequences of behavior to the behavior itself. The concept of behavior modification was developed by psychologist B. F. Skinner, who showed that there are two types of consequences that can modify behavior—reward and punishment. Skinner found that behavior that is rewarded will tend to be repeated, while behavior that is punished will tend to be eliminated. For example, employees who know that they will receive a bonus such as an expensive restaurant meal for making a sale over $2,000 may be more motivated to make sales. Workers who know they will be punished for being tardy are likely to make a greater effort to get to work on time.

However, the two strategies may not be equally effective. Punishing unacceptable behavior may provide quick results but may lead to undesirable long-term side effects, such as employee dissatisfaction and increased turnover. In general, rewarding appropriate behavior is a more effective way to modify behavior.

Job Design

Herzberg identified the job itself as a motivational factor. Managers have several strategies that they can use to design jobs to help improve employee motivation. These include job rotation, job enlargement, job enrichment, and flexible scheduling strategies.

job rotation
movement of employees from one job to another in an effort to relieve the boredom often associated with job specialization

Job Rotation.   **Job rotation** allows employees to move from one job to another in an effort to relieve the boredom that is often associated with job specialization. Businesses often turn to specialization in hopes of increasing productivity, but there is a negative side effect to this type of job design: Employees become bored and dissatisfied, and productivity declines. Job rotation reduces this boredom by allowing workers to undertake a greater variety of tasks and by giving them the opportunity to learn new skills. With job rotation, an employee spends a specified amount of time performing one job and then moves on to another, different job. The worker eventually returns to the initial job and begins the cycle again.

Job rotation is a good idea, but it has one major drawback. Because employees may eventually become bored with all the jobs in the cycle, job rotation does not totally eliminate the problem of boredom. Job rota- tion is extremely useful, however, in situations where a person is being trained for a position that requires an understanding of various units in an organization. Eli Lilly is a strong believer in the ben- efits of job rotation. The company leaves employees in their current jobs and asks them to take on addi- tional assignments outside their field of expertise or interest. The results of the process have been posi- tive, and Nokia is trying the same process with simi- lar outcomes.[15] Many executive training programs require trainees to spend time learning a variety of specialized jobs. Job rotation is also used to cross- train today's self-directed work teams.

Job Enlargement. **Job enlargement** adds more tasks to a job instead of treating each task as separate. Like job rotation, job enlargement was developed to overcome the boredom associated with specialization. The rationale behind this strategy is that jobs are more satisfying as the number of tasks performed by an individual increases. Employees sometimes enlarge, or craft, their jobs by noticing what needs to be done and then changing tasks and relationship boundaries to adjust. Individual orien- tation and motivation shape opportunities to craft new jobs and job relationships. Job enlargement strategies have been more successful in increasing job satisfaction than have job rotation strategies. IBM, AT&T, and Maytag are among the many com- panies that have used job enlargement to motivate employees.

Job Enrichment.   **Job enrichment** incorporates motivational factors such as opportunity for achieve- ment, recognition, responsibility, and advancement

Nucor Corporation's nonunion employees don't see themselves as ordinary steel workers. There are no special benefits or compensation plan for executives at Nucor. The company's flat organizational structure encourages employees to adopt the mindset of owner-operators.

into a job. It gives workers not only more tasks within the job, but more control and authority over the job. Job enrichment programs enhance a worker's feeling of responsibility and provide opportunities for growth and advancement when the worker is able to take on the more challenging tasks. Hyatt Hotels Corporation and General Foods use job enrichment to improve the quality of work life for their employees. The potential benefits of job enrichment are great, but it requires careful planning and execution.

Flexible Scheduling Strategies.   Many U.S. workers work a traditional 40-hour workweek consisting of five 8-hour days with fixed starting and ending times. Fac- ing problems of poor morale and high absenteeism as well as a diverse workforce with changing needs, many managers have turned to flexible scheduling strategies such as flextime, compressed workweeks, job sharing, part-time work, and telecom- muting. A survey by CareerBuilder.com showed that 40 percent of working fathers were offered flexible work schedules versus 53 percent of working mothers.[16]

job enlargement
the addition of more tasks to a job instead of treating each task as separate

job enrichment
the incorporation of motivational factors, such as opportunity for achievement, recognition, responsibility, and advancement, into a job

FIGURE 9.4

Flextime, Showing Core and Flexible Hours

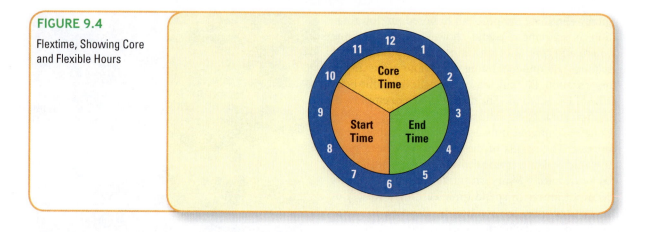

Flextime is a program that allows employees to choose their starting and ending times, as long as they are at work during a specified core period (Figure 9.4). It does not reduce the total number of hours that employees work; instead, it gives employees more flexibility in choosing which hours they work. A firm may specify that employees must be present from 10:00 a.m. to 3:00 p.m. One employee may choose to come in at 7:00 a.m. and leave at the end of the core time, perhaps to attend classes at a nearby college after work. Another employee, a mother who lives in the suburbs, may come in at 9:00 a.m. in order to have time to drop off her children at a day-care center and commute by public transportation to her job. Flextime provides many benefits, including improved ability to recruit and retain workers who wish to balance work and home life. Customers can be better served by allowing more coverage of customers over longer hours, workstations and facilities can be better utilized by staggering employee use, and rush hour traffic may be reduced. In addition, flexible schedules have been associated with an increase in healthy behaviors on the part of employees. More flexible schedules are associated with healthier lifestyle choices such as increased physical activity and healthier sleep habits.[17]

Related to flextime are the scheduling strategies of the compressed workweek and job sharing. The **compressed workweek** is a four-day (or shorter) period in which an employee works 40 hours. Under such a plan, employees typically work 10 hours per day for four days and have a three-day weekend. The compressed workweek reduces the company's operating expenses because its actual hours of operation are reduced. It is also sometimes used by parents who want to have more days off to spend with their families. The U.S. Bureau of Labor Statistics notes that the following career options provide greater flexibility in scheduling: medical transcriptionist, financial manager, nurse, database administrator, accountant, software developer, physical therapist assistant, paralegal, graphic designer, and private investigator.[18]

Job sharing occurs when two people do one job. One person may work from 8:00 a.m. to 12:30 p.m.; the second person comes in at 12:30 p.m. and works until 5:00 p.m. Job sharing gives both people the opportunity to work as well as time to fulfill other obligations, such as parenting or school. With job sharing, the company has the benefit of the skills of two people for one job, often at a lower total cost for salaries and benefits than one person working eight hours a day would be paid.

Two other flexible scheduling strategies attaining wider use include allowing full-time workers to work part time for a certain period and allowing workers to work at home either full or part time. Employees at some firms may be permitted to work part time for several months in order to care for a new baby or an elderly parent or just to slow down for a little while to "recharge their batteries." When the employees return to full-time work, they are usually given a position comparable to their original full-time position. Other firms are allowing employees to telecommute or telework (work at home a few days of the week), staying connected via computers, modems, and telephones. Today, 33.7 million Americans are teleworkers, working most often from home, a customer's business, or from their cars.[19] Table 9.5 shows the companies in the *Fortune* 100 Best Companies to Work For with the highest percentage of telecommuters.

REI, the outdoor-sporting company, encourages its workers to have a healthy work/life balance. Among other benefits, employees get paid to take a sabbatical after a number of years of service.

Although many employees ask for the option of working at home to ease the responsibilities of caring for family members, some have discovered that they are more productive at home without the distractions of the workplace. An assessment of 12 company telecommuting programs, including Apple, AT&T, and the state of California, found that positive productivity changes occurred. Traveler's Insurance Company reports its telecommuters to be 20 percent more productive than its traditional employees.[20] Other employees, however, have discovered that they are not suited for working at home. Human resource management executives are split as to whether telecommuting helps or hurts employees' careers. Thirty percent feel telecommuting helps their careers, 25 percent feel that it hurts, while 39 percent feel it does neither.[21] Still, work-at-home programs do help reduce overhead costs for businesses. For example, some companies used to maintain a surplus of office space but have reduced the surplus through employee telecommuting, "hoteling" (being assigned to a desk through a reservation system), and "hot-desking" (several people using the same desk but at different times).

Companies are turning to flexible work schedules to provide more options to employees who are trying to juggle their work duties with other responsibilities and

TABLE 9.5

Best Companies to Work For

Companies with Most Opportunities for Telecommuters in the *Fortune* "100 Best Companies to Work For"

Company	Best Companies Rank	Percent of "Regular" Telecommuters
Deloitte	61	90%
Cisco Systems	6	85
Juniper Networks	84	75
Accenture	97	67
Recreational Equipment (REI)	12	53
eBay	83	50
S.C. Johnson & Son	81	39
Southern Ohio Medical Center	68	37
Booz Allen Hamilton	52	36
American Fidelity Assurance	46	34

Source: http://money.cnn.com/magazines/fortune/bestcompanies/2009/benefits/telecommuting.html (accessed February 9, 2010).

Entrepreneurship in Action
Hudson Valley Fresh Helps Dairy Farmers Thrive

Sam Simon

Business: Hudson Valley Fresh

Founded: 2005.

Success: Helping struggling dairy farmers find a way to survive and sell their goods.

Hudson Valley Fresh is a dairy cooperative founded by Sam Simon, an orthopedic surgeon-turned dairy farmer. Simon gave up his successful medical practice in order to become a small-scale sustainable farmer. His coop is dedicated to more than selling milk products—it is dedicated to preserving and promoting an agricultural way of life in the Hudson River Valley of New York state. The farmers who supply Hudson Valley Fresh are all paid living wages and practice organic farming, which is better for the cows and the land. Another appeal of working for Hudson Valley Fresh is a chance to bypass the industrial milk producers system, which does not support or encourage small-scale production. Hudson Valley Fresh allows farmers to earn a better living and to raise their cows without using drugs and hormones to boost milk production. Simon hopes that this business model will help save a way of life for the small, traditional dairy farmer—something that has been dying out for a long time—while providing customers with highly superior products.[22]

needs. Preliminary results indicate that flexible scheduling plans increase job satisfaction, which, in turn, leads to increases in productivity. Some recent research, however, has indicated there are potential problems with telecommuting. Some managers are reluctant to adopt the practice because the pace of change in today's workplace is faster than ever, and telecommuters may be left behind or actually cause managers more work in helping them stay abreast of changes. Some employers also worry that telecommuting workers create a security risk by creating more opportunities for computer hackers or equipment thieves. Some employees have found that working outside the office may hurt career advancement opportunities, and some report that instead of helping them balance work and family responsibilities, telecommuting increases the strain by blurring the barriers between the office and home. Co-workers call at all hours, and telecommuters are apt to continue to work when they are not supposed to (after regular business hours or during vacation time).

Importance of Motivational Strategies

Motivation is more than a tool that managers can use to foster employee loyalty and boost productivity. It is a process that affects all the relationships within an organization and influences many areas such as pay, promotion, job design, training opportunities, and reporting relationships. Employees are motivated by the nature of the relationships they have with their supervisors, by the nature of their jobs, and by characteristics of the organization. Even the economic environment can change an employee's motivation. In a slow growth or recession economy, sales can flatten or decrease and morale can drop because of the need to cut jobs. In the most recent recession, many workers feared losing their jobs and increased the amount they were saving. The firm may have to work harder to keep good employees and to motivate all employees to work to overcome obstacles. In good economic times, employees may be more demanding and be on the lookout for better opportunities. New rewards or incentives may help motivate workers in such economies. Motivation tools, then, must be varied as well. Managers can further nurture motivation by being honest, supportive, empathetic, accessible, fair, and open. Motivating employees to increase satisfaction and productivity is an important concern for organizations seeking to remain competitive in the global marketplace.

So You Think You May Be Good at Motivating a Workforce

If you are good at mediation, smoothing conflict, and have a good understanding of motivation and human relations theories, then you might be a good leader, human resource manager, or training expert. Most organizations, especially as they grow, will need to implement human relations programs. These are necessary to teach employees about sensitivity to other cultures, religions, and beliefs, as well as for teaching the workforce about the organization so that they understand how they fit in the larger picture. Employees need to appreciate the benefits of working together to make the firm run smoothly, and they also need to understand how their contributions help the firm. To stay motivated, most employees need to feel like what they do each day contributes something of value to the firm. Disclosing information and including employees in decision-making processes will also help employees feel valuable and wanted within the firm.

There are many different ways employers can reward and encourage employees. However, employers must be careful when considering what kinds of incentives to use. Different cultures value different kinds of incentives more highly than others. For example, a Japanese worker would probably not like it if she were singled out from the group and given a large cash bonus as reward for her work. Japanese workers tend to be more group oriented, and therefore anything that singles out individuals would not be an effective way of rewarding and motivating. American workers, on the other hand, are very individualistic, and a raise and public praise might be more effective. However,

what might motivate a younger employee (bonuses, raises, and perks) may not be the same as what motivates a more seasoned, experienced, and financially successful employee (recognition, opportunity for greater influence, and increased training). Motivation is not an easy thing to understand, especially as firms become more global and more diverse.

Another important part of motivation is enjoying where you work and your career opportunities. Here is a list of the best places to do business and start careers in the United States, according to *Forbes* magazine. Chances are, workers who live in these places have encountered fewer frustrations than those places at the bottom of the list and, therefore, would probably be more content with where they work.[23]

Best Places for Business and Careers

Rank	Metro Area	Job Growth Rank	Metro Area Population (in thousands)
1.	Raleigh, NC	4	1,086
2.	Fort Collins, CO	45	292
3.	Durham, NC	30	487
4.	Fayetteville, AR	19	442
5.	Lincoln, NE	100	296
6.	Asheville, NC	39	411
7.	Des Moines, IA	41	553
8.	Austin, TX	8	1,645
9.	Boise, ID	13	601
10.	Colorado Springs, CO	85	614[24]

Review Your Understanding

Define human relations, and determine why its study is important.

Human relations is the study of the behavior of individuals and groups in organizational settings. Its focus is what motivates employees to perform on the job. Human relations is important because businesses need to understand how to motivate their increasingly diverse employees to be more effective, boost workplace morale, and maximize employees' productivity and creativity.

Summarize studies that laid the groundwork for understanding employee motivation.

Time and motion studies by Frederick Taylor and others helped them analyze how employees perform specific work tasks in an effort to improve their productivity. Taylor and the early practitioners of the classical theory of motivation felt that money and job security were the primary motivators of employees. However, the Hawthorne studies revealed that human factors also influence workers' behavior.

Compare and contrast the human-relations theories of Abraham Maslow and Frederick Herzberg.

Abraham Maslow defined five basic needs of all people and arranged them in the order in which they must be satisfied: physiological, security, social, esteem, and self-actualization. Frederick Herzberg divided characteristics of the job into hygiene factors and motivational factors. Hygiene factors relate to the work environment and must be present for employees to remain in a job. Motivational factors—recognition, responsibility, and advancement—relate to the work itself. They encourage employees to be productive. Herzberg's hygiene factors can be compared to Maslow's physiological and security needs; motivational factors may include Maslow's social, esteem, and self-actualization needs.

Investigate various theories of motivation, including Theories X, Y, and Z; equity theory; and expectancy theory.

Douglas McGregor contrasted two views of management: Theory X (traditional) suggests workers dislike work, while theory Y (humanistic) suggests that workers not only like work but seek out responsibility to satisfy their higher-order needs. Theory Z stresses employee participation in all aspects of company decision making, often through participative management programs and self-directed work teams. According to equity theory, how much people are willing to contribute to an organization depends on their assessment of the fairness, or equity, of the rewards they will receive in exchange. Expectancy theory states that motivation depends not only on how much a person wants something but also on the person's perception of how likely he or she is to get it.

Describe some of the strategies that managers use to motivate employees.

Strategies for motivating workers include behavior modification (changing behavior and encouraging appropriate actions by relating the consequences of behavior to the behavior itself) and job design. Among the job design strategies businesses use are job rotation (allowing employees to move from one job to another to try to relieve the boredom associated with job specialization), job enlargement (adding tasks to a job instead of treating each task as a separate job), job enrichment (incorporating motivational factors into a job situation), and flexible scheduling strategies (flextime, compressed work weeks, job sharing, part-time work, and telecommuting).

Critique a business's program for motivating its sales force.

Using the information presented in the chapter, you should be able to analyze and defend Eagle Pharmaceutical's motivation program in "Solve the Dilemma" on page 292 including the motivation theories the firm is applying to boost morale and productivity.

Revisit the World of Business

1. What has J.A. Frate done to set its business apart from the competition?
2. How does J.A. Frate keep its employees motivated and satisfied?
3. How did J.A. Frate handle layoffs? What this a good strategy for maintaining employee morale?

Learn the Terms

Check Your Progress

1. Why do managers need to understand the needs of their employees?
2. Describe the motivation process.
3. What was the goal of the Hawthorne studies? What was the outcome of those studies?
4. Explain Maslow's hierarchy of needs. What does it tell us about employee motivation?
5. What are Herzberg's hygiene and motivational factors? How can managers use them to motivate workers?
6. Contrast the assumptions of Theory X and Theory Y. Why has Theory Y replaced Theory X in management today?
7. What is Theory Z? How can businesses apply Theory Z to the workplace?
8. Identify and describe four job-design strategies.
9. Name and describe some flexible scheduling strategies. How can flexible schedules help motivate workers?
10. Why are motivational strategies important to both employees and employers?

Get Involved

1. Consider a person who is homeless: How would he or she be motivated and what actions would that person take? Use the motivation process to explain. Which of the needs in Maslow's hierarchy are likely to be most important? Least important?
2. View the video *Cheaper by the Dozen* (1950) and report on how the Gilbreths tried to incorporate their passion for efficiency into their family life.
3. What events and trends in society, technology, and economics do you think will shape human relations management theory in the future?

Build Your Skills

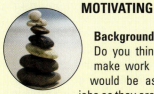

MOTIVATING

Background:
Do you think that, if employers could make work more like play, employees would be as enthusiastic about their jobs as they are about what they do in their leisure time? Let's see where this idea might take us.

Task:
After reading the "Characteristics of PLAY," place a √ in column one for those characteristics you have experienced in your leisure time activities. Likewise, check column three for those "Characteristics of WORK" you have experienced in any of the jobs you've held.

All That Apply	Characteristics of PLAY	All That Apply	Characteristics of WORK
	1. New games can be played on different days.		1. Job enrichment, job enlargement, or job rotation.
	2. Flexible duration of play.		2. Job sharing.
	3. Flexible time of when to play.		3. Flextime, telecommuting.
	4. Opportunity to express oneself.		4. Encourage and implement employee suggestions.
	5. Opportunity to use one's talents.		5. Assignment of challenging projects.
	6. Skillful play brings applause, praise, and recognition from spectators.		6. Employee-of-the-month awards, press releases, employee newsletter announcements.
	7. Healthy competition, rivalry, and challenge exist.		7. Production goals with competition to see which team does best.
	8. Opportunity for social interaction.		8. Employee softball or bowling teams.
	9. Mechanisms for scoring one's performance are available (feedback).		9. Profit sharing; peer performance appraisals.
	10. Rules ensure basic fairness and justice.		10. Use tactful and consistent discipline.

Discussion Questions

1. What prevents managers from making work more like play?
2. Are these forces real, or imagined?
3. What would be the likely (positive and negative) results of making work more like play?
4. Could others in the organization accept such creative behaviors?

Solve the Dilemma

MOTIVATING TO WIN

Eagle Pharmaceutical has long been recognized for its innovative techniques for motivating its salesforce. It features the salesperson who has been the most successful during the previous quarter in the company newsletter, "Touchdown." The salesperson also receives a football jersey, a plaque, and $1,000 worth of Eagle stock. Eagle's "Superbowl Club" is for employees who reach or exceed their sales goal, and a "Heisman Award," which includes a trip to the Caribbean, is given annually to the top 20 salespeople in terms of goal achievement.

Eagle employs a video conference hook-up between the honored salesperson and four regional sales managers to capture some of the successful tactics and strategies the winning salesperson uses to succeed. The managers summarize these ideas and pass them along to the salespeople they manage. Sales managers feel strongly that programs such as this are important and that, by sharing strategies and tactics with one another, they can be a successful team.

Discussion Questions

1. Which motivational theories are in use at Eagle?
2. What is the value of getting employees to compete against a goal instead of against one another?
3. Put yourself in the shoes of one of the four regional sales managers and argue against potential cutbacks to the motivational program.

Build Your Business Plan

MOTIVATING THE WORKFORCE

As you determine the size of your workforce, you are going to face the reality that you cannot provide the level of financial compensation that you would like to your employees, especially when you are starting your business.

Many employees are motivated by other things than money. Knowing that they are appreciated and doing a good job can bring great satisfaction to employees. Known as "stroking," it can provide employees with internal gratification that can be valued even more that financial incentives. Listening to your employees' suggestions, involving them in discussions about future growth and valuing their input, can go a long way toward building loyal employees and reducing employee turnover.

Think about what you could do in your business to motivate your employees without spending much money. Maybe you will have lunch brought in once a week or offer tickets to a local sporting event to the employee with the most sales. Whatever you elect to do, you must be consistent and fair with all your employees.

See for Yourself Videocase

VOLUNTEERING HELPS INCREASE PROFITS AND IMPROVE EMPLOYEE RETENTION

As part of an increasing focus on social responsibility, companies of all sizes are turning to volunteering. There's no doubt that well-publicized volunteering efforts help improve a company's reputation and look good on annual reports and in investor statements. Interestingly, these efforts also boost bottom line profits and enhance employee retention. Points of Light Foundation, an organization founded to help people find ways to make a difference in their communities, reports that over 80 percent of companies feel volunteering (especially in teams) increases profits. This may be mainly due to the fact that consumers increasingly demand that businesses be socially responsible. As information becomes more available on the decisions and conduct of companies, consumers seek out companies that share their values. Employees also tend to be more committed to companies that give back to communities and the environment. Often, this commitment is fueled by a sense that volunteering and socially responsible initiatives contribute a deeper sense of meaning to their work.

Small companies such as Milestone use team volunteering as a way to give employees an opportunity to contribute positively to their communities and to build skills that translate into better performance back to the office. The more employees are exposed to working together on meaningful tasks, the more likely it is they will work well together in a work environment.

Many large corporations use team volunteering as well. Microsoft participates in team events such as the United Way's annual Day of Caring and Seattle Works Day. Disney runs a volunteer program called voluntEARS. Employees participating in this program work with a number of local and national charities throughout the year.

New York Cares is one of a number of organizations set up to assist companies with finding volunteering opportunities. As of 2009, the company had assisted over 800 companies such as Credit Suisse Foundation, Barclays Capital, and L'Oreal. American Express has partnered with New York Cares for years cleaning parks, fixing public schools, leading jobs skills workshops for women reentering the workforce, taking children on field trips, and much more. New York Cares stresses that companies with volunteer programs are better perceived by the public than those without. All in all, companies have a lot to feel good about when they give back. Employees are happier and work better together, customer perception is often more positive, and earnings generally grow. What's not to love?

Discussion Questions

1. Why should managers investigate providing volunteer opportunities for employees? What are the advantages?

2. Why is team volunteering especially helpful for employees?

3. Do you see any potential downside to volunteering?

Remember to check out our Online Learning Center at www.mhhe.com/ferrell8e

Team Exercise

Form groups and outline a compensation package that you would consider ideal in motivating an employee, recognizing performance, and assisting the company in attaining its cost-to-performance objectives. Think about the impact of intrinsic and extrinsic motivation and recognition. How can flexible scheduling strategies be used effectively to motivate employees? Report your compensation package to the class.

Managing Human Resources

OBJECTIVES

After reading this chapter, you will be able to:

- Define human resources management, and explain its significance.

- Summarize the processes of recruiting and selecting human resources for a company.

- Discuss how workers are trained and their performance appraised.

- Identify the types of turnover companies may experience, and explain why turnover is an important issue.

- Specify the various ways a worker may be compensated.

- Discuss some of the issues associated with unionized employees, including collective bargaining and dispute resolution.

- Describe the importance of diversity in the workforce.

- Assess an organization's efforts to reduce its workforce size and manage the resulting effects.

Bringing Together 15,000 People across the Globe to Create "Our Brew"

Promoted to CEO in 2008, Molson Coors' Peter Swinburn had not been in the top spot long before he realized his company was missing something critical—namely, a cohesive team spirit. After a number of acquisitions and joint ventures (including the merger between the Adolph Coors Company and Molson Inc.), Molson Coors lacked a sense of unity. Each location was operating without considering overall company impact. Taking over as the economy began to take a downturn, Swinburn seized the opportunity to focus on developing a companywide culture. Molson Coors has 15,000 employees in more than 30 countries. Bringing them all together through a unifying structure, corporate culture, and vision required acknowledging many different cultures, work values, and languages.

Swinburn spent his first six months holding meetings with officials throughout the company and listening carefully to employee suggestions. As a result of one suggestion, for example, Swinburn signed his company up for Yammer (a private, Twitter-like site available to companies). Many employees now use the site to collaborate, discuss ideas, and more—some "chatting" across the globe. Swinburn's philosophy is that in order for employees to support the company, the company must also support the employees. Swinburn advocates putting the team first and believes that employees united by goals, vision, and approach view the end products as their own. He ensures the tools are in place to facilitate this goal and to open dialogue.

continued

ENTER THE WORLD OF BUSINESS

In turn, employees feel that Molson Coors' vision for the future has crystallized. Swinburn plans to continue with the expansion approach he inherited, but in the process will ensure that each new company welcomed into the Molson Coors family will be given the tools it needs to succeed while being incorporated into the overall culture.[1]

Introduction

If a business is to achieve success, it must have sufficient numbers of employees who are qualified and motivated to perform the required duties. Thus, managing the quantity (from hiring to firing) and quality (through training, compensating, and so on) of employees is an important business function. Meeting the challenge of managing increasingly diverse human resources effectively can give a company a competitive edge in a global marketplace.

This chapter focuses on the quantity and quality of human resources. First we look at how human resources managers plan for, recruit, and select qualified employees. Next we look at training, appraising, and compensating employees, aspects of human resources management designed to retain valued employees. Along the way, we'll also consider the challenges of managing unionized and diverse employees.

The Nature of Human Resources Management

human resources management (HRM)
all the activities involved in determining an organization's human resources needs, as well as acquiring, training, and compensating people to fill those needs

Chapter 1 defined human resources as labor, the physical and mental abilities that people use to produce goods and services. **Human resources management (HRM)** refers to all the activities involved in determining an organization's human resources needs, as well as acquiring, training, and compensating people to fill those needs. Human resources managers are concerned with maximizing the satisfaction of employees and motivating them to meet organizational objectives productively. In some companies, this function is called personnel management.

HRM has increased in importance over the last few decades, in part because managers have developed a better understanding of human relations through the work of Maslow, Herzberg, and others. Moreover, the human resources themselves are changing. Employees today are concerned not only about how much a job pays; they are concerned also with job satisfaction, personal performance, leisure, the environment, and their opportunities for advancement. Once dominated by white men, today's workforce includes significantly more women, African Americans, Hispanics, and

Today's workforce is becoming increasingly more diverse.

other minorities, as well as disabled and older workers. Human resources managers must be aware of these changes and leverage them to increase the productivity of their employees. Every manager practices some of the functions of human resources management at all times.

Planning for Human Resources Needs

When planning and developing strategies for reaching the organization's overall objectives, a company must consider whether it will have the human resources necessary to carry out its plans. After determining how many employees and what skills are needed to satisfy the overall plans, the human resources department (which may range from the owner in a small business to hundreds of people in a large corporation) ascertains how many employees the company currently has and how many will be retiring or otherwise leaving the organization during the planning period. With this information, the human resources manager can then forecast how many more employees the company will need to hire and what qualifications they must have, or determine if layoffs are required to meet demand more efficiently. HRM planning also requires forecasting the availability of people in the workforce who will have the necessary qualifications to meet the organization's future needs. The human resources manager then develops a strategy for satisfying the organization's human resources needs. Many experts believe that after the most recent global financial crisis, not all jobs lost to the downturn will return. Analysts anticipate that roughly 25 percent of the jobs eliminated during the recession will not come back. Human resource managers will need to follow the trend to see if their hiring needs will change or result in more outsourcing or greater automation of certain positions within the organization.[2]

Next, managers analyze the jobs within the organization so that they can match the human resources to the available assignments. **Job analysis** determines, through observation and study, pertinent information about a job—the specific tasks that comprise it; the knowledge, skills, and abilities necessary to perform it, and the environment in which it will be performed. Managers use the information obtained through a job analysis to develop job descriptions and job specifications.

A **job description** is a formal, written explanation of a specific job that usually includes job title, tasks to be performed (for instance, waiting on customers), relationship with other jobs, physical and mental skills required (such as lifting heavy boxes or calculating data), duties, responsibilities, and working conditions. A **job specification** describes the qualifications necessary for a specific job, in terms of education (some jobs require a college degree), experience, personal characteristics (ads frequently request outgoing, hardworking persons), and physical characteristics. Both the job description and job specification are used to develop recruiting materials such as newspaper, trade publications, and online advertisements.

Recruiting and Selecting New Employees

After forecasting the firm's human resources needs and comparing them to existing human resources, the human resources manager should have a general idea of how many new employees the firm needs to hire. With the aid of job analyses, management can then recruit and select employees who are qualified to fill specific job openings.

Recruiting

Recruiting means forming a pool of qualified applicants from which management can select employees. There are two sources from which to develop this pool of applicants—internal and external.

job analysis
the determination, through observation and study, of pertinent information about a job—including specific tasks and necessary abilities, knowledge, and skills

job description
a formal, written explanation of a specific job, usually including job title, tasks, relationship with other jobs, physical and mental skills required, duties, responsibilities, and working conditions

job specification
a description of the qualifications necessary for a specific job, in terms of education, experience, and personal and physical characteristics

recruiting
forming a pool of qualified applicants from which management can select employees

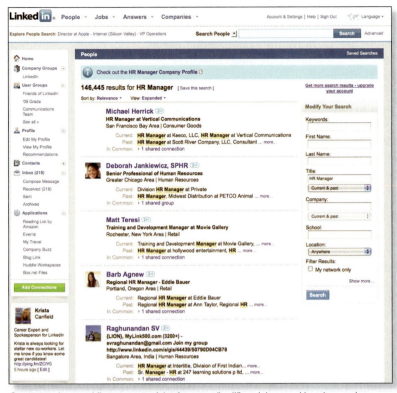

Some recruiters and firms use special software to "troll" social networking sites such as Linked In to find outstanding employees who might not be looking for a job but who could be successfully recruited.

Internal sources of applicants include the organization's current employees. Many firms have a policy of giving first consideration to their own employees—or promoting from within. The cost of hiring current employees to fill job openings is inexpensive when compared with the cost of hiring from external sources, and it is good for employee morale. However, hiring from within creates another job vacancy to be filled.

External sources consist of advertisements in newspapers and professional journals, employment agencies, colleges, vocational schools, recommendations from current employees, competing firms, unsolicited applications, and online. Internships are also a good way to solicit for potential employees. Many companies hire college students or recent graduates to low-paying internships that give them the opportunity to get hands-on experience on the job.

If the intern proves to be a good fit, an organization may then hire the intern as a full-time worker. Figure 10.1 illustrates some of the top benefits of becoming an intern. There are also hundreds of Web sites where employers can post job openings and job seekers can post their résumés, including Monster.com, Craigslist.org,

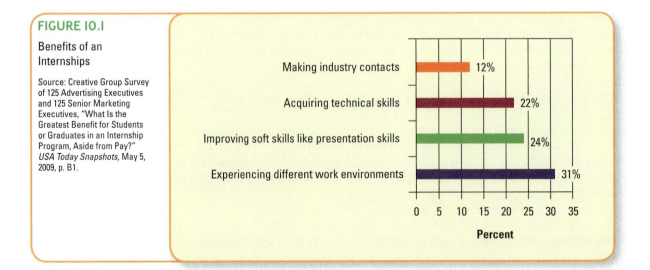

FIGURE 10.1

Benefits of an Internships

Source: Creative Group Survey of 125 Advertising Executives and 125 Senior Marketing Executives, "What Is the Greatest Benefit for Students or Graduates in an Internship Program, Aside from Pay?" *USA Today Snapshots,* May 5, 2009, p. B1.

and CareerBuilder.com. Theladders.com is a Web site that focuses on jobs starting at $100,000 a year. It seeks higher educated and more experienced individuals for high-paying positions. Employers looking for employees for specialized jobs can use more focused sites such as computerwork.com. Increasingly, companies can turn to their own Web sites for potential candidates: Nearly all of the *Fortune* 500 firms provide career Web sites where they recruit, provide employment information, and take applications. Using these sources of applicants is generally more expensive than hiring from within, but it may be necessary if there are no current employees who meet the job specifications or there are better-qualified people

The McGraw-Hill Companies has an online database of job offerings called "Strategic Talent Acquisition Resources," or STAR. STAR helps employees manage their careers by alerting them to employment opportunities within the company that match their experience. The system captures all résumés in a common database so that they can be shared nationwide.

outside of the organization. Recruiting for entry-level managerial and professional positions is often carried out on college and university campuses. For managerial or professional positions above the entry level, companies sometimes depend on employment agencies or executive search firms, sometimes called *headhunters,* which specialize in luring qualified people away from other companies.

Selection

Selection is the process of collecting information about applicants and using that information to decide which ones to hire. It includes the application itself, as well as interviewing, testing, and reference checking. This process can be quite lengthy and expensive. Procter & Gamble, for example, offers online applications for jobs in 80 countries. The first round of evaluation involves testing, and if this stage goes well, the candidate interviews in the region or country to which the applicant applied.[3] Such rigorous scrutiny is necessary to find those applicants who can do the work expected and fit into the firm's structure and culture. If an organization finds the "right" employees through its recruiting and selection process, it will not have to spend as much money later in recruiting, selecting, and training replacement employees.

selection
the process of collecting information about applicants and using that information to make hiring decisions

The Application. In the first stage of the selection process, the individual fills out an application form and perhaps has a brief interview. The application form asks for the applicant's name, address, telephone number, education, and previous work experience. The goal of this stage of the selection process is to get acquainted with the applicants and to weed out those who are obviously not qualified for the job. Most companies ask for the following information before contacting a potential candidate: current salary, reason for seeking a new job, years of experience, availability, and level of interest in the position. In addition to identifying obvious qualifications, the application can provide subtle clues about whether a person is appropriate for a particular job. For instance, an applicant who gives unusually creative answers may be perfect for a position at an advertising agency; a person who turns in a sloppy, hurriedly scrawled application probably would not be appropriate for a technical job requiring precise adjustments. Many companies now accept online applications. The online application for Borders Bookstore is designed not only to collect biographical data on the applicant, but also to create a picture of the applicant and how that person might contribute to the company. The completion time takes about 15 to 45 minutes, depending on the position. To get a better view of the fit between the applicant and the company, the online application contains several pages that ask applicants more specific questions, from how they might react in a certain situation to personality attributes like self-esteem or ability to interact with people.[5]

The Interview. The next phase of the selection process involves interviewing applicants. Interviews allow management to obtain detailed information about the applicant's experience and skills, reasons for changing jobs, attitudes toward the job, and an idea of whether the person would fit in with the company. Furthermore, the interviewer can answer the applicant's questions about the requirements for the job, compensation, working conditions, company policies, organizational culture, and so on. A potential employee's questions may be just as revealing as his or her answers. Table 10.1 provides some insights on finding the right work environment. Table 10.2 lists some of the most common questions asked by interviewers while Table 10.3 reveals mistakes candidates make in interviewing.

TABLE 10.1 Interviewing Tips	
	1. Evaluate the work environment. Do employees seem to get along and work well in teams?
	2. Evaluate the attitude of employees. Are employees happy, tense, or overworked?
	3. Are employees enthusiastic and excited about their work?
	4. What is the organizational culture, and would you feel comfortable working there?

Source: Adapted from "What to Look for During Office Visits," http://careercenter.tamu.edu/guides/interviews/lookforinoffice.cfm?sn=faculty (accessed March 16, 2010).

TABLE 10.2
Most Common Question Asked during the Interview

1. Tell me about yourself.
2. Why should I hire you?
3. Please tell me about your future objectives.
4. Has your education prepared you for your career?
5. Have you been a team player?
6. Did you encounter any conflict with your previous professors or employer? What are the steps that you have taken to resolve this issue?
7. What is your biggest weakness?
8. How would your professors describe you?
9. What are the qualities that a manager should possess?
10. If you could turn back time, what would you change?

Source: "Job Interview Skills Training: Top Ten Interview Questions for College Graduates," February 17, 2010, http://www.articlesbase.com/business-articles/job-interview-skills-training-top-ten-interview-questions-for-college-graduates-1871741.html (accessed March 13, 2010).

TABLE 10.3
Mistakes Made in Interviewing

1. Not taking the interview seriously.
2. Not dressing appropriately (dressing down).
3. Not appropriately discussing experience, abilities, and education.
4. Being too modest about your accomplishments.
5. Talking too much.
6. Too much concern about compensation.
7. Speaking negatively of a former employer.
8. Not asking enough or appropriate questions.
9. Not showing the proper enthusiasm level.
10. Not engaging in appropriate follow-up to the interview.

Source: "Avoid the Top 10 Job Interview Mistakes," All Business, http://www.allbusiness.com/human-resources/careers-job-interview/1611-2.html (March 16, 2010).

Testing. Another step in the selection process is testing. Ability and performance tests are used to determine whether an applicant has the skills necessary for the job. Aptitude, IQ, or personality tests may be used to assess an applicant's potential for a certain kind of work and his or her ability to fit into the organization's culture. One of the most commonly used tests is the Myers-Briggs Type Indicator. Myers-Briggs Type Indicator Test is used worldwide by millions of people each year. Although polygraph ("lie detector") tests were once a common technique for evaluating the honesty of applicants, in 1988 their use was restricted to specific government jobs and those involving security or access to drugs. Applicants may also undergo physical examinations to determine their suitability for some jobs, and many companies require applicants

Occasionally companies genetically test applicants to screen out people who may be more likely to develop illness if exposed to certain worksite substances. Recently, IBM became the first corporation to ban genetic testing in the interests of employee privacy.

TABLE 10.4

Top 10 Résumé Lies

1. Stretching dates of employment
2. Inflating past accomplishments and skills
3. Enhancing job titles and responsibilities
4. Education exaggeration and fabricating degrees
5. Unexplained gaps and periods of "self employment"
6. Omitting past employment
7. Faking credentials
8. Fabricating reasons for leaving previous job
9. Providing fraudulent references
10. Misrepresenting military record

Source: Christopher T. Marquet and Lisa J. B. Peterson, "Résumé Fraud: The Top 10 Lies," http://www. marquetinternational.com/pdf/Resume%20Fraud-Top%20Ten%20Lies.pdf (accessed March 13, 2010).

to be screened for illegal drug use. There are more than 11 million heavy drinkers and 16 million illegal drug users in the United States. Of this group, 75 percent are employed full time and around half work for small businesses. On average in small businesses, 1 out of 10 employees are either alcohol or drug abusers. Small businesses may have a higher percentage of these employees because they do not engage in systematic drug testing. If you employ a drug or alcohol abuser, you can expect a 33 percent loss in productivity from this employee, which costs employers roughly $7,000 annually. Overall, substance abuse costs American employers $160 billion each year through high employee turnover and absenteeism, workplace accidents, higher workers' compensation costs, higher medical costs, and workplace theft and violence.[6] Because computer knowledge is a requirement for many jobs today, certain companies also require an applicant to take a typing test or tests to determine their knowledge of MS Word, Excel, PowerPoint, and/or other necessary programs. Like the application form and the interview, testing serves to eliminate those who do not meet the job specifications.

Reference Checking.   Before making a job offer, the company should always check an applicant's references. Reference checking usually involves verifying educational background and previous work experience. Background checking is important because applicants may misrepresent themselves on their applications or résumés. The star of *Dinner: Impossible* on the Food Network fabricated portions of his résumé, including the claim that he cooked for Britain's Royal Family. The Food Network, upon learning of these errors, did not renew Robert Irvine's contract, indicating that viewers place trust in the network and the accuracy of information that it provides and that Irvine "challenged that trust."[7] Irvine had to work for months to apologize and set the record straight about his chef credentials. Food Network ultimately did rehire him to host *Dinner: Impossible*. As Table 10.4 illustrates, some of the most common types of résumé lies include the faking of credentials, overstatements of skills or accomplishments, lies concerning education/degrees, omissions of past employment, and the falsification of references.[8] Reference checking is a vital, albeit often overlooked, stage in the selection process. Managers charged with hiring should be aware, however, that many organizations will confirm only that an applicant is a former employee, perhaps with beginning and ending work dates, and will not release details about the quality of the employee's work.

Legal Issues in Recruiting and Selecting

Legal constraints and regulations are present in almost every phase of the recruitment and selection process, and a violation of these regulations can result in lawsuits and fines. Therefore, managers should be aware of these restrictions to avoid legal problems. Some of the laws affecting human resources management are discussed below.

Because one law pervades all areas of human resources management, we'll take a quick look at it now. **Title VII of the Civil Rights Act** of 1964 prohibits discrimination in employment. It also created the Equal Employment Opportunity Commission (EEOC), a federal agency dedicated to increasing job opportunities for women and minorities and eliminating job discrimination based on race, religion, color, sex, national origin, or handicap. As a result of Title VII, employers must not impose sex distinctions in job specifications, job descriptions, or newspaper advertisements. In 2009, workplace discrimination charges filed with the EEOC totaled 93,277. Monetary compensation for victims reached more than $376 million. Race discrimination charges made up 36 percent of the total, while sexual discrimination charges consisted of 30 percent.[9] Sexual harassment cases make up the largest number of claims the EEOC sees each day. The Civil Rights Act of 1964 also outlaws the use of discriminatory tests for applicants. Aptitude tests and other indirect tests must be validated; in other words, employers must be able to demonstrate that scores on such tests are related to job performance, so that no one race has an advantage in taking the tests. Although many hope for improvements in organizational diversity, in a survey of 357 global senior executives, 76 percent have one or no minorities among their top executives. Minorities make up 17 percent of the U.S. workforce, and that number should hit 20 percent by 2016. In spite of a lack of diversity, many of these companies indicate an initiative to support workplace diversity.[10]

Other laws affecting HRM include the Americans with Disabilities Act (ADA), which prevents discrimination against disabled persons. It also classifies people with AIDS as handicapped and, consequently, prohibits using a positive AIDS test as reason to deny an applicant employment. The Age Discrimination in Employment Act specifically outlaws discrimination based on age. Its focus is banning hiring practices that discriminate against people between the ages of 40 and 69, but it also outlaws policies that require employees to retire before the age of 70. Generally, when companies need employees, recruiters head to college campuses, and when downsizing is necessary, many older workers are offered early retirement. For instance, roughly 9 percent of retirees said they were forced to retire.[11] However, there are many benefits that companies are realizing in hiring older workers. Some of these benefits include the fact that they are more dedicated, punctual, honest, and detail-oriented; are good listeners; take pride in their work; exhibit good organizational skills; are efficient and confident; are mature; can be seen as role models; have good communication skills; and offer an opportunity for a reduced labor cost because of already having insurance plans.[12] The Equal Pay Act mandates that men and women who do equal work must receive the same wage. Wage differences are acceptable only if they are attributed to seniority, performance, or qualifications. In the United States, the typical full-time female employee earns 19 percent less than the average full-time male employee. In a study by PayScale, some of the biggest gender pay gaps can be found in positions such as chief executive (women earn 71 percent of what men earn), hospital administrator (women earn 77 percent of what men earn), and chief operating officer (women earn 80 percent of what men earn). Performance quality in these jobs is relatively subjective. Jobs like engineers, actuaries, or electricians, where

Title VII of the Civil Rights Act
prohibits discrimination in employment and created the Equal Employment Opportunity Commission

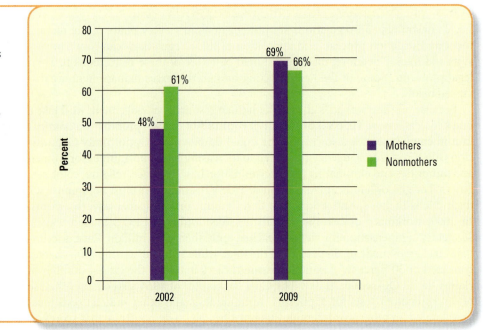

FIGURE 10.2

Women Who Want to
Move Up in Their Jobs

Source: Sue Shellenbarger,
"New Workplace Equalizer:
Ambition," *The Wall Street
Journal* March 25, 2009,
http://online.wsj.com/article/
SB123801512551141207.html
(accessed March 8, 2010).

the performance evaluation is more objective, result in greater salary parity between men and women.[13] However, despite the wage inequalities that still exist, women in the workplace are becoming increasingly accepted among both genders. The working mother is no longer a novelty; in fact, many working mothers seek the same amount of achievement as working men and women who are not mothers. As Figure 10.2 illustrates, 69 percent of young working mothers surveyed reported that they want to move up in their careers compared to 48 percent in 2002. Also, more and more men believe that a woman can be a good mother and still maintain a successful career. About 67 percent of the men surveyed believe that working women can still be good mothers compared to 49 percent in 1977. Figure 10.3 highlights these findings.[14]

Developing the Workforce

Once the most qualified applicants have been selected, have been offered positions, and have accepted their offers, they must be formally introduced to the organization and trained so they can begin to be productive members of the workforce. **Orientation** familiarizes the newly hired employees with fellow workers, company procedures, and the physical properties of the company. It generally includes a tour of the building; introductions to supervisors, co-workers, and subordinates; and the distribution of organizational manuals describing the organization's policy on vacations, absenteeism, lunch breaks, company benefits, and so on. Orientation also involves socializing the new employee into the ethics and culture of the new company. Many larger companies now show videotapes of procedures, facilities, and key personnel in the organization to help speed the adjustment process.

orientation
familiarizing newly hired
employees with fellow
workers, company
procedures, and the
physical properties of the
company

Training and Development
Although recruiting and selection are designed to find employees who have the knowledge, skills, and abilities the company needs, new employees still must

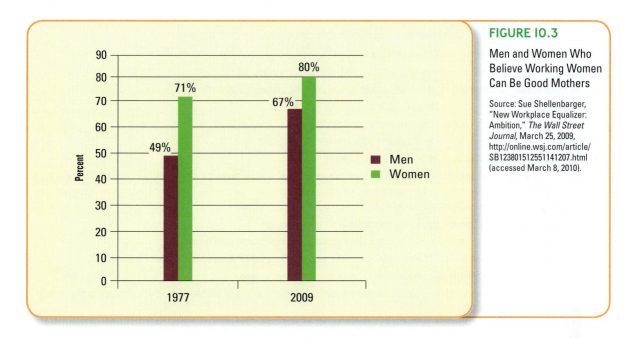

FIGURE 10.3

Men and Women Who Believe Working Women Can Be Good Mothers

Source: Sue Shellenbarger, "New Workplace Equalizer: Ambition," *The Wall Street Journal,* March 25, 2009, http://online.wsj.com/article/SB123801512551141207.html (accessed March 8, 2010).

undergo **training** to learn how to do their specific job tasks. *On-the-job training* allows workers to learn by actually performing the tasks of the job, while *classroom training* teaches employees with lectures, conferences, videotapes, case studies, and Web-based training. For instance, McDonald's trains those interested in company operations and leadership development at the Fred L. Turner Training Center, otherwise known as Hamburger University. Hamburger University employs 19 full-time professors to train students in a variety of topics, including crew development, restaurant management, middle management, and executive development. Training includes classroom instruction, hands-on instruction, and computer e-learning, with instruction available in 28 different languages.[15] **Development** is training that augments the skills and knowledge of managers and professionals. Training and development are also used to improve the skills of employees in their present positions and to prepare them for increased responsibility and job promotions. Training is therefore a vital function of human resources management. Companies are engaging in more experiential and involvement-oriented training exercises for employees. Use of role-plays, simulations, and online training methods are becoming increasingly popular in employee training.

training
teaching employees to do specific job tasks through either classroom development or on-the-job experience

development
training that augments the skills and knowledge of managers and professionals

Assessing Performance

Assessing an employee's performance—his or her strengths and weaknesses on the job—is one of the most difficult tasks for managers. However, performance appraisal is crucial because it gives employees feedback on how they are doing and what they need to do to improve. It also provides a basis for determining how to compensate and reward employees, and it generates information about the quality of the firm's selection, training, and development activities. Table 10.5 identifies 16 characteristics that may be assessed in a performance review.

Performance appraisals may be objective or subjective. An objective assessment is quantifiable. For example, a Westinghouse employee might be judged by how many circuit boards he typically produces in one day or by how many of his boards

---

TABLE 10.5   Performance Characteristics

- **Productivity**—rate at which work is regularly produced
- **Quality**—accuracy, professionalism, and deliverability of produced work
- **Job knowledge**—understanding of the objectives, practices, and standards of work
- **Problem solving**—ability to identify and correct problems effectively
- **Communication**—effectiveness in written and verbal exchanges
- **Initiative**—willingness to identify and address opportunities for improvement
- **Adaptability**—ability to become comfortable with change
- **Planning and organization skills**—reflected through the ability to schedule projects, set goals, and maintain organizational systems
- **Teamwork and cooperation**—effectiveness of collaborations with co-workers
- **Judgment**—ability to determine appropriate actions in a timely manner
- **Dependability**—responsiveness, reliability, and conscientiousness demonstrated on the job
- **Creativity**—extent to which resourceful ideas, solutions, and methods for task completion are proposed
- **Sales**—demonstrated through success in selling products, services, yourself, and your company
- **Customer service**—ability to communicate effectively with customers, address problems, and offer solutions that meet or exceed their expectations
- **Leadership**—tendency and ability to serve as a doer, guide, decision maker, and role model
- **Financial management**—appropriateness of cost controls and financial planning within the scope defined by the position

Source: "Performance Characteristics," Performance Review from http://www.salary.com/Careerresources/docs/related_performance_review_part2_popup .html (accessed June 12, 2001). Used with permission.

---

have defects. A Century 21 real estate agent might be judged by the number of houses she has shown or the number of sales she has closed. A company can also use tests as an objective method of assessment. Whatever method they use, managers must take into account the work environment when they appraise performance objectively.

When jobs do not lend themselves to objective appraisal, the manager must relate the employee's performance to some other standard. One popular tool used in subjective assessment is the ranking system, which lists various performance factors on which the manager ranks employees against each other. Although used by many large companies, ranking systems are unpopular with many employees. Qualitative criteria, such as teamwork and communication skills, used to evaluate employees are generally hard to gauge. Such grading systems have triggered employee lawsuits that allege discrimination in grade/ranking assignments. For example, one manager may grade a company's employees one way, while another manager grades a group more harshly depending on the managers' grading style. If layoffs occur, then employees graded by the second manager may be more likely to lose their jobs. Other criticisms of grading systems include unclear wording or inappropriate words that a manager may unintentionally write in a performance evaluation, like *young* or *pretty* to describe an employee's appearance. These liabilities can all be fodder for lawsuits should employees allege that they were treated unfairly. It is therefore crucial that managers use clear language in performance evaluations and be consistent with all employees. Several employee grading computer packages have been developed to make performance evaluations easier for managers and clearer for employees.[16]

Another performance appraisal method used by many companies is the 360-degree feedback system, which provides feedback from a panel that typically

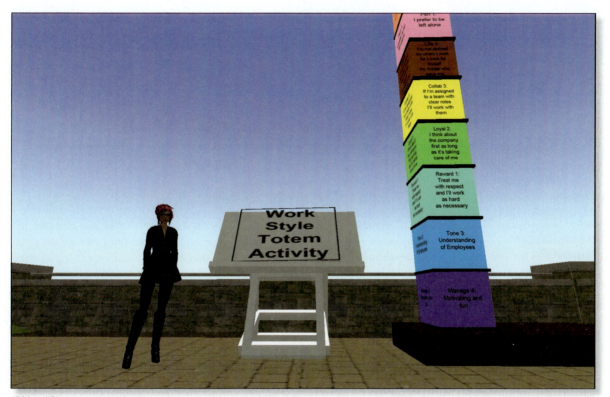

IBM and Cisco are among the companies now using customized applications in the virtual-reality game "Second Life" to train and develop their employees.

includes superiors, peers, and subordinates. Because of the tensions it may cause, peer appraisal appears to be difficult for many. However, companies that have success with 360-degree feedback tend to be open to learning and willing to experiment and are led by executives who are direct about the expected benefits as well as the challenges.[17] Managers and leaders with a high emotional intelligence (sensitivity to their own as well as others' emotions) assess and reflect upon their interactions with colleagues on a daily basis. In addition, they conduct follow-up analysis on their projects, asking the right questions and listening carefully to responses without getting defensive of their actions.[18]

Whether the assessment is objective or subjective, it is vital that the manager discuss the results with the employee, so that the employee knows how well he or she is doing the job. The results of a performance appraisal become useful only when they are communicated, tactfully, to the employee and presented as a tool to allow the employee to grow and improve in his or her position and beyond. Performance appraisals are also used to determine whether an employee should be promoted, transferred, or terminated from the organization.

Turnover

Turnover, which occurs when employees quit or are fired and must be replaced by new employees, results in lost productivity from the vacancy, fees to recruit replacement employees, management time devoted to interviewing, and training costs for new employees. Clarkston Consulting in Durham, North Carolina, was going

turnover
occurs when employees quit or are fired and must be replaced by new employees

through a phase where employees were dissatisfied, working more than the industry norm of 56 hours per week (not including travel), and turnover was increasing. The company engaged in intense training to improve skills and understand competitive and best practices, and it introduced a truncated travel schedule. The travel program allowed employees to leave home on Monday, stay in a hotel and work at the client's site for four days, and return to work at home on Friday. Removing large amounts of travel from evenings and weekends significantly improved morale, productivity, and satisfaction.[19] Part of the reason for turnover may be overworked employees as a result of downsizing and a lack of training and advancement opportunities.[20] Of course, turnover is not always an unhappy occasion when its takes the form of a promotion or transfer.

promotion
an advancement to a higher-level job with increased authority, responsibility, and pay

A **promotion** is an advancement to a higher-level job with increased authority, responsibility, and pay. In some companies and most labor unions, seniority—the length of time a person has been with the company or at a particular job classification—is the key issue in determining who should be promoted. Most managers base promotions on seniority only when they have candidates with equal qualifications: Managers prefer to base promotions on merit.

transfer
a move to another job within the company at essentially the same level and wage

A **transfer** is a move to another job within the company at essentially the same level and wage. Transfers allow workers to obtain new skills or to find a new position within an organization when their old position has been eliminated because of automation or downsizing.

separations
employment changes involving resignation, retirement, termination, or layoff

Separations occur when employees resign, retire, are terminated, or are laid off. Employees may be terminated, or fired, for poor performance, violation of work rules, absenteeism, and so on. Businesses have traditionally been able to fire employees *at will,* that is, for any reason other than for race, religion, sex, or age, or because an employee is a union organizer. However, recent legislation and court decisions now require that companies fire employees fairly, for just cause only. Managers must take care, then, to warn employees when their performance is unacceptable and may lead to dismissal. They should also document all problems and warnings in employees' work records. To avoid the possibility of lawsuits from individuals who may feel they have been fired unfairly, employers should provide clear, business-related reasons for any firing, supported by written documentation if possible. Employee disciplinary procedures should be carefully explained to all employees and should be set forth in employee handbooks. Table 10.6 illustrates what *not* to do when you are terminated.

Many companies have downsized in recent years, laying off tens of thousands of employees in their effort to become more productive and competitive. For example, due to the recession Chrysler underwent a restructuring plan that cut 3,000 jobs and three models, including the PT Cruiser, Dodge Durango, and Chrysler Aspen.

TABLE 10.6 What You Should Not Do When You Are Terminated

1. Do not tell off your boss and co-workers, even if you think they deserve it.
2. Do not damage company property or steal something.
3. Do not forget to ask for a reference.
4. Do not badmouth your employer or any of your co-workers to your replacement.
5. Do not badmouth your employer to a prospective employer when you go on a job interview.

Source: Dawn Rosenberg McKay, "Five Things Not to Do When You Leave Your Job," http://careerplanning.about.com/od/jobseparation/a/leave_mistakes.htm (accessed March 13, 2010).

TABLE 10.7   Job Areas for Which Employers Plan to Hire Recent MBA Graduates

	All Job Areas	Entry Level	Middle Level	Senior Level	Executive Level	Total
Finance other than investment banking	44%	57%	68%	17%	6%	100%
Marketing or sales	44	51	67	19	8	100
General management	29	46	73	25	9	100
Consulting	28	47	67	16	7	100
Business development	28	49	68	26	11	100
Accounting	26	63	65	18	8	100
Operations and logistics	21	53	70	2	12	100
Information technology or management information systems	16	57	66	27	10	100
Investment banking	15	61	59	17	11	100
Human resources or organization management	14	61	69	25	12	100
Other job areas	15	63	66	25	12	100

Source: "Corporate Recruiters Survey: 2009 General Data Report," Graduate Management Admission Council®, http://www.gmac.com/NR/rdonlyres/06C3E039-7335-4814-AD1D-16F501AB70E9/0/2009CRS_GeneralDataReport.pdf (accessed March 8, 2010).

The company also rejected hundreds of car dealership agreements, resulting in significant job losses.[21] Layoffs are sometimes temporary; employees may be brought back when business conditions improve. When layoffs are to be permanent, employers often help employees find other jobs and may extend benefits while the employees search for new employment. Such actions help lessen the trauma of the layoffs. Table 10.7, on the other hand, shows some industries that are planning to hire in the near future.

A well-organized human resources department strives to minimize losses due to separations and transfers because recruiting and training new employees is very expensive. Note that a high turnover rate in a company may signal problems either with the selection and training process, the compensation program, or even the type of company. To help reduce turnover, companies have tried a number of strategies, including giving employees more interesting job responsibilities (job enrichment), allowing for increased job flexibility, and providing more employee benefits.

Compensating the Workforce

People don't work for free, and how much they are paid for their work is a complicated issue. Also, designing a fair compensation plan is an important task because pay and benefits represent a substantial portion of an organization's expenses. Wages that are too high may result in the company's products being priced too high, making them uncompetitive in the market. Wages that are too low may damage employee morale and result in costly turnover. Remember that compensation is one of the hygiene factors identified by Herzberg.

Designing a fair compensation plan is a difficult task because it involves evaluating the relative worth of all jobs within the business while allowing for individual efforts. Compensation for a specific job is typically determined through a **wage/salary survey,** which tells the company how much compensation comparable firms are paying for specific jobs that the firms have in common. Compensation for individuals within a specific job category depends on both the compensation for that job and

wage/salary survey
a study that tells a company how much compensation comparable firms are paying for specific jobs that the firms have in common

the individual's productivity. Therefore, two employees with identical jobs may not receive exactly the same pay because of individual differences in performance.

Financial Compensation

wages
financial rewards based on the number of hours the employee works or the level of output achieved

Financial compensation falls into two general categories—wages and salaries. **Wages** are financial rewards based on the number of hours the employee works or the level of output achieved. Wages based on the number of hours worked are called time wages. The federal minimum wage increased to $7.25 per hour in 2009 for covered nonexempt workers.[23] Many states also mandate minimum wages; in the case where the two wages are in conflict, the higher of the two wages prevails. There may even be differences between city and state minimum wages. In New Mexico, the minimum wage is $7.50, whereas in the state capital of Santa Fe, the minimum wage is $9.85, due to a higher cost of living.[24] Table 10.8 compares wage and other information for Costco and Walmart, two well-known discount chains. Time wages are appropriate when employees are continually interrupted and when quality is more important than quantity. Assembly-line workers, clerks, and maintenance personnel are commonly paid on a time-wage basis. The advantage of time wages is the ease of computation. The disadvantage is that time wages provide no incentive to increase productivity. In fact, time wages may encourage employees to be less productive.

To overcome these disadvantages, many companies pay on an incentive system, using piece wages or commissions. Piece wages are based on the level of output achieved. A major advantage of piece wages is that they motivate employees to supervise their own activities and to increase output. Skilled craftworkers are often paid on a piece-wage basis.

TABLE 10.8   Costco versus Walmart

	Costco	Walmart
Number of employees	147,000	2,100,000₊
2009 revenues	$71.4 billion	$405 billion
Average hourly wage	$19	$11.24
World's Most Admired Companies ranking	21	9
Strengths	Management quality; financial soundness; people management	Management quality; financial soundness; global competitiveness

Sources: "Fortune Global 500," *CNNMoney.com,* http://money.cnn.com/magazines/fortune/global500/2009/snapshots/2255.html (accessed March 9, 2010); "World's Most Admired Companies: Costco Wholesale," *CNNMoney.com,* http://money.cnn.com/magazines/fortune/mostadmired/2010/snapshots/2649 .html (accessed March 9, 2010); "World's Most Admired Companies: Walmart Stores," *CNNMoney.com,* http://money.cnn.com/magazines/fortune/mostad-mired/2010/snapshots/2255.html (accessed March 9, 2010); Edward Teach, "Because It's the Right Thing to Do," *CFO Magazine,* March 1, 2010, http://www .cfo.com/article.cfm/14476783/1/c_14477052?f=insidecfo (accessed March 9, 2010); "Walmart," nyjobsource.com, http://nyjobsource.com/walmart.html (accessed March 9, 2010).

The other incentive system, **commission,** pays a fixed amount or a percentage of the employee's sales. Kele & Co Jewelers in Plainfield, Illinois, make sterling silver jewelry and offer semi-precious and gemstones at affordable prices. Their handcrafted jewelry is sold through the Internet (www.keleonline.com) and through independent sales representatives (ISRs) all over the country. The unique aspect of Kele's sales process is their innovative sales and commission structure. ISRs have no minimum sales quotas, sales are shared among team members during training and after being promoted, and there is no requirement to purchase inventory as jewelry is shipped from Kele headquarters. ISRs receive a 30 percent commission on sales. Kele also pays for the design, development, and maintenance of a Web site to support ISRs. The goal is to increase the profit margin and earning potential of the salespeople. The company's goal is to become the largest direct sales company in the industry.[25] This method motivates employees to sell as much as they can. Some companies also combine payment based on commission with time wages or salaries.

A **salary** is a financial reward calculated on a weekly, monthly, or annual basis. Salaries are associated with white-collar workers such as office personnel, executives, and professional employees. Although a salary provides a stable stream of income, salaried workers may be required to work beyond usual hours without additional financial compensation.

In addition to the basic wages or salaries paid to employees, a company may offer **bonuses** for exceptional performance as an incentive to increase productivity further. Many workers receive a bonus as a "thank you" for good work and an incentive to continue working hard. Many owners and managers are recognizing that simple bonuses and perks foster happier employees and reduce turnover.

Another form of compensation is **profit sharing,** which distributes a percentage of company profits to the employees whose work helped to generate those profits. Some profit-sharing plans involve distributing shares of company stock to employees. Usually referred to as *ESOPs*—employee stock ownership plans— they have been gaining popularity in recent years. One reason for the popularity of ESOPs is the sense of partnership that they create between the organization

commission
an incentive system that pays a fixed amount or a percentage of the employee's sales

salary
a financial reward calculated on a weekly, monthly, or annual basis

bonuses
monetary rewards offered by companies for exceptional performance as incentives to further increase productivity

profit sharing
a form of compensation whereby a percentage of company profits is distributed to the employees whose work helped to generate them

and employees. Profit sharing can also motivate employees to work hard, because increased productivity and sales mean that the profits or the stock dividends will increase. Many organizations offer employees a stake in the company through stock purchase plans, ESOPs, or stock investments through 401(k) plans. Employees below senior management levels rarely received stock options, until recently. Companies are adopting broad-based stock option plans to build a stronger link between employees' interests and the organization's interests. ESOPs have met with enormous success over the years, even during the most recent recession. In 2009, for example, 5 of the top 15 workplaces in *The Wall Street Journal* were employee owned. Additionally, employee-owned stock has also outperformed the stock market during certain years. Many businesses have found employee stock options a great way to boost productivity and increase morale. As of 2009, there were more than 9,000 ESOPs in the United States.[26]

Benefits

benefits
nonfinancial forms of compensation provided to employees, such as pension plans, health insurance, paid vacation and holidays, and the like

Benefits are nonfinancial forms of compensation provided to employees, such as pension plans for retirement; health, disability, and life insurance; holidays and paid days off for vacation or illness; credit union membership; health programs; child care; elder care; assistance with adoption; and more. According to the Bureau of Labor Statistics, employer costs for employee compensation for civilian workers in the United States average $27.42 per hour worked. Wages and salaries account for approximately 70.8 percent of those costs, while benefits account for 29.2 percent of the cost. Legally required benefits (Social Security, Medicare, federal and state employment insurance, and workers' compensation) account for 7.7 percent of total compensation.[27] Such benefits increase employee security and, to a certain extent, their morale and motivation.

Table 10.9 lists some of the benefits Internet search engine Google offers its employees. Although health insurance is a common benefit for full-time employees, rising health care costs have forced a growing number of employers to trim this benefit. Even government workers, whose wages and benefits used to be virtually guaranteed safe, have seen reductions in health care and other benefits. For example, the City Council of Pensacola, Florida, voted to sharply reduce city workers' benefits and wages in order to deal with a budget shortfall after the most recent recession left the city scrambling to make ends meet.[28]

A benefit increasingly offered is the employee assistance program (EAP). Each company's EAP is different, but most offer counseling for and assistance with those employees'personal problems that might hurt their job performance if not addressed. The most common counseling services offered include drug- and alcohol-abuse treatment programs, fitness programs, smoking cessation clinics, stress-management clinics, financial counseling, family counseling, and career counseling. EAPs help reduce costs associated with poor productivity, absenteeism, and other workplace issues by helping employees deal with personal problems that contribute to these issues. For example, exercise and fitness programs reduce health insurance costs by helping employees stay healthy. Family counseling may help workers trying to cope with a divorce or other personal problems better focus on their jobs.

Companies try to provide the benefits they believe their employees want, but diverse people may want different things. In recent years, some single workers have felt that co-workers with spouses and children seem to get "special breaks" and extra time off to deal with family issues. Some companies use flexible benefit

• Health insurance:
– Employee medical insurance (spouse and domestic-partner insurance also available)
– Dental insurance
– Vision insurance
• Vacation (15 days per year for one–three years' employment; 20 days off for four–five years' employment; 25 days for more than six years' employment)
• Twelve paid holidays/year
• Savings plans
– 401(k) retirement plan, matched by Google up to $2,500/year
– Flexible spending accounts
• Disability and life insurance
• Employee Assistance Program
• Free lunches, breakfast foods, and snacks
• Massages, gym membership, hair stylist, fitness class, and bike repair
• Weekly activities
• Maternity and parental leave
• Adoption assistance
• Tuition reimbursement
• Employee referral plan
• On-site doctor
• Google child care center and backup child care
• Ski trip, company movie day, summar picnic, health fair, credit union, sauna, roller hockey, discounts for local attractions

TABLE 10.9

Google's Employees' Benefits

Source: "Google Benefits" http://www.google.com/intl/en/jobs/lifeatgoogle/benefits (accessed March 16, 2010).

programs to allow employees to choose the benefits they would like, up to a specified amount.

Fringe benefits include sick leave, vacation pay, pension plans, health plans, as well as any other extra compensation. Soft benefits include perks that help balance life and work. They include onsite child care, spas, food service, and even laundry services and hair salons. These soft benefits motivate employees and give them more time to focus on their job.

Cafeteria benefit plans provide a financial amount to employees so that they can select the specific benefits that fit their needs. The key is making benefits flexible, rather than giving employees identical benefits. As firms go global, the need for cafeteria or flexible benefit plans becomes even more important. For some employees, benefits are a greater motivator and differentiator in jobs than wages. For many Starbucks employees who receive health insurance when working part time, this benefit could be the most important compensation.

Over the last two decades, the list of fringe benefits has grown dramatically, and new benefits are being added every year.

Managing Unionized Employees

Employees who are dissatisfied with their working conditions or compensation have to negotiate with management to bring about change. Dealing with management on an individual basis is not always effective, however, so employees may organize

FIGURE 10.4

Union Membership
Rates by State

Source: U.S. Bureau of Labor
Statistics, February 17, 2010,
http://www.bls.gov/ro3/unionva.
htm (accessed March 9, 2010).

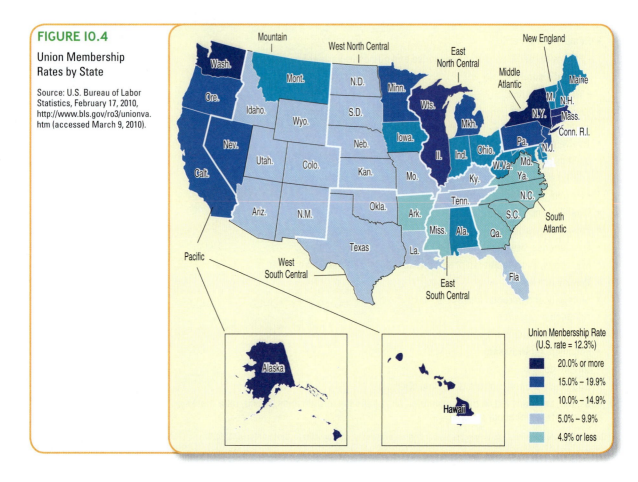

labor unions

employee organizations
formed to deal with
employers for achieving
better pay, hours, and
working conditions

themselves into **labor unions** to deal with employers and to achieve better pay, hours, and working conditions. Organized employees are backed by the power of a large group that can hire specialists to represent the entire union in its dealings with management. Union workers make significantly more than nonunion employees. The United States has a roughly 13.6 percent unionization rate. Figure 10.4 displays unionization rates by state. On average, unionized workers have 15 percent higher hourly wages, a 19 percent higher rate of employer health insurance coverage, and a 24 percent increase in employee-sponsored retirement plans than nonunionized employees in similar positions.[29]

However, union growth has slowed in recent years, and prospects for growth do not look good. One reason is that most blue-collar workers, the traditional members of unions, have already been organized. Factories have become more automated and need fewer blue-collar workers. The United States has shifted from a manufacturing to a service economy, further reducing the demand for blue-collar workers. Moreover, in response to foreign competition, U.S. companies are scrambling to find ways to become more productive and cost efficient. Job enrichment programs and participative management have blurred the line between management and workers. Because workers' say in the way plants are run is increasing, their need for union protection is decreasing.

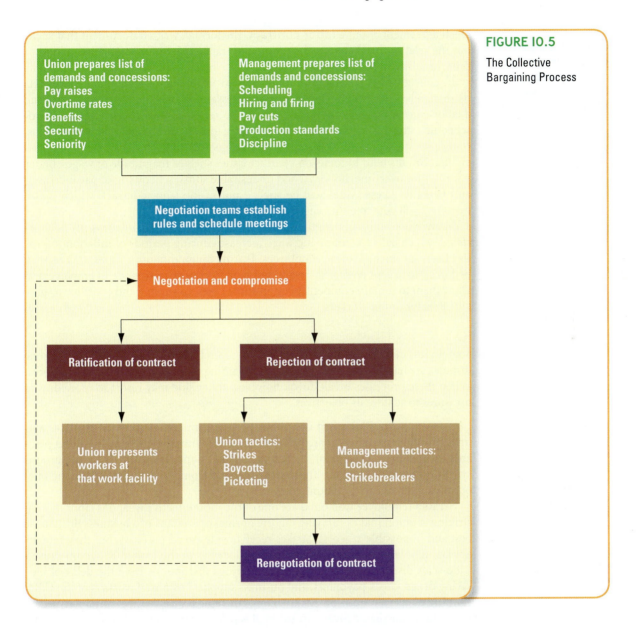

FIGURE 10.5

The Collective
Bargaining Process

Nonetheless, labor unions have been successful in organizing blue-collar manufacturing, government, and health care workers, as well as smaller percentages
of employees in other industries. Consequently, significant aspects of HRM, particularly compensation, are dictated to a large degree by union contracts at many
companies. Therefore, we'll take a brief look at collective bargaining and dispute
resolution in this section.

Collective Bargaining

Collective bargaining is the negotiation process through which management
and unions reach an agreement about compensation, working hours, and working
conditions for the bargaining unit (Figure 10.5). The objective of negotiations is to

collective bargaining
the negotiation
process through which
management and unions
reach an agreement
about compensation,
working hours, and
working conditions for the
bargaining unit

labor contract
the formal, written document that spells out the relationship between the union and management for a specified period of time—usually two or three years

reach agreement about a **labor contract,** the formal, written document that spells out the relationship between the union and management for a specified period of time, usually two or three years.

In collective bargaining, each side tries to negotiate an agreement that meets its demands; compromise is frequently necessary. Management tries to negotiate a labor contract that permits the company to retain control over things like work schedules; the hiring and firing of workers; production standards; promotions, transfers, and separations; the span of management in each department; and discipline. Unions tend to focus on contract issues such as magnitude of wages; better pay rates for overtime, holidays, and undesirable shifts; scheduling of pay increases; and benefits. These issues will be spelled out in the labor contract, which union members will vote to either accept (and abide by) or reject.

Many labor contracts contain a *cost-of-living escalator* (or *adjustment*) *(COLA) clause,* which calls for automatic wage increases during periods of inflation to protect the "real" income of the employees. During tough economic times, unions may be forced to accept *givebacks*—wage and benefit concessions made to employers to allow them to remain competitive or, in some cases, to survive and continue to provide jobs for union workers.

Resolving Disputes

Sometimes, management and labor simply cannot agree on a contract. Most labor disputes are handled through collective bargaining or through grievance procedures. When these processes break down, however, either side may resort to more drastic measures to achieve its objectives.

picketing
a public protest against management practices that involves union members marching and carrying antimanagement signs at the employer's plant

Labor Tactics.   **Picketing** is a public protest against management practices and involves union members marching (often waving antimanagement signs and placards) at the employer's plant. Picketing workers hope that their signs will arouse sympathy for their demands from the public and from other unions. Picketing may occur as a protest or in conjunction with a strike.

strikes
employee walkouts; one of the most effective weapons labor has

Strikes (employee walkouts) are one of the most effective weapons labor has. By striking, a union makes carrying out the normal operations of a business difficult at best and impossible at worst. Strikes receive widespread publicity, but they remain a weapon of last resort. For example, postal strikes in the United Kingdom caused wide-scale disruption. Among the more serious disruptions were the delay of life-saving drugs, check payments, and business supplies. As postal workers of the U.K.'s Royal Mail service went on strike, many consumers switched to its private-sector competitors for mail delivery. Royal Mail was forced to strike a deal with the Communication Workers Union to increase pay and job security for workers along with cutting the workweek.[30] The threat of a strike is often enough to get management to back down. In fact, the number of worker-days actually lost to strikes is less than the amount lost to the common cold.

boycott
an attempt to keep people from purchasing the products of a company

A **boycott** is an attempt to keep people from purchasing the products of a company. In a boycott, union members are asked not to do business with the boycotted organization. Some unions may even impose fines on members who ignore the boycott. To gain further support for their objectives, a union involved in a boycott may also ask the public—through picketing and advertising—not to purchase the products of the picketed firm.

lockout
management's version of a strike, wherein a work site is closed so that employees cannot go to work

Management Tactics.   Management's version of a strike is the **lockout;** management actually closes a work site so that employees cannot go to work. Lockouts

Employees have been known to do more than just strike. During the latest economic downturn, some French workers, angered by job losses, went so far as to hold their managers hostage.

are used, as a general rule, only when a union strike has partially shut down a plant and it seems less expensive for the plant to close completely. In 2009, five major work stoppages involving 1,000 or more U.S. employees participating in strikes and lockouts occurred, the lowest since 1947. The stoppages idled 13,000 workers with 124,000 lost workdays.[31]

Strikebreakers, called "scabs" by striking union members, are people hired by management to replace striking employees. Managers hire strikebreakers to continue operations and reduce the losses associated with strikes—and to show the unions that they will not bow to their demands. Strikebreaking is generally a last-resort measure for management because it does great damage to the relationship between management and labor.

Outside Resolution.   Management and union members normally reach mutually agreeable decisions without outside assistance. Sometimes though, even after lengthy negotiations, strikes, lockouts, and other tactics, management and labor still cannot resolve a contract dispute. In such cases, they have three choices: conciliation, mediation, and arbitration. **Conciliation** brings in a neutral third party to keep labor and management talking. The conciliator has no formal power over union representatives or over management. The conciliator's goal is to get both parties to focus on the issues and to prevent negotiations from breaking down. Like conciliation, **mediation** involves bringing in a neutral third party, but the mediator's role is to suggest or propose a solution to the problem. Mediators have no formal power over either labor or management. With **arbitration,** a neutral third party is brought in to settle the dispute, but the arbitrator's solution is legally binding and enforceable. Generally, arbitration takes place on a voluntary basis—management and labor must agree to it, and they usually split the cost (the arbitrator's fee and expenses) between them. Occasionally, management and labor submit to *compulsory arbitration,*

strikebreakers
people hired by management to replace striking employees; called "scabs" by striking union members

conciliation
a method of outside resolution of labor and management differences in which a third party is brought in to keep the two sides talking

mediation
a method of outside resolution of labor and management differences in which the third party's role is to suggest or propose a solution to the problem

arbitration
settlement of a labor/management dispute by a third party whose solution is legally binding and enforceable

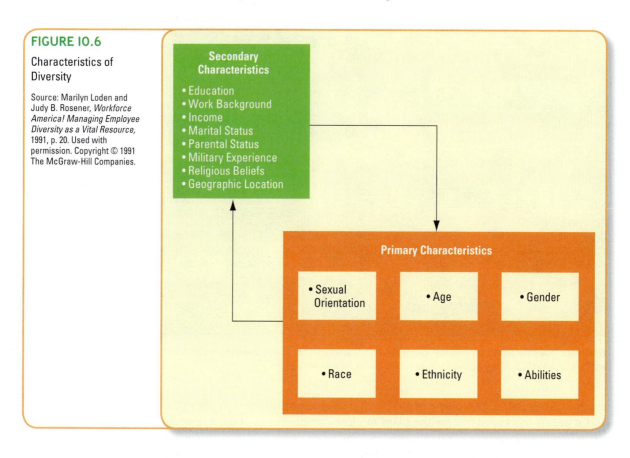

FIGURE IO.6

Characteristics of Diversity

Source: Marilyn Loden and Judy B. Rosener, *Workforce America! Managing Employee Diversity as a Vital Resource,* 1991, p. 20. Used with permission. Copyright © 1991 The McGraw-Hill Companies.

in which an outside party (usually the federal government) requests arbitration as a means of eliminating a prolonged strike that threatens to disrupt the economy.

The Importance of Workforce Diversity

Customers, employees, suppliers—all the participants in the world of business—come in different ages, genders, races, ethnicities, nationalities, and abilities, a truth that business has come to label **diversity.** Understanding this diversity means recognizing and accepting differences as well as valuing the unique perspectives such differences can bring to the workplace.

The Characteristics of Diversity

diversity
the participation of different ages, genders, races, ethnicities, nationalities, and abilities in the workplace

When managers speak of diverse workforces, they typically mean differences in gender and race. While gender and race are important characteristics of diversity, others are also important. We can divide these differences into primary and secondary characteristics of diversity. In the lower segment of Figure 10.6, age, gender, race, ethnicity, abilities, and sexual orientation represent *primary characteristics* of diversity which are inborn and cannot be changed. In the upper section of Figure 10.6 are eight *secondary characteristics* of diversity—work background, income, marital status, military experience, religious beliefs, geographic location, parental status, and education—which *can* be changed. We acquire, change, and discard them as we progress through our lives.

Consider Ethics and Social Responsibility
Companies Change Compensation Packages

Is it ethical for corporations to reward executives with high compensation packages even when the company performs poorly? In light of recent corporate scandals, this question has caused many companies to reevaluate how they reward their executives. High pay attracts the best candidates and is often used as an incentive to encourage good performance. However, stockholders and the American public are now questioning the value of giving large compensation packages if corporate performance is low.

Executive compensation packages are often based on short-term financial goals. While this may create financial gains, it does not encourage executives to work toward successful long-term strategies. This was what caused many companies to become bankrupt during the recent recession; by only looking at short-term gains, they took risks without considering what might happen in the long-term.

To help solve this problem, many companies are still providing large compensation packages but are reducing or eliminating cash bonuses. Morgan Stanley restructured its year-end compensation packages, with the executive committee receiving 75 percent of their year-end pay in deferred compensation like stocks and options. Its CEO received a compensation package based on a variety of stocks and options. The total package could be worth almost $9 million. Many of the units are tied to his performance, such as meeting financial and corporate goals and remaining at Morgan Stanley for the length of his contract. JPMorgan Chase's total employee compensation for the fourth quarter of 2009 was $1.3 billion less than previous quarters; however, the average banker still received $378,600.

Excessive compensation packages remain a major ethical issue among the public and, if not addressed properly by companies, could cause the government to intervene. It is therefore essential for businesses to come up with ways to reward effective executives and provide less compensation to executives with sub-par performance.[32]

Discussion Questions
1. Do you think executives deserve high compensation packages? If the firm is doing well? If the firm fares poorly?
2. What are some of the unintended consequences of basing executive pay on short-term goals?
3. What do you suggest companies do to help align executive compensation and long-term corporate health?

Defining characteristics of diversity as either primary or secondary enhances our understanding, but we must remember that each person is defined by the interrelation of all characteristics. In dealing with diversity in the workforce, managers must consider the complete person—not one or a few of a person's differences.

Why Is Diversity Important?

The U.S. workforce is becoming increasingly diverse. Once dominated by white men, today's workforce includes significantly more women, African Americans, Hispanics, and other minorities, as well as disabled and older workers. Table 10.10 presents some of the population data from the Census Bureau. It is estimated that within the next 50 years, Hispanics will represent 24 percent of the population, while African Americans and Asians/Pacific Islanders will comprise 15 percent and 9 percent, respectively.[33] These groups have traditionally faced discrimination and higher unemployment rates and have been denied opportunities to assume leadership roles in corporate America. Consequently, more and more companies are trying to improve HRM programs to recruit, develop, and retain more diverse employees to better serve their diverse customers. Some firms are providing special programs such as sponsored affinity groups, mentoring programs, and special career development opportunities. Sodexo has implemented a diversity score-card index that uses both quantitative and qualitative measurements to measure the company's progress in the recruitment, retaining, and promotion of women and minority employees. In 2002, Sodexo began to hold managers responsible for

TABLE 10.10	**Ethnic Group**	**Percentages**	**Total**
Population by Race	Total population	100%	307,212,123 (2009 estimate)
	White	79.96 (2007 estimate)	245,646,814
	Black	12.85 (2007 estimate)	39,476,758
	Asian	4.43 (2007 estimate)	13,609,497
	Amerindian or Alaskan Native	0.97 (2007 estimate)	2,979,958
	Hawaiian or Pacific Islander	0.18 (2007 estimate)	552,982
	Two or more races	1.61 (2007 estimate)	4,946,115
	Hispanic	15.1 (2007 estimate)[*]	46,389,031[*]

[*] The U.S. Census Bureau does not include a separate listing for Hispanic origin. The 15.1 percent who are classified as Hispanic are included in the given segments (they may be classified as white, black, etc., depending on origins). This is why the percentages will come out greater than 100 percent.

Source: "United States," *CIA World Factbook,* https://www.cia.gov/library/publications/the-world-factbook/geos/us.html (accessed March 9, 2010).

diversity by creating a link between scorecard results and management bonuses. The result was a 23 percent increase of minority employees in the company since the implementation of the scorecard and an 11 percent increase in female employees.[34] Table 10.11 shows the top 20 companies for minorities according to a study by *Diversity, Inc.* Effectively managing diversity in the workforce involves cultivating and valuing its benefits and minimizing its problems.

The Benefits of Workforce Diversity

There are a number of benefits to fostering and valuing workforce diversity, including the following:

1. More productive use of a company's human resources.
2. Reduced conflict among employees of different ethnicities, races, religions, and sexual orientations as they learn to respect each other's differences.
3. More productive working relationships among diverse employees as they learn more about and accept each other.
4. Increased commitment to and sharing of organizational goals among diverse employees at all organizational levels.
5. Increased innovation and creativity as diverse employees bring new, unique perspectives to decision-making and problem-solving tasks.
6. Increased ability to serve the needs of an increasingly diverse customer base.[35]

Companies that do not value their diverse employees are likely to experience greater conflict, as well as prejudice and discrimination. Among individual employees, for example, racial slurs and gestures, sexist comments, and other behaviors by co-workers harm the individuals at whom such behavior is directed. The victims of such behavior may feel hurt, depressed, or even threatened and suffer from lowered self-esteem, all of which harm their productivity and morale. In such cases, women and minority employees may simply leave the firm, wasting the time, money, and

TABLE IO.II

The *Diversity Inc.*
Top 50 Companies for Diversity

1. Johnson & Johnson	26. Henry Ford Health System
2. AT&T	27. Colgate-Palmolive
3. Ernst & Young	28. Ford Motor Co.
4. Marriott International	29. The Walt Disney Co.
5. PricewaterhouseCoopers	30. Comerica Bank
6. Sodexo	31. Wells Fargo & Co.
7. Kaiser Permanente	32. Blue Cross and Blue Shield of Florida
8. Merck & Co.	33. Deloitte
9. The Coca-Cola Co.	34. HSBC — North America
10. IBM Corp.	35. Xerox Corp.
11. Procter & Gamble	36. Monsanto Co.
12. Verizon Communications	37. AARP
13. American Express Co.	38. Time Warner Cable
14. Bank of America	39. Starwood Hotels & Resorts Worldwide
15. JPMorgan Chase	40. Toyota Motor North America
16. Abbott	41. MasterCard Worldwide
17. Cox Communications	42. Cummins
18. Pepsi Bottling Group	43. MetLife
19. MGM MIRAGE	44. WellPoint
20. Novartis Pharmaceuticals Corp.	45. Prudential Financial
21. KPMG	46. SC Johnson
22. Health Care Service Corp.	47. General Mills
23. Accenture	48. Aetna
24. PepsiCo	49. CSX Corp.
25. Capital One Financial Corp.	50. KeyBank

Source: "The 2009 DiversityInc Top 50 Companies for Diversity ®," *DiversityInc*, http://diversityinc.com/department/289/ (accessed March 5, 2010).

other resources spent on hiring and training them. When discrimination comes from a supervisor, employees may also fear for their jobs. A discriminatory atmosphere not only can harm productivity and increase turnover, but it may also subject a firm to costly lawsuits and negative publicity.

Astute businesses recognize that they need to modify their human resources management programs to target the needs of *all* their diverse employees as well as the needs of the firm itself. They realize that the benefits of diversity are long term in nature and come only to those organizations willing to make the commitment. Most importantly, as workforce diversity becomes a valued organizational asset, companies spend less time managing conflict and more time accomplishing tasks and satisfying customers, which is, after all, the purpose of business.

Affirmative Action

Many companies strive to improve their working environment through **affirmative action programs,** legally mandated plans that try to increase job opportunities for minority groups by analyzing the current pool of workers, identifying areas where women and minorities are underrepresented, and establishing specific hiring and promotion goals along with target dates for meeting those goals to resolve the

affirmative action programs
legally mandated plans that try to increase job opportunities for minority groups by analyzing the current pool of workers, identifying areas where women and minorities are underrepresented, and establishing specific hiring and promotion goals, with target dates, for addressing the discrepancy

discrepancy. Affirmative action began in 1965 as Lyndon B. Johnson issued the first of a series of presidential directives. It was designed to make up for past hiring and promotion prejudices, to overcome workplace discrimination, and to provide equal employment opportunities for blacks and whites. Since then, minorities have made solid gains.

Legislation passed in 1991 reinforces affirmative action but prohibits organizations from setting hiring quotas that might result in reverse discrimination. Reverse discrimination occurs when a company's policies force it to consider only minorities or women instead of concentrating on hiring the person who is best qualified. More companies are arguing that affirmative action stifles their ability to hire the best employees, regardless of their minority status. Because of these problems, affirmative action became politically questionable.

So You Want to Work in Human Resources

Managing human resources is a challenging and creative facet of a business. It is the department that handles the recruiting, hiring, training, and firing of employees. Because of the diligence and detail required in hiring and the sensitivity required in firing, human resource managers have a broad skill set. Human resources, therefore, is vital to the overall functioning of the business because without the right staff a firm will not be able to effectively carry out its plans. Like in basketball, a team is only as strong as its individual players, and those players must be able to work together and to enhance strengths and downplay weaknesses. In addition, a good human resource manager can anticipate upcoming needs and changes in the business, hiring in line with the dynamics of the market and organization.

Once a good workforce is in place, human resource managers must ensure that employees are properly trained and oriented and that they clearly understand some elements of what the organization expects. Hiring new people is expensive, time consuming, and turbulent; thus, it is imperative that all employees are carefully selected, trained, and motivated so that they will remain committed and loyal to the company. This is not an easy task, but it is one of the responsibilities of the human resources manager. Because even with references, a résumé, background checks, and an interview, it can be hard to tell how a person will fit in the organization—the HR manager needs to have skills to be able to anticipate how every individual will "fit in." Human resource jobs include compensation, labor relations, benefits, training, ethics, and compliance

managers. All of the tasks associated with the interface with hiring, developing, and maintaining employee motivation come into play in human resource management. Jobs are diverse and salaries will depend on responsibilities, education, and experience.

One of the major considerations for an HR manager is workforce diversity. A multicultural, multiethnic workforce consisting of men and women will help to bring a variety of viewpoints and improve the quality and creativity of organizational decision making. Diversity is an asset and can help a company from having blindspots or harmony in thought, background, and perspective, which stifles good team decisions. However, a diverse workforce can present some management challenges. Human resource management is often responsible for managing diversity training and compliance to make sure employees do not violate the ethical culture of the organization or break the law. Different people have different goals, motivations, and ways of thinking about issues that are informed by their culture, religion, and the people closest to them. No one way of thinking is more right or more wrong than others, and they are all valuable. A human resource manager's job can become very complicated, however, because of diversity. To be good at human resources, you should be aware of the value of differences, strive to be culturally sensitive, and ideally should have a strong understanding and appreciation of different cultures and religions. Human resource managers' ability to manage diversity and those differences will affect their overall career success.

Review Your Understanding

Define human resources management, and explain its significance.

Human resources, or personnel management refers to all the activities involved in determining an organization's human resources needs and acquiring, training, and compensating people to fill those needs. It is concerned with maximizing the satisfaction of employees and improving their efficiency to meet organizational objectives.

Summarize the processes of recruiting and selecting human resources for a company.

First, the human resources manager must determine the firm's future human resources needs and develop a strategy to meet them. Recruiting is the formation of a pool of qualified applicants from which management will select employees; it takes place both internally and externally. Selection is the process of collecting information about applicants and using that information to decide which ones to hire; it includes the application, interviewing, testing, and reference checking.

Discuss how workers are trained and their performance appraised.

Training teaches employees how to do their specific job tasks; development is training that augments the skills and knowledge of managers and professionals, as well as current employees. Appraising performance involves identifying an employee's strengths and weaknesses on the job. Performance appraisals may be subjective or objective.

Identify the types of turnover companies may experience, and explain why turnover is an important issue.

A promotion is an advancement to a higher-level job with increased authority, responsibility, and pay. A transfer is a move to another job within the company at essentially the same level and wage. Separations occur when employees resign, retire, are terminated, or are laid off. Turnovers due to separation are expensive because of the time, money, and effort required to select, train, and manage new employees.

Specify the various ways a worker may be compensated.

Wages are financial compensation based on the number of hours worked (time wages) or the number of units produced (piece wages). Commissions are a fixed amount or a percentage of a sale paid as compensation. Salaries are compensation calculated on a weekly, monthly, or annual basis, regardless of the number of hours worked or the number of items produced. Bonuses and profit sharing are types of financial incentives. Benefits are nonfinancial forms of compensation, such as vacation, insurance, and sick leave.

Discuss some of the issues associated with unionized employees, including collective bargaining and dispute resolution.

Collective bargaining is the negotiation process through which management and unions reach an agreement on a labor contract—the formal, written document that spells out the relationship written between the union and management. If labor and management cannot agree on a contract, labor union members may picket, strike, or boycott the firm, while management may lock out striking employees, hire strikebreakers, or form employers' associations. In a deadlock, labor disputes may be resolved by a third party—a conciliator, mediator, or arbitrator.

Describe the importance of diversity in the workforce.

When companies value and effectively manage their diverse workforces, they experience more productive use of human resources, reduced conflict, better work relationships among workers, increased commitment to and sharing of organizational goals, increased innovation and creativity, and enhanced ability to serve diverse customers.

Assess an organization's efforts to reduce its workforce size and manage the resulting effects.

Based on the material in this chapter, you should be able to answer the questions posed in "Solve the Dilemma" on page 326 and evaluate the company's efforts to manage the human consequences of its downsizing.

Revisit the World of Business

1. What were some of the problems at Molson Coors when Swinburn took over as CEO?

2. What did Swinburn do to help turn the company around and improve performance?

3. Do you think it is important, even in corporations as large as Molson Coors, to have a coherent corporate culture that pervades the entire organization? Why or why not?

Learn the Terms

affirmative action programs   321
arbitration   317
benefits   312
bonuses   311
boycott   316
collective bargaining   315
commission   311
conciliation   317
development   305
diversity   318
human resources management
   (HRM)   296

job analysis   297
job description   297
job specification   297
labor contract   316
labor unions   314
lockout   316
mediation   317
orientation   304
picketing   316
profit sharing   311
promotion   308
recruiting   297

salary   311
selection   299
separations   308
strikebreakers   317
strikes   316
Title VII of the Civil Rights Act   303
training   305
transfer   308
turnover   307
wage/salary survey   309
wages   310

Check Your Progress

1. Distinguish among job analysis, job descriptions, and job specifications. How do they relate to planning in human resources management?

2. What activities are involved in acquiring and maintaining the appropriate level of qualified human resources? Name the stages of the selection process.

3. What are the two types of training programs? Relate training to kinds of jobs.

4. What is the significance of performance appraisal? How do managers appraise employees?

5. Why does turnover occur? List the types of turnover. Why do businesses want to reduce turnover due to separations?

6. Relate wages, salaries, bonuses, and benefits to Herzberg's distinction between hygiene and motivation factors. How does the form of compensation relate to the type of job?

7. What is the role of benefits? Name some examples of benefits.

8. Describe the negotiation process through which management and unions reach an agreement on a contract.

9. Besides collective bargaining and the grievance procedures, what other alternatives are available to labor and management to handle labor disputes?

10. What are the benefits associated with a diverse workforce?

Get Involved

1. Although many companies screen applicants and test employees for illegal drug use, such testing is somewhat controversial. Find some companies in your community that test applicants and/or employees for drugs. Why do they have such a policy? How do the employees feel about it? Using this information, debate the pros and cons of drug testing in the workplace.

2. If collective bargaining and the grievance procedures have not been able to settle a current labor dispute, what tactics would you and other employees adopt? Which tactics would be best for which situations? Give examples.

3. Find some examples of companies that value their diverse workforces, perhaps some of the companies mentioned in the chapter. In what ways have these firms derived benefits from promoting cultural diversity? How have they dealt with the problems associated with cultural diversity?

Build Your Skills

APPRECIATING AND VALUING DIVERSITY

Background:
Here's a quick self-assessment to get you to think about diversity issues and evaluate the behaviors you exhibit that reflect your level of appreciation of other cultures:

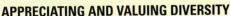

Do you . . .	Regularly	Sometimes	Never
1. Make a conscious effort not to think stereotypically?			
2. Listen with interest to the ideas of people who don't think like you do?			
3. Respect other people's opinions, even when you disagree?			
4. Spend time with friends who are not your age, race, gender, or the same economic status and education?			
5. Believe your way is *not* the only way?			
6. Adapt well to change and new situations?			
7. Enjoy traveling, seeing new places, eating different foods, and experiencing other cultures?			
8. Try not to offend or hurt others?			
9. Allow extra time to communicate with someone whose first language is not yours?			
10. Consider the effect of cultural differences on the messages you send and adjust them accordingly?			

Scoring

Number of **Regularly** checks _____ multiplied by 5 = _____
Number of **Sometimes** checks _____ multiplied by 3 = _____
Number of **Never** checks _____ multiplied by 0 = _____
                                                    TOTAL _____

Indications from score

40–50   You appear to understand the importance of valuing diversity and exhibit behaviors that support your appreciation of diversity.

26–39   You appear to have a basic understanding of the importance of valuing diversity and exhibit some behaviors that support that understanding.

13–25   You appear to lack a thorough understanding of the importance of valuing diversity and exhibit only some behaviors related to valuing diversity.

0–12   You appear to lack an understanding of valuing diversity and exhibit few, if any, behaviors of an individual who appreciates and values diversity.

Task:

In a small group or class discussion, share the results of your assessment. After reading the following list of ways you can increase your knowledge and understanding of other cultures, select one of the items that you have done and share how it helped you learn more about another culture. Finish your discussion by generating your own ideas on other ways you can learn about and understand other cultures and fill in those ideas on the blank lines on page 326.

- Be alert to and take advantage of opportunities to talk to and get to know people from other races and ethnic groups. You can find them in your neighborhood, in your classes, at your fitness center, at a concert or sporting event—just about anywhere you go. Take the initiative to strike up a conversation and show a genuine interest in getting to know the other person.

- Select a culture you're interested in and immerse yourself in that culture. Read novels, look at art, take courses, see plays.

- College students often have unique opportunities to travel inexpensively to other countries—for example, as a member of a performing arts group, with a humanitarian mission group, or as part of a college course studying abroad. Actively seek out travel opportunities that will expose you to as many cultures as possible during your college education.

- Study a foreign language.

- Expand your taste buds. The next time you're going to go to a restaurant, instead of choosing that old familiar favorite, use the Yellow Pages to find a restaurant that serves ethnic food you've never tried before.

- Many large metropolitan cities sponsor ethnic festivals, particularly in the summertime, where you can go and take in the sights and sounds of other cultures. Take advantage of these opportunities to have a fun time learning about cultures that are different from yours.

- _____

  _____

- _____

  _____

Solve the Dilemma

MORALE AMONG THE SURVIVORS

Medallion Corporation manufactures quality carpeting and linoleum for homes throughout the United States. A recession and subsequent downturn in home sales has sharply cut the company's sales. Medallion found itself in the unenviable position of having to lay off hundreds of employees in the home office (the manufacturing facilities) as well as many salespeople. Employees were called in on Friday afternoon and told about their status in individual meetings with their supervisors. The laid-off employees were given one additional month of work and a month of severance pay, along with the opportunity to sign up for classes to help with the transition, including job search tactics and résumé writing.

Several months after the cutbacks, morale was at an all-time low for the company, although productivity had improved. Medallion brought in consultants, who suggested that the leaner, flatter organizational structure would be suitable for more team activities. Medallion therefore set up task forces and teams to deal with employee concerns, but the diversity of the workforce led to conflict and misunderstandings among team members. Medallion is evaluating how to proceed with this new team approach.

Discussion Questions

1. What did Medallion's HRM department do right in dealing with the employees who were laid off?

2. What are some of the potential problems that must be dealt with after an organization experiences a major trauma such as massive layoffs?

3. What can Medallion do to make the team approach work more smoothly? What role do you think diversity training should play?

Build Your Business Plan

MANAGING HUMAN RESOURCES

Now is the time to start thinking about the employees you will need to hire to implement your business plan. What kinds of background/skills are you going to look for in potential employees? Are you going to require a certain amount of work experience?

When you are starting a business you are often only able to hire part-time employees because you cannot afford to pay the benefits for a full time employee. Remember at the end of the last chapter we discussed how important it is to think of ways to motivate your employees when you cannot afford to pay them what you would like.

You need to consider how you are going to recruit your employees. When you are first starting your business, it is often a good idea to ask people you respect (and not necessarily members of your family) for any recommendations of potential employees they might have. You probably won't be able to afford to advertise in the classifieds, so announcements in sources such as church bulletins or community bulletin boards should be considered as an excellent way to attract potential candidates with little, if any, investment.

Finally, you need to think about hiring employees from diverse backgrounds. Especially if you are considering targeting diverse segments. The more diverse your employees, the greater the chance you will be able to draw in diverse customers.

See for Yourself Videocase

BLUEWOLF, INC., UTILIZES HUMAN RESOURCE SAVVY

All companies must manage human resources in order to maximize productivity while keeping employees satisfied and loyal. Bluewolf, Inc., is an IT consulting firm dedicated to assisting clients in harnessing cloud computing. It offers the unusual benefit of unrestricted vacation time. The company's 175 employees may take time off to travel, volunteer, participate in other ventures, attend their children's events, and for many other reasons. When an employee is away, other employees step in to cover; it is understood that the favor will be returned. At Bluewolf, the focus is on outcome rather than on time spent at a desk. This benefits generosity helps to maintain highly loyal employees.

Do not be mistaken, however. This flexible vacation policy does not mean that employees may literally take as much time off as they like. Because they are not judged based on hours spent in the office, Bluewolf employees are evaluated on whether or not they meet goals set by the company. A company spokesman says it would be challenging to meet these goals and take more than three to four weeks vacation time (the average logged be individuals each year). The company does, however, offer extended unpaid leave for those employees in need of significant amounts of time off. In order to make this policy succeed, Bluewolf hires driven and confident individuals willing to think in nontraditional ways and able to tackle

problems with unique solutions. In other words, the company focuses on hiring people driven to be leaders and who think like entrepreneurs.

For Bluewolf, this policy has decided advantages. Employees are loyal and dedicated to a high level of performance, in spite of their vacation time freedom. The company's turnover rate hovers around a very low three percent. The vacation policy plays a large role in Bluewolf's being able to draw young, highly skilled workers. While one might think it would be expensive to offer such a generous vacation package, the company has found that it actually saves money because it avoids paying staff to track employee hours; the policy also helps reduce burnout among employees. Clearly, this type of flex time is not a good fit for all companies. For Bluewolf, however, it works like a charm. Profits and the client list are expanding and employees love their jobs.[36]

Discussion Questions

1. Why does Bluewolf offer such flexible vacation time?
2. What is the result of Bluewolf's unusual approach to human resources? Are employees satisfied?
3. What are some industries for which this arrangement would not be a good fit?

Remember to check out our Online Learning Center at www.mhhe.com/ferrell8e.

Team Exercise

Form groups and go to monster.com and look up job descriptions for positions in business (account executive in advertising, marketing manager, human resource director, production supervisor, financial analyst, bank teller, etc). What are the key requirements for the position that

you have been assigned (education, work experience, language/computer skills, etc.)? Does the position announcement provide a thorough understanding of the job? Was any key information that you would have expected omitted? Report your findings to the class.

Appendix C

Personal Career Plan

The tools and techniques used in creating a business plan are just as useful in designing a plan to help sell yourself to potential employers. The outline in this appendix is designed to assist you in writing a personalized plan that will help you achieve your career goals. While this outline follows the same general format found in Appendix A, it has been adapted to be more relevant to career planning. Answering the questions presented in this outline will enable you to:

1. Organize and structure the data and information you collect about job prospects, the overall job market, and your competition.
2. Use this information to better understand your own personal strengths and weaknesses, as well as recognize the opportunities and threats that exist in your career development.
3. Develop goals and objectives that will capitalize on your strengths.
4. Develop a personalized strategy that will give you a competitive advantage.
5. Outline a plan for implementing your personalized strategy.

As you work through the following outline, it is very important that you be honest with yourself. If you do not possess a strength in a given area, it is important to recognize that fact. Similarly, do not overlook your weaknesses. The viability of your SWOT analysis and your strategy depend on how well you have identified all of the relevant issues in an honest manner.

I. Summary
If you choose to write a summary, do so after you have written the entire plan. It should provide a brief overview of the strategy for your career. State your career objectives and what means you will use to achieve those objectives.

II. Situation Analysis
A. The External Environment
   1. **Competition**
     a) Who are your major competitors? What are their characteristics (number and growth in the number of graduates, skills, target employers)? Competitors to consider include peers at the same college or in the same degree field, peers at different colleges or in different degree fields, and graduates of trade, technical, or community colleges.
     b) What are the key strengths and weaknesses of the total pool of potential employees (or recent college graduates)?
     c) What are other college graduates doing in terms of developing skills, networking, showing a willingness to relocate, and promoting themselves to potential employers?
     d) What are the current trends in terms of work experience versus getting an advanced degree?
     e) Is your competitive set likely to change in the future? If so, how? Who are these new competitors likely to be?

   2. **Economic conditions**
     a) What are the general economic conditions of the country, region, state, and local area in which you live or in which you want to relocate?
     b) Overall, are potential employers optimistic or pessimistic about the economy?
     c) What is the overall outlook for major job/career categories? Where do potential employers seem to be placing their recruitment and hiring emphasis?
     d) What is the trend in terms of starting salaries for major job/career categories?

3. **Political trends**
   a) Have recent elections changed the political landscape so that certain industries or companies are now more or less attractive as potential employers?

4. **Legal and regulatory factors**
   a) What changes in international, federal, state, or local laws and regulations are being proposed that would affect your job/career prospects?
   b) Have recent court decisions made it easier or harder for you to find employment?
   c) Have global trade agreements changed in any way that makes certain industries or companies more or less attractive as potential employers?

5. **Changes in technology**
   a) What impact has changing technology had on potential employers in terms of their need for employees?
   b) What technological changes will affect the way you will have to work and compete for employment in the future?
   c) What technological changes will affect the way you market your skills and abilities to potential employers?
   d) How do technological advances threaten to make your skills and abilities obsolete?

6. **Cultural trends**
   a) How are society's demographics and values changing? What effect will these changes have on your:
      (1) Skills and abilities:
      (2) Career/lifestyle choices:
      (3) Ability to market yourself:
      (4) Willingness to relocate:
      (5) Required minimum salary:
   b) What problems or opportunities are being created by changes in the cultural diversity of the labor pool and the requirements of potential employers?
      c) What is the general attitude of society regarding the particular skills, abilities, and talents that you possess and the career/lifestyle choices that you have made?

B. **The Employer Environment**
   1. **Who are your potential employers?**
      a) Identifying characteristics: industry, products, size, growth, profitability, hiring practices, union/nonunion, employee needs, etc.
      b) Geographic characteristics: home office, local offices, global sites, expansion, etc.
      c) Organizational culture: mission statement, values, priorities, employee training, etc.
      d) In each organization, who is responsible for recruiting and selecting new employees?

   2. **What do your potential employers look for in new employees?**
      a) What are the basic or specific skills and abilities that employers are looking for in new employees?
      b) What are the basic or specific needs that are fulfilled by the skills and abilities that you *currently* possess and that other potential employees currently possess?
      c) How well do your skills and abilities (and those of your competitors) currently meet the needs of potential employers?
      d) How are the needs of potential employers expected to change in the future?

   3. **What are the recent hiring practices of your potential employers?**
      a) How many employees are being hired? What combination of skills and abilities do these new hires possess?
      b) Is the growth or decline in hiring related to the recent expansion or downsizing of markets and/or territories? Changes in technology?
      c) Are there major hiring differences between large and small companies? If so, why?

4. **Where and how do your potential employers recruit new employees?**
   a) Where do employers make contact with potential employees?
      (1) College placement offices:
      (2) Job/career fairs:
      (3) Internship programs:
      (4) Headhunting firms:
      (5) Unsolicited applications:
      (6) The Internet:
   b) Do potential employers place a premium on experience or are they willing to hire new graduates without experience?
5. **When do your potential employers recruit new employees?**
   a) Does recruiting follow a seasonal pattern or do employers recruit new employees on an ongoing basis?

C. **Personal Assessment**
1. **Review of personal goals, objectives, and performance**
   a) What are your personal goals and objectives in terms of employment, career, lifestyle, geographic preferences, etc.?
   b) Are your personal goals and objectives consistent with the realities of the labor market? Why or why not?
   c) Are your personal goals and objectives consistent with recent changes in the external or employer environments? Why or why not?
   d) How are your current strategies for success working in areas such as course performance, internships, networking, job leads, career development, interviewing skills, etc.?
   e) How does your current performance compare to that of your peers (competitors)? Are they performing well in terms of course performance, internships, networking, job leads, career development, interviewing skills, etc.?
   f) If your performance is declining, what is the most likely cause?

   g) If your performance is improving, what actions can you take to ensure that your performance continues in this direction?
2. **Inventory of personal skills and resources**
   a) What do you consider to be your marketable skills? This list should be as comprehensive as possible and include areas such as interpersonal skills, organizational skills, technological skills, communication skills (oral and written), networking/teambuilding skills, etc.
   b) Considering the current and future needs of your potential employers, what important skills are you lacking?
   c) Other than personal skills, what do you consider to be your other career enhancing resources? This list should be as comprehensive as possible and include areas such as financial resources (to pay for additional training, if necessary), personal contacts or "connections" with individuals who can assist your career development, specific degrees or certificates you hold, and intangible resources (family name, prestige of your educational institution, etc.).
   d) Considering the current and future needs of your potential employers, what important resources are you lacking?

III. **SWOT Analysis (your personal strengths and weaknesses and the opportunities and threats that may impact your career)**
A. **Personal Strengths**
1. Three key strengths
   a) Strength 1:
   b) Strength 2:
   c) Strength 3:
2. How do these strengths allow you to meet the needs of your potential employers?
3. How do these strengths compare to those of your peers/competitors? Do

these strengths give you an advantage relative to your peers/competitors?

B. Personal Weaknesses
1. Three key weaknesses
   a) Weakness 1:
   b) Weakness 2:
   c) Weakness 3:
2. How do these weaknesses cause you to fall short of meeting the needs of your potential employers?
3. How do these weaknesses compare to those of your peers/competitors? Do these weaknesses put you at a disadvantage relative to your peers/competitors?

C. Career Opportunities
1. Three key career opportunities
   a) Opportunity 1:
   b) Opportunity 2:
   c) Opportunity 3:
2. How are these opportunities related to serving the needs of your potential employers?
3. What actions must be taken to capitalize on these opportunities in the short-term? In the long-term?

D. Career Threats
1. Three key career threats
   a) Threat 1:
   b) Threat 2:
   c) Threat 3:
2. How are these threats related to serving the needs of your potential employers?
3. What actions must be taken to prevent these threats from limiting your capabilities in the short-term? In the long-term?

E. The SWOT Matrix

F. Matching, Converting, Minimizing, and Avoiding Strategies
1. How can you match your strengths to your opportunities to better serve the needs of your potential employers?
2. How can you convert your weaknesses into strengths?
3. How can you convert your threats into opportunities?
4. How can you minimize or avoid those weaknesses and threats that cannot be converted successfully?

IV. Resources

A. Financial
1. Do you have the financial resources necessary to undertake and successfully complete this plan (that is, preparation/duplication/mailing of a résumé; interviewing costs, including proper attire; etc.)?

B. Human
1. Is the industry in which you are interested currently hiring? Are companies in your area currently hiring?

C. Experience and Expertise
1. Do you have experience from either part-time or summer employment that could prove useful in your current plan?
2. Do you have the required expertise or skills to qualify for a job in your desired field? If not, do you have the resources to obtain them?

V. Strategies

A. Objective(s)
1. Potential employer A:
   a) Descriptive characteristics:
   b) Geographic locations:
   c) Culture/values/mission:
   d) Basic employee needs:
   e) Recruiting/hiring practices:
   f) Employee training/compensation practices:
   g) Justification for selection:
2. Potential employer B:
   a) Descriptive characteristics:
   b) Geographic locations:
   c) Culture/values/mission:
   d) Basic employee needs:
   e) Recruiting/hiring practices:
   f) Employee training/compensation practices:
   g) Justification for selection:

B. Strategy(ies) for Using Capabilities and Resources
1. Strategy A (to meet the needs of potential employer A)
   a) Personal skills, abilities, and resources
      (1) Description of your skills and abilities:

(2) Specific employer needs that your skills/abilities can fulfill:

(3) Differentiation relative to peers/competitors (why should *you* be hired?):

(4) Additional resources that you have to offer:

(5) Needed or expected starting salary:

(6) Expected employee benefits:

(7) Additional employer-paid training that you require:

(8) Willingness to relocate:

(9) Geographic areas to target:

(10) Corporate divisions or offices to target:

(11) Summary of overall strategy:

(12) Tactics for standing out among the crowd of potential employees:

(13) Point of contact with potential employer:

(14) Specific elements
- *(a)* Résumé:
- *(b)* Internships:
- *(c)* Placement offices:
- *(d)* Job fairs:
- *(e)* Personal contacts:
- *(f)* Unsolicited:

(15) Specific objectives and budget:

2. Strategy B (to meet the needs of potential employer B)

a) Personal skills, abilities, and resources

(1) Description of your skills and abilities:

(2) Specific employer needs that your skills/abilities can fulfill:

(3) Differentiation relative to peers/competitors (why should *you* be hired?):

(4) Additional resources that you have to offer:

(5) Needed or expected starting salary:

(6) Expected employee benefits:

(7) Additional employer-paid training that you require:

(8) Willingness to relocate:

(9) Geographic areas to target:

(10) Corporate divisions or offices to target:

(11) Summary of overall strategy:

(12) Tactics for standing out among the crowd of potential employees:

(13) Point of contact with potential employer:

(14) Specific elements
- *(a)* Résumé:
- *(b)* Internships:
- *(c)* Placement offices:
- *(d)* Job fairs:
- *(e)* Personal contacts:
- *(f)* Unsolicited:

(15) Specific objectives and budget:

C. Strategy Summary

1. How does strategy A (B) give you a competitive advantage in serving the needs of potential employer A (B)?

2. Is this competitive advantage sustainable? Why or why not?

VI. Financial Projections and Budgets

A. Do you have a clear idea of your budgetary requirements (for example, housing, furnishings, clothing, transportation, food, other living expenses)?

B. Will the expected salaries/benefits from potential employers meet these requirements? If not, do you have an alternative plan (that is, a different job choice, a second job, requesting a higher salary)?

VII. Controls and Evaluation

A. Performance Standards

1. What do you have to offer? Corrective actions that can be taken if your skills, abilities, and resources do not match the needs of potential employers:

2. Are you worth it? Corrective actions that can be taken if potential employers do not think your skills/abilities are worth your asking price:

3. Where do you want to go Corrective actions that can be taken if potential employers do not offer you

a position in a preferred geographic location:

4. How will you stand out among the crowd?

Corrective actions that can be taken if your message is not being heard by potential employers or is not reaching the right people:

B. Monitoring Procedures

1. What types and levels of formal control mechanisms are in place to ensure the proper implementation of your plan?

   a) Are your potential employers hiring?

   b) Do you need additional training/ education?

   c) Have you allocated sufficient time to your career development?

   d) Are your investments in career development adequate?

      (1) Training/education:

      (2) Networking/making contacts:

      (3) Wardrobe/clothing:

      (4) Development of interviewing skills:

   e) Have you done your homework on potential employers?

   f) Have you been involved in an internship program?

   g) Have you attended job/career fairs?

   h) Are you using the resources of your placement center?

   i) Are you committed to your career development?

C. Performance Analysis

1. Number/quality/potential of all job contacts made:

2. Number of job/career fairs attended and quality of the job leads generated:

3. Number of résumés distributed:

   a) Number of potential employers who responded:

   b) Number of negative responses:

4. Number of personal interviews:

5. Number/quality of job offers:

part

5

Marketing: Developing Relationships

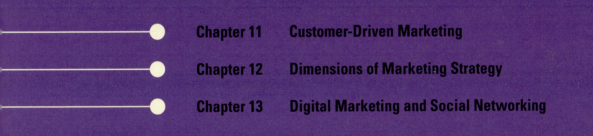

Customer-Driven Marketing

OBJECTIVES

After reading this chapter, you will be able to:

- Define marketing, and describe the exchange process.

- Specify the functions of marketing.

- Explain the marketing concept and its implications for developing marketing strategies.

- Examine the development of a marketing strategy, including market segmentation and marketing mix.

- Investigate how marketers conduct marketing research and study buying behavior.

- Summarize the environmental forces that influence marketing decisions.

- Assess a company's marketing plans, and propose a solution for resolving its problem.

Target Goes Downstream to Compete with Walmart

Target enjoyed great success during the decade beginning in 2000. The company found the perfect mix of low prices, hip styling, and a fun image. Walmart, in spite of its ongoing success, has not been able to replicate the cheap-chic image attained by Target. However, during the most recent recession, consumers were more concerned about simply cheap and less so about chic. The tide turned in Walmart's favor, leaving Target to follow Walmart's lead. Thanks to the unstable economy starting in late 2008, many consumers turned to Walmart for their shopping needs. In a change of strategy, Walmart began promoting its good values over cheap prices. Walmart stores have the added advantage of offering fresh grocery goods, making it one-stop shopping. Walmart saw sales continue to rise during the recession, while Target and other big-box retailers watched them fall.

Target executives acknowledge that they have lost some ground to Walmart, but insist they have learned from the experience. The retailer's target market has long been the 40-year-old mom who is stylish on a budget. However, Target had to reformulate its marketing strategy to acknowledge its target market's changing needs. Super Targets seek to imitate the one-stop shopping appeal of Walmart stores. The company has plans to eventually offer full-service grocery sections in all stores. Starting in 2010, Target slowed its expansion efforts to concentrate on enhancing consumers' experience at current locations. Walmart has responded by unveiling its own revamped stores that improve the shopping experience. Both retailers also have plans for smaller stores in urban markets. To make this succeed, both

continued

ENTER THE WORLD OF BUSINESS

must consider the differing needs of urban dwellers versus suburbanites and choose their merchandise accordingly. It will take years for both chains in implement their new strategies—until then, it's anyone's guess who will end up on top.[1]

Introduction

Marketing involves planning and executing the development, pricing, promotion, and distribution of ideas, goods, and services to create exchanges that satisfy individual and organizational goals. These activities ensure that the products consumers want to buy are available at a price they are willing to pay and that consumers are provided with information about product features and availability. Organizations of all sizes and objectives engage in these activities.

In this chapter, we focus on the basic principles of marketing. First we define and examine the nature of marketing. Then we look at how marketers develop marketing strategies to satisfy the needs and wants of their customers. Next we discuss buying behavior and how marketers use research to determine what consumers want to buy and why. Finally we explore the impact of the environment on marketing activities.

Nature of Marketing

marketing
a group of activities designed to expedite transactions by creating, distributing, pricing, and promoting goods, services, and ideas

A vital part of any business undertaking, **marketing** is a group of activities designed to expedite transactions by creating, distributing, pricing, and promoting goods, services, and ideas. These activities create value by allowing individuals and organizations to obtain what they need and want. A business cannot achieve its objectives unless it provides something that customers value. But just creating an innovative product that meets many users' needs isn't sufficient in today's volatile global marketplace. Products must be conveniently available, competitively priced, and uniquely promoted.

Marketing is an important part of a firm's overall strategy. Other functional areas of the business—such as operations, finance, and all areas of management—must be coordinated with marketing decisions. Businesses try to respond to consumer wants and needs and to anticipate changes in the environment. Unfortunately, it is difficult to understand and predict what consumers want: Motives are often unclear; few principles can be applied consistently; and markets tend to fragment, each desiring customized products, new value, or better service.

It is important to note what marketing is not: It is not manipulating consumers to get them to buy products they do not want. It is not just selling and advertising; it is a systematic approach to satisfying consumers. Marketing focuses on the many activities—planning, pricing, promoting, and distributing products—that foster exchanges.

The Exchange Relationship

exchange
the act of giving up one thing (money, credit, labor, goods) in return for something else (goods, services, or ideas)

At the heart of all business is the **exchange,** the act of giving up one thing (money, credit, labor, goods) in return for something else (goods, services, or ideas). Businesses exchange their goods, services, or ideas for money or credit supplied by customers in a voluntary *exchange relationship,* illustrated in Figure 11.1. The buyer

Martha Stewart tries to facilitate the "exchange relationship" with her customers by tweeting them daily about her company's products and promotional events, such as her book signings.

must feel good about the purchase, or the exchange will not continue. If your cell phone service works everywhere, you will probably feel good about using its services. But if you have a lot of dropped calls, you will probably use another phone service next time.

For an exchange to occur, certain conditions are required. As indicated by the arrows in Figure 11.1, buyers and sellers must be able to communicate about the "something of value" available to each. An exchange does not necessarily take place just because buyers and sellers have something of value to exchange. Each participant must be willing to give up his or her respective "something of value" to receive the "something" held by the other. You are willing to exchange your "something of value"—your money or credit—for soft drinks, football tickets, or new shoes because you consider those products more valuable or more important than holding on to your cash or credit potential.

When you think of marketing products, you may think of tangible things—cars, stereo systems, or books, for example. What most consumers want, however, is a way to get a job done, solve a problem, or gain some enjoyment. You may purchase a Hoover vacuum cleaner not because you want a vacuum cleaner but because you want clean carpets. Starbucks serves coffee drinks at a premium price, providing convenience, quality, and an inviting environment. Therefore, the tangible product

FIGURE II.I

The Exchange Process:
Giving Up One Thing in
Return for Another

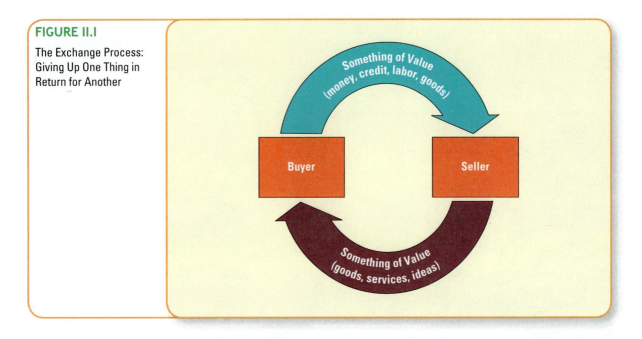

itself may not be as important as the image or the benefits associated with the product. This intangible "something of value" may be capability gained from using a product or the image evoked by it, or even the brand name. Good examples of brand names that are easy to remember include Avon's Skin So Soft, Tide detergent, and the Ford Mustang. The label or brand name may also offer the added bonus of being a conversation piece in a social environment, such as Dancing Bull or Smoking Loon wine.

Functions of Marketing

Marketing focuses on a complex set of activities that must be performed to accomplish objectives and generate exchanges. These activities include buying, selling, transporting, storing, grading, financing, marketing research, and risk taking.

Buying.   Everyone who shops for products (consumers, stores, businesses, governments) decides whether and what to buy. A marketer must understand buyers' needs and desires to determine what products to make available.

Selling.   The exchange process is expedited through selling. Marketers usually view selling as a persuasive activity that is accomplished through promotion (advertising, personal selling, sales promotion, publicity, and packaging).

Transporting.   Transporting is the process of moving products from the seller to the buyer. Marketers focus on transportation costs and services.

Storing.   Like transporting, storing is part of the physical distribution of products and includes warehousing goods. Warehouses hold some products for lengthy periods in order to create time utility. Time utility has to do with being able to satisfy demand in a timely manner. This especially pertains to a seasonal good such as orange juice. Fresh oranges are only available for a few months annually, but consumers demand juice throughout the entire year. Sellers must arrange for cold storage of orange juice concentrate so that they can maintain a steady supply all of the time.

Grading.   Grading refers to standardizing products by dividing them into subgroups and displaying and labeling them so that consumers clearly understand their nature and quality. Many products, such as meat, steel, and fruit, are graded according to a set of standards that often are established by the state or federal government.

Financing.   For many products, especially large items such as automobiles, refrigerators, and new homes, the marketer arranges credit to expedite the purchase.

Marketing Research.   Through research, marketers ascertain the need for new goods and services. By gathering information regularly, marketers can detect new trends and changes in consumer tastes.

Risk Taking.   Risk is the chance of loss associated with marketing decisions. Developing a new product creates a chance of loss if consumers do not like it enough to buy it. Spending money to hire a sales force or to conduct marketing research also involves risk. The implication of risk is that most marketing decisions result in either success or failure.

Creating Value with Marketing[2]

Value is an important element of managing long-term customer relationships and implementing the marking concept. We view **value** as a customer's subjective assessment of benefits relative to costs in determining the worth of a product (customer value = customer benefits − customer costs).

value
A customer's subjective assessment of benefits relative to costs in determining the worth of a product

Customer benefits include anything a buyer receives in an exchange. Hotels and motels, for example, basically provide a room with a bed and bathroom, but each firm provides a different level of service, amenities, and atmosphere to satisfy its guests. Hampton Inn offers the minimum services necessary to maintain a quality, efficient, low-price overnight accommodation. In contrast, the Ritz-Carlton provides every imaginable service a guest might desire and strives to ensure that all service is of the highest quality. Customers judge which type of accommodation offers them the best value according to the benefits they desire and their willingness and ability to pay for the costs associated with the benefits.

Customer costs include anything a buyer must give up to obtain the benefits the product provides. The most obvious cost is the monetary price of the product, but nonmonetary costs can be equally important in a customer's determination of value. Two nonmonetary costs are the time and effort customers expend to find to find and purchase desired products. To reduce time and effort, a company can increase product availability, thereby making it more convenient for buyers to purchase the firm's products. Another nonmonetary cost is risk, which can be reduced by offering good basic warranties for an additional charge. Another risk-reduction strategy is increasingly popular in today's catalog/telephone/Internet shopping environment. L.L. Bean, for example, uses a guarantee to reduce the risk involved in ordering merchandise from its catalogs.

In developing marketing activities, it is important to recognize that customers receive benefits based on their experiences. For example, many computer buyers consider services such as fast delivery, ease of installation, technical advice, and training assistance to be important elements of the product. Customers also derive benefits from the act of shopping and selecting products. These benefits can be affected by the atmosphere or environment of a store, such as Red Lobster's nautical/seafood theme.

Entrepreneurship in Action
Casttoos Make Breaking a Limb a Little More Fashionable

Jessica Smith

Business: Casttoos

Founded: 2006

Success: Smith recently penned a deal with corporate giant 3M, giving Casttoos access to the international arena.

Breaking a bone is rarely a positive event, unless you're artist Jessica Smith. In 2006, Smith broke her arm while riding her bike. During her healing process, she decorated her entire cast. When she returned to her doctor's office, the doctor raved about her designs, saying he would market a product that could create that look on a cast. Smith took him seriously, launching Casttoos six months later. Casttoos are placed on adhesive film and transferred to casts via heat. Encouraged by her doctor's interest, Smith initially marketed her wares at medical gatherings, and hospitals and clinics quickly jumped on board. Currently, Casttoos are sold individually for $20 to $40 (depending on size) and in a clinic and hospital kit selling for $525 to $550. Smith and her company recently signed an agreement with 3M, which will allow them to reach a much wider market.[3]

The Marketing Concept

marketing concept
the idea that an organization should try to satisfy customers' needs through coordinated activities that also allow it to achieve its own goals

A basic philosophy that guides all marketing activities is the **marketing concept,** the idea that an organization should try to satisfy customers' needs through coordinated activities that also allow it to achieve its own goals. According to the marketing concept, a business must find out what consumers desire and then develop the good, service, or idea that fulfills their needs or wants. The business must then get the product to the customer. In addition, the business must continually alter, adapt, and develop products to keep pace with changing consumer needs and wants. McDonald's faces increasing pressure to provide more healthful fast-food choices. The company has eliminated supersized fries and soft drinks from its menu to address these concerns.[4] McDonald's was also the first fast-food chain to put nutritional information on its food packaging.[5] In 2008, the company took a further step to address its health commitment by switching to trans-fat-free cooking oils. Now all of McDonald's french fries, pies, and cookies distributed in the United States and Canada are trans-fat free.[6] The Health Care Reform Act of 2010 will require all restaurants with 20 locations or more to post nutritional information. Over the years, the fast-food giant has experimented with healthier fare, but consumers often have rejected these items. To remain competitive, the company must be prepared to add to or adapt its menu to satisfy customers' desires for new fads or changes in eating habits. Each business must determine how best to implement the marketing concept, given its own goals and resources.

Trying to determine customers' true needs is increasingly difficult because no one fully understands what motivates people to buy things. However, Estée Lauder, founder of her namesake cosmetics company, had a pretty good idea. When a prestigious store in Paris rejected her perfume in the 1960s, she "accidentally" dropped a bottle on the floor where nearby customers could get a whiff of it. So many asked about the scent that Galeries Lafayette was obliged to place an order. Lauder ultimately built an empire using then-unheard-of tactics like free samples and gifts with purchases to market her "jars of hope."[7]

Although customer satisfaction is the goal of the marketing concept, a business must also achieve its own objectives, such as boosting productivity, reducing costs, or achieving a percentage of a specific market. If it does not, it will not survive. For example, Dell could sell computers for $50 and give customers a lifetime guarantee, which would be great for customers but not so great for Dell. Obviously, the company must strike a balance between achieving organizational objectives and satisfying customers.

To implement the marketing concept, a firm must have good information about what consumers want, adopt a consumer orientation, and coordinate its efforts throughout the entire organization; otherwise, it may be awash with goods, services, and ideas that consumers do not want or need. Successfully implementing the marketing concept requires that a business view the customer's perception of value as the ultimate measure of work performance and improving value, and the rate at which this is done, as the measure of success.[8] Everyone in the organization who interacts with customers—*all* customer-contact employees—must know what customers want. They are selling ideas, benefits, philosophies, and experiences—not just goods and services.

Someone once said that if you build a better mousetrap, the world will beat a path to your door. Suppose you do build a better mousetrap. What will happen? Actually, consumers are not likely to beat a path to your door because the market is so competitive. A coordinated effort by everyone involved with the mousetrap is needed to sell the product. Your company must reach out to customers and tell them about your mousetrap, especially how your mousetrap works better than those offered by competitors. If you do not make the benefits of your product widely known, in most cases, it will not be successful. Consider Apple's 273 national and international retail stores, which market computers and electronics in a way unlike any other computer manufacturer or retail establishments. The upscale stores, located in high-rent shopping districts, show off Apple's products in airy, stylish settings to encourage consumers to try new things—like making a movie on a computer. The stores also offer special events like concerts and classes to give customers ideas on how to maximize their use of Apple's products.[9] You must also find—or create—stores willing to sell your mousetrap to consumers. You must implement the marketing concept by making a product with satisfying benefits and making it available and visible.

Orville Wright said that an airplane is "a group of separate parts flying in close formation." This is what most companies are trying to accomplish: They are striving for a team effort to deliver the right good or service to customers. A breakdown at any point in the organization—whether it be in production, purchasing, sales, distribution, or advertising—can result in lost sales, lost revenue, and dissatisfied customers.

Evolution of the Marketing Concept

The marketing concept may seem like the obvious approach to running a business and building relationships with customers. However, businesspeople are not always focused on customers when they create and operate businesses. Many companies fail to grasp the importance of customer relationships and fail to implement customer strategies. A firm's marketing department needs to share information about customers and their desires with the entire organization. Our society and economic system have changed over time, and marketing has become more important as markets have become more competitive.

The Production Orientation.   During the second half of the 19th century, the Industrial Revolution was well under way in the United States. New technologies, such as electricity, railroads, internal combustion engines, and mass-production techniques, made it possible to manufacture goods with ever increasing efficiency. Together with new management ideas and ways of using labor, products poured into the marketplace, where demand for manufactured goods was strong.

The Sales Orientation.   By the early part of the 20th century, supply caught up with and then exceeded demand, and businesspeople began to realize they would have to "sell" products to buyers. During the first half of the 20th century, business-people viewed sales as the primary means of increasing profits, and this period came to have a sales orientation. They believed the most important marketing activities were personal selling and advertising. Today some people still inaccurately equate marketing with a sales orientation.

The Market Orientation.   By the 1950s, some businesspeople began to recognize that even efficient production and extensive promotion did not guarantee sales. These businesses, and many others since, found that they must first determine what customers want and then produce it, rather than making the products first and then trying to persuade customers that they need them. Managers at General Electric first suggested that the marketing concept was a companywide philosophy of doing business. As more organizations realized the importance of satisfying customers' needs, U.S. businesses entered the marketing era, one of marketing orientation.

A **market orientation** requires organizations to gather information about customer needs, share that information throughout the entire firm, and use it to help build long-term relationships with customers. Top executives, marketing managers, nonmarketing managers (those in production, finance, human resources, and so on), and customers all become mutually dependent and cooperate in developing and carrying out a market orientation. Nonmarketing managers must communicate with marketing managers to share information important to understanding the customer. Consider the 117-year history of Wrigley's gum. In 1891 it was given away to promote sales of baking powder. The gum was launched as a product in 1893, and after four generations of Wrigley family CEOs, the company continues to reinvent itself and focus on consumers. In 2008, the family made the decision to sell the company to Mars. Wrigley now functions as a stand-alone subsidiary of Mars. The deal combined such popular brands as Wrigley's gums and Life Savers with Mars' M&Ms, Snickers, and Skittles to form the world's largest confectionary company.

Trying to assess what customers want, difficult to begin with, is further complicated by the rate at which trends, fashions, and tastes can change. Businesses today want to satisfy customers and build meaningful long-term relationships with them. It is more efficient and less expensive for the company to retain existing customers and even increase the amount of business each customer provides the organization than to find new customers. Most companies' success depends on increasing the amount of repeat business; therefore, relationship building between company and customer is key. Many companies are turning to technologies associated with customer relationship management to help build relationships and boost business with existing customers.

Communication remains a major element of any strategy to develop and manage long-term customer relationships. By providing multiple points of interactions with customers—that is, Web sites, telephone, fax, e-mail, and personal contact—companies can personalize customer relationships.[10] Like many online retailers, Amazon.com stores and analyzes purchase data in an attempt to understand each customer's interests. This information helps the retailer improve its ability to satisfy individual customers and thereby increase sales of books, music, movies,

market orientation
an approach requiring organizations to gather information about customer needs, share that information throughout the firm, and use that information to help build long-term relationships with customers

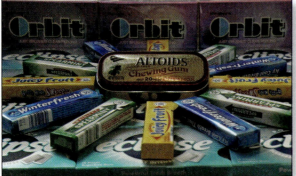

Wrigley originally gave gum away to promote its baking powder. The company continues to reorient and reinvent itself. In 2008, it merged with the candy maker Mars.

and other products to each customer. The ability to identify individual customers allows marketers to shift their focus from targeting groups of similar customers to increasing their share of an individual customer's purchases. Regardless of the medium through which communication occurs, customers should ultimately be the drivers of marketing strategy because they understand what they want. Customer relationship management systems should ensure that marketers listen to customers in order to respond to their needs and concerns and build long-term relationships.

Developing a Marketing Strategy

To implement the marketing concept and customer relationship management, a business needs to develop and maintain a **marketing strategy,** a plan of action for developing, pricing, distributing, and promoting products that meet the needs of specific customers. This definition has two major components: selecting a target market and developing an appropriate marketing mix to satisfy that target market.

Selecting a Target Market

A **market** is a group of people who have a need, purchasing power, and the desire and authority to spend money on goods, services, and ideas. A **target market** is a more specific group of consumers on whose needs and wants a company focuses its marketing efforts. Dell targets kindergarten to eighth-grade students with its notebook computers, which sell at very low prices. The computers are brightly colored with a grippable rubber surface. A light on the lid of the computer informs teachers if students are online.[11]

Marketing managers may define a target market as a relatively small number of people within a larger market, or they may define it as the total market (Figure 11.2). Rolls Royce, for example, targets its products at a very exclusive, high-income market—people who want the ultimate in prestige in an automobile. On the other hand, Ford Motor Company manufactures a variety of vehicles including Lincolns, Mercurys, and Ford Trucks in order to appeal to varied tastes, needs, and desires.

Some firms use a **total-market approach,** in which they try to appeal to everyone and assume that all buyers have similar needs and wants. Sellers of salt, sugar, and many agricultural products use a total-market approach because everyone is a potential consumer of these products. Most firms, though, use **market segmentation** and divide the total market into groups of people. A **market segment** is a collection of individuals, groups, or organizations who share one or more characteristics and thus have relatively similar product needs and desires. Women are the largest market segment, with 51 percent of the U.S. population. In addition, 10.1 million privately held companies are majority owned (75 percent or more) by women.[12] At the household level, segmentation can unlock each woman's social, cultural, and stage in life to determine preferences and needs. One market segment on which many marketers are focusing is the growing Hispanic population. Olive Garden launched a campaign to make Italian food more appealing to Hispanic diners. The restaurant chain created a Spanish version of its Web site, provided all locations with menus in Spanish, and even sponsored several segments on Univision television shows.[13] One of the challenges for marketers in the future will be to effectively address an increasingly racially diverse United States. The minority population of the United States is about 104.6 million (34 percent of the total population).[14] In future decades, the purchasing power of minority market segments is set

marketing strategy
a plan of action for developing, pricing, distributing, and promoting products that meet the needs of specific customers

market
a group of people who have a need, purchasing power, and the desire and authority to spend money on goods, services, and ideas

target market
a specific group of consumers on whose needs and wants a company focuses its marketing efforts

total-market approach
an approach whereby a firm tries to appeal to everyone and assumes that all buyers have similar needs

market segmentation
a strategy whereby a firm divides the total market into groups of people who have relatively similar product needs

market segment
a collection of individuals, groups, or organizations who share one or more characteristics and thus have relatively similar product needs and desires

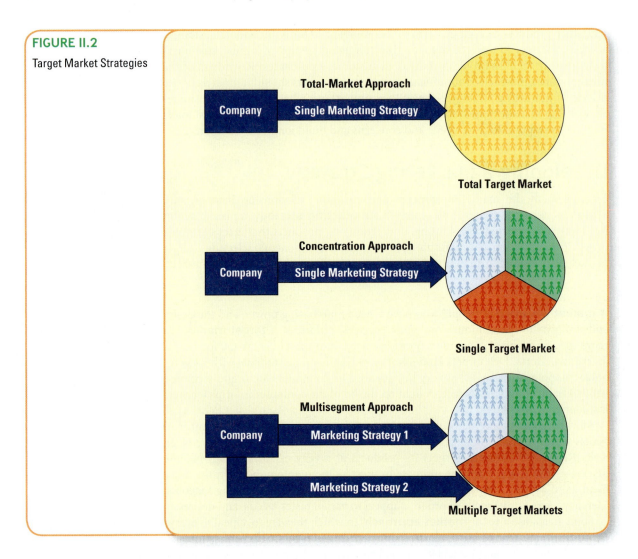

FIGURE II.2

Target Market Strategies

to grow by leaps and bounds. Table 11.1 shows the buying power and market share percentages of four market segments. Companies will have to learn how to most effectively reach these growing segments. Companies use market segmentation to focus their efforts and resources on specific target markets so that they can develop

TABLE II.I

U.S. Buying Power Statistics by Race

	1990	2000	2009	2014
Total	4,270.5	7,187.6	10,717.8	13,097.1
White	3,816.2	6,231.2	9,125.2	11,032.7
Black	318.1	590.2	910.4	1,136.8
American Indian	19.7	39.1	64.7	82.7
Asian	116.5	268.7	508.6	696.5
Multiracial	N/A	58.4	108.9	148.3

Source: Jeffrey M. Humphreys, "The Multicultural Economy 2009," *GBEC* 69 (3rd Quarter, 2009), p. 3, http://www.terry.uga.edu/selig/docs/GBEC0903q.pdf (accessed March 30, 2010).

a productive marketing strategy. Two common approaches to segmenting markets are the concentration approach and the multisegment approach.

Market Segmentation Approaches.   In the **concentration approach,** a company develops one marketing strategy for a single market segment. The concentration approach allows a firm to specialize, focusing all its efforts on the one market segment. Porsche, for example, directs all its marketing efforts toward high-income individuals who want to own high-performance vehicles. A firm can generate a large sales volume by penetrating a single market segment deeply. The concentration approach may be especially effective when a firm can identify and develop products for a segment ignored by other companies in the industry.

In the **multisegment approach,** the marketer aims its marketing efforts at two or more segments, developing a marketing strategy for each. Many firms use a multisegment approach that includes different advertising messages for different segments. Companies also develop product variations to appeal to different market segments. The U.S. Post Office, for example, offers personalized stamps; clothing company J.Crew sells jeans customization kits; various on-demand television services ensure that consumers only watch what they want to watch; and LEGO toy

company offers a service through its Web site wherein children can design their own sets. Companies also develop product variations to appeal to different market segments. For example, Samsung has widened its range of smart phones to appeal to the high-end and lower-end consumer. The company offers models for those who want a smart phone with the maximum capabilities. However, Samsung has also developed an ultra-cheap model targeted at consumers in developing countries, where consumers have not traditionally been able to afford smart phones.[15] Many other firms also attempt to use a multisegment approach to market segmentation, such as the manufacturer of Raleigh bicycles, which has designed separate marketing strategies for racers, tourers, commuters, and children.

Niche marketing is a narrow market segment focus when efforts are on one small, well-defined group that has a unique, specific set of needs. Many airlines cater to first-class flyers, who comprise only 10 percent of international air travelers. To meet the needs of these elite customers, airlines include special perks along with the spacious seats. Continental offers business passengers traveling overseas an in-flight menu featuring broiled beef tenderloin and seafood-filled pastry blossoms, and Delta is installing flat-bed seats on dozens of airplanes.[16]

For a firm to successfully use a concentration or multisegment approach to market segmentation, several requirements must be met:

1. Consumers' needs for the product must be heterogeneous.
2. The segments must be identifiable and divisible.

concentration approach
a market segmentation approach whereby a company develops one marketing strategy for a single market segment

Procter & Gamble uses a multisegment marketing strategy around the globe. In China, it offers an advanced laundry detergent formula for the high end of the market, a mid-priced brand for the medium end of the market, and a basic inexpensive product for the low end of the market.

multisegment approach
a market segmentation approach whereby the marketer aims its efforts at two or more segments, developing a marketing strategy for each

Responding to Business Challenges
Bringing Back Barbie

Barbie debuted in 1959 and instantly filled a gap in a doll market filled with baby dolls. After decades of popularity (Barbie hit her peak in 2002 with $1.52 billion in sales), Barbie sales have fallen close to 30 percent. Barbie has always had her critics. For example, feminists object to a number of Barbie's incarnations such as Miss America Barbie and Flight Attendant Barbie. However, Barbie has also run for president, gone to space, and won Olympic medals, among other accomplishments. The true issue seems to be that for many years, Barbie had little competition. Today, she competes against Bratz dolls (recently awarded to Mattel as part of a lawsuit), Liv dolls, and Moxie dolls.

Given the competition, Richard Dickson (the general manager and senior vice president, who is leading the move to revive the Barbie brand) believes Mattel needs to stop customizing products for retailers, and manufacture fewer dolls of better quality. In addition, Dickson has approached Barbie's revival as one would the revival of a high-fashion label such as Gucci. According to Mattel, Barbie has always been a fashion icon, so the comparison makes sense. Mattel recently opened its flagship Barbie store in Shanghai—House of Barbie—a six-story edifice dedicated to all things Barbie. It also celebrated Barbie's recent 50th birthday with a fashion show in New York City and launched the Heidi Klum Barbie. High fashion appears to be a key component setting Barbie apart from her competition. Whether or not Barbie soars to the top of the doll market, she is willing to work (with incarnations like Fire Fighter Barbie, NASCAR Barbie, or Doctor Barbie) and shows no sign of giving up. The question is: Can high fashion save the Barbie brand?[17]

Discussion Questions

1. Why is Barbie less popular with girls today than she was a generation ago?
2. What do you think of the strategy to market Barbie as more of a high-fashion doll? Is it a good strategy?
3. What are other ways Mattel could help the Barbie brand regain market share?

3. The total market must be divided in a way that allows estimated sales potential, cost, and profits of the segments to be compared.

4. At least one segment must have enough profit potential to justify developing and maintaining a special marketing strategy.

5. The firm must be able to reach the chosen market segment with a particular market strategy.

J&D Foods caters to the niche group of bacon lovers. Started on a lark by Justin Esch and Dave Lefkow, a couple of former tech employees, the company makes bacon-flavored mayonnaise (Baconnaise®), salt (Bacon Salt®), microwave popcorn (BaconPOP®), and even lip balm (Bacon Lip Balm™).

Bases for Segmenting Markets. Companies segment markets on the basis of several variables:

1. *Demographic*—age, sex, race, ethnicity, income, education, occupation, family size, religion, social class. These characteristics are often closely related to customers' product needs and purchasing behavior, and they can be readily measured. For example, deodorants are often segmented by sex: Secret and Soft n' Dri for women; Old Spice and Mennen for men.

2. *Geographic*—climate, terrain, natural resources, population density, subcultural values. These influence consumers' needs and product usage. Climate, for example, influences consumers' purchases of clothing, automobiles, heating and air conditioning equipment, and leisure activity equipment.

3. *Psychographic*—personality characteristics, motives, lifestyles. Soft-drink marketers

provide their products in several types of packaging, including two-liter bottles and cases of cans, to satisfy different lifestyles and motives.

4. *Behavioristic*—some characteristic of the consumer's behavior toward the product. These characteristics commonly involve some aspect of product use.

Developing a Marketing Mix

The second step in developing a marketing strategy is to create and maintain a satisfying marketing mix. The **marketing mix** refers to four marketing activities—product, price, distribution, and promotion—that the firm can control to achieve specific goals within a dynamic marketing environment (Figure 11.3). The buyer or the target market is the central focus of all marketing activities.

Product.   A product—whether a good, a service, an idea, or some combination—is a complex mix of tangible and intangible attributes that provide satisfaction and benefits. A *good* is a physical entity you can touch. A Porsche Cayenne, a Hewlett-Packard printer, and a kitten available for adoption at an animal shelter are examples of goods. A *service* is the application of human and mechanical efforts to people or objects to provide intangible benefits to customers. Air travel, dry cleaning, haircuts, banking, insurance, medical care, and day care are examples of services. *Ideas* include concepts, philosophies, images, and issues. For instance, an attorney, for a fee, may advise you about what rights you have in the event that the IRS decides to audit your tax return. Other marketers of ideas include political parties, churches, and schools.

A product has emotional and psychological, as well as physical characteristics, that include everything that the buyer receives from an exchange. This definition includes supporting services such as installation, guarantees, product information, and promises of repair. Products usually have both favorable and unfavorable attributes; therefore, almost every purchase or exchange involves trade-offs as consumers try to maximize their benefits and satisfaction and minimize unfavorable attributes.

Products are among a firm's most visible contacts with consumers. If they do not meet consumer needs and expectations, sales will be difficult, and product life spans

marketing mix
the four marketing activites—product, price, promotion, and distribution—that the firm can control to achieve specific goals within a dynamic marketing environment

FIGURE II.3

The Marketing Mix: Product, Price, Promotion, and Distribution

will be brief. The product is an important variable—often the central focus—of the marketing mix; the other variables (price, promotion, and distribution) must be coordinated with product decisions.

price
a value placed on an object exchanged between a buyer and a seller

Price.   Almost anything can be assessed by a **price,** a value placed on an object exchanged between a buyer and a seller. Although the seller usually establishes the price, it may be negotiated between buyer and seller. The buyer usually exchanges purchasing power—income, credit, wealth—for the satisfaction or utility associated with a product. Because financial price is the measure of value commonly used in an exchange, it quantifies value and is the basis of most market exchanges.

Marketers view price as much more than a way of assessing value, however. It is a key element of the marketing mix because it relates directly to the generation of revenue and profits. Prices can also be changed quickly to stimulate demand or respond to competitors' actions. The sudden increase in the cost of commodities such as oil can create price increases or a drop in consumer demand for a product. When gas prices rise, consumers purchase more fuel-efficient cars; when prices fall, consumers return to larger vehicles with a smaller price tag.[19]

> **Did You Know?**   During its first year of operation, sales of Coca-Cola averaged just nine drinks per day for total first-year sales of $50. Today, Coca-Cola products are consumed at the rate of 1.6 billion drinks per day.[18]

distribution
making products available to customers in the quantities desired

Distribution.   **Distribution** (sometimes referred to as "place" because it helps to remember the marketing mix as the "4 Ps") is making products available to customers in the quantities desired. For example, consumers can rent DVDs and videogames from a physical store, a vending machine, or an online service. Intermediaries, usually wholesalers and retailers, perform many of the activities required to move products efficiently from producers to consumers or industrial buyers. These activities involve transporting, warehousing, materials handling, and inventory control, as well as packaging and communication.

Critics who suggest that eliminating wholesalers and other middlemen would result in lower prices for consumers do not recognize that eliminating intermediaries would not do away with the need for their services. Other institutions would have to perform those services, and consumers would still have to pay for them. In addition, in the absence of wholesalers, all producers would have to deal directly with retailers or customers, keeping voluminous records and hiring extra people to deal with customers.

promotion
a persuasive form of communication that attempts to expedite a marketing exchange by influencing individuals, groups, and organizations to accept goods, services, and ideas

Promotion.   **Promotion** is a persuasive form of communication that attempts to expedite a marketing exchange by influencing individuals, groups, and organizations to accept goods, services, and ideas. Promotion includes advertising, personal selling, publicity, and sales promotion, all of which we will look at more closely in Chapter 12.

The aim of promotion is to communicate directly or indirectly with individuals, groups, and organizations to facilitate exchanges. When marketers use advertising and other forms of promotion, they must effectively manage their promotional resources and understand product and target-market characteristics to ensure that these promotional activities contribute to the firm's objectives.

Most major companies have set up Web sites on the Internet to promote themselves and their products. The home page for Betty Crocker, for example, offers recipes; meal planning; blogs and message boards; the company's history; descriptions for its products; online shopping for complementary items such as dinnerware, linens, and gifts; and the ability to print a shopping list based on recipes chosen or

When KFC launched its grilled chicken, it offered customers free coupons on Oprah.com. The promotion was so successful that KFC risked running out of chicken just 24 hours after the coupons were uploaded to the Web site.

ingredients on hand in the consumer's kitchen. The Web sites for The Gap and Old Navy provide consumers with the opportunity to purchase clothing and other items from the convenience of their homes or offices. Some sites, however, simply promote a company's products but do not offer them for sale online.

Marketing Research and Information Systems

Before marketers can develop a marketing mix, they must collect in-depth, up-to-date information about customer needs. **Marketing research** is a systematic, objective process of getting information about potential customers to guide marketing decisions. Such information might include data about the age, income, ethnicity, gender, and educational level of people in the target market, their preferences for product features, their attitudes toward competitors' products, and the frequency with which they use the product. For example, demand for most carbonated beverages has been declining for several years as consumers turn away from high-calorie bottled beverages. Experts predict that soft-drink sales will continue to fall at least 1.5 percent each year for the next 5 to 10 years. This shift in consumer preferences is already changing the way companies produce and market bottled beverages.[20] Marketing research is vital because the marketing concept cannot be implemented without information about customers.

marketing research
a systematic, objective process of getting information about potential customers to guide marketing decisions

Pick our panel.

When it comes to picking the right panel for your research project, there are a lot of boogers out there. If you're looking for the one destination you can count on to deliver high quality panel at a price that won't leave a bad taste in your mouth, you've come to the right place. Our actively managed panel can help you kick any sized project faster than you can say, "mmmgood."

Pick a winner.

Opinion Outpost®
Your destination for online panel

(801)373-7735

a service of

Western Wats

To get in touch with what consumers want, companies often utilize online panels, like Opinion Outpost from Western Wats, to ask survey-panel respondents to share their opinions on various products and services.

primary data
marketing information that is observed, recorded, or collected directly from respondents

secondary data
information that is compiled inside or outside an organization for some purpose other than changing the current situation

A marketing information system is a framework for accessing information about customers from sources both inside and outside the organization. Inside the organization, there is a continuous flow of information about prices, sales, and expenses. Outside the organization, data are readily available through private or public reports and census statistics, as well as from many other sources. Computer networking technology provides a framework for companies to connect to useful databases and customers with instantaneous information about product acceptance, sales performance, and buying behavior. This information is important to planning and marketing strategy development.

Two types of data are usually available to decision makers. **Primary data** are observed, recorded, or collected directly from respondents. If you've ever participated in a telephone survey about a product, recorded your TV viewing habits for A. C. Nielsen or Arbitron, or even responded to a political opinion poll, you provided the researcher with primary data. Primary data must be gathered by researchers who develop a method to observe phenomena or research respondents. Many companies use "mystery shoppers" to visit their retail establishments and report on whether the stores were adhering to the companies' standards of service. These undercover customers document their observations of store appearance, employee effectiveness, and customer treatment. Mystery shoppers provide valuable information that helps companies improve their organizations and refine their marketing strategies.[21] Table 11.2 provides the results of an online mystery shopping study of several retailers. Companies also use surveys and focus groups to gauge customer opinion. A weakness of surveys is that respondents are sometimes untruthful in order to avoid seeming foolish or ignorant.

Some methods for marketing research use passive observation of consumer behavior and open-ended questioning techniques. Called ethnographic or observational research, the approach can help marketers determine what consumers really think about their products and how different ethnic or demographic groups react to them.

Secondary data are compiled inside or out-side the organization for some purpose other than changing the current situation. Marketers typically use information compiled by the U.S. Census Bureau and other government agencies, databases created by marketing research firms, as well as sales and other internal reports, to gain information about customers.

Online Marketing Research

The marketing of products and collecting of data about buying behavior—information on what people actually buy and how they buy it—represents marketing

	Number of Hours for E-mail Response	Customer Service Rep Knowledge[a]	Number of Clicks from Product Selection through Checkout	Number of Business Days for Delivery	
Blue Nile	0.22	2.0	5.0	3.0	**TABLE II.2**
Brooks Brothers	3.07	3.0	5.0	3.0	Online Mystery Shopping Study: Customer Service Leaders
Coach	2.48	2.0	4.0	3.0	
Crutchfield	1.27	3.0	5.0	3.0	
Green Mountain	19.73	3.0	5.0	3.0	
Museum of Modern Art	20.48	2.0	4.0	4.0	
Lands' End	6.52	2.5	4.0	3.0	
REI	0.37	2.0	5.0	3.0	
Saks Fifth Avenue	0.88	3.0	5.0	4.0	
Zappos	0.98	3.0	3.0	1.0	
Average of 100 retailers	20.69	2.24	5.42	4.05	

[a] Based on a scale of 1 to 3, with 3 being the most knowledgeable.

Source: "E-retailers Reach Out to Engage Shoppers," *Internet Retailer,* April 2010, http://www.internetretailer.com/article.asp?id=34189 (accessed April 1, 2010).

research of the future. New information technologies are changing the way businesses learn about their customers and market their products. Interactive multimedia research, or *virtual testing,* combines sight, sound, and animation to facilitate the testing of concepts as well as packaging and design features for consumer products. The evolving development of telecommunications and computer technologies is allowing marketing researchers quick and easy access to a growing number of online services and a vast database of potential respondents.

Marketing research can use digital media and social networking sites to gather useful information for marketing decision. Sites such as Twitter, Facebook, MySpace and LinkedIn can be a good substitute for focus groups. Online surveys can serve as an alternative to mail, telephone, or personal interviews.

Social networks are a great way to obtain information from consumers who are willing to share their experiences about products and companies. In a way, this process identifies those consumers who develop an identity or passion for certain products, as well as those consumers who have concerns about quality or performance. It is possible for firms to tap into existing online social networks and simply 'listen' to what consumers have on their mind. Firms can also identify consumers to join a community or group so that they can share their opinions with the business.

A good outcome from using social networks is the opportunity to reach new voices and gain varied perspectives on the creative process of developing new products and promotions. Websites, such as 99designs.com, assist with product design. Victorandspoils.com provides information to help in the development of a complete advertising campaign. To some extent, social networking is democratizing design by welcoming consumer to join in the development process for new products.[22]

There is no end to the opportunities to gain information and insights from consumers that can be used in developing new products and marketing strategies. For example, Rupert Barksfield developed the Multi-Pet Feeder to end pet feeding-time frenzy where one greedy pet eats the other pet's food. He paid $99 and posted his concept along with some of his drawings at quirky.com, and 30,000 people passed judgment on his idea.[23]

Procter & Gamble views social networking as an important marketing research tool that allows the company into consumers' lives and the environments in which they are spending their time. For example, they develop Facebook fan pages for brands. The Pringles fan page has more than 2 million global fans. The company views Twitter as a valuable marketing research tool, with consumers able to ask questions that can be converted into understanding of product interest and issues that need to be resolved.[24]

Twitter and Facebook are putting small businesses on the same level as Starbucks and Dell when it comes to gathering information. Cordarounds, a small clothing company in San Francisco, utilized Twitter to learn about the needs of consumers in the Bay area. Employees realized that a large number of commuters used their bikes to get to work and needed bike-friendly work clothing. The company created its "Bike-to-work pants" with built in reflective material to make it safe to ride home at night.[25]

Buying Behavior

buying behavior
the decision processes and actions of people who purchase and use products

Carrying out the marketing concept is impossible unless marketers know what, where, when, and how consumers buy; marketing research into the factors that influence buying behavior helps marketers develop effective marketing strategies. **Buying behavior** refers to the decision processes and actions of people who purchase and use products. It includes the behavior of both consumers purchasing products for personal or household use as well as organizations buying products for business use. Marketers analyze buying behavior because a firm's marketing strategy should be guided by an understanding of buyers. People view pets as part of their families, and they want their pets to have the best of everything. Iams, which markets the Iams and Eukanuba pet food brands, recognized this trend and shifted its focus. Today, it markets high-quality pet food, fancy pet treats, sauces, and other items. Both psychological and social variables are important to an understanding of buying behavior.

Psychological Variables of Buying Behavior

perception
the process by which a person selects, organizes, and interprets information received from his or her senses

Psychological factors include the following:

- **Perception** is the process by which a person selects, organizes, and interprets information received from his or her senses, as when hearing an advertisement on the radio or touching a product to better understand it.

motivation
inner drive that directs a person's behavior toward goals

- **Motivation,** as we said in Chapter 9, is an inner drive that directs a person's behavior toward goals. A customer's behavior is influenced by a set of motives rather than by a single motive. A buyer of a home computer, for example, may be motivated by ease of use, ability to communicate with the office, and price.

learning
changes in a person's behavior based on information and experience

- **Learning** brings about changes in a person's behavior based on information and experience. If a person's actions result in a reward, he or she is likely to behave the same way in similar situations. If a person's actions bring about a negative result, however—such as feeling ill after eating at a certain restaurant—he or she will probably not repeat that action.

- **Attitude** is knowledge and positive or negative feelings about something. For example, a person who feels strongly about protecting the environment may refuse to buy products that harm the earth and its inhabitants.

- **Personality** refers to the organization of an individual's distinguishing character traits, attitudes, or habits. Although market research on the relationship between personality and buying behavior has been inconclusive, some marketers believe that the type of car or clothing a person buys reflects his or her personality.

Social Variables of Buying Behavior

Social factors include **social roles,** which are a set of expectations for individuals based on some position they occupy. A person may have many roles: mother, wife, student, executive. Each of these roles can influence buying behavior. Consider a woman choosing an automobile. Her father advises her to buy a safe, gasoline-efficient car, such as a Volvo. Her teenaged daughter wants her to buy a cool car, such as a Ford Mustang; her young son wants her to buy a Ford Explorer to take on camping trips. Some of her colleagues at work say she should buy a hybrid Prius to help the environment. Thus, in choosing which car to buy, the woman's buying behavior may be affected by the opinions and experiences of her family and friends and by her roles as mother, daughter, and employee.

Other social factors include reference groups, social classes, and culture.

- **Reference groups** include families, professional groups, civic organizations, and other groups with whom buyers identify and whose values or attitudes they adopt. A person may use a reference group as a point of comparison or a source of information. A person new to a community may ask other group

attitude
knowledge and positive or negative feelings about something

personality
the organization of an individual's distinguishing character traits, attitudes, or habits

social roles
a set of expectations for individuals based on some position they occupy

reference groups
groups with whom buyers identify and whose values or attitudes they adopt

355

People's cultures have a big impact on what they buy. The food-seller Goya Foods sells more than three dozen types of beans to U.S. supermarkets because people with different cultural roots demand different types of beans. Which products are delivered to which stores depends on the heritage of those living in each area.

social classes
a ranking of people into higher or lower positions of respect

culture
the integrated, accepted pattern of human behavior, including thought, speech, beliefs, actions, and artifacts

members to recommend a family doctor, for example.

- **Social classes** are determined by ranking people into higher or lower positions of respect. Criteria vary from one society to another. People within a particular social class may develop common patterns of behavior. People in the upper-middle class, for example, might buy a Lexus or a Cadillac as a symbol of their social class.
- **Culture** is the integrated, accepted pattern of human behavior, including thought, speech, beliefs, actions, and artifacts. Culture determines what people wear and eat and where they live and travel. Many Hispanic Texans and New Mexicans, for example, buy *masa trigo,* the dough used to prepare flour tortillas, which are basic to Southwestern and Mexican cuisine.

Understanding Buying Behavior

Although marketers try to understand buying behavior, it is extremely difficult to explain exactly why a buyer purchases a particular product. The tools and techniques for analyzing consumers are not exact. Marketers may not be able to determine accurately what is highly satisfying to buyers, but they know that trying to understand consumer wants and needs is the best way to satisfy them. After the economic recession in 2009, consumer behavior shifted from conspicuous consumption to more responsible purchasing. Consumers became more price conscious and increased their use of coupons and other promotions even after the immediate financial threat of the recession had passed. Retailers had to adjust to meet the new needs of consumers.[27]

The Marketing Environment

A number of external forces directly or indirectly influence the development of marketing strategies; the following political, legal, regulatory, social, competitive, economic, and technological forces comprise the marketing environment.

- *Political, legal, and regulatory forces*—laws and regulators' interpretation of laws; law enforcement and regulatory activities; regulatory bodies, legislators and legislation, and political actions of interest groups. Specific laws, for example, require that advertisements be truthful and that all health claims be documented.
- *Social forces*—the public's opinions and attitudes toward issues such as living standards, ethics, the environment, lifestyles, and quality of life. For example, social concerns have led marketers to design and market safer toys for children.
- *Competitive and economic forces*—competitive relationships, unemployment, purchasing power, and general economic conditions (prosperity, recession, depression, recovery, product shortages, and inflation).

Marketers like Benetton want their ads to appeal to the consumer's self-image. The message: "I want to be like them, so I should buy Benetton's products."

- *Technological forces*—computers and other technological advances that improve distribution, promotion, and new-product development.

Marketing requires creativity and consumer focus because environmental forces can change quickly and dramatically. Changes can arise from social concerns and economic forces such as price increases, product shortages, and altering levels of demand for commodities. Recently, the concern about climate change, global warming, and the impact of carbon emissions on our environment has developed social concerns leading businesses to rethink marketing strategies. Possibly the most important concern is to make businesses, consumers, and governments consider carbon emissions and the effect their purchases have. Escalating fossil fuel use in economies such as China and India has placed strong upward pressure on oil prices. China's fast development has made it the planet's largest contributor to greenhouse gases. For example, 75 percent of new energy electricity generation in China in 2009 was derived from coal, while coal generates only 45 percent of the total electricity in the United States. China's pollution will create an environmental catastrophe unless there is increased pressure to utilize alternate energy sources.[28]

The average American generates about five tons of greenhouse gases annually. Many people are disturbed by this statistic and have resolved to take actions that reduce their energy usage and their impact on the environment through the use of carpooling, driving hybrid cars, using Energy Star products, and even washing their clothes in cold water instead of hot. In addition to fueling the demand for low-energy products, these developments are also accelerating the development of renewable energy such as solar and wind.[29] If there is a cap on carbon emissions in the United States, the prices would rise for fossil fuels such as coal, oil, and gas. More expensive renewable energy sources such as solar, wind, and biofuels would have a better chance for growth. For example, if turbine wind farms and transmission lines were built in Montana and the Dakotas, the region would have enough wind to provide 886 million megawatt hours a year, which would generate billions of dollars in revenue and improve prosperity.[30]

Because such environmental forces are interconnected, changes in one may cause changes in others. Consider that because of evidence linking children's consumption of soft drinks and fast foods to health issues such as obesity, diabetes, and osteoporosis, marketers of such products have experienced negative publicity and calls for legislation regulating the sale of soft drinks in public schools.

Although the forces in the marketing environment are sometimes called uncontrollables, they are not totally so. A marketing manager can influence some environmental variables. For example, businesses can lobby legislators to dissuade them from passing unfavorable legislation. Figure 11.4 shows the variables in the marketing environment that affect the marketing mix and the buyer.

FIGURE 11.4

The Marketing Mix and the Marketing Environment

Political, Legal, and Regulatory Forces

Social Forces

Technological Forces

Competitive and Economic Forces

Product

Promotion   Customer   Price

Distribution

Marketing Environment

So You Want a Job in Marketing

You probably did not think as a child how great it would be to grow up and become a marketer. That's because often marketing is associated with sales jobs, but opportunities in marketing, public relations, product management, advertising, e-marketing, and customer relationship management and beyond represent almost one-third of all jobs in today's business world. To enter any job in the marketing field, you must balance an awareness of customer needs with business knowledge while mixing in creativity and the ability to obtain useful information to make smart business decisions.

Marketing starts with understanding the customer. Marketing research is a vital aspect in marketing decision making and presents many job opportunities. Market researchers survey customers to determine their habits, preferences, and aspirations. Activities include concept testing, product testing, package testing, test-market research, and new-product research. Salaries vary, depending on the nature and level of the position as well as the type, size, and location of the firm. An entry-level market analyst may make between $24,000 and $50,000, while a market research director may earn from $75,000 to $200,000 or more.

One of the most dynamic areas in marketing is direct marketing, where a seller solicits a response from a consumer using direct communications methods such as telephone, online communication, direct mail, or catalogs. Jobs in direct marketing include buyers, catalog managers, research/mail-list managers, or order fulfillment managers. Most positions in direct marketing involve planning and market analysis. Some require the use of databases to sort and analyze customer information and sales history.

Use of the Internet for retail sales is growing, and the Internet continues to be very useful for business-to-business sales, so e-marketing offers many career opportunities, including customer relationship management (CRM). CRM helps companies market to customers through relationships, maintaining customer loyalty. Information technology plays a huge role in such marketing jobs, as you need to combine technical skills and marketing knowledge to effectively communicate with customers. Job titles include e-marketing manager, customer relationship manager, and e-services manager. A CRM customer service manager may receive a salary in the $40,000 to $45,000, and experienced individuals in charge of online product offerings may earn up to $100,000.

A job in any of these marketing fields will require a strong sense of the current trends in business and marketing. Customer service is vital to many aspects of marketing, so the ability to work with customers and to communicate their needs and wants is important. Marketing is everywhere, from the corner grocery or local nonprofit organization to the largest multinational corporations, making it a shrewd choice for an ambitious and creative person. We will provide additional job opportunities in marketing in Chapter 12.

Review Your Understanding

Define marketing, and describe the exchange process.

Marketing is a group of activities designed to expedite transactions by creating, distributing, pricing, and promoting goods, services, and ideas. Marketing facilitates the exchange, the act of giving up one thing in return for something else. The central focus of marketing is to satisfy needs.

Specify the functions of marketing.

Marketing includes many varied and interrelated activities: buying, selling, transporting, storing, grading, financing, marketing research, and risk taking.

Explain the marketing concept and its implications for developing marketing strategies.

The marketing concept is the idea that an organization should try to satisfy customers' needs through coordinated activities that also allow it to achieve its goals. If a company does not implement the marketing concept by providing products that consumers need and want while achieving its own objectives, it will not survive.

Examine the development of a marketing strategy, including market segmentation and marketing mix.

A marketing strategy is a plan of action for creating a marketing mix (product, price, distribution, promotion) for a specific target market (a specific group of consumers on whose needs and wants a company focuses its marketing efforts). Some firms use a total-market approach, designating everyone as the target market. Most firms divide the total market into segments of people who have relatively similar product needs. A company using a concentration approach develops one marketing strategy for a single market segment, whereas a multisegment approach aims marketing efforts at two or more segments, developing a different marketing strategy for each.

Investigate how marketers conduct marketing research and study buying behavior.

Carrying out the marketing concept is impossible unless marketers know what, where, when, and how consumers buy; marketing research into the factors that influence buying behavior helps marketers develop effective marketing strategies. Marketing research is a systematic, objective process of getting information about potential customers to guide marketing decisions. Buying behavior is the decision processes and actions of people who purchase and use products.

Summarize the environmental forces that influence marketing decisions.

There are several forces that influence marketing activities: political, legal, regulatory, social, competitive, economic, and technological.

Assess a company's marketing plans, and propose a solution for resolving its problem.

Based on the material in this chapter, you should be able to answer the questions posed in "Solve the Dilemma" on page 362 and help the business understand what went wrong and how to correct it.

Revisit the World of Business

1. What changed in the business environment to cause the change in dynamics between Target and Walmart?

2. Why did consumers switch allegiance from Target to Walmart during the most recent economic recession?

3. What is Target doing to gain competitive advantage over Walmart? Do you think this will be a good strategy in the long run?

Learn the Terms

Check Your Progress

1. What is marketing? How does it facilitate exchanges?

2. Name the functions of marketing. How does an organization use marketing activities to achieve its objectives?

3. What is the marketing concept? Why is it so important?

4. What is a marketing strategy?

5. What is market segmentation? Describe three target market strategies.

6. List the variables in the marketing mix. How is each used in a marketing strategy?

7. Why are marketing research and information systems important to an organization's planning and development of strategy?

8. Briefly describe the factors that influence buying behavior. How does understanding buying behavior help marketers?

9. Discuss the impact of technological forces and political and legal forces on the market.

Get Involved

1. With some or all of your classmates, watch several hours of television, paying close attention to the commercials. Pick three commercials for products with which you are somewhat familiar. Based on the commercials, determine who the target market is. Can you surmise the marketing strategy for each of the three?

2. Discuss the decision process and influences involved in purchasing a personal computer.

Build Your Skills

THE MARKETING MIX

Background:
You've learned the four variables—product, promotion, price, and distribution—that the marketer can select to achieve specific goals within a dynamic marketing environment. This exercise will give you an opportunity to analyze the marketing strategies of some well-known companies to determine which of the variables received the most emphasis to help the company achieve its goals.

Task:
In groups of three to five students, discuss the examples below and decide which variable received the most emphasis.

A. Product
B. Distribution
C. Promotion
D. Price

_____ 1. Starbucks Coffee began selling bagged premium specialty coffee through an agreement with Kraft Foods to gain access to more than 30,000 supermarkets.

_____ 2. Skype is a software application that allows consumers to make telephone calls over the Web. Calls to Skype subscribers are free, while calls to land line and mobile phones cost around 2 cents per minute.

_____ 3. Amid great anticipation, Apple released its iPad, selling over 3 million within 3 months.

The slim tablet computer is a major step forward in reading e-books, watching movies, and playing games.

_____ 4. After decades on the market, WD-40 is in about 80 percent of U.S. households—more than any other branded product. Although WD-40 is promoted as a product that can stop squeaks, protect metal, loosen rusted parts, and free sticky mechanisms, the WD-40 Company has received letters from customers who have sprayed the product on bait to attract fish, on pets to cure mange, and even on people to cure arthritis. Despite more than 200 proposals to expand the WD-40 product line and ideas to change the packaging and labeling, the company stands firmly behind its one highly successful and respected original product.

_____ 5. Southwest Airlines makes flying fun. Flight attendants try to entertain passengers, and the airline has an impeccable customer service record. Employees play a key role and take classes that emphasize that having fun translates into great customer service.

_____ 6. Hewlett Packard offered a $100 rebate on a $799 HP LaserJet printer when purchased with an HP LaserJet toner cartridge. To receive the rebate, the buyer had to return a mail-in certificate to certify the purchase. A one-page ad with a coupon was used in

USA Today stating, "We're taking $100 off the top."

_____ **7.** Denny's, the largest full-service family restaurant chain in the United States, serves more than 1 million customers a day. The restaurants offer the Grand Slam Breakfast

for about $3, lunch basket specials for $4–$6, and a dinner of prime rib for about $7.

Solve the Dilemma

WILL IT GO?

Ventura Motors makes midsized and luxury automobiles in the United States. Best selling models include its basic four-door sedans (priced from $20,000 to $25,000) and two-door and four-door luxury automobiles (priced from $40,000 to $55,000). The success of two-seat sports cars like the Mazda RX-8 started the company evaluating the market for a two-seat sports car priced midway between the moderate and luxury market. Research found that there was indeed significant demand and that Ventura needed to act quickly to take advantage of this market opportunity.

Ventura took the platform of the car from a popular model in its moderate line, borrowing the internal design from its luxury line. The car was designed, engineered, and produced in just over two years, but the coordination needed to bring the design together resulted in higher than anticipated costs. The price for this two-seat car, the Olympus, was set at $32,000. Dealers were anxious to take

delivery on the car, and salespeople were well trained on techniques to sell this new model.

However, initial sales have been slow, and company executives are surprised and concerned. The Olympus was introduced relatively quickly, made available at all Ventura dealers, priced midway between luxury and moderate models, and advertised heavily since its introduction.

Discussion Questions

1. What do you think were the main concerns with the Olympus two-door sports coupe? Is there a market for a two-seat, $32,000 sports car when the RX-8 sells for significantly less?

2. Evaluate the role of the marketing mix in the Olympus introduction.

3. What are some of the marketing strategies auto manufacturers use to stimulate sales of certain makes of automobiles?

Build Your Business Plan

CUSTOMER-DRIVEN MARKETING

The first step is to develop a marketing strategy for your product or service. Who will be the target market you will specifically try to reach? What group(s) of people has the need, ability and willingness to purchase this product? How will you segment customers within your target market? Segmenting by demographic and geographic variables are often the easiest segmentation strategies to attempt. Remember that you would like to have the customers in your segment be as homogeneous and accessible as possible. You might target several segments if you feel your product or service has broad appeal.

The second step in your marketing strategy is to develop the marketing mix for your product or service.

Whether you are dealing with an established product or you are creating your own product or service, you need to think about what is the differential advantage your product offers. What makes it unique? How should it be priced? Should the product be priced below, above, or at the market? How will you distribute the product? And last but certainly not least, you need to think about the promotional strategy for your product.

What about the uncontrollable variables you need to be aware of? Is your product something that can constantly be technologically advanced? Is your product a luxury that will not be considered by consumers when the economy is in a downturn?

See for Yourself Videocase

NEW BELGIUM BREWERY SERVES CONSUMERS WHAT THEY WANT

Not everyone may recognize the name New Belgium Brewery, but many people are familiar with Fat Tire beer. New Belgium founder Jeff Lebesch first began brewing beer with a roommate in his basement. Although the first attempts failed, he and his wife, Kim Jordan, continued basement brewing, eventually creating the now famous Fat Tire—named after the tires Lebesch used to mountain bike through European villages famous for beer. The basement brewery officially went commercial in 1991, selling first to friends, family, and neighbors. A quality product, concern for employees, and commitment to environmental stewardship have led to fast sales growth, making New Belgium the third largest craft brewer in the United States.

For Lebesch and Jordon, the basement brewery turned out to be a blessing. Jordon became the brewery's first bottler, sales representative, distributor, marketer, and financial planner. (Today, she is the CEO.) This, combined with the low overhead, allowed Lebesch the freedom to experiment with creative beer formulas and innovative techniques without worry about investor expectations or paying off large bank loans. New Belgium's customers are drawn to the company's care over naming, labeling, and producing its beer as much as they are by all that the brewery represents. Lebesch and his team are constantly coming up with new products, such New Belgium's "Skinny Dip" beer—so named for the company's involvement in water advocacy.

From the beginning, Lebesch and Jordon have been concerned with the brewery's impact on the environment and have made every effort to minimize that impact. When they grew beyond the basement and created what is today's New Belgium brewery, they continued to put this concern at the forefront of all business operations. Today, the company is dedicated to balancing profitability with social and environmental responsibility—something its loyal consumers appreciate. The company has used 100 percent wind-powered electricity since 1999, using sun-tubes, light shelves and evaporative coolers to reduce energy consumption. New Belgium is now using aluminum cans for some of its Fat Tire beer. Not only are aluminum cans more convenient for customers because they can be taken to places glass cannot, like baseball parks and other outdoor venues, but they are environmentally friendly as well. Although many in the business world believe that to aid the environment is to destroy a business and to profit is to destroy the environment, New Belgium is an example of how a business can truly succeed financially while maintaining a dedication to the environment. The company's environmental practices have become synonymous with its brand, distinguishing it from other specialty beer on the market and creating customer loyalty through shared commitment.

New Belgium began with innovation and a dedication to the environment and has stayed true to these elements throughout. As the company continues to grow, it focuses on the balance between producing a great product, profit, and environmental stewardship. Ever dedicated to bringing great, unique, and creative beer to its customers, today New Belgium is also striving to reduce its carbon footprint by 50 percent, reduce water usage by 10 percent, and increase waste stream diversion rate from 70–80 percent. Customers remain as loyal to New Belgium as it is to its roots.[31]

Discussion Question

1. Why is environmental stewardship so important at New Belgium Brewery?

2. How does a strong commitment to environmental and social responsibility help to attract new customers and maintain old ones?

3. Who do you think is New Belgium's target market?

Remember to check out our Online learning Center at www.mhhe.com/ferrell8e.

Team Exercise

Form groups and assign the responsibility of finding examples of companies that excel in one dimension of the marketing mix (price, product, promotion, and distribution). Provide several company and product examples, and defend why this would be an exemplary case. Present your research to the class.

chapter 12

Dimensions of Marketing Strategy

OBJECTIVES

After reading this chapter, you will be able to:

- Describe the role of product in the marketing mix, including how products are developed, classified, and identified.

- Define price, and discuss its importance in the marketing mix, including various pricing strategies a firm might employ.

- Identify factors affecting distribution decisions, such as marketing channels and intensity of market coverage.

- Specify the activities involved in promotion, as well as promotional strategies and promotional positioning.

- Evaluate an organization's marketing strategy plans.

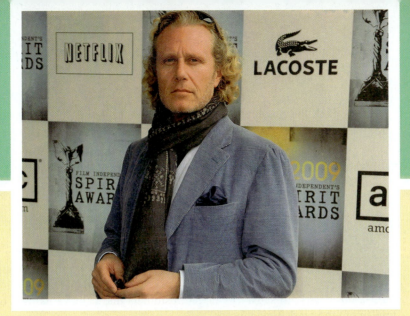

Product Placement Is Popular as a Marketing Tactic

Watch a movie or television show carefully and you will likely identify several familiar product brands. These products are not there by accident. In fact, master of product placement Ruben Igielko-Herrlich of Propaganda Global Entertainment Marketing (GEM) makes it his business to help companies place their products in such media. While working as a sales executive, Igielko-Herrlich was approached by MGM. The film studio wanted to use one of his products in a film. After brokering the deal, Igielko-Herrlich and partner Anders Granath founded Propaganda GEM in 1991. Today the international marketing agency boasts 11 offices worldwide. The company also handles promotion, events, outreach, public relations, and endorsements.

While product placement seems simple enough, making it unobtrusive is challenging. This is where Igielko-Herrlich comes in. He made his mark with the first *Matrix* movie. Knowing that Nokia was launching one of the first Web-connected mobile phones, he approached the directors and convinced them to make the new phone a portal through which Keanu Reeves entered the Matrix. After the movie release, sales of the new Nokia phone soared. Igielko-Herrlich is also responsible for placing the Audi R8 in *Transformers: Revenge of the Fallen*, creating buzz around the speedy car. Many companies seek his services as part of their advertising campaigns, citing the finesse with which he places products.

Igielko-Herrlich offers clients a valuable opportunity. As more viewers bypass television commercials, inserting the products directly in TV shows

continued

and movies may be one of the best ways to garner notice. Product placement can become part of a pull promotional strategy used to launch a new product or to revive interest in existing products. So, next time you watch your favorite TV show or head to the movies, check out the unsung stars—the products.[1]

Introduction

The key to developing a marketing strategy is selecting a target market and maintaining a marketing mix that creates long-term relationships with customers.

Getting just the right mix of product, price, promotion, and distribution is critical if a business is to satisfy its target customers and achieve its own objectives (implement the marketing concept).

In Chapter 11, we introduced the concept of marketing and the various activities important in developing a marketing strategy. In this chapter, we'll take a closer look at the four dimensions of the marketing mix—product, price, distribution, and promotion—used to develop the marketing strategy. The focus of these marketing mix elements is a marketing strategy that builds customer relationships and satisfaction.

The Marketing Mix

The marketing mix is the part of marketing strategy that involves decisions regarding controllable variables. To develop meaningful customer relationships, marketers have to develop and manage the dimensions of the marketing mix to give their firm an advantage over competitors. Successful companies offer at least one dimension of value that surpasses all competitors in the marketplace in meeting customer expectations. However, this does not mean that a company can ignore the other dimensions of the marketing mix; it must maintain acceptable, and if possible distinguishable, differences in the other dimensions as well.

> **Did You Know?** Less than 10 percent of new products succeed in the marketplace, and 90 percent of successes come from a handful of companies.[2]

Walmart, for example, emphasizes price ("Save money, live better"). Procter & Gamble is well known for its promotion of top consumer brands such as Tide, Cheer, Crest, Ivory, and Head & Shoulders. Dell Computers' efficient distribution and customization processes explain why it has secured such a large share of the computer industry.[3]

Product Strategy

As mentioned previously, the term *product* refers to goods, services, and ideas. Because the product is often the most visible of the marketing mix dimensions, managing product decisions is crucial. In this section, we'll consider product development, classification, mix, life cycle, and identification.

Developing New Products

Each year thousands of products are introduced, but few of them succeed. For instance, The Coca-Cola Company spent two years to develop Coke Blak, a Coca-Cola coffee drink aimed at an older audience. The product failed to take off in the United

While attending Yale in 1966, FedEx founder Fred Smith studied a mathematical discipline called topology, which inspired his vision for creating the company. Realizing the potential efficiencies of connecting all points on a network through a central hub, Smith used what he learned to get FedEx off the ground.

States and was discontinued less than two years after its launch.[4] Figure 12.1 shows the different steps in the product development process. Before introducing a new product, a business must follow a multistep process: idea development, the screening of new ideas, business analysis, product development, test marketing, and commercialization. A firm can take considerable time to get a product ready for the market: It took more than 20 years for the first photocopier, for example. Although the Chevy Volt was announced in 2007, it was not released until 2010. This did not stop the Volt from winning the Green Car Vision Award in 2009, more than a year before it was released.[5]

Idea Development.   New ideas can come from marketing research, engineers, and outside sources such as advertising agencies and management consultants. Microsoft has a separate division—Microsoft Research—where scientists devise technology of the future. The division has more than 800 researchers who work in a universitylike research atmosphere. Research teams then present their ideas to Microsoft engineers who are developing specific products. As we said in Chapter 11, ideas sometimes come from customers, too. Other sources are brainstorming and intracompany incentives or rewards for good ideas. New ideas can even create a company. Las Vegas–based Shuffle Master, for example, grew out of entrepreneur John Breeding's idea for a card-shuffling machine. The Shuffle Master has more than 22,000 shuffling units installed around the world.[6]

New Idea Screening.   The next step in developing a new product is idea screening. In this phase, a marketing manager should look at the organization's resources

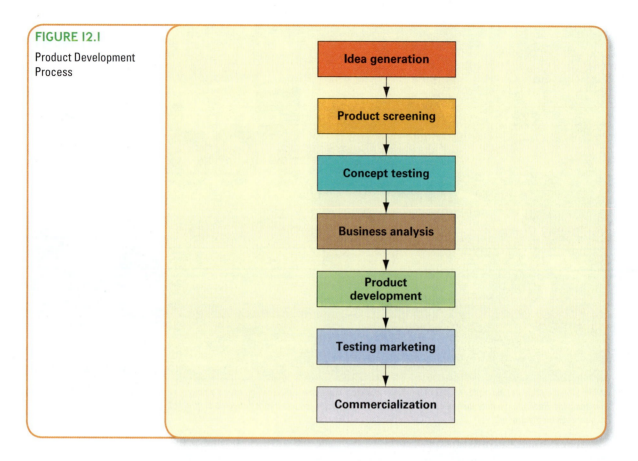

FIGURE 12.1

Product Development
Process

- Idea generation
- Product screening
- Concept testing
- Business analysis
- Product development
- Testing marketing
- Commercialization

and objectives and assess the firm's ability to produce and market the product. Important aspects to be considered at this stage are consumer desires, the competition, technological changes, social trends, and political, economic, and environmental considerations. Basically, there are two reasons new products succeed: They are able to meet a need or solve a problem better than products already available or they add variety to the product selection currently on the market. Bringing together a team of knowledgeable people including design, engineering, marketing and customers is a great way to screen ideas. Using the Internet to encourage collaboration represents a rich opportunity for marketers to screen ideas. Most new-product ideas are rejected during screening because they seem inappropriate or impractical for the organization.

Business Analysis.   Business analysis is a basic assessment of a product's compatibility in the marketplace and its potential profitability. Both the size of the market and competing products are often studied at this point. The most important question relates to market demand: How will the product affect the firm's sales, costs, and profits?

Product Development.   If a product survives the first three steps, it is developed into a prototype that should reveal the intangible attributes it possesses as perceived by the consumer. Product development is often expensive, and few product ideas make it to this stage. New product research and development costs vary. Adding a new color to an existing item may cost $100,000 to $200,000, but launching a

FIGURE 12.2

ACNielsen Market Decisions

Source: "Test Marketing," ACNielsen (n.d.), www.acnielsen.com/services/testing/test1.htm (accessed June 5, 2004). Reprinted with permission of ACNielsen Market Decisions.

completely new product can cost millions of dollars. The Coca-Cola Co. reduced the time and cost of product development research by 50 percent when it created an online panel of 100 teenagers and asked them how to remake its Powerade sports drink.[7] During product development, various elements of the marketing mix must be developed for testing. Copyrights, tentative advertising copy, packaging, labeling, and descriptions of a target market are integrated to develop an overall marketing strategy.

Test Marketing.   **Test marketing** is a trial minilaunch of a product in limited areas that represent the potential market. It allows a complete test of the marketing strategy in a natural environment, giving the organization an opportunity to discover weaknesses and eliminate them before the product is fully launched. Consider Tide Basic, a product released by Procter & Gamble to appeal to money-conscious consumers during the most recent recession. Tide Basic is a stripped-down version of the company's Tide laundry detergent that costs 20 percent less. It was meant to appeal to consumers who needed to save money but still wanted the same basic benefits that Tide had to offer. P&G started out by testing it in limited markets and then initially introduced the new product into only 100 stores in the South. This cautious strategy allowed the company to carefully measure the product's success before P&G introduced it on a wider scale.[8] ACNielsen assists companies in test-marketing their products. Figure 12.2 shows the permanent sites as well as custom locations for test marketing.

test marketing
a trial minilaunch of a product in limited areas that represent the potential market

Commercialization.   **Commercialization** is the full introduction of a complete marketing strategy and the launch of the product for commercial success. During commercialization, the firm gears up for full-scale production, distribution, and

commercialization
the full introduction of a complete marketing strategy and the launch of the product for commercial success

When consumers are shopping for specialty products such as rare antiques, they go to great lengths to get what they want and often aren't willing to accept substitutes.

consumer products
products intended for household or family use

business products
products that are used directly or indirectly in the operation or manufacturing processes of businesses

Industrial supply company Grainger is able to supply business customers with an array of more than one million products to keep their facilities up and running. The company serves two million businesses and institutions in 153 countries.

promotion. To compete more effectively against coffee chains like Starbucks, McDonald's introduced its first American McCafé in Chicago in 2001. In 2007, the company introduced iced coffee to its menu and began testing its new line of espresso-based beverages. However, it was not until 2009 that McDonald's implemented nationwide commercialization of its McCafés. The launch was McDonald's largest in 30 years.[9]

Classifying Products

Products are usually classified as either consumer products or industrial products. **Consumer products** are for household or family use; they are not intended for any purpose other than daily living. They can be further classified as convenience products, shopping products, and specialty products on the basis of consumers' buying behavior and intentions.

- *Convenience products,* such as eggs, milk, bread, and newspapers, are bought frequently, without a lengthy search, and often for immediate consumption. Consumers spend virtually no time planning where to purchase these products and usually accept whatever brand is available.
- *Shopping products,* such as furniture, audio equipment, clothing, and sporting goods, are purchased after the consumer has compared competitive products and "shopped around." Price, product features, quality, style, service, and image all influence the decision to buy.
- *Specialty products,* such as ethnic foods, designer clothing and shoes, art, and antiques, require even greater research and shopping effort. Consumers know what they want and go out of their way to find it; they are not willing to accept a substitute.

Business products are used directly or indirectly in the operation or manufacturing processes of businesses. They are usually purchased for the operation of an organization or the production of other products; thus, their purchase is tied to specific goals and objectives. They too can be further classified:

- *Raw materials* are natural products taken from the earth, oceans, and recycled solid waste. Iron ore, bauxite, lumber, cotton, and fruits and vegetables are examples.
- *Major equipment* covers large, expensive items used in production. Examples include earth-moving equipment, stamping machines, and robotic equipment used on auto assembly lines.
- *Accessory equipment* includes items used for production, office, or management purposes, which

usually do not become part of the final product. Computers, fax machines, calculators, and hand tools are examples.

- *Component parts* are finished items, ready to be assembled into the company's final products. Tires, window glass, batteries, and spark plugs are component parts of automobiles.
- *Processed materials* are things used directly in production or management operations but are not readily identifiable as component parts. Varnish, for example, is a processed material for a furniture manufacturer.
- *Supplies* include materials that make production, management, and other operations possible, such as paper, pencils, paint, cleaning supplies, and so on.
- *Industrial services* include financial, legal, marketing research, security, janitorial, and exterminating services. Purchasers decide whether to provide these services internally or to acquire them from an outside supplier.

Product Line and Product Mix

Product relationships within an organization are of key importance. A **product line** is a group of closely related products that are treated as a unit because of similar marketing strategy. At Colgate-Palmolive, for example, the oral-care product line includes Colgate toothpaste, toothbrushes, and dental floss. A **product mix** is all the products offered by an organization. Figure 12.3 displays a sampling of the product mix and product lines of the Colgate-Palmolive Company.

Product Life Cycle

Like people, products are born, grow, mature, and eventually die. Some products have very long lives. Ivory Soap was introduced in 1879 and is still popular. In contrast, a new computer chip is usually outdated within a year because of technological breakthroughs and rapid changes in the computer industry. There are four stages in

product line
a group of closely related products that are treated as a unit because of similar marketing strategy, production, or end-use considerations

product mix
all the products offered by an organization

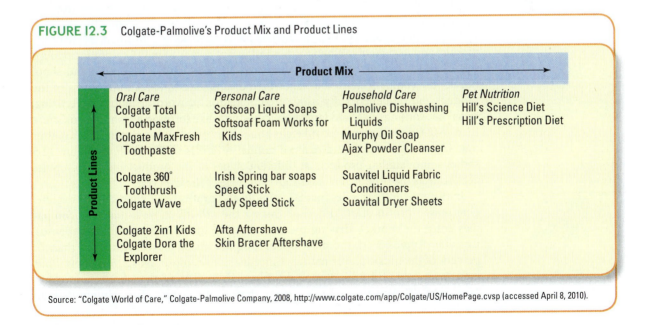

FIGURE I2.3   Colgate-Palmolive's Product Mix and Product Lines

Source: "Colgate World of Care," Colgate-Palmolive Company, 2008, http://www.colgate.com/app/Colgate/US/HomePage.cvsp (accessed April 8, 2010).

FIGURE 12.4

The Life Cycle of a Product

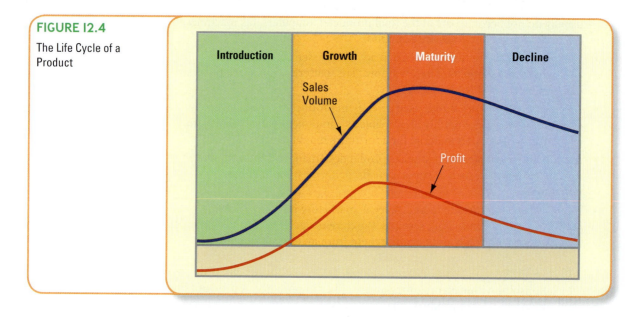

the life cycle of a product: introduction, growth, maturity, and decline (Figure 12.4). The stage a product is in helps determine marketing strategy. While pickup trucks have historically sold very well in the United States, sales have reached the maturity stage, declining after a peak in 2004. The percentage of new vehicles sold reveals more car sales than truck sales. As oil prices continue to fluctuate and carbon outputs become more of a concern, consumers are looking for better gas mileage and the demand for fuel-efficient cars is on the rise. Hybrid vehicles are in the introductory stage, with around 3 percent of market share, but with continued demand will quickly pass into the growth stage.[10]

In the *introductory stage,* consumer awareness and acceptance of the product are limited, sales are zero, and profits are negative. Profits are negative because the firm has spent money on research, development, and marketing to launch the product. During the introductory stage, marketers focus on making consumers aware of the product and its benefits. When former restaurant owner Sean O'Connor introduced Batter Blaster, a canned organic pancake and waffle batter mix with a point-and-shoot nozzle, the company started a major media campaign to spread awareness of the product and its benefits. By using a combination of word-of-mouth advertising, social networking sites, and large publicity stunts like forming a team to cook more than 76,000 pancakes in a record eight hours, the company has gotten Batter Blaster into 13,000 U.S. outlets and realized annual revenues of $15 million. Figure 12.5 shows some familiar products at different stages of the product life cycle.[11] Sales accelerate as the product enters the growth stage of the life cycle.

In the *growth stage,* sales increase rapidly and profits peak, then start to decline. One reason profits start to decline during the growth stage is that new companies enter the market, driving prices down and increasing marketing expenses. Consider Apple's iPod, the most popular digital music player with more than 70 percent of the music player market. Since its launch, more than 225 million iPods have been sold, 1.8 billion apps downloaded, and more than 8.5 billion songs purchased. Its App Store also has more than 21,000 games. To maintain its high

Introduction	Growth	Maturity	Decline	FIGURE 12.5
3D television	DVRs	Flat-screen televisions	AM/FM radios	Products at Different Stages of the Life Cycle
YouTube movies	Netflix	Laptop computers	VCRs	
Electric cars	Tablet computers	Netbook computers	Desktop computers	

growth, Apple has also introduced the iTunes 9, the iPod Classic, and the iPod Touch.[12] During the growth stage, the firm tries to strengthen its position in the market by emphasizing the product's benefits and identifying market segments that want these benefits.

Sales continue to increase at the beginning of the *maturity stage,* but then the sales curve peaks and starts to decline while profits continue to decline. This stage is characterized by severe competition and heavy expenditures. In the highly competitive snack food industry, Quaker is converting mature products to single serve lower-calorie treats. Because 100-calorie packs were a smash success for Quaker and competitor Kraft, rivals across the industry are introducing 90-, 80-, even 60-calorie versions of mature products in hopes of maintaining sales.[13]

During the *decline stage,* sales continue to fall rapidly. Profits also decline and may even become losses as prices are cut and necessary marketing expenditures are made. As profits drop, firms may eliminate certain models or items. To reduce expenses and squeeze out any remaining profits, marketing expenditures may be cut back, even though such cutbacks accelerate the sales decline. Finally, plans must be made for phasing out the product and introducing new ones to take its place. In 2010, General Motors sold its final Hummer SUVs at steeply reduced prices. The company discontinued the brand because of its poor fuel economy, negative public opinion, and plummeting sales. GM also phased out its Saturn and Pontiac brands.

At the same time, it should be noted that product stages do not always go one way. Some products that have moved to the maturity stage or to the decline stage can still rebound through redesign or new uses for the product. One prime example is baking soda. Originally, baking soda was only used for cooking, which meant it reached the maturity stage very quickly. However, once it was discovered that baking soda could be used as a deodorizer, sales shot up and bumped baking soda back into the growth stage.[14] Similarly, Mattel is trying to make a comeback with Barbie by releasing new lines of redesigned dolls. For example, their "fashionista" dolls have 12 movable joints and wear clothes similar to what is found on the runway. Mattel also released So in Style, its first line of black dolls, in 2009.[15]

Identifying Products

Branding, packaging, and labeling can be used to identify or distinguish one product from others. As a result, they are key marketing activities that help position a product appropriately for its target market.

Branding.   **Branding** is the process of naming and identifying products. A *brand* is a name, term, symbol, design, or combination that identifies a product and distinguishes it from other products. Consider that Google, iPod, and TiVo are

branding
the process of naming and identifying products

Are gigantic houses becoming a thing of the past? To appeal to consumers concerned about the environment and overextending their finances, the nation's leading homebuilder, D.R. Horton, has begun building smaller homes.

trademark
a brand that is registered with the U.S. Patent and Trademark Office and is thus legally protected from use by any other firm

manufacturer brands
brands initiated and owned by the manufacturer to identify products from the point of production to the point of purchase

private distributor brands
brands, which may cost less than manufacturer brands, that are owned and controlled by a wholesaler or retailer

brand names that are used to identify entire product categories, much like Xerox has become synonymous with photocopying and Kleenex with tissues. Protecting a brand name is important in maintaining a brand identity. The world's 10 most valuable brands are shown in Table 12.1. The brand name is the part of the brand that can be spoken and consists of letters, words, and numbers—such as WD-40 lubricant. A *brand mark* is the part of the brand that is a distinctive design, such as the silver star on the hood of a Mercedes or McDonald's golden arches logo. A **trademark** is a brand that is registered with the U.S. Patent and Trademark Office and is thus legally protected from use by any other firm.

Two major categories of brands are manufacturer brands and private distributor brands. **Manufacturer brands** are brands initiated and owned by the manufacturer to identify products from the point of production to the point of purchase. Kellogg's, Sony, and Texaco are examples. **Private distributor brands,** which may be less expensive than manufacturer brands, are owned and controlled by a wholesaler or retailer, such as Kenmore appliances (Sears) and Sam's grocery products (Walmart and Sam's Wholesale Club). The names of private brands do not usually identify their manufacturer. While private-label brands were once considered cheaper and of poor quality, such as Walmart's Ol' Roy dog food, many private-label brands are increasing quality and image and competing with national brands.

TABLE 12.1

The 10 Most Valuable
Brands in the World

Rank	Brand	Brand Value ($ Billions)	Brand Value Change
1.	Google	$100,039	16%
2.	Microsoft	76,249	8
3.	Coca-Cola	67,625	16
4.	IBM	66,622	20
5.	McDonald's	66,575	34
6.	Apple	63,113	14
7.	China Mobile	61,283	7
8.	GE	59,793	−16
9.	Vodafone	53,727	45
10.	Marlboro	49,460	33

Source: "Brandz Top 100 Most Valuable Global Brands 2009," Milward Brown Optimor, http://www.millwardbrown.com/
Sites/Optimor/Media/Pdfs/en/BrandZ/BrandZ-2009-Report.pdf (accessed March 29, 2010).

For instance, several companies are hiring professional designers to design their private-label brands, replacing the traditional two-color packaging schemes often associated with private-label products. In fact, the grocery retailer Tesco has four types of private-label brands, and its branding strategy has performed so effectively that consumers may end up paying more for Tesco's own products than for branded goods.[16] Manufacturer brands are fighting hard against private distributor brands.

Another type of brand that has developed is **generic products**—products with no brand name at all. They often come in plain simple packages that carry only the generic name of the product—peanut butter, tomato juice, aspirin, dog food, and so on. They appeal to consumers who may be willing to sacrifice quality or product consistency to get a lower price.

generic products
products with no brand name that often come in simple packages and carry only their generic name

Companies use two basic approaches to branding multiple products. In one, a company gives each product within its complete product mix its own brand name. Warner-Lambert, for example, sells many well-known consumer products—Dentyne, Chiclets, Listerine, Halls, Rolaids, and Trident—each individually branded. This branding policy ensures that the name of one product does not affect the names of others, and different brands can be targeted at different segments of the same market, increasing the company's market share (its percentage of the sales for the total market for a product). Another approach to branding is to develop a family of brands with each of the firm's products carrying the same name or at least part of the name. Gillette, Sara Lee, and IBM use this approach. Finally, consumers may react differently to domestic versus foreign brands. Table 12.2 provides a snapshot of the most popular car brands. Notice that they are all Japanese and American brands.

Packaging.   The **packaging,** or external container that holds and describes the product, influences consumers' attitudes and their buying decisions. In a Harris Interactive Panel, three-fourths of respondents replied they would be willing to pay more money for certain packaging attributes. Some of the more important attributes cited included reusability, "staying fresh longer," and stating that the product is "made in the United States."[17] It is estimated that consumers' eyes linger only 2.5 seconds on each product on an average shopping trip; therefore, product packaging should be designed to attract and hold consumers' attention.

packaging
the external container that holds and describes the product

Ranking	Car Model	Country of Origin
1	Ford F-Series Pickup	United States
2	Toyota Camry/Solara	Japan
3	Chevrolet Silverado	United States
4	Toyota Corolla/Matrix	Japan
5	Honda Accord	Japan
6	Nissan Altima	Japan
7	Ford Escape	United States
8	Honda CR-V	Japan
9	Ford Fusion	United States
10	Honda Civic	Japan

TABLE 12.2 Best-Selling Cars

Source: Joann Muller, "In Pictures: Top 10 Cars of 2009," *Forbes,* December 23, 2009, http://www.forbes.com/2009/12/23/best-selling-cars-business-autos-ford-toyota_slide_2.html (accessed March 31, 2010).

A package can perform several functions including protection, economy, convenience, and promotion. Beverage manufacturers have been redesigning their bottles to make them more convenient for consumers and to promote them to certain markets. Scientists videotaped people drinking from different types of bottles and made plaster casts of their hands. They found that the average gulp is around 1 ounce and that half the population would rather suck liquid through a pop-up top than sip it. Since the early 1990s, soft drinks in 20-ounce plastic bottles revitalized U.S. sales for Coca-Cola and PepsiCo by getting Americans to drink larger servings. Recent concerns about health and the desire for lower-priced options have led both companies to test a variety of smaller container sizes to win back lost customers.[18]

labeling
the presentation of important information on a package

Labeling.   **Labeling,** the presentation of important information on the package, is closely associated with packaging. The content of labeling, often required by law, may include ingredients or content, nutrition facts (calories, fat, etc.), care instructions, suggestions for use (such as recipes), the manufacturer's address and toll-free number, Web site, and other useful information. This information can have a strong impact on sales. The labels of many products, particularly food and drugs, must carry warnings, instructions, certifications, or manufacturers' identifications.

quality
the degree to which a good, service, or idea meets the demands and requirements of customers

Product Quality.   **Quality** reflects the degree to which a good, service, or idea meets the demands and requirements of customers. Quality products are often referred to as reliable, durable, easily maintained, easily used, a good value, or a trusted brand name. The level of quality is the amount of quality that a product possesses, and the consistency of quality depends on the product maintaining the same level of quality over time.

Quality of service is difficult to gauge because it depends on customers' perceptions of how well the service meets or exceeds their expectations. In other words, service quality is judged by consumers, not the service providers. A bank may define service quality as employing friendly and knowledgeable employees, but the bank's customers may be more concerned with waiting time, ATM access, security, and statement accuracy. Similarly, an airline traveler considers on-time arrival, on-board food service, and satisfaction with the ticketing and boarding process. The American Customer Satisfaction Index produces customer satisfaction scores

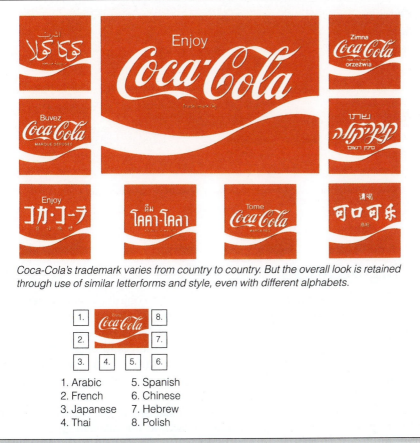

Coca-Cola's trademark varies from country to country. But the overall look is retained through use of similar letterforms and style, even with different alphabets.

1. Arabic   5. Spanish
2. French   6. Chinese
3. Japanese   7. Hebrew
4. Thai   8. Polish

Coca-Cola is one of the most valuable brands in the world.

for 10 economic sectors, 44 industries, and more than 200 companies. The latest results show that overall customer satisfaction was 76.0 (out of a possible 100), with increases in some industries balancing drops in others. Customer satisfaction with the wireless telephone industry reached its highest point, while the satisfaction score for the cable and satellite television industry went down 1.6 percent.[19] Table 12.3 shows the top 10 airlines in the Airline Quality Rankings. Hawaiian Airlines took the top ranking, while US Airways had the highest consumer complaint rate.[20]

The quality of services provided by businesses on the Internet can be gauged by consumers on such sites as ConsumerReports.org and BBBOnline. The subscription service offered by ConsumerReports.org provides consumers with a view of e-commerce sites' business, security, and privacy policies, while BBBOnline is dedicated to promoting responsibility online. As consumers join in by posting business and product reviews on the Internet on sites such as Yelp, the public can often get a much better idea of the quality of certain goods and services. Quality can also be associated with where the product is made. For example, "Made in U.S.A." labeling can be perceived as a different value and quality. For instance, there are differences in the perception of quality and value between the U.S. consumers and Europeans when comparing products made in the United States, Japan, Korea and China.[21]

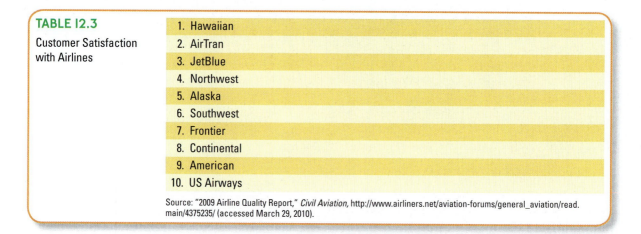

TABLE 12.3

Customer Satisfaction with Airlines

1. Hawaiian
2. AirTran
3. JetBlue
4. Northwest
5. Alaska
6. Southwest
7. Frontier
8. Continental
9. American
10. US Airways

Source: "2009 Airline Quality Report," *Civil Aviation,* http://www.airliners.net/aviation-forums/general_aviation/read. main/4375235/ (accessed March 29, 2010).

Pricing Strategy

Previously, we defined price as the value placed on an object exchanged between a buyer and a seller. Buyers' interest in price stems from their expectations about the usefulness of a product or the satisfaction they may derive from it. Because buyers have limited resources, they must allocate those resources to obtain the products they most desire. They must decide whether the benefits gained in an exchange are worth the buying power sacrificed. Almost anything of value can be assessed by a price. Many factors may influence the evaluation of value, including time constraints, price levels, perceived quality, and motivations to use available information about prices.[22] Figure 12.6 illustrates a method for calculating the value of your product. Indeed, consumers vary in their response to price: Some focus solely on the lowest price, while others consider quality or the prestige associated with a product and its price. Some types of consumers are increasingly "trading up" to more status-conscious products, such as automobiles, home appliances, restaurants, and even pet food, yet remain price-conscious for other products such as

FIGURE 12.6   Calculating the Value of Your Product

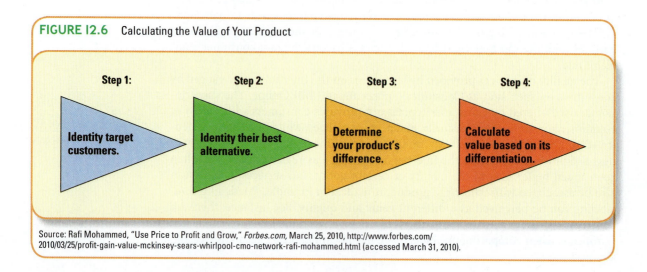

Source: Rafi Mohammed, "Use Price to Profit and Grow," *Forbes.com,* March 25, 2010, http://www.forbes.com/ 2010/03/25/profit-gain-value-mckinsey-sears-whirlpool-cmo-network-rafi-mohammed.html (accessed March 31, 2010).

cleaning and grocery goods. In setting prices, marketers must consider not just a company's cost to produce a product or service, but the perceived value of that item in the marketplace. Products' perceived value has benefited marketers at Starbucks, Sub-Zero, BMW, and Petco—which can charge premium prices for high-quality, prestige products—as well as Sam's Clubs and Costco—which offer basic household products at everyday low prices.

Price is a key element in the marketing mix because it relates directly to the generation of revenue and profits. In large part, the ability to set a price depends on the supply of and demand for a product. For most products, the quantity demanded goes up as the price goes down, and as the price goes up, the quantity demanded goes down. Changes in buyers' needs, variations in the effectiveness of other marketing mix variables, the presence of substitutes, and dynamic environmental factors can influence demand. New demand has greatly increased prices for industrial-grade diamonds as jewelers have turned to the impure gems, typically used for drill bits and saws, as a fashion statement. Even diamond giant De Beers has turned to the fashion, with its Talisman collection of rough-cut and uncut diamond jewelry capitalizing on ancient beliefs of the power and allure of uncut diamonds.[23]

Price is probably the most flexible variable in the marketing mix. Although it may take years to develop a product, establish channels of distribution, and design and implement promotion, a product's price may be set and changed in a few minutes. Under certain circumstances, of course, the price may not be so flexible, especially if government regulations prevent dealers from controlling prices. Of course, price also depends on the cost to manufacture a good or provide a service or idea. A firm may temporarily sell products below cost to match competition, to generate cash flow, or even to increase market share, but in the long run it cannot survive by selling its products below cost.

Pricing Objectives

Pricing objectives specify the role of price in an organization's marketing mix and strategy. They usually are influenced not only by marketing mix decisions but also by finance, accounting, and production factors. Maximizing profits and sales, boosting market share, maintaining the status quo, and survival are four common pricing objectives.

Specific Pricing Strategies

Pricing strategies provide guidelines for achieving the company's pricing objectives and overall marketing strategy. They specify how price will be used as a variable in the marketing mix. Significant pricing strategies relate to the pricing of new products, psychological pricing, and price discounting.

Apple used a price-skimming strategy when it first launched the iPhone. The device initially cost $599. By pricing their products high, companies like Apple can recover the high costs of developing them more quickly by selling them to consumers who consider them to be status symbols.

price skimming
charging the highest possible price that buyers who want the product will pay

Pricing New Products.   Setting the price for a new product is critical: The right price leads to profitability; the wrong price may kill the product. In general, there are two basic strategies to setting the base price for a new product. **Price skimming**

Going Green
General Mills Breaks into Organic Foods under a New Name

General Mills is stepping into the fast-growing organic foods industry. In 1999, it became the owner of the organic brand Cascadian Farm. However, you will not find the General Mills name on Cascadian Farm packaging or on its Web site. General Mills has chosen to maintain the Cascadian Farm name and take advantage of the brand equity associated with it.

Cascadian Farm was founded in 1972 by Gene Kahn. Located in the Northern Cascade Mountains of Washington, Kahn's organic farm gained support in farmer's markets and grocery stores. In 1998, the company merged with Muir Glen, becoming Small Planet Foods, and in 1999, Kahn sold the company to General Mills for an undisclosed amount. He then joined General Mills and was promoted to vice president and global sustainability officer in 2007.

Kahn believes that joining General Mills has allowed for a more diverse distribution strategy for his organic products and has allowed him to spread the word on a much larger scale, thanks to General Mills' larger collection of resources. These same resources make Cascadian Farm products available in stores such as Walmart, where they are sold at more affordable prices. However, some organic food enthusiasts are not

so optimistic. In one study, several participants judged the Cascadian Farm brand favorably. Yet when it was announced that Cascadian Farm was owned by General Mills, the energy of the group dropped, with some individuals claiming they would never again purchase Cascadian Farm products. They thought they were purchasing products produced at a small farm rather than what some termed an "agribusiness." This brings up the issue of authenticity—has the Cascadian Farm brand been compromised by its association with General Mills? This issue reinforces the care that marketers must take when choosing a particular type of branding strategy.[24]

Discussion Questions:

1. Why did General Mills choose to keep the Cascadian Farms brand name separate? Do you think it was a good idea?
2. What was the advantage to General Mills of acquiring an organic foods line?
3. Do you think General Mills has compromised the authenticity of the Cascadian Farm brand? Keep in mind that Gene Kahn remains highly involved in the brand.

---

is charging the highest possible price that buyers who want the product will pay. Starbuck's new Via coffee, for example, sells at a price of $2.95 for a trio of single-serve packets and $9.95 for 12 packets. Per serving, Via is priced four times higher than market leader Nestlé.[25] This strategy allows the company to generate much-needed revenue to help offset the costs of research and development. Conversely, a **penetration price** is a low price designed to help a product enter the market and gain market share rapidly. For example, when Industrias Añaños introduced Kola Real to capitalize on limited penetration of Coca-Cola and Pepsi Cola in Peru, it set an ultralow penetration price to appeal to the poor who predominate in the region. Kola Real quickly secured one-fifth of the Peruvian market and has since made significant gains in Ecuador, Venezuela, and Mexico, forcing larger soft-drink marketers to cut prices.[26] Penetration pricing is less flexible than price skimming; it is more difficult to raise a penetration price than to lower a skimming price. Penetration pricing is used most often when marketers suspect that competitors will enter the market shortly after the product has been introduced.

penetration price
a low price designed to help a product enter the market and gain market share rapidly

psychological pricing
encouraging purchases based on emotional rather than rational responses to the price

Psychological Pricing. **Psychological pricing** encourages purchases based on emotional rather than rational responses to the price. For example, the assumption behind *even/odd pricing* is that people will buy more of a product for $9.99 than $10 because it seems to be a bargain at the odd price. The assumption behind *symbolic/prestige pricing* is that high prices connote high quality. Thus the prices of certain fragrances are set artificially high to give the impression of superior quality. Some over-the-counter drugs are priced high because consumers associate a drug's price with potency.

Price Discounting. Temporary price reductions, or **discounts,** are often employed to boost sales. Although there are many types, quantity, seasonal, and promotional discounts are among the most widely used. Quantity discounts reflect the economies of purchasing in large volume. Seasonal discounts to buyers who purchase goods or services out of season help even out production capacity. Promotional discounts attempt to improve sales by advertising price reductions on selected products to increase customer interest. Often promotional pricing is geared toward increased profits. Taco Bell, with its reputation for value, has been labeled the "best-positioned U.S. brand" to do well in a recession economy as consumers look for cheaper fast-food options. Taco Bell offers a Why Pay More? menu with selections priced at 79¢, 89¢, and 99¢. KFC, Wendy's, and McDonald's all offer Value Menus as well, with items priced around $1.

discounts
temporary price reductions, often employed to boost sales

Distribution Strategy

The best products in the world will not be successful unless companies make them available where and when customers want to buy them. In this section, we will explore dimensions of distribution strategy, including the channels through which products are distributed, the intensity of market coverage, and the physical handling of products during distribution.

Marketing Channels

A **marketing channel,** or channel of distribution, is a group of organizations that moves products from their producer to customers. Marketing channels make products available to buyers when and where they desire to purchase them. Organizations that bridge the gap between a product's manufacturer and the ultimate consumer are called *middlemen,* or intermediaries. They create time, place, and ownership utility. Two intermediary organizations are retailers and wholesalers.

Retailers buy products from manufacturers (or other intermediaries) and sell them to consumers for home and household use rather than for resale or for use in producing other products. Toys 'Я' Us, for example, buys products from Mattel and other manufacturers and resells them to consumers. Retailing usually occurs in a store, but the Internet, vending machines, mail-order catalogs, and entertainment, such as going to a Chicago Bulls basketball game, also provide opportunities for retailing. With more than 340 million Americans and a high Internet access rate, U.S. e-commerce sales were approximately $132 billion in 2009.[27] By bringing together an assortment of products from competing producers, retailers create utility. Retailers arrange for products to be moved from producers to a convenient retail establishment (place utility). They maintain hours of operation for their retail stores to make merchandise available when consumers want it (time utility). They also assume the risk of ownership of inventories (ownership utility). Table 12.4 describes various types of general merchandise retailers.

Today, there are too many stores competing for too few customers, and, as a result, competition between similar retailers has never been more intense. In addition, retailers face challenges such as shoplifting, as indicated in Table 12.5. Further, competition between different types of stores is changing the nature of retailing. Supermarkets compete with specialty food stores, wholesale clubs, and discount stores. Department stores compete with nearly every other type of store including specialty stores, off-price chains, category killers, discount stores, and online retailers. Many traditional retailers, such as Walmart and Macy's, have created online shopping sites

marketing channel
a group of organizations that moves products from their producer to customers; also called a channel of distribution

retailers
intermediaries who buy products from manufacturers (or other intermediaries) and sell them to consumers for home and household use rather than for resale or for use in producing other products

TABLE I2.4   General Merchandise Retailers

Type of Retailer	Description	Examples
Department store	Large organization offering wide product mix and organized into separate departments	Macy's, JCPenney, Sears
Discount store	Self-service, general merchandise store offering brand name and private brand products at low prices	Walmart, Target
Supermarket	Self-service store offering complete line of food products and some nonfood products	Kroger, Albertson's, Winn-Dixie
Superstore	Giant outlet offering all food and nonfood products found in supermarkets, as well as most routinely purchased products	Walmart Supercenters
Hypermarket	Combination supermarket and discount store, larger than a superstore	Carrefour
Warehouse club	Large-scale, members-only establishments combining cash-and-carry wholesaling with discount retailing	Sam's Club, Costco
Warehouse showroom	Facility in a large, low-cost building with large on-premises inventories and minimum service	Ikea
Catalog showroom	Type of warehouse showroom where consumers shop from a catalog and products are stored out of buyers' reach and provided in manufacturer's carton	Service Merchandise

Source: William M. Pride and O. C. Ferrell, *Marketing: Concepts and Strategies,* 2008, p. 428. Copyright 2008 by Houghton Mifflin Company. Reprinted with permission.

TABLE I2.5

Statistics on Shoplifting in the United States

Shoplifters in the United States	27 million (1 in 11 people)
Amount retailers lose per year	More than $13 billion (more than $35 million per day)
Percent of shoplifters who are adults	75%
Percent of adult shoplifters that started in their teens	55%
Habitual shoplifters steal on average	About 1.6 times per week

Source: "Shoplifting Statistics," National Association for Shoplifting Prevention, http://www.shopliftingprevention.org/ WhatNASPOffers/NRC/PublicEducStats.htm (accessed March 31, 2010).

to retain customers and compete with online-only retailers. One of the best-known online-only, or cyber, merchants is Amazon.com. Amazon offers millions of products from which to choose, all from the privacy and convenience of the purchaser's home. In some cases, Web merchants offer wide selections, ultra-convenience, superior service, knowledge, and the best products.

Wholesalers are intermediaries who buy from producers or from other wholesalers and sell to retailers. They usually do not sell in significant quantities to ultimate consumers. Wholesalers perform the functions listed in Table 12.6.

Wholesalers are extremely important because of the marketing activities they perform, particularly for consumer products. Although it is true that wholesalers can be eliminated, their functions must be passed on to some other entity, such as the producer, another intermediary, or even the customer. Wholesalers help

wholesalers
intermediaries who buy from producers or from other wholesalers and sell to retailers

TABLE 12.6   Major Wholesaling Functions

Supply chain management	Creating long-term partnerships among channel members
Promotion	Providing a sales force, advertising, sales promotion, and publicity
Warehousing, shipping, and product handling	Receiving, storing, and stockkeeping Packaging Shipping outgoing orders Materials handling Arranging and making local and long distance shipments
Inventory control and data processing	Processing orders Controlling physical inventory Recording transactions Tracking sales data for financial analysis
Risk taking	Assuming responsibility for theft, product obsolescence, and excess inventories
Financing and budgeting	Extending credit Making capital investments Forecasting cash flow
Marketing research and information systems	Providing information about market Conducting research studies Managing computer networks to facilitate exchanges and relationships

Source: William M. Pride and O. C. Ferrell, *Marketing: Concepts and Strategies,* 2008, p. 389. Copyright 2008 by Houghton Mifflin Company. Reprinted with permission.

consumers and retailers by buying in large quantities, then selling to retailers in smaller quantities. By stocking an assortment of products, wholesalers match products to demand.

Supply Chain Management.   In an effort to improve distribution channel relationships among manufacturers and other channel intermediaries, supply chain management creates alliances between channel members. In Chapter 8, we defined supply chain management as connecting and integrating all parties or members of the distribution system in order to satisfy customers. It involves long-term partnerships among marketing channel members working together to reduce costs, waste, and unnecessary movement in the entire marketing channel in order to satisfy customers. It goes beyond traditional channel members (producers, wholesalers, retailers, customers) to include *all* organizations involved in moving products from the producer to the ultimate customer. In a survey of business managers, a disruption in the supply chain was viewed as the number-one crisis that could decrease revenue.[28]

The focus shifts from one of selling to the next level in the channel to one of selling products *through* the channel to a satisfied ultimate customer. Information, once provided on a guarded, "as needed" basis, is now open, honest, and ongoing. Perhaps most importantly, the points of contact in the relationship expand from one-on-one at the salesperson–buyer level to multiple interfaces at all levels and in all functional areas of the various organizations.

Channels for Consumer Products.   Typical marketing channels for consumer products are shown in Figure 12.7. In Channel A, the product moves from the producer directly to the consumer. Farmers who sell their fruit and vegetables to consumers at roadside stands use a direct-from-producer-to-consumer marketing channel.

FIGURE I2.7

Marketing Channels for
Consumer Products

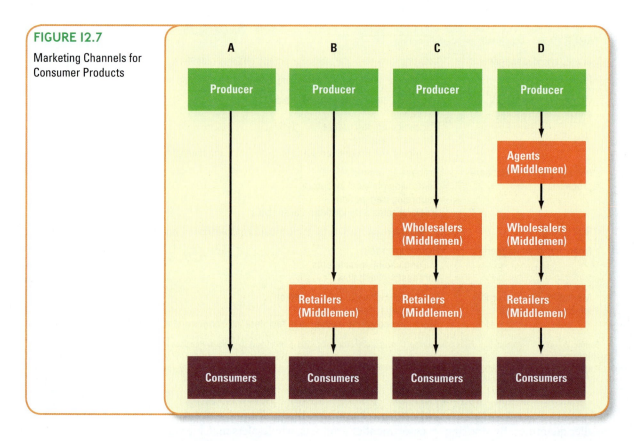

In Channel B, the product goes from producer to retailer to consumer. This type of channel is used for products such as college textbooks, automobiles, and appliances. In Channel C, the product is handled by a wholesaler and a retailer before it reaches the consumer. Producer-to-wholesaler-to-retailer-to-consumer marketing channels distribute a wide range of products including refrigerators, televisions, soft drinks, cigarettes, clocks, watches, and office products. In Channel D, the product goes to an agent, a wholesaler, and a retailer before going to the consumer. This long channel of distribution is especially useful for convenience products. Candy and some produce are often sold by agents who bring buyers and sellers together.

Services are usually distributed through direct marketing channels because they are generally produced *and* consumed simultaneously. For example, you cannot take a haircut home for later use. Many services require the customer's presence and participation: The sick patient must visit the physician to receive treatment; the child must be at the day care center to receive care; the tourist must be present to sightsee and consume tourism services.

Channels for Business Products.   In contrast to consumer goods, more than half of all business products, especially expensive equipment or technically complex products, are sold through direct marketing channels. Business customers like to communicate directly with producers of such products to gain the technical assistance and personal assurances that only the producer can offer. For this reason, business buyers prefer to purchase expensive and highly complex mainframe computers directly from IBM, Cray, and other mainframe producers. Other business products

Ruan is a trucking company that helps other firms keep their supply chains moving efficiently.

may be distributed through channels employing wholesaling intermediaries such as industrial distributors and/or manufacturer's agents.

Intensity of Market Coverage

A major distribution decision is how widely to distribute a product—that is, how many and what type of outlets should carry it. The intensity of market coverage depends on buyer behavior, as well as the nature of the target market and the competition. Wholesalers and retailers provide various intensities of market coverage and must be selected carefully to ensure success. Market coverage may be intensive, selective, or exclusive.

Intensive distribution makes a product available in as many outlets as possible. Because availability is important to purchasers of convenience products such as bread, milk, gasoline, soft drinks, and chewing gum, a nearby location with a minimum of time spent searching and waiting in line is most important to the consumer. To saturate markets intensively, wholesalers and many varied retailers try to make the product available at every location where a consumer might desire to purchase it. Zoom Systems provides robotic vending machines for products beyond candy and drinks. Zoom has more than a thousand machines in airports and hotels across the United States, some selling items such as Apple iPods, Neutrogena hair and skin products, and Sony products. The vending machines accept credit cards and allow

intensive distribution
a form of market coverage whereby a product is made available in as many outlets as possible

Redbox has made inroads against competitors like Blockbuster using an intensive distribution. Its movie-rental machines are conveniently located where consumers congregate—in restaurants, grocery stores, and drugstores.

selective distribution
a form of market coverage whereby only a small number of all available outlets are used to expose products

exclusive distribution
the awarding by a manufacturer to an intermediary of the sole right to sell a product in a defined geographic territory

sales to occur in places where storefronts would be impossible.[29] Through partnering with different companies, today's ZoomShops sell a variety of brands including products from Sephora, Best Buy, Macy's, and Rosetta Stone.[30]

Selective distribution uses only a small number of all available outlets to expose products. It is used most often for products that consumers buy only after shopping and comparing price, quality, and style. Many products sold on a selective basis require salesperson assistance, technical advice, warranties, or repair service to maintain consumer satisfaction. Typical products include automobiles, major appliances, clothes, and furniture.

Exclusive distribution exists when a manufacturer gives an intermediary the sole right to sell a product in a defined geographic territory. Such exclusivity provides an incentive for a dealer to handle a product that has a limited market. Exclusive distribution is the opposite of intensive distribution in that products are purchased and consumed over a long period of time, and service or information is required to develop a satisfactory sales relationship. Products distributed on an exclusive basis include high-quality musical instruments, yachts, airplanes, and high-fashion leather goods.

Physical Distribution

physical distribution
all the activities necessary to move products from producers to customers—inventory control, transportation, warehousing, and materials handling

Physical distribution includes all the activities necessary to move products from producers to customers—inventory control, transportation, warehousing, and materials handling. Physical distribution creates time and place utility by making products available when they are wanted, with adequate service and at minimum cost. Both goods and services require physical distribution. Many physical distribution activities are part of supply chain management, which we discussed in Chapter 8; we'll take a brief look at a few more now.

Transportation.   **Transportation,** the shipment of products to buyers, creates time and place utility for products, and thus is a key element in the flow of goods and services from producer to consumer. The five major modes of transportation used to move products between cities in the United States are railways, motor vehicles, inland waterways, pipelines, and airways.

Railroads offer the least expensive transportation for many products. Heavy commodities, foodstuffs, raw materials, and coal are examples of products carried by railroads. Trucks have greater flexibility than railroads because they can reach more locations. Trucks handle freight quickly and economically, offer door-to-door service, and are more flexible in their packaging requirements than are ships or airplanes. Air transport offers speed and a high degree of dependability but is the most expensive means of transportation; shipping is the least expensive and slowest form. Pipelines are used to transport petroleum, natural gas, semiliquid coal, wood chips, and certain chemicals. Many products can be moved most efficiently by using more than one mode of transportation.

Factors affecting the selection of a mode of transportation include cost, capability to handle the product, reliability, and availability, and, as suggested, selecting transportation modes requires trade-offs. Unique characteristics of the product and consumer desires often determine the mode selected.

transportation
the shipment of products to buyers

Warehousing.   **Warehousing** is the design and operation of facilities to receive, store, and ship products. A warehouse facility receives, identifies, sorts, and dispatches goods to storage; stores them; recalls, selects, or picks goods; assembles the shipment; and finally, dispatches the shipment.

Companies often own and operate their own private warehouses that store, handle, and move their own products. They can also rent storage and related physical distribution services from public warehouses. Regardless of whether a private or a public warehouse is used, warehousing is important because it makes products available for shipment to match demand at different geographic locations.

warehousing
the design and operation of facilities to receive, store, and ship products

Materials Handling.   **Materials handling** is the physical handling and movement of products in warehousing and transportation. Handling processes may vary significantly due to product characteristics. Efficient materials-handling procedures increase a warehouse's useful capacity and improve customer service. Well-coordinated loading and movement systems increase efficiency and reduce costs.

materials handling
the physical handling and movement of products in warehousing and transportation

Importance of Distribution in a Marketing Strategy

Distribution decisions are among the least flexible marketing mix decisions. Products can be changed over time; prices can be changed quickly; and promotion is usually changed regularly. But distribution decisions often commit resources and establish contractual relationships that are difficult if not impossible to change. As a company attempts to expand into new markets, it may require a complete change in distribution. Moreover, if a firm does not manage its marketing channel in the most efficient manner and provide the best service, then a new competitor will evolve to create a more effective distribution system.

Promotion Strategy

The role of promotion is to communicate with individuals, groups, and organizations to facilitate an exchange directly or indirectly. It encourages marketing exchanges by attempting to persuade individuals, groups, and organizations to accept goods, services, and ideas. Promotion is used not only to sell products but also to influence opinions and attitudes toward an organization, person, or cause. The state of Texas, for example, has successfully used promotion to educate people about the costs of highway litter and thereby reduce littering. Most people probably equate promotion with advertising, but it also includes personal selling, publicity, and sales promotion. The role that these elements play in a marketing strategy is extremely important.

The Promotion Mix

Advertising, personal selling, publicity, and sales promotion are collectively known as the promotion mix because a strong promotion program results from the careful selection and blending of these elements. The process of coordinating the promotion mix elements and synchronizing promotion as a unified effort is called **integrated marketing communications.** When planning promotional activities, an integrated marketing communications approach results in the desired message for customers. Different elements of the promotion mix are coordinated to play their appropriate roles in delivery of the message on a consistent basis.

integrated marketing communications
coordinating the promotion mix elements and synchronizing promotion as a unified effort

Advertising.   Perhaps the best-known form of promotion, **advertising** is a paid form of nonpersonal communication transmitted through a mass medium, such as television commercials, magazine advertisements or online ads. Even Google, one of the most powerful brands in the world, advertises. Google has turned to outdoor advertising on buses, trains, and ballparks in San Francisco and Chicago to promote its Google Maps feature.[32] Commercials featuring celebrities, customers, or unique creations (the Energizer Bunny, for example) serve to grab viewers' attention and pique their interest in a product. Table 12.7 shows companies that spent more than $1 billion on ads in the United States in one year.

advertising
a paid form of nonpersonal communication transmitted through a mass medium, such as television commercials or magazine advertisements

An **advertising campaign** involves designing a series of advertisements and placing them in various media to reach a particular target audience. The basic content and form of an advertising campaign are a function of several factors. A product's features, uses, and benefits affect the content of the campaign message and individual ads. Characteristics of the people in the target audience—gender, age, education,

advertising campaign
designing a series of advertisements and placing them in various media to reach a particular target market

race, income, occupation, lifestyle, and other attributes—influence both content and form. When Procter & Gamble promotes Crest toothpaste to children, the company emphasizes daily brushing and cavity control, whereas it promotes tartar control and whiter teeth when marketing to adults. To communicate effectively, advertisers use words, symbols, and illustrations that are meaningful, familiar, and attractive to people in the target audience.

An advertising campaign's objectives and platform also affect the content and form of its messages. If a firm's advertising objectives involve large sales increases, the message may include hard-hitting, high-impact language and symbols. When campaign objectives aim at increasing brand awareness, the message may use much repetition of the brand name and words and illustrations associated with it. Thus, the advertising platform is the foundation on which campaign messages are built.

Advertising media are the vehicles or forms of communication used to reach a desired audience. Print media include newspapers, magazines, direct mail, and billboards, while electronic media include television, radio, and cyber ads. Newspapers,television, and direct mail are the most widely used advertising media.

Choice of media obviously influences the content and form of the message. Effective outdoor displays and short broadcast spot announcements require concise, simple messages. Magazine and newspaper advertisements can include considerable detail and long explanations. Because several kinds of media offer geographic selectivity, a precise message can be tailored to a particular geographic

Organization	Advertising Expenditure ($ Millions)
1. Procter & Gamble Co.	$4,838.1
2. Verizon Communications	3,700.0
3. AT&T	3,073.0
4. General Motors Co.	2,901.1
5. Johnson & Johnson	2,529.2
6. Unilever	2,422.6
7. Walt Disney Corp.	2,217.6
8. Time Warner	2,207.7
9. General Electric Co.	2,019.3
10. Sears Holdings Corp.	1,864.9

TABLE 12.7

Top 10 Leading National Advertisers

Source: "Marketer Trees 2009," *Advertising Age,* http://adage.com/marketertrees09/ (accessed March 29, 2010).

Responding to Business Challenges
People across America Catch the Twitter Bug

Businesses big and small are discovering tweeting as a way to inform the world about their companies. By asking the question "What are you doing?" Twitter allows users to tell their followers about moments in their daily lives. Twitter users post messages of up to 140 characters through SMS, instant messaging, or the Twitter Web site. Based out of a South Park, San Francisco warehouse, Twitter was founded by Biz Stone and Evan Williams. It started as a podcasting company but quickly morphed into its current social networking form. People use Twitter for everything from "I'm catching some zzz's in class," to President Obama's "We just made history" on election night, to a San Francisco writer tweeting that his house was being broken into.

Many marketers have been quick to jump on the Twitter bandwagon, finding it to be an effective communications tool for attracting consumers. For example, Bradsdeals.com, a site that identifies online shopping deals, started posting company updates on Twitter. Within two months, the company had attracted 2,500 followers. NASA tweets to inform people about its space shuttle flights. Bakeries are even tweeting to tell customers when fresh cookies are available.

Of course, with the success of Twitter comes criticism as well. Some feel that many Twitter users post mundane details of their lives just to kill time. Yet these complaints have not dulled Twitter's success. With two-thirds of online users visiting social networking sites like Twitter, the Twitter craze is continuing at full force.[33]

Discussion Questions

1. Why is Twitter appealing to companies?
2. How could Twitter be used as a tool to strengthen customer relationships and to gather consumer feedback?
3. What are some of the drawbacks of using Twitter as a marketing tool?

---

section of the target audience. For example, a company advertising in *Time* might decide to use one message in the New England region and another in the rest of the nation. A company may also choose to advertise in only one region. Such geographic selectivity lets a firm use the same message in different regions at different times.

The use of online advertising is increasing. However, advertisers are demanding more for their ad dollars and proof that they are working. Certain types of ads are more popular than pop-up ads and banner ads that consumers find annoying. One technique is to blur the lines between television and online advertising. TV commercials may point viewers to a Web site for more information, where short "advertainment" films continue the marketing message. When godaddy.com's 2008 Super Bowl commercial was rejected by Fox for being too racy, it left the racy version on its Web site. The TV commercial that aired showed people watching the original commercial featuring racecar driver Danica Patrick online.[34]

Infomercials—typically 30-minute blocks of radio or television air time featuring a celebrity or upbeat host talking about and demonstrating a product—have evolved as an advertising method. Toll-free numbers and Web site addresses are usually provided so consumers can conveniently purchase the product or obtain additional information. Although many consumers and companies have negative feelings about infomercials, apparently they get results.

personal selling
direct, two-way communication with buyers and potential buyers

Personal Selling. **Personal selling** is direct, two-way communication with buyers and potential buyers. For many products—especially large, expensive ones with specialized uses, such as cars, appliances, and houses—interaction between a salesperson and the customer is probably the most important promotional tool.

Personal selling is the most flexible of the promotional methods because it gives marketers the greatest opportunity to communicate specific information that might trigger a purchase. Only personal selling can zero in on a prospect and attempt to persuade that person to make a purchase. Although personal selling has a lot of advantages, it is one of the most costly forms of promotion. A sales call on an industrial customer can cost as much as $200 or $300.

There are three distinct categories of salespersons: order takers (for example, retail sales clerks and route salespeople), creative salespersons (for example, automobile, furniture, and insurance salespeople), and support salespersons (for example, customer educators and goodwill builders who usually do not take orders). For most of these salespeople, personal selling is a six-step process:

1. *Prospecting:* Identifying potential buyers of the product.
2. *Approaching:* Using a referral or calling on a customer without prior notice to determine interest in the product.
3. *Presenting:* Getting the prospect's attention with a product demonstration.
4. *Handling objections:* Countering reasons for not buying the product.
5. *Closing:* Asking the prospect to buy the product.
6. *Following up:* Checking customer satisfaction with the purchased product.

Publicity.   **Publicity** is nonpersonal communication transmitted through the mass media but not paid for directly by the firm. A firm does not pay the media cost for publicity and is not identified as the originator of the message; instead, the message is presented in news story form. Obviously, a company can benefit from publicity by releasing to news sources newsworthy messages about the firm and its involvement with the public. Many companies have *public relations* departments to try to gain favorable publicity and minimize negative publicity for the firm.

publicity
nonpersonal communication transmitted through the mass media but not paid for directly by the firm

Although advertising and publicity are both carried by the mass media, they differ in several major ways. Advertising messages tend to be informative, persuasive, or both; publicity is mainly informative. Advertising is often designed to have an immediate impact or to provide specific information to persuade a person to act; publicity describes what a firm is doing, what products it is launching, or other newsworthy information, but seldom calls for action. When advertising is used, the organization must pay for media time and select the media that will best reach target audiences. The mass media willingly carry publicity because they believe it has general public interest. Advertising can be repeated a number of times; most publicity appears in the mass media once and is not repeated.

Advertising, personal selling, and sales promotion are especially useful for influencing an exchange directly. Publicity is extremely important when communication focuses on a company's activities and products and is directed at interest groups, current and potential investors, regulatory agencies, and society in general.

A variation of traditional advertising is buzz marketing, in which marketers attempt to create a trend or acceptance of a product. Companies seek out trendsetters in communities and get them to "talk up" a brand to their friends, family, coworkers, and others. For example, until recently, there was only one place in Japan where you could purchase a McDonald's Quarter Pounder burger. To promote its quarter pounders at other shops in Japan, McDonald's launched a buzz marketing campaign by replacing the Golden Arches sign out front of two Japanese restaurants with the signs "Quarter Pounder." Inside the restaurant, dim lighting and dark walls made it appear more like a disco, and the menu only had two items available: a double Quarter Pounder meal or a single Quarter Pounder.[35] Other marketers using the buzz technique include Hebrew National ("mom squads" grilled the company's hot dogs), and Chrysler (its retro PT Cruiser was planted in rental fleets). The idea behind buzz marketing is that an accepted member of a particular social group will be more credible than any form of paid communication.[36] The concept works best as part of an integrated marketing communication program that also includes traditional advertising, personal selling, sales promotion, and publicity.

A related concept is viral marketing, which describes the concept of getting Internet users to pass on ads and promotions to others. For example, the restaurant Kogi, which operates Korean taco trucks that traverse the Los Angeles area, was dubbed by *Newsweek* as "America's First Viral Restaurant" after it began using Twitter and the Web to announce the whereabouts of its taco trucks.[37]

sales promotion
direct inducements offering added value or some other incentive for buyers to enter into an exchange

Sales Promotion.   **Sales promotion** involves direct inducements offering added value or some other incentive for buyers to enter into an exchange. Sales promotions are generally easier to measure and less expensive than advertising. The major tools of sales promotion are store displays, premiums, samples and demonstrations, coupons, contests and sweepstakes, refunds, and trade shows. Coupon-clipping in particular has become more common during the recent recession. While coupons in the past decade traditionally had a fairly low redemption rate, with about 2 percent being redeemed, the recent recession caused an upsurge in coupon usage. In one marketing research study, 60 percent of respondents under the age of 35 reported using coupons during a six-month period. The Web site "Coupon Mom" also saw a significant rise in membership, from a membership of 100,000 per month to 1.5 million per month one year later.[38] While coupons can be a valuable tool in sales promotion, they cannot be relied upon to stand, but should be part of an overall promotion mix. Sales promotion stimulates customer purchasing and increases dealer effectiveness in selling products. It is used to enhance and supplement other forms of promotion. Test drives allow salespersons to demonstrate vehicles, which can help purchase decisions. Sampling a product may also encourage consumers to buy. PepsiCo, for example, used sampling to promote its Sierra Mist soft drink to reach more than 5 million potential consumers at well-traveled sites such as Times Square and Penn Station.[39] In a given year, almost three-fourths of consumer product companies may use sampling.

Promotion Strategies: To Push or To Pull

push strategy
an attempt to motivate intermediaries to push the product down to their customers

pull strategy
the use of promotion to create consumer demand for a product so that consumers exert pressure on marketing channel members to make it available

In developing a promotion mix, organizations must decide whether to fashion a mix that pushes or pulls the product (Figure 12.8). A **push strategy** attempts to motivate intermediaries to push the product down to their customers. When a push strategy is used, the company attempts to motivate wholesalers and retailers to make the product available to their customers. Sales personnel may be used to persuade intermediaries to offer the product, distribute promotional materials, and offer special promotional incentives for those who agree to carry the product. For example, Kimberly Clark has begun partnering with its retailers to create a "win–win situation" for both types of companies. By sharing point-of-sales data with retailers and running more effective promotions, Kimberly Clark hopes to create favorable relationships with its intermediaries to push its products through the system.[40] A **pull strategy** uses promotion to create consumer demand for a product so that consumers exert pressure on marketing channel members to

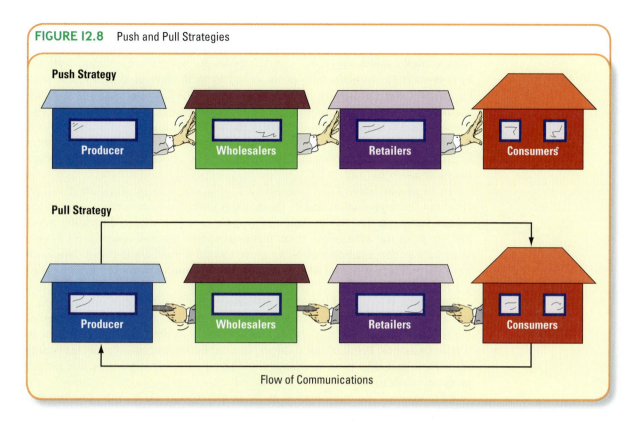

FIGURE I2.8   Push and Pull Strategies

Push Strategy

Producer → Wholesalers → Retailers → Consumers

Pull Strategy

Producer → Wholesalers → Retailers → Consumers

Flow of Communications

make it available. For example, when the Coca-Cola Company launched its hybrid energy soda VAULT, the company gave away samples throughout the United States via sampling teams in VAULT-branded International CXTs, the world's largest production pickup trucks. They distributed ice-cold VAULT at concerts and targeted retail outlets, sporting events, and other locations.[41] Such sampling prior to a product rollout encourages consumers to request the product from their favorite retailer.

A company can use either strategy, or it can use a variation or combination of the two. The exclusive use of advertising indicates a pull strategy. Personal selling to marketing channel members indicates a push strategy. The allocation of promotional resources to various marketing mix elements probably determines which strategy a marketer uses.

Objectives of Promotion

The marketing mix a company uses depends on its objectives. It is important to recognize that promotion is only one element of the marketing strategy and must be tied carefully to the goals of the firm, its overall marketing objectives, and the other elements of the marketing strategy. Firms use promotion for many reasons, but typical objectives are to stimulate demand, to stabilize sales, and to inform, remind, and reinforce customers.

Increasing demand for a product is probably the most typical promotional objective. Stimulating demand, often through advertising and sales promotion, is particularly important when a firm is using a pull strategy.

Another goal of promotion is to stabilize sales by maintaining the status quo—that is, the current sales level of the product. During periods of slack or decreasing sales, contests, prizes, vacations, and other sales promotions are sometimes offered to customers to maintain sales goals. Advertising is often used to stabilize sales by making customers aware of slack use periods. For example, auto manufacturers often provide rebates, free options, or lower-than-market interest rates to stabilize sales and thereby keep production lines moving during temporary slowdowns. A stable sales pattern allows the firm to run efficiently by maintaining a consistent level of production and storage and utilizing all its functions so that it is ready when sales increase.

An important role of any promotional program is to inform potential buyers about the organization and its products. A major portion of advertising in the United States, particularly in daily newspapers, is informational. Providing information about the availability, price, technology, and features of a product is very important in encouraging a buyer to move toward a purchase decision. Nearly all forms of promotion involve an attempt to help consumers learn more about a product and a company.

Promotion is also used to remind consumers that an established organization is still around and sells certain products that have uses and benefits. Often advertising reminds customers that they may need to use a product more frequently or in certain situations. Pennzoil, for example, has run television commercials reminding car owners that they need to change their oil every 3,000 miles to ensure proper performance of their cars.

Reinforcement promotion attempts to assure current users of the product that they have made the right choice and tells them how to get the most satisfaction from the product. Also, a company could release publicity statements through the news media about a new use for a product. Additionally, firms can have salespeople communicate with current and potential customers about the proper use and maintenance of a product—all in the hope of developing a repeat customer.

Promotional Positioning

promotional positioning
the use of promotion to create and maintain an image of a product in buyers' minds

Promotional positioning uses promotion to create and maintain an image of a product in buyers' minds. It is a natural result of market segmentation. In both promotional positioning and market segmentation, the firm targets a given product or brand at a portion of the total market. A promotional strategy helps differentiate the product and make it appeal to a particular market segment. For example, to appeal to safety-conscious consumers, Volvo heavily promotes the safety and crashworthiness of Volvo automobiles in its advertising. Volkswagen has done the same thing with its edgy ads showing car crashes. Promotion can be used to change or reinforce an image. Effective promotion influences customers and persuades them to buy.

So You Want to Be a Marketing Manager

Many jobs in marketing are closely tied to the marketing mix functions: distribution, product, promotion, and price. Often the job titles could be sales manager, distribution or supply chain manager, advertising account executive, or store manager.

A distribution manager arranges for transportation of goods within firms and through marketing channels. Transportation can be costly, and time is always an important factor, so minimizing their effects is vital to the success of a firm. Distribution managers must choose one or a combination of transportation modes from a vast array of options, taking into account local, federal, and international regulations for different freight classifications; the weight, size, and fragility of products to be shipped; time schedules; and loss and damage ratios. Manufacturing firms are the largest employers of distribution managers.

A product manager is responsible for the success or failure of a product line. This requires a general knowledge of advertising, transportation modes, inventory control, selling and sales management, promotion, marketing research, packaging, and pricing. Frequently, several years of selling and sales management experience are prerequisites for such a position as well as college training in business administration. Being a product manager can be rewarding both financially and psychologically.

Some of the most creative roles in the business world are in the area of advertising. Advertising pervades our daily lives, as businesses and other organizations try to grab our attention and tell us about what they have to offer. Copywriters, artists, and account executives in advertising must have creativity, imagination, artistic talent, and expertise in expression and persuasion. Advertising is an area of business in which a wide variety of educational backgrounds may be useful, from degrees in advertising itself, to journalism or liberal arts degrees. Common entry-level positions in an advertising agency are found in the traffic department, account service (account coordinator), or the media department (media assistant). Advertising jobs are also available in many manufacturing or retail firms, nonprofit organizations, banks, professional associations, utility companies, and other arenas outside of an advertising agency.

Although a career in retailing may begin in sales, there is much more to retailing than simply selling. Many retail personnel occupy management positions, focusing on selecting and ordering merchandise, promotional activities, inventory control, customer credit operations, accounting, personnel, and store security. Many specific examples of retailing jobs can be found in large department stores. A section manager coordinates inventory and promotions and interacts with buyers, salespeople, and consumers. The buyer's job is fast-paced, often involving much travel and pressure. Buyers must be open-minded and foresighted in their hunt for new, potentially successful items. Regional managers coordinate the activities of several retail stores within a specific geographic area, usually monitoring and supporting sales, promotions, and general procedures. Retail management can be exciting and challenging. Growth in retailing is expected to accompany the growth in population and is likely to create substantial opportunities in the coming years.

While a career in marketing can be very rewarding, marketers today agree that the job is getting tougher. Many advertising and marketing executives say the job has gotten much more demanding in the past 10 years, viewing their number-one challenge as balancing work and personal obligations. Other challenges include staying current on industry trends or technologies, keeping motivated/inspired on the job, and measuring success. If you are up to the challenge, you may find that a career in marketing is just right for you to utilize your business knowledge while exercising your creative side as well.

Review Your Understanding

Describe the role of product in the marketing mix, including how products are developed, classified, and identified.

Products (goods, services, ideas) are among a firm's most visible contacts with consumers and must meet consumers' needs and expectations to ensure success.

New-product development is a multistep process: idea development, the screening of new ideas, business analysis, product development, test marketing, and commercialization. Products are usually classified as either consumer or business products. Consumer products can be further classified as convenience, shopping, or specialty products. The business product classifications are raw materials, major equipment, accessory equipment, component parts, processed materials, supplies, and industrial services. Products also can be classified by the stage of the product life cycle (introduction, growth, maturity, and decline). Identifying products includes branding (the process of naming and identifying products); packaging (the product's container); and labeling (information, such as content and warnings, on the package).

Define price, and discuss its importance in the marketing mix, including various pricing strategies a firm might employ.

Price is the value placed on an object exchanged between a buyer and a seller. It is probably the most flexible variable of the marketing mix. Pricing objectives include survival, maximization of profits and sales volume, and maintaining the status quo. When a firm introduces a new product, it may use price skimming or penetration pricing. Psychological pricing and price discounting are other strategies.

Identify factors affecting distribution decisions, such as marketing channels and intensity of market coverage.

Making products available to customers is facilitated by middlemen, or intermediaries, who bridge the gap between the producer of the product and its ultimate user. A marketing channel is a group of marketing organizations that directs the flow of products from producers to consumers. Market coverage relates to the number and variety of outlets that make products available to customers; it may be intensive, selective, or exclusive. Physical distribution is all the activities necessary to move products from producers to consumers, including inventory planning and control, transportation, warehousing, and materials handling.

Specify the activities involved in promotion, as well as promotional strategies and promotional positioning.

Promotion encourages marketing exchanges by persuading individuals, groups, and organizations to accept goods, services, and ideas. The promotion mix includes advertising (a paid form of nonpersonal communication transmitted through a mass medium), personal selling (direct, two-way communication with buyers and potential buyers), publicity (nonpersonal communication transmitted through the mass media but not paid for directly by the firm), and sales promotion (direct inducements offering added value or some other incentive for buyers to enter into an exchange). A push strategy attempts to motivate intermediaries to push the product down to their customers, whereas a pull strategy tries to create consumer demand for a product so that consumers exert pressure on marketing channel members to make the product available. Typical promotion objectives are to stimulate demand, stabilize sales, and inform, remind, and reinforce customers. Promotional positioning is the use of promotion to create and maintain in the buyer's mind an image of a product.

Evaluate an organization's marketing strategy plans.

Based on the material in this chapter, you should be able to answer the questions posed in "Solve the Dilemma" on page 398 and evaluate the company's marketing strategy plans, including its target market and marketing mix.

Revisit the World of Business

1. Why has product placement become more popular in recent years?
2. What are some of the challenges of using product placement in television or movies?
3. What are some of the marketing benefits of using product placements over more traditional ad spots?

Learn the Terms

advertising   388
advertising campaign   388
branding   373
business products   370
commercialization   369
consumer products   370
discounts   381
exclusive distribution   386
generic products   375

integrated marketing communications   388
intensive distribution   385
labeling   376
manufacturer brands   374
marketing channel   381
materials handling   387
packaging   375
penetration price   380
personal selling   390

physical distribution   386
price skimming   379
private distributor brands   374
product line   371
product mix   371
promotional positioning   394
psychological pricing   380
publicity   391
pull strategy   392
push strategy   392

Check Your Progress

1. What steps do companies generally take to develop and introduce a new product?

2. What is the product life cycle? How does a product's life cycle stage affect its marketing strategy?

3. Which marketing mix variable is probably the most flexible? Why?

4. Distinguish between the two ways to set the base price for a new product.

5. What is probably the least flexible marketing mix variable? Why?

6. Describe the typical marketing channels for consumer products.

7. What activities are involved in physical distribution? What functions does a warehouse perform?

8. How do publicity and advertising differ? How are they related?

9. What does the personal selling process involve? Briefly discuss the process.

10. List the circumstances in which the push and pull promotional strategies are used.

Get Involved

1. Pick three products you use every day (either in school, at work, or for pleasure—perhaps one of each). Determine what phase of the product life cycle each is in. Evaluate the marketer's strategy (product, price, promotion, and distribution) for the product and whether it is appropriate for the life-cycle stage.

2. Design a distribution channel for a manufacturer of stuffed toys.

3. Pick a nearby store, and briefly describe the kinds of sales promotion used and their effectiveness.

Build Your Skills

ANALYZING MOTEL 6'S MARKETING STRATEGY

Background:
Made famous through the well-known radio and TV commercials spoken in the distinctive "down-home" voice of Tom Bodett, the Dallas-based Motel 6 chain of budget motels is probably familiar to you. Based on the information provided here and any personal knowledge you may have about the company, you will analyze the marketing strategy of Motel 6.

Task:
Read the following paragraphs, then complete the questions that follow.

Motel 6 was established in 1962 with the original name emphasizing its low-cost, no-frills approach. Rooms at that time were $6 per night. Today, Motel 6 has more than 760 units, and the average nightly cost is $34. Motel 6 is the largest company-owned and operated lodging chain in the United States. Customers receive HBO, ESPN, free morning coffee, and free local phone calls, and most units have pools and some business services. Motel 6 has made a name for itself by offering clean, comfortable rooms at the lowest prices of any national motel chain and by standardizing both its product offering and its operating policies and procedures. The company's national spokesperson, Tom Bodett, is featured in radio and television commercials that use humorous stories to show why it makes sense to stay at Motel 6 rather than a pricey hotel.

In appealing to pleasure travelers on a budget as well as business travelers looking to get the most for their dollar, one commercial makes the point that all hotel and motel rooms look the same at night when the lights are out—when customers are getting what they came for, a good night's sleep. Motel 6 location sites are selected based on whether they provide convenient access to the highway system and whether they are close to areas such as shopping centers, tourist attractions, or business districts.

1. In SELECTING A TARGET MARKET, which approach is Motel 6 using to segment markets?
   a. concentration approach
   b. multisegment approach
2. In DEVELOPING A MARKETING MIX, identify in the second column of the table what the current strategy is and then identify any changes you think Motel 6 should consider for carrying it successfully through the next five years.

Marketing Mix Variable	Current Strategy	5-Year Strategy
a. Product		
b. Price		
c. Distribution		
d. Promotion		

Solve the Dilemma

BETTER HEALTH WITH SNACKS

Deluxe Chips is one of the leading companies in the salty-snack industry, with almost one-fourth of the $10 billion market. Its Deluxos tortilla chips are the number-one selling brand in North America, and its Ridgerunner potato chip is also a market share leader. Deluxe Chips wants to stay on top of the market by changing marketing strategies to match changing consumer needs and preferences. Promoting specific brands to market segments with the appropriate price and distribution channel is helping Deluxe Chips succeed.

As many middle-aged consumers modify their snacking habits, Deluxe Chips is considering a new product line of light snack foods with less fat and cholesterol and targeted at the 35- to 50-year-old consumer who enjoys snacking but wants to be more health conscious.

Marketing research suggests that the product will succeed as long as it tastes good and that consumers may be willing to pay more for it. Large expenditures on advertising may be necessary to overcome the competition. However, it may be possible to analyze customer profiles and retail store characteristics and then match the right product with the right neighborhood. Store-specific micromarketing would allow Deluxe Chips to spend its promotional dollars more efficiently.

Discussion Questions
1. Design a marketing strategy for the new product line.
2. Critique your marketing strategy in terms of its strengths and weaknesses.
3. What are your suggestions for implementation of the marketing strategy?

Build Your Business Plan

DIMENSIONS OF MARKETING STRATEGY

If you think your product/business is truly new to or unique to the market, you need to substantiate your claim. After a thorough exploration on the Web, you want to make sure there has not been a similar business/service recently launched in your community. Check with your Chamber of Commerce or Economic Development Office that might be able to provide you with a history of recent business failures. If you are not confident about the ability or willingness of customers to try your new product or service, collecting your own primary data to ascertain demand is highly advisable.

The decision of where to initially set your prices is a critical one. If there are currently similar products in the market, you need to be aware of the competitors' prices before you determine yours. If your product/service is new to the market, you can price it high (market skimming strategy) as long as you realize that the high price will probably attract competitors to the market more quickly (they will think they can make the same product for less), which will force you to drop your prices sooner than you would like. Another strategy to consider is market penetration pricing, a strategy that sets price lower and discourages competition from entering the market as quickly. Whatever strategy you decide to use, don't forget to examine your product/service's elasticity.

At this time you need to start thinking about how to promote your product. Why do you feel your product/service is different or new to the market? How do you want to position your product/service so customers view it favorably? Remember this is all occurring *within the consumer's mind.*

See for Yourself Videocase

OBERWEIS DAIRY FOCUSES ON ITS CUSTOMERS

Oberweis, an ice cream and dairy business, is renowned for its high-quality dairy products. The company started by accident in 1915 when Peter Oberweis sold excess milk from his dairy cows to his neighbors. Twelve years later, Oberweis partnered with Big Woods Dairy (which he later purchased), which allowed him to launch a full scale home delivery service. In 1951, Peter's son, Joe, opened the first Oberweis retail store and began producing ice cream and other products. For decades, Oberweis only had the one dairy store and its home delivery business. In the 1990s the company expanded by opening several new stores, entering the wholesale market, and continuing its home delivery service. As Oberweis Dairy has grown, its marketing strategies have adapted.

One thing has never changed. The company has always focused on its relationship with its customers. Oberweis tries to keep their needs in mind throughout all phases of product development and marketing. During product development, the company analyzes current trends and consumer desires. It carefully assesses its pricing strategy and the best way to distribute the product to the customer. Oberweis also conducts primary marketing research. Employees and managers talk with customers in stores in order to learn more about their opinions. Oberweis also conducts surveys, often offering new products free to customers who volunteer to fill out a short questionnaire.

Oberweis believes strongly in conducting marketing research and understanding the needs of each of its target market segments. The company chooses store locations based on demographic research. Social variables also factor heavily into Oberweis's marketing strategies. The company uses its Moola loyalty card to track customer buying behavior. This data allows Oberweis to divide its customers into two categories—those who primarily purchase milk and those who primarily purchase ice cream and other treats. Using this information, the company can customize its marketing strategy for each customer. Oberweis often sends coupons and other promotional materials so that customers will try other products in the company's product line.

Oberweis' commitment to quality products and excellent service is at the heart of its marketing strategy. The company strives to create a marketing mix in which the products, prices, distribution, and promotions keep the customer in mind. The success of over 50 dairy store locations, a home delivery service that boasts over 10,000 customers, and a successful wholesale operation all indicate that putting the customer first pays off.[42]

Discussion Questions

1. How did a company like Oberweis have to change its marketing strategy as the company grew from one retail store to over 10,000 customers and many stores?

2. What is the value of marketing research to Oberweis?

3. What represents the heart of Oberweis' marketing strategy?

Remember to check out our Online Learning Center at www.mhhe.com/ferrell8e.

Team Exercise

Form groups and search for examples of convenience products, shopping products, specialty products, and business products. How are these products marketed? Provide examples of any ads that you can find to show examples of the promotional strategies for these products. Report your findings to the class.

Digital Marketing and Social Networking

OBJECTIVES

After reading this chapter, you will be able to:

• Define *digital media* and *digital marketing* and recognize their increasing value in strategic planning.

• Understand the characteristics of digital media and how they differentiate these methods from traditional marketing activities.

• Demonstrate the role of digital marketing and social networking in today's business environment.

• Show how digital media affect the marketing mix.

• Define social networking and illustrate how businesses can use different types of social networking media.

• Identify legal and ethical considerations in digital media.

NASCAR Turns to Social Media

NASCAR (the National Association for Stock Car Auto Racing), was founded in 1948 by Bill France Sr. as a sanctioning body for stock car racing and held its first race less than a week later. In the early 1970s, when television coverage of sports exploded, corporations began marketing their products by sponsoring NASCAR events and drivers. Today, NASCAR racing is the United States's most popular spectator sport and the second most popular television sport.

Whether you watch NASCAR or not, you have likely seen that the cars and drivers' jumpsuits are covered in advertisements. In 2009, the organization also announced a three-year deal to run ads in movie theaters. All this has worked out well—statistics show that NASCAR fans do patronize its sponsor companies. Recently, NASCAR and its sponsors have looked to the future and are now using online social media as well.

NASCAR.com is a popular site that features links to sponsors via Facebook, Twitter, and YouTube. Sprint, one of NASCAR's cup sponsors, created Facebook and Twitter "Miss Sprint Cup" accounts, which have just over 100,000 fans. Miss Sprint Cup representatives travel the NASCAR circuit and post updates to their pages. NASCAR fans tune in to these posts for information about favorite drivers and images from races that Miss Sprint Cup representatives post. Extending one step further, NASCAR recently reviewed independent NASCAR fan sites and awarded journalist status to some, giving selected fan bloggers access to media events and resources and even press boxes. NASCAR was awarded the Forrester Groundswell Award for business-to-consumer listening based on the handling of its NASCAR Fan Council, an online community founded to learn more about its fans.[1]

ENTER THE WORLD OF BUSINESS

Introduction[2]

The Internet and information technology have dramatically changed the environment for business. Marketers' new ability to convert all types of communications into digital media has created efficient, inexpensive ways of connecting businesses and consumers and improved the flow and the usefulness of information. Businesses have the information they need to make more informed decisions, and consumers have access to a greater variety of products and more information about choices and quality.

The defining characteristic of information technology in the 21st century is accelerating change. New systems and applications advance so rapidly that it is almost impossible to keep up with the latest developments. Startup companies emerge that quickly overtake existing approaches to digital media. When Google first arrived on the scene, a number of search engines were fighting for dominance, including Excite, Infoseek, Lycos, and Webcrawler. With its fast, easy-to-use search engine, Google became number one and is now challenging many industries, including advertising, newspapers, mobile phones, and book publishing. Social networking continues to advance as the channel most observers believe will dominate digital communication in the near future. Today, people spend more time on social networking sites, such as Facebook, than they spend on e-mail.

In this chapter we first provide some key definitions related to digital marketing and social networking. Next we discuss using digital media in business and digital marketing. We look at marketing mix considerations when using digital media and pay special attention to social networking. Then we focus on digital marketing strategies—particularly new communication channels like social networks—and consider how consumers are changing their information searches and consumption behavior to fit emerging technologies and trends. Finally, we examine the legal and social issues associated with information technology, digital media, and e-business.

What Is Digital Marketing?

Let's start with a clear understanding of our focus in this chapter. First, we can distinguish **e-business** from traditional business by noting that conducting e-business means carrying out the goals of business through the use of the Internet. **Digital media** are electronic media that function using digital codes—when we refer to digital media, we mean media available via computers and other digital devices, including mobile and wireless ones like cell phones and smart phones.

Digital marketing uses all digital media, including the Internet and mobile and interactive channels, to develop communication and exchanges with customers. Digital marketing is a term we will use often, because we are interested in all types of digital communications, regardless of the electronic channel that transmits the data.

Growth and Benefits of Digital Communication

The Internet has created tremendous opportunities for businesses to forge relationships with consumers and business customers, target markets more precisely, and even reach previously inaccessible markets at home and around the world. The

e-business
carrying out the goals of business through utilization of the Internet

digital media
electronic media that function using digital codes via computers, cellular phones, smart phones, and other digital devices that have been released in recent years

digital marketing
uses all digital media, including the Internet and mobile and interactive channels, to develop communication and exchanges with customers

Internet also facilitates business transactions, allowing companies to network with manufacturers, wholesalers, retailers, suppliers, and outsource firms to serve customers more quickly and more efficiently. The telecommunication opportunities created by the Internet have set the stage for digital marketing's development and growth.

Digital communication offers a completely new dimension in connecting with others. Some of the characteristics that distinguish digital from traditional communication are addressability, interactivity, accessibility, connectivity, and control. Let's look at what these mean and how they enhance marketing.

The ability of a business to identify customers before they make a purchase is **addressability.** Digital media make it possible for visitors on a Web site like Amazon.com to provide information about their needs and wants before they buy. A social network such as Facebook lets users create a profile to keep in touch or to build a network of identified contacts including friends, colleagues, and businesses. Companies such as Procter & Gamble create social network accounts to share information with consumers and find out their opinions about products and reactions to new ideas.

addressability
the ability of a business to identify customers before they make purchases

Interactivity allows customers to express their needs and wants directly to the firm in response to its communications. In traditional one-way forms of communications, such as television advertising, the customer must contact the company by phone or other means. Interactivity relies on digital media that can make a conversation between the firm and the customer happen without any delay; thus real relationships become possible. Digital media such as blogs and social networks allow marketers to engage with customers, shape their expectations and perceptions, and benefit from broader market reach at lower cost.

interactivity
allows customers to express their needs and wants directly to the firm in response to its communications

Accessibility allows consumers to find information about competing products, prices, and reviews and become more informed about a firm and the relative value of its products. Mobile devices—including smart phones, mobile computing devices like the iPad, and PDAs—allow customers to leave their desktops and access digital networks from anywhere. Thanks to the popularity of the iPhone and Black-Berry, businesses and their customers can stay in constant touch. Benjamin Moore & Co. has an iPhone app (application) that allows customers to match anything, such as their own home-decorating color samples and photographs with shades of Benjamin Moore® paint. Many companies are adopting a digital media philosophy of open communication with customers; for example, a firm can go to a site such as GeniusRocket.com, a marketing firm that provides customized services linking businesses with customers, to request ideas for new products.

accessibility
allows consumers to find information about competing products, prices, and reviews and become more informed about a firm and the relative value of its products

Connectivity keeps customers, employees, and businesses connected with each other. It involves the use of digital networks to provide linkages between information providers and users. Social networking is a key form of connectivity made easier on a global scale by Facebook, MySpace, LinkedIn, Twitter, and other networking sites. Facebook has a larger audience than any television network that has ever existed. Firms can also target precise markets through local social networking sites such as Rokut, a Google-owned service operating in India and Brazil.

connectivity
the use of digital networks to provide linkages between information providers and users

Control refers to consumers' ability to regulate the information they receive via the Internet, and the rate and sequence of their exposure to that information. Consumers choose the Web sites they view, the blogs they follow, and the social networking sites to which they belong. This trend toward a consumer-controlled market requires marketers to approach their jobs in a different way than they did in traditional marketing.

control
consumers' ability to regulate the information they receive via the Internet, and the rate and sequence of their exposure to that information

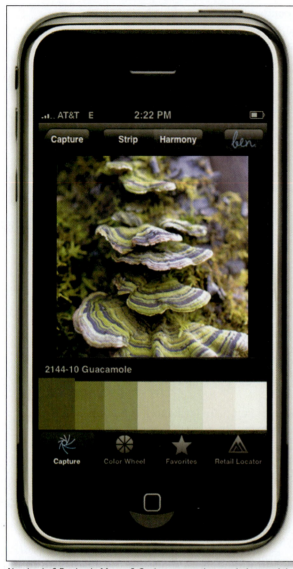

Need paint? Benjamin Moore & Co. has an app that can help you pick out the perfect color on your iPhone.

Using Digital Media in Business

The phenomenal growth of digital media has provided new ways of conducting business. Given almost instant communication with precisely defined consumer groups, firms can use real-time exchanges to create to stimulate interactive communication, forge closer relationships, and learn more accurately about consumer and supplier needs. With $19.2 billion in annual revenue, Amazon.com is one of the most successful e-businesses, ranked 130th on the *Fortune* 500 list in 2009. Amazon is a true global e-business, and was one of the early success stories in the industry, getting 50 percent of its revenue from international sales. The United Kingdom, Japan, and Germany each account for 10 percent.[3] Many of you may not remember a world before Amazon because it has completely transformed how many people shop. Previously, consumers had to travel store to store in order to find goods and compare prices.

Because it is fast and inexpensive, digital communication is making it easier for businesses to conduct marketing research, provide and obtain price and product information, and advertise, as well as to fulfill their business goals by selling goods and services online. Even the U.S. government engages in digital marketing activities—marketing everything from Treasury bonds and other financial instruments to oil-drilling leases and wild horses. Procter & Gamble uses the Internet as a fast, cost-effective means for marketing research, judging consumer demand for potential new products by inviting online consumers to sample new-product prototypes and provide feedback. If a product gets rave reviews from the samplers, the company might decide to introduce it. By testing concepts online, companies can save significant time and money in getting new products to market.

New businesses and even industries are evolving that would not exist without digital media. Hulu is a video Web site that lets consumers watch a broad collection of premium videos from more than 190 content companies, any time and from anywhere. The company has partnered with several companies to advertise on their sites, including Johnson & Johnson and Best Buy. In fact, Hulu's growing popularity is allowing it to compete with YouTube.[4]

The reality, however, is that Internet markets are more similar to traditional markets than they are different. Thus, successful e-business strategies, like traditional business strategies, focus on creating products that customers need or want, not merely developing a brand name or reducing the costs associated with online transactions. Instead of changing all industries, e-business has had much more impact in certain industries where the cost of business and customer transactions has been very high. For example, investment trading is less expensive online because customers can buy and sell investments, such as stocks and mutual funds, on their own. Firms such as Charles Schwab Corp., the biggest online brokerage firm, have been innovators in promoting online trading. Traditional brokers such as Merrill Lynch have had to follow with online trading for their customers.

Because the Internet lowers the cost of communication, it can contribute significantly to any industry or activity that depends on the flow of digital information such as entertainment, health care, government services, education, and computer services like software development. The publishing industry is transitioning away from print newspapers, magazines, and books as more consumers purchase e-readers, like the Kindle or iPad, or read the news online. Even your textbook is available electronically. Because publishers save money on paper, ink, and shipping, many times electronic versions of books are cheaper than their paper counterparts.

Most universities now offer enough online courses for complete degree programs. Many utilize open-university courseware, which makes the courses free to anyone who wants to access the materials. Yale University has launched several open courses made up of complete videotaped lectures. Apple's U Web site allows free access to audio and video lectures supplied by dozens of universities.[5]

Digital media can reduce the cost of both customer and business transactions, and they can also improve communication within and between businesses. In the future, most significant gains will come from productivity improvements within businesses. Communication is a key business function, and improving the speed and clarity of communication can help businesses save time and improve employee problem-solving abilities. Digital media can be a communications backbone that helps to store knowledge, information, and records in management information systems so co-workers can access it when faced with a problem to solve. A well-designed management information system that utilizes digital technology can, therefore, help reduce confusion, improve organization and efficiency, and facilitate clear communications. Given the crucial role of communication and information in business, the long-term impact of digital media on economic growth is substantial, and it will inevitably grow over time.

Firms also need to control access to their digital communication systems to ensure worker productivity. This can be a challenge. For example, in companies across the United States, employees are surfing the Internet for as much as an hour during each workday. Many firms are trying to curb this practice by limiting employees' access to instant messaging services, streaming music, and Web sites with adult content.[6]

Digital Media and the Marketing Mix

While digital marketing shares some similarities with conventional marketing techniques, a few valuable differences stand out. First, digital media make customer communications richer, faster, and interactive. Second, digital media help companies reach new target markets more easily, affordably, and quickly than ever before. Finally, digital media help marketers utilize new resources in seeking out and communication with customers. One of the most important benefits of digital marketing is the ability of marketers and customers to easily share information. Through Web sites, social networks, and other digital media, consumers can learn about everything they consume and use in their lives, ask questions, voice complaints, indicate preferences, and otherwise communicate about their needs and desires. Many marketers use e-mail, mobile phones, social networking, wikis, video sharing, podcasts, blogs, videoconferencing, and other technologies to coordinate activities and communicate with employees, customers, and suppliers. Twitter, considered both a social network and a micro blog that has a limit on characters per post, illustrates how these digital technologies can combine to create new communication opportunities.

Nielsen Marketing Research revealed that consumers now spend more time on social networking sites than they do on e-mail, and social network use is still growing. The most avid online social networkers are Australians, followed by British, Italian, and U.S. users. In 2009, the average U.S. adult spent around six hours a day surfing social networking sites, almost three times as long as two years earlier.[7] With digital media, even small businesses can reach new markets through these inexpensive communication channels. Brick-and-mortar companies like Walmart utilize online catalogs and company Web sites and blogs to supplement their retail stores. Internet companies like Amazon.com and Zappos.com that lack physical stores let customers post reviews of their purchases on their Web sites, creating company-sponsored communities.

One aspect of marketing that has not changed with digital media is the importance of achieving the right marketing mix. Product, distribution, promotion, and pricing are as important as ever for successful online marketing strategies. More than one-fourth of the world's population now uses the Internet.[8] That means it is essential for businesses large and small to use digital media effectively, not only to grab or maintain market share but also to streamline their organizations and offer customers entirely new benefits and convenience. Let's look at how businesses are using digital media to create effective marketing strategies on the Web.

Product Considerations. Like traditional marketers, digital marketers must anticipate consumer needs and preferences, tailor their products and services to meet these needs, and continually upgrade them to remain competitive. The connectivity created by digital media provide the opportunity for adding services and can enhance product benefits. Some products, such as online games, applications and virtual worlds are only available via digital media. Netflix offers a much wider array of movies and games than the average movie rental stores, along with a two-week free trial, quick delivery and easy returns, online video streaming of some movies, and no late fees. Netflix also prides itself on its recommendation engine, which recommends movies for users based on their previous rental history and how they rate movies they have seen. To stay ahead of the competition and keep consumers satisfied, Netflix recently ran a contest that awarded a consumer team $1 million for an algorithm the company will use to improve its product recommendations by 10 percent. The Internet can make it much easier to anticipate consumer needs. However, fierce competition makes quality product and service offerings more important than ever.[9]

Distribution Considerations. The Internet is a new distribution channel for making products available at the right time, at the right place, and in the right quantities. Marketers' ability to process orders electronically and increase the speed of communications via the Internet reduces inefficiencies, costs, and redundancies while increasing speed throughout the marketing channel. Shipping times and costs have become an important consideration in attracting customers, prompting many companies to offer consumers low shipping costs or next-day delivery. For example, Walmart is attempting to take market share away from e-marketers like Amazon.com

Netflix is determined to improve its customers' online experiences with the company. In 2009, it awarded the group shown here $1 million for developing an algorithm the company used to improve its movie recommendations to customers.

by reducing delivery time and creating a "site to store" system that eliminates shipping costs for consumers who pick up their deliveries in the store. This offer has the increased benefit of getting customer into the store, where they might make add-on purchases. Walmart has even tested a new distribution concept to complement store pickups: a drive-through window that allows customers to pick up the products they ordered through Walmart's Web site. Through even more sophisticated distribution systems, Walmart hopes to overtake online retailers to become the biggest online merchant.[10]

Promotion Considerations.   Perhaps one of the best ways businesses can utilize digital media is for promotion purposes—whether they are increasing brand awareness, connecting with consumers, or taking advantage of social networks or virtual worlds (discussed later) to form relationships and generate positive publicity or "buzz" about their products. Thanks to online promotion, consumers can be more informed than ever, including reading customer-generated content before making purchasing decisions. Consumer consumption patterns are radically changing, and marketers must adapt their promotional efforts to meet them.

These effects are not limited to the developed world. In a revolutionary shift in China, where online shopping had not been widely adopted by consumers, businesses are now realizing the benefits of marketing online. One of the first adopters of Internet selling was the Chinese company Taobao, a consumer auction site that also features sections for Chinese brands and retailers. Taobao provides online

Going Green
Social Networking Sites Advance Sustainability

It seems natural that online marketing should be more sustainable than paper-based media outlets. For one thing, it saves paper and generates lower greenhouse gas emissions. Doing away with paper-oriented banking transactions alone can save 6.6 pounds of paper, 4.5 gallons of gasoline, 63 gallons of wastewater, and 171 pounds of greenhouse gas emissions per household per year. While it still takes energy and resources to manufacture and power up your computer, imagine the impact businesses can have by reducing wastepaper and transportation-related pollution through the use of social networking sites to conduct marketing activities. Social networks can be a great place for companies to establish their green reputation, gather information about customers, and even discover new markets.

Care2.com is a "green" social network with almost 13 million members. The site features four basic categories of information: causes and news, healthy and green living, actions to take, and community and fun. Member and nonmember visitors can sign petitions on a wide variety of issues such as animal rights, global warming, and more.

Care2.com is funded by advertising. While it certainly supports advertisers that are eco-friendly, it also allows companies to advertise that are promoting and working toward sustainability. Treehugger.com is another social networking site supported by advertising, which offers advertisers a wide variety of ad choices. The same seems to apply to greenwala.com. On the site, you can participate in contests that sponsor the site and its partners, purchase green items, and view advertising. All the sites are heavily involved in promoting both their messages and their revenue streams, although each site uses a slightly different technique. For all things green, and to avoid that paper trail, these are sites worth visiting.[11]

Discussion Questions

1. What are the advantages of doing more marketing online?
2. Why do you think many consumers have not switched to online bill-paying and banking systems?
3. How do the online organizations featured in this box generate revenue? Do you think they have sustainable marketing strategies?

---

promotion of retailers and products featured on its site. Taobao has been enormously successful; the majority of online sales in China take place there.[12] Consumer trends like these demonstrate that the shift to digital media promotion is well under way worldwide.

Pricing Considerations. Price is the most flexible element of the marketing mix. Digital marketing can enhance the value of products by providing extra benefits such as service, information and convenience. Through digital media, discounts and other promotions can be quickly communicated. As consumers have become better informed about their options, the demand for low-priced products has grown, leading to the creation of deal sites where consumers can directly compare prices. Expedia.com, for instance, provides consumers with a wealth of travel information about everything from flights to hotels that lets them compare benefits and prices. Many marketers offer buying incentives like online coupons or free samples to generate consumer demand for their products.

Social Networking

social network
a Web-based meeting place for friends, family, co-workers, and peers that lets users create a profile and connect with others users for a wide range of purposes

A **social network** is "a web-based meeting place for friends, family, co-workers and peers that lets users create a profile and connect with other users for the purposes that range from getting acquainted, to keeping in touch, to building a work related network."[13] Social networks are a valued part of marketing because they are changing the way consumers communicate with each other and with firms. Sites such as Facebook, MySpace, Twitter, and LinkedIn have emerged as opportunities for marketers to build communities, provide product information, and learn about consumer needs. By the time you read this, it is possible there will be new social network sites that continue to advance digital communication and opportunities for marketers.

You might be surprised to know that social networks have existed in some form or other for 40 years. The precursors of today's social networks began in the 1970s as online bulletin boards that allowed users with common interests to interact with one another. The first modern social network was Six Degrees.com, launched in 1997. This system permitted users to create a profile and connect with friends—the core attributes of today's networks.[14] Although Six Degrees eventually shut down for lack of interest, the seed of networking had been planted.[15] Other social networks followed, including early efforts like LiveJournal, Friendster, and Hi5.[16] Each new generation of social network has been increasingly sophisticated. Today's sites offer a multitude of consumer benefits, including the ability to download music, games, and applications; upload photos and videos; join groups; find and chat with friends; comment on friends' posts; and post and update status messages.

NASCAR stays in touch with its fans in numerous ways, including via Twitter and Facebook.

As the number of social network users increases, interactive marketers are finding opportunities to reach out to consumers in new target markets. MyYearBook.com is a social networking site that offers teenagers a forum in which to write about particular subjects important to them, including sensitive topics facing today's younger generation. Its popularity with teenagers is rising; the site's traffic has increased 36 percent annually, with most users coming from the United States. For advertisers, the site is an opportunity to connect with teens and young adults, a demographic that is difficult to reach with traditional marketing. Advertisers from Nikon and Paramount Pictures have both made deals to advertise through MyYearBook.com.[17] We'll have more to say about how marketers utilize social networks later in this chapter.

Types of Consumer-Generated Marketing and Digital Media

While digital marketing has generated exciting opportunities for companies to interact with their customers, digital media are also more consumer-driven than traditional media. Internet users are creating and reading consumer-generated content as never before and having a profound effect on marketing in the process.

Two factors have sparked the rise of consumer-generated information:

1. The increased tendency of consumers to publish their own thoughts, opinions, reviews, and product discussions through blogs or digital media. These "creators" accounted for almost one-fifth of U.S. adult online users by 2007.[18]

2. Consumers' tendencies to trust other consumers over corporations. Consumers often rely on the recommendations of friends, family, and fellow consumers when making purchasing decisions.

Marketers who know where online users are likely to express their thoughts and opinions can use these forums to interact with them, address problems, and promote their companies. Types of digital media in which Internet users are likely to participate include blogs, wikis, video sharing sites, podcasts, social networking sites, virtual reality sites, and mobile applications. Let's look a little more closely at each.

Blogs and Wikis

Today's marketers must recognize that the impact of consumer-generated material like blogs and wikis and their significance to online consumers have increased a great deal. **Blogs** (short for web logs) are Web-based journals in which writers can editorialize and interact with other Internet users. Two-thirds of Internet users read blogs, and more than half of bloggers say they blog about topics and brands about which they feel strongly.[19] The blogging phenomenon is not limited to North America. In South Korea, for example, more than two-thirds of the online population creates blogs or similar material.[20]

blog
a Web-based journal in which a writer can editorialize and interact with other Internet users

Blogs give consumers power, sometimes more than companies would like. Bloggers can post whatever they like about a company or its products, whether their opinions are positive or negative and even whether the content of their posts is true or false. When a Korean Dunkin' Donuts worker created a blog alleging that a company factory had unsanitary conditions, the company forced him to delete the blog. However, readers had already created copies of it and spread it across the Internet after the original's removal.[22] The company was not able to thwart the power of the Internet user. In other cases, a positive review of a product or service posted on a popular blog can result in large increases in sales. Thus, blogs can represent a potent threat or opportunity to marketers.

Rather than trying to eliminate blogs that cast their companies in a negative light, some firms are using their own blogs, or employee blogs, to answer consumer concerns or defend their corporate reputations. Boeing operates a corporate blog to highlight company news and to post correspondence from Boeing enthusiasts from all over the world.[23] As blogging changes the face of media, smart companies are using it to build enthusiasm for their products and create relationships with consumers.

wiki
software that creates an interface that enables users to add or edit the content of some types of Web sites

Wikis are Web sites where users can add to or edit the content of posted articles. One of the best-known is Wikipedia.com, an online encyclopedia with more than 15 million articles (3.2 million in English) on nearly every subject imaginable. Wikipedia is one of the 10 most popular sites on the Web, and because much of its content can be edited by anyone, it is easy for online consumers to add detail and supporting evidence and to correct inaccuracies in content. Wikipedia used to be completely open to editing, but in order to stop vandalism, the site had to make some topics off-limits that are now editable only by a small group of experts.

Like all digital media, wikis have advantages and disadvantages for companies. Wikis about controversial companies like Walmart and Nike often contain negative publicity, such as about workers' rights violations. However, monitoring relevant wikis can provide companies with a better idea of how consumers feel about the company or brand.

Some companies have begun to use wikis as internal tools for teams working on projects that require a great deal of documentation (e.g., a book project with many collaborators may use an internal wiki to help make the writing and editing processes more efficient).[24]

There is too much at stake financially for marketers to ignore wikis and blogs. Despite this fact, less than one-fifth of *Fortune* 500 companies have a blog.[25]

Marketers who want to form better customer relationships and promote their company's products must not underestimate the power of these two media outlets.

Video Sharing

Video sharing sites allow virtually anybody to upload videos, from professional marketers at *Fortune* 500 corporations to the average Internet user. The most popular video sharing site on the Internet is YouTube; its users upload 20 hours worth of video each minute.[26] YouTube is the king of video-sharing websites, but Video.Yahoo.com and Metacafe.com also attract millions of visitors, giving companies the opportunity to upload ads and informational videos about their products. There are hundreds of smaller video-sharing sites on the Internet, available in dozens of languages. A few videos become viral at any given time, and although many of these gain popularity because they embarrass the subject in some way, others reach viral status because people find them entertaining. Many videos become viral, which occurs when a message gets sent from person to person. **Viral marketing** can be an extremely effective tool for marketers—particularly on the Internet, where one click can send a message to dozens or hundreds of people simultaneously. However, viral marketing often requires marketers to develop an offbeat sense of humor and creativity in order to catch the viewer's attention—something with which some marketers may not be comfortable. For instance, IBM created a series of six videos called "The Art of the Sale," which presents three attributes of the company's mainframe computer in a humorous format reminiscent of episodes of *The Office*. Though some wrote off the video as a forced attempt at humorous marketing, it received nearly 300,000 hits on YouTube.[27]

viral marketing
a marketing tool that uses the Internet, particularly social networking and video sharing sites, to spread a message and create brand awareness.

Joel Levinson, an amateur videographer, trekked to the Arctic Circle to shoot a video for the "What Would You Do for a Klondike Bar?" contest. Levinson won the contest and its $100,000 grand prize. (To see more of Joel's winning videos, visit www.happyjoel.com. You can see all of the Klondike video entries on YouTube or at www.KlondikeContest.com.)

Businesses have also begun to utilize consumer-generated video content; saving money they would have spent on hiring advertising firms to develop professional advertising campaigns. After an initially disappointing ad campaign for its Flip video camera, Cisco Systems launched 10-second television and Web clips that showed both celebrities and ordinary consumers using the Flip camera to record aspects of their daily lives. Consumers enjoyed the opportunity to showcase their talent. Submissions included videos ranging from a baby with spaghetti dangling from her mouth to singer Lenny Kravitz brushing his teeth—all filmed with the Flip camera. Marketers believe consumer videos appear more authentic and create enthusiasm for the product among consumer participants.

Google is so confident video-sharing sites will revolutionize online marketing that it purchased YouTube for $1.65 billion in 2006.[28] If Google is correct in its predictions, then online videos clips—both corporate-sponsored and consumer-generated—are likely to revolutionize the marketing industry.

Photo Sharing

Flickr is owned by Yahoo and is the most popular photo sharing site on the Internet. It allows users to upload and share their photos and short videos with the world. Other popular photo sharing sites are SmugMug and Webshots. A Flickr user can upload images, edit them, classify the images, create photo albums, and share photos or with friends without having to email bulky image files or send photos through the mail. Flickr is so popular that the site experiences thousands of new image uploads every minute. Most users have free accounts, that allow users to upload 2 videos and 100 MB of photos per month, but for around $25 a year, users can open an unlimited Pro account.[29] Photo sharing represents an opportunity for companies to market themselves visually by displaying snapshots of company events, company staff, and/or company products. Companies can direct viewers to their photostreams (their sets of photographs) by marking their pictures with the appropriate keywords, or tags.[30] Tags are essential for marketing on Flickr as they help direct traffic to the corporate photostreams.

Many businesses with pictures on Flickr have a link connecting their Flickr photostreams to their corporate websites.[31] General Motors, for example, uses Flickr not only to showcase its cars and important events, but also to provide links that connect users to GM's blog and to *The Lab,* GM's "interactive research community" where the company test markets designs and project ideas on consumers.[32] In addition to the White House's stream of photos by official White House photographers, President Obama has his own Flickr photostream, which he used to post images that related directly to the health care bill he signed into law in March 2010.[33]

Picasa Web Albums is a Google photo sharing site that developed out of Google's photo-editing program, called Picasa. The program has grown rapidly and is growing in popularity, as it provides more features than Flickr and some of the other major photo sharing websites. Picasa Web Albums is free, and generates revenues through ads shown on the site. If users want to use more than 1 GB of storage space, they can rent additional space up to 16 TBs.

As one web marketer puts it, companies that use photo sharing "add a personal touch to their businesses".[34] Although it is too early to gauge the effects of marketing through photo sharing sites, more and more marketers will likely use the site as an inexpensive way to reach their audience.

Podcasting

Podcasts are audio or video files that can be downloaded from the Internet via a subscription that automatically delivers new content to listening devices or personal computers. Podcasting offers the benefit of convenience, giving users the ability to listen to or view content when and where they choose.

Podcasting is rapidly gaining in popularity. Dozens of online programs, such as Apple's iPodderX and Podcast Studio or Android's dPod, offer podcasting services. Other companies, such as Yodio, combine podcasting with photos to create customized online greeting card-style messages. It is estimated that by 2013, more than 37 million U.S. consumers will be downloading podcasts every month. Most current podcast users are between 18 and 29 years of age, making podcasts a good marketing tool for reaching this demographic.[35] The Student Loan Network offers a free weekly Financial Aid Podcast to college-age students. It gives advice on affordable college education, credit cards, and other financial subjects important to young people. Listeners also have the added benefit of making comments and offering feedback on the podcasts.[36]

As podcasting continues to catch on, radio stations and television networks like CBC Radio, NPR, MSNBC, and PBS are creating podcasts of their shows to profit from this growing trend. Many companies hope to use podcasts to create brand awareness, promote their products, and encourage customer loyalty.

podcast
an audio or video file that can be downloaded from the Internet with a subscription that automatically delivers new content to listening devices or personal computers

Social Networks

It is estimated that two-thirds of consumers in the United States have visited social networks or blogs.[37] One in three South Korean and one in five Japanese Internet users participate in social networks.[38] As social networks evolve, both marketers and the owners of social networking sites are realizing the opportunities such networks offer—an influx of advertising dollars for site owners and a large reach for the advertiser. As a result, marketers have begun investigating and experimenting with promotion on social networks. Four of the most prominent sites are MySpace, Facebook, LinkedIn, and Twitter.

MySpace.   MySpace offers users the chance to create a profile and connect with other MySpace members across the world. Users can invite people to be their MySpace friends, watch videos, listen to and promote music, instant message their friends, write on various topics (called forums), network with friends and colleagues, and play games. Since 2006, MySpace has been accessible in a variety of languages, including Swedish, Chinese, Spanish, Portuguese, and Turkish. Alternate versions also exist depending on the locality. MySpace receives approximately 59 million monthly viewers.[39]

Businesses have come up with unique ways to utilize MySpace to interact with consumers. Burger King created a fictional profile for its mascot, The King, on MySpace to appeal to the 18- to 34-year-old age group. Financial institutions like American Express and Citigroup have also created MySpace pages to better connect with customers.[40] By allowing consumers to become "friends," businesses can provide updates to everyone in their network and permit users to post comments. Marketers should be warned, however, that not all comments from users will be positive. MySpace is home to hundreds of profiles specifically created to boycott certain businesses. Yet if marketers are willing to take the risk and address negative feedback, using MySpace can be an effective and creative way to generate customer loyalty and interest.

Facebook.   In April 2008, the social networking site Facebook surpassed MySpace in its number of members, becoming the most popular social networking site in the world.[41] It is estimated that nearly a third of Internet users have visited the site.[42] Facebook users create profiles, which they can make public or private, and then search the network for people with whom to connect. Users must be a "friend" of the person whose profile they are trying to view before they can see that user's personal information. Many believe Facebook appeals to a broader demographic than does MySpace, attracting parents and grandparents as well as teens and college students.[43] In fact, the fastest-growing group on Facebook is women 55 and over.[44]

For this reason, many marketers are turning to Facebook to market products, interact with consumers, and gain free publicity. It is possible for a consumer to become a "fan" of a major company like Starbucks by clicking on the "Become a Fan" icon on the coffee retailer's Facebook page. Companies are also using Facebook to generate excitement about new products. BMW created a Facebook contest in which users shared their own drawings of a BMW-1 car with others. This tactic created excitement for the product, a sense of personal involvement, and greater recognition for the brand.[45]

Social networking sites are also useful for small businesses. Hansen Cakes in Beverly Hills uses interactive marketing on a social networking outlet to drum up more business.[46] One of the bakery's cake decorators provides updates on her current projects and offers free cake samples to local Facebook users. Facebook lets companies better engage in relationship marketing, or the creation of relationships that mutually benefit the marketing business and the customer. Other companies that have utilized relationship marketing to help consumers feel more connected to their products are Pepsi and Procter & Gamble. The Pepsi Refresh project invites consumers to suggest local charities that are making a positive impact. Consumers vote for their favorites, and Pepsi donates money to the winning causes. The company utilized Facebook, Twitter, and blogging to spread the word about the Refresh Project.[47] Procter & Gamble responded to a fall in market share for its Prilosec OTC heartburn medication by turning to new digital media, as well as by sponsoring causes and companies important to its customers to make them feel more connected and loyal to the product. Prilosec declared itself the "official sponsor of everything" and aimed to strike 1,000 sponsorship deals worth $1,000 each. The brand largely relied on word-of-mouth publicity via social networking sites to spread the word about its unique campaign.[48]

LinkedIn.   LinkedIn is a social networking site geared toward professionals from all over the world. With more than 55 million members, including executives from all the *Fortune* 500 companies, it is the fifth-largest social networking site and logs several million visitors a month.[49]

A LinkedIn profile resembles a résumé. It contains information about past and current job experiences, qualifications, goals, and educational background. Like all social networking sites, it lets users locate and connect with other members and join groups, which are often professional organizations. Perhaps most beneficial, LinkedIn facilitates job searches and allows companies to search the network for potential employees with the necessary skills. Microsoft, Target, eBay, and Netflix have all used the LinkedIn network to recruit new employees.[50]

Although a professional networking site like LinkedIn seems more like a recruiting site than a marketing tool, companies do use it to familiarize users with their business. In addition to listing job openings, Target's LinkedIn page also offers stock

Entrepreneurship in Action
Desert Blends Creates Unique Products with a Regional Flair

Toni Leigh

Business: Desert Blends of Taos

Founded: 2000

Success: Desert Blend now has distribution through Whole Foods and works closely with high-end spas and hotels to custom create products and brands to meet their clients' needs.

If you're a small business operating out of Taos, New Mexico, how do you create awareness of your personal care products, which use a unique Ayurvedic blend of infused, wildcrafted sage and herbal extracts from the mountains in the region? Just ask Toni Leigh, founder and owner/operator of Desert Blends of Taos. Leigh's skin care products use desert plants chosen for their micronutrients that not only revitalize and renourish the skin, but also strengthen the vital centers of the body and enhance a sense of well-being. Educating consumers about the benefit of plants and extracts used by Native Americans for healing and purification is perhaps Leigh's biggest challenge. To create awareness of her innovative products, she maintains a stream of communications with her current and potential customers through Facebook, offering information about ingredients in her products and their restorative, healing benefits as well as sharing periodic discounts. Social networking works for Desert Blends and many other small businesses.[51]

information, a link to the company Web site, some background on the business, and links to news updates on company activities and products. Procter & Gamble has a LinkedIn page that allows users to locate professionals, research careers, and get updates about the company. Smart marketers can, therefore, use LinkedIn to reach professionals not only for recruiting purposes, but also to spread information about and interest in the company.

Twitter.   Twitter is a hybrid of a social networking site and a micro-blogging site that asks users one simple question: "What are you doing?" Members can post answers of up to 140 characters, which are then available for their registered "followers" to read. It sounds simple enough, but Twitter's effect on digital media has been immense. The site quickly progressed from a novelty to a social networking staple, attracting millions of viewers each month.[52] About 11 percent of Internet users have used a micro-blogging site like Twitter.[53]

The thrill of Twitter is that users get to tell the world about their daily lives in short messages, known as "tweets." These tweets can be mundane, such as "I'm eating a sandwich," to the highly significant. President Obama used Twitter to announce "We just made history" when he won the 2008 presidential election. Twitter has allowed people to report information fast—even scooping major news networks on important topics, as in the 2008 Mumbai shootings when those in the area used Twitter to provide details about the incident almost immediately. Twitter quickly transformed from novelty to serious marketing tool, with the company announcing plans to generate revenue through sponsored tweets and working to make the service more user-friendly at its 2010 annual conference.[54]

Although 140 characters may not seem like enough for companies to send an effective message, some have become experts at micro-blogging. Tupelo, a restaurant in Cambridge, Massachusetts, used Twitter to transmit updates before it even opened on everything from what would be on the menu to its health inspections. The restaurant claims that at least half the customers present on opening night were there as a result of its Twitter activity.[55]

Like other social networking tools, Twitter is also being used to build, or in some cases rebuild, customer relationships. Perhaps the most notable example is banks, which used Twitter to reach out to consumers and try to restore their trust in financial institutions after the most recent Wall Street financial crisis. Wells Fargo and Bank of America tweeted about customer benefits and their companies' services, as well to address customer concerns.[56] Social networking has helped to personalize what many consider an impersonal business.

Finally, companies are using Twitter to gain a competitive advantage. Microsoft's search engine Bing developed a partnership with Twitter in which Bing sorts the millions of tweets by relevance and the popularity of the person tweeting. By doing a Bing-Twitter search, Twitter fans can get the most important tweets in real time. Not to be outdone, Google created its own deal with Twitter shortly afterward.[57] The race is on among companies that want to use Twitter to gain a competitive edge.

Virtual Worlds

Games and programs allowing viewers to develop avatars that exist in an online virtual world have exploded in popularity in the 21st century. Second Life is a social network with a twist. It is a virtual, three-dimensional game world created by users that features its own economy, its own lands, and residents of every shape and size. Internet users who participate in Second Life choose a fictional persona, called an *avatar,* to communicate with one another, purchase goods with virtual Linden dollars (convertible to real dollars at a rate of around 250 Linden dollars per $1), and even own virtual businesses. For entertainment purposes, residents can shop, attend concerts, or travel to virtual environments—all while spending real money. Farmville provides a similar virtual world experience, except it is limited to life on a farm. Second Life has the most potential for marketers, given that avatars can purchase property, goods, and services.

While the businesses in Second Life are virtual ones, real-world marketers and organizations have been eager to capitalize on the site's popularity. Second Life allows businesses to reach consumers in ways that are creative and fun. For instance, to connect with consumers and build brand loyalty, car companies like Toyota and General Motors began selling virtual cars to Second Life residents.[58] Other businesses are looking toward Second Life to familiarize consumers with their products and services. Sun Microsystems Chief Researcher John Gage held a Second Life press conference in which his avatar announced the opening of a Sun Microsystems facility in Second Life, complete with video kiosks to show recent Sun Microsystems projects and innovations.[59] Large corporations like Best Buy and H&R Block even offer support services on Second Life.

Second Life has become so popular that even professors are using it as a way to connect with their students. Ulrike Schultz is a business professor at Southern Methodist University. Students can choose to attend her real-world class, the virtual one, or both. Schultz sees virtual worlds as the next step in communications and feels that it is a great way to connect with young people who are accustomed to being wired for most of their waking hours.[60] Schultz sees great potential for businesses in virtual environments, not only to promote and sell products, but also in engaging in virtual teamwork between physically distant employees and in role-playing exercises. Prestigious universities like the University of Texas, Harvard Law School, Bowling Green State University, and the University of California at Davis all have virtual classrooms in Second Life. Companies are also using Second Life to encourage residents to participate in company activities. CNN created a virtual news hub and began encouraging residents to submit stories that occur in this virtual world.[61] Such firms are not only creating brand loyalty by connecting with Second Life residents, they are also using consumer knowledge and money to earn virtual and real-world profits. Although the presence of real-world companies in virtual worlds is still in the experimental stages, virtual worlds like Second Life offer a creative and novel way for marketers to interact with consumers.

Mobile Marketing

As digital marketing becomes increasingly sophisticated, consumers are beginning to utilize mobile devices like smart phones as a highly functional communication method. The iPhone and BlackBerry have changed the way consumers communicate, and a growing number of travelers, for instance, are using their smart phones to find online maps, travel guides, and taxis. In industries such as hotels, airlines, and car rental, mobile phones have become a primary method for booking reservations and communicating about services. They can act as airline boarding passes, GPS devices, and even hotel room keys. Travel companies are collecting personal information so they can send consumers relevant updates about travel opportunities. FARELOGIX, a travel software company, is working with a number of airlines to introduce features that allow airlines to sell services such as priority boarding. While airlines already make these services available on their Web sites, they also want to communicate with travelers who experience unexpected changes on their trips. Other marketing uses of mobile phones include sending shoppers timely messages related to discounts and shopping opportunities.[62]

Marketing over mobile devices has been made possible largely by mobile applications or apps—programs that can be loaded onto certain mobile devices to allow users to perform a variety of functions, from playing games to comparing product prices from different stores. The latter is becoming particularly useful for consumers. The smart phone's ability to find retailers and entertainment and to organize an itinerary is changing the nature of consumer and business relationships. Large hotels, such as Hilton Hotels, are increasingly using iPhone apps that allow guests to check in early, order room service so food is waiting for them when they arrive, and even specify bed and pillow type.

The most important feature of apps such as price comparison programs is the convenience and cost savings they offer the consumer. To remain competitive, companies are beginning to use mobile marketing to offer additional customer incentives, with some success. Jiffy Lube offered coupons for one of its franchises

Yowza!!, a mobile phone app, uses the GPS devices in cell phones to locate consumers and send them coupons from retailers in that area.

over mobile devices. The company estimated that 50 percent of the new customers who came to the franchise did so as a result of its mobile marketing.[63]

Another app that benefits both consumers and retailers is the mobile app known as Yowza!!. Yowza!! uses the GPS devices in many cell phones to locate consumers and send them coupons from retailers in that area.[64] Imagine walking by a Starbucks and immediately having a coupon for a mocha latte appear on your cell phone. Mobile apps are making this possible, introducing a whole new layer to digital marketing.

Using Digital Media to Reach Consumers

We've seen that customer-generated communications and digital media connect consumers as never before. These connections let consumers share information and experiences without company interference so they get more of the "real story" on a product or company feature. In many ways, these media take some of the professional marketer's power to control and dispense information and place it in the hands of the consumer.

However, this shift does not have to spell doom for marketers, who can choose to utilize the power of the consumer and Internet technology to their advantage. While consumers use digital media to access more product information, marketers can use the same sites to get better and more targeted information about the consumer—often more than they could gather through traditional marketing venues. Marketers increasingly use consumer-generated content to aid their own marketing efforts, even going so far as to incorporate Internet bloggers in their publicity campaigns. Finally, marketers are also beginning to use the Internet to track the success of their online marketing campaigns, creating an entirely new way of gathering marketing research.

The challenge for digital media marketers is to constantly adapt to new technologies and changing consumer patterns. Unfortunately, the attrition rate for digital media channels is very high, with some dying off each year as new ones emerge. Social networks are no exception: the earliest ones, like Six Degrees, disappeared when they failed to catch on with the general public, and Friendster, though still active, has been far surpassed by newer networks. As time passes, digital media are becoming more sophisticated so as to reach consumers in more effective ways. Those that are not able to adapt and change eventually fail.

Mastering digital media presents a daunting task for businesses, particularly those used to more traditional means of marketing. For this reason, it is essential that marketers focus on the changing social behaviors of consumers, the ways in which they gather and use information, and the way the Internet is enabling them to get involved in the marketing process.

Charlene Li and Josh Bernoff of Forrester Research, a technology and market research company, emphasize need for marketers to understand these changing relationships in the online media world. By grouping consumers into different segments based on how they utilize digital media, marketers can gain a better understanding of the online market and how best to proceed.[65]

Table 13.1 shows six ways to group consumers based on their Internet activity (or lack thereof). The categories are not mutually exclusive; online consumers can participate in more than one at a time.

Creators are consumers who create their own media outlets, such as blogs, podcasts, consumer-generated videos, and wikis.[66] Consumer-generated media are

Creators	• Publish a blog
	• Publish your own Web pages
	• Upload video you created
	• Upload audio/music you created
	• Write articles or stories and post them
Critics	• Post ratings/reviews of products or services
	• Comment on someone else's blog
	• Contribute to online forums
	• Contribute to/edit articles in a wiki
Collectors	• Use RSS feeds
	• Add tags to Web pages or photos
	• "Vote" for Web sites online
Joiners	• Maintain profile on a social networking site
	• Visit social networking sites
Spectators	• Read blogs
	• Watch video from other users
	• Listen to podcasts
	• Read online forums
	• Read customer ratings/reviews
Inactives	• None of the activities

TABLE 13.1

Social Technographics

Source: Charlene Li and Josh Bernoff, *Groundswell* (Boston: Harvard Business Press, 2008), p. 43.

increasingly important to online marketers as a conduit for addressing consumers directly. The second category, *critics,* consists of people who comment on blogs or post ratings and reviews. Because many online shoppers read ratings and reviews to aid their purchasing decision, critics should be a primary component in a company's digital marketing strategy. *Collectors* are the most recently recognized category. They collect information and organize content generated by critics and creators.[67] Because collectors are active members of the online community, a company story or site that catches the eye of a collector is likely to be posted about, discussed on collector sites, and made available to other online users looking for information.

Joiners include all who become users of MySpace, Twitter, Facebook, or other social networking sites. It is not unusual for consumers to be members of several social networking sites at once. Joiners use these sites to connect and network with other users, but as we've seen, marketers too can take significant advantage of these sites to connect with consumers and form customer relationships.[68] The last two segments are Spectators and Inactives. *Spectators,* who read online information but do not join groups or post anywhere, are the largest group in most countries. *Inactives* are online users who do not participate in any digital online media, but their numbers are dwindling.

Marketers who want to capitalize on social and digital media marketing need to consider what proportion of online consumers are creating, rating, collecting, joining, or simply reading online materials. As in traditional marketing efforts, they need to know their target market. For instance, where spectators make up the majority of the online population, companies should post their own corporate messages through blogs and Web sites promoting their organizations.

Responding to Business Challenges

Open Source Hardware: In the Age of Social Networking, Even Manufacturing Benefits from Shared Information

Most businesses believe that protecting their proprietary information and intellectual property allows them to maintain a competitive edge. However, a new breed of entrepreneur is taking an entirely different approach to competitiveness: the use of open-source technology. Open source is a technology that emerged with the rise of the Internet. It allows free access to a product's source codes, meaning that anyone with the desire and knowledge to take a certain program or device, replicate it, and enhance it can do so. Open-source technology, whether for software or hardware, requires a more collaborative and less protective approach to developing new products. While it may make some producers nervous, those who embrace it argue that allowing for replication is a more certain way of speeding up innovation. If manufacturers start to openly share knowledge, they can learn from each other's mistakes.

One example of this new approach is the Arduino, a microcontroller board produced by Smart Projects of Scarmagno, Italy. The Arduino board costs only $30 and can be programmed to do a range of different things, from making lights blink to automatically turning electronics on and off. Smart Projects also offers licensing agreements to companies that want to carry the Arduino name on their products.

The beauty of open-source hardware and software is that anyone can take the basic idea and customize it to fit their purposes. Many open-source advocates do not see the need for copyrighting in the tech industry anymore. By the time you have secured a copyright for your work or a patent for your product, your technology will likely be outdated.[69]

Discussion Questions

1. What is open-source hardware and software? What are their advantages and disadvantages?
2. How do companies that make open-source hardware and software generate revenue?
3. Do you agree that copyrights are becoming less useful over time and that information sharing is the way of the future?

Using Digital Media to Learn about Consumers

Marketing research and information systems can use digital media and social networking sites to gather useful information about consumers and their preferences. Sites such as Twitter, Facebook, MySpace, and LinkedIn can be a good substitute for focus groups. Online surveys can serve as an alternative to mail, telephone, or personal interviews.

Crowdsourcing describes how marketers use digital media to find out the opinions or needs of the crowd (or potential markets). Communities of interested consumers join sites like threadless.com, which designs T-shirts, or crowdspring.com, which creates logos and print and Web designs. These companies give interested consumers an opportunity to contribute and give feedback on product ideas. Crowdsourcing lets companies gather and utilize consumers' ideas in an interactive way when creating new products. There are even sites that crowdsource entire advertising campaigns, like victorandspoils.com. Mobile phone brand LG offered the public more than $80,000 for ideas about what the mobile phone should look like in 2, 5, or 10 years. Barilla, the Italian pasta brand, gets consumers involved in designing new pasta for little expense—far less than the cost of banner ads on Web sites.

There is no end to the opportunities to gain information, insights, and new-product ideas from consumers. Rupert Barksfield developed the Multi-Pet Feeder to end pet feeding-time frenzy when one greedy pet eats the other pet's food. Barksfield paid $99 to post a concept and some drawings at quirky.com, and 30,000 people passed judgment on his idea.[70]

Twitter and Facebook are putting small businesses on the same level as giants like Starbucks and Dell when it comes to information-gathering power. After spending time on Twitter, the employees at Cordaround.com, a small U.S. clothing company, found that many people use bicycles to get to work. The firm responded by producing a line of "Bike-to-work-pants" with built-in reflective material for safer nighttime riding.[71]

Consumer feedback is an important part of the digital media equation. Some of the oldest forms of digital media are online forums, where participants post and respond to messages and discuss specific topics. About one-fifth of U.S. and Japanese Internet users participate in discussion forums, whose topics can range from consumer products to movies. Ratings and reviews have become exceptionally popular; 25 percent of the U.S. online population reads this type of consumer-generated feedback.[72] Retailers such as Amazon, Netflix, and Priceline allow consumers to post comments on their sites about the books, movies, and travel arrangements they sell. Today, most online shoppers search the Internet for ratings and reviews before making major purchase decisions.

About three-quarters of people shopping on the Web read online ratings and reviews before making a purchasing decision.

While consumer-generated content about a firm can be either positive or negative, digital media forums do allow businesses to closely monitor what their customers are saying. In the case of negative feedback, businesses can communicate with consumers to address problems or complaints much more easily than through traditional communication channels. Yet despite the ease and obvious importance of online feedback, many companies do not yet take full advantage of the digital tools at their disposal.

Legal and Social Issues in Internet Marketing

The extraordinary growth of information technology, the Internet, and e-business has generated many legal and social issues for consumers and businesses. These issues include privacy concerns, the risk of identity theft and online fraud, and the need to protect intellectual property. The U.S. Federal Trade Commission (FTC) compiles an annual list of consumer complaints related to the Internet and digital media. Figure 13.1 outlines the major sources of complaints. We discuss each of these in this section, as well as steps individuals, companies, and the government have taken to address them.

Privacy

Businesses have long tracked consumers' shopping habits with little controversy. However, observing the contents of a consumer's shopping cart or the process a consumer goes through when choosing a box of cereal generally does not result in the collection of specific, personally identifying data. Although by using credit cards, shopping cards, and coupons consumers give up a certain degree of anonymity in the traditional shopping process, they can still choose to remain anonymous by paying cash. Shopping on the Internet, however, allows businesses to track them on a far more personal level, from the contents of their online purchases to the Web sites they favor. Current technology has made it possible for marketers to amass vast quantities of personal information, often without consumers' knowledge, and

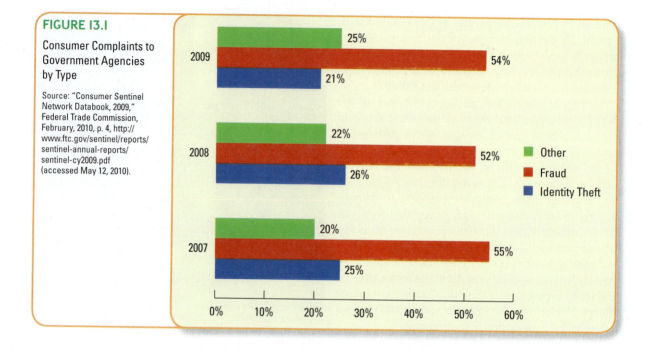

FIGURE 13.1

Consumer Complaints to
Government Agencies
by Type

Source: "Consumer Sentinel
Network Databook, 2009,"
Federal Trade Commission,
February, 2010, p. 4, http://
www.ftc.gov/sentinel/reports/
sentinel-annual-reports/
sentinel-cy2009.pdf
(accessed May 12, 2010).

to share and sell this information to interested third parties. Privacy has, therefore, become one of Web users' biggest concerns.

How is personal information collected on the Web? Many sites follow users online by storing a "cookie," or an identifying string of text, on users' computers. Cookies permit Web site operators to track how often a user visits the site, what he or she looks at while there, and in what sequence. They also allow Web site visitors to customize services, such as virtual shopping carts, as well as the particular content they see when they log onto a Web page. Users have the option of turning off cookies on their machines, but nevertheless the potential for misuse has left many consumers uncomfortable with this technology.

Some measure of protection of personal privacy is provided by the U.S. Constitution, as well as by Supreme Court rulings and federal laws (see Table 13.2). Some of these laws relate specifically to Internet privacy, while others protect privacy both on and off the Internet. The FTC also regulates and enforces privacy standards and monitors Web sites to ensure compliance.

In response to consumer worries, the Federal Trade Commission is considering regulations that would limit the amount of consumer information companies can gather online. Federal regulation could pose a significant threat to Web advertisers, who use consumer information to better target advertisements. Many are attempting to regulate themselves in order to stay ahead of the game. Trade groups such as American Association of Advertising Agencies, the Association of National Advertisers, the Direct Marketing Association, and the Interactive Advertising Bureau are trying to implement new policies that give consumers more control over how companies will use their online information. One proposal is to place icons on company Web pages that provide information about how information will be gathered and give consumers a choice to opt out of such collection efforts.[73]

Several nonprofit organizations have also stepped in to help companies develop privacy policies. Among the best known are TRUSTe and the Better Business Bureau

TABLE 13.2   A Timeline of Internet-Related Privacy Policies

Year	Legislation	Major Provisions
1986	Electronic Communications Privacy Act	Extended laws on wiretaps to electronic transmissions.
1987	Computer Security Act	Improved the regulation of public information by making the National Institute of Standards and Technology (NIST) responsible for the standardization of communication protocols, data structures, and interfaces in telecommunications and computer systems.
1988	Computer Matching and Privacy Protection Act	Amended the 1986 Privacy Act by regulating the use of computer matching, the computerized comparison of individual information for purposes of determining eligibility for federal benefits programs.
1996	Digital Millenium Copyright Act	Refined copyright laws to protect digital versions of copyrighted materials, including music and movies.
1998	European Union Directive	Required companies to explain how the personal information they collect will be used and to obtain the individual's permission.
1999	Anti-Cyber Squatting Consumer Protection Act	Made it illegal to register others' trademarks as domain names in order to profit from the sale or transfer of the domain name, tarnish the trademark owner's reputation, or mislead consumers.
1999	Uniform Electronic Transactions Act	Set guidelines for electronic transactions, including the retention of records, electronic contracts, and electronic signatures.
2000	Children's Online Privacy and Protection Act (COPPA)	Regulated the online collection of personally identifiable information (name, address, e-mail address, hobbies, interests, or information collected through cookies) from children under 13.
2004	Controlling the Assault of Non-Solicited Pornography and Marketing Act (CAN-SPAM)	Banned fraudulent or deceptive unsolicited commercial e-mail and required senders to provide information about how recipients can opt out of receiving additional messages.

Sources: "Federal Statutes Relevant in the Information Sharing Environment (ISE)," Justice Information Sharing: U.S. Department of Justice, Office of Justice Programs, February 27, 2009, http://www.it.ojp.gov/default.aspx?area=privacy&page=1285- (accessed February 18, 2010); Report to Congress: The Anticybersquatting Consumer Protection Act of 1999, section 3006 concerning the abusive registration of domain names, http://www.uspto.gov/web/offices/dcom/olia/tmcybpiracy/repcongress.pdf (accessed February 18, 2010).

Online. TRUSTe is a nonprofit organization devoted to promoting global trust in Internet technology. Companies that agree to abide by TRUSTe's privacy standards may display a "trustmark" on their Web sites; thousands of Web sites currently do so.[74] The BBBOnLine program provides verification, monitoring and review, consumer dispute resolution, a compliance seal, enforcement mechanisms, and an educational component. It is managed by the Council of Better Business Bureaus, an organization with considerable experience in conducting self-regulation and dispute-resolution programs, and it employs guidelines and requirements outlined by the FTC and the U.S. Department of Commerce.[75] The hope among online marketers is that widespread adoption of these privacy policies may prevent regulation that could make it more difficult to advertise effectively online.

Identity Theft

Identity theft occurs when criminals obtain personal information that allows them to impersonate someone else in order to use the person's credit to access financial accounts and make purchases. In 2009 it was estimated that security and data breaches cost organizations more than $6 million each time they occurred.

identity theft
when criminals obtain personal information that allows them to impersonate someone else in order to use their credit to access financial accounts and make purchases

Many of these breaches occur at banks, universities, and other businesses that contain sensitive consumer information.[76] This requires organizations to implement increased security measures to prevent database theft. As you can see in Figure 13.2, the most common complaints related to credit card fraud, followed by utility fraud, bank fraud, employment-related fraud, government document fraud, and loan fraud.

The Internet's relative anonymity and speed make possible both legal and illegal access to databases containing Social Security numbers, drivers' license numbers, dates of birth, mothers' maiden names, and other information that can be used to establish a credit card or bank account in another person's name in order to make fraudulent transactions. One growing scam used to initiate identity theft fraud is the practice of *phishing*, whereby con artists counterfeit a well-known Web site and send out e-mails directing victims to it. There visitors find instructions to reveal sensitive information such as their credit card numbers. Phishing scams have faked Web sites for PayPal, AOL, and the Federal Deposit Insurance Corporation.

Some identity theft problems are resolved quickly, while other cases take weeks and hundreds of dollars before a victim's bank balances and credit standings are restored. The Javelin Strategy and Research 2009 Identity Fraud Survey Report indicated that 11 million U.S. adults were victims of identity theft in 2009.[77] To deter identity theft, the National Fraud Center wants financial institutions to implement new technologies such as digital certificates, digital signatures, and biometrics—the use of fingerprinting or retina scanning.

online fraud
any attempt to conduct fraudulent activities online

Online Fraud

Online fraud includes any attempt to conduct fraudulent activities online, such as by deceiving consumers into releasing personal information. It is becoming a major

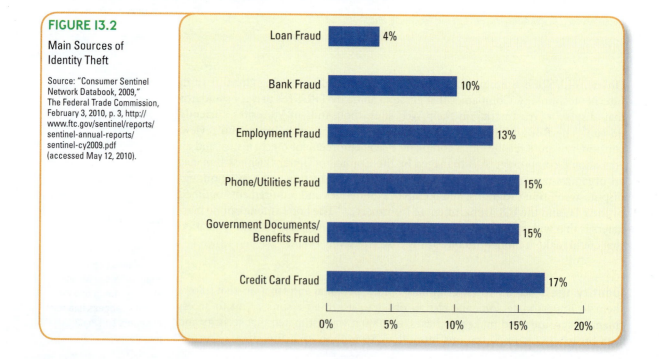

FIGURE 13.2

Main Sources of Identity Theft

Source: "Consumer Sentinel Network Databook, 2009," The Federal Trade Commission, February 3, 2010, p. 3, http://www.ftc.gov/sentinel/reports/sentinel-annual-reports/sentinel-cy2009.pdf (accessed May 12, 2010).

Loan Fraud 4%
Bank Fraud 10%
Employment Fraud 13%
Phone/Utilities Fraud 15%
Government Documents/Benefits Fraud 15%
Credit Card Fraud 17%

source of frustration among users of social networking sites, because cybercriminals are finding new ways to use sites like Facebook and Twitter to commit fraudulent activities. For instance, they will create profiles under a company's name to either damage the company's reputation (particularly larger, more controversial companies) or lure that company's customers into releasing personal information the perpetrators can use for monetary gain.

Another tactic is to copy a blog entry from a reputable company and repost it with a link that connects the user to the criminal's own fraudulent site, where he or she attempts to sell the user goods (under the reputable company's name) or collect personal information. For instance, a fraudster may repost a blog written by a professional sport organization with a fraudulent link that connects users to a site that sells unlicensed sporting goods.[78] Criminals may also use social networking sites to pose as charitable institutions. After the 2010 earthquake in Haiti, fraudsters set up fake accounts to scam Facebook users into donating money for the fraudsters' own financial gain.[79]

Despite any number of safeguards, the best protection for consumers is to be careful when they divulge information online. The surest way to stay out of trouble is never to give out personal information, like a Social Security or credit card number, unless it is a site you trust and that you know is legitimate.

Intellectual Property

In addition to protecting personal privacy, Internet users and others want to protect their rights to property they may create, including songs, movies, books, and software. Such intellectual property consists of the ideas and creative materials developed to solve problems, carry out applications, and educate and entertain others.

Although intellectual property is generally protected by patents and copyrights, each year losses from the illegal copying of computer programs, music, movies, compact discs, and books reaches billions of dollars in the United States alone. This has become a particular problem for social networking sites that use consumer-generated materials. YouTube often faces lawsuits over its users' possible infringement of other company's copyrights. In one case, Viacom Inc. sued YouTube's owner, Google, claiming Google had violated its copyrights by allowing users to post protected film clips on YouTube.[80] Although YouTube is responsible for the video content shown on its sites, it can be difficult for Google to monitor and remove all the videos that may contain copyrighted content, given the many millions of clips that are loaded onto YouTube daily.

Illegal sharing of content is another major intellectual property problem. Consumers rationalize the pirating of software, videogames, movies, and music for a number of reasons. First, many feel they just don't have the money to pay for what they want. Second, because their friends engage in piracy and swap digital content, some users feel influenced to engage in this activity. Others enjoy the thrill of getting away with something with a low risk of consequences. And finally, some people feel being tech-savvy allows them to take advantage of the opportunity to pirate content.[81]

The software industry loses about $53 billion globally each year due to theft and illegal use of software products, according to the Business Software Alliance. About 90 percent of illegal software copying is actually done by businesses. For example, a firm may obtain a license to install a specific application on 100 of its computers but actually installs it on 300. In some cases, software is illegally made available through

Because anyone can upload videos to YouTube, the company, owned by Google, is frequently sued by people and firms claiming videos on the site violate their copyrights. Although Google tries to monitor YouTube and take down copyrighted material, it's tough to keep up with the amount of content uploaded every day.

the Internet by companies that have taken the software from the producer and set up their own distribution system.

Digital Media's Impact on Marketing

To be successful in business, you need to know much more than how to use a social networking site to communicate with friends. Developing a strategic understanding of how digital marketing can make business more efficient and productive is increasingly necessary. If you are thinking of becoming an entrepreneur, then the digital world can open doors to new resources and customers. Smart phones, mobile broadband, and Webcams are among the tools that can make the most of an online business world, creating greater efficiency at less cost. For example, rather than using traditional phone lines, Skype helps people make and receive calls via the Internet and provides free video calling and text messaging for about 10 percent of the cost of a land line.[82] Increased cell phone and wireless Internet coverage have helped to connect more consumers in the developing world than ever before. It is up to businesses and entrepreneurs to develop strategies that achieve business success using existing and future technology, software, and networking opportunities.

Traditional businesses accustomed to using print media can find the transition to digital challenging. New media may require employees with new skills or additional training for current employees. There is often a gap between technical knowledge of how to develop sites and how to develop effective digital marketing strategies to enhance business success. Determining the correct blend of traditional and new media requires careful consideration; the mix will vary depending on the business, its size, and its target market. Future career opportunities will require skills in both traditional and digital media areas so that marketers properly understand and implement marketing strategies that help businesses achieve a competitive advantage.

So You Want to Be a Digital Marketer

The business world has grown increasingly dependent on digital marketing to maintain communication with stakeholders. Reaching customers is often a major concern, but digital marketing can also be used to communicate with suppliers, concerned community members, and special interest groups about issues related to sustainability, safety practices, and philanthropic activities. Many types of jobs exist: account executive directors of social media and director of marketing for digital products, as well as digital advertisers, online marketers, global digital marketers, and brand managers are prominently listed on career opportunity Web sites.

Entrepreneurs are taking advantage of the low cost of digital marketing, building social networking sites to help market their products. In fact, some small businesses such as specialty publishing, personal health and beauty, and other specialty products can use digital marketing as the primary channel for reaching consumers. Many small businesses are posting signs outside their stores with statements such as "Follow us on Twitter" or "Check out our Facebook page."

To utilize digital marketing, especially social networking, requires more than information technology skills related to constructing Web sites, graphics, videos, podcasts, etc. Most importantly, one must be able to determine how digital media can be used in implementing a marketing strategy. All marketing starts with identifying a target market and developing a marketing mix to satisfy customers. Digital marketing is just another way to reach customers, provide information, and develop relationships. Therefore, your opportunity for a career in this field is greatly based on understanding the messages, desired level of interactivity, and connectivity that helps achieve marketing objectives.

As social media use skyrockets, digital marketing professionals will be in demand. The experience of many businesses and research indicate digital marketing is a powerful way to increase brand exposure and generate traffic. In fact, a study conducted on Social Media Examiner found that 85 percent of marketers surveyed believe generating exposure for their business is their number-one advantage in Internet marketing. As consumers use social networking for their personal communication, they will be more open to obtaining information about products through this channel. Digital marketing could be the fastest-growing opportunity in business.

To prepare yourself for a digital marketing career, learn not only the technical aspects, but also how social media can be used to maximize marketing performance. A glance at careerbuilder.com indicates that management positions such as account manager, digital marketing manager, and digital product manager can pay from $60,000 to $170,000 or more per year.

Review Your Understanding

Define digital media *and* digital marketing *and recognize their increasing value in strategic planning.*

Digital media are electronic media that function using digital codes and are available via computers, cellular phones, smart phones, and other digital devices. Digital marketing refers to the strategic process of distributing, promoting, pricing products, and discovering the desires of customers in the virtual environment of the Internet. Because they can enhance the exchange of information between the marketer and the customer, digital media have become an important component of firms' marketing strategies.

Understand the characteristics of digital media—and how they differentiate these methods from traditional marketing activities.

The ability of a marketer to identify customers before they make a purchase is called addressability. Interactivity allows customers to express their needs and wants directly to the firm in response to its marketing communications. Connectivity keeps customers, employees, and businesses connected with each other, even on a global level, via social networking. Control refers to customers' ability to regulate the information they view and the rate and sequence of their exposure to that information. The ability to obtain information is accessibility.

Demonstrate the role of digital marketing and social networking in today's business environment.

Digital communication facilitates marketing research and lowers the cost of communication and consumer service and support. Through Web sites, social networks, and other digital media, consumers can learn about everything they purchase and use in life and businesses can reach new markets through inexpensive and interactive communication channels. Social networking is expanding so fast that no business can ignore its impact on customer relationships.

Show how digital media affect the marketing mix.

The ability to process orders electronically and increase the speed of communications via the Internet has reduced many distribution inefficiencies, costs, and redundancies while increasing speed throughout the marketing channel. Digital media help firms increase brand awareness, connect with consumers, form relationships, and spread positive publicity about their products. Because consumers are more informed than ever and consumer consumption patterns are changing, marketers must adapt their promotional efforts. The Internet gives consumers access to more information about costs and prices.

Define social networking and illustrate how businesses can use different types of social networking media.

Social networking occurs when online consumers interact with other users on a Web-based platform to discuss or view topics of interest. Types of social networking media include blogs, wikis, photo- and video-sharing sites, podcasts, social networking sites, virtual reality sites, and mobile applications.

Blogs give consumers power but also allow companies to answer consumer concerns and obtain free publicity. Wikis give marketers a better understanding of how consumers feel about their companies. Photo posting sites enable companies to share images of their businesses or products with consumers and often have links that connect users to company-sponsored blogs. Video sharing is allowing many businesses to engage in viral marketing. Amateur filmmakers are also becoming a potential low-cost, effective marketing venue for companies. Podcasts are audio or video files that can be downloaded from the Internet with a subscription that automatically delivers new content to listening devices or personal computers.

Marketers have begun joining and advertising on social networking sites like Facebook and Twitter due to their global reach. Virtual realities can be fun and creative ways to reach consumers, create brand loyalty, and use consumer knowledge to benefit companies. Mobile apps can be anything from games, to news updates, to shopping assistance. They provide a way for marketers to reach consumers via their cell phones. Apps can help consumers to perform services and make purchases more easily, such as checking in at a hotel or comparing and contrasting the price of appliances or a new dress.

Identify legal and ethical considerations in digital media.

Increasing consumer concerns about privacy are prompting the FTC to look into regulating the types of information marketers can gather from Internet users, while many Web advertisers and trade groups try to engage in self-regulation to prevent the passage of new Internet privacy laws. Online fraud includes any attempt to conduct fraudulent activities online. Intellectual property losses cost the U.S. billions of dollars and have become a particular problem for sites such as YouTube, which often finds it hard to monitor the millions of videos uploaded to its site for copyright infringement.

Based on the material in this chapter, you should be able to answer the questions posed in "Solve the Dilemma" on page 430 and evaluate where the company's marketing strategy has failed. How could Paul utilize new digital media to help promote his product and gather data on how to improve it?

Revisit the World of Business

1. How are NASCAR and its sponsors using social media to connect with fans?

2. How is NASCAR encouraging fans to contribute their own material?

3. Why do you think fans are responding so favorably to NASCAR social media and fan sites?

Learn the Terms

accessibility   403
addressability   403
blogs   410
connectivity   403
control   403

digital marketing   402
digital media   402
e-business   402
identity theft   423
interactivity   403

online fraud   424
podcast   413
social network   408
viral marketing   411
wikis   410

Check Your Progress

1. What is digital marketing?

2. How can marketers utilize digital media to improve business?

3. Define *accessibility, addressability, connectivity,* and *control.* What do these terms have to do with digital marketing?

4. What is e-business?

5. How is the Internet changing the practice of marketing?

6. What impact do digital media have on the marketing mix?

7. How can businesses utilize new digital and social networking channels in their marketing campaigns?

8. What are some of the privacy concerns associated with the Internet and e-business? How are these concerns being addressed in the United States?

9. What is identity theft? How can consumers protect themselves from this crime?

10. Why do creators want to protect their intellectual property? Provide an example on the Internet where intellectual property may not be protected or where a copyright has been infringed.

Get Involved

1. Amazon.com is one of the most recognized e-businesses. Visit the site (www.amazon.com) and identify the types of products the company sells. Explain its privacy policy.

2. Visit some of the social networking sites identified in this chapter. How do they differ in design, audience, and features? Why do you think some social networking sites like Facebook are more popular than others?

3. It has been stated that digital technology and the Internet is to business today what manufacturing was to business during the Industrial Revolution. The technology revolution requires a strategic understanding greater than learning the latest software and programs or determining which computer is the fastest. Leaders in business can no longer delegate digital media to specialists and must be the connectors and the strategists of how digital media will be used in the company. Outline a plan for how you will prepare yourself to function in a business world where digital marketing knowledge will be important to your success.

Build Your Skills

PLANNING A DIGITAL MARKETING AND SOCIAL NETWORKING SITE

Background

Many companies today utilize new digital media in a way that reflects their images and goals. They can also help to improve customer service, loyalty and satisfaction while reaching out to new target markets. Companies use these sites in a variety of ways, sometimes setting up Facebook pages or Twitter accounts to gather customer feedback, to promote new products, or even to hold competitions.

The U.S. economy has experienced many ups and downs in recent decades, but e-commerce has been an area that has continued to grow throughout economic ups and downs. Many dot-com companies and social networking sites have risen and collapsed. Others, such as Amazon.com, Ebay, Facebook, MySpace, and Twitter have not only survived, but thrived. Many that succeed are "niche players"; that is, they cater to a very specific

market that a "brick-and-mortar" business (existing only in a physical marketplace) would find hard to reach. Others are able to compete with brick and mortar stores because they offer a wider variety of products, lower prices, or better customer service. Many new digital media outlets help companies compete on these fronts.

As a manager of Biodegradable Packaging Products Inc., a small business that produces packaging foam from recycled agricultural waste (mostly corn), you want to expand into e-business by using digital media to help market your product. Your major customers are other businesses and could include environmentally friendly companies like Tom's of Maine (natural toothpaste) and Celestial Seasonings (herbal tea). Your first need is to develop a social networking site or blog that will help you reach your potential customers. You must decide who your target market is and which medium will attract them the best.

Task:

Plan a digital media marketing campaign using online social networking sites, blogs, or another digital media outlet using the template below.

Social networking/ Blog/ other site: _____

Overall image and design of your site: _____

Strategy for attracting followers to your site: _____

Potential advertising partners to draw in more customers: _____

Solve the Dilemma

DEVELOPING SUCCESSFUL FREEWARE

Paul Easterwood, a recent graduate of Colorado State University with a degree in computer science, entered the job market during a slow point in the economy. Tech sector positions were hard to come by, and Paul felt he wouldn't be making anywhere near what he was worth. The only offer he received was from an entrepreneurial firm, Pentaverate Inc., that produced freeware. Freeware, or public domain software, is offered to consumers free of charge in exchange for revenues generated later. Makers of freeware (such as Adobe and Netscape) can earn high profits through advertisements their sites carry, from purchases made on the freeware site, or, for more specialized software, through fee-based tutorials and workshops offered to help end users. Paul did some research and found an article in *Worth* magazine documenting the enormous success of freeware.

Pentaverate Inc. offered compensation mainly in the form of stock options, which had the potential to be highly profitable if the company did well. Paul's job would be to develop freeware that people could download from the Internet and that would generate significant income for Pentaverate. With this in mind, he decided to accept the position, but he quickly realized he knew very little about business. With no real experience in marketing, Paul was at a loss to know what software he should produce that would make the company money. His first project, IOWatch, was designed to take users on virtual tours of outer space, especially the moons of Jupiter (Paul's favorite subject), by continually searching the Internet for images and video clips associated with the cosmos and downloading them directly to a PC. The images would then appear as soon as the person logged on. Advertisements would accompany each download, generating income for Pentaverate.

However, IOWatch experienced low end-user interest and drew little advertising income as a result. Historically at Pentaverate, employees were fired after two failed projects. Desperate to save his job, Paul decided to hire a consultant. He needed to figure out what customers might want so he could design some useful freeware for his second project. He also needed to know what went wrong with IOWatch, because he loved the software and couldn't figure out why it had failed to find an audience. The job market has not improved, so Paul realizes how important it is for his second project to succeed.

Discussion Questions

1. As a consultant, what would you do to help Paul figure out what went wrong with IOWatch?

2. What ideas for new freeware can you give Paul? What potential uses will the new software have?

3. How will it make money?

Build Your Business Plan

DIGITAL MARKETING AND SOCIAL NETWORKING

If you are considering developing a business plan for an established product or service, find out whether it is currently is marketed digitally. If it is not, think about why that is the case. Can you think of how you might overcome any obstacles and engage in digital marketing on the Internet?

If you are thinking about introducing a new product or service, now is the time to think about whether you might want to market this product on the Internet. Remember, you do not have to have a brick-and-mortar store to open your own business anymore. Perhaps you might want to consider click instead of brick!

See for Yourself Videocase

SHOULD EMPLOYEES USE FACEBOOK AT WORK?

As Facebook and other social media sites have gained popularity and expanded, managing their use at work has become an increasingly hot topic. Studies on the use of social media in the workplace conflict over how much it inhibits productivity. Should employees be allowed to access social media at work? Many offices have banned access to the site. The results are as mixed as the research. Recently, Nielsen reported that 87.25 million Facebook users spent an average of just under five hours daily on the site, both at home and at work. Many managers are conflicted as to whether this constitutes enough of a problem to be banned outright.

A study conducted by Nucleus Research (an IT research company) revealed a 1.5 percent loss of productivity for businesses allowing social media access. It found that 77 percent of Facebook users used the site during work for as much as two hours a day; 87 percent of those surveyed admitted they were using social media sites to waste time. However, an outright ban could cause problems. Some younger employees have expressed that they do not want to work for companies without social media access; they view restricting or eliminating access like removing a benefit. Employees at companies with an outright ban often resent the lack of trust associated with

such a move and feel that management is censuring their activities.

An Australian study indicates that employees taking time out to pursue Facebook and other social media were actually 9 percent more productive than those who did not. Brent Coker, the study's author and University of Melbourne faculty member, says people are more productive when they take time to "zone out" throughout the work day. Doing so can improve concentration. Coker's study focused on those using less than 20 percent of the workday on such breaks.

Some companies actually encourage employees to use social networking as part of their integrated marketing strategy. For example, Patrick Hoover Law Offices charges employees with the responsibility to use social media in ways that the employees believe can benefit the company. Although this does potentially allow employees to use social media for personal purposes rather than for work, this tactic has been effective in getting new clients and publicizing the organization. By trusting its employees and giving them leeway to use social media in ways they see fit, Patrick Hoover Law Offices has taken a potential problem and reworked it to its own advantage.

Despite the benefits that companies like Patrick Hoover Law Offices have received from allowing their employees to use social media, 54 percent of companies have gone ahead with social media bans. Robert Half Technology surveyed 1,400 companies and only 10 percent allowed unrestricted use of these sites.

Companies all need to ask, "Can management use social media to benefit the company?" If so, it may be more advantageous to take the risks of employees using social media for personal use if they can also be encouraged to use social networks to publicize their organizations, connect with customers, and view consumer comments or complaints. By restricting social media use, companies may be forfeiting an effective marketing tool.[83]

Discussion Questions

1.   Why do you think results are so mixed on the use of social networking in the workplace?

2.   What are some possible upsides to utilizing social media as part of an integrated marketing strategy, especially in digital marketing?

3.   What are the downsides to restricting employee access to social networking sites?

Remember to check out our Online Learning Center at www.mhhe.com/ferrell8e

Team Exercise

Develop a digital marketing promotion for a local sports team. Use Twitter, Facebook, and other social networking media to promote ticket sales for next season's schedule. In your plan, provide specific details and ideas for the content you would use on the sites. Also, describe how you would encourage fans and potential fans to go to your site. How would you use digital media to motivate sports fans to purchase tickets and merchandise and attend games?

part 6

Financing the Enterprise

Accounting and Financial Statements

OBJECTIVES

After reading this chapter, you will be able to:

- Define accounting, and describe the different uses of accounting information.

- Demonstrate the accounting process.

- Examine the various components of an income statement in order to evaluate a firm's "bottom line."

- Interpret a company's balance sheet to determine its current financial position.

- Analyze the statement of cash flows to evaluate the increase and decrease in a company's cash balance.

- Assess a company's financial position using its accounting statements and ratio analysis.

Fannie Mae and Freddie Mac: Poor Decisions Contributed to Crisis

Fannie Mae and Freddie Mac will go down in history as major players in the most recent mortgage crisis. Fannie Mae is a stockholder-owned corporation created to purchase and securitize mortgages. Freddie Mac buys and sells mortgages on the secondary market and resells them as mortgage-backed securities. This increases the money available for mortgage lending and home purchases. Before 2008, Fannie Mae and Freddie Mac guaranteed about half of the $12 trillion in the mortgage market. Yet with the economic downturn, homeowners could not afford their houses. Houses were foreclosed, and soon supply exceeded demand. The shares of Fannie Mae and Freddie Mac plummeted and the government had to intervene. In 2008, James Lockhart of the Federal Housing Finance Agency (FHFA) announced that Fannie Mae and Freddie Mac would be put into a conservatorship, meaning it was subject to the legal control of the FHFA.

While they were a popular instrument in the early 21st century, subprime loans were long known to be troublesome. They are high-risk loans given to people who cannot obtain loans at the "prime" rate, meaning they have to pay a higher interest rate. In 1999 *The New York Times* predicted that subprime loans could cause trouble during a recession. Yet, because of the high interest rates, the loans were highly profitable and warnings were largely ignored. In 2007 the government passed rules allowing Fannie Mae and Freddie Mac to carry $200 billion more in subprime loans than they were allowed to previously. Problems surfaced the next year.

Fannie Mae's problems went beyond bad decision making. Civil charges had already been filed against Fannie Mae's CEO, CFO, and the former controller,

continued

who allegedly manipulated earnings to increase bonuses. Similarly, in 2003 Freddie Mac announced that it had underreported earnings by more than $5 billion, which was the largest corporate restatement in history—and the result of irresponsible accounting decisions. It was later forced to pay $3.8 million for making illegal campaign contributions between 2000 and 2003. In 2008, CEOs Daniel Mudd and Ryan Syron were investigated for lying to investors about earnings. Bad decisions and managerial misconduct contributed to these companies' downfall and to the financial crisis of 2008–2009.[1]

Introduction

Accounting, the financial "language" that organizations use to record, measure, and interpret all of their financial transactions and records, is very important in business. All businesses—from a small family farm to a giant corporation—use the language of accounting to make sure they use their money wisely and to plan for the future. Nonbusiness organizations such as charities and governments also use accounting to demonstrate to donors and taxpayers how well they are using their funds and meeting their stated objectives.

This chapter explores the role of accounting in business and its importance in making business decisions. First, we discuss the uses of accounting information and the accounting process. Then, we briefly look at some simple financial statements and accounting tools that are useful in analyzing organizations worldwide.

The Nature of Accounting

accounting
the recording, measurement, and interpretation of financial information

Simply stated, **accounting** is the recording, measurement, and interpretation of financial information. Large numbers of people and institutions, both within and outside businesses, use accounting tools to evaluate organizational operations. The Financial Accounting Standards Board has been setting the principles standards of financial accounting and reporting in the private sector since 1973. Its mission is to establish and improve standards of financial accounting and reporting for the guidance and education of the public, including issuers, auditors, and users of financial information. However, the accounting scandals at the turn of the last century resulted when many accounting firms and businesses failed to abide by generally accepted accounting principles, or GAAP. Consequently, the federal government has taken a greater role in making rules, requirements, and policies for accounting firms and businesses through the Securities and Exchange Commission's (SEC) Public Company Accounting Oversight Board. For example, Ernst & Young, a leading accounting firm, was barred from undertaking new audit clients for six months as penalty for abusing the agency's auditor-independence rules.[2]

To better understand the importance of accounting, we must first understand who prepares accounting information and how it is used.

Accountants

Many of the functions of accounting are carried out by public or private accountants.

Public Accountants.   Individuals and businesses can hire a **certified public accountant (CPA),** an individual who has been certified by the state in which he or she practices to provide accounting services ranging from the preparation of financial records and the filing of tax returns to complex audits of corporate financial records. Certification gives a public accountant the right to express, officially, an unbiased opinion regarding the accuracy of the client's financial statements. Most public accountants are either self-employed or members of large public accounting firms such as Ernst & Young, KPMG, Deloitte Touche Tohmatsu and PricewaterhouseCoopers, together referred to as "the Big Four." In addition, many CPAs work for one of the second-tier accounting firms that are much smaller than the Big Four firms, as illustrated in Table 14.1.

While there will always be companies and individual money managers who can successfully hide illegal or misleading accounting practices for a while, eventually they are exposed. After the accounting scandals of Enron and Worldcom in the early 2000s, Congress passed the Sarbanes-Oxley Act, which required firms to be more rigorous in their accounting and reporting practices. Sarbanes-Oxley made accounting firms separate their consulting and auditing businesses and punished corporate executives with potential jail sentences for inaccurate, misleading, or illegal accounting statements. This seemed to reduce the accounting errors among non-financial companies, but declining housing prices exposed some of the questionable practices by banks and mortgage companies. In 2008–2009, the world experienced a financial crisis—part of which was due to excessive risk taking and inappropriate accounting practices. Many banks failed to understand the true state of their financial health. Banks developed questionable lending practices and investments based on subprime mortgages made to individuals who had poor credit. When housing prices declined and people suddenly found that they owed more on their mortgages than their homes were worth, they began to default. To prevent a depression, the government intervened and bailed out some of the United States' largest banks.

certified public accountant (CPA)
an individual who has been state certified to provide accounting services ranging from the preparation of financial records and the filing of tax returns to complex audits of corporate financial records

Company	2009 Revenues ($Millions)	2010 Vault Accounting Firm Prestige Rankings
"Big Four"		
PricewaterhouseCoopers	$26,200	7.813
Ernst & Young	21,400	7.744
Deloitte Touche Tohmatsu	26,100	7.613
KPMG	20,110	7.129
"Second-Tier Firms"		
Grant Thornton	3,600	6.670
Moss Adams LLP	731	6.080
McGladrey & Pullen	150	6.014

TABLE 14.1

Leading Accounting Firms

Source: "Accounting Firm Rankings, 2010," Vault's Top 40 Accounting Firms, http://www.vault.com/wps/portal/usa/companies/rankings?rankingId1=178&rankingId2=178&rankings=1&rankingYear=2010&regionId=0&showVaultAllRankingPortlet=true&showVaultRegionalRankingPortlet=true&routerSignalFromVaultAllRankingPortlet=false&routerSignalFromViewRankingIndexPage=false&routerControllerName=selectRankingIndividualController (accessed April 2, 2010).

Congress is continuing to work on legislation that will strengthen the oversight of financial institutions. Most likely this legislation will limit the types of assets commercial banks can buy; the amount of capital they must maintain; and the use of derivative instruments such as options, futures, and structured investment products.

A growing area for public accountants is *forensic accounting,* which is accounting that is fit for legal review. It involves analyzing financial documents in search of fraudulent entries or financial misconduct. Functioning as much like detectives as accountants, forensic accountants have been used since the 1930s. In the wake of the accounting scandals of the early 2000s, many auditing firms are rapidly adding or expanding forensic or fraud-detection services. Additionally, many forensic accountants root out evidence of "cooked books" for federal agencies like the Federal Bureau of Investigation or the Internal Revenue Service. The Association of Certified Fraud Examiners, which certifies accounting professionals as *certified fraud examiners (CFEs),* has grown to more than 45,000 members.[4]

Did You Know?   Corporate fraud costs are estimated at $994 billion annually.[3]

Private Accountants.   Large corporations, government agencies, and other organizations may employ their own **private accountants** to prepare and analyze their financial statements. With titles such as controller, tax accountant, or internal auditor, private accountants are deeply involved in many of the most important financial decisions of the organizations for which they work. Private accountants can be CPAs and may become **certified management accountants (CMAs)** by passing a rigorous examination by the Institute of Management Accountants.

private accountants
accountants employed by large corporations, government agencies, and other organizations to prepare and analyze their financial statements

certified management accountants (CMAs)
private accountants who, after rigorous examination, are certified by the National Association of Accountants and who have some managerial responsibility

Accounting or Bookkeeping?

The terms *accounting* and *bookkeeping* are often mistakenly used interchangeably. Much narrower and far more mechanical than accounting, bookkeeping is typically limited to the routine, day-to-day recording of business transactions. Bookkeepers are responsible for obtaining and recording the information that accountants require to analyze a firm's financial position. They generally require less training than accountants. Accountants, on the other hand, usually complete course work beyond their basic four- or five-year college accounting degrees. This additional training allows accountants not only to record financial information, but to understand, interpret, and even develop the sophisticated accounting systems necessary to classify and analyze complex financial information.

The Uses of Accounting Information

Accountants summarize the information from a firm's business transactions in various financial statements (which we'll look at in a later section of this chapter) for a variety of stakeholders, including managers, investors, creditors, and government agencies. Many business failures may be directly linked to ignorance of the information "hidden" inside these financial statements. Likewise, most business successes can be traced to informed managers who understand the consequences of their decisions. While maintaining and even increasing short-run profits is desirable, the failure to plan sufficiently for the future can easily lead an otherwise successful company to insolvency and bankruptcy court.

Basically, managers and owners use financial statements (1) to aid in internal planning and control and (2) for external purposes such as reporting to the Internal Revenue Service, stockholders, creditors, customers, employees, and other interested parties. Figure 14.1 shows some of the users of the accounting information generated by a typical corporation.

Internal Uses. **Managerial accounting** refers to the internal use of accounting statements by managers in planning and directing the organization's activities. Perhaps management's greatest single concern is **cash flow,** the movement of money through an organization over a daily, weekly, monthly, or yearly basis. Obviously, for any business to succeed, it needs to generate enough cash to pay its bills as they fall due. However, it is not at all unusual for highly successful and rapidly growing companies to struggle to make payments to employees, suppliers, and lenders because of an inadequate cash flow. One common reason for a so-called cash crunch, or shortfall, is poor managerial planning.

Managerial accountants also help prepare an organization's **budget,** an internal financial plan that forecasts expenses and income over a set period of time. It is not unusual for an organization to prepare separate daily, weekly, monthly, and yearly budgets. Think of a budget as a financial map, showing how the company expects to move from Point A to Point B over a specific period of time. While most companies prepare *master budgets* for the entire firm, many also prepare budgets for smaller segments of the organization such as divisions, departments, product lines, or projects. "Top-down" master budgets begin at the upper management level and filter down to the individual department level, while "bottom-up" budgets start at the department or project level and are combined at the chief executive's office. Generally, the larger and more rapidly growing an organization, the greater will be the likelihood that it will build its master budget from the ground up.

Regardless of focus, the principal value of a budget lies in its breakdown of cash inflows and outflows. Expected operating expenses (cash outflows such as wages, materials costs, and taxes) and operating revenues (cash inflows in the form of payments from customers) over a set period of time are carefully forecast and subsequently compared with actual results. Deviations between the two serve as a "trip wire" or "feedback loop" to launch more detailed financial analyses in an effort to pinpoint trouble spots and opportunities.

External Uses. Managers also use accounting statements to report the business's financial performance to outsiders. Such statements are used for filing income taxes, obtaining credit from lenders, and reporting results to the firm's stockholders. They become the basis for the information provided in the official corporate **annual report,** a summary of the firm's financial information, products, and growth plans for owners and potential investors. While frequently presented between slick, glossy covers prepared by major advertising firms, the single most important component of an annual report is the signature of a certified public accountant attesting that the required financial statements are an accurate reflection of the underlying financial condition of the firm. Financial statements meeting these conditions are termed *audited.* The primary external users of audited accounting information are

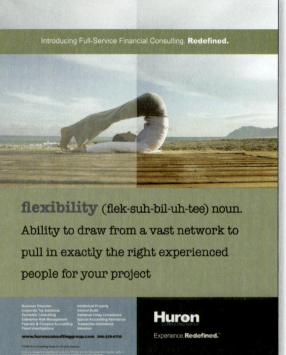

External suppliers, such as Huron Consulting Group, can help firms make better managerial decisions.

managerial accounting
the internal use of accounting statements by managers in planning and directing the organization's activities

cash flow
the movement of money through an organization over a daily, weekly, monthly, or yearly basis

budget
an internal financial plan that forecasts expenses and income over a set period of time

annual report
summary of a firm's financial information, products, and growth plans for owners and potential investors

Even profitable businesses can go bust if they don't manage their cash flows carefully.

government agencies, stockholders and potential investors, and lenders, suppliers, and employees.

During the global financial crisis it turns out that Greece had also been engaging in deceptive accounting practices, with the help of U.S. investment banks. Greece was using financial techniques that hid massive amounts of debt from its public balance sheets. Eventually the markets figured out the country was up to its ears in debt and might not be able to pay off its creditors. The European Union and the International Monetary Fund came up with a plan to give Greece some credit relief, but tied to this was the message to "get your financial house in order."

To top this off, *The New York Times* reported that many states, such as Illinois and California, seem to have the same problems as Greece—debt overload. These states have "budgets that will not balance, accounting that masks debt, the use of derivatives to plug holes, and armies of retired public workers who are counting on benefits that are proving harder and harder to pay." Clearly, the financial crisis will have some lasting effects that need clear accounting solutions.[5]

Financial statements evaluate the return on stockholders' investment and the overall quality of the firm's management team. As a result, poor performance, as documented in the financial statements, often results in changes in top management. Potential investors study the financial statements in a firm's annual report to

FIGURE 14.1

The Users of Accounting Information

Source: Belverd E. Needles, Henry R. Anderson, and James C. Caldwell, *Principles of Accounting,* 4th edition. Copyright © 1990 by Houghton Mifflin Company. Reprinted with permission.

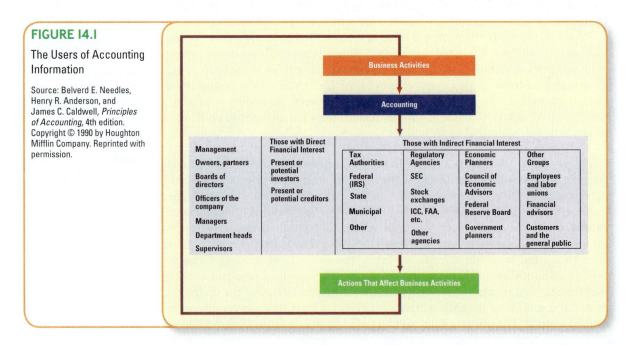

Going Green
Frog's Leap Winery Cares about Wine and the Environment

John Williams, founder of Frog's Leap Winery in Napa Valley, California, cares about wine, the environment, and his company's bottom line. Transparency and a free and open attitude are hallmarks of the company. Frog's Leap has been organic since 1988 and produces handcrafted Zinfandel, Merlot, Cabernet, Petite Syrah, Riesling, Rosé, and Rutherford on 200 acres. Williams believes healthy soil results in healthy vines and great grapes. Using pesticides to kill weeds alters the balance of microbes in the soil, forcing farmers to compensate with more fertilizer and water. His dry farming methods help the soil retain more moisture and requires less watering. Williams also saves money on inputs and can garner a higher profit margin on his wines.

Williams believes that the entire farming environment must be healthy to create good wine; he avoids pollutants like diesel-fueled tractors and takes good care of employees, too. The winery is 100-percent solar powered, which cost the winery $1.2 million to install, but which should reduce fossil fuel consumption by 1,600 tons over 30 years. At the time of installation, Williams figured the system would pay itself off in six years. Frog's Leap also has a geothermal energy system for heating and cooling, which is installed under its parking lot, which will also pay for itself in six to seven years. The winery is pursuing LEED (a green building rating system) certification for its buildings, and it built a LEED-certified hospitality center that incorporated recycled and renewable materials.

At Frog's Leap, the mantra is *reduce, reuse, recycle, renew, retain, and reverse,* which has served Williams well. By displaying a dedication to the environment and green practices, he is caring for the earth, saving money in the long run, and building a loyal customer base through its fun approach to wine making and sustainability initiatives.[6]

Discussion Questions
1. What has Frog's Leap Winery done to be profitable and reduce its carbon footprint?
2. Have these moves to become organic and sustainable helped or hurt the company's financial position?
3. What should Frog's Leap do in the future to maintain its competitive advantage in the rapidly growing organic alcohol industry?

determine whether the company meets their investment requirements and whether the returns from a given firm are likely to compare favorably with other similar companies.

Banks and other lenders look at financial statements to determine a company's ability to meet current and future debt obligations if a loan or credit is granted. To determine this ability, a short-term lender examines a firm's cash flow to assess its ability to repay a loan quickly with cash generated from sales. A long-term lender is more interested in the company's profitability and indebtedness to other lenders.

Labor unions and employees use financial statements to establish reasonable expectations for salary and other benefit requests. Just as firms experiencing record profits are likely to face added pressure to increase employee wages, so too are employees unlikely to grant employers wage and benefit concessions without considerable evidence of financial distress.

Financial statements help people both inside and outside of a firm assess its strengths.

The Accounting Process

Many view accounting as a primary business language. It is of little use, however, unless you know how to "speak" it. Fortunately, the fundamentals—the accounting equation and the double-entry bookkeeping system—are not difficult to learn.

These two concepts serve as the starting point for all currently accepted accounting principles.

The Accounting Equation

Accountants are concerned with reporting an organization's assets, liabilities, and owners' equity. To help illustrate these concepts, consider a hypothetical floral shop called Anna's Flowers, owned by Anna Rodriguez. A firm's economic resources, or items of value that it owns, represent its **assets**—cash, inventory, land, equipment, buildings, and other tangible and intangible things. The assets of Anna's Flowers include counters, refrigerated display cases, flowers, decorations, vases, cards, and other gifts, as well as something known as "goodwill," which in this case is Anna's reputation for preparing and delivering beautiful floral arrangements on a timely basis. **Liabilities,** on the other hand, are debts the firm owes to others. Among the liabilities of Anna's Flowers are a loan from the Small Business Administration and money owed to flower suppliers and other creditors for items purchased. The **owners' equity** category contains all of the money that has ever been contributed to the company that never has to be paid back. The funds can come from investors who have given money or assets to the company, or it can come from past profitable operations. In the case of Anna's Flowers, if Anna were to sell off, or liquidate, her business, any money left over after selling all the shop's assets and paying off its liabilities would comprise her owner's equity. The relationship between assets,

assets
a firm's economic resources, or items of value that it owns, such as cash, inventory, land, equipment, buildings, and other tangible and intangible things

liabilities
debts that a firm owes to others

owners' equity
equals assets minus liabilities and reflects historical values

The owner's equity portion of a balance sheet includes the money a company's owners have invested in the firm.

liabilities, and owners' equity is a fundamental concept in accounting and is known as the **accounting equation:**

Assets = Liabilities + Owner's equity

accounting equation assets equal liabilities plus owners' equity

Double-Entry Bookkeeping

Double-entry bookkeeping is a system of recording and classifying business transactions in separate accounts in order to maintain the balance of the accounting equation. Returning to Anna's Flowers, suppose Anna buys $325 worth of roses on credit from the Antique Rose Emporium to fill a wedding order. When she records this transaction, she will list the $325 as a liability or a debt to a supplier. At the same time, however, she will also record $325 worth of roses as an asset in an account known as "inventory." Because the assets and liabilities are on different sides of the accounting equation, Anna's accounts increase in total size (by $325) but remain in balance:

double-entry bookkeeping a system of recording and classifying business transactions that maintains the balance of the accounting equation

Assets = Liabilities + Owner's equity
$325 = $325

Thus, to keep the accounting equation in balance, each business transaction must be recorded in two separate accounts.

In the final analysis, all business transactions are classified as either assets, liabilities, or owners' equity. However, most organizations further break down these three accounts to provide more specific information about a transaction. For example, assets may be broken down into specific categories such as cash, inventory, and equipment, while liabilities may include bank loans, supplier credit, and other debts.

Figure 14.2 shows how Anna used the double-entry bookkeeping system to account for all of the transactions that took place in her first month of business. These transactions include her initial investment of $2,500, the loan from the Small

FIGURE 14.2 The Accounting Equation and Double-Entry Bookkeeping for Anna's Flowers

	Assets			= Liabilities		+ Owners' Equity
	Cash	Equipment	Inventory	Debts to suppliers	Loans	Equity
Cash invested by Anna	$2,500.00					$2,500.00
Loan from SBA	$5,000.00				$5,000.00	
Purchase of furnishings	–$3,000.00	$3,000.00				
Purchase of inventory	–$2,000.00		$2,000.00			
Purchase of roses			$325.00	$325.00		
First month sales	$2,000.00		–$1,500.00			$500.00
Totals	$4,500.00	$3,000.00	$825.00	$325.00	$5,000.00	$3,000.00

$8,325 = $5,325 + $3,000

$8,325 Assets = $8,325 (Liabilities + Owners' Equity)

Business Administration, purchases of equipment and inventory, and the purchase of roses on credit. In her first month of business, Anna generated revenues of $2,000 by selling $1,500 worth of inventory. Thus, she deducts, or (in accounting notation that is appropriate for assets) *credits,* $1,500 from inventory and adds, or *debits,* $2,000 to the cash account. The difference between Anna's $2,000 cash inflow and her $1,500 outflow is represented by a credit to owners' equity, because it is money that belongs to her as the owner of the flower shop.

The Accounting Cycle

In any accounting system, financial data typically pass through a four-step procedure sometimes called the **accounting cycle.** The steps include examining source documents, recording transactions in an accounting journal, posting recorded transactions, and preparing financial statements. Figure 14.3 shows how Anna works through them. Traditionally, all of these steps were performed using paper, pencils, and erasers (lots of erasers!), but today the process is often fully computerized.

accounting cycle
the four-step procedure of an accounting system: examining source documents, recording transactions in an accounting journal, posting recorded transactions, and preparing financial statements

Step One: Examine Source Documents.   Like all good managers, Anna Rodriguez begins the accounting cycle by gathering and examining source documents— checks, credit-card receipts, sales slips, and other related evidence concerning specific transactions.

Step Two: Record Transactions.   Next, Anna records each financial transaction in a **journal,** which is basically just a time-ordered list of account transactions. While most businesses keep a general journal in which all transactions are recorded, some classify transactions into specialized journals for specific types of transaction accounts.

journal
a time-ordered list of account transactions

Step Three: Post Transactions.   Anna next transfers the information from her journal into a **ledger,** a book or computer program with separate files for each account. This process is known as *posting.* At the end of the accounting period (usually yearly, but occasionally quarterly or monthly), Anna prepares a *trial balance,* a summary of the balances of all the accounts in the general ledger. If, upon totalling, the trial balance doesn't (that is, the accounting equation is not in balance), Anna or her accountant must look for mistakes (typically an error in one or more of the ledger entries) and correct them. If the trial balance is correct, the accountant can then begin to prepare the financial statements.

ledger
a book or computer file with separate sections for each account

Step Four: Prepare Financial Statements.   The information from the trial balance is also used to prepare the company's financial statements. In the case of public corporations and certain other organizations, a CPA must *attest,* or certify, that the organization followed generally accepted accounting principles in preparing the financial statements. When these statements have been completed, the organization's books are "closed," and the accounting cycle begins anew for the next accounting period.

Financial Statements

The end result of the accounting process is a series of financial statements. The income statement, the balance sheet, and the statement of cash flows are the best-known examples of financial statements. They are provided to stockholders and potential investors in a firm's annual report as well as to other relevant outsiders such as creditors, government agencies, and the Internal Revenue Service.

FIGURE 14.3   The Accounting Process for Anna's Flowers

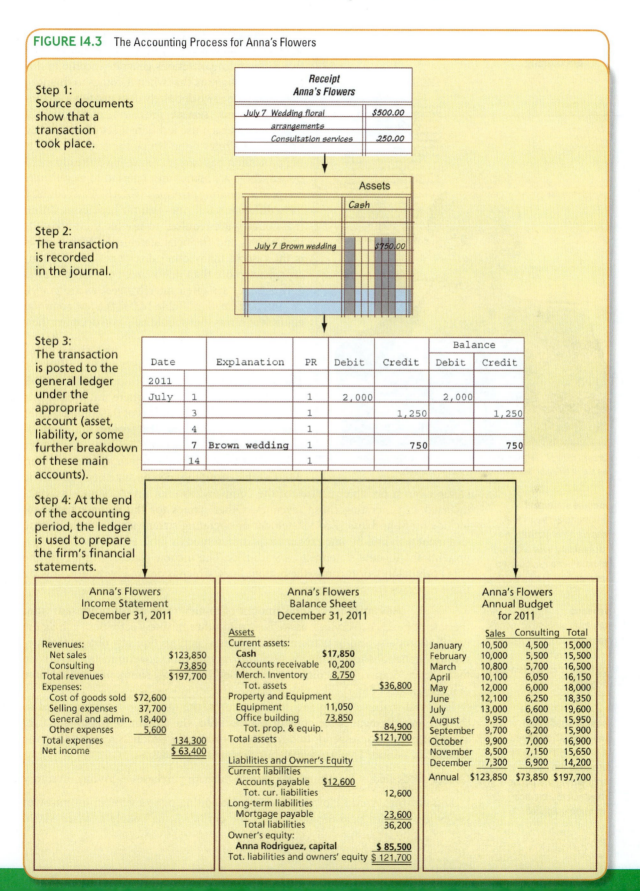

Step 1: Source documents show that a transaction took place.

Receipt
Anna's Flowers

July 7 Wedding floral arrangements	$500.00
Consultation services	250.00

Step 2: The transaction is recorded in the journal.

Assets

Cash

July 7 Brown wedding $750.00

Step 3: The transaction is posted to the general ledger under the appropriate account (asset, liability, or some further breakdown of these main accounts).

						Balance	
Date		Explanation	PR	Debit	Credit	Debit	Credit
2011							
July	1		1	2,000		2,000	
	3		1		1,250		1,250
	4		1				
	7	Brown wedding	1		750		750
	14		1				

Step 4: At the end of the accounting period, the ledger is used to prepare the firm's financial statements.

Anna's Flowers
Income Statement
December 31, 2011

Revenues:		
Net sales		$123,850
Consulting		73,850
Total revenues		$197,700
Expenses:		
Cost of goods sold	$72,600	
Selling expenses	37,700	
General and admin.	18,400	
Other expenses	5,600	
Total expenses		134,300
Net income		$ 63,400

Anna's Flowers
Balance Sheet
December 31, 2011

Assets		
Current assets:		
Cash	**$17,850**	
Accounts receivable	10,200	
Merch. Inventory	8,750	
Tot. assets		$36,800
Property and Equipment		
Equipment	11,050	
Office building	73,850	
Tot. prop. & equip.		84,900
Total assets		$121,700
Liabilities and Owner's Equity		
Current liabilities		
Accounts payable	$12,600	
Tot. cur. liabilities		12,600
Long-term liabilities		
Mortgage payable		23,600
Total liabilities		36,200
Owner's equity:		
Anna Rodriguez, capital		**$ 85,500**
Tot. liabilities and owners' equity		$ 121,700

Anna's Flowers
Annual Budget
for 2011

	Sales	Consulting	Total
January	10,500	4,500	15,000
February	10,000	5,500	15,500
March	10,800	5,700	16,500
April	10,100	6,050	16,150
May	12,000	6,000	18,000
June	12,100	6,250	18,350
July	13,000	6,600	19,600
August	9,950	6,000	15,950
September	9,700	6,200	15,900
October	9,900	7,000	16,900
November	8,500	7,150	15,650
December	7,300	6,900	14,200
Annual	$123,850	$73,850	$197,700

Grant Thornton LLP provides comprehensive accounting services such as the auditing of financial statements to its clients.

It is important to recognize that not all financial statements follow precisely the same format. The fact that different organizations generate income in different ways suggests that when it comes to financial statements, one size definitely does not fit all. Manufacturing firms, service providers, and nonprofit organizations each use a different set of accounting principles or rules upon which the public accounting profession has agreed. As we have already mentioned, these are sometimes referred to as *generally accepted accounting principles (GAAP)*. Each country has a different set of rules that the businesses within that country are required to use for their accounting process and financial statements. Moreover, as is the case in many other disciplines, certain concepts have more than one name. For example, *sales* and *revenues* are often interchanged, as are *profits, income,* and *earnings*. Table 14.2 lists a few common equivalent terms that should help you decipher their meaning in accounting statements.

The Income Statement

The question, "What's the bottom line?" derives from the income statement, where the bottom line shows the overall profit or loss of the company after taxes. Thus, the **income statement** is a financial report that shows an organization's profitability over a period of time, be that a month, quarter, or year. By its very design, the income statement offers one of the clearest possible pictures of the company's overall revenues and the costs incurred in generating those revenues. Other names for the income statement include profit and loss (P&L) statement or operating statement. A sample income statement with line-by-line explanations is presented in Table 14.3, while Table 14.4 presents the income statement of Starbucks. The income statement indicates the firm's profitability or income (the bottom line), which is derived by subtracting the firm's expenses from its revenues.

Revenue.   **Revenue** is the total amount of money received (or promised) from the sale of goods or services, as well as from other business activities such as the rental of property and investments. Nonbusiness entities typically obtain revenues through donations from individuals and/or grants from governments and private foundations. Starbucks' income statement (see Table 14.4) shows one main source of income: sales of Starbucks' products.

For most manufacturing and retail concerns, the next major item included in the income statement is the **cost of goods sold,** the amount of money the firm spent (or promised to spend) to buy and/or produce the products it sold during the accounting period. This figure may be calculated as follows:

Cost of goods sold = Beginning inventory + Interim purchases − Ending inventory

Let's say that Anna's Flowers began an accounting period with an inventory of goods for which it paid $5,000. During the period, Anna bought another $4,000

income statement
a fianancial report that shows an organization's profitability over a period of time—month, quarter, or year

revenue
the total amount of money received from the sale of goods or services, as well as from related business activities

cost of goods sold
the amount of money a firm spent to buy or produce the products it sold during the period to which the income statement applies

Term	Equivalent Term
Revenues	Sales
	Goods or services sold
Gross profit	Gross income
	Gross earnings
Operating income	Operating profit
	Earnings before interest and taxes (EBIT)
	Income before interest and taxes (IBIT)
Income before taxes (IBT)	Earnings before taxes (EBT)
	Profit before taxes (PBT)
Net income (NI)	Earnings after taxes (EAT)
	Profit after taxes (PAT)
Income available to common stockholders	Earnings available to common stockholders

TABLE 14.2

Equivalent Terms in Accounting

worth of goods, giving the shop a total inventory available for sale of $9,000. If, at the end of the accounting period, Anna's inventory was worth $5,500, the cost of goods sold during the period would have been $3,500 ($5,000 + $4,000 − $5,500 = $3,500). If Anna had total revenues of $10,000 over the same period of time, subtracting the cost of goods sold ($3,500) from the total revenues of $10,000 yields the store's **gross income or profit** (revenues minus the cost of goods sold required to generate the revenues): $6,500. As indicated in Table 14.4, the cost of goods sold was just over $4.3 billion in 2009. Notice that Starbucks calls it cost of sales, rather than cost of goods sold. This is because Starbucks buys raw materials and supplies and produces drinks.

gross income (or profit) revenues minus the cost of goods sold required to generate the revenues

Expenses.   **Expenses** are the costs incurred in the day-to-day operations of an organization. Three common expense accounts shown on income statements are (1) selling, general, and administrative expenses; (2) research, development, and engineering expenses; and (3) interest expenses (remember that the costs directly attributable to selling goods or services are included in the cost of goods sold). Selling expenses include advertising and sales salaries. General and administrative expenses include salaries of executives and their staff and the costs of owning and maintaining the general office. Research and development costs include scientific, engineering, and marketing personnel and the equipment and information used to design and build prototypes and samples. Interest expenses include the direct costs of borrowing money.

expenses the costs incurred in the day-to-day operations of an organization

The number and type of expense accounts vary from organization to organization. Included in the general and administrative category is a special type of expense known as **depreciation,** the process of spreading the costs of long-lived assets such as buildings and equipment over the total number of accounting periods in which they are expected to be used. Consider a manufacturer that purchases a $100,000 machine expected to last about 10 years. Rather than showing an expense of $100,000 in the first year and no expense for that equipment over the next nine years, the manufacturer is allowed to report depreciation expenses of $10,000 per year in each of the next 10 years because that better matches the cost of the machine to the years the machine is used. Each time this depreciation is "written off" as an

depreciation the process of spreading the costs of long-lived assets such as buildings and equipment over the total number of accounting periods in which they are expected to be used

TABLE 14.3   Sample Income Statement

The following exhibit presents a sample income statement with all the terms defined and explained.

Company Name for the Year Ended December 31	
Revenues (sales)	Total dollar amount of products sold (includes income from other business services such as rental-lease income and interest income).
Less: Cost of goods sold	The cost of producing the goods and services, including the cost of labor and raw materials as well as other expenses associated with production.
Gross profit	The income available after paying all expenses of production.
Less: Selling and administrative expense	The cost of promoting, advertising, and selling products as well as the overhead costs of managing the company. This includes the cost of management and corporate staff. One non-cash expense included in this category is depreciation, which approximates the decline in the value of plant and equipment assets due to use over time. In most accounting statements, depreciation is not separated from selling and administrative expenses. However, financial analysts usually create statements that include this expense.
Income before interest and taxes (operating income or EBIT)	This line represents all income left over after operating expenses have been deducted. This is sometimes referred to as operating income since it represents all income after the expenses of operations have been accounted for. Occasionally, this is referred to as EBIT, or earnings before interest and taxes.
Less: Interest expense	Interest expense arises as a cost of borrowing money. This is a financial expense rather than an operating expense and is listed separately. As the amount of debt and the cost of debt increase, so will the interest expense. This covers the cost of both short-term and long-term borrowing.
Income before taxes (earnings before taxes—EBT)	The firm will pay a tax on this amount. This is what is left of revenues after subtracting all operating costs, depreciation costs, and interest costs.
Less: Taxes	The tax rate is specified in the federal tax code.
Net income	This is the amount of income left after taxes. The firm may decide to retain all or a portion of the income for reinvestment in new assets. Whatever it decides not to keep it will usually pay out in dividends to its stockholders.
Less: Preferred dividends	If the company has preferred stockholders, they are first in line for dividends. That is one reason why their stock is called "preferred."
Income to common stockholders	This is the income left for the common stockholders. If the company has a good year, there may be a lot of income available for dividends. If the company has a bad year, income could be negative. The common stockholders are the ultimate owners and risk takers. They have the potential for very high or very poor returns since they get whatever is left after all other expenses.
Earnings per share	Earnings per share is found by taking the income available to the common stockholders and dividing by the number of shares of common stock outstanding. This is income generated by the company for each share of common stock.

expense, the book value of the machine is also reduced by $10,000. The fact that the equipment has a zero value on the firm's balance sheet when it is fully depreciated (in this case, after 10 years) does not necessarily mean that it can no longer be used or is economically worthless. Indeed, in some industries, machines used every day have been reported as having no book value whatsoever for more than 30 years.

net income
the total profit (or loss) after all expenses, including taxes, have been deducted from revenue; also called net earnings

Net Income.   **Net income** (or net earnings) is the total profit (or loss) after all expenses including taxes have been deducted from revenue. Generally, accountants divide profits into individual sections such as operating income and earnings before interest and taxes. Starbucks, for example, lists earnings before income taxes, net

Fiscal Year Ended	Sep 27, 2009	Sep 28, 2008	Sep 30, 2007
Net revenues:			
Company-operated retail	$8,180.1	$8,771.9	$7,998.3
Specialty:			
Licensing	1,222.3	1,171.6	1,026.3
Foodservice and other	372.2	439.5	386.9
Total specialty	1,594.5	1,611.1	1,413.2
Total net revenues	9,774.6	10,383.0	9,411.5
Cost of sales including occupancy costs	4,324.9	4,645.3	3,999.1
Store operating expenses	3,425.1	3,745.1	3,215.9
Other operating expenses	264.4	330.1	294.2
Depreciation and amortization expenses	534.7	549.3	467.2
General and administrative expenses	453.0	456.0	489.2
Restructuring charges	332.4	266.9	—
Total operating expenses	9,334.5	9,992.7	8,465.6
Income from equity investees	121.9	113.6	108.0
Operating income	562.0	503.9	1,053.9
Interest income and other, net	36.3	9.0	40.4
Interest expense	(39.1)	(53.4)	(38.0)
Earnings before income taxes	559.2	459.5	1,056.3
Income taxes	168.4	144.0	383.7
Net earnings	$ 390.8	$ 315.5	$ 672.6
Per common share:			
Net earnings—basic	$ 0.53	$ 0.43	$ 0.90
Net earnings—diluted	$ 0.52	$ 0.43	$ 0.87
Weighted average shares outstanding:			
Basic	738.7	731.5	749.8
Diluted	745.9	741.7	770.1

Source: Starbucks 2009 Annual Report, p. 40.

TABLE 14.4

Starbucks Corporation Consolidated Statements of Earnings (in millions, except earnings per share)

earnings, and earnings per share of outstanding stock (see Table 14.4). Like most companies, Starbucks presents not only the current year's results but also the previous two years' income statements to permit comparison of performance from one period to another.

Temporary Nature of the Income Statement Accounts.   Companies record their operational activities in the revenue and expense accounts during an accounting period. Gross profit, earnings before interest and taxes, and net income are the results of calculations made from the revenues and expenses accounts; they are not actual accounts. At the end of each accounting period, the dollar amounts in all the revenue and expense accounts are moved into an account called "Retained Earnings," one of the owners' equity accounts. Revenues increase owners' equity, while expenses decrease it. The resulting change in the owners' equity account is exactly equal to the net income. This shifting of dollar values from the revenue and expense

Entrepreneurship in Action
PayItGreen Helps Consumers Go Online and Save Paper

Business: PayItGreen Alliance

Founded: 2007

Success: A coalition of businesses dedicated to reducing paper waste. PayItGreen helps member businesses convert to paper-free, which saves trees and money.

Online banking first started to become popular in the early 2000s. It is convenient, but also a great way to reduce paper usage. Doing away with paper statements, converting to direct deposit, using online banking services, and ditching receipts and deposit envelopes are all ways that consumers can become more eco-friendly. According to payitgreen.org, one household can save 6.6 pounds of paper and avoid the use of 4.5 gallons of gasoline, the release of 63 gallons of wastewater, and the production of 171 pounds of greenhouse gas emissions annually by making the switch. If 20 percent of households got involved, it would save 150,939,615 pounds of paper and avoid using 102,945,600 gallons of gasoline and the production of 3,920,802,916 pounds of greenhouse gas emissions.

Why are three out of four households still receiving so many paper statements and bills? A possible reason is that customer confusion resulting from a lack of information and suggests that banks push green banking and help their customers make the switch. The PayItGreen Alliance—made up of companies and financial institutions of all sizes—aims to do just this by offering assistance and information via payitgreen.org. As an added bonus, online bankers are more likely to spot fraud and identity theft than those using paper. At a time when protecting the earth is critical, it's great to know that making a small change can have such a large impact—bank online and go green![7]

accounts allows the firm to begin the next accounting period with zero balances in those accounts. Zeroing out the balances enables a company to count how much it has sold and how many expenses have been incurred during a period of time. The basic accounting equation (Assets = Liabilities + Owners' equity) will not balance until the revenue and expense account balances have been moved or "closed out" to the owners' equity account.

One final note about income statements: You may remember that corporations may choose to make cash payments called dividends to shareholders out of their net earnings. When a corporation elects to pay dividends, it decreases the cash account (in the assets category of the balance sheet) as well as a capital account (in the owners' equity category of the balance sheet). During any period of time, the owners' equity account may change because of the sale of stock (or contributions/withdrawals by owners), the net income or loss, or from the dividends paid.

The Balance Sheet

balance sheet
a "snapshot" of an organization's financial position at a given moment

The second basic financial statement is the **balance sheet,** which presents a "snapshot" of an organization's financial position at a given moment. As such, the balance sheet indicates what the organization owns or controls and the various sources of the funds used to pay for these assets, such as bank debt or owners' equity.

The balance sheet takes its name from its reliance on the accounting equation: Assets *must* equal liabilities plus owners' equity. Table 14.5 provides a sample balance sheet with line-by-line explanations. Unlike the income statement, the balance sheet does not represent the result of transactions completed over a specified accounting period. Instead, the balance sheet is, by definition, an accumulation of all financial transactions conducted by an organization since its founding. Following long-established traditions, items on the balance sheet are listed on the basis of their original cost less accumulated depreciation, rather than their present values.

Balance sheets are often presented in two different formats. The traditional balance sheet format placed the organization's assets on the left side and its liabilities and owners' equity on the right. More recently, a vertical format, with assets on top

TABLE 14.5   Sample Balance Sheet

The following exhibit presents a balance sheet in word form with each item defined or explained.

Typical Company December 31	
Assets	This is the major category for all physical, monetary, or intangible goods that have some dollar value.
Current assets	Assets that are either cash or are expected to be turned into cash within the next 12 months.
Cash	Cash or checking accounts.
Marketable securities	Short-term investments in securities that can be converted to cash quickly (liquid assets).
Accounts receivable	Cash due from customers in payment for goods received. These arise from sales made on credit.
Inventory	Finished goods ready for sale, goods in the process of being finished, or raw materials used in the production of goods.
Prepaid expense	A future expense item that has already been paid, such as insurance premiums or rent.
Total current assets	The sum of the above accounts.
Fixed assets	Assets that are long term in nature and have a minimum life expectancy that exceeds one year.
Investments	Assets held as investments rather than assets owned for the production process. Most often the assets include small ownership interests in other companies.
Gross property, plant, and equipment	Land, buildings, and other fixed assets listed at original cost.
Less: Accumulated depreciation	The accumulated expense deductions applied to all plant and equipment over their life. Land may not be depreciated. The total amount represents in general the decline in value as equipment gets older and wears out. The maximum amount that can be deducted is set by the U.S. Federal Tax Code and varies by type of asset.
Net property, plant, and equipment	Gross property, plant, and equipment minus the accumulated depreciation. This amount reflects the book value of the fixed assets and not their value if sold.
Other assets	Any other asset that is long term and does not fit into the above categories. It could be patents or trademarks.
Total assets	The sum of all the asset values.
Liabilities and Stockholders' Equity	This is the major category. Liabilities refer to all indebtedness and loans of both a long-term and short-term nature. Stockholders' equity refers to all money that has been contributed to the company over the life of the firm by the owners.
Current liabilities	Short-term debt expected to be paid off within the next 12 months.
Accounts payable	Money owed to suppliers for goods ordered. Firms usually have between 30 and 90 days to pay this account, depending on industry norms.
Wages payable	Money owned to employees for hours worked or salary. If workers receive checks every two weeks, the amount owed should be no more than two weeks' pay.
Taxes payable	Firms are required to pay corporate taxes quarterly. This refers to taxes owed based on earnings estimates for the quarter.
Notes payable	Short-term loans from banks or other lenders.
Other current liabilities	The other short-term debts that do not fit into the above categories.
Total current liabilities	The sum of the above accounts.

(continued)

TABLE 14.5 Sample Balance Sheet *(Continued)*

Long-term liabilities	All long-term debt that will not be paid off in the next 12 months.
Long-term debt	Loans of more than one year from banks, pension funds, insurance companies, or other lenders. These loans often take the form of bonds, which are securities that may be bought and sold in bond markets.
Deferred income taxes	This is a liability owed to the government but not due within one year.
Other liabilities	Any other long-term debt that does not fit the above two categories.
Stockholders' equity	The following categories are the owners' investment in the company.
Common stock	The tangible evidence of ownership is a security called common stock. The par value is stated value and does not indicate the company's worth.
Capital in excess of par (a.k.a. contributed capital)	When shares of stock were sold to the owners, they were recorded at the price at the time of the original sale. If the price paid was $10 per share, the extra $9 per share would show up in this account at 100,000 shares times $9 per share, or $900,000.
Retained earnings	The total amount of earnings the company has made during its life and not paid out to its stockholders as dividends. This account represents the owners' reinvestment of earnings into company assets rather than payments of cash dividends. This account does not represent cash.
Total stockholders' equity	This is the sum of the above equity accounts representing the owner's total investment in the company.
Total liabilities and stockholders' equity	The total short-term and long-term debt of the company plus the owner's total investment. This combined amount *must* equal total assets.

followed by liabilities and owners' equity, has gained wide acceptance. Starbucks' balance sheet for 2008 and 2009 is presented in Table 14.6. In the sections that follow, we'll briefly describe the basic items found on the balance sheet; we'll take a closer look at a number of these in Chapter 16.

Assets. All asset accounts are listed in descending order of *liquidity*—that is, how quickly each could be turned into cash. **Current assets,** also called short-term assets, are those that are used or converted into cash within the course of a calendar year. Cash is followed by temporary investments, accounts receivable, and inventory, in that order. **Accounts receivable** refers to money owed the company by its clients or customers who have promised to pay for the products at a later date. Accounts receivable usually includes an allowance for bad debts that management does not expect to collect. The bad-debts adjustment is normally based on historical collections experience and is deducted from the accounts receivable balance to pre-sent a more realistic view of the payments likely to be received in the future, called net receivables. Inventory may be held in the form of raw materials, work-in-progress, or finished goods ready for delivery.

Long-term, or fixed assets represent a commitment of organizational funds of at least one year. Items classified as fixed include long-term investments, plant and equipment, and intangible assets, such as corporate "goodwill," or reputation, as well as patents and trademarks.

Liabilities. As seen in the accounting equation, total assets must be financed either through borrowing (liabilities) or through owner investments (owners' equity). **Current liabilities** include a firm's financial obligations to short-term creditors, which must be repaid within one year, while long-term liabilities have longer repayment terms. **Accounts payable** represents amounts owed to suppliers

current assets
assets that are used or converted into cash within the course of a calendar year

accounts receivable
money owed a company by its clients or customers who have promised to pay for the products at a later date

current liabilities
a firm's financial obligations to short-term creditors, which must be repaid within one year

accounts payable
the amount a company owes to suppliers for goods and services purchased with credit

TABLE 14.6   Starbucks Corporation Consolidated Balance Sheets (in millions, except per share data)

Fiscal Year Ended	Sep 27, 2009	Sep 28, 2008
Assets		
Current assets:		
Cash and cash equivalents	$ 599.8	$ 269.8
Short-term investments—available-for-sale securities	21.5	3.0
Short-term investments—trading securities	44.8	49.5
Accounts receivable, net	271.0	329.5
Inventories	664.9	692.8
Prepaid expenses and other current assets	147.2	169.2
Deferred income taxes, net	286.6	234.2
Total current assets	2,035.8	1,748.0
Long-term investments—available-for-sale securities	71.2	71.4
Equity and cost investments	352.3	302.6
Property, plant and equipment, net	2,536.4	2,956.4
Other assets	253.8	261.1
Other intangible assets	68.2	66.6
Goodwill	259.1	266.5
Total Assets	$5,576.8	$5,672.6
Liabilities and Shareholders' Equity		
Current liabilities:		
Commercial paper and short-term borrowings	$ —	$ 713.0
Accounts payable	267.1	324.9
Accrued compensation and related costs	307.5	253.6
Accrued occupancy costs	188.1	136.1
Accrued taxes	127.8	76.1
Insurance reserves	154.3	152.5
Other accrued expenses	147.3	164.4
Deferred revenue	388.7	368.4
Current portion of long-term debt	0.2	0.7
Total current liabilities	1,581.0	2,189.7
Long-term debt	549.3	549.6
Other long-term liabilities	400.8	442.4
Total liabilities	2,531.1	3,181.7
Shareholders' equity:		
Common stock ($0.001 par value)—authorized, 1,200.0 shares; issued and outstanding, 742.9 and 735.5 shares, respectively (includes 3.4 common stock units in both periods)	0.7	0.7
Additional paid-in capital	147.0	—
Other additional paid-in-capital	39.4	39.4
Retained earnings	2,793.2	2,402.4
Accumulated other comprehensive income	65.4	48.4
Total shareholders' equity	3,045.7	2,490.9
Total Liabilities and Shareholders' Equity	$5,576.8	$5,672.6

Source: Starbucks 2009 Annual Report, p. 41.

for goods and services purchased with credit. For example, if you buy gas with a BP credit card, the purchase represents an account payable for you (and an account receivable for BP). Other liabilities include wages earned by employees but not yet paid and taxes owed to the government. Occasionally, these accounts are consolidated into an **accrued expenses** account, representing all unpaid financial obligations incurred by the organization.

accrued expenses
is an account representing all unpaid financial obligations incurred by the organization

Owners' Equity.   Owners' equity includes the owners' contributions to the organization along with income earned by the organization and retained to finance continued growth and development. If the organization were to sell off all of its assets and pay off all of its liabilities, any remaining funds would belong to the owners. Not surprisingly, the accounts listed as owners' equity on a balance sheet may differ dramatically from company to company. Corporations sell stock to investors, who then become the owners of the firm. Many corporations issue two, three, or even more different classes of common and preferred stock, each with different dividend payments and/or voting rights. Because each type of stock issued represents a different claim on the organization, each must be represented by a separate owners' equity account, called contributed capital.

The Statement of Cash Flows

statement of cash flows
explains how the company's cash changed from the beginning of the accounting period to the end

The third primary financial statement is called the **statement of cash flows,** which explains how the company's cash changed from the beginning of the accounting period to the end. Cash, of course, is an asset shown on the balance sheet, which provides a snapshot of the firm's financial position at one point in time. However, many investors and other users of financial statements want more information about the cash flowing into and out of the firm than is provided on the balance sheet in order to better understand the company's financial health. The statement of cash flows takes the cash balance from one year's balance sheet and compares it with the next while providing detail about how the firm used the cash. Table 14.7 presents Starbucks' statement of cash flows.

The change in cash is explained through details in three categories: cash from (used for) operating activities, cash from (used for) investing activities, and cash from (used for) financing activities. *Cash from operating activities* is calculated by combining the changes in the revenue accounts, expense accounts, current asset accounts, and current liability accounts. This category of cash flows includes all the accounts on the balance sheet that relate to computing revenues and expenses for the accounting period. If this amount is a positive number, as it is for Starbucks, then the business is making extra cash that it can use to invest in increased long-term capacity or to pay off debts such as loans or bonds. A negative number may indicate a business that is in a declining position with regards to operations. Negative cash flow is not always a bad thing, however. It may indicate that a business is growing, with a very negative cash flow indicating rapid growth.

Cash from investing activities is calculated from changes in the long-term or fixed asset accounts. If this amount is negative, as is the case with Starbucks, the company is purchasing long-term assets for future growth. A positive figure indicates a business that is selling off existing long-term assets and reducing its capacity for the future.

Finally, *cash from financing activities* is calculated from changes in the long-term liability accounts and the contributed capital accounts in owners' equity. If this amount is negative, the company is likely paying off long-term debt or returning contributed capital to investors. As in the case of Starbucks, if this amount is positive, the company is either borrowing more money or raising money from investors by selling more shares of stock.

Ratio Analysis: Analyzing Financial Statements

The income statement shows a company's profit or loss, while the balance sheet itemizes the value of its assets, liabilities, and owners' equity. Together, the two statements provide the means to answer two critical questions: (1) How much did the

TABLE 14.7   Starbucks Corporation Consolidated Statements of Cash Flows (in millions)

Fiscal Year Ended	Sep 27, 2009	Sep 28, 2008	Sep 30, 2007
Operating Activities:			
Net earnings	$ 390.8	$ 315.5	$ 672.6
Adjustments to reconcile net earnings to net cash provided by operating activities:			
Depreciation and amortization	563.3	604.5	491.2
Provision for impairments and asset disposals	224.4	325.0	26.0
Deferred income taxes	(69.6)	(117.1)	(37.3)
Equity in income of investees	(78.4)	(61.3)	(65.7)
Distributions of income from equity investees	53.0	52.6	65.9
Stock-based compensation	83.2	75.0	103.9
Tax benefit from exercise of stock options	2.0	3.8	7.7
Excess tax benefit from exercise of stock options	(15.9)	(14.7)	(93.1)
Other	5.4	(0.1)	0.7
Cash provided/(used) by changes in operating assets and liabilities:			
Inventories	28.5	(0.6)	(48.6)
Accounts payable	(53.0)	(63.9)	36.1
Accrued taxes	57.2	7.3	86.4
Deferred revenue	16.3	72.4	63.2
Other operating assets	120.5	(11.2)	(92.7)
Other operating liabilities	61.3	71.5	114.9
Net cash provided by operating activities	1,389.0	1,258.7	1,331.2
Investing Activities:			
Purchase of available-for-sale securities	(129.2)	(71.8)	(237.4)
Maturities and calls of available-for-sale securities	111.0	20.0	178.2
Sales of available-for-sale securities	5.0	75.9	47.5
Acquisitions, net of cash acquired	—	(74.2)	(53.3)
Net purchases of equity, other investments and other assets	(4.8)	(52.0)	(56.6)
Additions to property, plant and equipment	(445.6)	(984.5)	(1,080.3)
Proceeds from sale of property, plant and equipment	42.5	—	—
Net cash used by investing activities	(421.1)	(1,086.6)	(1,201.9)

(continued)

TABLE 14.7 Starbucks Corporation Consolidated Statements of Cash Flows (In millions) *(Continued)*

Financing Activities:			
Proceeds from issuance of commercial paper	20,965.4	65,770.8	17,311.1
Repayments of commercial paper	(21,378.5)	(66,068.0)	(16,600.9)
Proceeds from short-term borrowings	1,338.0	528.2	770.0
Repayments of short-term borrowings	(1,638.0)	(228.8)	(1,470.0)
Proceeds from issuance of common stock	57.3	112.3	176.9
Excess tax benefit from exercise of stock options	15.9	14.7	93.1
Proceeds from issuance of long-term debt	—	—	549.0
Principal payments on long-term debt	(0.7)	(0.6)	(0.8)
Repurchase of common stock	—	(311.4)	(996.8)
Other	(1.6)	(1.7)	(3.5)
Net cash used by financing activities	(642.2)	(184.5)	(171.9)
Effect of exchange rate changes on cash and cash equivalents	4.3	0.9	11.3
Net increase/(decrease) in cash and cash equivalents	330.0	(11.5)	(31.3)
Cash and Cash Equivalents:			
Beginning of period	269.8	281.3	312.6
End of period	$ 599.8	$ 269.8	$ 281.3
Supplemental Disclosure of Cash Flow Information:			
Net change in short-term borrowings and commercial paper for the period	$ (713.1)	$ 2.2	$ 10.2
Cash paid during the period for:			
Interest, net of capitalized interest	$ 39.8	$ 52.7	$ 35.3
Income taxes	$ 162.0	$ 259.5	$ 342.2

Source: Starbucks 2009 Annual Report, p. 42.

ratio analysis
calculations that measure an organization's financial health

firm make or lose? and (2) How much is the firm presently worth based on historical values found on the balance sheet? **Ratio analysis,** calculations that measure an organization's financial health, brings the complex information from the income statement and balance sheet into sharper focus so that managers, lenders, owners, and other interested parties can measure and compare the organization's productivity, profitability, and financing mix with other similar entities.

You can look on Web sites like Yahoo! Finance under a company's "key statistics" link to find financial ratios such as the firm's return on assets, return on equity, and current ratios. Other ratios require a closer look at the company's actual financial statements.

As you know, a ratio is simply one number divided by another, with the result showing the relationship between the two numbers. Financial ratios are used to weigh and evaluate a firm's performance. An absolute value such as earnings of $70,000 or accounts receivable of $200,000 almost never provides as much useful information as a well-constructed ratio. Whether those numbers are good or bad depends on their relation to other numbers. If a company earned $70,000 on $700,000 in sales (a 10 percent return), such an earnings level might be quite satisfactory. The president of a company earning this same $70,000 on sales of $7 million (a 1 percent return), however, should probably start looking for another job!

Ratios by themselves are not very useful. It is the relationship of the calculated ratios to both prior organizational performance and the performance of the organization's "peers," as well as its stated goals, that really matters. Remember, while the profitability, asset utilization, liquidity, debt ratios, and per share data we'll look at here can be very useful, you will never see the forest by looking only at the trees.

Profitability Ratios

Profitability ratios measure how much operating income or net income an organization is able to generate relative to its assets, owners' equity, and sales. The numerator (top number) used in these examples is always the net income after taxes. Common profitability ratios include profit margin, return on assets, and return on equity. The following examples are based on the 2009 income statement and balance sheet for Starbucks, as shown in Tables 14.4 and 14.6. Except where specified, all data are expressed in millions of dollars.

The **profit margin,** computed by dividing net income by sales, shows the overall percentage profits earned by the company. It is based solely upon data obtained from the income statement. The higher the profit margin, the better the cost controls within the company and the higher the return on every dollar of revenue. Starbucks' profit margin is calculated as follows:

$$\text{Profit margin} = \frac{\text{Net income (Net earnings)}}{\text{Sales (Total net revenues)}} = \frac{\$390.8}{\$9,774.6} = 4.00\%$$

Thus, for every $1 in sales, Starbucks generated profits of just over 4 cents.

Return on assets, net income divided by assets, shows how much income the firm produces for every dollar invested in assets. A company with a low return on assets is probably not using its assets very productively—a key managerial failing. For its construction, the return on assets calculation requires data from both the income statement and the balance sheet.

$$\text{Return on assets} = \frac{\text{Net income (Net earnings)}}{\text{Total assets}} = \frac{\$390.8}{\$5,576.8} = 7.01\%$$

In the case of Starbucks, every $1 of assets generated a return of around 7 percent, or profits of around 7 cents per dollar.

Stockholders are always concerned with how much money they will make on their investment, and they frequently use the return on equity ratio as one of their key performance yardsticks. **Return on equity** (also called return on investment [ROI]), calculated by dividing net income by owners' equity, shows how much income is generated by each $1 the owners have invested in the firm. Obviously, a low return on equity means low stockholder returns and may indicate a need for immediate managerial attention. Because some assets may have been financed with debt not contributed by the owners, the value of the owners' equity is usually considerably lower than the total value of the firm's assets. Starbucks' return on equity is calculated as follows:

$$\text{Return on equity} = \frac{\text{Net income}}{\text{Stockholders' equity}} = \frac{\$390.8}{\$2,490} = 15.69\%$$

For every dollar invested by Starbucks stockholders, the company earned around a 15.7 percent return, or 15.69 cents per dollar invested.

profitability ratios
ratios that measure the amount of operating income or net income an organization is able to generate relative to its assets, owners' equity, and sales

profit margin
net income divided by sales

return on assets
net income divided by assets

return on equity
net income divided by owner's equity; also called return on investment (ROI)

Consider Ethics and Responsibility
Was Mark-to-Market Accounting at the Root of the Financial Crisis?

Mark-to-market accounting attributed to the problems banks faced in the 2008–2009 financial crisis. It requires companies to mark their assets to the market price that existed on that day, which makes sense for futures traders because they buy assets at a fixed future price. However, mark-to-market accounting has been abused recently, most notably by Enron. Enron misused mark-to-market by tabulating anticipated future profits as real, thereby driving up the company's appearance of profitability. This was clearly a misuse of the accounting technique.

Mark-to-market also does not work well when trading stops because a market price cannot be determined based on the price of other trades. When a market dries up, as the mortgage-backed securities market did in late 2008, no active trading occurs and comparison prices do not exist. Banks had mortgages and other assets and debts that were technically marketable, but investors perceived that there was a high level of risk involved and did not want to invest. If the banks marked their assets to zero or 20 cents on the dollar, they would be grossly undervaluing these instruments. Unfortunately, banks were forced to write down assets based on the mark-to-market rule—and wrote off billions of dollars of losses.

To help with the problems on Wall Street, Congress pressured the Securities and Exchange Commission and Federal Accounting Standards Board to relax the mark-to-market rules, which they did to allow the use of discounted cash flow models to value these assets. These models allow banks more accounting flexibility so that they do not have to drastically mark down valuations in times of crisis.[8]

Discussion Questions

1. How would you describe the mark-to-market account method (in your own words)?
2. How did mark-to-market accounting methods so greatly affect the value of companies during the financial crisis?
3. Is it a good idea to relax mark-to-market rules in order to give companies more flexibility with accounting procedures during times of crisis?

Asset Utilization Ratios

asset utilization ratios
ratios that measure how well a firm uses its assets to generate each $1 of sales

Asset utilization ratios measure how well a firm uses its assets to generate each $1 of sales. Obviously, companies using their assets more productively will have higher returns on assets than their less efficient competitors. Similarly, managers can use asset utilization ratios to pinpoint areas of inefficiency in their operations. These ratios (receivables turnover, inventory turnover, and total asset turnover) relate balance sheet assets to sales, which are found on the income statement.

receivables turnover
sales divided by accounts receivable

The **receivables turnover,** sales divided by accounts receivable, indicates how many times a firm collects its accounts receivable in one year. It also demonstrates how quickly a firm is able to collect payments on its credit sales. Obviously, no payments means no profits. Starbucks collected its receivables 36 times per year. The reason the number is so high is that most of Starbucks' sales are for cash and not credit.

$$\text{Receivables turnover} = \frac{\text{Sales (Total net revenues)}}{\text{Receivables}} = \frac{\$9,774.6}{\$271.0} = 36.07 \times$$

inventory turnover
sales divided by total inventory

Inventory turnover, sales divided by total inventory, indicates how many times a firm sells and replaces its inventory over the course of a year. A high inventory turnover ratio may indicate great efficiency but may also suggest the possibility of lost sales due to insufficient stock levels. Starbucks' inventory turnover indicates that it replaced its inventory 14.7 times last year, or more than once a month.

$$\text{Inventory turnover} = \frac{\text{Sales (Total net revenues)}}{\text{Inventory}} = \frac{\$9,774.6}{\$664.9} = 14.70 \times$$

total asset turnover
sales divided by total assets

Total asset turnover, sales divided by total assets, measures how well an organization uses all of its assets in creating sales. It indicates whether a company is using its assets productively. Starbucks generated $1.75 in sales for every $1 in total corporate assets.

$$\text{Total asset turnover} = \frac{\text{Sales (Total net revenues)}}{\text{Total assets}} = \frac{\$9,774.6}{\$5,576.8} = 1.75 \times$$

Liquidity Ratios

Liquidity ratios compare current (short-term) assets to current liabilities to indicate the speed with which a company can turn its assets into cash to meet debts as they fall due. High liquidity ratios may satisfy a creditor's need for safety, but ratios that are too high may indicate that the organization is not using its current assets efficiently. Liquidity ratios are generally best examined in conjunction with asset utilization ratios because high turnover ratios imply that cash is flowing through an organization very quickly—a situation that dramatically reduces the need for the type of reserves measured by liquidity ratios.

liquidity ratios ratios that measure the speed with which a company can turn its assets into cash to meet short-term debt

The **current ratio** is calculated by dividing current assets by current liabilities. Starbucks's current ratio indicates that for every $1 of current liabilities, the firm had $1.29 of current assets on hand. This number improved from previous years, and indicates that Starbucks has increased its liquidity as it restructures its business. Current liabilities decreased from 2008 to 2009 and current assets increased during this period making for a much improved current ratio. Additionally, accounts receivable has increased over the same time period.

current ratio current assets divided by current liabilities

$$\text{Current ratio} = \frac{\text{Current assets}}{\text{Current liabilities}} = \frac{\$2,035.8}{\$1,581.0} = 1.29 \times$$

The **quick ratio** (also known as the **acid test**) is a far more stringent measure of liquidity because it eliminates inventory, the least liquid current asset. It measures how well an organization can meet its current obligations without resorting to the sale of its inventory. In 2009, Starbucks had 87 cents invested in current assets (after subtracting inventory) for every $1 of current liabilities, an increase over previous years.

quick ratio (acid test) a stringent measure of liquidity that eliminates inventory

$$\text{Quick ratio} = \frac{\text{Current assets} - \text{Inventory}}{\text{Current liabilities}} = \frac{\$1,370.9}{\$1,581.0} = 0.87 \times$$

Debt Utilization Ratios

Debt utilization ratios provide information about how much debt an organization is using relative to other sources of capital, such as owners' equity. Because the use of debt carries an interest charge that must be paid regularly regardless of profitability, debt financing is much riskier than equity. Unforeseen negative events such as recessions affect heavily indebted firms to a far greater extent than those financed exclusively with owners' equity. Because of this and other factors, the managers of most firms tend to keep debt-to-asset levels below 50 percent. However, firms in very stable and/or regulated industries, such as electric utilities, often are able to carry debt ratios well in excess of 50 percent with no ill effects.

debt utilization ratios ratios that measure how much debt an organization is using relative to other sources of capital, such as owners' equity

The **debt to total assets ratio** indicates how much of the firm is financed by debt and how much by owners' equity. To find the value of Starbucks' total debt, you must add current liabilities to long-term debt and other liabilities.

debt to total assets ratio a ratio indicating how much of the firm is financed by debt and how much by owners' equity

$$\text{Debt to total assets} = \frac{\text{Debt (Total liabilities)}}{\text{Total assets}} = \frac{\$2,531.0}{\$5,576.8} = 45\%$$

Thus, for every $1 of Starbucks' total assets, 45 percent is financed with debt. The remaining 55 percent is provided by owners' equity.

The **times interest earned ratio,** operating income divided by interest expense, is a measure of the safety margin a company has with respect to the interest payments it must make to its creditors. A low times interest earned ratio indicates that even a small decrease in earnings may lead the company into financial straits. Because Starbucks has more interest income than interest expense, it would appear that their times interest earned ratio is not able to be calculated by using the income statement. However, in the statement of cash flows in Table 14.7 on the second line from the bottom, we can see that Starbucks paid $39.8 million in interest expense, an amount that was covered nearly 14.37 times by income before interest and taxes. A lender would probably not have to worry about receiving interest payments.

$$\text{Times interest earned} = \frac{\text{EBIT (Operating income)}}{\text{Interest}} = \frac{\$562.0}{\$39.1} = 14.37 \times$$

Per Share Data

Investors may use **per share data** to compare the performance of one company with another on an equal, or per share, basis. Generally, the more shares of stock a company issues, the less income is available for each share.

Earnings per share is calculated by dividing net income or profit by the number of shares of stock outstanding. This ratio is important because yearly changes in earnings per share, in combination with other economywide factors, determine a company's overall stock price. When earnings go up, so does a company's stock price—and so does the wealth of its stockholders.

$$\text{Diluted earnings per share} = \frac{\text{Net income}}{\text{Number of shares outstanding (diluted)}}$$

$$= \frac{\$390.8}{745.9} = \$0.52$$

We can see from the income statement that Starbucks' basic earnings per share decreased dramatically from $0.90 in 2007 to $0.43 in 2008, then recovered slightly in 2009 to $0.52. Notice that Starbucks lists diluted earnings per share, calculated here, of $0.43 per share in 2008 and $0.53 per share in 2009. You can see from the income statement that diluted earnings per share include more shares than the basic calculation; this is because diluted shares include potential shares that could be issued due to the exercise of stock options or the conversion of certain types of debt into common stock. Investors generally pay more attention to diluted earnings per share than basic earnings per share.

Dividends per share are paid by the corporation to the stockholders for each share owned. The payment is made from earnings after taxes by the corporation but is taxable income to the stockholder. Thus, dividends result in double taxation: The corporation pays tax once on its earnings, and the stockholder pays tax a second time on his or her dividend income. Starbucks has never paid a dividend, so the calculation of dividends per share does not apply in this case.

$$\text{Dividends per share} = \frac{\text{Dividends paid}}{\text{Number of shares outstanding}} = \frac{\$0}{746} = \$0.00$$

Industry Analysis

We have used McDonald's as a comparison to Starbucks because there are no real national and international coffee houses that compete with Starbucks on the same scale. While McDonald's is almost four times larger than Starbucks in terms of sales, they both have a national and international presence and to some extent compete for the consumer's dollars. Table 14.8 shows that McDonald's dominates Starbucks in all areas of profitability. Since 2007, McDonald's has almost doubled its profitability, while Starbucks has stumbled. Coffee prices went up, which increased costs, and the economic recession caused coffee drinkers to look for lower cost alternatives. Both companies have very little accounts receivable relative to the size of their sales, and so the ratios are very high, indicating a lot of cash sales and credit card sales. McDonald's pushes off much of its inventory holding costs on its suppliers, and so has much less inventory per sales dollar compared with Starbucks and, therefore, has a much higher inventory turnover ratio. Both have current ratios about the same, but because McDonald's has less inventory, its quick ratio is higher than Starbucks. Fortunately for Starbucks, its inventory is highly liquid and can be turned into cash quickly. The difference in the quick ratios is of little consequence to the financial analyst or lender because both companies have high times interest earned ratios. Starbucks' earnings have suffered over the past three years, and Howard Schultz, the founder, has come back as CEO to lead a restructuring of the company. Starbucks has closed unprofitable stores and introduced new products and seem to be on its way to a recovery. On the other hand, McDonald's has increased its earnings per share from $1.93 in 2007 to $4.11 in 2009. McDonald's has also increased its dividend over this time period from $1.50 per share to $2.05 per share, while Starbucks has continued to pay no dividend, choosing instead to reinvest in the company's expansion and debt reduction. Both companies are in good financial health, but McDonald's is winning the race for stockholder returns. One thing is for sure: If Starbucks could earn the same profit margin as McDonald's, it would improve its other profitability ratios and its stock price.

	Starbucks	McDonald's
Profit margin	4.00%	20.01%
Return on assets	7.01%	15.06%
Return on equity	15.69%	32.43%
Receivables turnover	36.07	21.38
Inventory turnover	14.7×	214.17×
Total asset turnover	1.75×	0.75×
Current ratio	1.29×	1.14×
Quick ratio	0.87×	1.11×
Debt to total assets	45.00%	54.00%
Times interest earned	14.37×	14.46×
Diluted earnings per share	$0.52	$4.11
Dividends per share	$0.00	$2.05

Source: Data calculated from 2009 annual reports.

TABLE 14.8

Industry Analysis, Year Ending 2009

Accounting and the Impact of the Financial Crisis

The financial crisis of 2007–2009 provided another example of failed accounting audits. Banks and other financial institutions often held assets off their books by manipulating their accounts. In 2010, the examiner for the Lehman Brothers' bankruptcy found that the most common example of removing assets or liabilities from the books was entering into what is called a "repurchase agreement." In a repurchase agreement, assets are transferred to another entity with the contractual promise of buying them back at a set price. In the case of Lehman Brothers and other companies, repurchase agreements were used as a method of "cooking the books" that allowed them to manipulate accounting statements so that their ratios looked better than they actually were. If the accountants, the SEC, and the bank regulators had been more careful, these types of transactions would have been discovered and corrected. The public discovered that the audit system failed with Lehman Brothers and many other major financial firms during the 2008 crisis on Wall Street.

Banks and other financial companies blamed much of the problem on the accounting rule of mark-to-market, which was also used by Enron to make it look more profitable. (Mark-to-market accounting is discussed in the Ethics and Social Responsibility Box in this chapter.) This rule meant that assets on the books have to be carried on the books at the current market price. As the financial markets deteriorated, the value of many assets (such as mortgages) could not be valued accurately. What happens when a market is so unhealthy that it basically ceases to function? Is the asset worth zero? Because the value of the assets held on their books determined a bank's capital adequacy ratios, the decline in value that resulted from using the mark-to-market accounting method made banks' capital appear to shrink dramatically. Investors determined that these banks were suddenly risky investments. The government determined that it had to step in and allow banks to revalue assets. Many think this was helpful in stemming the deterioration of banks' capital. Some accountants, however, argued that the mark-to-market rule creates a more honest balance sheet and true value of a company's worth. This may be true under normal circumstances, where markets are not frozen and investors continue to trade and trust the financial stability of their trading partners. These issues will continue to be addressed by the government in future financial reform.

So You Want to Be an Accountant

Do you like numbers and finances? Are you detail oriented, a perfectionist, and highly accountable for your decisions? If so, accounting may be a good field for you. If you are interested in accounting, there are always job opportunities available no matter the state of the economy. Accounting is one of the most secure job options in business. Of course, becoming an accountant is not easy. You will need at least a bachelor's degree in accounting to get a job, and many positions require additional training. Many states demand coursework beyond the 120 to 150 credit hours collegiate programs require for an accounting degree. If you are really serious about getting into the accounting field, you will probably want to consider getting your master's in accounting and taking the CPA exam. The field of accounting can be complicated, and the extra training provided through a master's in accounting program will prove invaluable when you go out looking for a good job. Accounting is a volatile discipline affected by changes in legislative initiatives.

With corporate accounting policies changing constantly and becoming more complex, accountants are needed to help keep a business running smoothly and within the bounds of the law. In fact, the number of jobs in the accounting and auditing field are expected to increase 22 percent between 2008 and 2018, with more than 1.5 million jobs in the United States alone by 2018. Jobs in accounting tend to pay quite well, with the national average salary standing at just over $59,000 annually. If you go on to get your master's degree in accounting, expect to see an even higher starting wage. In 2009, accountants with a bachelor's degree received an average opening offer of $48,993, while employees with master's degrees were offered $49,786 starting. Of course, your earnings could be higher or lower than these averages, depending on where you work, your level of experience, the firm, and your particular position.

Accountants are needed in the public and the private sectors, in large and small firms, in for-profit and not-for-profit organizations. Accountants in firms are generally in charge of preparing and filing tax forms and financial reports. Public-sector accountants are responsible for checking the veracity of corporate and personal records in order to prepare tax filings. Basically, any organization that has to deal with money and/or taxes in some way or another will be in need of an accountant, either for in-house service or occasional contract work. Requirements for audits under the Sarbanes Oxley Act and rules from the Public Company Accounting Oversight Board are creating more jobs and increased responsibility to maintain internal controls and accounting ethics. The fact that accounting rules and tax filings tend to be complex virtually assures that the demand for accountants will never decrease.[9]

Review Your Understanding

Define accounting, and describe the different uses of accounting information.

Accounting is the language businesses and other organizations use to record, measure, and interpret financial transactions. Financial statements are used internally to judge and control an organization's performance and to plan and direct its future activities and measure goal attainment. External organizations such as lenders, governments, customers, suppliers, and the Internal Revenue Service are major consumers of the information generated by the accounting process.

Demonstrate the accounting process.

Assets are an organization's economic resources; liabilities, debts the organization owes to others; owners' equity, and the difference between the value of an organization's assets and liabilities. This principle can be expressed as the accounting equation: Assets = Liabilities − Owners' equity. The double-entry bookkeeping system is a system of recording and classifying business transactions in accounts that maintain the balance of the accounting equation. The accounting cycle involves examining source documents, recording transactions in a journal, posting transactions, and preparing financial statements on a continuous basis throughout the life of the organization.

Decipher the various components of an income statement in order to evaluate a firm's "bottom line."

The income statement indicates a company's profitability over a specific period of time. It shows the "bottom line," the total profit (or loss) after all expenses (the costs incurred in the day-to-day operations of the organization) have been deducted from revenue (the total amount of money received from the sale of goods or services and other business activities). The cash flow statement details how much cash is moving through the firm and thus adds insight to a firm's "bottom line."

Interpret a company's balance sheet to determine its current financial position.

The balance sheet, which summarizes the firm's assets, liabilities, and owners' equity since its inception, portrays its financial position as of a particular point in time. Major classifications included in the balance sheet are current assets (assets that can be converted to cash within one calendar year), fixed assets (assets of greater than one year's duration), current liabilities (bills owed by the organization within one calendar year), long-term liabilities (bills due more than one year hence), and owners' equity (the net value of the owners' investment).

Analyze financial statements, using ratio analysis, to evaluate a company's performance.

Ratio analysis is a series of calculations that brings the complex information from the income statement and

balance sheet into sharper focus so that managers, lenders, owners, and other interested parties can measure and compare the organization's productivity, profitability, and financing mix with other similar entities. Ratios may be classified in terms of profitability (measure dollars of return for each dollar of employed assets), asset utilization (measure how well the organization uses its assets to generate $1 in sales), liquidity (assess organizational risk by comparing current assets to current liabilities), debt utilization (measure how much debt the organization is using relative to other sources of capital), and per share data (compare the performance of one company with another on an equal basis).

Assess a company's financial position using its accounting statements and ratio analysis.

Based on the information presented in the chapter, you should be able to answer the questions posed in "Solve the Dilemma" on page 466 formulate a plan for determining BrainDrain's bottom line, current worth, and productivity.

Revisit the World of Business

1. How did accounting misconduct and bad financial statements contribute to the demises of Fannie Mae and Freddie Mac?

2. Why was accounting at Fannie Mae and Freddie Mac so important for external use by stakeholders?

3. Why is it essential for Fannie Mae and Freddie Mac to have accurate financial records and accounting statements?

Learn the Terms

Check Your Progress

1. Why are accountants so important to a corporation? What function do they perform?
2. Discuss the internal uses of accounting statements.
3. What is a budget?
4. Discuss the external uses of financial statements.
5. Describe the accounting process and cycle.
6. The income statements of all corporations are in the same format. True or false? Discuss.
7. Which accounts appear under "current liabilities"?
8. Together, the income statement and the balance sheet answer two basic questions. What are they?
9. What are the five basic ratio classifications? What ratios are found in each category?
10. Why are debt ratios important in assessing the risk of a firm?

Get Involved

1. Go to the library or the Internet and get the annual report of a company with which you are familiar. Read through the financial statements, then write up an analysis of the firm's performance using ratio analysis. Look at data over several years and analyze whether the firm's performance is changing through time.
2. Form a group of three or four students to perform an industry analysis. Each student should analyze a company in the same industry, and then all of you should compare your results. The following companies would make good group projects:

Automobiles: DaimlerChrysler, Ford, General Motors

Computers: Apple, IBM, Dell

Brewing: Anheuser-Busch, Molson Coors, G. Heileman

Chemicals: Du Pont, Dow Chemical, Monsanto

Petroleum: Chevron, ExxonMobil, Amoco

Pharmaceuticals: Merck, Lilly, UpJohn

Retail: Sears, JCPenney, Kmart, The Limited

Build Your Skills

FINANCIAL ANALYSIS

Background:
The income statement for Western Grain Company, a producer of agricultural products for industrial as well as consumer markets, is shown below. Western Grain's total assets are $4,237.1 million, and its equity is $1,713.4 million.

Consolidated Earnings and Retained Earnings Year Ended December 31

(Millions)	2010
Net sales	$6,295.4
Cost of goods sold	2,989.0
Selling and administrative expense	2,237.5
Operating profit	1,068.9
Interest expense	33.3
Other income (expense), net	(1.5)
Earnings before income taxes	1,034.1
Income taxes	353.4
Net earnings	680.7
(Net earnings per share)	$2.94
Retained earnings, beginning of year	3,033.9
Dividends paid	(305.2)
Retained earnings, end of year	$3,409.4

Task:

Calculate the following profitability ratios: profit margin, return on assets, and return on equity. Assume that the industry averages for these ratios are as follows: profit margin, 12 percent; return on assets, 18 percent; and return on equity, 25 percent. Evaluate Western Grain's profitability relative to the industry averages. Why is this information useful?

Solve the Dilemma

EXPLORING THE SECRETS OF ACCOUNTING

You have just been promoted from vice president of marketing of BrainDrain Corporation to president and CEO! That's the good news. Unfortunately, while you know marketing like the back of your hand, you know next to nothing about finance. Worse still, the "word on the street" is that BrainDrain is in danger of failure if steps to correct large and continuing financial losses are not taken immediately. Accordingly, you have asked the vice president of finance and accounting for a complete set of accounting statements detailing the financial operations of the company over the past several years.

Recovering from the dual shocks of your promotion and feeling the weight of the firm's complete accounting report for the very first time, you decide to attack the problem systematically and learn the "hidden secrets" of the company, statement by statement. With Mary Pruitt, the firm's trusted senior financial analyst, by your side, you delve into the accounting statements as never before. You resolve to "get to the bottom" of the firm's financial problems and set a new course for the future—a course that will take the firm from insolvency and failure to financial recovery and perpetual prosperity.

Discussion Questions

1. Describe the three basic accounting statements. What types of information does each provide that can help you evaluate the situation?

2. Which of the financial ratios are likely to prove to be of greatest value in identifying problem areas in the company? Why? Which of your company's financial ratios might you expect to be especially poor?

3. Discuss the limitations of ratio analysis.

Build Your Business Plan

ACCOUNTING AND FINANCIAL STATEMENTS

After you determine your initial *reasonable selling price,* you need to estimate your sales forecasts (in terms of units and dollars of sales) for the first year of operation. Remember to be conservative and set forecasts that are more modest.

While customers may initially try your business, many businesses have seasonal patterns. A good budgeting/planning system allows managers to anticipate problems, coordinate activities of the business (so that subunits within the organization are all working toward the common goal of the organization), and control operations (how do we know whether spending is "in line").

The first financial statement you need to prepare is the income statement. Beginning with your estimated sales revenue, determine what expenses will be necessary to generate that level of sales revenue.

The second financial statement you need to create is your balance sheet. Your balance sheet is a snapshot of your financial position in a moment in time. Refer to Table 14.6 to assist you in listing your assets, liabilities and owner's equity.

The last financial statement, the cash flow statement, is the most important one to a bank. It is a measure of your ability to get and repay the loan from the bank. Referring to Table 14.7, be as realistic as possible as you are completing it. Allow yourself enough cash on hand until the point in which the business starts to support itself.

See for Yourself Videocase

ARENA FOOTBALL RETURNS FROM THE BRINK OF BANKRUPTCY

The Arena Football League (AFL) seemed to have everything going for it. About 13,000 people flocked to see its games in 2008, and revenues poured in. Yet less than a year later, the AFL filed for bankruptcy and suspended operations for a year. In late 2009, the Arena Football One League acquired the assets of the AFL in a $61 million bankruptcy settlement.

The AFL was founded in 1987 by former National Football League executive Jim Foster, who first conceived the idea while watching a soccer game. Unlike traditional football games, arena football is played inside on a smaller field with eight players on each side and slightly different rules. Over the years, AFL gained a loyal fan following and increased significantly in popularity.

AFL's failure had more to do with poor business management than with a lack of fans. It expanded quickly into unprofitable markets, and revenues could not keep up with costs. In one year, the AFL team Chicago Rush spent $6 million but only generated $4.7 million in revenues. Player salaries were excessively high, with an AFL-union mandate of at least $1,800 per game. The AFL also took on the well-established National Football League, which was a costly decision. According to Mike Polisky, President of the Chicago Rush team, investments in arena football may not generate profits for several years. This often deters investors who are looking to profit immediately. Arena football teams must also compete against more well-known national football teams for investors and fans.

To generate more money, the AFL teams have begun to create a new niche. The sport has experienced significant growth in the past few years while other sports markets have begun to stagnate. However, without enough revenue, the AFL could not pay back its debts. After its bankruptcy filing, the AFL was acquired by Arena Football One. The new league will retain the original name but will take a different approach to ensure its financial survival.

The AFL teams are managing their financial operations. Several ratios are utilized to measure the financial health of the organization and make adjustments for any monetary issues. For example, liquidity ratios determine how quickly assets can be turned into cash to pay immediate debts. Many companies face cash flow problems, and AFL teams are attempting to avoid this trap by ensuring that enough of its assets can be quickly converted to cash as

needed to prevent the stockpiling of debt. Additionally, the league is adopting a single-entity business model, which allows the franchises to be owned by the league itself. Investors who want to assume ownership must pay the league to operate the teams. The league will also pay less for player salaries. In the process, the AFL can use the extra revenue provided by team owners and the reduced salaries to keep the league financially healthy.

The original AFL fell into the same traps as many failed organizations: not having enough money on hand to pay debts, expanding too quickly, and incurring out-of-control expenses. However, arena football now has the opportunity to thrive once more. The league strategy expanded (albeit more slowly) beginning in 2011. With effective oversight and financial management, arena football may soon be giving competitors a run for their money.[10]

Discussion Questions

1. What marketing and financial decisions did the AFL make that forced it to declare bankruptcy?

2. What financial ratios does Arena Football use to help it assess the financial health of the organization? What is the purpose of these different ratios?

3. What is the AFL doing differently now that has helped it to regain financial solvency?

Remember to check out our Online Learning Center at www.mhhe.com/ferrell8e.

Team Exercise

You can look at Web sites such as Yahoo! Finance (http://finance.yahoo.com/), under the company's 'key statistics' link, to find many of its financial ratios, such as return on assets and return on equity. Have each member of your team look up a different company, and explain why you think there are differences in the ratio analysis for these two ratios among the selected companies.

Money and the Financial System

OBJECTIVES

After reading this chapter, you will be able to:

- Define money, its functions, and its characteristics.

- Describe various types of money.

- Specify how the Federal Reserve Board manages the money supply and regulates the American banking system.

- Compare and contrast commercial banks, savings and loan associations, credit unions, and mutual savings banks.

- Distinguish among nonbanking institutions such as insurance companies, pension funds, mutual funds, and finance companies.

- Investigate the challenges ahead for the banking industry.

- Recommend the most appropriate financial institution for a hypothetical small business.

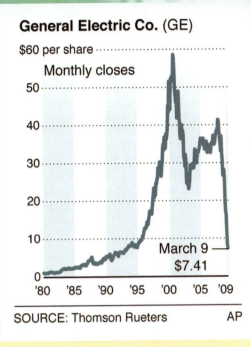

General Electric Co. (GE)

$60 per share

Monthly closes

March 9 — $7.41

'80 '85 '90 '95 '00 '05 '09

SOURCE: Thomson Rueters   AP

General Electric, the Financial Giant

Most people think of General Electric as a maker of light bulbs or appliances. GE also makes jet engines, power turbines, and medical-imaging machines and owns NBC. General Electric Capital, a division of GE, is one of the largest financial companies in the United States. It is the second-largest leaser of airplanes in the world and one of the largest commercial and consumer lenders. It currently accounts for 37 percent of GE's revenue and 33 percent of profits. The commercial lending and leasing division alone accounts for about $230 billion in assets, while consumer finance (which includes private-label credit cards) accounted for $183 billion in assets.

General Electric Capital is not regulated by the Federal Reserve. It has the ability to use money from its industrial divisions to shore up its lending and financial arm. During the financial meltdown, investors became more and more worried that GE would go the way of Bank America and Citibank. For example, Bank of America's common stock price went from a high of $55 in 2007 to a low of $3 in March 2009 and CitiGroup's stock went from a high of $57 to a low of $0.97 during the same time period. General Electric's common stock went from a high of $42 in 2007 to $5.73 in March 2009. Investors were worried that GE didn't have enough capital and might default on its loans. Even though GE raised more than $50 billion in capital through public markets, investors were still nervous. GE had more than $45 billion in cash on its balance sheet, but that wasn't enough to calm the market. By May 2009, the stock had rallied to $13, signaling a strong rebound in investor trust.[1]

Introduction

finance
the study of money; how it's made, how it's lost, and how it's managed

From Wall Street to Main Street, both overseas and at home, money is the one tool used to measure personal and business income and wealth. **Finance** is the study of money: how it's made, how it's lost, and how it's managed. This chapter introduces you to the role of money and the financial system in the economy. Of course, if you have a checking account, automobile insurance, a college loan, or a credit card, you already have personal experience with some key players in the financial world.

We begin our discussion with a definition of money and then explore some of the many forms money may take. Next, we examine the roles of the Federal Reserve Board and other major institutions in the financial system. Finally, we explore the future of the finance industry and some of the changes likely to occur over the course of the next several years.

Money in the Financial System

money
anything generally accepted in exchange for goods and services

Strictly defined, **money,** or *currency,* is anything generally accepted in exchange for goods and services. Materials as diverse as salt, cattle, fish, rocks, shells, cloth, as well as precious metals such as gold, silver, and copper have long been used by various cultures as money. Most of these materials were limited-supply commodities that had their own value to society (for example, salt can be used as a preservative and shells and metals as jewelry). The supply of these commodities therefore determined the supply of "money" in that society. The next step was the development of "IOUs," or slips of paper that could be exchanged for a specified supply of the underlying commodity. "Gold" notes, for instance, could be exchanged for gold, and the money supply was tied to the amount of gold available. While paper money was first used in North America in 1685 (and even earlier in Europe), the concept of *fiat money*—a paper money not readily convertible to a precious metal such as gold—did not gain full acceptance until the Great Depression in the 1930s. The U.S. abandoned its gold-backed currency standard largely in response to the Great Depression and converted to a fiduciary, or fiat, monetary system. In the United States, paper money is really a government "note" or promise, worth the value specified on the note.

Functions of Money

No matter what a particular society uses for money, its primary purpose is to enable a person or organization to transform a desire into an action. These desires may be for entertainment actions, such as party expenses; operating actions, such as paying for rent, utilities, or employees; investing actions, such as buying property or equipment; or financing actions, such as for starting or growing a business. Money serves three important functions: as a medium of exchange, a measure of value, and a store of value.

Medium of Exchange.   Before fiat money, the trade of goods and services was accomplished through *bartering*—trading one good or service for another of similar value. As any school-age child knows, bartering can become quite inefficient—particularly in the case of complex, three-party transactions involving peanut butter sandwiches, baseball cards, and hair barrettes. There had to be a simpler way, and that was to decide on a single item—money—that can be freely converted to any other good upon agreement between parties.

Measure of Value.   As a measure of value, money serves as a common standard or yardstick of the value of goods and services. For example, $2 will buy a dozen large eggs and $25,000 will buy a nice car in the United States. In Japan, where the currency is known as the yen, these same transactions would cost about 185 yen and 2.3 million yen, respectively. Money, then, is a common denominator that allows people to compare the different goods and services that can be consumed on a particular income level. While a star athlete and a "burger-flipper" are paid vastly different wages, each uses money as a measure of the value of their yearly earnings and purchases.

For centuries people on the Micronesian island of Yap have used giant round stones, like the ones shown here, for money. The stones aren't moved, but their ownership can change.

Store of Value.   As a store of value, money serves as a way to accumulate wealth (buying power) until it is needed. For example, a person making $500 per week who wants to buy a $500 computer could save $50 per week for each of the next 10 weeks. Unfortunately, the value of stored money is directly dependent on the health of the economy. If, due to rapid inflation, all prices double in one year, then the purchasing power value of the money "stuffed in the mattress" would fall by half. On the other hand, "mattress savings" buy more when prices fall as they did for more than 52 months in Hong Kong between 1999 and 2005.

Characteristics of Money

To be used as a medium of exchange, money must be acceptable, divisible, portable, stable in value, durable, and difficult to counterfeit.

Acceptability.   To be effective, money must be readily acceptable for the purchase of goods and services and for the settlement of debts. Acceptability is probably the most important characteristic of money: If people do not trust the value of money, businesses will not accept it as a payment for goods and services, and consumers will have to find some other means of paying for their purchases.

Divisibility.   Given the widespread use of quarters, dimes, nickels, and pennies in the United States, it is no surprise that the principle of divisibility is an important one. With barter, the lack of divisibility often makes otherwise preferable trades impossible, as would be an attempt to trade a steer for a loaf of bread. For money to serve effectively as a measure of value, all items must be valued in terms of comparable units—dimes for a piece of bubble gum, quarters for laundry machines, and dollars (or dollars and coins) for everything else.

Portability.   Clearly, for money to function as a medium of exchange, it must be easily moved from one location to the next. Large colored rocks could be used as money, but you couldn't carry them around in your wallet. Paper currency and metal coins, on the other hand, are capable of transferring vast purchasing power into small, easily carried (and hidden!) bundles. Few Americans realize it, but more U.S. currency is in circulation outside the United States than within. Currently,

Inflation erodes the value of money. Zimbabwe's inflation recently became so bad that the value of its currency began falling by half its value on a daily basis.

about $829 billion of U.S. currency is in circulation, and the majority is held outside the United States.[2]

Stability.   Money must be stable and maintain its declared face value. A $10 bill should purchase the same amount of goods or services from one day to the next. The principle of stability allows people who wish to postpone purchases and save their money to do so without fear that it will decline in value. As mentioned earlier, money declines in value during periods of inflation, when economic conditions cause prices to rise. Thus, the same amount of money buys fewer and fewer goods and services. In some countries, people spend their money as fast as they can in order to keep it from losing any more of its value. Instability destroys confidence in a nation's money and its ability to store value and serve as an effective medium of exchange. Ultimately, people faced with spiraling price increases avoid the increasingly worthless paper money at all costs, storing all of their savings in the form of real assets such as gold and land.

Durability.   Money must be durable. The crisp new dollar bills you trade at the music store for the hottest new CD will make their way all around town for about 20 months before being replaced (see Table 15.1). Were the value of an old, faded bill to fall in line with the deterioration of its appearance, the principles of stability and universal acceptability would fail (but, no doubt, fewer bills would pass through the washer!). Although metal coins, due to their much longer useful life, would appear to be an ideal form of money, paper currency is far more portable than metal because of its light weight. Today, coins are used primarily to provide divisibility.

Difficulty to Counterfeit.   Finally, to remain stable and enjoy universal acceptance, it almost goes without saying that money must be very difficult to counterfeit—that is, to duplicate illegally. Every country takes steps to make counterfeiting difficult. Most use multicolored money, and many use specially watermarked papers that are virtually impossible to duplicate. Counterfeit bills represent less than 0.03 percent of the currency in circulation in the United States,[4] but it is becoming increasingly easier for counterfeiters to print money with just a modest inkjet printer. This illegal printing of money is fueled by hundreds of people who often circulate only small amounts of counterfeit bills. To thwart the problem of counterfeiting, the U.S. Treasury Department redesigned the U.S. currency, starting with the $20 bill in 2003, the $50 bill in 2004, the $10 bill in 2006, the $5 bill in 2008, and the $100 bill in 2010. For the first time, U.S. money includes subtle colors in addition to the traditional green, as well as enhanced security features, such as a watermark, security thread, and color-shifting ink.[5] In 2006 the new Jefferson nickel was introduced, showing a profile of the nation's third president. Due to the increased price of

Did You Know?   Around 75 percent of counterfeit currency is found and destroyed before it ever reaches the public.[3]

The U.S. government redesigns currency in order to stay ahead of counterfeiters and protect the public.

metals, it costs 5.79 cents to make the 5 cent piece.[6] President Lincoln was the first president to appear on a coin when the Lincoln penny was introduced in 1909. As Figure 15.1 indicates it costs more than a penny to manufacture a penny, resulting in a call to discontinue it.

Types of Money

While paper money and coins are the most visible types of money, the combined value of all of the printed bills and all of the minted coins is actually rather insignificant when compared with the value of money kept in checking accounts, savings accounts, and other monetary forms.

You probably have a **checking account** (also called a *demand deposit*), money stored in an account at a bank or other financial institution that can be withdrawn without advance notice. One way to withdraw funds from your account is by writing a *check,* a written order to a bank to pay the indicated individual or business the amount specified on the check from money already on deposit. Figure 15.2 explains the significance of the numbers found on a typical U.S. check. As legal instruments, checks serve as a substitute for currency and coins and are preferred for many transactions due to their lower risk of loss. If you lose a $100 bill, anyone who finds or steals it can spend it. If you lose a blank check, however, the risk of catastrophic loss

checking account
money stored in an account at a bank or other financial institution that can be withdrawn without advance notice; also called a demand deposit

Denomination of Bill	Life Expectancy (Years)
$1	1.8
$5	1.3
$10	1.5
$20	2.0
$50	4.6
$100	7.4

TABLE 15.1

The Life Expectancy of Paper Currency

Source: "How Currency Gets into Circulation", Federal Reserve Bank of Bank of New York, http://www.newyorkfed.org/aboutthefed/fedpoint/fed01.html (accessed on March 31, 2010).

FIGURE 15.1

Cost to Produce a Penny

Source: "US Mint Cost to Produce the Penny and Nickel," *Coin Update News,* http://news.coinupdate.com/us-mint-cost-to-produce-the-penny-and-nickel-0137 (accessed March, 31, 2009).

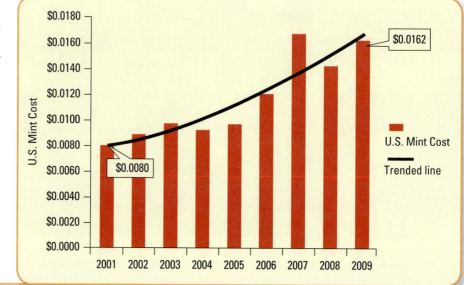

savings accounts
accounts with funds that usually cannot be withdrawn without advance notice; also known as time deposits

money market accounts
accounts that offer higher interest rates than standard bank rates but with greater restrictions

certificates of deposit (CDs)
savings accounts that guarantee a depositor a set interest rate over a specified interval as long as the funds are not withdrawn before the end of the period—six months or one year, for example

credit cards
means of access to preapproved lines of credit granted by a bank or finance company

is quite low. Not only does your bank have a sample of your signature on file to compare with a suspected forged signature, but you can render the check immediately worthless by means of a stop-payment order at your bank.

There are several types of checking accounts, with different features available for different monthly fee levels or specific minimum account balances. Some checking accounts earn interest (a small percentage of the amount deposited in the account that the bank pays to the depositor). One such interest-bearing checking account is the *NOW (Negotiable Order of Withdrawal) account* offered by most financial institutions. The interest rate paid on such accounts varies with the interest rates available in the economy but is typically quite low (ranging between 2 and 5 percent).

Savings accounts (also known as *time deposits*) are accounts with funds that usually cannot be withdrawn without advance notice and/or have limits on the number of withdrawals per period. While seldom enforced, the "fine print" governing most savings accounts prohibits withdrawals without two or three days' notice. Savings accounts are not generally used for transactions or as a medium of exchange, but their funds can be moved to a checking account or turned into cash.

Money market accounts are similar to interest-bearing checking accounts, but with more restrictions. Generally, in exchange for slightly higher interest rates, the owner of a money market account can write only a limited number of checks each month, and there may be a restriction on the minimum amount of each check.

Certificates of deposit (CDs) are savings accounts that guarantee a depositor a set interest rate over a specified interval of time as long as the funds are not withdrawn before the end of the interval—six months, one year, or seven years, for example. Money may be withdrawn from these accounts prematurely only after paying a substantial penalty. In general, the longer the term of the CD, the higher is the interest rate it earns. As with all interest rates, the rate offered and fixed at the time the account is opened fluctuates according to economic conditions.

Credit cards allow you to promise to pay at a later date by using preapproved lines of credit granted by a bank or finance company. They are a popular substitute for cash payments because of their convenience, easy access to credit, and acceptance

FIGURE 15.2   A Check

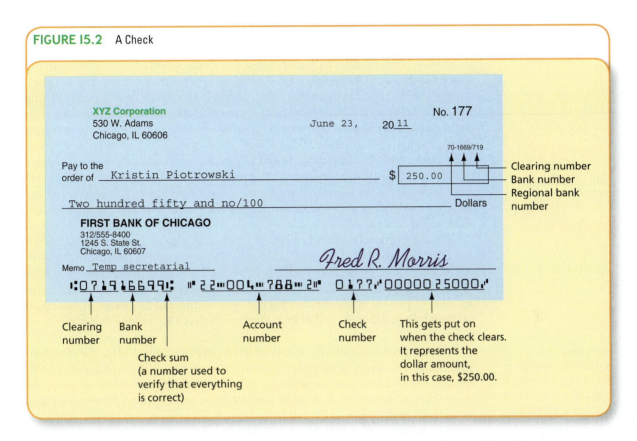

by merchants around the world. The institution that issues the credit card guarantees payment of a credit charge to merchants and assumes responsibility for collecting the money from the cardholders. Card issuers charge a transaction fee to the merchants for performing the credit check, guaranteeing the payment and collecting the payment. The fee is typically between 2 and 5 percent, depending on the type of card. American Express fees are usually higher than Visa and MasterCard.

The original American Express cards require full payment at the end of each month, but American Express now offers credit cards similar to Visa, MasterCard, and Discover that allow cardholders to make installment payments and carry a maximum balance. There is a minimum monthly payment with interest charged on the remaining balance. Some people pay off their credit cards monthly, while other make monthly payments. Charges for unpaid balances can run 18 percent or higher at an annual rate, making credit card debt one of the most expensive ways to borrow money.

Besides the major credit card companies, many stores—Target, Saks Fifth Avenue, Macy's, Bloomingdales, Sears, and others—have their own branded credit

High interest rates on credit cards and the most recent recession have led the bulk of Americans to reduce credit card balances for the first time in years.

cards. They use credit rating agencies to check the credit of the cardholders and they generally make money on the finance charges.

In May 2009, President Obama signed the Credit CARD (Card Accountability Responsibility and Disclosure) Act of 2009 into law, primarily to regulate the practices of credit card companies that were coming under attack by consumers during the recession of 2007–2009. Without going into the details, the law limited the ability of card issuers to raise interest rates, limited credit to young adults, gave people more time to pay bills, required that if there were various levels of interest rates that the balances with the highest rate would be paid off first, and made clearer due dates on billing cycles, along with several other provisions. For college students, the most important part of the law is that young adults under the age of 21 will have to have an adult co-signer or show proof that they have enough income to handle the debt limit on the card.

This act is important to all companies and cardholders. There were more than 609.8 million credit cards held by U.S. consumers at the end of 2009, with the average cardholder having between three and four cards. The top 10 issuers held close to 87 percent of the market share of close to $1 trillion of general-purpose credit cards. In 2008, 41 percent of college students had credit cards, and 65 percent of them paid off their bills in full at the end of each month, which is a higher rate than the general population.[7]

debit card
a card that looks like a credit card but works like a check; using it results in a direct, immediate, electronic payment from the cardholder's checking account to a merchant or third party

A **debit card** looks like a credit card but works like a check. The use of a debit card results in a direct, immediate, electronic payment from the cardholder's checking account to a merchant or other party. While they are convenient to carry and profitable for banks, they lack credit features, offer no purchase "grace period," and provide no hard "paper trail." Debit cards are gaining more acceptance with merchants, and consumers like debit cards because of the ease of getting cash from an increasing number of ATM machines. Financial institutions also want consumers to use debit cards because they reduce the number of teller transactions and check processing costs. Some cash management accounts at retail brokers like Merrill Lynch offer deferred debit cards. These act like a credit card but debit to the cash management account once a month. During that time, the cash earns a money market return.

Traveler's checks, money orders, and cashier's checks are other common forms of "near money." Although each is slightly different from the others, they all share a common characteristic: A financial institution, bank, credit company, or neighborhood currency exchange issues them in exchange for cash and guarantees that the purchased note will be honored and exchanged for cash when it is presented to the institution making the guarantee.

The American Financial System

The U.S. financial system fuels our economy by storing money, fostering investment opportunities, and making loans for new businesses and business expansion as well as for homes, cars, and college educations. This amazingly complex system includes banking institutions, nonbanking financial institutions such as finance companies, and systems that provide for the electronic transfer of funds throughout the world. Over the past 20 years, the rate at which money turns over, or changes hands, has increased exponentially. Different cultures place unique values on saving, spending, borrowing, and investing. The combination of this increased turnover rate and increasing interactions with people and organizations from other countries has created a complex money system. First, we need to meet the guardian of this complex system.

The Federal Reserve System

The guardian of the American financial system is the **Federal Reserve Board,** or "the Fed," as it is commonly called, an independent agency of the federal government established in 1913 to regulate the nation's banking and financial industry. The Federal Reserve System is organized into 12 regions, each with a Federal Reserve Bank that serves its defined area (Figure 15.3). All the Federal Reserve banks except those in Boston and Philadelphia have regional branches. The Cleveland Federal Reserve Bank, for example, is responsible for branch offices in Pittsburgh and Cincinnati.

The Federal Reserve Board is the chief economic policy arm of the United States. Working with Congress and the president, the Fed tries to create a positive economic environment capable of sustaining low inflation, high levels of employment, a balance in international payments, and long-term economic growth. To this end, the Federal Reserve Board has four major responsibilities: (1) to control the supply of money, or monetary policy; (2) to regulate banks and other financial institutions; (3) to manage regional and national checking account procedures, or check clearing; and (4) to supervise the federal deposit insurance programs of banks belonging to the Federal Reserve System.

Federal Reserve Board an independent agency of the federal government established in 1913 to regulate the nation's banking and financial industry

---

FIGURE 15.3   Federal Reserve System

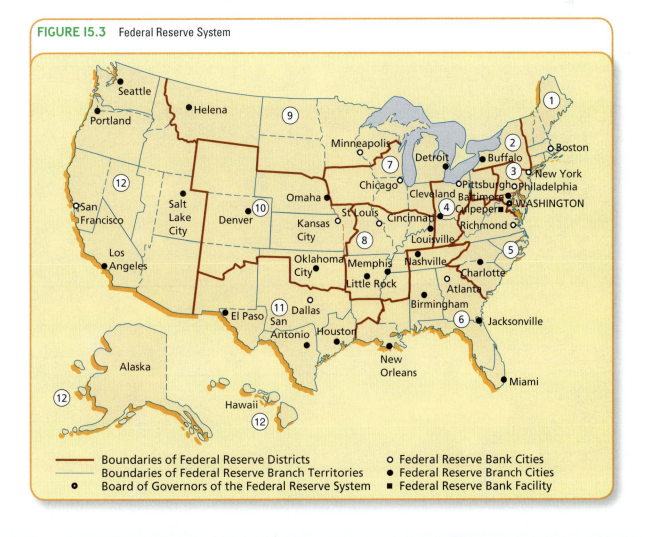

—— Boundaries of Federal Reserve Districts
—— Boundaries of Federal Reserve Branch Territories
• Board of Governors of the Federal Reserve System
○ Federal Reserve Bank Cities
• Federal Reserve Branch Cities
■ Federal Reserve Bank Facility

Monetary Policy.   The Fed controls the amount of money available in the economy through **monetary policy.** Without this intervention, the supply of and demand for money might not balance. This could result in either rapid price increases (inflation) because of too little money or economic recession and a slow-down of price increases (disinflation) because of too little growth in the money supply. In very rare cases (the depression of the 1930s) the United States has suf-fered from deflation, where the actual purchasing power of the dollar has increased as prices declined. To effectively control the supply of money in the economy, the Fed must have a good idea of how much money is in circulation at any given time. This has become increasingly challenging because the global nature of our economy means that more and more U.S. dollars are circulating overseas. Using several differ-ent measures of the money supply, the Fed establishes specific growth targets which, presumably, ensure a close balance between money supply and money demand. The Fed fine-tunes money growth by using four basic tools: open market operations, reserve requirements, the discount rate, and credit controls (see Table 15.2). There is generally a log of 6 to 18 months before the effect of these charges shows up in economic activity.

Open market operations refer to decisions to buy or sell U.S. Treasury bills (short-term debt issued by the U.S. government; also called T-bills) and other investments in the open market. The actual purchase or sale of the investments is performed by the New York Federal Reserve Bank. This monetary tool, the most

monetary policy
means by which the Fed controls the amount of money available in the economy

open market operations
decisions to buy or sell U.S. Treasury bills (short-term debt issued by the U.S. government) and other investments in the open market

One of the roles of the Federal Reserve is to use its policies to keep money flowing. Money is the lifeblood of the economy. If banks become too protective of their funds and stop lending money, the economy can grind to a halt.

Activity	Effect on the Money Supply and the Economy
Buy government securities	The money supply increases; economic activity increases.
Sell government securities	The money supply decreases; economic activity slows down.
Raise discount rate	Interest rates increase; the money supply decreases; economic activity slows down.
Lower discount rate	Interest rates decrease; the money supply increases; economic activity increases.
Increase reserve requirements	Banks make fewer loans; the money supply declines; economic activity slows down.
Decrease reserve requirements	Banks make more loans; the money supply increases; economic activity increases.
Relax credit controls	More people are encouraged to make major purchases, increasing economic activity.
Restrict credit controls	People are discouraged from making major purchases, decreasing economic activity.

TABLE 15.2

Fed Tools for Regulating the Money Supply

commonly employed of all Fed operations, is performed almost daily in an effort to control the money supply.

When the Fed buys securities, it writes a check on its own account to the seller of the investments. When the seller of the investments (usually a large bank) deposits the check, the Fed transfers the balance from the Federal Reserve account into the seller's account, thus increasing the supply of money in the economy and, hopefully, fueling economic growth. The opposite occurs when the Fed sells investments. The buyer writes a check to the Federal Reserve, and when the funds are transferred out of the purchaser's account, the amount of money in circulation falls, slowing economic growth to a desired level.

The second major monetary policy tool is the **reserve requirement,** the percentage of deposits that banking institutions must hold in reserve ("in the vault," as it were). Funds so held are not available for lending to businesses and consumers. For example, a bank holding $10 million in deposits, with a 10 percent reserve requirement, must have reserves of $1 million. If the Fed were to reduce the reserve requirement to, say, 5 percent, the bank would need to keep only $500,000 in reserves. The bank could then lend to customers the $500,000 difference between the old reserve level and the new lower reserve level, thus increasing the supply of money. Because the reserve requirement has such a powerful effect on the money supply, the Fed does not change it very often, relying instead on open market operations most of the time.

The third monetary policy tool, the **discount rate,** is the rate of interest the Fed charges to loan money to any banking institution to meet reserve requirements. The Fed is the lender of last resort for these banks. When a bank borrows from the Fed, it is said to have borrowed at the "discount window," and the interest rates charged there are often higher than those charged on loans of comparable risk elsewhere in the economy. This added interest expense, when it exists, serves to discourage banks from borrowing from the Fed.

When the Fed wants to expand the money supply, it lowers the discount rate to encourage borrowing. Conversely, when the Fed wants to decrease the money

reserve requirement
the percentage of deposits that banking institutions must hold in reserve

discount rate
the rate of interest the Fed charges to loan money to any banking institution to meet reserve requirements

supply, it raises the discount rate. The increases in interest rates that occurred in the United States from 2003 through 2006 were the result of more than 16 quarter-point (0.25 percent) increases in the Fed discount rate. The purpose was to keep inflation under control and to raise rates to a more normal level as the economy recovered from the recession of 2001. During the most recent recession, which started in 2007, the Fed lowered interest rates to nearly zero in order to encourage borrowing. In an environment where credit markets were nearly frozen, the Fed utilized monetary policy to stimulate spending. Not surprisingly, economists watch changes in this sensitive interest rate as an indicator of the Fed's monetary policy.

credit controls
the authority to establish and enforce credit rules for financial institutions and some private investors

The final tool in the Fed's arsenal of weapons is **credit controls**—the authority to establish and enforce credit rules for financial institutions and some private investors. For example, the Fed can determine how large a down payment individuals and businesses must make on credit purchases of expensive items such as automobiles, and how much time they have to finish paying for the purchases. By raising and lowering minimum down payment amounts and payment periods, the Fed can stimulate or discourage credit purchases of "big ticket" items. The Fed also has the authority to set the minimum down payment investors must use for the credit purchases of stock. Buying stock with credit—"buying on margin"—is a popular investment strategy among individual speculators. By altering the margin requirement (currently set at 50 percent of the price of the purchased stocks), the Fed can effectively control the total amount of credit borrowing in the stock market.

Regulatory Functions.   The second major responsibility of the Fed is to regulate banking institutions that are members of the Federal Reserve System. Accordingly, the Fed establishes and enforces banking rules that affect monetary policy and the overall level of the competition between different banks. It determines which non-banking activities, such as brokerage services, leasing, and insurance, are appropriate for banks and which should be prohibited. The Fed also has the authority to approve or disapprove mergers between banks and the formation of bank holding companies. In an effort to ensure that all rules are enforced and that correct accounting procedures are being followed at member banks, surprise bank examinations are conducted by bank examiners each year.

Check Clearing.   The Federal Reserve provides national check processing on a huge scale. Divisions of the Fed known as check clearinghouses handle almost all the checks written against a bank in one city and presented for deposit to a bank in a second city. Any banking institution can present the checks it has received from others around the country to its regional Federal Reserve Bank. The Fed passes the checks to the appropriate regional Federal Reserve Bank, which then sends the checks to the issuing bank for payment. With the advance of electronic payment systems and the passage of the Check Clearing for the 21st Century Act (Check 21 Act), checks can now be processed in a day. The Check 21 Act allows banks to clear checks electronically by presenting an electronic image of the check. This eliminates mail delays and time-consuming paper processing.

Depository Insurance.   The Fed is also responsible for supervising the federal insurance funds that protect the deposits of member institutions. These insurance funds will be discussed in greater detail in the following section.

Banking Institutions

Banking institutions accept money deposits from and make loans to individual consumers and businesses. Some of the most important banking institutions include commercial banks, savings and loan associations, credit unions, and mutual savings banks. Historically, these have all been separate institutions. However, new hybrid forms of banking institutions that perform two or more of these functions have emerged over the last two decades. The following all have one thing in common: They are businesses whose objective is to earn money by managing, safeguarding, and lending money to others. Their sales revenues come from the fees and interest that they charge for providing these financial services.

commercial banks
the largest and oldest of all financial institutions, relying mainly on checking and savings accounts as sources of funds for loans to businesses and individuals

Commercial Banks.   The largest and oldest of all financial institutions are **commercial banks,** which perform a variety of financial services. They rely mainly on checking and savings accounts as their major source of funds and use only a portion of these deposits to make loans to businesses and individuals. Because it is unlikely that all the depositors of any one bank will want to withdraw all of their funds at the same time, a bank can safely loan out a large percentage of its deposits.

Today, banks are quite diversified and offer a number of services. Commercial banks make loans for virtually any conceivable legal purpose, from vacations to cars, from homes to college educations. Banks in many states offer *home equity loans,* by which home owners can borrow against the appraised value of their already purchased homes. Banks also issue Visa and MasterCard credit cards and offer CDs and trusts (legal entities set up to hold and manage assets for a beneficiary). Many banks rent safe deposit boxes in bank vaults to customers who want to store jewelry, legal documents, artwork, and other valuables. In 1999 Congress passed the Financial Services Modernization Act, also known as the Gramm-Leach-Bliley Bill. This act repealed the Glass Stegal Act, which was enacted in 1929 after the

The bank bailouts of 2008–2009 might have prevented a deeper recession, but they weren't popular among the public. The Worthington Bank, a small Texas lender, ran billboards like these after the bailout and received millions in new deposits from the disenchanted customers of big banks.

stock market crash and prohibited commercial banks from being in the insurance and investment banking business. This puts U.S. commercial banks on the same competitive footing as European banks and provides a more level playing field for global banking competition. As commercial banks and investment banks have merged, the financial landscape has changed. Consolidation remains the norm in the U.S. banking industry. For example JPMorgan Chase completed a merger with Bank One in 2004, making it the second largest bank in the United States behind Citigroup. JPMorgan was created through a merger with Chase Manhattan Bank and JPMorgan, and Bank One acquired many Midwestern banks, with its biggest acquisition being First Chicago Corp. The financial crisis and the economic recession only accelerated the consolidation as large, healthy banks ended up buying weak banks that were in trouble. JPMorgan Chase bought Wachovia and the investment bank Bear Stearns Wells Fargo bought Washington Mutual; PNC bought National City Bank, and Bank of America bought Countrywide Credit and Merrill Lynch. Most of these purchases were made with financial help from the U.S. Treasury and Federal Reserve.

savings and loan associations (S&Ls)
financial institutions that primarily offer savings accounts and make long-term loans for residential mortgages; also called "thrifts"

Savings and Loan Associations.   **Savings and loan associations (S&Ls),** often called "thrifts," are financial institutions that primarily offer savings accounts

Going Green
Bank of America Stakeholders Support Sustainability

Bank of America, along with many other major banks, faced a difficult financial situation during the most recent financial crisis. In the midst of a global banking crisis, BofA was forced to accept a government rescue. Shareholders were concerned about the quality of leadership and decision making at BofA, and they approved a proposal to split the positions of chairman of the board and CEO. This came in response to the financial crisis and BofA's decision to acquire failing Merrill Lynch and Countrywide Financial. At the same time, a scandal erupted involving $3.6 billion in bonuses paid to Merrill executives at the same time the bank was experiencing huge losses. Ultimately, the federal government intervened with a $20 billion bailout.

For two decades, BofA has focused on energy efficiency, reducing emissions, and limiting waste, even in the wake of its financial meltdown–related troubles. BofA maintains a strong commitment to sustainability in addition to addressing concerns over its financial performance, a stance shareholders support. The company offers customers eco-friendly products and services such as the Brighter Planet™ Visa® and online banking to reduce paper waste. BofA is active in communities, promoting energy efficiency and environmental responsibility. The company committed $20 billion over 10 years to aid businesses addressing global climate change, to create loans for companies developing renewable energy, and to create new jobs. BofA won California's Governor's Environmental and Economic Leadership Award (GEELA) for its focus on melding environmental stewardship with long-term company management. This award was issued to BofA because of its involvement in solar school initiatives, the creation of Clean Renewable Energy Bonds, and its preservation efforts with redwood forests.

Although BofA admits that its focus on protecting the environment is for profit and economic growth, it also acknowledges it is the responsible stance to take. BofA intends to maintain its sustainability efforts even through recessionary times.[8]

Discussion Questions

1. How does BofA balance sustainability with performance during a difficult financial time?
2. What does BofA gain from continuing to invest in sustainability?
3. Do you think that being recognized and winning environmental awards will help BofA become more profitable?

and make long-term loans for residential mortgages. A mortgage is a loan made so that a business or individual can purchase real estate, typically a home; the real estate itself is pledged as a guarantee (called *collateral*) that the buyer will repay the loan. If the loan is not repaid, the savings and loan has the right to repossess the property. Prior to the 1970s, S&Ls focused almost exclusively on real estate lending and accepted only savings accounts. Today, following years of regulatory changes, S&Ls compete directly with commercial banks by offering many types of services.

Savings and loans have gone through a metamorphosis since the early 1990s, after having almost collapsed in the 1980s. Today, many of the largest savings and loans have merged with commercial banks. This segment of the financial services industry plays a diminished role in the mortgage lending market.

credit union
a financial institution owned and controlled by its depositors, who usually have a common employer, profession, trade group, or religion

Credit Unions.   A **credit union** is a financial institution owned and controlled by its depositors, who usually have a common employer, profession, trade group, or religion. The Aggieland Credit Union in College Station, Texas, for example, provides banking services for faculty, employees, and current and former students of Texas A&M University. A savings account at a credit union is commonly referred to as a share account, while a checking account is termed a share draft account. Because the credit union is tied to a common organization, the members (depositors) are allowed to vote for directors and share in the credit union's profits in the form of higher interest rates on accounts and/or lower loan rates.

While credit unions were originally created to provide depositors with a short-term source of funds for low-interest consumer loans for items such as cars, home

appliances, vacations, and college, today they offer a wide range of financial services. Generally, the larger the credit union, the more sophisticated its financial service offerings will be.

Mutual Savings Banks.   **Mutual savings banks** are similar to savings and loan
associations, but, like credit unions, they are owned by their depositors. Among the
oldest financial institutions in the United States, they were originally established to
provide a safe place for savings of particular groups of people, such as fishermen.
Found mostly in New England, they are becoming more popular in the rest of the
country as some S&Ls have converted to mutual savings banks to escape the stigma
created by the widespread S&L failures in the 1980s.

mutual savings banks
financial institutions that
are similar to savings and
loan associations but, like
credit unions, are owned
by their depositors

Insurance for Banking Institutions.   The **Federal Deposit Insurance
Corporation (FDIC),** which insures individual bank accounts, was established in
1933 to help stop bank failures throughout the country during the Great Depression. Today, the FDIC insures personal accounts up to a maximum of $250,000 at
nearly 8,000 FDIC member institutions.[9] While most major banks are insured by the
FDIC, small institutions in some states may be insured by state insurance funds or
private insurance companies. Should a member bank fail, its depositors can recover
all of their funds, up to $250,000. Amounts over $250,000, while not legally covered
by the insurance, are in fact usually covered because the Fed understands very well
the enormous damage that would result to the financial system should these large
depositors withdraw their money. When the financial crisis occurred, the FDIC was
worried about people taking their money out of banks, so they increased the deposit
insurance amount from $100,000 to $250,000. The amount is scheduled to revert
back to $100,000 on December 31, 2013. The *Federal Savings and Loan Insurance
Corporation (FSLIC)* insured thrift deposits prior to its insolvency and failure during
the S&L crisis of the 1980s. Now, the insurance functions once overseen by the FSLIC
are handled directly by the FDIC through its Savings Association Insurance Fund.
The **National Credit Union Association (NCUA)** regulates and charters credit
unions and insures their deposits through its National Credit Union Insurance Fund.

**Federal Deposit Insurance
Corporation (FDIC)**
an insurance fund
established in 1933 that
insures individual bank
accounts

**National Credit Union
Association (NCUA)**
an agency that regulates
and charters credit unions
and insures their deposits
through its National Credit
Union Insurance Fund

*Bank runs like this one
at Indymac still occur. To
re-instill confidence in banks
following the economic
meltdown, in 2008, the FDIC
temporarily increased the
deposit insurance from
$100,000 to $250000 per
depositor.*

TABLE 15.3				
Leading Diversified Financial Services Firms	**Company**	**2009 Revenues (in millions)**	**Company**	**2009 Revenues (in millions)**
	General Electric	$183,207	Aon	$8,406
	Citigroup	112,372	SLM	7,689
	GMAC	35,445	Ameriprise Financial	7,149
	Fannie Mae	22,652	AmeriCredit	2,543
	International Assets Holding	18,359	Annaly Capital Management	2,366
	Marsh & McLennan	11,587	Moody's	1,755

Source: "Industry: Diversified Financials," Fortune 500 2009, *Fortune*, http://money.cnn.com/magazines/fortune/fortune500/2009/industries/31/index.html (accessed March 31, 2010).

When they were originally established, Congress hoped that these insurance funds would make people feel secure about their savings so that they would not panic and withdraw their money when news of a bank failure was announced. The "bank run" scene in the perennial Christmas movie *It's a Wonderful Life,* when dozens of Bailey Building and Loan depositors attempted to withdraw their money (only to have the reassuring figure of Jimmy Stewart calm their fears), was not based on mere fiction. During the Great Depression, hundreds of banks failed and their depositors lost everything. The fact that large numbers of major financial institutions failed in the 1980s and 1990s—without a single major banking panic—underscores the effectiveness of the current insurance system. While the future may yet bring unfortunate surprises, most depositors go to sleep every night without worrying about the safety of their savings.

Nonbanking Institutions

Nonbank financial institutions offer some financial services, such as short-term loans or investment products, but do not accept deposits. These include insurance companies, pension funds, mutual funds, brokerage firms, nonfinancial firms, and finance companies. Table 15.3 lists some other diversified financial services firms.

Diversified Firms.   Recently, a growing number of traditionally nonfinancial firms have moved onto the financial field. These firms include manufacturing organizations, such as General Motors and General Electric, that traditionally confined their financial activities to financing their customers' purchases. GE was once so successful in the financial arena that its credit subsidiary accounted for more than 40 percent of the company's revenues and earnings. Unfortunately, GE Capital became a liability to GE during the financial crisis, and the stock price fell from $42 per share to less than $8 per share. It is in the process of recovery as GE cuts the size of its finance unit and writes off billions of dollars in bad loans. Other nonfinancial firms have been also been unsuccessful in their financial ventures. Sears, the retail giant, once commanded an imposing financial network composed of real estate (Coldwell Banker), credit card (Discover Card), and brokerage (Dean Witter Reynolds) companies, but losses of hundreds of millions of dollars forced Sears to dismantle its network. The very prestigious brokerage firm Morgan Stanley acquired Dean Witter Discover, thus creating one of the largest investment firms in the country—in a league with Smith Barney and Merrill Lynch. Perhaps the moral of the story for firms like Sears is "stick to what you know."

Insurance Companies.

Insurance companies are businesses that protect their clients against financial losses from certain specified risks (death, injury, disability, accident, fire, theft, and natural disasters, for example) in exchange for a fee, called a premium. Because insurance premiums flow into the companies regularly, but major insurance losses cannot be timed with great accuracy (though expected risks can be assessed with considerable precision), insurance companies generally have large amounts of excess funds. They typically invest these or make long-term loans, particularly to businesses in the form of commercial real estate loans.

Pension Funds.

Pension funds are managed investment pools set aside by individuals, corporations, unions, and some nonprofit organizations to provide retirement income for members. One type of pension fund is the *individual retirement account (IRA)*, which is established by individuals to provide for their personal retirement needs. IRAs can be invested in a variety of financial assets, from risky commodities such as oil or cocoa to low-risk financial "staples" such as U.S. Treasury securities. The choice is up to each person and is dictated solely by individual objectives and tolerance for risk. The interest earned by all of these investments may be deferred tax-free until retirement.

In 1997, Congress revised the IRA laws and created a Roth IRA. Although similar to a traditional IRA in that investors may contribute $5,000 per year, the money in a Roth IRA is considered an after-tax contribution. When the money is withdrawn at retirement, no tax is paid on the distribution. The Roth IRA is beneficial to young people who can allow a long time for their money to compound and who may be able to have their parents or grandparents fund the Roth IRA with gift money.

Most major corporations provide some kind of pension plan for their employees. Many of these are established with bank trust departments or life insurance companies. Money is deposited in a separate account in the name of each individual employee, and when the employee retires, the total amount in the account can be either withdrawn in one lump sum or taken as monthly cash payments over some defined time period (usually for the remaining life of the retiree).

Social Security, the largest pension fund, is publicly financed. The federal government collects Social Security funds from payroll taxes paid by both employers and employees. The Social Security Administration then takes these monies and makes payments to those eligible to receive Social Security benefits—the retired, the disabled, and the young children of deceased parents.

Mutual Funds.

A **mutual fund** pools individual investor dollars and invests them in large numbers of well-diversified securities. Individual investors buy shares in a mutual fund in the hope of earning a high rate of return and in much the same way as people buy shares of stock. Because of the large numbers of people investing in any one mutual fund, the funds can afford to invest in hundreds (if not thousands) of securities at any one time, minimizing the risks of any single security that does not do well. Mutual funds provide professional financial management

---

insurance companies
businesses that protect their clients against financial losses from certain specified risks (death, accident, and theft, for example)

pension funds
managed investment pools set aside by individuals, corporations, unions, and some nonprofit organizations to provide retirement income for members

mutual fund
an investment company that pools individual investor dollars and invests them in large numbers of well-diversified securities

Rather than buying individual stocks and bonds themselves, small investors often purchase mutual funds run by professional managers who decide which stocks to purchase for the fund.

for people who lack the time and/or expertise to invest in particular securities, such as government bonds. While there are no hard-and-fast rules, investments in one or more mutual funds are one way for people to plan for financial independence at the time of retirement.

A special type of mutual fund called a *money market fund* invests specifically in short-term debt securities issued by governments and large corporations. Although they offer services such as check-writing privileges and reinvestment of interest income, money market funds differ from the money market accounts offered by banks primarily in that the former represent a pool of funds, while the latter are basically specialized, individual checking accounts. Money market funds usually offer slightly higher rates of interest than bank money market accounts.

brokerage firms
firms that buy and sell stocks, bonds, and other securities for their customers and provide other financial services

Brokerage Firms and Investment Banks. **Brokerage firms** buy and sell stocks, bonds, and other securities for their customers and provide other financial services. Larger brokerage firms like Merrill Lynch, Charles Schwab, and Edward Jones offer financial services unavailable at their smaller competitors. Merrill Lynch, for example, offers the Merrill Lynch Cash Management Account (CMA), which pays interest on deposits and allows clients to write checks, borrow money, and withdraw cash much like a commercial bank. The largest of the brokerage firms (including Merrill Lynch) have developed so many specialized services that they may be considered financial networks—organizations capable of offering virtually all of the services traditionally associated with commercial banks.

investment banker
underwrites new issues of securities for corporations, states, and municipalities

Most brokerage firms are really part financial conglomerates that provide many different kinds of services besides buying and selling securities for clients. For example, Merrill Lynch also is an investment banker, as is Morgan Stanley, Smith Barney, and Goldman Sachs. The **investment banker** underwrites new issues of securities for corporations, states, and municipalities needed to raise money in the capital markets. The new issue market is called a *primary market* because the sale of the securities is for the first time. After the first sale, the securities trade in the *secondary markets* by brokers. The investment banker advises on the price of the new securities and generally guarantees the sale while overseeing the distribution of the securities through the selling brokerage houses. Investment bankers also act as dealers who make markets in securities. They do this by offering to sell the securities at an asked price (which is a higher rate) and buy the securities at a bid price (which is a lower rate)—the difference in the two prices represents the profit for the dealer.

Finance Companies.   **Finance companies** are businesses that offer short-term loans at substantially higher rates of interest than banks. Commercial finance companies make loans to businesses, requiring their borrowers to pledge assets such as equipment, inventories, or unpaid accounts as collateral for the loans. Consumer finance companies make loans to individuals. Like commercial finance companies, these firms require some sort of personal collateral as security against the borrower's possible inability to repay their loans. Because of the high interest rates they charge and other factors, finance companies typically are the lender of last resort for individuals and businesses whose credit limits have been exhausted and/or those with poor credit ratings.

finance companies
businesses that offer short-term loans at substantially higher rates of interest than banks

Electronic Banking

Since the advent of the computer age, a wide range of technological innovations has made it possible to move money all across the world electronically. Such "paperless" transactions have allowed financial institutions to reduce costs in what has been, and continues to be, a virtual competitive battlefield. **Electronic funds transfer (EFT)** is any movement of funds by means of an electronic terminal, telephone, computer, or magnetic tape. Such transactions order a particular financial institution to subtract money from one account and add it to another. The most commonly used forms of EFT are automated teller machines, automated clearinghouses, and home banking systems.

electronic funds transfer (EFT)
any movement of funds by means of an electronic terminal, telephone, computer, or magnetic tape

Automated Teller Machines.   Probably the most familiar form of electronic banking is the **automated teller machine (ATM),** which dispenses cash, accepts deposits, and allows balance inquiries and cash transfers from one account to another. ATMs provide 24-hour banking services—both at home (through a local bank) and far away (via worldwide ATM networks such as Cirrus and Plus). Rapid growth, driven by both strong consumer acceptance and lower transaction costs for banks (about half the cost of teller transactions), has led to the installation of hundreds of thousands of ATMs worldwide. Table 15.4 presents some interesting statistics about ATMs.

automated teller machine (ATM)
the most familiar form of electronic banking, which dispenses cash, accepts deposits, and allows balance inquiries and cash transfers from one account to another

- The first ATM was introduced in 1969.
- 17 percent of Americans use ATMs as their primary banking method.
- The United States has more than 425,000 ATMs.
- More than 11.8 billion ATM transactions take place annually.
- The top five ATM owners are Cardtronics, Payment Alliance, Bank of America, JPMorganChase, and Wells Fargo.

TABLE 15.4

Facts about ATM Use

Source: Tyler Metzger, "ATM Use in the United States," *CreditCards.com*, http://www.creditcards.com/credit-card-news/atm-use-statistics-3372.php (accessed April 2, 2010).

automated clearinghouses (ACHs)
a system that permits payments such as deposits or withdrawals to be made to and from a bank account by magnetic computer tape

Automated Clearinghouses. **Automated clearinghouses (ACHs)** permit payments such as deposits or withdrawals to be made to and from a bank account by magnetic computer tape. Most large U.S. employers, and many others worldwide, use ACHs to deposit their employees' paychecks directly to the employees' bank accounts. While direct deposit is used by only 50 percent of U.S. workers, nearly 100 percent of Japanese workers and more than 90 percent of European workers utilize it. The largest user of automated clearinghouses in the United States is the federal government, with 99 percent of federal government employees and 65 percent of the private workforce receiving their pay via direct deposit. And, more than 82 percent of all Social Security payments are made through an ACH system.

The advantages of direct deposits to consumers include convenience, safety, and potential interest earnings. It is estimated that more than 4 million paychecks are lost or stolen annually, and FBI studies show that 2,000 fraudulent checks are cashed every day in the United States. Checks can never be lost or stolen with direct deposit. The benefits to businesses include decreased check-processing expenses and increased employee productivity. Research shows that businesses that use direct deposit can save more than $1.25 on each payroll check processed. Productivity could increase by $3 to $5 billion annually if all employees were to use direct deposit rather than taking time away from work to deposit their payroll checks.

Some companies also use ACHs for dividend and interest payments. Consumers can also use ACHs to make periodic (usually monthly) fixed payments to specific creditors without ever having to write a check or buy stamps. The estimated number of bills paid annually by consumers is 20 billion, and the total number paid through ACHs is estimated at only 8.5 billion. The average consumer who writes 10 to 15 checks each month would save $41 to $62 annually in postage alone.[11]

Online Banking.   Many banking activities are now conducted on a computer at home or at work, or through wireless devices such as cell phones and PDAs anywhere there is a wireless "hot point." Consumers and small businesses can now make a bewildering array of financial transactions at home or on the go 24 hours a day. Functioning much like a vast network of personal ATMs, companies like Google and Apple provide online banking services through mobile phones, allowing subscribers to make sophisticated banking transactions, buy and sell stocks and bonds, and purchase products and airline tickets without ever leaving home or speaking to another human being. Many banks allow customers to log directly into their accounts to check balances, transfer money between accounts, view their account statements, and pay bills via home computer or other Internet-enabled devices. Computer and advanced telecommunications technology have revolutionized world commerce; 25 percent of adults list Internet banking as their preferred banking method, making it the most popular banking method in the United States.[12]

Banking in the Future and the Impact of the Financial Crisis

Rapid advances and innovations in technology are challenging the banking industry and requiring it to change. As we said earlier, more and more banks, both large and small, are offering electronic access to their financial services. ATM technology is rapidly changing, with machines now dispensing more than just cash. Online financial services, ATM technology, and bill presentation are just a few of the areas where rapidly changing technology is causing the banking industry to change as well. The premise that banks will get bigger over the next 10 years is uncertain. During 2007–2008, the financial markets collapsed under the weight of declining housing prices,

Computers and handheld devices have made online banking extremely convenient. However, hackers have stolen millions from banking customers by tricking them into visiting Web sites and downloading malicious software that gives the hackers access to their passwords.

subprime mortgages (mortgages with low-quality borrowers), and risky securities backed by these subprime mortgages. Because the value of bank assets declined dramatically, most large banks like CitiBank, Bank of America and Wachovia had a shrinking capital base. That is, the amount of debt in relation to their equity was so high that they were below the minimum required capital requirements. This was a financial environment where banks did not trust the counterparties to their loans and asset-backed securities. In this environment, the markets ceased to function in an orderly fashion.

To keep the banking system from total collapse, the U.S. Treasury and the Federal Reserve created the TARP program, an acronym for Troubled Asset Relief Program. This program allowed the Treasury to purchase up to $250 billion of senior preferred shares of bank securities.[13] The preferred shares were used because they were not voting securities but were considered Tier 2 capital by the regulators. Capital was divided into Tier 1 capital (common equity) and Tier 2 (preferred equity). The minimum Tier 1 ratio was 4 percent and Tier 2 ratio was 2 percent. A total capital ratio of 6 percent was the minimum, and banks at this level were considered high risk; regulators were more comfortable with 8 to 10 percent capital ratios.

Most of the big banks either needed to take the cash infusion from the U.S. Treasury or were forced to sell preferred stock to the Treasury. The rationale from the

Entrepreneurship in Action
MicroWind Technologies, LLC, Makes Wind Pay Off

Michael Easton

Business: MicroWind Technologies, LLC

Founded: 2008

Success: Easton's Lamppost and Residential turbines are being tested and his work is garnering press.

Michael Easton, a 20-something graduate of the Tufts University School of Engineering, has been spending a lot of time in his parents' basement. But he's not playing videogames; he's working on designing and perfecting a series of small wind turbines that he hopes will help us combat global warming.

His goal is to reinvent, in an earth-friendly fashion, how individuals and businesses receive their electricity. To date, Easton has completed prototypes of his Lamppost and Residential turbines and is in development on his Commercial turbine. The Lamppost is set to go into beta testing and should be available within a year. The Residential turbine has been in beta testing and results are due for release soon. In order to fund his work, Easton is exploring different options such as the Ignite Clean Energy business plan competition. As he develops, he will need to pay close attention to compiling financial statements and to money management.[14]

government's point of view was that it didn't want to signal to the financial community which banks were strong and which ones were weak for fear that depositors would move massive amounts of money from weak banks to strong banks. This phenomenon actually occurred several times and forced banks like Wachovia to be merged with Wells Fargo.

The total amount of preferred stock bought amounted to $204 billion. In the case of Citibank (Citigroup), its Tier 1 capital ratio fell under the minimum because it had to write off billions of dollars in bad loans, which reduced its asset base. This forced Citibank to give the Treasury common stock in exchange for the preferred stock, and so, as of spring 2010, the U.S. government was the largest stockholder in Citigroup. As 2010 progressed, the Treasury intended to sell its common stock in Citigroup, and it is estimated that the Treasury might make a profit of more than $7 to $8 billion on the transaction. All in all, many of the loans that were made have been paid back, and it is estimated that after the sale of Citigroup stock, the government will have been repaid $160 billion of the $204 billion it used to rescue the banks.[15]

During this period, the Federal Reserve took unprecedented actions that included buying up troubled assets from the banks and lending money at the discount window to nonbanks such as investment banks and brokers. The Fed also entered into the financial markets by making markets in commercial paper and other securities where the markets had ceased to function in an orderly fashion. Additionally, the Fed began to pay interest on reserves banks kept at the Fed and finally, it kept interest rates low to stimulate the economy and to help the banks regain their health. Because banks make money by the spread between their borrowing and lending rates, the Fed managed the spread between long- and short-term rates to generate a fairly large spread for the banks.

Lastly, the future of the structure of the banking system is in the hands of the U.S. Congress. In reaction to the financial meltdown and severe recession, the politicians have promised new financial regulations that will limit the ability of banks to create this type of problem again. There are proposals to limit the size of banks; proposals for more regulation; proposals to eliminate the Gramm-Leach-Bliley Act, which did away with some major consumer protections and contributed to deregulation of the financial and banking industries; and more proposals than we can name. Only time will tell what is in store for the U.S. banking system.

So You're Interested in Financial Systems or Banking

You think you might be interested in going into finance or banking, but it is so hard to tell when you are a full-time student. Classes that seem interesting when you take them might not translate in an interesting work experience after you graduate. A great way to see if you would excel at a career in finance is to get some experience in the industry. Internships, whether they are paid or unpaid, not only help you figure out what you might really want to do after you graduate but they are also a great way to build up your résumé, put your learning to use, and start generating connections within the field.

For example, for the past four years, Pennsylvania's Delaware County District Attorney's Office has been accepting business students from Villanova University for a six-month internship. The student works in the economic-crime division, analyzing documents of people under investigation for financial crimes ranging from fraud to money laundering. The students get actual experience in forensic accounting and have the chance to see whether this is the right career path. On top of that, the program has saved the county an average of $20,000 annually on consulting and accounting fees, not to mention that detectives now have more time to take on larger caseloads. Michael Busby, a student who completed the program, spent his six months

investigating a case in which the owner of a sewage treatment company had embezzled a total of $1 million over the course of nine years. Busby noted that the experience helped him gain an understanding about how different companies handle their financial statements, as well as how accounting can be applied in forensics and law enforcement.

Internship opportunities are plentiful all over the country, although you may need to do some research to find them. To start, talk to your program advisor and your professors about opportunities. Also, you can check company Web sites where you think you might like to work to see if they have any opportunities available. City, state, or federal government offices often provide student internships as well. No matter where you end up interning, the real-life skills you pick up, as well as the résumé boost you get, will be helpful in finding a job after you graduate. When you graduate, commercial banks and other financial institutions offer major employment opportunities. In 2008–2009, a major downturn in the financial industry resulted in mergers, acquisitions, and financial restructuring for many companies. While the immediate result was a decrease in job opportunities, as the industry recovers, there will be many challenging job opportunities available.[16]

Review Your Understanding

Define money, its functions, and its characteristics.

Money is anything generally accepted as a means of payment for goods and services. Money serves as a medium of exchange, a measure of value, and a store of wealth. To serve effectively in these functions, money must be acceptable, divisible, portable, durable, stable in value, and difficult to counterfeit.

Describe various types of money.

Money may take the form of currency, checking accounts, or other accounts. Checking accounts are funds left in an account in a financial institution that can be withdrawn (usually by writing a check) without advance notice. Other types of accounts include savings accounts (funds left in an interest-earning account that usually cannot be withdrawn without advance notice), money market accounts (an interest-bearing checking account that is invested in short-term debt instruments), certificates of deposit

(deposits left in an institution for a specified period of time at a specified interest rate), credit cards (access to a pre-approved line of credit granted by a bank or company), and debit cards (means of instant cash transfers between customer and merchant accounts), as well as traveler's checks, money orders, and cashier's checks.

Specify how the Federal Reserve Board manages the money supply and regulates the American banking system.

The Federal Reserve Board regulates the U.S. financial system. The Fed manages the money supply by buying and selling government securities, raising or lowering the discount rate (the rate of interest at which banks may borrow cash reserves from the Fed), raising or lowering bank reserve requirements (the percentage of funds on deposit at a bank that must be held to cover expected depositor withdrawals), and adjusting down payment and repayment terms for credit purchases. It also regulates banking

56292

practices, processes checks, and oversees federal depository insurance for institutions.

Compare and contrast commercial banks, savings and loan associations, credit unions, and mutual savings banks.

Commercial banks are financial institutions that take and hold deposits in accounts for and make loans to individuals and businesses. Savings and loan associations are financial institutions that primarily specialize in offering savings accounts and mortgage loans. Credit unions are financial institutions owned and controlled by their depositors. Mutual savings banks are similar to S&Ls except that they are owned by their depositors.

Distinguish among nonbanking institutions such as insurance companies, pension funds, mutual funds, and finance companies.

Insurance companies are businesses that protect their clients against financial losses due to certain circumstances, in exchange for a fee. Pension funds are investments set aside by organizations or individuals to meet retirement needs. Mutual funds pool investors' money and invest in large numbers of different types of securities. Brokerage firms buy and sell stocks and bonds for investors. Finance companies make short-term loans at higher interest rates than do banks.

Investigate the challenges ahead for the banking industry.

Future changes in financial regulations are likely to result in fewer but larger banks and other financial institutions.

Recommend the most appropriate financial institution for a hypothetical small business.

Using the information presented in this chapter, you should be able to answer the questions in "Solve the Dilemma" on page 493 and find the best institution for Hill Optometrics.

Revisit the World of Business

1. Why were investors so concerned about the future of GE Capital?
2. Why do you think investors provided GE Capital with $50 billion through public markets, even during the 2008–2009 financial crisis?
3. Look up the price of GE stock today and use it to evaluate current investor confidence.

Learn the Terms

automated clearinghouses (ACHs) 488
automated teller machine (ATM) 487
brokerage firms 486
certificates of deposit (CDs) 474
checking account 473
commercial banks 481
credit cards 474
credit controls 480
credit union 482
debit card 476

discount rate 479
electronic funds transfer (EFT) 487
Federal Deposit Insurance Corporation (FDIC) 483
Federal Reserve Board 477
finance 470
finance companies 487
insurance companies 485
investment banker 486
monetary policy 478
money 470

money market accounts 474
mutual fund 485
mutual savings banks 483
National Credit Union Association (NCUA) 483
open market operations 478
pension funds 485
reserve requirement 479
savings accounts 474
savings and loan associations (S&Ls) 481

Check Your Progress

1. What are the six characteristics of money? Explain how the U.S. dollar has those six characteristics.
2. What is the difference between a credit card and a debit card? Why are credit cards considerably more popular with U.S. consumers?
3. Discuss the four economic goals the Federal Reserve must try to achieve with its monetary policy.
4. Explain how the Federal Reserve uses open market operations to expand and contract the money supply.

5. What are the basic differences between commercial banks and savings and loans?

6. Why do credit unions charge lower rates than commercial banks?

7. Why do finance companies charge higher interest rates than commercial banks?

8. How are mutual funds, money market funds, and pension funds similar? How are they different?

9. What are some of the advantages of electronic funds transfer systems?

Get Involved

1. Survey the banks, savings and loans, and credit unions in your area, and put together a list of interest rates paid on the various types of checking accounts. Find out what, if any, restrictions are in effect for NOW accounts and regular checking accounts. In which type of account and in what institution would you deposit your money? Why?

2. Survey the same institutions as in question one, this time inquiring as to the rates asked for each of their various loans. Where would you prefer to obtain a car loan? A home loan? Why?

Build Your Skills

MANAGING MONEY

Background:
You have just graduated from college and have received an offer for your dream job (annual salary: $35,000). This premium salary is a reward for your hard work, perseverance, and good grades. It is also a reward for the social skills you developed in college doing service work as a tutor for high school students and interacting with the business community as the program chairman of the college business fraternity, Delta Sigma Pi. You are engaged and plan to be married this summer. You and your spouse will have a joint income of $60,000, and the two of you are trying to decide the best way to manage your money.

Task:
Research available financial service institutions in your area, and answer the following questions.

1. What kinds of institutions and services can you use to help manage your money?

2. Do you want a full service financial organization that can take care of your banking, insurance, and investing needs or do you want to spread your business among individual specialists? Why have you made this choice?

3. What retirement alternatives do you have?

Solve the Dilemma

SEEING THE FINANCIAL SIDE OF BUSINESS

Dr. Stephen Hill, a successful optometrist in Indianapolis, Indiana, has tinkered with various inventions for years. Having finally developed what he believes is his first saleable product (a truly scratch-resistant and lightweight lens), Hill has decided to invest his life savings and open Hill Optometrics to manufacture and market his invention.

Unfortunately, despite possessing true genius in many areas, Hill is uncertain about the "finance side" of business and the various functions of different types of financial institutions in the economy. He is, however, fully aware that he will need financial services such as checking and savings accounts, various short-term investments that can easily and quickly be converted to cash as needs dictate, and sources of borrowing capacity—should the need for either short- or long-term loans arise. Despite having read mounds of brochures from various local and national financial institutions, Hill is still somewhat unclear about the merits and capabilities of each type of financial institution. He has turned to you, his 11th patient of the day for help.

Discussion Questions

1. List the various types of U.S. financial institutions and the primary function of each.

2. What services of each financial institution is Hill's new company likely to need?

3. Which single financial institution is likely to be best able to meet Hill's small company's needs now? Why?

Build Your Business Plan

MONEY AND THE FINANCIAL SYSTEM

This chapter provides you with the opportunity to think about money and the financial system and just how many new businesses fail every year. In some industries the failure rate is as high as 80 percent. One reason for such a high failure rate is the inability to manage the finances of the organization. From the start of the business, financial planning plays a key role. Try getting a loan without an accompanying budget/forecast of earnings and cash flow.

While obtaining a loan from a family member may be the easiest way to fund your business, it may cause more problems for you later on if you are unable to pay the money back as scheduled. Before heading to a lending officer at a bank, contact your local SBA center to see what assistance they might provide.

See for Yourself Videocase

THE MOST RECENT RECESSION MADE CREDIT HARD TO COME BY

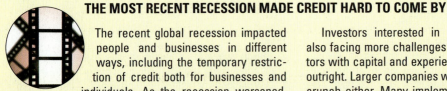

The recent global recession impacted people and businesses in different ways, including the temporary restriction of credit both for businesses and individuals. As the recession worsened, banks turned inward and significantly reduced or stopped lending money and businesses began having difficulty accessing credit. Bank credit usually falls under a business's notes payable or long-term debt. This increases liabilities on the balance sheet because businesses must pay off this debt over a certain time period. A company that depends too much on credit might incur long-term debt that they will be unable to pay off, resulting in bankruptcy. However, during the recession, the opposite problem occurred: a severe reduction in credit and loans. While credit does result in debt, it is usually necessary in order for small business owners to have the necessary funds available to start a business. Indeed, small business owners were among those most impacted by the loss of credit, which in turn harmed the economy. It is estimated that the U.S. alone supports 27 million small businesses, making up roughly 50 percent of the economy. Many small businesses that rely on credit to survive were forced to lay off employees or shut down altogether, resulting in the loss of hundreds of thousands of jobs. A business that suffered from loss of credit is Capitol Hill Bikes. The company flourished pre-recession, but once the recession hit, the bank reduced the shop's credit and consumer traffic flow decreased. Owner Denise D'Amour could not afford her rent. Eventually, the business ran out of credit and began running through cash reserves. The company had to struggle to stay afloat.

Investors interested in launching businesses were also facing more challenges than ever. Even those investors with capital and experience were being turned down outright. Larger companies were not immune to this credit crunch either. Many implemented massive layoffs and a number filed for bankruptcy. Technology giant IBM laid off roughly 10,000 employees in 2009 alone and General Motors was among those that filed for bankruptcy.

The credit crunch impacted individuals as well. Student loans were harder to get and more expensive, as were auto loans and mortgages. The main roadblock that faced people seeking these types of loans was their credit score. Banks hesitated to lend to anyone with a credit score of less than 700 out of 850, while the average credit score hovers around 680. Financial experts advise individuals to focus on improving their credit scores as a critical component of financial security. Additionally, a healthy amount of current assets that are liquid—easily converted to cash—is advisable for businesses, which can then use this cash to pay for inventory, equipment, or debt in case credit becomes unavailable.

Although the recession negatively impacted many businesses and individuals, some benefitted. Among businesses that do well in recessions are pawn shops, thrift stores, consignment shops, and people who repair high ticket items such as cars and appliances. These types of businesses are particularly targeted to those consumers looking to save money. In the case of cars and high-end appliances, many people are choosing to go to repair shops instead of purchasing new products. They are looking to save all the money they can. If businesses and individuals alike are to learn from the recession, it would seem that the message is to manage debt and operate within their means.[17]

Discussion Questions
1. While it does involve taking on debt, why is credit so important for businesses to function?

2. How do you think people can improve their credit scores in order to look more attractive for loans?

3. Why do some industries thrive during recessions while others falter?

Remember to check out our Online Learning Center at: www.mhhe.com/ferrell8e.

Team Exercise

Mutual funds pool individual investor dollars and invest them in a number of different securities. Go to http://finance.yahoo.com/ and select some top-performing funds using criteria such as sector, style, or strategy. Assume that your group has $100,000 to invest in mutual funds. Select five funds in which to invest, representing a balanced (varied industries, risk, etc.) portfolio, and defend your selections.

Financial Management and Securities Markets

OBJECTIVES

After reading this chapter, you will be able to:

- Describe some common methods of managing current assets.

- Identify some sources of short-term financing (current liabilities).

- Summarize the importance of long-term assets and capital budgeting.

- Specify how companies finance their operations and manage fixed assets with long-term liabilities, particularly bonds.

- Discuss how corporations can use equity financing by issuing stock through an investment banker.

- Describe the various securities markets in the United States.

- Critique the short-term asset and liabilities position of a small manufacturer, and recommend corrective action.

Y Combinator Is a Venture Firm Specializing in Startups

During the most recent recession, the media focused much of their attention on failing companies. Success stories in this difficult economic climate were more difficult to come by. Y Combinator and the companies it assists are among those thriving in a recessionary environment. Founder Paul Graham (famous in tech circles for creating Viaweb—sold to Yahoo! in 1998 for $49 million) launched Y Combinator in 2005. His method is somewhat like a school for start-ups, and his funding is similar to financial aid. Graham gathers entrepreneurs for three-month periods, during which time he provides them with small loans (typically under $20,000) to meet basic needs, allowing them to focus on developing their fledgling companies. In exchange, Y Combinator receives a 2 to 10 percent company stake.

Graham offers something more valuable than a simple loan—an experienced eye, solid advice, and a positive and creative environment. Y Combinator focuses on tech startups, with an emphasis on Web-based applications. Graham's experience allows him to help direct, or redirect, founders toward workable concepts attractive to larger investors. His business motto is, "Make something people want." Graham also addresses running businesses, handling investors, and dealing with acquisitions.

Small businesses like those funded by Y Combinator are making some *Fortune* 500 companies nervous. For example, eBay, for all of its success, does not often update its auction system. This leaves room for a small startup to gain market share if it can provide a superior service. These small companies are often less expensive and more flexible, making them better equipped

continued

to do well in a recession. Although Graham takes a risk with each startup, graduates such as Scribd (which partnered with literary giants and received more than $12 million in venture capital funding) and Omnisio (purchased by Google for more than $15 million) make it all worthwhile. Some of the companies flourish—and when they do, Graham makes a substantial profit.[1]

Introduction

While it's certainly true that money makes the world go around, financial management is the discipline that makes the world turn more smoothly. Indeed, without effective management of assets, liabilities, and owners' equity, all business organizations are doomed to fail—regardless of the quality and innovativeness of their products. Financial management is the field that addresses the issues of obtaining and managing the funds and resources necessary to run a business successfully. It is not limited to business organizations: All organizations, from the corner store to the local nonprofit art museum, from giant corporations to county governments, must manage their resources effectively and efficiently if they are to achieve their objectives.

In this chapter, we look at both short- and long-term financial management. First, we discuss the management of short-term assets, which companies use to generate sales and conduct ordinary day-to-day business operations. Next we turn our attention to the management of short-term liabilities, the sources of short-term funds used to finance the business. Then, we discuss the management of long-term assets such as plants, equipment, and the use of common stock (equity) and bonds (long-term liability) to finance these long-term corporate assets. Finally, we look at the securities markets, where stocks and bonds are traded.

Managing Current Assets and Liabilities

Managing short-term assets and liabilities involves managing the current assets and liabilities on the balance sheet (discussed in Chapter 14). Current assets are short-term resources such as cash, investments, accounts receivable, and inventory. Current liabilities are short-term debts such as accounts payable, accrued salaries, accrued taxes, and short-term bank loans. We use the terms *current* and *short term* interchangeably because short-term assets and liabilities are usually replaced by new assets and liabilities within three or four months, and always within a year. Managing short-term assets and liabilities is sometimes called **working capital management** because short-term assets and liabilities continually flow through an organization and are thus said to be "working."

working capital management
the managing of short-term assets and liabilities

Managing Current Assets

The chief goal of financial managers who focus on current assets and liabilities is to maximize the return to the business on cash, temporary investments of idle cash, accounts receivable, and inventory.

Managing Cash. A crucial element facing any financial manager is effectively managing the firm's cash flow. Remember that cash flow is the movement of money through an organization on a daily, weekly, monthly, or yearly basis. Ensuring that

Going Green
The Ups and Downs of Investing in First Solar

First Solar Inc. has been working to perfect an affordable alternative to fossil fuels since 1999. By tapping into solar energy, First Solar has more than $6 billion in contracts to provide solar project developers, system integrators, and public utilities with its cadmium telluride solar cells and panels. Much of First Solar's early business focused on Germany, which is the world's leader in solar power, however, it is growing rapidly in the United States as well.

While it may be obvious that a company devoted to developing alternative and renewable energy products would be committed to the environment, First Solar surpasses many of its peers. Solar energy conserves natural resources and reduces greenhouse gas emissions. However, many companies use perfluorinated gases such as nitrogen triflouride, which emit high levels of greenhouse gas, to manufacture solar cells. First Solar does not use these gases, focusing instead on less harmful options. The company also manages the entire life cycle of its products, from raw material sourcing through the collection and recycling of old products.

First Solar's management is determined to eliminate all unnecessary costs, which has generally yielded success beyond even Wall Street's or even the company's own predictions. First Solar's financial results have been generally good. During the most recent recession, the company stock fluctuated between $85 and $301, but generally increased in value. With cheaper solar energy and innovations on the horizon, as well as a president in office who supports clean energy, the future seems bright for companies like First Solar.[2]

Discussion Questions

1. Why did First Solar stock fluctuate over such a wide range in 2008 and 2009?
2. Because First Solar sells a product that is important to sustainability, does that mean its stock might be considered to have added value?
3. Look up the stock price of First Solar (FSLR), and evaluate current stock performance.

---

sufficient (but not excessive) funds are on hand to meet the company's obligations is one of the single most important facets of financial management.

Idle cash does not make money, and corporate checking accounts typically do not earn interest. As a result, astute money managers try to keep just enough cash on hand, called **transaction balances,** to pay bills—such as employee wages, supplies, and utilities—as they fall due. To manage the firm's cash and ensure that enough cash flows through the organization quickly and efficiently, companies try to speed up cash collections from customers.

To facilitate collection, some companies have customers send their payments to a **lockbox,** which is simply an address for receiving payments, instead of directly to the company's main address. The manager of the lockbox, usually a commercial bank, collects payments directly from the lockbox several times a day and deposits them into the company's bank account. The bank can then start clearing the checks and get the money into the company's checking account much more quickly than if the payments had been submitted directly to the company. However, there is no free lunch: The costs associated with lockbox systems make them worthwhile only for those companies that receive thousands of checks from customers each business day.

Large firms with many stores or offices around the country, such as HSBC Finance Corporation, formerly known as Household International, frequently use electronic funds transfer to speed up collections. HSBC Finance Corporation's local offices deposit checks received each business day into their local banks and, at the end of the day, HSBC Finance Corporation's corporate office initiates the transfer of all collected funds to its central bank for overnight investment. This technique is especially attractive for major international companies, which face slow and sometimes uncertain physical delivery of payments and/or less-than-efficient check-clearing procedures.

transaction balances
cash kept on hand by a firm to pay normal daily expenses, such as employee wages and bills for supplies and utilities

lockbox
an address, usually a commercial bank, at which a company receives payments in order to speed collections from customers

More and more companies are now using electronic funds transfer systems to pay and collect bills online. Companies generally want to collect cash quickly but pay out cash slowly. When companies use electronic funds transfers between buyers and suppliers, the speed of collections and disbursements increases to one day. Only with the use of checks can companies delay the payment of cash by three or four days until the check is presented to their bank and the cash leaves their account.

Investing Idle Cash.   As companies sell products, they generate cash on a daily basis, and sometimes cash comes in faster than it is needed to pay bills. Organizations often invest this "extra" cash, for periods as short as one day (overnight) or for as long as one year, until it is needed. Such temporary investments of cash are known as **marketable securities.** Examples include U.S. Treasury bills, certificates of deposit, commercial paper, and Eurodollar deposits. Table 16.1 summarizes a number of different marketable securities used by businesses and some sample interest rates on these investments as of June 23, 2006, and March 22, 2010. The safety rankings are relative. While all of the listed securities are very low risk, the U.S. government securities are the safest. You can see from the table that interest rates have declined during the two periods presented.

You may never see interest rates this low in your lifetime. The Fed used monetary policy to lower interest rates to stimulate borrowing and investment during the severe recession of 2007–2009 and continued to maintain low rates into 2010 in order to stimulate employment.

Many large companies invest idle cash in U.S. **Treasury bills (T-bills),** which are short-term debt obligations the U.S. government sells to raise money. Issued weekly by the U.S. Treasury, T-bills carry maturities of between one week to one year. U.S. T-bills are generally considered to be the safest of all investments and are called risk free because the U.S. government will not default on its debt.

Commercial certificates of deposit (CDs) are issued by commercial banks and brokerage companies. They are available in minimum amounts of $100,000 but are typically in units of $1 million for large corporations investing excess cash. Unlike consumer CDs (discussed in Chapter 15), which must be held until maturity, commercial CDs may be traded prior to maturity. Should a cash shortage occur, the organization can simply sell the CD on the open market and obtain needed funds.

One of the most popular short-term investments for the largest business organizations is **commercial paper**—a written promise from one company to another to pay a specific amount of money. Because commercial paper is backed only by

marketable securities temporary investment of "extra" cash by organizations for up to one year in U.S. Treasury bills, certificates of deposit, commercial paper, or Eurodollar loans

Treasury bills (T-bills) short-term debt obligations the U.S. government sells to raise money

commercial certificates of deposit (CDs) certificates of deposit issued by commercial banks and brokerage companies, available in minimum amounts of $100,000, which may be traded prior to maturity

commercial paper a written promise from one company to another to pay a specific amount of money

TABLE 16.1   Short-Term Investment Possibilities for Idle Cash

Type of Security	Maturity	Seller of Security	Interest Rate 6/23/2006	3/22/2010	Safety Level
U.S. Treasury bills	90 days	U.S. government	4.80%	0.17%	Excellent
U.S. Treasury bills	180 days	U.S. government	5.05	0.24	Excellent
Commercial paper	30 days	Major corporations	5.14	0.23	Very good
Certificates of deposit	90 days	U.S. commercial banks	5.40	0.23	Very good
Certificates of deposit	180 days	U.S. commercial banks	5.43	0.34	Very good
Eurodollars	90 days	European commercial banks	5.48	0.40	Very good

Source: "Selected Interest Rates," *Federal Reserve Statistical Release,* March 29, 2010, http://www.federalreserve.gov/releases/h15/current (accessed March 31, 2010).

Firms and individuals can buy and redeem T-bills and other government securities from the U.S. Department of the Treasury at www. treasurydirect.com.

the name and reputation of the issuing company, sales of commercial paper are restricted to only the largest and most financially stable companies. As commercial paper is frequently bought and sold for durations of as short as one business day, many "players" in the market find themselves buying commercial paper with excess cash on one day and selling it to gain extra money the following day.

During 2007 and 2008, the commercial paper market simply stopped functioning. Investors no longer trusted the IOUs of even the best companies. Companies that had relied on commercial paper to fund short-term cash needs had to turn to the banks for borrowing. Those companies who had existing lines of credit at their bank were able to draw on their line of credit. Others were in a tight spot. Eventually, the Federal Reserve entered the market to buy and sell commercial paper for its own portfolio. This is something the Fed was not in the habit of doing. But it rescued the market.

Some companies invest idle cash in international markets such as the **eurodollar market,** a market for trading U.S. dollars in foreign countries. Because the Eurodollar market was originally developed by London banks, any dollar-denominated deposit in a non-U.S. bank is called a eurodollar deposit, regardless of whether the issuing bank is actually located in Europe, South America, or anyplace else. For example, if you travel overseas and deposit $1,000 in a German bank, you will have "created" a eurodollar deposit in the amount of $1,000. Because the U.S. dollar is accepted by most countries for international trade, these dollar deposits can be used by international companies to settle their accounts. The market created for trading such investments offers firms with extra dollars a chance to earn a slightly higher rate of return with just a little more risk than they would face by investing in U.S. Treasury bills.

eurodollar market
a market centered in London for trading U.S. dollars in foreign countries

Maximizing Accounts Receivable.   After cash and marketable securities, the balance sheet lists accounts receivable and inventory. Remember that accounts receivable is money owed to a business by credit customers. For example, if you charge your

Shell gasoline purchases, until you actually pay for them with cash or a check, they represent an account receivable to Shell. Many businesses make the vast majority of their sales on credit, so managing accounts receivable is an important task.

Each credit sale represents an account receivable for the company, the terms of which typically require customers to pay the full amount due within 30, 60, or even 90 days from the date of the sale. To encourage quick payment, some businesses offer some of their customers discounts of between 1 to 2 percent if they pay off their balance within a specified period of time (usually between 10 and 30 days). On the other hand, late payment charges of between 1 and 1.5 percent serve to discourage slow payers from sitting on their bills forever. The larger the early payment discount offered, the faster customers will tend to pay their accounts. Unfortunately, while discounts increase cash flow, they also reduce profitability. Finding the right balance between the added advantages of early cash receipt and the disadvantages of reduced profits is no simple matter. Similarly, determining the optimal balance between the higher sales likely to result from extending credit to customers with less than sterling credit ratings and the higher bad-debt losses likely to result from a more lenient credit policy is also challenging. Information on company credit ratings is provided by local credit bureaus, national credit-rating agencies such as Dun and Bradstreet, and industry trade groups.

Optimizing Inventory. While the inventory that a firm holds is controlled by both production needs and marketing considerations, the financial manager has to coordinate inventory purchases to manage cash flows. The object is to minimize the firm's investment in inventory without experiencing production cutbacks as a result of critical materials shortfalls or lost sales due to insufficient finished goods inventories. Every dollar invested in inventory is a dollar unavailable for investment in some other area of the organization. Optimal inventory levels are determined in large part by the method of production. If a firm attempts to produce its goods just in time to meet sales demand, the level of inventory will be relatively low. If, on the other hand, the firm produces materials in a constant, level pattern, inventory increases when sales decrease and decreases when sales increase. One way that companies are attempting to optimize inventory is through the use of radio frequency identification (RFID) technology. Companies such as Walmart are attempting to better manage their inventories by using RFID tags. An RFID tag, which contains a silicon chip and an antenna, allows a company to use radio waves to track and identify the products to which the tags are attached. These tags are primarily used to track inventory shipments from the manufacturer to the buyer's warehouses and then to the individual stores.

Dell holds as little inventory as possible. Many of its suppliers are located right next to the computer maker's assembly facilities and provide it with parts only after the firm receives orders for computers.

The automobile industry is an excellent example of an industry driven almost solely by inventory levels. Because it is inefficient to continually lay off workers in slow times and call them back in better times, Ford, General Motors, and Chrysler try to set and stick to quarterly production quotas. Automakers typically try to keep a 60-day supply of unsold cars. During particularly slow periods, however, it is not unusual for inventories to exceed 100 days of sales.

Although less publicized, inventory shortages can be as much of a drag on potential profits as too much inventory. Not having an item on hand may send the customer to a competitor—forever. Complex computer inventory models are frequently employed to determine the optimum level of inventory a firm should hold to support a given level of sales. Such models can indicate how and when parts inventories should be ordered so that they are available exactly when required—and not a day before. Developing and maintaining such an intricate production and inventory system is difficult, but it can often prove to be the difference between experiencing average profits and spectacular ones.

Managing Current Liabilities

While having extra cash on hand is a delightful surprise, the opposite situation—a temporary cash shortfall—can be a crisis. The good news is that there are several potential sources of short-term funds. Suppliers often serve as an important source through credit sales practices. Also, banks, finance companies, and other organizations offer short-term funds through loans and other business operations.

Accounts Payable.   Remember from Chapter 14 that accounts payable is money an organization owes to suppliers for goods and services. Just as accounts receivable must be actively managed to ensure proper cash collections, so too must accounts payable be managed to make the best use of this important liability.

The most widely used source of short-term financing, and therefore the most important account payable, is **trade credit**—credit extended by suppliers for the purchase of their goods and services. While varying in formality, depending on both the organizations involved and the value of the items purchased, most trade credit agreements offer discounts to organizations that pay their bills early. A supplier, for example, may offer trade terms of "1/10 net 30," meaning that the purchasing organization may take a 1 percent discount from the invoice amount if it makes payment by the 10th day after receiving the bill. Otherwise, the entire amount is due within 30 days. For example, pretend that you are the financial manager in charge of payables. You owe Ajax Company $10,000, and it offers trade terms of 2/10 net 30. By paying the amount due within 10 days, you can save 2 percent of $10,000, or $200. Assume you place orders with Ajax once per month and have 12 bills of $10,000 each per year. By taking the discount every time, you will save 12 times $200, or $2,400, per year. Now assume you are the financial manager of Gigantic Corp., and it has monthly payables of $100 million per month. Two percent of $100 million is $2 million per month. Failure to take advantage of such trade discounts can add up to large opportunity losses over the span of a year.

Bank Loans.   Virtually all organizations—large and small—obtain short-term funds for operations from banks. In most instances, the credit services granted these firms take the form of a line of credit or fixed dollar loan. A **line of credit** is an arrangement by which a bank agrees to lend a specified amount of money to the organization upon request—provided that the bank has the required funds to make

trade credit
credit extended by suppliers for the purchase of their goods and services

line of credit
an arrangement by which a bank agrees to lend a specified amount of money to an organization upon request

Because both businesses and individuals want to keep their financing costs to a minimum, when interest rates drop, their investment in assets tends to increase.

the loan. In general, a business line of credit is very similar to a consumer credit card, with the exception that the preset credit limit can amount to millions of dollars.

In addition to credit lines, banks also make **secured loans**—loans backed by collateral that the bank can claim if the borrowers do not repay the loans—and **unsecured loans**—loans backed only by the borrowers' good reputation and previous credit rating. Both individuals and businesses build their credit rating from their history of borrowing and repaying borrowed funds on time and in full. The three national credit-rating services are Equifax, TransUnion, and Experian. A lack of credit history or a poor credit history can make it difficult to get loans from financial institutions. The *principal* is the amount of money borrowed; *interest* is a percentage of the principal that the bank charges for use of its money. As we mentioned in Chapter 15, banks also pay depositors interest on savings accounts and some checking accounts. Thus, banks charge borrowers interest for loans and pay interest to depositors for the use of their money. In addition, these loans may include origination fees.

One of the complaints from borrowers during the financial meltdown and recession was that banks weren't willing to lend. There were several causes. Banks were trying to rebuild their capital, and they didn't want to take the extra risk that lending offers in an economic recession. They were drowning in bad debts and were not sure how future loan losses would affect their capital. The banks' lack of lending caused problems for small businesses.

secured loans
loans backed by collateral that the bank can claim if the borrowers do not repay them

unsecured loans
loans backed only by the borrowers' good reputation and previous credit rating

prime rate
the interest rate that commercial banks charge their best customers (usually large corporations) for short-term loans

The **prime rate** is the interest rate commercial banks charge their best customers (usually large corporations) for short-term loans. While for many years, loans at the prime rate represented funds at the lowest possible cost, the rapid development of the market for commercial paper has dramatically reduced the importance of commercial banks as a source of short-term loans. Today, most "prime" borrowers are actually small- and medium-sized businesses.

The interest rates on commercial loans may be either fixed or variable. A variable, or floating-rate loan offers an advantage when interest rates are falling but represents a distinct disadvantage when interest rates are rising. Between 1999 and 2004, interest rates plummeted, and borrowers refinanced their loans with low-cost fixed-rate loans. Nowhere was this more visible than in the U.S. mortgage markets, where homeowners lined up to refinance their high-percentage home mortgages with lower-cost loans, in some cases as low as 5 percent on a 30-year loan. These mortgage interest rates had returned to 6.5 percent by mid-2006, but by 2009 they had declined to less than 5.0 percent and were slowly moving back up during spring of 2010. Individuals and corporations have the same motivation: to minimize their borrowing costs.

Nonbank Liabilities. Banks are not the only source of short-term funds for businesses. Indeed, virtually all financial institutions, from insurance companies to pension funds, from money market funds to finance companies, make short-term loans to many organizations. The largest U.S. companies also actively engage in borrowing money from the eurodollar and commercial paper markets. As noted earlier, both of these funds' sources are typically slightly less expensive than bank loans.

In some instances, businesses actually sell their accounts receivable to a finance company known as a **factor,** which gives the selling organizations cash and assumes responsibility for collecting the accounts. For example, a factor might pay $60,000 for receivables with a total face value of $100,000 (60 percent of the total). The factor profits if it can collect more than what it paid for the accounts. Because the selling organization's customers send their payments to a lockbox, they may have no idea that a factor has bought their receivables.

Companies don't just pay income taxes. They pay many other types of taxes as well, including property taxes, unemployment taxes for their workers, sales taxes, and many others.

Additional nonbank liabilities that must be efficiently managed to ensure maximum profitability are taxes owed to the government and wages owed to employees. Clearly, businesses are responsible for many different types of taxes, including federal, state, and local income taxes, property taxes, mineral rights taxes, unemployment taxes, Social Security taxes, workers' compensation taxes, excise taxes, and more. While the public tends to think that the only relevant taxes are on income and sales, many industries must pay other taxes that far exceed those levied against their income. Taxes and employees' wages represent debt obligations of the firm, which the financial manager must plan to meet as they fall due.

factor
a finance company to which businesses sell their accounts receivable—usually for a percentage of the total face value

Managing Fixed Assets

Up to this point, we have focused on the short-term aspects of financial management. While most business failures are the result of poor short-term planning, successful ventures must also consider the long-term financial consequences of their actions. Managing the long-term assets and liabilities and the owners' equity portion of the balance sheet is important for the long-term health of the business.

Long-term (fixed) assets are expected to last for many years—production facilities (plants), offices, equipment, heavy machinery, furniture, automobiles, and so on. In today's fast-paced world, companies need the most technologically advanced, modern facilities and equipment they can afford. Automobile, oil refining, and transportation companies are dependent on fixed assets.

Modern and high-tech equipment carry high price tags, and the financial arrangements required to support these investments are by no means trivial. Leasing is just one approach to financing. Obtaining major long-term financing can be challenging for even the most profitable organizations. For less successful firms, such challenges can prove nearly impossible. One approach is leasing

long-term (fixed) assets
production facilities (plants), offices, and equipment—all of which are expected to last for many years

assets such as equipment, machines, and buildings. Leasing involves paying a fee for usage rather than owning the asset. There are two kinds of leases: capital leases and operating leases. A capital lease is a long-term contract and shows up on the balance sheet as an asset and liability. The operating lease is a short-term cancelable lease and does not show up on the balance sheet. We'll take a closer look at long-term financing in a moment, but first let's address some issues associated with fixed assets, including capital budgeting, risk assessment, and the costs of financing fixed assets.

Capital Budgeting and Project Selection

One of the most important jobs performed by the financial manager is to decide what fixed assets, projects, and investments will earn profits for the firm beyond the costs necessary to fund them. The process of analyzing the needs of the business and selecting the assets that will maximize its value is called **capital budgeting,** and the capital budget is the amount of money budgeted for investment in such long-term assets. But capital budgeting does not end with the selection and purchase of a particular piece of land, equipment, or major investment. All assets and projects must be continually reevaluated to ensure their compatibility with the organization's needs. Financial executives believe most budgeting activities are occasionally or frequently unrealistic or irrelevant. If a particular asset does not live up to expectations, then management must determine why and take necessary corrective action. Budgeting is not an exact process, and managers must be flexible when new information is available.

capital budgeting
the process of analyzing the needs of the business and selecting the assets that will maximize its value

Assessing Risk

Every investment carries some risk. Figure 16.1 ranks potential investment projects according to estimated risk. When considering investments overseas, risk assessments must include the political climate and economic stability of a region. The decision to introduce a product or build a manufacturing facility in England would be much less risky than a decision to build one in the Middle East, for example.

The longer a project or asset is expected to last, the greater its potential risk because it is hard to predict whether a piece of equipment will wear out or become obsolete in 5 or 10 years. Predicting cash flows one year down the road is difficult, but projecting them over the span of a 10-year project is a gamble.

The level of a project's risk is also affected by the stability and competitive nature of the marketplace and the world economy as a whole. IBM's latest high-technology computer product is far more likely to become obsolete overnight than is a similar $10 million investment in a manufacturing plant. Dramatic changes in the marketplace are not uncommon. Indeed, uncertainty created by the rapid devaluation of Asian currencies in the late 1990s wrecked a host of assumptions in literally hundreds of projects worldwide. Financial managers must constantly consider such issues when making long-term decisions about the purchase of fixed assets.

Pricing Long-Term Money

The ultimate profitability of any project depends not only on accurate assumptions of how much cash it will generate, but also on its financing costs. Because a business must pay interest on money it borrows, the returns from any project must cover not only the costs of operating the project but also the interest expenses for the debt used to finance its construction. Unless an organization can effectively cover all of its costs—both financial and operating—it will eventually fail.

Clearly, only a limited supply of funds is available for investment in any given enterprise. The most efficient and profitable companies can attract the lowest-cost funds because they typically offer reasonable financial returns at very low relative risks. Newer and less prosperous firms must pay higher costs to attract capital because these companies tend to be quite risky. One of the strongest motivations for companies to manage their financial resources wisely is that they will, over time, be able to reduce the costs of their funds and in so doing increase their overall profitability.

In our free-enterprise economy, new firms tend to enter industries that offer the greatest potential rewards for success. However, as more and more companies enter an industry, competition intensifies, eventually driving profits down to average levels. The digital music player market of the early 2000s provides an excellent example of the changes in profitability that typically accompany increasing competition. The sign of a successful capital budgeting program is that the new products create higher than normal profits and drive sales and the stock price up. This has certainly been

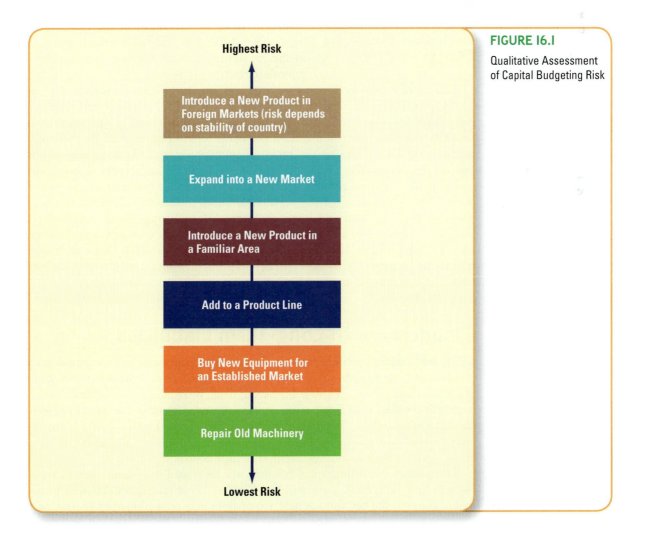

FIGURE 16.1

Qualitative Assessment of Capital Budgeting Risk

IBM got out of the computer business by selling its Personal Computing Division, which included highly recognized products like the ThinkPad line of laptops, to Lenovo. Today IBM focuses on its consulting business.

true for Apple. It introduced the first iPod in 2001, and after many enhancements it continued to sell 8.3 million iPods in 2007. Its sales have grown from $6.2 billion in 2003 to $36.5 billion in 2009, while its earnings per share have increased from $0.10 per share to $6.29 during the same time frame. From a low price of $6.36 per share in 2003, its stocks rose to a high of $279 on June 21, 2010. Note that $1,000 invested in Apple at its low point in 2003 would be worth approximately $44,000 on June 21, 2010, at $279 per share.[3]

The success of the iPod and iTunes was followed up with the introduction of the iPhone in 2007. The iPhone was followed by the successful introduction of the iPad tablet in April 2010. The combination of these products and the ease of synchronization with the iMac computers caused a complementary sales effect for Apple computers. Even with a well-planned capital budgeting program, it may be difficult for Apple to stay ahead of the competition because it is difficult to maintain market dominance in the consumer electronics industry for extended periods of time.

The same is true in the personal computer market. With increasing competition, prices have fallen dramatically since the 1990s. Even Dell and Gateway, with their low-cost products, have moved into other markets such as servers and televisions in order to maintain growth in a maturing market. Weaker companies have failed, leaving the most efficient producers/marketers scrambling for market share. The expanded market for personal computers dramatically reduced the financial returns generated by each dollar invested in productive assets. The "glory days" of the personal computer industry—the time in which fortunes could be won and lost in the space of an average-sized garage—have long since passed into history. Personal computers have essentially become commodity items, and profit margins for companies in this industry have shrunk as the market matures. With sales falling and profits falling faster. Hewlett-Packard and Compaq merged to gain the economies of scale that saved money and created efficiencies.

Financing with Long-Term Liabilities

As we said earlier, long-term assets do not come cheaply, and few companies have the cash on hand to open a new store across town, build a new manufacturing facility, research and develop a new life-saving drug, or launch a new product worldwide. To develop such fixed assets, companies need to raise low-cost long-term funds to finance them. Two common choices for raising these funds are attracting new owners (*equity financing*), which we'll look at in a moment, and taking on long-term liabilities (*debt financing*), which we'll look at now.

Long-term liabilities are debts that will be repaid over a number of years, such as long-term bank loans and bond issues. These take many different forms, but in the end, the key word is *debt*. Companies may raise money by borrowing it

long-term liabilities
debts that will be repaid over a number of years, such as long-term loans and bond issues

from commercial banks or other financial institutions in the form of lines of credit, short-term loans, or long-term loans. Many corporations acquire debt by borrowing money from pension funds, mutual funds, or life-insurance funds.

Companies that rely too heavily on debt can get into serious trouble should the economy falter; during these times, they may not earn enough operating income to make the required interest payments (remember the times-interest-earned ratio in Chapter 14). In severe cases when the problem persists too long, creditors will not restructure loans but will instead sue for the interest and principal owed and force the company into bankruptcy.

Bonds: Corporate IOUs

Much long-term debt takes the form of **bonds,** which are debt instruments that larger companies sell to raise long-term funds. In essence, the buyers of bonds (bondholders) loan the issuer of the bonds cash in exchange for regular interest payments until the loan is repaid on or before the specified maturity date. The bond itself is a certificate, much like an IOU, that represents the company's debt to the bondholder. Bonds are issued by a wide variety of entities, including corporations; national, state, and local governments; public utilities; and nonprofit corporations. Most bondholders need not hold their bonds until maturity; rather, the existence of active secondary markets of brokers and dealers allows for the quick and efficient transfer of bonds from owner to owner.

bonds
debt instruments that larger companies sell to raise long-term funds

The bond contract, or *indenture,* specifies all of the terms of the agreement between the bondholders and the issuing organization. The indenture, which can run more than 100 pages, specifies the basic terms of the bond, such as its face value, maturity date, and the annual interest rate. Table 16.2 briefly explains how to determine these and more things about a bond from a bond quote, as it might appear in *The Financial Times.* The face value of the bond, its initial sales price, is typically $1,000. After this, however, the price of the bond on the open market will fluctuate along with changes in the economy (particularly, changes in interest rates) and in the creditworthiness of the issuer. Bondholders receive the face value of the bond along with the final interest payment on the maturity date. The annual interest rate (often called the *coupon rate*) is the guaranteed percentage of face value that the company will pay to the bond owner every year. For example, a $1,000 bond with a coupon rate of 7 percent would pay $70 per year in interest. In most cases, bond indentures specify that interest payments be made every six months. In the example above, the $70 annual payment would be divided into two semiannual payments of $35.

In addition to the terms of interest payments and maturity date, the bond indenture typically covers other important topics, such as repayment methods, interest payment dates, procedures to be followed in case the organization fails to make the interest payments, conditions for the early repayment of the bonds, and any conditions requiring the pledging of assets as collateral.

An IBM bond certificate.

TABLE 16.2

Bonds—Global Investment Grade quoted in US $

30-Mar-10	Red Date[a]	Coupon[b]	S[c]	M[c]	F[c]	Bid Price[d]	Bid Yield[e]	Spread vs. Govts.[f]
GE Capital	01/16	5.00	AA+	Aa3	AA−	103.7	4.01	1.56
AT&T Wireless	03/31	8.75	A	A2	A	128.2	6.3	1.53
Goldman Sachs	02/33	6.13	A	A1	A+	98.29	6.27	1.49

[a]Red Date—the month and year that the bond matures and must pay back the borrowed amount.

[b]Coupon—the percentage in interest payment that the bond pays based on a $1,000 bond. For example, the GE Capital bond pays 5 percent on $1,000 or $50 per year while the AT&T bond pays $87.50.

[c]S-M-F—the ratings provided by the three major rating agenices: S (Standard and Poor's), M (Moody's), and F (Fitch). Using Standard and Poor's as an example, a rating of AAA would be the highest quality and lowest risk bond. Any bond in the A category is investment grade and considered high quality.

[d]Bid Price—the price as a percentage of par value ($1,000) that investors are willing to pay for a bond. For example, the GE capital bond has a bid price of 103.69, which would translate into 103% of $1,000 or a price of $1,036.90.

[e]Bid Yield—the annual rate of return the investor would receive if he or she held the bond to maturity. For example, with the GE bond you would get $50 per year until the bond matured in January 2016, and you would receive $1,000 par value at maturity. Because you paid $1,036.90, you would lose $36.90 on your investment. The 4.01 percent bid yield reflects both the income from the interest payment and the loss on the investment.

[f]Spread vs. Govts.—represents the premium yield the corporate bond pays over a U.S. government bond of equal maturity. Because corporate bonds are riskier than government bonds, an investor would expect the corporation to pay more than a risk-free government bond. In the case of GE Capital, the premium the company pays is an extra 1.56 percent.

Source: *The Financial Times*, March 31, 2010, p. 23.

Types of Bonds

unsecured bonds
debentures, or bonds that are not backed by specific collateral

Not surprisingly, there are a great many different types of bonds. Most are **unsecured bonds,** meaning that they are not backed by collateral; such bonds are termed *debentures.* **Secured bonds,** on the other hand, are backed by specific collateral that must be forfeited in the event that the issuing firm defaults. Whether secured or unsecured, bonds may be repaid in one lump sum or with many payments spread out over a period of time. **Serial bonds,** which are different from secured bonds, are actually a sequence of small bond issues of progressively longer maturity. The firm pays off each of the serial bonds as they mature. **Floating-rate bonds** do not have fixed interest payments; instead, the interest rate changes with current interest rates otherwise available in the economy.

secured bonds
bonds that are backed by specific collateral that must be forfeited in the event that the issuing firm defaults

serial bonds
a sequence of small bond issues of progressively longer maturity

In recent years, a special type of high-interest-rate bond has attracted considerable attention (usually negative) in the financial press. High-interest bonds, or **junk bonds** as they are popularly known, offer relatively high rates of interest because they have higher inherent risks. Historically, junk bonds have been associated with companies in poor financial health and/or startup firms with limited track records. In the mid-1980s, however, junk bonds became a very attractive method of financing corporate mergers; they remain popular today with many investors as a result of their very high relative interest rates. But higher risks are associated with those higher returns (upward of 12 percent per year in some cases) and the average investor would be well-advised to heed those famous words: Look before you leap!

floating-rate bonds
bonds with interest rates that change with current interest rates otherwise available in the economy

junk bonds
a special type of high interest-rate bond that carries higher inherent risks

Financing with Owners' Equity

A second means of long-term financing is through equity. Remember from Chapter 14 that owners' equity refers to the owners' investment in an organization. Sole proprietors and partners own all or a part of their businesses outright, and their equity includes the money and assets they have brought into their ventures. Corporate owners, on the other hand, own stock or shares of their companies, which they hope will provide them with a return on their investment. Stockholders' equity includes common stock, preferred stock, and retained earnings.

Common stock (introduced in Chapter 4) is the single most important source of capital for most new companies. On the balance sheet, the common stock account is separated into two basic parts—common stock at par and capital in excess of par. The *par value* of a stock is simply the dollar amount printed on the stock certificate and has no relation to actual *market value*—the price at which the common stock is currently trading. The difference between a stock's par value and its offering price is called *capital in excess of par*. Except in the case of some very low-priced stocks, the capital in excess of par account is significantly larger than the par value account. Table 16.3 briefly explains how to gather important information from a stock quote, as it might appear in *The Wall Street Journal* or on the NASDAQ Web site.

Preferred stock was defined in Chapter 14 as corporate ownership that gives the stockholder preference in the distribution of the company's profits but not the voting and control rights accorded to common stockholders. Thus, the primary advantage of owning preferred stock is that it is a safer investment than common stock.

All businesses exist to earn profits for their owners. Without the possibility of profit, there can be no incentive to risk investors' capital and succeed. When a corporation has profits left over after paying all of its expenses and taxes, it has the choice of retaining all or a portion of its earnings and/or paying them out to its shareholders in the form of dividends. **Retained earnings** are reinvested in the assets of the firm and belong to the owners in the form of equity. Retained

retained earnings earnings after expenses and taxes that are reinvested in the assets of the firm and belong to the owners in the form of equity

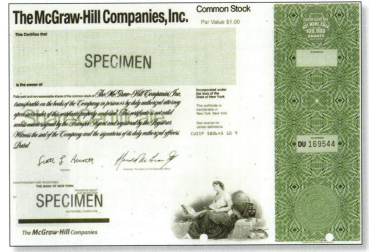

A McGraw-Hill stock certificate.

TABLE 16.3 A Basic Stock Quote

1		2	3	4	5	6	7	8
Stock Price 52 Week								
High	Low	Stock	Symbol	Dividend	Dividend Yield (%)	Volume	Close	Net Change
45.02	75.35	Nike	NKE	1.08	1.50%	2,546,930	73.89	+0.32
6.25	37.74	Skechers USA	SKX	0.00	0.00	1,231,908	37.40	+1.17
11.49	21.67	Timberland	TBL	0.00	0.00	726,583	20.98	−0.04
14.86	29.76	Wolverine Worldwide	WWW	0.44	1.50%	337,498	29.40	+0.28

1. The **52-week high and low**—the highest and lowest prices, respectively, paid for the stock in the last year; for Nike stock, the highest was $75.35 and the lowest price, $45.02.

2. **Stock**—the name of the issuing company. When followed by the letters "pf", the stock is a preferred stock.

3. **Symbol**—the ticker tape symbol for the stock; NKE.

4. **Dividend**—the annual cash dividend paid to stockholders; Nike paid a dividend of $1.08 per share of stock outstanding.

5. **Dividend yield**—the dividend return on one share of common stock; 1.50 percent.

6. **Volume**—the number of shares traded on this day; Nike, 2,546,930

7. **Close**—Nike's last sale of the day was for $73.89.

8. **Net Change**—the difference between the previous day's close and the close on the day being reported; Nike was up $0.32.

Source: Yahoo! Finance, http://finance.yahoo.com/q?s (accessed March 26, 2010).

earnings are an important source of funds and are, in fact, the only long-term funds that the company can generate internally.

When the board of directors distributes some of a corporation's profits to the owners, it issues them as cash dividend payments. But not all firms pay dividends. Many fast-growing firms retain all of their earnings because they can earn high rates of return on the earnings they reinvest. Companies with fewer growth opportunities typically pay out large proportions of their earnings in the form of dividends, thereby allowing their stockholders to reinvest their dividend payments in higher-growth companies. Table 16.4 presents a sample of companies and the dividend each paid on a single share of stock. As shown in the table, when the dividend is divided by the price the result is the **dividend yield**. The dividend yield is the cash return as a percentage of the price but does not reflect the total return an investor earns on the individual stock. If the dividend yield is 3.2 percent on Campbell Soup and the stock price increases by 10 percent from $34.92 to $38.41, then the total return would be 13.2 percent. It is not clear that stocks with high dividend yields will be preferred by investors to those with little or no dividends. Most large companies pay their stockholders dividends on a quarterly basis.

dividend yield
the dividend per share divided by the stock price

Investment Banking

A company that needs more money to expand or take advantage of opportunities may be able to obtain financing by issuing stock. The first-time sale of stocks and bonds directly to the public is called a *new issue*. Companies that already have stocks or bonds outstanding may offer a new issue of stock to raise additional funds for specific projects. When a company offers its stock to the public for the very first time, it is said to be "going public," and the sale is called an *initial public offering.*

New issues of stocks and bonds are sold directly to the public and to institutions in what is known as the **primary market**—the market where firms raise financial capital. The primary market differs from **secondary markets,** which are stock exchanges and over-the-counter markets where investors can trade their securities with other investors rather than the company that issued the stock or bonds. Primary market transactions actually raise cash for the issuing corporations, while secondary market transactions do not.

primary market
the market where firms raise financial capital

> **Did You Know?**   If you bought one share of Microsoft stock when the company went public in 1986, it would be worth almost $8,000 today, after allowing for stock splits and adjustments.[5]

Investment banking, the sale of stocks and bonds for corporations, helps such companies raise funds by matching people and institutions who have money to invest with corporations in need of resources to exploit new opportunities. Corporations usually employ an investment banking firm to help sell their securities in the primary market. An investment banker helps firms establish appropriate offering prices for their securities. In addition, the investment banker takes care of the myriad details and securities regulations involved in any sale of securities to the public.

secondary markets
stock exchanges and over-the-counter markets where investors can trade their securities with others

Just as large corporations such as IBM and Microsoft have a client relationship with a law firm and an accounting firm, they also have a client relationship with an investment banking firm. An investment banking firm such as Merrill Lynch, Goldman Sachs, or Morgan Stanley Smith Barney can provide advice about financing plans, dividend policy, or stock repurchases, as well as advice on mergers and acquisitions. Many now offer additional banking services, making them "one-stop shopping" banking centers. When Pixar merged with Disney, both companies used investment bankers to help them value the transaction. Each firm wanted an

investment banking
the sale of stocks and bonds for corporations

Ticker Symbol	Company Name	Price Per Share	Dividend Per Share	Dividend Yield	Earnings Per Share (*)	Price Earnings Ratio$^{P/E}$
AEO	American Eagle	$19.26	$0.40	2.10%	$0.81	23.87
AXP	American Express	41.12	0.72	1.70	1.54	26.72
AAPL	Apple	230.90	0.00	0.00	10.27	22.49
CPB	Campbell Soup	34.92	1.10	3.20	2.30	15.17
DIS	Disney	35.31	0.35	1.00	1.76	20.11
F	Ford	13.86	0.00	0.00	0.86	16.04
HOG	Harley Davidson	27.92	0.40	1.40	−0.24	N/A (**)
HD	Home Depot	32.75	0.95	2.90	$1.57	20.82
MCD	McDonald's	67.26	2.20	3.30	$4.11	16.36
PG	Procter & Gamble	63.69	1.76	2.80	$4.20	15.17
LUV	Southwest Airlines	13.00	0.02	0.15	0.19	68.42
SBUX	Starbucks	24.59	0.40	1.70	0.76	32.57

TABLE 16.4

Estimated Common Stock Price-Earnings Ratios and Dividends for Selected Companies

*Earnings per share are for the latest 12-month period and do not necessarily match year-end numbers.

**N/A—not applicable because of negative earnings

Source: http://finance.yahoo.com/q?s (accessed March 22, 2010).

outside opinion about what it was worth to the other. Sometimes mergers fall apart because the companies cannot agree on the price each company is worth or the structure of management after the merger. The advising investment banker, working with management, often irons out these details. Of course, investment bankers do not provide these services for free. They usually charge a fee of between 1 and 1.5 percent of the transaction. A $20 billion merger can generate between $200 and $300 million in investment banking fees. The merger mania of the late 1990s allowed top investment bankers to earn huge sums. Unfortunately, this type of fee income is dependent on healthy stock markets, which seem to stimulate the merger fever among corporate executives.

The Securities Markets

securities markets
the mechanism for buying and selling securities

Securities markets provide a mechanism for buying and selling securities. They make it possible for owners to sell their stocks and bonds to other investors. Thus, in the broadest sense, stocks and bonds markets may be thought of as providers of liquidity—the ability to turn security holdings into cash quickly and at minimal expense and effort. Without liquid securities markets, many potential investors would sit on the sidelines rather than invest their hard-earned savings in securities. Indeed, the ability to sell securities at well-established market prices is one of the very pillars of the capitalistic society that has developed over the years in the United States.

Unlike the primary market, in which corporations sell stocks directly to the public, secondary markets permit the trading of previously issued securities. There are many different secondary markets for both stocks and bonds. If you want to purchase 100 shares of Google common stock, for example, you must purchase this stock from another investor or institution. It is the active buying and selling by many thousands of investors that establishes the prices of all financial securities. Secondary market trades may take place on organized exchanges or in what is known as the over-the-counter market. Many brokerage houses exist to help investors with financial decisions, and many offer their services through the Internet. One such broker is Charles Schwab. Its site offers a wealth of information and provides educational material to individual investors.

Stock Markets

Stock markets exist around the world in New York, Tokyo, London, Frankfort, Paris, and other world locations. The two biggest stock markets in the United States are the New York Stock Exchange (NYSE) and the NASDAQ market. The American Stock Exchange is now part of the New York Exchange, and NASDAQ bought both the Boston and Philadelphia regional exchanges. The Chicago Stock Exchange still exists as a regional exchange, but it has a difficult time justifying its existence as a stand-alone exchange.

Exchanges used to be divided into organized exchanges and over-the-counter markets, but during the last several years, dramatic changes have occurred in the markets. Both the NYSE and NASDAQ became publicly traded companies. They were previously not-for-profit organizations but are now for-profit companies. Additionally both exchanges bought or merged with electronic exchanges, the NYSE with Archipelago and the NASDAQ with Instinet. Electronic trading is faster and less expensive than floor trading (where brokers meet to transact business) and now accounts for most of the stock trading done worldwide.

In an attempt to expand their markets, NASDAQ acquired the OMX, a Nordic stock exchange headquartered in Sweden, and the New York Stock Exchange merged with Euronext, a large European electronic exchange that trades options and futures contracts as well as common stock. Both the NYSE and NASDAQ have expanded their reach, their product line, and their ability to trade around the world. What we are witnessing is the globalization of the world's financial markets.

Traditionally, the NASDAQ market has been an electronic market, and many of the large technology companies such as Microsoft, Oracle, and Apple Computer trade on the NASDAQ market. The NASDAQ operates through dealers who buy and sell common stock (inventory) for their own accounts. The NYSE has traditionally been a floor-traded market, where brokers meet at trading posts on the floor of the New York Stock Exchange to buy and sell common stock. The brokers act as agents for their clients and do not own their own inventory. This traditional division between the two markets is becoming less significant as the exchanges become electronic.

The Over-the-Counter Market

Unlike the organized exchanges, the **over-the-counter (OTC) market** is a network of dealers all over the country linked by computers, telephones, and Teletype machines. It has no central location. Today, the OTC market consists of small stocks, illiquid bank stocks, penny stocks, and companies whose stocks trade on the "pink sheets." Once NASDAQ was classified as an exchange by the SEC, it was no longer part of the OTC market. Further, because most corporate bonds and all U.S. securities are traded over the counter, the OTC market regularly accounts for the largest total dollar value of all of the secondary markets.

over-the-counter (OTC) market
a network of dealers all over the country linked by computers, telephones, and Teletype machines

Measuring Market Performance

Investors, especially professional money managers, want to know how well their investments are performing relative to the market as a whole. Financial managers also need to know how their companies' securities are performing when compared with their competitors'. Thus, performance measures—averages and indexes—are very important to many different people. They not only indicate the performance of a particular securities market but also provide a measure of the overall health of the economy.

Indexes and averages are used to measure stock prices. An *index* compares current stock prices with those in a specified base period, such as 1944, 1967, or 1977. An *average* is the average of certain stock prices. The averages used are usually not simple calculations, however. Some stock market averages (such as the Standard & Poor's Composite Index) are weighted averages, where the weights employed are the total market values of each stock in the index (in this case 500). The Dow Jones Industrial Average is a price-weighted average. Regardless of how they are constructed, all market averages of stocks move together closely over time.

Many investors follow the activity of the Dow Jones Industrial Average to see whether the stock market has gone up or down. Table 16.5 lists the 30 companies that currently make up the Dow. Although these companies are only a small fraction of the total number of companies listed on the New York Stock Exchange, because of their size they account for about 25 percent of the total value of the NYSE.

The numbers listed in an index or average that tracks the performance of a stock market are expressed not as dollars but as a number on a fixed scale. If you know, for example, that the Dow Jones Industrial Average climbed from 860 in

Consider Ethics and Social Responsibility
The Hershey Trust Considers the Hershey School an Important Part of Doing Business

No matter where you live, you have probably eaten Hershey's chocolate products before. However, did you know that every product you purchase contributes to the Hershey School? Founded by Milton and Catherine Hershey in 1909, the school was originally dedicated to educating orphan boys. In 1918, Milton Hershey donated almost his entire fortune to a trust for the school—the Hershey Trust Company. Today, the school serves needy children from preschool through high school. The school is supported in part by Hershey stock (the trust holds the largest block of Hershey shares), and this is where you and the performance of Hershey come into play.

Any financial decisions The Hershey Company makes (including expansions, divestments, mergers, and acquisitions) must take the school's funding into account. The school's trust board must also consider carefully how it interacts with The Hershey Company. In 2007, when The Hershey Company was struggling, the school's trust board came close to selling its stock in order to diversify. At the last minute the board opted to take a greater role in The Hershey Company by replacing some Hershey board members and the then-CEO and chairman, Richard Lenny. This move gave the trust board greater control over the company's decisions.

In addition to its financial relationship with the school, The Hershey Company frequently invites Hershey School students to intern. This program gives students job prospects after they graduate. It also runs Project Fellowship—a partnership between the company and the school through which students and employees build relationships. It's clear that The Hershey Company's choices are deeply intertwined with the Milton Hershey School, forcing the company to assess risk with the school in mind.[6]

Discussion Questions
1. What is the goal of the Hershey School?
2. Does the Hershey School do anything to advance the company's financial position in any way?
3. Do you think that philanthropic efforts like the Hershey School can enhance a brand in the eyes of the consumer? How?

August 1982 to a high of 11,497 at the beginning of 2000, you can see clearly that the value of the Dow Jones Average increased more than 10 times in this 19-year period, making it one of the highest rate of return periods in the history of the stock market.

Unfortunately, prosperity did not last long once the Internet bubble burst. Technology stocks and new Internet companies were responsible for the huge increase in stock prices. Even companies with few sales and no earnings were selling at prices that were totally unreasonable. It is always easier to realize that a bubble existed after

TABLE 16.5

The 30 Stocks in the Dow Jones Industrial Average

3M Co	Du Pont	McDonald's
Alcoa Inc.	ExxonMobil	Merck
American Express Co	General Electric	Microsoft
AT&T Inc.	Hewlett-Packard	Pfizer
Bank of America	Home Depot	Procter & Gamble
Boeing	Intel	Travelers Companies
Caterpiller	IBM	United Technologies
Chevron	Johnson & Johnson	Verizon
Cisco Systems	JPMorgan Chase	Walmart
Coca-Cola	Kraft Foods	Walt Disney

Source: "Dow Jones Industrial Average," *Yahoo! Finance,* http://finance.yahoo.com/q/cp?s=%5EDJI (accessed March 26, 2010).

it has popped. By September 2002, the Dow Jones Industrial Average hit 7,461. The markets stabilized and the economy kept growing; investors were euphoric when the Dow Jones Industrial Average hit an all time high of 14,198 in October 2007. However, once the housing bubble burst, the economy and the stock market went into a free fall. The Dow Jones Industrial Average bottomed out at 6,470 in March 2009. The market entered a period of wild fluctuations, and by April 2010, it hit a new high for the year of 10,975. Perhaps this roller coaster ride indicates why some people are afraid to enter the market and buy common stocks. If you look at the long-term trend and long-term returns in common stocks, they far outdistance bonds and government securities. When you are young, you should be playing the long-term trends, and as you get older your investments should become more conservative.

Recognizing financial bubbles can be difficult. It is too easy to get caught up in the enthusiasm that accompanies rising markets. Knowing what something is worth in economic terms is the test of true value. During the housing bubble, banks made loans to subprime borrowers to buy houses. (Remember that the prime rate is the rate for the highest quality borrowers and subprime loans are generally made to those who do not qualify for regular ones.) As more money poured into the housing market, the obvious supply and demand relationship from economics would indicate that housing prices would rise. As prices rose, speculators entered the real estate market trying to make a fast buck. States such as Florida, Arizona, Nevada, and California were the favorite speculative spots and the states with the largest decline in house prices. To make matters worse, banks had created the home equity loan years ago so that borrowers could take out a second mortgage against their house and deduct the interest payment for tax purposes. Many

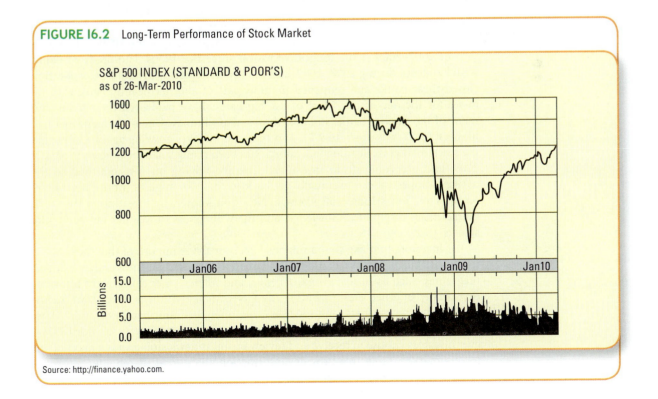

FIGURE 16.2   Long-Term Performance of Stock Market

Source: http://finance.yahoo.com.

homeowners no longer thought about paying off their mortgages but instead used the increase in the price of their houses to borrow more money. This behavior was unsustainable.

The bankers engaged in risky financial behavior packaged up billions of dollars of mortgages into securitized assets. In other words, an investor could buy a pool of assets and collect the interest income and eventually get a payment at the end of the life of the product. This technique allowed banks to make a mortgage, collect a fee, package the mortgage, and collect another fee. These securitized mortgages were sold to the market as asset-backed securities with a AAA credit rating off their books and replaced with cash to make more loans. In this case, when the bubble broke, it had extremely severe consequences for the economy, workers, and investors.

People defaulted on loans when they could no longer afford to pay the mortgage. Many of these people shouldn't have been able to borrow in the first place. The defaults caused housing prices to fall, and some people who had home equity loans no longer had any equity left in their house. Some homeowners owed the bank more than the house was worth, and they started walking away from their mortgage. As the same time, investors realized that the mortgage-backed securities they owned were probably not worth what they thought they were worth, and prices of these assets plummeted. Banks and other financial service firms that had these assets on their books suffered a double whammy. They had loan losses and losses on mortgage-backed securities that another division of the bank had bought for investment purposes. Soon, many banks were close to violating their capital requirement, and the U.S. Treasury and Federal Reserve stepped in—with the help of funding from Congress—to make banks loans, buy securities that were illiquid, and invest in the capital of the banks by buying preferred stocks.

The consensus of most economists is that through the actions of the U.S. Treasury, and the Federal Reserve, the U.S. economy escaped what might have been another depression equal to or worse than the depression of the 1930s. The recession of 2007–2009 is the longest recession since the 1930s. Hundreds of banks went bankrupt during 2008–2009, and the Federal Deposit Insurance Corporation closed these banks and reopened them as part of another healthy bank with no losses for the depositors. Most of the big banks have paid back their loans, but many of the smaller banks still owe the Treasury money. Unemployment that had hit over 10.4% was down to 9.7% and the economy was growing again. Given that the stock market is a leading indicator, it has been rising since the bottom in March 2009, and everyone—from investors to people relying on pensions tied to the market—hopes we can eventually get back to the 2007 high of more than 14,000 on the Dow Jones Industrial Average. Now you know why investing in the stock market takes discipline, knowledge, and the willingness to weather out economic storms. (See Figure 16.2.)

For investors to make sound financial decisions, it is important that they stay in touch with business news, markets, and indexes. Of course, business and investment magazines, such as *BusinessWeek, Fortune,* and *Money,* offer this type of information. Many Internet sites, including the CNN/*Money, Business Wire, USA Today,* other online newspapers, and *PR Newswire,* offer this information, as well. Many sites offer searchable databases of information by topic, company, or keyword. However investors choose to receive and review business news, doing so is a necessity in today's market. Table 16.6 Provides information about total shareholder return by industry over the past 10 years.

1 Year	Annual Rate of Return (%)
1 Food services	−5.8
2 Health care: pharmacy and other services	−9.2
3 Pharmaceuticals	−12.7
4 Railroads	−15.3
5 Food consumer products	−16.6
6 Household and personal products	−17.5
7 Information technology services	−20.8
8 Utilities: gas and electric	−23
9 Specialty retailers	−24
10 Airlines	−26.6
5 Years	**Annual Rate of Return 2003–2008 (%)**
1 Mining, crude-oil production	16
2 Railroads	15.3
3 Engineering, construction	15.1
4 Petroleum refining	14.3
5 Health care: pharmacy and other services	13.9
6 Metals	13
7 Food services	10.8
8 Wholesalers: diversified	9.4
9 Oil, gas equipment, services	8.1
10 Utilities: gas and electric	7.9
10 Years	**Annual Rate of Return 1998–2008 (%)**
1 Engineering, construction	16.8
2 Mining, crude-oil production	16.3
3 Oil, gas equipment, services	12.4
4 Petroleum refining	12
5 Health care: insurance and managed care	10.3
6 Construction and farm machinery	10.2
7 Wholesalers: diversified	8.3
8 Food services	8.2
9 Railroads	8.1
10 Metals	7

TABLE I6.6

Annual Total Return to Shareholders by Industry Rankings (1998–2008)

Source: "Fortune 500 Top Performers: Best Investments by Industry," *Fortune,* http://money.cnn.com/magazines/fortune/fortune500/2009/performers/industries/bestinv (accessed March 26, 2010).

So You Want to Work in Financial Management or Securities

Taking classes in financial and securities management can provide many career options, from managing a small firm's accounts receivables to handling charitable giving for a multinational to investment banking to stock brokerage. We have entered into a less certain period for finance and securities jobs, however. In the world of investment banking, the past few years have been especially challenging. Tens of thousands of employees from Wall Street firms have lost their jobs. This phenomenon is not confined to New York City either, leaving the industry with a lot fewer jobs around the country. This type of phenomenon is not isolated to the finance sector. In the early 2000s, the tech sector experienced a similar downturn, from which it has subsequently largely recovered. Undoubtedly, markets will bounce back and job creation in finance and securities will increase again—but until that happens the atmosphere across finance and securities will be more competitive than it has been in the past. However, this does not mean that there are no jobs. All firms need financial analysts to determine whether a project should be implemented, when to issue stocks or bonds, or when to initiate loans. These and other forward-looking questions such as how to invest excess cash must be addressed by financial managers. Economic uncertainty in the financial and securities market has made for more difficulty in finding the most desirable jobs.

Why this sudden downturn in financial industry prospects? A lot of these job cuts came in response to the subprime lending fallout and subsequent bank failures such as Bear Stearns, which alone lost around 7,000 employees. All of these people will be looking for new jobs in new organizations, increasing the competitive level in a lot of different employment areas. For young jobseekers with relatively little experience, this may result in a great deal of frustration. On the other hand, by the time you graduate, the job market for finance majors could be in recovery and rebuilding with new employees. Uncertainty results in hiring freezes and layoffs, but leave firms lean and ready to grow when the cycle turns around, resulting in hiring from the bottom up.

Many different industries require people with finance skills. So do not despair if you have a difficult time finding a job in exactly the right firm. Most students switch companies a number of times over the course of their careers. Many organizations require individuals trained in forecasting, statistics, economics, and finance. Even unlikely places like museums, aquariums, and zoos need people who are good at numbers. It may require some creativity, but if you are committed to a career in finance, look to less obvious sources—not just the large financial firms.[7]

Review Your Understanding

Describe some common methods of managing current assets.

Current assets are short-term resources such as cash, investments, accounts receivable, and inventory, which can be converted to cash within a year. Financial managers focus on minimizing the amount of cash kept on hand and increasing the speed of collections through lockboxes and electronic funds transfer and investing in marketable securities. Marketable securities include U.S. Treasury bills, certificates of deposit, commercial paper, and money market funds. Managing accounts receivable requires judging customer creditworthiness and creating credit terms that encourage prompt payment. Inventory management focuses on determining optimum inventory levels that minimize the cost of storing and ordering inventory without sacrificing too many lost sales due to stockouts.

Identify some sources of short-term financing (current liabilities).

Current liabilities are short-term debt obligations that must be repaid within one year, such as accounts payable, taxes payable, and notes (loans) payable. Trade credit is extended by suppliers for the purchase of their goods and services. A line of credit is an arrangement by which a bank agrees to lend a specified amount of money to a business whenever the business needs it. Secured loans are backed by collateral; unsecured loans are backed only by the borrower's good reputation.

Summarize the importance of long-term assets and capital budgeting.

Long-term, or fixed, assets are expected to last for many years, such as production facilities (plants), offices, and equipment. Businesses need modern, up-to-date equipment to succeed in today's competitive environment. Capital budgeting is the process of analyzing company needs and selecting the assets that will maximize its value; a capital budget is the amount of money budgeted for the purchase of fixed assets. Every investment in fixed assets carries some risk.

Specify how companies finance their operations and manage fixed assets with long-term liabilities, particularly bonds.

Two common choices for financing are equity financing (attracting new owners) and debt financing (taking on long-term liabilities). Long-term liabilities are debts that will be repaid over a number of years, such as long-term bank loans and bond issues. A bond is a long-term debt security that an organization sells to raise money. The bond indenture specifies the provisions of the bond contract—maturity date, coupon rate, repayment methods, and others.

Discuss how corporations can use equity financing by issuing stock through an investment banker.

Owners' equity represents what owners have contributed to the company and includes common stock, preferred stock, and retained earnings (profits that have been reinvested in the assets of the firm). To finance operations, companies can issue new common and preferred stock through an investment banker that sells stocks and bonds for corporations.

Describe the various securities markets in the United States.

Securities markets provide the mechanism for buying and selling stocks and bonds. Primary markets allow companies to raise capital by selling new stock directly to investors through investment bankers. Secondary markets allow the buyers of previously issued shares of stock to sell them to other owners. The major secondary markets are the New York Stock Exchange, the American Stock Exchange, and the over-the-counter market. Investors measure stock market performance by watching stock market averages and indexes such as the Dow Jones Industrial Average and the Standard and Poor's (S&P) Composite Index.

Critique the short-term asset and liabilities position of a small manufacturer, and recommend corrective action.

Using the information presented in this chapter, you should be able to "Solve the Dilemma" on page 523 presented by the current bleak working capital situation of Glasspray Corporation.

Revisit the World of Business

1. Why has Y Combinator succeeded while many other firms in the financial industry have failed?
2. What are the risks involved in creating a business like Y Combinator?
3. What are the rewards for Graham in taking a risk in small tech startups?

Learn the Terms

Check Your Progress

1. Define working capital management.
2. How can a company speed up cash flow? Why should it?
3. Describe the various types of marketable securities.
4. What does it mean to have a line of credit at a bank?
5. What are fixed assets? Why is assessing risk important in capital budgeting?
6. How can a company finance fixed assets?
7. What are bonds and what do companies do with them?
8. How can companies use equity to finance their operations and long-term growth?
9. What are the functions of securities markets?
10. What were some of the principal causes of the most recent recession?

Get Involved

1. Using your local newspaper or *The Wall Street Journal,* find the current rates of interest on the following marketable securities. If you were a financial manager for a large corporation, which would you invest extra cash in? Which would you invest in if you worked for a small business?

   a. Three-month T-bills
   b. Six-month T-bills
   c. Commercial certificates of deposit
   d. Commercial paper
   e. Eurodollar deposits
   f. Money market deposits

2. Select five of the Dow Jones Industrials from Table 16.5. Look up their earnings, dividends, and prices for the past five years. What kind of picture is presented by this information? Which stocks would you like to have owned over this past period? Do you think the next five years will present a similar picture?

Build Your Skills

CHOOSING AMONG PROJECTS

Background:
As the senior executive in charge of exploration for High Octane Oil Co., you are constantly looking for projects that will add to the company's profitability—without increasing the company's risk. High Octane Oil is an international oil company with operations in Latin America, the Middle East, Africa, the United States, and Mexico. The company is one of the world's leading experts in deep-water exploration and drilling. High Octane currently produces 50 percent of its oil in the United States, 25 percent in the Middle East, 5 percent in Africa, 10 percent in Latin America, and 10 percent in Mexico. You are considering six projects from around the world.

Project 1—Your deep-water drilling platform in the Gulf of Mexico is producing at maximum capacity from the Valdez oil field, and High Octane's geological engineers think there is a high probability that there is oil in the Sanchez field, which is adjacent to Valdez. They recommend drilling a new series of wells. Once commercial quantities of oil have been discovered, it will take two more years to build the collection platform and pipelines. It will be four years before the discovered oil gets to the refineries.

Project 2—The Brazilian government has invited you to drill on some unexplored tracts in the middle of the central jungle region. There are roads to within 50 miles of the tract and British Petroleum has found oil 500 miles away from this tract. It would take about three years to develop this property and several more years to build pipelines and pumping stations to carry the oil to the refineries. The Brazilian government wants 20 percent of all production as its fee for giving High Octane Oil Co. the drilling rights or a $500 million up-front fee and 5 percent of the output.

Project 3—Your fields in Saudi Arabia have been producing oil for 50 years. Several wells are old, and the pressure has diminished. Your engineers are sure that if you were to initiate high-pressure secondary recovery procedures, you would increase the output of these existing wells by 20 percent. High-pressure recovery methods pump water at high pressure into the underground limestone formations to enhance the movement of petroleum toward the surface.

Project 4—Your largest oil fields in Alaska have been producing from only 50 percent of the known deposits. Your geological engineers estimate that you could open up 10 percent of the remaining fields every two years and offset your current declining production from existing wells. The pipeline capacity is available and, while you can only drill during six months of the year, the fields could be producing oil in three years.

Project 5—Some of High Octane's west Texas oil fields produce in shallow stripper wells of 2,000- to 4,000-foot depths. Stripper wells produce anywhere from 10 to 2,000 barrels per day and can last for six months or 40 years. Generally, once you find a shallow deposit, there is an 80 percent chance that offset wells will find more oil. Because these wells are shallow, they can be drilled quickly at a low cost. High Octane's engineers estimate that in your largest tract, which is closest to the company's Houston refinery, you could increase production by 30 percent for the next 10 years by increasing the density of the wells per square mile.

Project 6—The government of a republic in Russia has invited you to drill for oil in Siberia. Russian geologists think that this oil field might be the largest in the world, but there have been no wells drilled and no infrastructure exists to carry oil if it should be found. The republic has no money to help you build the infrastructure but if you find oil, it will let you keep the first five years' production before taking its 25 percent share. Knowing that oil fields do not start producing at full capacity for many years after initial production, your engineers are not sure that your portion the first five years of production will pay for the infrastructure they must build to get the oil to market. The republic also has been known to have a rather

unstable government, and the last international oil company that began this project left the country when a new government demanded a higher than originally agreed-upon percentage of the expected output. If this field is in fact the largest in the world, High Octane's supply of oil would be ensured well into the 21st century.

Task:
1. Working in groups, rank the six projects from lowest risk to highest risk.
2. Given the information provided, do the best you can to rank the projects from lowest cost to highest cost.
3. What political considerations might affect your project choice?
4. If you could choose one project, which would it be and why?
5. If you could choose three projects, which ones would you choose? In making this decision, consider which projects might be highly correlated to High Octane Oil's existing production and which ones might diversify the company's production on a geographical basis.

Solve the Dilemma

SURVIVING RAPID GROWTH

Glasspray Corporation is a small firm that makes industrial fiberglass spray equipment. Despite its size, the company supplies to a range of firms from small mom-and-pop boatmakers to major industrial giants, both overseas and here at home. Indeed, just about every molded fiberglass resin product, from bathroom sinks and counters to portable spas and racing yachts, is constructed with the help of one or more of the company's machines.

Despite global acceptance of its products, Glasspray has repeatedly run into trouble with regard to the management of its current assets and liabilities as a result of extremely rapid and consistent increases in year-to-year sales. The firm's president and founder, Stephen T. Rose, recently lamented the sad state of his firm's working capital

position: "Our current assets aren't, and our current liabilities are!" Rose shouted in a recent meeting of the firm's top officers. "We can't afford any more increases in sales! We're selling our way into bankruptcy! Frankly, our *working* capital doesn't!"

Discussion Questions
1. Normally, rapidly increasing sales are a good thing. What seems to be the problem here?
2. List the important components of a firm's working capital. Include both current assets and current liabilities.
3. What are some management techniques applied to current liabilities that Glasspray might use to improve its working capital position?

Build Your Business Plan

FINANCIAL MANAGEMENT AND SECURITIES MARKET

This chapter helps you realize that once you are making money, you need to be careful in determining how to invest it. Meanwhile, your team should consider

the pros and cons of establishing a line of credit at the bank.

Remember the key to building your business plan is to be realistic!!

See for Yourself Videocase

MORNINGSTAR, INC., MAKES INVESTING EASIER

Many individuals find stocks and bonds to be confusing, but Joe Mansueto has begun to change that by making investing easier to understand. In 1984, Mansueto founded Morningstar, Inc., which provides independent investment research to individuals, financial advisers, and institutional advisers. The company's top asset is that it is independent and its assessments are based on impartial research. Although it works with advisers, its main focus is on individuals. From the beginning, Mansueto, a former stock analyst, aimed to take the chaos of the investment world and create tools that would help individuals make sense of it. With so much investment information and opportunities available, it is easy for the average person to feel lost.

The idea for Morningstar began when Mansueto realized that in order to compare funds and get enough information to begin investing effectively he would have to order prospectuses from each individual fund. The amount of information needed was overwhelming. Mansueto thought that if he could create a compendium of information for the different funds out there, it would make it much easier for the average person to invest intelligently. In 1984 Mansueto founded Morningstar, Inc., and began by focusing on mutual funds. He created the Mutual Fund Sourcebook, a compilation of information on roughly 400 different mutual funds. Over two decades later, Morningstar assists over 6 million individual investors with mutual funds, stocks, bonds, and more. The company employs almost 200 fund and/or stock analysts who research, write up, and rate investments along with guiding individuals toward making wise business decisions. Morningstar is dedicated to serving investors. It does not charge the companies that it rates and prides itself on maintaining an independent view. Analysts regularly compile data on more than 325,000 global investment offerings.

The company focuses on offering information for three different types of investment choices: mutual funds, stocks, and bonds. Mutual funds are pools of investments (often called portfolios) selected by fund managers. A mutual fund can be good for someone wanting less risk. The idea is to offset the high risk investments by investing in multiple securities. Mutual funds are also well-suited for investors who do not want to take the time or who lack the expertise to invest in individual securities. Morningstar also works with stocks and bonds. Stocks are ownerships, or stakes, in a particular company whereas a bond is like a company IOU. A bond investor basically loans a company money with the understanding that the company will pay back the money with interest. Bonds generally carry less risk than stocks do.

Multiply all this information by the thousands of mutual funds, stocks, and bonds out there, and it is easy to see why someone might become confused when deciding where to invest. Morningstar has even geared its website toward new investors, with features such as the investing classroom, analyst picks, data tools, and articles. In a post-Enron, post-recession world, it is more critical than ever that people understand how to manage their finances and keep their debt in check. Mansueto believes firmly that investing is a key component to financial solvency. He recommends investing early, even suggesting that high school students take the plunge. According to him, it is not the amount of money a person invests that matters; it is getting started early, being consistent, and patiently waiting for initial investments to grow.[8]

Discussion Questions

1. What is it about investing that Mansueto discovered is so confusing for the average investor?
2. How does Morningstar, Inc., make investing easier for individuals?
3. Why does Mansueto recommend investing early in life, even in high school?

Remember to check out our Online Learning Center at www.mhhe.com/ferrell8e.

Team Exercise

Compare and contrast financing with long-term liabilities, such as bonds versus financing with owner's equity, typically retained earnings, common stock, and preferred stock. Form groups and suggest a good mix of long-term liabilities and owner's equity for a new firm that makes wind turbines for generating alternate energy and would like to grow quickly.

Personal Financial Planning*

The Financial Planning Process

Personal financial planning is the process of managing your finances so that you can achieve your financial goals. By anticipating future needs and wants, you can take appropriate steps to prepare for them. Your needs and wants will undoubtedly change over time as you enter into various life circumstances. Although financial planning is not entirely about money management, a large part of this process is concerned with decisions related to expenditures, investments, and credit.

Although every person has unique needs, everyone can benefit from financial planning. Even if the entire financial plan is not implemented at once, the process itself will help you focus on what is important. With a little forethought and action, you may be able to achieve goals that you previously thought were unattainable. Table D.1 shows how teens handle finances.

The steps in development and implementation of an effective financial plan are:

- Evaluate your financial health.
- Set short-term and long-term financial goals.

- Create and adhere to a budget.
- Manage credit wisely.
- Develop a savings and investment plan.
- Evaluate and purchase insurance.
- Develop an estate plan.
- Adjust your financial plan to new circumstances.

Evaluate Your Financial Health

Just as businesses make use of financial reports to track their performance, good personal financial planning requires that individuals keep track of their income and expenses and their overall financial condition. Several software packages are readily available to help track personal finances (for example, Quicken and Microsoft Money), but all that is really needed is a simple spreadsheet program. This appendix includes some simple worksheets that can be reproduced to provide a starting point for personal financial planning. Comprehensive financial planning sites are also available on the Internet. For example, **www.moneycentral.msn.com** and **www. smartmoney.com** both provide information and tools to simplify this process.

		TABLE D.I
Learned about money from their parents	87%	Teens and Money
Agree that saving and investing can help you achieve the freedom to do what you want in life	89%	
Feel that it's more important as a teen to save money than to spend it	20%	
Know how to use a debit card/credit card	54%/48%	
Get money from a job	57%	
Get money from a credit card	20% parents' card; 14% own card	
Are in debt either to a person or a company	31%	
Would like to learn more about money management in school	76%	

Source: Charles Schwab Foundation, "Teens & Money 2006 Survey Findings," "Insights into Money Attitudes Behaviors and Concerns of Teens," www.aboutschwab.com/teensurvey2006.pdf (accessed May 15, 2006).

*This appendix was contributed by Dr. Vickie Bajtelsmit.

While it is possible to track all kinds of information over time, the two most critical elements of your finances are your personal net worth and your personal cash flow. The information necessary for these two measures is often required by lending institutions on loan applications, so keeping it up-to-date can save you time and effort later.

The Personal Balance Sheet

For businesses, net worth is usually defined as *assets minus liabilities,* and this is no different for individuals. **Personal net worth** is simply the total value of all personal assets less the total value of unpaid debts or liabilities. Although a business could not survive with a negative net worth since it would be technically insolvent, many students have negative net worth. As a student, you probably are not yet earning enough to have accumulated significant assets, such as a house or stock portfolio, but you are likely to have incurred various forms of debt, including student loans, car loans, and credit card debt.

At this stage in your life, negative net worth is not necessarily an indication of poor future financial prospects. Current investment in your "human capital" (education) is usually considered to have a resulting payoff in the form of better job opportunities and higher potential lifetime income, so this "upside-down" balance sheet should not stay that way forever. Unfortunately, there are many people in the United States who have negative net worth much later in their lives. This can result from unforeseen circumstances, like divorce, illness, or disability, but the easy availability of credit in the last couple of decades has also been blamed for the heavy debt loads of many American families. No matter the immediate trigger, it is usually poor financial planning—the failure to prepare in advance for those unforeseen circumstances—that makes the difference between those who fail and those who survive. It is interesting to note that we could say the exact same thing about business failures. Most are attributable to poor financial planning. If your net worth is negative, you should definitely include debt reduction on your list of short and/or long-term goals.

You can use Table D.2 to estimate your net worth. On the left-hand side of the balance sheet, you

TABLE D.2 Personal Net Worth

Assets	$	Liabilities	$
Checking accounts	___	Credit cards balances (list)	___
Savings accounts	___	1 ___	___
Money market accounts	___	2 ___	___
Other short-term investment	___	3 ___	___
	___	Personal Loans	___
Market value of investments (stocks, bonds, mutual funds)	___	Student loans	___
	___	Car Loans	___
Value of retirement funds	___	Home mortgage balance	___
College savings plan	___	Home equity loans	___
Other savings plans	___	Other real estate loans	___
Market value of real estate	___	Alimony/child support owed	___
Cars	___	Taxes owed (above withholding)	___
Home furnishings	___	Other investment loans	___
Jewelry/art/collectibles	___	Other liabilities/debts	___
Clothing/personal assets	___		___
Other assets	___		___
TOTAL ASSETS	___	TOTAL LIABILITIES	___

PERSONAL NET WORTH = TOTAL ASSETS MINUS TOTAL LIABILITIES = $ ___

should record the value of *assets,* all the things you own that have value. These include checking and savings account balances, investments, furniture, books, clothing, vehicles, houses, and the like. As with business balance sheets, assets are usually arranged from most liquid (easily convertible to cash) to least liquid. If you are a young student, it should not be surprising to find that you have little, if anything, to put on this side of your balance sheet. You should note that balance sheets are sensitive to the point in time chosen for evaluation. For example, if you always get paid on the first day of the month, your checking balance will be greatest at that point but will quickly be depleted as you pay for rent, food, and other needs. You may want to use your average daily balance in checking and savings accounts as a more accurate reflection of your financial condition. The right-hand side of the balance sheet is for recording *liabilities,* amounts of money that you owe to others. These include bank loans, mortgages, credit card debt, and other personal loans and are usually listed in order of how soon they must be paid back to the lender.

The Cash Flow Statement

Businesses forecast and track their regular inflows and outflows of cash with a cash budget and summarize annual cash flows on the statement of cash flows. Similarly, individuals should have a clear understanding of their flow of cash as they budget their expenditures and regularly check to be sure that they are sticking to their budget.

What is cash flow? Anytime you receive cash or pay cash (including payments with checks), the dollar amount that is moving from one person to another is a **cash flow.** For students, the most likely cash inflows will be student loans, grants, and income from part-time jobs. Cash outflows will include rent, food, gas, car payments, books, tuition, and personal care expenses. Although it may seem obvious that you need to have enough inflows to cover the outflows, it is very common for people to estimate incorrectly and overspend. This may result in hefty bank overdraft charges or increasing debt as credit lines are used to make up the difference. Accurate forecasting of cash inflows and outflows allows you to make arrangements to cover estimated shortfalls before they occur. For students, this can be particularly valuable when cash inflows primarily occur at the beginning of the semester (for example, student loans) but outflows are spread over the semester.

How should you treat credit card purchases on your cash flow worksheet? Because credit purchases do not require payment of cash *now,* your cash flow statement should not reflect the value of the purchase as an outflow until you pay the bill. Take for example the purchase of a television set on credit. The $500 purchase will increase your assets and your liabilities by $500 but will only result in a negative cash flow of a few dollars per month, since payments on credit cards are cash outflows when they are made. If you always pay your credit card balances in full each month, the purchases are really the same thing as cash, and your balance sheet will never reflect the debt. But if you purchase on credit and only pay minimum balances, you will be living beyond your means, and your balance sheet will get more and more "upside down." A further problem with using credit to purchase assets that decline in value is that the liability may still be there long after the asset you purchased has no value.

Table D.3 can be used to estimate your cash flow. The purpose of a cash flow worksheet for your financial plan is to heighten your awareness of where the cash is going. Many people are surprised to find that they are spending more than they make (by using too much credit) or that they have significant "cash leakage"—those little expenditures that add up to a lot without their even noticing. Examples include afternoon lattes or snacks, too many nights out at the local pub, eating lunch at the Student Center instead of packing a bag, and regularly paying for parking (or parking tickets) instead of biking or riding the bus to school. In many cases, plugging the little leaks can free up enough cash to make a significant contribution toward achieving long-term savings goals.

Set Short-Term and Long-Term Financial Goals

Just as a business develops its vision and strategic plan, individuals should have a clear set of financial goals. This component of your financial plan is the road map that will lead you to achieving your short-term and long-term financial goals.

Short-term goals are those that can be achieved in two years or less. They may include saving for particular short-term objectives, such as a new car, a down payment for a home, a vacation, or other major consumer purchase. For many people, short-term

TABLE D.3   Personal Cash Flow

Cash Inflows	Monthly	Annual
Salary/wage income (gross)	$ _____	$ _____
Interest/dividend income	_____	_____
Other income (self-employment)	_____	_____
Rental income (after expenses)	_____	_____
Capital gains	_____	_____
Other income	_____	_____
Total income	_____	_____
Cash Outflows	**Monthly**	**Annual**
Groceries	$ _____	$ _____
Housing	_____	_____
Mortgage or rent	_____	_____
House repairs/expenses	_____	_____
Property taxes	_____	_____
Utilities	_____	_____
Heating	_____	_____
Electric	_____	_____
Water and sewer	_____	_____
Cable/phone/satellite/Internet	_____	_____
Car loan payments	_____	_____
Car maintenance/gas	_____	_____
Credit card payments	_____	_____
Other loan payments	_____	_____
Income and payroll taxes	_____	_____
Other taxes	_____	_____
Insurance	_____	_____
Life	_____	_____
Health	_____	_____
Auto	_____	_____
Disability	_____	_____
Other insurance	_____	_____
Clothing	_____	_____
Gifts	_____	_____
Other consumables (TVs,etc)	_____	_____
Child care expenses	_____	_____
Sports-related expenses	_____	_____
Health club dues	_____	_____
Uninsured medical expenses	_____	_____
Education	_____	_____
Vacations	_____	_____
Entertainment	_____	_____
Alimony/child support	_____	_____
Charitable contributions	_____	_____
Required pension contributions	_____	_____
Magazine subscriptions/books	_____	_____
Other payments/expenses	_____	_____
Total Expenses	$ _____	$ _____

NET PERSONAL CASH FLOW = TOTAL INCOME − TOTAL EXPENSES = $ _____

financial goals should include tightening up on household spending patterns and reducing outstanding credit.

Long-term goals are those that require substantial time to achieve. Nearly everyone should include retirement planning as a long-term objective. Those who have or anticipate having children will probably consider college savings a priority. Protection of loved ones from the financial hazards of your unexpected death, illness, or disability is also a long-term objective for many individuals. If you have a spouse or other dependents, having adequate insurance and an estate plan in place should be part of your longterm goals.

Create and Adhere to a Budget

Whereas the cash flow table you completed in the previous section tells you what you are doing with your money currently, a **budget** shows what you plan to do with it in the future. A budget can be for any period of time, but it is common to budget in monthly and/or annual intervals.

Developing a Budget

You can use the cash flow worksheet completed earlier to create a budget. Begin with the amount of income you have for the month. Enter your

Do you know whether your expenses are going up or down? Use a budget to track them.

nondiscretionary expenditures (that is, bills you *must* pay, such as tuition, rent, and utilities) on the worksheet and determine the leftover amount. Next list your discretionary expenditures, such as entertainment and cable TV, in order of importance. You can then work down your discretionary list until your remaining available cash flow is zero.

An important component of your budget is the amount that you allocate to savings. If you put a high priority on saving and you do not use credit to spend beyond your income each month, you will be able to accumulate wealth that can be used to meet your short-term and long-term financial goals. In the bestseller *The Millionaire Next Door,* authors Thomas J. Stanley and William D. Danko point out that most millionaires have achieved financial success through hard work and thriftiness as opposed to luck or inheritance. You cannot achieve your financial goals unless your budget process places a high priority on saving and investing.

Tracking Your Budgeting Success

Businesses regularly identify budget items and track their variance from budget forecasts. People who follow a similar strategy in their personal finances are better able to meet their financial goals as well. If certain budgeted expenses routinely turn out to be under or over your previous estimates, then it is important to either revise the budget estimate or develop a strategy for reducing that expense.

College students commonly have trouble adhering to their budget for food and entertainment expenses. A strategy that works fairly well is to limit yourself to cash payments. At the beginning of the week, withdraw an amount from checking that will cover your weekly budgeted expenses. For the rest of the week, leave your checkbook, ATM card, and debit and credit cards at home. When the cash is gone, don't spend any more. While this is easier said than done, after a couple of weeks, you will learn to cut down on the cash leakage that inevitably occurs without careful cash management.

A debit card looks like a credit card but works like a check. For example, in the Netherlands almost no one writes a check, and everything is paid by debit card, which drafts directly from a checking account. You do not build up your credit rating when using a debit card. Figure D.1 indicates that the use of debit cards is growing rapidly in the United States. On the other hand, credit cards allow you to promise to pay

FIGURE D.I   Number of Debit Card Transactions

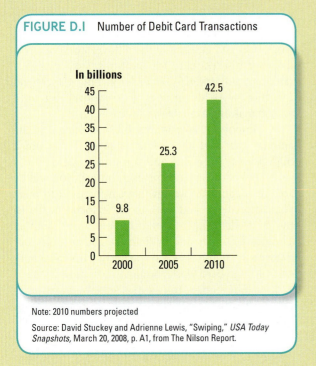

In billions

Note: 2010 numbers projected

Source: David Stuckey and Adrienne Lewis, "Swiping," *USA Today Snapshots,* March 20, 2008, p. A1, from The Nilson Report.

for something at a later date by using preapproved lines of credit granted by a bank or finance company. Credit cards are easy to use and are accepted by most retailers today.

Manage Credit Wisely

One of the cornerstones of your financial plan should be to keep credit usage to a minimum and to work at reducing outstanding debt. The use of credit for consumer and home purchases is well entrenched in our culture and has arguably fueled our economy and enabled Americans to better their standard of living as compared to earlier generations. Nevertheless, credit abuse is a serious problem in this country, and the most recent economic downturn undoubtedly pushed many households over the edge into bankruptcy as a result.

To consider the pros and cons of credit usage, compare the following two scenarios. In the first case, Joel takes an 8 percent fixed-rate mortgage to purchase a house to live in while he is a college student. The mortgage payment is comparable to alternative monthly rental costs, and his house appreciates 20 percent in value over the four years he is in college. At the end of college, Joel will be able to sell his house and reap the return, having invested only a small amount of his own cash. For example, if he made an initial 5 percent down payment on a $100,000 home that is now worth $120,000 four years later, he has earned $12,800 (after a 6 percent commission to the real estate agent) on an investment of $5,000. This amounts to a sizable return on investment of more than 250 percent over four years. This example is oversimplified in that we did not take into account the principal that has been repaid over the four years, and we did not consider the mortgage payment costs or the tax deductibility of interest paid during that time. However, the point is still clear; borrowing money to buy an asset that appreciates in value by more than the cost of the debt is a terrific way to invest.

In the second case, Nicole uses her credit card to pay for some of her college expenses. Instead of paying off the balance each month, Nicole makes only the minimum payment and incurs 16 percent interest costs. Over the course of several years of college, Nicole's credit card debt is likely to amount to several thousand dollars, typical of college graduates in the United States. The beer and pizza Nicole purchased have long ago been digested, yet the debt remains, and the payments continue. If Nicole continues making minimum payments, it will take many years to pay back that original debt, and in the meantime the interest paid will far exceed the original amount borrowed. Credit card debt in the amount of $1,000 will usually require a minimum payment of at least $15 per month. At this payment level, it will take 166 months (almost 14 years) to pay the debt in full, and the total interest paid will be more than $1,400!

So when is borrowing a good financial strategy? A rule of thumb is that you should borrow only to buy assets that will appreciate in value or when your financing charges are less than what you are earning on the cash that you would otherwise use to make the purchase. This rule generally will limit your borrowing to home purchases and investments.

Use and Abuse of Credit Cards

Credit cards should be used only as a cash flow management tool. If you pay off your balance every month, you avoid financing charges (assuming no annual fee), you have proof of expenditures, which may be necessary for tax or business reasons, and you may be able to better match your cash inflows and outflows over the course of the month. There are several aspects of credit cards that you should be familiar with.

- *Finance charges.* Credit card companies make money by lending to you at a higher rate than it costs them to obtain financing. Since many of their customers don't pay back their debts in a timely fashion (default), they must charge enough to cover the risk of default as well. Interest is usually calculated on the average daily balance over the month, and payments are applied to old debts first. Although there are "teaser" rates that may be less than 5 percent, most credit cards regularly charge 13 to 24 percent annual interest. The low introductory rates are subject to time limitations (often six months or less), and they revert to the higher rates if you don't pay on time.

- *Annual fee.* Many credit cards assess an annual fee that may be as low as $15 or as much as $100 per year. If you regularly carry a very low balance, this amounts to the equivalent of a very high additional interest charge. For example, a $50 annual fee is the equivalent of an additional 5 percent on your annual interest rate if your balance is $1,000. Because the cards with fees do not generally provide you with different services, it is best to choose no-annual-fee credit cards.

- *Credit line.* The credit line is the maximum you are allowed to borrow. This may begin with a small amount for a new customer, perhaps as low as $300. As the customer shows the ability and intent to repay (by doing so in a timely fashion), the limit can increase to many thousands of dollars.

- *Grace period.* The grace period for most credit cards is 25 days. This may amount to twice as long a period of free credit depending on when your purchase date falls in the billing cycle. For example, if you used your card on January 1 and your billing cycle goes from the 1st to the 31st, then the bill for January purchases will arrive the first week in February and will be due on February 25. If you pay it in full on the last possible day, you will have had 55 days of free credit. Keep in mind that the lender considers the bill paid when the check is *received,* not when it is mailed.

- *Fees and penalties.* In addition to charging interest and annual fees, credit card companies charge extra for late payments and for going over the stated limit on the card. These fees have been on the rise in the last decade and $25 or higher penalties are now fairly common.

- *ATM withdrawals.* Most credit cards can be used to obtain cash from ATMs. Although this may be convenient, it contributes to your increasing credit card balance and may result in extra expenditures that you would otherwise have avoided. In addition, these withdrawals may have hidden costs. Withdrawing cash from a machine that is not owned by your credit card lender will usually cause you to incur a fee of $1 or $1.50. The effective interest that this represents can be substantial if you are withdrawing small amounts of cash. A $1 charge on a withdrawal of $50 is the equivalent of 2 percent interest in addition to any interest you might pay to the credit card lender.

- *Perks.* Most credit cards provide a number of additional services. These may include a limitation on your potential liability in the event your card is lost or stolen or trip insurance. Some cards promise "cash back" in the form of a small rebate based on dollar volume of credit purchases. Many credit card companies offer the opportunity to participate in airline mileage programs. The general rule of thumb is that none of these perks is worth the credit card interest that is charged. If, however, you use your credit card as a cash management tool only, paying off your balance every month, then these perks are truly free to you.

Student Loans

Student loans are fairly common in today's environment of rising college tuition and costs. These loans can be a great deal, offering lower interest rates than other loans and terms that allow deferral of repayment until graduation. Furthermore, the money is being borrowed to pay for an asset that is expected to increase in value—your human capital. Don't underestimate, however, the monthly payments that will be required upon graduation. Students today graduate with average student loan debt of more than $19,000. Table D.4 shows the monthly payments required to repay the debt under various term and interest scenarios. For larger outstanding debt amounts, new college graduates in entry-level positions find that it is difficult to make the necessary payments without help.

TABLE D.4   How Much Will It Take to Pay That Debt?

Months to Pay	Interest Rate	Amount of Debt			
		$1,000	$2,500	$5,000	$10,000
12	15%	$90.26	$225.65	$451.29	$902.58
	18%	$91.68	$229.20	$458.40	$916.80
	21%	$93.11	$232.78	$465.57	$931.14
24	15%	$48.49	$121.22	$242.43	$484.87
	18%	$49.92	$124.81	$249.62	$499.24
	21%	$51.39	$128.46	$256.93	$513.86
36	15%	$34.67	$86.66	$173.33	$346.65
	18%	$36.15	$90.38	$180.76	$361.52
	21%	$37.68	$94.19	$188.38	$376.75
48	15%	$27.83	$69.58	$139.15	$278.31
	18%	$29.37	$73.44	$146.87	$293.75
	21%	$30.97	$77.41	$154.83	$309.66
60	15%	$23.79	$59.47	$118.95	$237.90
	18%	$25.39	$63.48	$126.97	$253.93
	21%	$27.05	$67.63	$135.27	$270.53
72	15%	$21.15	$52.86	$105.73	$211.45
	18%	$22.81	$57.02	$114.04	$228.08
	21%	$24.54	$61.34	$122.68	$245.36

Develop a Savings and Investment Plan

The next step to achieving your financial goals is to decide on a savings plan. A common recommendation of financial planners is to "pay yourself first." What this means is that you begin the month by setting aside an amount of money for your savings and investments, as compared to waiting until the end of the month and seeing what's left to save or invest. The budget is extremely important for deciding on a reasonable dollar amount to apply to this component of your financial plan.

As students, you might think that you cannot possibly find any extra dollars in your budget for saving, but, in fact, nearly everyone can stretch their budget a little. Some strategies for students might include taking public transportation several times a week and setting aside the gas or parking dollars you would have spent, buying regular coffees instead of Starbucks lattes, or eating at home one more night per week.

Understanding the Power of Compounded Returns

Even better, if you are a college student living on a typically small budget, you should be able to use this experience to help jump-start a viable savings program after graduation. If you currently live on $10,000 per year and your first job pays $30,000, it should be easy to "pay yourself" $2,000 or more per year. Putting the current maximum of $3,000 in an individual retirement account (IRA) will give you some tax advantages and can result in substantial wealth accumulation over time. An investment of only $2,000 per year from age 22 to retirement at 67 at 6 percent return per year will result in $425,487 at the retirement date. An annual contribution of $5,000 for 45 years will result in retirement wealth of about $1 million, not considering any additional tax benefits you might qualify for. If you invest that $5,000 per year for only 10 years and discontinue your contributions, you will still have about half a million dollars at age 67. And that assumes only a 6 percent return on investment!

What happens if you wait 10 years to start, beginning your $5,000 annual savings at age 32? By age 67, you will have only about a half million. Thirty-five years of investing instead of 45 doesn't sound like a big difference, but it cuts your retirement wealth in half. These examples illustrate an important point about long-term savings and wealth accumulation—the earlier you start, the better off you will be.

The Link between Investment Choice and Savings Goals

Once you have decided how much you can save, your choice of investment should be guided by your financial goals and the investment's risk and return and whether it will be long-term or short-term.

In general, investments differ in risk and return. The types of risk that you should be aware of are:

- Liquidity risk—How easy/costly is it to convert the investment to cash without loss of value?
- Default risk—How likely are you to receive the promised cash flows?
- Inflation risk—Will changes in purchasing power of the dollar over time erode the value of future cash flows your investment will generate?
- Price risk—How much might your investment fluctuate in value in the short run and the long run?

In general, the riskier an investment, the higher the return it will generate to you. Therefore, even though individuals differ in their willingness to take risk, it is important to invest in assets that expose you to at least moderate risk so that you can accumulate sufficient wealth to fund your long-term goals. To illustrate this more clearly, consider a $1 investment made in 1926. If this dollar had been invested in short-term Treasury bills, at the end of 2000 it would have grown to only $16.57. If the dollar had been invested in the S&P 500 index, which includes a diversified mix of stocks, the investment would be worth $2,586 in 2000 and about the same value in 2008, almost 200 times more than an investment in Treasury bills. But this gain was not without risk. In some of those 70 years, the stock market lost money and your investment would have actually declined in value.

Short-Term versus Long-Term Investment

Given the differences in risk exposure across investments, your investment time horizon plays an important role in choice of investment vehicle. For example, suppose you borrow $5,000 on a student loan today but the money will be needed to pay tuition six months from now. Because you cannot afford to lose *any* of this principal in the short run, your investment should be in a low-risk security such as a bank certificate of deposit. These types of accounts promise that the original $5,000 principal plus promised interest will be available to you when your tuition is due. During the bull market of the 1990s, many students were tempted to take student loans and invest in the stock market in the hopes of doubling their money (although this undoubtedly violated their lender's rules). However, in the recent bear market, this strategy might have reduced the tuition funds by 20 percent or more.

In contrast to money that you are saving for near-term goals, your retirement is likely to be many decades away, so you can afford to take more risk for greater return. The average return on stocks over the last 25 years has been around 17 percent. In contrast, the average return on long-term corporate bonds, which offer regular payments of interest to investors, has been around 10 percent. Short-term, low-risk debt securities have averaged 7 percent but are lower in 2010. The differences in investment returns between these three categories is explainable based on the difference in risk imposed on the owners. Stock is the most risky. Corporate bonds with their regular payments of interest are less risky to you since you do not have to wait until you sell your investment to get some of your return on the investment. Because they are less risky, investors expect a lower percentage return.

Investment Choices

There are numerous possible investments, both domestic and international. The difficulty lies in deciding which ones are most appropriate for your needs and risk tolerance.

Savings Accounts and Certificates of Deposit.
The easiest parking spot for your cash is in a savings account. Unfortunately, investments in these low-risk (FDIC-insured), low-return accounts will barely keep up with inflation. If you have a need for liquidity but not necessarily immediate access to cash, a certificate of deposit wherein you promise to leave the money in the bank for six months or more will give you a slightly higher rate of return.

Bonds. Corporations regularly borrow money from investors and issue bonds, which are securities that contain the firm's promise to pay regular interest and to repay principal at the end of the loan period, often 20 or more years in the future. These investments provide higher return to investors than short-term, interest-bearing accounts, but they also expose investors to price volatility, liquidity, and default risk.

A second group of bonds are those offered by government entities, commonly referred to as municipal bonds. These are typically issued to finance government projects, such as roads, airports, and bridges. Like corporate bonds, municipal bonds will pay interest on a regular basis, and the principal amount will be paid back to the investor at the end of a stated period of time, often 20 or more years. This type of bond has fewer interested investors and therefore has more liquidity risk.

Stocks. A share of stock represents proportionate ownership interest in a business. Stockholders are thus exposed to all the risks that impact the business environment—interest rates, competition from other firms, input and output price risk, and others. In return for being willing to bear this risk, shareholders may receive dividends and/or capital appreciation in the value of their share(s). In any given year, stocks may fare better or worse than other investments, but there is substantial evidence that for long holding periods (20-plus years) stocks tend to outperform other investment choices.

Mutual Funds. For the novice investor with a small amount of money to invest, the best choice is mutual funds. A mutual fund is a pool of funds from many investors that is managed by professionals who allocate the pooled dollars among various investments that meet the requirements of the mutual fund investors. There are literally thousands of these funds from which to choose, and they differ in type of investment (bonds, stocks, real estate, etc.), management style (active versus passive), and fee structure. Although even small investors have access to the market for individual securities, professional investors spend 100 percent of their time following the market and are likely to have more information at their disposal to aid in making buy and sell decisions.

Purchase of a Home. For many people, one of the best investments is the purchase of a home. With a small up-front investment (your down payment)

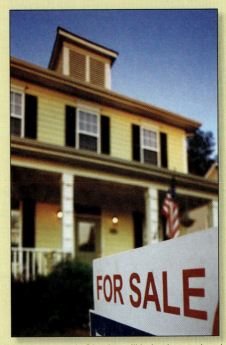

Want to buy a home someday? Lenders will look at how you have handled your past debts before loaning you money.

and relatively low borrowing costs, modest appreciation in the home's value can generate a large return on investment. This return benefits from the tax deductibility of home mortgage interest and capital gains tax relief at the point of sale. And to top it off, you have a place to live and thus save any additional rental costs you would incur if you invested your money elsewhere. There are many sources of information about home ownership for investors on the Internet. How much house can you afford? What mortgage can you qualify for? How much difference does investment choice make?

Everyone needs to have a place to live, and two-thirds of Americans own their own homes. Nevertheless, owning a home is not necessarily the best choice for everyone. The decision on when and how to buy a house and how much to spend must be made based on a careful examination of your ability to pay the mortgage and to cover the time and expense of maintenance and repair. A home is probably the largest purchase you will ever make in your life. It is also one of the best investments you can make. As in the example given earlier, the ability to buy with a small down payment and to deduct the cost of interest paid from your taxable income provides financial benefits that are not available with any other investment type.

Few people could afford to buy homes at young ages if they were required to pay the full purchase price on their own. Instead, it is common for people to borrow most of the money from a financial institution and pay it back over time. The process of buying a home can begin with your search for the perfect home or it can begin with a visit to your local lender, who can give you an estimate of the amount of mortgage for which you can qualify. Mortgage companies and banks have specific guidelines that help them determine your creditworthiness. These include consideration of your ability and willingness to repay the loan in a timely fashion, as well as an estimate of the value of the house that will be the basis for the loan.

A **mortgage** is a special type of loan that commonly requires that you make a constant payment over time to repay the lender the original money you borrowed (**principal**) together with **interest,** the amount that the lender charges for your use of its money. In the event that you do not make timely payments, the lender has the right to sell your property to get its money back (a process called **foreclosure).**

Mortgage interest rates in the last decade have ranged from 5 to 10 percent per year, depending on the terms and creditworthiness of the borrower. There are many variations on mortgages, some that lock in an interest rate for the full term of the loan, often 30 years, and others that allow the rate to vary with market rates of interest. In low-interest-rate economic circumstances, it makes sense to lock in the mortgage at favorable low rates.

Several measures are commonly applied to assess your *ability to repay* the loan. In addition to requiring some work history, most lenders will apply two ratio tests. First, the ratio of your total mortgage payment (including principal, interest, property taxes, and homeowners insurance) to your gross monthly income can be no more than a prespecified percentage that varies from lender to lender but is rarely greater than 28 percent. Second, the ratio of your credit payments (including credit cards, car loan or lease payments, and mortgage payment) to your gross monthly income is limited to no more than 36 percent. More restrictive lenders will have lower limits on both of these ratios.

Lenders also consider your *willingness to repay* the loan by looking at how you have managed debt obligations in the past. The primary source of information will be a credit report provided by one of the large credit reporting agencies. Late payments and

defaulted loans will appear on that report and may result in denial of the mortgage loan. Most lenders, however, will overlook previously poor credit if more recent credit management shows a change in behavior. This can be helpful to college students who had trouble paying bills before they were gainfully employed.

The value of the home is important to the lender since it is the **collateral** for the loan; that is, in the event that you default on the loan (don't pay), the lender has the right to take the home in payment of the loan. To ensure that they are adequately covered, lenders will rarely lend more than 95 percent of the appraised value of the home. If you borrow more than 80 percent of the value, you will usually be required to pay a mortgage insurance premium with your regular payments. This will effectively increase the financing costs by ½ percent per year.

To illustrate the process of buying a home and qualifying for a mortgage, consider the following example. Jennifer graduated from college two years ago and has saved $7,000. She intends to use some of her savings as a down payment on a home. Her current salary is $36,000. She has a car payment of $250 per month and credit card debt that requires a minimum monthly payment of $100 per month. Suppose that Jennifer has found her dream home, which has a price of $105,000. She intends to make a down payment of $5,000 and borrow the rest. Can she qualify for the $100,000 loan at a rate of 7 percent?

Using Table D.5, her payment of principal and interest on a loan of $100,000 at 7 percent annual

TABLE D.5   Calcualting Monthly Mortgage Payments
(30 year loan, principal and interest only)

Annual Interest %	Amount Borrowed			
	$75,000	$100,000	$125,000	$150,000
6.0	$450	$600	$749	$899
6.5	$474	$632	$790	$948
7.0	$499	$665	$832	$998
7.5	$524	$699	$874	$1,049
8.0	$550	$734	$917	$1,101
8.5	$577	$769	$961	$1,153
9.0	$603	$805	$1,006	$1,207
9.5	$631	$841	$1,051	$1,261
10.0	$658	$878	$1,097	$1,316

interest will be $665. With an additional $150 per month for property taxes and insurance (which may vary substantially in different areas of the country), her total payment will be $815. Since her gross monthly income is $3,000, the ratio of her payment to her income is 27 percent. Unless her lender has fairly strict rules, this should be acceptable. Her ratio of total payments to income will be ($815 + $250 + $150)/$3,000 = 40.5 percent. Unfortunately, Jennifer will not be able to qualify for this loan in her current financial circumstances.

So what can she do? The simplest solution is to use some of her remaining savings to pay off her credit card debt. By doing this, her debt ratio will drop to 35.5 percent and she will be accomplishing another element of good financial planning—reducing credit card debt and investing in assets that increase in value.

Planning for a Comfortable Retirement

Although it may seem like it's too early to start thinking about retirement when you are still in college, this is actually the best time to do so. In the investment section of this Appendix, you learned about the power of compound interest over long periods of time. The earlier you start saving for long-term goals, the easier it will be to achieve them.

How Much to Save.   There is no "magic number" that will tell you how much to save. You must determine, based on budgeted income and expenses, what amount is realistic to set aside for this important goal. Several factors should help to guide this decision:

- Contributions to qualified retirement plans can be made before tax. This allows you to defer the payment of taxes until you retire many years from now.
- Earnings on retirement plan assets are tax deferred. If you have money in nonretirement vehicles, you will have to pay state and federal taxes on your earnings, which will significantly reduce your ending accumulation.
- If you need the money at some time before you reach age 59½, you will be subject to a withdrawal penalty of 10 percent, and the distribution will also be subject to taxes at the time of withdrawal.

In planning for your retirement needs, keep in mind that inflation will erode the purchasing power

of your money. You should consider your ability to replace preretirement income as a measure of your success in retirement preparation. You can use the Social Security Administration Web site (**www.ssa.gov**) to estimate your future benefits from that program. In addition, most financial Web sites provide calculators to aid you in forecasting the future accumulations of your savings.

Employer Retirement Plans.   Many employers offer retirement plans as part of their employee benefits package. **Defined benefit plans** promise a specific benefit at retirement (for example, 60 percent of final salary). More commonly, firms offer **defined contribution plans,** where they promise to put a certain amount of money into the plan in your name every pay period. The plan may also allow you to make additional contributions or the employer may base its contribution on your contribution (for example, by matching the first 3 percent of salary that you put in). Employers also may make it possible for their employees to contribute additional amounts toward retirement on a tax-deferred basis. Many plans now allow employees to specify the investment allocation of their plan contributions and to shift account balances between different investment choices.

Some simple rules to follow with respect to employer plans include the following:

- If your employer offers you the opportunity to participate in a retirement plan, you should do so.
- If your employer offers to match your contributions, you should contribute as much as is necessary to get the maximum match, if you can afford to. Every dollar that the employer matches is like getting a 100 percent return on your investment in the first year.
- If your plan allows you to select your investment allocation, do not be too conservative in your choices if you still have many years until retirement.

Individual Retirement Accounts (IRAs).   Even if you do not have an employer-sponsored plan, you can contribute to retirement through an individual retirement account (IRA). There are two types of IRAs with distinctively different characteristics (which are summarized in Table D.6). Although previously subject to a $2,000 maximum annual contribution limit, tax reform in 2001 increases that limit gradually to $5,000 by 2008. The critical difference between Roth

TABLE D.6   Comparing Individual Retirement Account Options

	Roth IRA	Traditional IRA
2008–2010 allowable contribution	$5,000	$5,000
Contributions deductible from current taxable income	No	Yes
Current tax on annual investment earnings	No	No
Tax due on withdrawal in retirement	No	Yes
10% penalty for withdrawal before age 59½	Yes	Yes
Mandatory distribution before age 70½	No	Yes
Tax-free withdrawals allowed for first-time homebuyers	Yes	No

IRAs and traditional IRAs is the taxation of contributions and withdrawals. Roth IRA contributions are taxable, but the withdrawals are tax-free. Traditional IRAs are deductible, but the withdrawals are taxable. Both types impose a penalty of 10 percent for withdrawal before the qualified retirement age of 59½, subject to a few exceptions.

Social Security.   Social Security is a public pension plan sponsored by the federal government and paid for by payroll taxes equally split between employers and employees. In addition to funding the retirement portion of the plan, Social Security payroll taxes pay for Medicare insurance (an old-age health program), disability insurance, and survivors benefits for the families of those who die prematurely.

The aging of the U.S. population has created a problem for funding the current Social Security system. Whereas it has traditionally been a pay-as-you-go program, with current payroll taxes going out to pay current retiree benefits, the impending retirement of baby boomers is forecast to bankrupt the system early in this century if changes are not made in a timely fashion. To understand the problem, consider that when Social Security began, there were 17 workers for each retiree receiving benefits. There are currently fewer than four workers per beneficiary. After the baby boom retirement, there will be only two workers to pay for each retiree. Obviously, that equation cannot work.

Does that mean that Social Security will not be around when you retire? Contrary to popular belief, it is unlikely that this will happen. There are simply too many voters relying on the future of Social Security for Congress to ever take such a drastic action. Instead, it is likely that the current system will be revised to help it balance. Prior to the heavy declines in the stock market in 2008–2009 there was some general support for a plan that would divert some of the current payroll taxes to fund individual retirement accounts that could be invested in market assets. In addition, it seems likely that the retirement age will increase gradually to age 67. Other possible changes are to increase payroll taxes or to limit benefits payable to wealthier individuals. The proposed solutions are all complicated by the necessity of providing a transition program for those who are too old to save significant additional amounts toward their retirement. Figure D.2 indicates that most people are saving more because they are concerned about the future of Social Security.

Evaluate and Purchase Insurance

The next step in personal financial planning is the evaluation and purchase of insurance. Insurance policies are contracts between you and an insurance company wherein the insurer promises to pay you money in the event that a particular event occurs. Insurance is important, not only to protect your own assets from claims but also to protect your loved ones and dependents. The most common types of insurance for individuals are identified and briefly described below.

Automobile Insurance
In most states, drivers are required by law to carry a minimum amount of **auto liability insurance.** In the event that you are in a car accident, this coverage promises to pay claims against you for injuries to persons or property, up to a maximum per person and per accident. The basic liability policy will also cover your own medical costs. If you want to insure against damage to your own vehicle, you must purchase an additional type of coverage called **auto physical damage insurance.** If you have a car loan, the lender will require that you carry this type of insurance, since the value of the car is the collateral

FIGURE D.2   Social Security and Retirement

Are you saving more than you planned because you're concerned about Social Security?

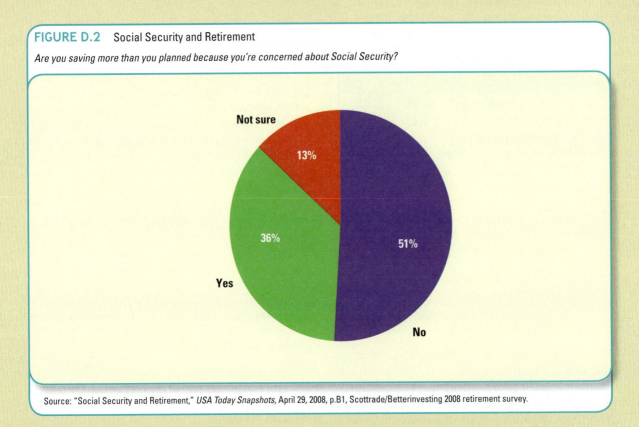

Source: "Social Security and Retirement," *USA Today Snapshots,* April 29, 2008, p.B1, Scottrade/Betterinvesting 2008 retirement survey.

for that loan and the lender wants to be sure that you can afford to fix any damage to the vehicle following an accident. The minimum limits in most states are too low to cover typical claim levels. Good financial planning requires that you pay for insurance coverage with much higher limits.

Auto physical damage insurance coverage is always subject to a **deductible.** A deductible is an amount that you must pay before the insurance company will pay. To illustrate this, suppose your policy has a $250 deductible. You back into your garage door and damage your bumper, which will cost $750 to fix. The insurer will only pay $500, because you are responsible for the first $250. Once you receive the check from the insurer, you are free to try to get it fixed for less than the full $750.

Homeowners/Renters Insurance

Homeowners insurance provides coverage for liability and property damage in your home. For example, if someone slips and falls on your front steps and sues you for medical expenses, this insurance policy will pay the claim (or defend you against the claim if the insurer thinks it is not justified). If your house

and/or property are damaged in a fire, the insurance will pay for lost property and the costs of repair. It is a good idea to pay extra for replacement cost insurance, since otherwise the insurance company is only obligated to pay you the depreciated value, which won't be enough to replace your belongings.

Renters insurance is similar to homeowners in that it covers you for liability on your premises (for example, if your dog bites someone) and for damage to your personal property. Because you do not own the house, your landlord needs to carry separate insurance for his building. This insurance is very cheap and is well worth the cost, since your landlord's insurance will not pay anything to you in the event that the house burns down and you lose all your belongings.

Life Insurance

As compared to other types of insurance, the primary purpose of life insurance is to provide protection for others. **Life insurance** pays a benefit to your designated beneficiary (usually your spouse or other family members) in the event that you die during the coverage period. Life insurance premiums will depend on the face amount of the policy, your age and health, your habits (smoker versus nonsmoker), and the type of policy (whether it includes an investment component in addition to the death benefit).

The simplest type of life insurance is **term insurance.** This policy is usually for one year and the insurer promises to pay your designated beneficiary only the face amount of the policy in the event that you die during the year of coverage. Because the probability of dying at a young age is very small, the cost of providing this promise to people in their 20s and 30s is very inexpensive, and premiums are fairly low. Term insurance becomes more expensive at older ages, since the probability of dying is much higher and insurers must charge more.

Other types of life insurance usually fall into a category often called **permanent insurance,** because they are designed to provide you with insurance protection over your lifetime. To provide lifetime coverage at a reasonable cost, premiums will include an investment component. While there are many variations, typically in the early years of the policy you are paying a lot more than the actual cost of providing the death protection. The insurer takes that extra cost and invests it so that when you are older, the company has sufficient funds to cover your death risk. The primary difference between different types of permanent insurance is the way that they treat the investment component. Some policies allow the buyer to direct the investment choice and others do not.

Health Insurance

Health insurance pays the cost of covered medical expenses during the policy period, which is usually six months or one year. Most health insurance is provided under group policies through employers, but it is possible to purchase an individual policy. Because those who want to buy individual insurance are likely to be people who anticipate medical expenses, individual policies can be very expensive and are usually subject to exclusions, high coinsurance (the percentage of each dollar of expenses that you must pay out of pocket), and deductibles (the amount you must pay in full before the insurance pays).

From a financial-planning perspective, the type of health coverage that is most important is that which will protect you and your family from unexpected large medical costs. The usual checkups, shots, and prescription drugs are all budgetable expenses so need not be insured. At a minimum, you should

Medical costs can be astronomical. Part of keeping your finances in order is making sure you have health insurance.

have a policy that covers hospitalization and care for major disease or injury. This can be accomplished at relatively low cost by contracting for a large deductible (e.g., you pay the first $1,000 of costs per year).

The two main types of health insurance plans are *fee-for-service* and *managed care*. In a fee-for-service arrangement, the insurer simply pays for whatever covered medical costs you incur, subject to the deductible and coinsurance. Blue Cross and Blue Shield plans are the best known of this type. Managed care includes health maintenance organizations (HMOs) and preferred provider organizations (PPOs). In these health insurance arrangements, your health insurer pays all your costs (subject sometimes to small co-pays for office visits), but the care you receive is determined by your physician, who has contracted with the health insurer and has incentives to control overall costs. You are often limited in your choice of physician and your ability to seek specialist care under these plans.

Disability Insurance

One of the most overlooked types of insurance is **disability insurance,** which pays replacement income to you in the event you are disabled under the definition in your policy. One in three people will be disabled for a period of three months or more during their lifetime, so disability insurance should be a component of the financial plan for anyone without sufficient financial resources to weather a period of loss of income.

Develop an Estate Plan

As with retirement planning, it is difficult to think about estate planning when you are young. In fact, you probably don't need to think much about it yet. If you have no dependents, there is little point in doing so. However, if you are married or have other dependents, you should include this as a necessary part of your financial plan. The essential components of an **estate plan** are

- Your will, including a plan for guardianship of your children.
- Minimization of taxes on your estate.
- Protection of estate assets.

Estate planning is a complicated subject that is mired in legal issues. As such, appropriate design and implementation of an estate plan requires the assistance of a qualified professional.

The Importance of Having a Will

There are several circumstances that necessitate having a will. If you have a spouse and/or dependent children, if you have substantial assets, or if you have specific assets that you would like to give to certain individuals in the event of your death, you *should* have a will. On the other hand, if you are single with no assets or obligations (like many students), a will is probably not necessary—yet.

Having a valid will makes the estate settlement simpler for your spouse. If your children are left parentless, will provisions specify who will take guardianship of the children and direct funds for their support. You might also like to include a *living will*, which gives your family directions for whether to keep you on life support in the event that an illness or injury makes it unlikely for you to survive without extraordinary interventions. Lastly, you may want to make a will so that you can give your CD collection to your college roommate or Grandma's china to

---

Gender Differences Create Special Financial Planning Concerns

Although most people would agree that there are some essential differences between men and women, it is not as clear why their financial planning needs should be different. After all, people of both sexes need to invest for future financial goals like college educations for their children and retirement income for themselves. In the last few years, professionals have written articles considering this subject. The results are both controversial and eye-opening.

- Even though 75 percent of women in the United States are working, they still have greater responsibility for household chores, child care, and care of aging parents than their husbands. This leaves less time for household finances.
- Women still earn much less than men, on average.
- Women are much less likely to have a pension sponsored through their employer. Only one-third of all working women have one at their current employer.
- Women are more conservative investors than men. Although there is evidence that women are gradually getting smart about taking a little more risk in their portfolios, on average they allocate half as much as men do to stocks.
- Most women will someday be on their own, either divorced or widowed.

Because women live an average of five years longer than men, they actually need to have saved more to provide a comparable retirement income. The combined impact of these research findings makes it difficult but not impossible for women to save adequately for retirement. Much of the problem lies in education. Women need to be better informed about investing in order to make choices early in life that will pay off in the end. If they don't take the time to become informed about their finances or can't due to other obligations, in the end they will join the ranks of many women over age 65 who are living in poverty. But when women earn less, they don't have access to an employer pension, and they invest too conservatively, it is no surprise that women have so little wealth accumulation.

In her book, *The Busy Woman's Guide to Financial Freedom,* Dr. Vickie Bajtelsmit, an associate professor at Colorado State University, provides a road map for women who are interested in taking charge of their financial future. With simple-to-follow instructions for all aspects of financial planning, from investing to insurance to home buying, the book provides information for women to get on the right financial track.

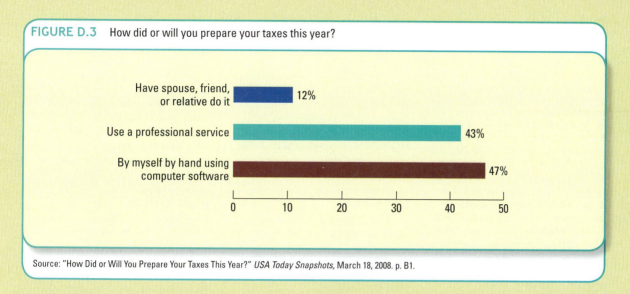

FIGURE D.3   How did or will you prepare your taxes this year?

Have spouse, friend, or relative do it — 12%
Use a professional service — 43%
By myself by hand using computer software — 47%

Source: "How Did or Will You Prepare Your Taxes This Year?" *USA Today Snapshots,* March 18, 2008. p. B1.

your daughter. Absent such provisions, relatives and friends have been known to take whatever they want without regard to your specific desires.

Avoiding Estate Taxes

As students, it will likely be many years before you will have accumulated a large enough estate (all your "worldly possessions") to have to worry about estate taxes. Although recent federal tax law changes eliminated the estate tax in 2010, the tax was reinstated and raised to a maximum of 55% in 2011. This is an area of law that frequently changes. Because no one can predict the date of his or her death, this implies that estate tax planning should be done assuming the worst-case scenario. Current estate taxes can take a big bite out of your family's inheritance for wealthy taxpayers. Thus, much of estate planning is actually tax-avoidance planning. Professionals can help set up trust arrangements that allow all or part of your estate to pass to your heirs without incurring taxes.

Adjust Your Financial Plan to New Circumstances

Finally, to ensure the success of your overall financial plan, it is vital that you evaluate it on a periodic basis and adjust it to accommodate changes in your life, such as marriage, children, or the addition or deletion of a second income from your spouse. You may be preparing income tax returns now, but as your income increases you may have to make a decision about professional assistance. Figure D.3 indicates that most people prepare their own taxes, but many taxpayers use a professional service. Your plan also must be adjusted as your financial goals change (for example, desires to own a home, make a large purchase, or retire at an early age). Whatever your goals may be, the information and worksheets provided here will help with your personal financial planning.

Notes

Chapter 1

1. Max Chafkin, "At 10 O'Clock in the Morning Markus Frind Leaves His Apartment and Heads to Work," *Inc.,* January/February 2009, pp. 64–69; Randall Stross, "From 10 Hours a Week, $10 Million a Year," *The New York Times,* January 13, 2008, **http://www.nytimes. com/2008/01/13/business/13digi.html? ex=1357966800&en=0d6823d6b616b6a8 &ei=5124&partner=permalink&exprod= permalink** (accessed February 22, 2010); Plenty of Fish Web site, plentyoffish.com (accessed February 23, 2010).

2. Debbie Thorne, O. C. Ferrell, and Linda Ferrell, *Business and Society* (Mason, OH: South-Western Cengage Learning, 2011), p. 304.

3. "GMAC® Diversity Initiatives," The Graduate Management Admissions Council, **http://www.gmac.com/ gmac/SchoolServices/Diversity/ GMACDiversityInitiatives.htm** (accessed February 22, 2010).

4. Liz Clarke, "While Nascar Takes Stock, Racing's Popularity Wanes," *The Washington Post,* November 4, 2007, p. D3.

5. Miriko Yash, "Sony and Samsung Strategic Split," *BusinessWeek,* January 18, 2010, p. 52.

6. Elizabeth M. Whelan, "Kellogg's: A Sad Cereal Sellout," *The New York Post,* June 17, 2007. **http://www.nypost. com/seven/06172007/postopinion/ opedcolumnists/kelloggs__a_sad_ cereal_sellout_opedcolumnists_ elizabeth_m__whelan.htm** (accessed February 23, 2010).

7. Bruce Horowitz, "Unilever Gets All the Trans Fat Out of Its Margarines," *USA Today,* July 27, 2009, **http://www. usatoday.com/money/industries/ food/2009-07-26-trans-fat-unilever_N. htm?csp=34** (accessed February 23, 2010).

8. "Got Milk?" **http://www.whymilk.com/ celeb.php** (accessed February 25, 2010).

9. "About Bill Daniels," **http://www. danielsfund.org/BillDaniels/index.asp** (accessed February 23, 2010).

10. "Venecuba, A Single Nation," *Economist,* February 13–19, 2010, p. 40.

11. "Reforms Please Cubans, But Is It Communism?" *Associated Press,* April 2, 2008, **http://www.msnbc.msn.com/ id/23925259** (accessed April 18, 2008).

12. James T. Areddy and Craig Karmin, "China Stocks Once Frothy, Fall by Half in Six Months," *The Wall Street Journal,* April 16, 2008, pp. 1, 7.

13. John D. Sutter and Doug Gross, "Apple Unveils the 'Magical' iPad," *CNN Tech,* January 28, 2010, **http://www.cnn. com/2010/TECH/01/27/apple.tablet/ index.html?section=cnn_latest** (accessed February 3, 2010).

14. Steve Hamm, "Into Africa: Capitalism from the Ground Up," *BusinessWeek,* May 4, 2009, pp. 60–61; "Uzuri African Blend," Peet's Coffee & Tea, **http://www.peets.com/shop/ coffee_detail.asp?id=1853&cid=1000145** (accessed February 11, 2010); TechnoServe Homepage, **http:// technoserve.org** (accessed February 11, 1010); "TechnoServe Coffee Initiative," TechnoServe, **http://www. technoserve.org/assets/documents/ jan2009coffeeinitiativefactsheet.pdf** (accessed February 11, 2010).

15. U.S. Patent Statistics, Calendar Years 1963–2008, **http://www.uspto.gov/web/ offices/ac/ido/oeip/taf/us_stat.pdf** (accessed February 3, 2010).

16. "Zimbabwe," *CIA—The World Factbook,* **https://www.cia.gov/library/ publications/the-world-factbook/geos/ zi.html#** (accessed February 3, 2010).

17. "Monthly Statement of the Public Debt of the United States," Treasury Public Debt, December 31, 2009, **http:// www.treasurydirect.gov/govt/reports/ pd/mspd/2009/2009_dec.htm** (accessed February 3, 2010).

18. Jon Birger, "Field General," *Fortune,* July 6, 2009, pp. 86–89; Christopher Jensen, "Ethanol Industry's 15% Solution Raises Concerns," *The New York Times,* May 8, 2009, **www.nytimes.com/2009/05/10/ automobiles/10ETHANOL. html?pagewanted=1&_r=1** (accessed February 23, 2010); "EPA Notifies Industry Group on Status of Ethanol Waiver Request," December 1, 2009, **yosemite.epa.gov/opa/admpress.nsf/0/ A4A8C42F54552D3C8525767F00515 DED** (accessed February 23, 2010)

19. "Facts about Working Women," *Women Employed,* **http://www. womenemployed.org/index.php?id=20** (accessed February 23, 2010).

20. Liz Welch, "Wolfgang Puck: From Potato Peeler to Gourmet-Pizza Tycoon," *Inc.,* October 2009, pp. 87–88.

21. "About the Hershey Company," The Hershey Company, **http://www. thehersheycompany.com/** (accessed February 15, 2010).

22. "Fortune Global 500," *CNNMoney. com,* **http://money.cnn.com/magazines/ fortune/global500/2009/snapshots/2255. html** (accessed February 19, 2010); Anthony Bianco and Wendy Zellner, "Is Wal-Mart Too Powerful?" *BusinessWeek,* October 6, 2003, pp. 100–10; "Wal Mart Stores, Inc. Business Information, Profile, and History," **http://companies.jrank. org/pages/4725/Wal-Mart-Stores-Inc. html** (accessed February 23, 2010).

23. "Our Story," NadaMoo!, **http://www. nadamoo.com/story.html** (accessed February 15, 2010); Kate Thornberry, "NadaMoo!," *The Austin Chronicle,* May 29, 2009, **www.austinchronicle.com/ gyrobase/Issue/story?oid=787037** (accessed February 15, 2010); Gina Bastone, "Interview: Amy Ramm of NadaMoo," *Austin Decider,* **http://www. avclub.com/austin/articles/amy-ramm- of-nadamoo,25945/** (accessed February 15, 2010).

24. Dennis Schaal, "100 Best Corporate Citizens 2008," *The CRO,* **http://www. thecro.com/node/615** (accessed February 23, 2010).

25. 2003 National Business Ethics Survey (n.d.), **www.ethics.org/nbes/2003/ 1003nbes_summary.html** (accessed January 6, 2004). "2007 National Business Ethics Survey: An Inside View of Private Sector Ethics," Ethics Resources Center, 2007.

26. Lindsey Gerdes, "Where Undergrads Dream of Working," *BusinessWeek Online,* May 23, 2008, **http://www.business**

week.com/managing/content/may2008/ ca20080523_988667.htm?chan=search (accessed June 19, 2008).

27. Joel Holland, "Save the World, Make a Million," *Entrepreneur,* April 2010, **http:// www.entrepreneur.com/magazine/ entrepreneur/2010/april/205556.html** (accessed April 20, 2010); iContact, **http:// www.icontact.com** (accessed April 24, 2010).

Chapter 2

1. John Hechinger, "FTC Criticizes College-Themed Cans in Anheuser-Busch Marketing Efforts," *The Wall Street Journal,* August 25, 2009, pp. B1, B4; Steve Wieberg and Steve Berkowitz, "Has College Sports Marketing Gone Too Gar?" *USA Today,* April 2, 2009, pp. 1A–2A; Xorje Olivares, "'Fan Can' Beers Come in School Colors of 26 Universities: Invites Binge Drinking?," *ABC News,* August 28, 2009, **http://abcnews.com/Business/ anheuser-buschs-bud-light-markets-beer-college-students/story?id=8418866** (accessed January 22, 2010); David Wharton and William Donovan, "Socially Responsible Investing Blog," About.com, August 23, 2009, **http://socialinvesting. about.com/b/2009/08/23/bud-lights-fan-cans-and-social-responsibility. html** (accessed January 23, 2010); Annie Thomas, "University Puts Halt to Bud Light 'Fan Can' Gimmick," *The Michigan Daily,* September 6, 2009, **www.michigandaily.com/content/ university-puts-halt-bud-light-fan-can-gimmick?page=0,1** (accessed January 23, 2010); "NCAA Reportedly Finally Interviews Reggie Bush," *SportingNews,* January 11, 2010, **www.sportingnews. com/college-football/article/2010-01-11/ ncaa-reportedly-finally-interviews-reggie-bush** (accessed January 24, 2010); **www.ncaa.org** (accessed January 24, 2010).

2. "New US Consumer Survey Shows High Distrust of Financial Services Companies," Cohn & Wolfe newsroom, January 20, 2009, **http://www.cohnwolfe. com/en/news/new-us-consumer-survey-shows-high-distrust-financial-services-companies** (accessed January 27, 2010).

3. "PWC Accounting Firm Reaches $97 Million Settlement with Ohio in AIG Case," *Insurance Journal,* **http:// www.insurancejournal.com/news/ national/2008/10/06/94335.htm** (accessed January 27, 2010).

4. Jonathan D. Rockoff, "J&J Is Accused of Kickbacks to Omnicare on Drug Sales," *The Wall Street Journal,* January 16, 2010, **http://online.wsj.com/article/ SB10001424052748703657604575004902853166786.html** (accessed January 27, 2010).

5. Ronald Alsop, "Corporate Scandals Hit Home," *The Wall Street Journal,* February 19, 2004, via **http://www. driversofloyalty.com/services/ pubs/The_Wall_Street_Journal_ CorporateScandalsHitHome_2004.pdf** (accessed February 5, 2010).

6. Chad Bray, "Recorded Music Price-Fixing Suit Reinstated," *The Wall Street Journal,* January 14, 2010, **http://online. wsj.com/article/SB100014240527487 04675104575001152036653136.html** (accessed January 27, 2010).

7. O. C. Ferrell, John Fraedrich, and Linda Ferrell, *Business Ethics: Ethical Decision Making and Cases,* 8th ed. (Mason, OH: South-Western Cengage Learning, 2011), p. 7.

8. David Callahan, as quoted in Archie Carroll, "Carroll: Do We Live in a Cheating Culture?" *Athens Banner-Herald,* February 21, 2004, **www. onlineathens.com/stores/022204/ bus_20040222028.shtml** (accessed February 25, 2010).

9. Jenny Anderson, "3 Executives Under Fire on Exit Pay," *The New York Times,* March 8, 2008, pp. B1, B4.

10. Rick Pearson and Ray Long, "Senate Votes Unanimously," *Chicago Tribune,* January 30, 2009, **http://www. chicagotribune.com/news/local/chi-blagojevich-mainbarjan30,0,923624. story** (accessed January 28, 2010).

11. Marcus Walker and David Crawford, "Prosecutors Blow Whistle on Soccer Betting Scandal," *The Wall Street Journal,* December 2, 2009, **http://online.wsj.com/ article/SB1000142405274870330050 4574565962716863996.html** (accessed January 27, 2010).

12. Ferrell, Fraedrich, and Ferrell, *Business Ethics.*

13. Bobby White, "The New Workplace Rules: No Video Watching," *The New York Times,* March 3, 2008, p. B1.

14. "Proper Use of Company, Customer, and Supplier Resources," Boeing, November 19, 2009, **http://www.boeing. com/companyoffices/aboutus/ethics/ pro10.pdf** (accessed January 28, 2010).

15. Stop Workplace Bullying! **http:// www.bullyfreeworkplace.org** (accessed February 25, 2010).

16. Peter Lattman, "Boeing's Top Lawyer Spotlights Company's Ethical Lapses," *The Wall Street Journal,* Law Blog, January 30, 2006, **http://blogs.wsj.com/ law/2006/01/31/boeings-top-lawyer-rips-into-his-company/tab/article/** (accessed February 25, 2010).

17. Barbara Kiviat, "A Bolder Approach to Credit-Agency Rating Reform," *Time,* September 18, 2009, **http://curiouscapitalist.blogs.time. com/2009/09/18/a-bolder-approach-to-credit-rating-agency-reform/** (accessed January 28, 2010).

18. Evan Perez and Brent Kendall, "Twenty-Two Arrested in U.S. Bribery Probe," *The Wall Street Journal,* January 20, 2010, **http://www.google.com/ search?q=%22Twnety-two+arrested+ in+U.S.+bribery+probe%22&rls=com. microsoft:en-us&ie=UTF-8&oe=UTF-8&startIndex=&startPage=1** (accessed January 27, 2010).

19. "Corruption Perceptions Index 2009," Transparency International, **http://www. transparency.org/policy_research/ surveys_indices/cpi/2009/cpi_2009_ table,** (accessed January 22, 2010).

20. "Nearly 20 Percent of U.S. Workers Have Taken Office Supplies for Personal Use, Despite Most Feeling it is Wrong to Do So," *PR Newswire,* June 10, 2008. **http://www2.prnewswire.com/cgi-bin/ stories.pl?ACCT=104&STORY=/www/ story/06-10-2008/0004829858&EDATE=** (accessed January 22, 2010).

21. David Whelan, "Only the Paranoid Resurge," *Forbes,* April 10, 2006, **http:// www.forbes.com/forbes/2006/0410/042. html** (accessed February 4, 2010).

22. Reuters, "Intel Pays AMD $1.25 billion To Settle All Disputes," *Wired,* November 12, 2009, **http://www.wired. com/epicenter/2009/11/intel-pays-amd-125-billion-to-settle-all-disputes/** (accessed January 29, 2010); Jordan Robertson, "Intel Hit with More Antitrust Charges in FTC Suit," Yahoo! Finance, December 16, 2009, **http://finance. yahoo.com/news/Intel-hit-with-more-antitrust-apf-642649616.html?x=0,** (accessed January 29, 2010).

23. Jennifer Corbett Dooren, "Regulators Turn Cautious on Bisphenol A," *The Wall Street Journal,* January 16, 2010, **http://**

online.wsj.com/article/SB100014240527
487036576045750052116583938110.html
(accessed January 27, 2010).

24. Michael Josephson, "The Ethics
of American Youth 2008," Josephson
Institute of Ethics, press release, **http://
charactercounts.org/programs/
reportcard/2008/index.html** (accessed
February 25, 2010).

25. "Teens Respect Good Business
Ethics," *USA Today,* Snapshots, December
12, 2005, p. 13-1.

26. Al Lewis, "Lying, Cheating,
Violence—All Ingredients for Success,
Teen Survey Says," *Denver Post,* December
5, 2007, **http://blogs.denverpost.com/
lewis/2007/12/05/lying-cheating-
violence-all-ingredients-for-success-
teen-survey-says/** (accessed February 25,
2010).

27. James Vaznis, "Charter School
Cheating Detailed," *The Boston Globe,*
January 23, 2010, **http://www.boston.
com/news/education/k_12/mcas/
articles/2010/01/23/springfield_charter_
school_staff_admits_helping_on_mcas/**
(accessed January 28, 2010).

28. Michael Schmidt, "Guilty Plea in
Sale of Products with Steroids," *The
New York Times,* January 20, 2010,
**http://www.nytimes.com/2010/01/21/
business/21steroids.html** (accessed
January 28, 2010).

29. "Campaign Warns about Drugs from
Canada," *CNN,* February 5, 2004, **www.
cnn.com;** Gardiner Harris and Monica
Davey, "FDA Begins Push to End Drug
Imports," *The New York Times,* January 23,
2004, p. C1.

30. James Bandler and Nicholas
Varchaver with Doris Burke, "How Bernie
Did It," *Fortune,* May 11, 2009, p. 50–71;
Tom Hays, "Trustee: Nearly 9,000 Claims
in Madoff Case," *The Associated Press,*
May 15, 2009, **http://www.google.com/
hostednews/ap/article/ALeqM5iVRa
RYcWFCQgMxBfNtbcfT98Zr4QD986
AALO1** (accessed May 15, 2009);
Robert Frank and Tom Lauricella,
"Madoff Created Air of Mystery,"
The Wall Street Journal, December
20, 2008, **http://online.wsj.com/
article/SB122973208705022949.
html** (accessed December 23, 2008);
Aaron Smith, "Madoff's Victims,
One Year Later," CNNMoney.com,
December 10, 2009, **http://money.cnn.
com/2009/12/10/news/companies/**
madoff_ponzi_victims/index.htm
(accessed February 4, 2010).

31. Marc C. Willemsen, "The New
EU Cigarette Health Warnings Benefit
Smokers Who Want to Quit the Habit:
Results from the Dutch Continuous
Survey of Smoking Habits," *The European
Journal of Public Health* 15, no. 4 (2005),
pp. 389–92.

32. Ethics Resource Center, *2005 National
Business Ethics Survey* (Washington, DC:
Ethics Resource Center, 2005), p. 43.

33. Thomas M. Jones, "Ethical Decision
Making by Individuals in Organizations:
An Issue-Contingent Model," *Academy of
Management Review* 2 (April 1991), pp.
371–73.

34. Sir Adrian Cadbury, "Ethical
Managers Make Their Own Rules,"
Harvard Business Review 65 (September–
October 1987), p. 72.

35. Ferrell, Fraedrich, and Ferrell,
Business Ethics, pp. 174–75.

36. Ethics Resource Center, *2009 National
Business Ethics Survey* (Washington, DC:
Ethics Resource Center, 2009), p. 41.

37. Ibid., p. 9.

38. Jennifer Levitz, "Shielding the
Whistleblower," *The New York Times,*
December 1, 2009, **http://online.wsj.com/
article/SB10001424052748703939404
574568272685253690.html** (accessed
January 28, 2010).

39. Ferrell, Fraedrich, and Ferrell,
Business Ethics, p. 13.

40. John Galvin, "The New Business
Ethics," *SmartBusinessMag.com,* June
2000, p. 99.

41. Archie B. Carroll, "The Pyramid of
Corporate Social Responsibility: Toward
the Moral Management of Organizational
Stakeholders," *Business Horizons* 34 (July/
August 1991), p. 42.

42. Bryan Walsh, "Why Green Is the New
Red, White and Blue," *Time,* April 28,
2008, p. 46.

43. Adam Shriver, "Not Grass-Fed, But
at Least Pain-Free," *The New York Times,*
February 18, 2010, **http://www.nytimes.
com/2010/02/19/opinion/19shriver.
html?scp=4&sq=animal%20rights&st=
cse** (accessed February 25, 2010).

44. Walsh, "Why Green Is the New Red,
White and Blue," p. 54.

45. Alan Beattie, "Countries Rush to
Restrict Trade in Basic Foods," *Financial
Times,* April 2, 2008, p. 1.

46. Laura Petrecca, "Marketing Efforts
May End Up in a Green Blur," *USA Today,*
April 22, 2008, 10B.

47. Alexandra Zendrian, "Workers:
Employers Not Green Enough," *Inc.,* April
17, 2008, **http://www.inc.com/news/
articles,2008/04/green.html** (accessed
February 25, 2010).

48. Indra Nooyi, "The Responsible
Company," *The Economist, The World in
2008 Special Edition,* March 2008, p. 132.

49. Ferrell, Fraedrich, and Ferrell,
Business Ethics, pp. 13–19.

50. Matthew Dolan, "Ford to Begin
Hiring at New Wages," *The New York
Times,* January 26, 2010, **http://online.
wsj.com/article/SB100014240527487
04762904575025420550494324.html**
(accessed January 28, 2010).

51. Beth Cooney, "Stew Leonard Tells
His Life Story in New Book," News
Times, November 20, 2009, **http://www.
newstimes.com/news/article/Stew-
Leonard-tells-his-life-story-in-new-
book-259361.php** (accessed January 17,
2010); "Company Story," Stew Leonard's,
**http://www.stewleonards.com/html/
about.cfm** (accessed January 21, 2010).

52. Jeff Harrington, "Outback Steakhouse
Settle Class-Action Sex Discrimination
Case for $19M," *St. Petersburg Times,*
December 30, 2009; **http://www.
tampabay.com/news/business/
corporate/outback-steakhouse-settles-
class-action-sex-discrimination-case-
for-19m/1061920** (accessed May 4, 2010).

53. "Year after Fatal Walmart Stampede,
Black Friday Gets Makeover," *The
Associated Press,* November 25, 2009,
via **http://www.nola.com/business/
index.ssf/2009/11/year_after_walmart_
stampede_bl.html** (accessed January 28,
2010).

54. Miguel Bustillo, "Walmart to Assign
New 'Green Ratings,'" *The Wall Street
Journal,* July 16, 2009, **http://online.wsj.
com/article/SB124766892562645475.
html** (accessed July 30, 2009); Jeffrey
Ball, "What Can Green Labels Tell Us,"
The Wall Street Journal, July 16, 2009; p.
A10; Sandra M. Jones, "Walmart Keen to
Define Green," Chicago Tribune, July 16,
2009, **www.chicagotribune.com/features/
lifestyle/green/chi-thu-Walmart-
ecolabel-0716-jul16,0,7878172.story**
(accessed July 30, 2009); Alex Salkever,
"Walmart's eco-labeling mandate,"
dailyfinance.com, July 16, 2009,

www.dailyfinance.com/2009/07/16/Walmarts-eco-labeling-mandate/?icid=main|aimzones|dl2|link5|http%3A%2F%2Fwww.dailyfinance.com%2F2009%2F07%2F16%2FWalmarts-eco-labeling-mandate%2F (accessed July 30, 2009).

55. Todd Littman, "Win-Win Emissions Reductions Strategies," Victoria Transport Policy Institute, http://www.vtpi.org/wwclimate.pdf (accessed February 25, 2010).

56. Lauren Etter, "Earth Day: 36 Years on, Plenty of Concerns Remain," *The Wall Street Journal,* April 22–23, 2006, p. A7.

57. Cornelia Dean, "Drugs Are in the Water, Does It Matter?" *The New York Times,* April 3, 2007, HEALTH, http://www.nytimes.com/2007/04/03/science/earth/03water.html?_r=1&scp=55&sq=%22cornelia+dean%22&st=nyt&oref=slogin (accessed February 25, 2010).

58. Michael Grunwald, "The Clean Energy Scam," *Time,* April 7, 2008, http://www.time.com/time/magazine/article/0,9171,1725975,00.html (accessed February 25, 2010).

59. "Diamant Corporation Furthers National Consumer Awareness Efforts as British Prime Minister Gordon Brown Announces Tougher Measures to Drastically Reduce the Society's Dependence on Single-Use Plastic Bags," *CNN Money,* March 25, 2008, http://money.cnn.com/news/newsfeeds/articles/marketwire/0379140.htm (accessed February 25, 2010).

60. Matthew Knight, "Plastic Bags Fly into Environmental Storm," *CNN.com,* March 17, 2008, http://edition.cnn.com/2007/TECH/11/14/fsummit.climate.plasticbags/index.html (accessed February 25, 2010).

61. "Whole Foods to Sack Disposable Plastic Grocery Bags," January 22, 2008, http://www.wholefoodsmarket.com/cgi-bin/print10pt.cgi?url=/pressroom/pr_01-22-08.html (accessed February 25, 2010).

62. Josh Glasser, "T. Boone Pickens on Natural Gas: You Can't Beat it," *Fortune,* July 14, 2009, http://bigtech.blogs.fortune.cnn.com/2009/07/14/news/economy/pickens_natural_gas.fortune/?postversion=2009071415 (accessed January 28, 2010).

63. "U.S. Stimulus Boosts Renewables, Energy Efficiency, and Smart Grids," Energy Envirofinland." Source originally taken from *Reuters,* February 14, 2009, http://www.energy-enviro.fi/index.php?PAGE=2427 (accessed January 28, 2010).

64. Alan K. Reichert, Marion S. Webb, and Edward G. Thomas, "Corporate Support for Ethical and Environmental Policies: A Financial Management Perspective," *Journal of Business Ethics* 25 (2000), pp. 53–64.

65. David J. Lynch, "Corporate American Warms to Fight Against Global Warming," *USA Today,* June 1, 2006, p. B1.

66. Jim Rogers, "Point of View: A New Model for Energy Efficiency," *The News & Observer,* February 19. 2008, http://www.newsobserver.com/print/tuesday/opinion/story/951188.html (accessed February 25, 2010).

67. "GreenChoice: The #1 Green Power Program in America," Austin Energy (n.d.), www.austinenergy.com/Energy%20Efficiency/Programs/Green%20Choice/index.htm (accessed February 25, 2010).

68. "Certification," Home Depot, www.homedepot.com/HDUS/EN_US/corporate/corp_respon/certification.shtml (accessed February 25, 2010).

69. Chiquita, Bananalink, http://www.bananalink.org.uk/content/view/62/22/lang,en/ (accessed February 25, 2010).

70. "US Charitable Giving Estimated to Be $307.65 Billion in 2008," Press Release, Giving USA, http://www.aafrc.org/press_releases/gusa/GivingReaches300billion.pdf (accessed February 25, 2010).

71. Mark Calvey, "Profile: Safeway's Grants Reflect Its People," *San Francisco Business Times,* July 14, 2003, http://sanfrancisco.bizjournals.com/sanfrancisco/stories/2003/07/14/focus9.html (accessed February 25, 2010).

72. "About Avon," Avon (n.d.), www.avoncompany.com/about/ (accessed February 25, 2010); "The Avon Breast Cancer Crusade," Avon, www.avoncompany.com/women/avoncrusade/ (accessed February 25, 2010).

73. "Take Charge of Education," Target (n.d.), http://target.com/common/page.jhtml;jsessionid=GWORM5AQSLBLDLARAAVWW4FMCEACU1IX?content=target_cg_take_charge_of_education (accessed February 25, 2010).

74. "Who Really Pays for CSR Initiatives," *Environmental Leader,* February 15, 2008, http://www.environmentalleader.com/2008/02/15/who-really-pays-for-csr-initiatives/ (accessed February 25, 2010); "Global Fund," http://www.joinred.com/globalfund (accessed February 25, 2010); Reena Jana, "The Business of Going Green," *Business-Week Online,* June 22, 2007, http://www.businessweek.com/innovate/content/jun2007/id20070622_491833.htm?chan=search (accessed June 19, 2008).

75. Permission granted by the author of *Gray Matters,* George Sammet Jr., Vice President, Office of Corporate Ethics, Lockheed Martin Corporation, Orlando, Florida, to use these portions of *Gray Matters: The Ethics Game* © 1992. If you would like more information about the complete game, call 1-800-3ETHICS.

76. information from video; Jessica Silver-Greenberg, Tara Kalwarski, and Alexis Leondis, "CEO Pay Drops, But...Cash is King," *Bloomberg BusinessWeek,* April 5, 2010, pp. 50–56; "The Dynamics of Public Trust in Business—Emerging Opportunities for Leaders," Arthur W. Page Society and Business Roundtable Institute for Corporate Ethics, http://www.corporate-ethics.org/pdf/public_trust_in_Business.pdf (accessed May 4, 2010).

77. M.P. McQueen, "Agency Misses Chance to Curb Lead in Jewelry," *The Wall Street Journal,* February 12, 2008, p. D1.

78. Avery Johnson, "Pfizer Will Pull Some Lipitor Ads in Wake of Probe." *The Wall Street Journal,* February 26, 2008, p. B5, http://online.wsj.com/article/SB120396972593291395.html; Vanessa Aristide, "Pfizer Voluntarily Withdraws Lipitor Advertising Featuring Dr. Robert Jarvik." *Pfizer Press Release,* February 25, 2008, http://www.pfizer.com/news/press_releases/pfizer_press_releases.jsp?rssUrl=http://mediaroom.pfizer.com/portal/site/pfizer/index.jsp?ndmViewId=news_view&ndmConfigId=1010794&newsId=20080225006247&newsLang=en; *Better Business Bureau,* http://us.bbb.org/WWWRoot/SitePage.aspx?site=113&id=8e20ba59-acb8-4dcfa1e2-0cc3ab9cfbb4, Section 14.

79. "5 Major Corporate Bankruptcies of 2009," BankruptcyHome.com, http://www.bankruptcyhome.com/Five-Major-Corporate-Bankruptcies-2009.htm (accessed January 28, 2010).

80. Jessica E. Vascallero, "Google Book-Search Pact Draws Antitrust Scrutiny," *The Wall Street Journal,* April 29, 2009, **http://online.wsj.com/article/SB124095639971465549.html** (accessed January 28, 2010); Catherine Holahan, "Google's Antitrust Trouble," *BusinessWeek,* September 15, 2008, **http://www.businessweek.com/bwdaily/dnflash/content/sep2008/db20080914_683068.htm** (accessed January 28, 2010); "Ending Our Agreement with Yahoo!," The Official Google Blog, November 5, 2008, **http://googleblog.blogspot.com/2008/11/ending-our-agreement-with-yahoo.html** (accessed January 28, 2010).

81. Maureen Dorney, "Congress Passes Federal Anti-Spam Law: Preempts Most State Anti-Spam Laws," *DLA Piper,* December 3, 2003, **http://franchiseagreements.com/global/publications/detail.aspx?pub=622** (accessed February 25, 2010).

82. Larry Barrett, "Data Breach Costs Surge in 2009: Study," eSecurityPlanet, January 26, 2010, **http://www.esecurityplanet.com/features/article.php/3860811/Data-Breach-Costs-Surge-in-2009-Study.htm** (accessed January 28, 2010).

Chapter 3

1. R. Jai Krishna, "Nokia to Offer Phone Installments in India," *The Wall Street Journal,* August 19, 2009, p. B7; Mark Bordon, "iPhone Envy? You Must Be Jöking," *Fast Company,* September 2009, pp. 68–73, 106; Adam Smith, "Nokia Calling," *Time,* August 3, 2009, **www.time.com/time/magazine/article/0,9171,1912307,00.html** (accessed February 2, 2010); **www.wireless.att.com** (accessed February 2, 2010); **www.verizonwireless.com** (accessed February 2, 2010).

2. Tim Kelly, "Squash the Caterpillar," *Forbes,* April 21, 2008, p. 136.

3. "FAQs," McDonald's Canada, **http://www.mcdonalds.ca/en/aboutus/faq.aspx** (accessed February 19, 2010).

4. "Company Profile," Starbucks, **http://assets.starbucks.com/assets/company-profile-feb10.pdf** (accessed March 3, 2010).

5. Elisabeth Sullivan, "Choose Your Words Wisely," *Marketing News,* February 15, 2008, p. 22.

6. Dexter Roberts and David Rocks, "China: Let a Thousand Brands Bloom," *BusinessWeek,* October 17, 2005, pp. 58, 60.

7. Sullivan, "Choose Your Words Wisely."

8. "2009 Annual Trade Highlights, Dollar Change from Prior Year," *U.S. Census Bureau, Foreign Trade Statistics,* **http://www.census.gov/foreign-trade/statistics/highlights/annual.html** (accessed February 17, 2010).

9. Roberts and Rocks, "China: Let a Thousand Brands Bloom."

10. Joseph O'Reilly, "Global Logistics: In China, Bigger Bull's-eye Better," *Inbound Logistics,* April 2008, p. 26.

11. "2009 Annual Trade Highlights, Dollar Change from Prior Year."

12. Ibid.

13. "Trade in Goods (Imports, Exports and Trade Balance) with China," *U.S. Census Bureau: Foreign Trade Statistics,* **http://www.census.gov/foreign-trade/balance/c5700.html** (accessed February 17, 2010).

14. Jeanne Whalen, "Novartis Invests in Chinese Vaccines." *The Wall Street Journal,* November 5, 2009, p. B2.

15. "Japan Finance Minister Steps Down," *BBC News,* February 17, 2009, **http://news.bbc.co.uk/2/hi/asia-pacific/7893924.stm** (accessed February 20, 2010).

16. O'Reilly, "Global Logistics: New Tax Treaty Raises U.S. Stakes in Belgium's Lowlands," p. 24.

17. Eric Bellman, "Walmart Exports Big-Box Concept to India," *The Wall Street Journal,* May 28, 2009, **http://online.wsj.com/article/SB124346697277260377.html** (accessed February 16, 2010); Nandini Lakshman, "Why Walmart's First India Store Isn't a Walmart," *Time,* May 15, 2009, **www.time.com/time/world/article/0,8599,1898823,00.html** (accessed March 3, 2010); "Walmart in India Fact Sheet," **http://walmartstores.com/FactsNews/FactSheets/** (accessed June 12, 2009); "Walmart Scales Up Expansion Plan," *The Telegraph—Calcutta, India,* November 8, 2009, **http://www.telegraphindia.com/1091109/jsp/business/story_11717096.jsp** (accessed November 24, 2009).

18. "Zambia Bans Foreign Currency Use," *PressTV,* March 22, 2009, **http://www.presstv.com/detail.aspx?id=89362&sectionid=351020506** (accessed February 20, 2010); Garth Theunissen, "Zambia to Ban Kwacha Loans to Non-Residents, Central Bank Says," *Bloomberg.com,* March 6, 2009, **http://www.bloomberg.com/apps/news?pid=20601116&sid=aDOPdoYArL8M&refer=africa** (accessed February 20, 2010).

19. "Sixth Annual BSA and IDC Global Software Piracy Study," Business Software Alliance, May 2009, **http://global.bsa.org/globalpiracy2008/index.html** (accessed February 20, 2010).

20. Kitty Bean Yancey and Laura Bly, "Door May Be Inching Open for Tourism," *USA Today,* February 20, 2008, p. A5; Sue Kirchhoff and Chris Woodyard, "Cuba Trade Gets 'New Opportunity,'" *USA Today,* February 20, 2008, p. B1.

21. "Obama Move on China Tires Could Spur More Requests," *Reuters,* September 14, 2009, **http://www.reuters.com/article/idUKTRE58D3Y120090914** (accessed February 23, 2010).

22. "Our Story," EcoMom, **http://www.ecomom.com/page/our-story-1** (accessed February 17, 2010); "World Nomination: The EcoMom Alliance Is Saving the Planet One Mother at a Time," The Family Groove, May 2009, **www.thefamilygroove.com/may09_CharityMonth.htm** (accessed March 3, 2010); Mary Jane Smetanka, "EcoMom Alliance: For the Children," *Star Tribune,* June 15, 2008, **http://www.startribune.com/local/west/19962324.html** (accessed March 3, 2010).

23. Julie Bennett, "Product Pitfalls Proliferate in Global Cultural Maze," *The Wall Street Journal,* May 14, 2001, p. B11.

24. Ann Blackman Moscow, Moscow's Big Mac Attack, *Time,* February 5, 1990, **http://www.time.com/time/magazine/article/0,9171,969321,00.html** (accessed March 8, 2010.

25. Slogans Gone Bad, Joe-ks, **www.joe-ks.com/archives_apr2004/slogans_gone_bad.htm** (accessed March 3, 2010).

26. David Ricks, *Blunders in International Business,* 4th ed. (Malden, MA: Blackwell Publishing, 2006), p. 70. Downloaded from Google Books, **http://books.google.com/books?id=S4L3ntwgs-8C&pg=PA68&lpg=PA68&dq=Mountain+Bell+company,+Saudi+advertisement&source=bl&ots=9apNX6s3hy&sig=Z5BEVaLe4-2p39kNYMlBd5sOX-GA&hl=en&ei=XJGFS6rfNpPKsAODk5zEDw&sa=X&oi=book_result&ct=result&resnum=5&ved=0CBcQ6AEwBA#v=onepage&**

q=airline&f=false (accessed February 24, 2010).

27. J. Bonasia, "For Web, Global Reach Is Beauty—and Challenge," *Investor's Business Daily,* June 13, 2001, p. A6.

28. Chris Foresman, "While PC Market Rebounds, Apple Slips into 5th Place in US," *Ars Technica,* January 14, 2010, **http://arstechnica.com/hardware/news/2010/01/while-pc-market-rebounds-apple-slips-into-5th-place-in-us.ars** (accessed February 24, 2010).

29. "What Is the WTO," World Trade Organization (n.d.), **http://www.wto.org/english/thewto_e/whatis_e/whatis_e.htm** (accessed March 3, 2010).

30. August Cole and Peter Sanders, "Air Force Resumes Tanker Contest," *The Wall Street Journal,* September 25, 2009, B3.

31. "North America: Canada," *CIA—World Factbook,* **https://www.cia.gov/library/publications/the-world-factbook/geos/ca.html** (accessed February 24, 2010).

32. "Trade in Goods (Imports, Exports and Trade Balance) with Canada," U.S. Census Bureau, **http://www.census.gov/foreign-trade/balance/c1220.html** (accessed February 24, 2010); "North America: Canada," *CIA—World Factbook,* **https://www.cia.gov/library/publications/the-world-factbook/geos/ca.html** (accessed February 24, 2010).

33. "America's Biggest Partners," *CNBC.com,* **http://www.cnbc.com/id/31064179?slide=11** (accessed February 24, 2010).

34. "North America: Mexico," *CIA—World Factbook,* **https://www.cia.gov/library/publications/the-world-factbook/geos/mx.html** (February 24, 2010); "Trade in Goods (Imports, Exports and Trade Balance) with Mexico," U.S. Census Bureau, **http://www.census.gov/foreign-trade/balance/c2010.html#2009** (accessed February 24, 2010).

35. "Current Population Survey, 2008," U.S. Census Bureau, **http://www.census.gov/hhes/www/cpstables/032009/hhinc/new01_009.htm** (accessed March 3, 2010); Felipe Calderón Hinojosa, "Mexico's Road," *The Economist,* November 15, 2007, p. 48.

36. Pete Engardio and Geri Smith, "Business Is Standing Its Ground," *BusinessWeek,* April 20, 2009, p.34–39.

37. "Country Comparison: GDP (purchasing power parity)," *CIA—World Factbook,* **https://www.cia.gov/library/publications/the-world-factbook/rankorder/2001rank.html?countryName=United%20States&countryCode=us&regionCode=na&rank=2#us** (accessed February 3, 2010).

38. "A Tale of Two Mexicos: North and South," *The Economist,* April 26, 2008, pp. 53–54.

39. "Antecedents of the FTAA Process," Free Trade Area of the Americas (n.d.), **www.ftaa-alca.org/View_e.asp** (accessed March 10, 2010); "FTAA Fact Sheet," Market Access and Compliance, U.S. Department of Commerce (n.d.), **www.mac.doc.gov/ftaa2005/ftaa_fact_sheet.html** (accessed November 3, 2003).

40. "Economy Will Be Top Issue at 5th Americas Summit: U.S. Official," *China View,* March 14, 2009, **http://news.xinhuanet.com/english/2009-03/14/content_11008994.htm** (accessed February 25, 2010); "Frequently Asked Questions," Fifth Summit of the Americas, March 3, 2009, **http://www.fifthsummitoftheamericas.org/faqs.htm** (accessed February 25, 2010).

41. "Archer Daniels to File NAFTA Claim Against Mexico," *Inbound Logistics,* October 2003, p. 30.

42. Geri Smith and Cristina Lindblad, "Mexico: Was NAFTA Worth It?," *BusinessWeek,* December 23, 2003, **http://www.businessweek.com/magazine/content/03_51/b3863008.htm** (accessed May 5, 2010).

43. Pete Engardio and Geri Smith, "Business Is Standing Its Ground," *BusinessWeek,* April 20, 2009, p. 34–39.

44. "Europe in 12 Lessons," **http://europa.eu/abc/12lessons/lesson_2/index_en.htm** (accessed March 3, 2010).

45. "Europe: European Union," *CIA—World Factbook,* **https://www.cia.gov/library/publications/the-world-factbook/geos/ee.html** (accessed February 25, 2010).

46. Stanley Reed, with Ariane Sains, David Fairlamb, and Carol Matlack, "The Euro: How Damaging a Hit?" *BusinessWeek,* September 29, 2003, p. 63; "The Single Currency," *CNN* (n.d.), **www.cnn.com/SPECIALS/2000/eurounion/story/currency/** (accessed July 3, 2001).

47. "EU Slaps a Record Fine on Intel," *BBC News,* May 13, 2009, **http://news.bbc.co.uk/2/hi/business/8047546.stm** (accessed February 25, 2010).

48. "About APEC," Asia-Pacific Economic Cooperation, **http://www.apec.org/apec/about_apec.html** (accessed February 25, 2010).

49. Smith and Lindblad, "Mexico: Was NAFTA Worth It?"

50. "China Economic Growth Accelerates," *BBC News,* October 22, 2009, **http://news.bbc.co.uk/2/hi/business/8319706.stm** (accessed February 25, 2010).

51. James T. Areddy, James Hookway, John Lyons, and Marcus Walker, "U.S. Slump Takes Toll Across Globe," *The Wall Street Journal,* April 3, 2008, p. A1; Pam Woodall, "The New Champions," *The Economist,* November 15, 2008, p. 55; Matt Jenkins, "A Really Inconvenient Truth," *Miller-McCune,* April/May 2008, p. 42.

52. Peter Collins, "A Special Report on Vietnam: Halfway from Rags to Riches," *The Economist,* April 26, 2008, p 3–16.

53. "Tackling Current Challenges," International Monetary Fund, **http://www.imf.org/external/about/onagenda.htm** (accessed February 25, 2010).

54. David J. Lynch, "The IMF is . . . Tired Fund Struggles to Reinvent Itself," *USA Today,* April 19, 2006. p. B1.

55. Ilan Brat and Paul Kiernan, "Heinz Seeks to Tap Mexico's Taste for Ketchup," *The Wall Street Journal,* November 24, 2009, pp. B1–B2.

56. Ben Worthen, "The Crazy World of Outsourcing," *WSJ.com,* February 25, 2008. **http://blogs.wsj.com/biztech/2008/02/25/the-crazy-world-ofoutsourcing/?mod=relevancy** (accessed May 6, 2008).

57. Walter B. Wriston, "Ever Heard of Insourcing?" Commentary, *The Wall Street Journal,* March 24, 2004, p. A20.

58. Nick Heath, "Banks: Offshoring, Not Outsourcing," *BusinessWeek,* March 10, 2009, **http://www.businessweek.com/globalbiz/content/mar2009/gb20090310_619247.htm** (accessed February 25, 2010); Coomi Kapoor, "What Now after the Satyam Fraud?" *Asia News Network,* December 1, 2009, **http://www.asianewsnet.net/news.php?id=3368&sec=3&t=** (accessed February 25, 2010).

59. Barclays Wealth, **http://www.census.gov/hhes/www/cpstables/032009/hhinc/new01_009.htm** (accessed March 3, 2010); Nick Heath, "Banks: Offshoring,

Not Outsourcing," *BusinessWeek,* March 10, 2009, **http://www.businessweek. com/globalbiz/content/mar2009/ gb20090310_619247.htm** (accessed March 3, 2010).

60. "About Us," Carrefour: Arab Republic of Egypt, **http://www.carrefour.com. eg/aboutus.aspx** (accessed February 25, 2010).

61. "What We're About," NUMI (n.d.), **www.numi.com/co_info.html** (accessed February March 1, 2010).

62. Sharon Silk Carty, "Ford Plans to Park Jaguar, Land Rover with Tata Motors," *USA Today,* March 26, 2008, p B1.

63. O. C. Ferrell, John Fraedrich, and Linda Ferrell, *Business Ethics,* 6th ed. (Boston: Houghton Mifflin, 2005), pp. 227–30.

64. Pete Engardio, "Cradle of a Green Revolution," *BusinessWeek,* November 2, 2009, pp. 40–41; Bryan Walsh, "Electric Cars: China's Power Play," *Time,* August 31, 2009, **www.time.com/ time/printout/0,8816,1917647,00.html** (accessed March 3, 2010); Daniel K. Gardner, "Meet China's Green Crusader," *The New York Times,* November 1, 2009, **www.nytimes.com/2009/02/11/ opinion/11iht-edgardner.1.20105872. html** (accessed March 3, 2010); Ben Elgin and Bruce Einhorn, "China's Carbon-Credit Hustle," *BusinessWeek,* December 21, 2009, pp. 18–21; "China Gets Greener," *BusinessWeek,* January 11, 2010, p. 7; Adam Aston, "China's Surprising Clout in Cleantech," *BusinessWeek,* November 30, 2009, p. 56.

65. Export.gov, **http://www.export.gov/ about/index.asp** (accessed March 3, 2010), CIBER Web, **http://CIBERWEB. msu.edu** (accessed March 3, 2010).

66. Jeff Chu, "Happily Ever After?" *Time,* March 18, 2002, **http:// www.time.com/time/magazine/ article/0,9171,901020325-218398,00. html** (accessed May 6, 2010); Wendy Leung, ""Disney Set to Miss Mark on Visitors," *The Standard,* September 5, 2006, **http://www.thestandard.com. hk/news_detail.asp?pp_cat=11&art_ id=26614&sid=9732977&con_ type=1&d_str=20060905&sear_ year=2006** (accessed May 6, 2010); Brady MacDonal, "Hong Kong Disneyland expansion to add three new themed lands," LA Times, November 12, 2009, **http://travel.latimes.com/**

daily-deal-blog/index.php/hong-kong-disneyland-5811** (accessed April 22, 2010); Robert Mendick, "Race Against Time to Make That Disney Magic Work," *The London Independent,* February 6, 2000, **http://www.independent.co.uk/ news/uk/this-britain/race-against-time-to-make-that-new-disney-magic-work-726623.html** (accessed May 6, 2010); "The Narrative of Numbers," Disneyland Paris, **http://corporate. disneylandparis.com/about-our-company/the-narrative-of-numbers/ index.xhtml** (accessed April 20, 2010).

Chapter 4

1. David M. Ewalt, "Low-Dose Capitalism," *Forbes,* November 2, 2009, p. 40; **http://www.kiva.org** (accessed December 19, 2009); Leena Rao, "Kiva Brings Microlending Home to U.S. Entrepreneurs In Need," *TechCrunch,* June 10, 2009, **http:// www.techcrunch.com/2009/06/10/ kiva-brings-microlending-home-to-us-entrepreneurs-in-need** (accessed December 19, 2009); Alice Rawsthorn, "Winning Ways of Making a Better World," *The New York Times,* August 30, 2009, **http://www.nytimes. com/2009/08/31/fashion/3liht-designweb.html?_r=1** (accessed December 19, 2009); "40 Under 40: Business's Hottest Rising Stars," *Fortune,* 2009, **http://money.cnn.com/magazines/ fortune/40under40/2009/full_list/** (accessed January 20, 2010); Peter Greer and Phil Smith, *The Poor Will Be Glad* (Grand Rapids, MI: Zondervan, 2009), pp. 99, 107.

2. The Entrepreneurs' Help Page, **http://www.tannedfeet.com/sole_ proprietorship.htm** (accessed March 16, 2010); Kent Hoover, "Startups Down for Women Entrepreneurs, Up for Men," *SanFrancisco Business Times,* May 2, 2008, **http://sanfrancisco.bizjournals. com/sanfrancisco/stories/2008/05/05/ smallb2.html** (accessed March 16, 2010).

3. Maggie Overfelt, "Start-Me-Up: How the Garage Became a Legendary Place to Rev Up Ideas," *Fortune Small Business,* September 1, 2003, **http:// money.cnn.com/magazines/fsb/fsb_ archive/2003/09/01/350784/index.htm** (accessed March 16, 2010).

4. "Subway® Restaurant Chain Honors Brooklyn Franchisee," August 15, 2008, *FindLaw,* **http://news.corporate.**

findlaw.com/prnewswire/20080815/15 aug20081200.html** (accessed March 16, 2010); Richard Gibson, "Chain Reaction," *The Wall Street Journal,* October 13, 2008, p. R13; Subway, **http://www.subway.com** (accessed March 16, 2010).

5. Digital Artists Agency, **http://www.d-a-a.com/clients/clientindexframe.html** (accessed March 16, 2010).

6. Ben Rooney, "Dubai Selling off the Queen Elizabeth 2," February 9, 2010 **http://money.cnn.com/2010/02/09/ news/economy/Dubai_asset_sales/ index.htm** (accessed March 8, 2010).

7. Elizabeth Weise, "On Tiny Plots, a New Generation of Farmers Emerges," *USA Today,* July 14, 2009, pp. 1A–2A.

8. N. Kane Bennett, "Dispute between Business Partners Ends in Dissolution and Double Damages under Connecticut Wage Act," *Connecticut Business Litigation Blog,* September 13, 2009, **http:// www.connecticutbusinesslitigation. com/2009/09/articles/employment-1/ dispute-between-business-partners-ends-in-dissolution-and-double-damages-under-connecticut-wage-act** (accessed March 8, 2010).

9. Jason Norman, "Best Buy to Stock E-Bikes in Select Stores," *Bicycle Retailer,* April 29, 2009, **http:// www.bicycleretailer.com/news/ newsDetail/2648.html** (accessed February 26, 2010); Christian Wust, "Making Everyman a Superman: Electric Bikes Gain Speed and Popularity," *Spiegal Online International,* May 15, 2009, **http://www.spiegel.de/international/ zeitgeist/0,1518,625181,00.html** (accessed February 26, 2010); "FAQ," ebikes.ca, **http://www.ebikes.ca/faq. shtml** (accessed February 26, 2010); "Electric Bikes," Schwinn Quality, **http://www.schwinnbike.com/usa/ eng/Products/Electric/All/** (accessed February 26, 2010); "A2B," Ultra Motor A2B, **http://sanfrancisco.goa2b.us/ products/a2b** (accessed May 19, 2009); "Our Vision," Ultra Motor A2B, **http:// www.ultramotor.com/uk/about_us/** (accessed February 26, 2010); Julio Ojeda-Zapata, "Riders of Electric Bicycles Plug in and Pedal," TwinCities.com, May 17, 2009, **http://www.twincities.com/ ci_12383680** (accessed February 26, 2010).

10. "America's Largest Privately-Owned Companies," *Forbes.com,* October 28, 2009, **http://www.forbes.com/**

lists/2009/21/private-companies-09_
Cargill_5ZUZ.html (accessed March 2,
2010).

11. "Global Brands," Mars, **http://www.
mars.com/global/global-brands.aspx**
(accessed March 8, 2010).

12. Deborah Orr, "The Secret World
of Mars," *Forbes,* April 28, 2008,
**http://www.forbes.com/2008/04/28/
billionaires-mars-wrigley-biz-billies-cz_
do_0428marsfamily.html** (accessed
March 16, 2010).

13. "*Fortune* 500: *Fortune*'s Annual
Ranking of America's Largest
Corporations," *Fortune,* **http://
money.cnn.com/magazines/fortune/
fortune500/2009/full_list/** (accessed
March 1, 2010).

14. Jay Hart, "Not His father's CEO,"
Yahoo! Sports, January 22, 2010, **http://
sports.yahoo.com/nascar/news?slug=jh-
france012209** (accessed March 2, 2010).

15. Scott DeCarlo, "The World's Biggest
Companies," *Forbes.com,* April 8, 2009,
**http://www.forbes.com/2009/04/08/
worlds-largest-companies-business-
global-09-global-intro.html** (accessed
March 2, 2010).

16. Eric Fox, "The Best IPOs of 2009,"
Investopedia, December 16, 2009,
**http://stocks.investopedia.com/stock-
analysis/2009/The-Best-IPOs-Of-2009-
DGW-CYOU-MJN-BPI-SWI1216.aspx**
(accessed March 2, 2010); Scott Austin,
"It's Official: SolarWinds Breaks Nine-
Month IPO Drought," *The Wall Street
Journal Blogs,* May 19, 2009, **http://blogs.
wsj.com/venturecapital/2009/05/19/its-
official-solarwinds-breaks-nine-month-
ipo-drought/tab/article** (accessed March
2, 2010).

17. Niraj Sheth and Jeff McCracken,
"RCN Is Sold to Firm in $535 Million
Deal," March 5, 2010, **http://online.wsj.
com/article/SB10001424052748703915204575103362665861820.html?KEYWORDS=private+equity+buy+out** (accessed
March 9, 2010).

18. O. C. Ferrell, John Fraedrich, and
Linda Ferrell, *Business Ethics: Ethical
Decision Making and Cases,* 8th ed.
(Mason, OH: South-Western Cengage
Learning, 2011), p. 109.

19. "Board Composition," P&G, **http://
www.pg.com/en_US/company/global_
structure_operations/governance/
board_composition.shtml** (accessed
March 3, 2010).

20. Joseph Nathan Kane, *Famous First
Facts,* 4th ed. (New York: The H. W.
Wilson Company, 1981), p. 202.

21. David Kaplan, "Dow Jones in Joint
Venture to Launch WSJ Japan Site,"
The Washington Post, May 7, 2009,
**http://www.washingtonpost.com/
wp-dyn/content/article/2009/05/07/
AR2009050703543.html** (accessed March
3, 2010).

22. Robert D. Hisrich and Michael P.
Peters, *Entrepreneurship,* 5th ed. (Boston:
McGraw-Hill, 2002), pp. 315–16.

23. Russell Gold, "Biomass Power
Generates Traction," *The Wall Street
Journal,* June 1, 2009, p. A4.

24. Leigh Buchanan, "Margot Fraser,
Birkenstock, Forty Years of Peace, Love,
and Clunky Sandals," *Inc.,* June 2009,
pp. 79–80; "About Birkenstock U.S.A.,"
Birkenstock, **http://www.birkenstockusa.
com/about** (accessed February 26, 2010);
"Green Steps," Birkenstock, **http://www.
birkenstockusa.com/about/green-steps**
(accessed February 26, 2010).

25. Kerry Capell and Dermot Doherty,
"What Novartis Sees in Eye Care,"
Bloomberg BusinessWeek, January 18,
2010, p. 26.

26. "CKE Restaurants Adopts Poison
Pill Plan," January 5, 2009, **http://www.
thestreet.com/story/10456052/cke-
restaurants-adopts-poison-pill-plan.
html** (accessed March 9, 2010).

27. New Belgium Brewing Company
Web site, **http://www.newbelgium.com**
(accessed June 22, 2010); Greg Owsley,
New Belgium Brewing marketing director,
"The Necessity for Aligning Brand
with Corporate Ethics," in Sheb True,
Linda Ferrell, O. C. Ferrell, *Fulfilling
our Obligation: Perspectives on Teaching
Business Ethics,* Kennesaw (Ga.) State
University, 2005; Bryan Simpson, New
Belgium Brewing, "New Belgium Brewing:
Brand Building through Advertising
and Public Relations," 2010 case and
interviews with Greg Owsley.

Chapter 5

1. Jonathan Fahey, "Fishing Expedition,"
Forbes, June 8, 2009, pp. 48–50; **www.
aquacopia.com** (accessed March 4, 2010);
Alessandra Bianchi, "The Next Seafood
Frontier: The Ocean," *CNNMoney.
com,* April 28, 2009, **http://money.
cnn.com/2009/04/27/smallbusiness/
farming_the_open_oceans.fsb/index.

htm?postversion=2009042806** (accessed
March 4, 2010).

2. "FAQs," U.S. Small Business
Administration, **http://web.sba.gov/
faqs/faqindex.cfm?areaID=24** (accessed
March 9, 2010).

3. "Environmentalism: What We Do,"
Patagonia, **http://www.patagonia.com/
web/us/patagonia.go?assetid=2329**
(accessed March 9, 2010).

4. "FAQs," U.S. Small Business
Administration.

5. "Nation's Women-Owned Firms
Contribute Nearly $3 Trillion to U.S.
Economy According to Groundbreaking
Research," Center for Women's Business
Research, October 2, 2009, **http://
www.womensbusinessresearchcenter.
org/Data/newsroom/
pressreleases/2009pressreleases/
economicimpactmeas/
cfwbreconomicimpact.release.100209.
pdf** (accessed March 9, 2010).

6. "The State of Minority Business,"
Minority Business Development Agency,
April 2008, **http://www.mbda.gov/index.
php?section_id=6&bucket_id=789#
bucket_852** (accessed March 9, 2010).

7. "FAQs," U.S. Small Business
Administration.

8. "Statistics about Business Size
(including Small Business)," U.S. Census
Bureau, **http://www.census.gov/epcd/
www/smallbus.html#EMpSize** (accessed
March 9, 2010).

9. "Bittersweet Synergy: Domestic
Outsourcing in India," *The Economist,*
October 22, 2009, p. 74.

10. Joseph Schumpeter, "Brand Royalty,"
The Economist, November 26, 2009, p. 78.

11. Lindsay Blakely, "One Man Brands,"
Money.CNN.com, July 6, 2007, **http://
money.cnn.com/galleries/2007/
biz2/0706/gallery.building_brands.
biz2/2.html** (accessed March 16, 2010).

12. "How to Finance a New Business,"
Consumer Reports, April 2008, **http://
www.consumerreports.org/cro/money/
credit-loan/how-to-finance-a-new-
business/overview/how-to-finance-a-
new-business-ov.htm** (accessed March 9,
2010).

13. "Moms 'Can't Live Without' the
Boppy® Pillow," Boppy Web site, Press
Release, October 6, 2009, **http://www.
boppy.com/news-releases/the-boppy-
pillow-wins-1** (accessed March 16,
2010).

14. "Service Sector Growing at Fastest Rate since 2008," *Associated Press,* March 3, 2010, **http://www.msnbc.msn.com/ id/35684642/ns/business-stocks_and_ economy** (accessed March 9, 2010).

15. "Midway USA, 2009 Award Recipient, Small Business Category," Baldrige Award Recipient Profile, **http://www.nist.gov/ public_affairs/releases/midway_profile. html** (accessed March 16, 2010).

16. "FAQs," U.S. Small Business Administration.

17. "Statistics," Facebook Press Room, **http://www.facebook.com/press/info. php?statistics** (accessed March 9, 2010).

18. Laurie Goodstein, "2 Entrepreneurs Help a Monastery Thrive," *The New York Times,* June 2, 2009, **http://www.nytimes. com/2009/06/02/us/02monks.html?_r= 1&scp=1&sq=2%20entrepreneurs%20 help%20a%20monastery%20to%20 thrive&st=cse** (accessed March 4, 2010); **www.lasermonks.com** (accessed March 4, 2010); "Monks Turn Office Products into $4.5M Business," *USA Today,* May 31, 2008, **www.usatoday.com/money/ companies/2008-05-31-lasermonks_ n.htm** (accessed March 4, 2010).

19. Dana Knight, "Big-Headed Guy Gets a Big Idea for Sunglasses Business," *USA Today,* March 21, 2006, p. 4B; Fatheadz, **http://wwwfatheadz. com** (accessed March 9, 2010); Dana Hunsinger, "Fatheadz Founder Thrilled That Retail Giant Wal-Mart Has Taken a Shine to His Sunglasses for Bigger Noggins," *The Indianapolis Star,* July 27, 2009, **http://www.fatheadz.com/ pressselect.php?sid=16** (accessed March 9, 2010).

20. "FAQs," U.S. Small Business Administration.

21. Peter Gott, "Don't Seek Help in Pyramid Sales of Chocolate Product," *Tulsa World,* August 22, 2008, **http://www.tulsaworld.com/news/ article.aspx?subjectID=17&articl eID=20080822_17_D6_DearDr515300** (accessed March 4, 2010); Debra Jopson, "Sweet Schemes: The Great Chocolate Rip-Off," *The Sydney Morning Herald,* August 2, 2008, **http://www.smh.com. au/articles/2008/08/01/1217097533797. html** (accessed March 4, 2010); Direct Selling Association, **http://www.dsa. org** (accessed March 4, 2010); MXI Corporation, **http://www.mxicorp. com** (accessed March 4, 2010); Michael

Wilson, "A Chocolate, with Amway Undertones, Networks Its Way into New York," *The New York Times,* May 9, 2009, **http://www.nytimes. com/2009/05/10/nyregion/10chocolate. html?pagewanted=1** (accessed March 4, 2010).

22. Jennifer Martin, "From Cow Pies to Cow Pots: A Creative Way to Manage Farm Waste," Cooperative State Research, Education, and Extension Service, July 17, 2007, **http://www.csrees.usda.gov/ newsroom/research/2007/cowpots.html** (accessed March 16, 2010).

23. Jena McGregor, "Second Acts: Trading Textbooks for Triple Crème," *Fortune,* February 19, 2010, **http://money. cnn.com/2010/02/18/news/companies/ fifth_town_cheese.fortune** (accessed March 16, 2010).

24. "Keep an Eye on These: Greentech Media's Top 50 Cleantech Startups," *eBoom,* March 8, 2010, **http://www. energyboom.com/emerging/keep- eye-these-greentech-medias-top-50- cleantech-startups** (accessed March 9, 2010).

25. Thomas W. Zimmerer and Norman M. Scarborough, *Essentials of Entrepreneurship and Small Business Management,* 6th ed. (Upper Saddle River, NJ: Pearson Prentice Hall, 2005), pp. 118–24.

26. Ibid.

27. "Dow, Algenol to Build Pilot Algae-Based Biorefinery," cleantech group, LLC, June 29, 2009, **http:// cleantech.com/news/4648/dow- algenol-build-pilot-algae-based** (accessed March 4, 2010); Timothy B. Wheeler, "Researchers in a Baltimore Lab Work to Tap the Energy Potential of a Bacterium," *The Baltimore Sun,* May 8, 2009, **http://www.baltimoresun. com/news/maryland/baltimore-city/ bal-te.md.algae08may08,0,2228536. story** (accessed March 4, 2010); **algenolbiofuels.com** (accessed March 4, 2010).

28. "Media Fact Sheet," SCORE, **http:// www.score.org/media_fact_sheet.html** (accessed March 16, 2010).

29. Adapted from "Tomorrow's Entrepreneur," *Inc. State of Small Business,* 23, no. 7 (2001), pp. 80–104.

30. Nanci Hellmich, "Baby Boomers by the Numbers: Census Reveals Trends," *USA Today,* November 10, 2009, **http:// www.usatoday.com/news/nation/**

census/2009-11-10-topblline10_ST_N. htm (accessed March 9, 2010).

31. Molly Smith, "Managing Generation Y as They Change the Workforce," *Reuters,* January 8, 2008, **http://www. reuters.com/article/pressRelease/ idUS129795+08-Jan-2008+BW20080108** (accessed March 16, 2010).

32. Jeffrey Passal and D'Vera Cohn, "Immigration to Play Lead Role in Future U.S. Growth," Pew Research, February 11, 2008, **http://pewresearch.org/pubs/729/ united-states-population-projections** (accessed March 16, 2010).

33. Daniel McGinn, "How I Did It: Arianna Huffington," *Inc.* February 10, 2010, p. 65, **http://www.inc.com/ magazine/20100201/how-i-did-it- arianna-huffington.html** (accessed March 16, 2010).

34. Gifford Pinchott III, *Intrapreneuring* (New York: Harper & Row, 1985), p. 34.

35. Paul Brown, "How to Cope with Hard Times," *The New York Times,* June 10, 2008, **http://www. nytimes.com/2008/06/10/business/ smallbusiness/10toolkit.html?_r=1& ref=smallbusiness&oref=slogin** (accessed March 10, 2010).

36. Adapted from Carol Kinsey Gorman, *Creativity in Business: A Practical Guide for Creative Thinking,* Crisp Publications Inc., 1989, pp. 5–6. © Crisp Publications Inc., 1200 Hamilton Court, Menlo Park, CA 94025.

37. video; **www.sonicdrivein.com** (accessed April 25, 2010); "Sonic Drive In Restaurant," Entrepreneur, 2010, **www.entrepreneur.com/franchises/ sonicdriveinrestaurants/282811-0. html** (accessed April 27, 2010); "Strictly Speaking," Sonic website, **http://www. sonicdrivein.com/business/franchise/ faq.jsp** (accessed May 6, 2010).

Chapter 6

1. Heidi Evans, "Ursula Burns to Head Xerox, Will Be the First Black Woman to Be CEO for Fortune 500 Company," nydailynews.com, May 23, 2009, **http://www.nydailynews.com/ money/2009/05/23/2009-05-23_1st_ black_woman_xerox_ceo.html** (accessed February 25, 2010); Jenny A. DiColo, "With Ursula Burns As CEO, Xerox Gets Tough Operator," *Dow Jones Newswire,* May 21, 2009, **http://www.nasdaq.com/aspx/stock- market-news-story.aspx?storyid=200905**

211629dowjonesdjonline000817&title=
with-ursula-burns-as-ceoxerox-gets-
tough-operator (accessed February 25,
2010); Nanette Byrnes and Roger O.
Crockett, "An Historic Succession at Xerox,"
BusinessWeek, June 8, 2009, pp. 18–22.

2. "Ford Fiesta," *Automobile,* April 2010,
p. 14.

3. "Letter to Stakeholders," General
Electric Ecomagination, **http://
ge.ecomagination.com/annual-reports/
letter-to-stakeholders.html** (accessed
March 9, 2010).

4. Jim Swift, "Austin Man Launches
Unique Limousine," *Austin News,* kxan.
com, June 16, 2009, **www.kxan.com/
dpp/news/local/Austin_man_launches_
unique_limousine** (accessed February 25,
2010); mobilejets.com (accessed February
25, 2010).

5. "Celestial Difference,"
Celestial Seasonings, **http://www.
celestialseasonings.ca/en/index.php/
celestial** (accessed March 8, 2010).

6. "Points of Light Institute Honors
Corporate America's Renewed Call to
Service," June 24, 2009, **http://www.
pointsoflight.org/press-releases/
points-light-institute-honors-corporate-
america%E2%80%99s-renewed-call-
service** (accessed February 25, 2010).

7. G. Tomas, M. Hult, David W. Cravens,
and Jagdish Sheth, "Competitive
Advantage in the Global Marketplace: A
Focus on Marketing Strategy," *Journal of
Business Research* 51 (January 2001), p. 1.

8. Jordan Zimmerman, "Plenty of Time
to Catch Up on His Sleep—When He
Dies," *Inc.,* March 2010, p. 69.

9. Telis Demos, "Bag Revolution,"
Fortune, May 12, 2008, p. 18.

10. Bill Vlasic, "Toyota's Slow
Awakening to a Deadly Problem,"
The New York Times, January
31, 2010. **http://www.nytimes.
com/2010/02/01/business/01toyota.
html?pagewanted=1&hpw** (accessed
March 2, 2010).

11. Stanley Reed, "Media Giant or Media
Muddle," *BusinessWeek,* May 12, 2008,
p. 47.

12. John Barfield, "Staffing Up for
Growth," *Fortune,* May 5, 2008, p. S10.

13. "Labor Force Statistics from the
Current Population Survey," Bureau of
Labor Statistics, **http://data.bls.gov/PDQ/
servlet/SurveyOutputServlet?series_**

id=LNS14000000 (accessed March 2,
2010).

14. "The Big Picture," *BusinessWeek,* July
16, 2001, p. 12.

15. Adam Lashinsky, "The Decade of
Steve," *Fortune,* November 23, 2009, pp.
92–100.

16. "About the IAPP," International
Association of Privacy Professionals,
**https://www.privacyassociation.org/
about_iapp/** (accessed March 12, 2010).

17. "Women CEOs," *Fortune* 500
2009, *Fortune,* **http://money.cnn.com/
magazines/fortune/fortune500/2009/
womenceos** (accessed March 4, 2010).

18. Joe Bel Bruno and Jessica Papini,
Morgan Stanley's Gorman: No Bonus,
but $9 Million Package, *The Wall Street
Journal,* January 23, 2010, **http://online.
wsj.com/article/SB100014240527487
0382240457501965017353
2966.html**
(accessed March 4, 2010).

19. Annie Finnigan, "Different Strokes,"
Working Woman, April 2001, p. 44.

20. W. Garrison Jackson, "Multicultural
Advertising," *Fortune,* May 5, 2008, p. S23.

21. Kim Reynolds, "Spark Versus
Ignition: In Which the Tiny Electric Car
Company from San Carlos, California,
Takes on What May Be Zuffenhausen's
Best Open Sports Car Ever. It Wins to 60
mph," *Motor Trend,* February 2010, pp.
40–48.

22. David Welch, "GM's Good News: A
$3 Billion Loss," *BusinessWeek,* May 12,
2008, p. O31.

23. " Chevy Volt FAQs," GM-Volt.com,
http://gm-volt.com/chevy-volt-faqs
(accessed March 11, 2010).

24. Google Management," **http://www.
google.com/intl/en/corporate/execs.
html** (accessed March 4, 2010); "The
Engineer's Life at Google," **http://www.
google.com/intl/en/jobs/lifeatgoogle/
englife** (accessed March 4, 2010).

25. "World's Most Admired Companies
2009," *Fortune,* **http://money.cnn.com/
magazines/fortune/mostadmired/2009/
snapshots/2184.html** (accessed February
25, 2010); Reena Jana, "Nike Quietly
Goes Green," *BusinessWeek,* June 11,
2009, **http://www.businessweek.
com/magazine/content/09_25/
b4136056155092.htm** (accessed February
25, 2010); "Nike Outlines Global
Strategy for Creating a More Sustainable
Business," January 22, ,2010, **http://www.**

nikebiz.com/media/pr/2010/01/22_
FY070809CRReport.html** (accessed
February 25, 2010).

26. "Bank of America Assumes
$16.6B in Countrywide Debt," *Dayton
Business Journal,* November 10, 2008,
**http://www.bizjournals.com/dayton/
stories/2008/11/10/daily7.html** (accessed
February 25, 2010); Carl Gutierrez,
"Countrywide's New Bad News," *Forbes,*
March 10, 2008, **http://www.forbes.
com/markets/2008/03/10/countrywide-
fbi-mortgage-markets-equity-cx_
cg_0310markets26.html** (accessed
February 25, 2010); "Judge Rules Mozilo
and Countrywide Execs Must Face
Multi-Million Dollar Federal Lawsuit,"
The New York Times, May 22, 2008,
**http://www.nytimes.com/2008/03/07/
business/07cnd-pay.html?_
r=1&oref=slogin** (accessed February 25,
2010); Maria Bartiromo, "Countrywide
Feels the Heat," *BusinessWeek,* August
29, 2007, **http://www.businessweek.
com/bwdaily/dnflash/content/aug2007/
db20070829_117563.htm?chan=search**
(accessed February 25, 2010); Eric Lipton,
"Ex-Leaders of Countrywide Profit
From Bad Loans," *The New York Times,*
March 3, 2009, **http://www.nytimes.
com/2009/03/04/business/04penny.html**
(accessed February 25, 2010).

27. Kerrie Unsworth, "Unpacking
Creativity," *Academy of Management
Review,* 26 (April 2001), pp. 289–97.

28. Pallavi Gogoi, "A Bittersweet Deal for
Wrigley," *BusinessWeek,* May 12, 2008, p.
O34.

29. *Harvard Business Review,* 60
(November–December 1982), p. 160.

30. Kris Maher, "The Jungle," *The Wall
Street Journal,* May 29, 2001, p. B16.

31. "The Passion to Perform," The
Nierenberg Group, **http://www.
selfmarketing.com/about.html** (accessed
March 11, 2010).

32. "Salary After Taxes," *Employment
Spot,* **http://www.employmentspot.com/
employment-articles/salary-after-taxes**
(accessed March 9, 2010).

33. Ibid.

34. Leslie Berlin, "Try, Try Again, or
Maybe Not," *The New York Times,* March
21, 2009, **www.nytimes.com/2009/03/22/
business/22proto.html** (accessed April
29, 2010); Bambi Francisco Roizen,
"Mark Pincus' lessons from Tribe-fail
fast," *vatornews,* April 27, 2009, **http://**

vator.tv/news/show/2009-04-27-mark-pincus-lessons-from-tribe-fail-fast (accessed May 1, 2010); Peter Burrows, "Apple's Endlessly Expanding Universe," *Bloomberg BusinessWeek,* April 26–May 2, 2010, pp. 92-99; Douglas MacMillan, "Zynga and Facebook. It's Complicated," *Bloomberg BusinessWeek,* April 26–May 2, 2010, pp. 47–48.

Chapter 7

1.   Quentin Hardy, "Carol Bartz," *Forbes,* September 7, 2009, pp. 84–88; Brian Womack, "Yahoo Opens Its Checkbook," *Bloomberg BusinessWeek,* January 25, 2010, p. 55; Associated Press, "On The Call: Yahoo CEO Carol Bartz," January 26, 2010, **http://news.yahoo.com/s/ap/20100127/ap_on_hi_te/us_on_the_call_yahoo** (accessed February 3, 2010); Brian Womack, "Yahoo! CEO Carol Bartz Rates Her First Year a B-Minus," *BusinessWeek,* January 8, 2010, **www.businessweek.com/technology/content/jan2010/tc2010018_388422.htm** (accessed February 3, 2010).

2.   Mina Kimes, "What Admired Firms Don't Have in Common," *CNNMoney.com,* March 6, 2009, **http://money.cnn.com/2009/03/06/news/companies/hay.survey.fortune/index.htm** (accessed February 22, 2010).

3.   Kelly K. Spors, "Top Small Workplaces 2008," *The Wall Street Journal,* February 22, 2009, **http://online.wsj.com/article/SB122347733961315417.html** (accessed March 11, 2010); "ATA Engineering Named as One of San Diego's 100 Fastest Growing Companies," ATA Engineering, October 2, 2008, **http://www.ata-engineering.com/news/news20081002.html** (accessed March 11, 2010); "This Year's Most Innovative Employee-Owned Companies Awarded in Chicago Last Week," The National Center for Employee Ownership and the Beyster Institute, **http://www.ata-engineering.com/news/Innovations_in_EO_Award_Winners_08_press_release.pdf** (accessed March 11, 2010); Michelle Strulzenberger, "Employee Ownership Results in Better Workplace for ATA Engineering Inc.," January 16, 2009, **http://www.axiomnews.ca/genarchives/456** (accessed March 11, 2010).

4.   Richard McGill Murphy, "Why Doing Good is Good for Business," *CNNMoney.com,* February 2, 2010, **http://money.cnn.com/2010/02/01/news/companies/dov_seidman_lrn.fortune/index.htm** (accessed February 22, 2010).

5.   "A New Future for Toms Shoes, Tweed Shire and Room to Read," Reputation Report, August 7, 2009, **http://www.reputationreport.com.au/2009/08/a-new-future-by-toms-shoes-tweed-shire-and-room-to-read/** (accessed March 9, 2010); "Our Movement," TOMS Shoes, **http://www.tomsshoes.com/content.asp?tid=271** (accessed March 9, 2010).

6.   Benjamin Fulford, "The Tortoise Jumps the Hare," *Forbes,* February 2, 2004, pp. 53–56.

7.   Gretchen Morgenson, "Inside the Countrywide Lending Spree," *The New York Times,* August 26, 2007, **http://www.nytimes.com/2007/08/26/business/yourmoney/26country.html** (accessed March 11, 2010).

8.   FSB 100, *CNNMoney.com,* **http://money.cnn.com/magazines/fsb/fsb100/2009/snapshots/72.html** (accessed March 3, 2010).

9.   Adam Smith, *Wealth of Nations* (New York: Modern Library, 1937; originally published in 1776).

10.   "Profile: Campbell Soup Company (CPB)," *Reuters,* **http://www.reuters.com/finance/stocks/companyProfile?symbol=CPB** (accessed March 3, 2010).

11.   "Al Dente Pasta Co.," **http://www.goodlifer.com/2009/09/al-dente-pasta-co** (accessed March 11, 2010); **http://www.aldentepasta.com** (accessed March 11, 2010); "Marcella Hazan," HarperCollins, **http://www.harpercollins.com/authors/4331/Marcella_Hazan/index.aspx** (accessed March 11, 2010).

12.   "Italy Critics Trash McDonald's Nationalist Food Bid," **http://af.reuters.com/article/oddlyEnoughNews/idAFTRE6143I720100205** (accessed February 11, 2010).

13.   "Why Work Here?" **http://www.wholefoodsmarket.com/careers/workhere.php** (accessed March 3, 2010).

14.   "PepsiCo Unveils New Organizational Structure, Names CEOs of Three Principle Operating Units," PepsiCo Media, November 5, 2007, **http://www.pepsico.com/PressRelease/PepsiCo-Unveils-New-Organizational-Structure-Names.html** (accessed May 19, 2010).

15.   Jon R. Katzenbach and Douglas K. Smith, "The Discipline of Teams," *Harvard Business Review* 71 (March–April 1993), 19.

16.   Ibid.

17.   Leah Buchanan, "When Absence Makes the Team Grow Stronger," *Inc.,* June 2008, p. 40.

18.   "How to Build a (Strong) Virtual Team," *CNNMoney.com,* **http://money.cnn.com/2009/11/19/news/companies/ibm_virtual_manager.fortune/index.htm** (accessed February 11, 2010).

19.   "Toyota Motor Corporation President Akio Toyoda Announces Global Quality Task Force," February 5, **http://money.cnn.com/news/newsfeeds/articles/globenewswire/183685.htm** (accessed March 3, 2010).

20.   Jerry Useem, "What's That Spell? TEAMWORK," *Fortune,* June 12, 2006, p. 66.

21.   Jia Lynnyang, "The Power of Number 4.6," *Fortune,* June 12, 2006, p. 122.

22.   "Combining Creativity and Education," **http://sfs.wsu.edu/facultystaff/clark/FoodProdDevTeam.html** (accessed February 12, 2010).

23.   Richard S. Wellins, William C. Byham, and Jeanne M. Wilson, *Empowered Teams: Creating Self-Directed Work Groups That Improve Quality, Productivity, and Participation* (San Francisco: Jossey-Bass Publishers, 1991), p. 5.

24.   Matt Krumrie, "Are Meetings a Waste of Time? Survey Says Yes," *Minneapolis Workplace Examiner,* May 12, 2009, **http://www.examiner.com/x-2452-Minneapolis-Workplace-Examiner~y2009m5d12-Are-meetings-a-waste-of-time-Survey-says-yes** (accessed March 11, 2010).

25.   "Top 10 Ideas: Making the Most of Your Corporate Intranet," **http://www.claromentis.com/blog/2009/04/top-10-ideas-making-the-most-of-your-corporate-intranet** (accessed February 12, 2010).

26.   Kelly K. Spors, "Top Small Workplaces 2008," *The Wall Street Journal,* February 22, 2009, **http://online.wsj.com/article/SB122347733961315417.html** (accessed May 12, 2009); Richard Donovan, "Rainforest Alliance Launches TREES," Forest Stewardship Council, **www.fscus.org/news/index.**

php?article=169 (accessed May 29, 2009); "Rainforest Alliance," Wikipedia, **http://en.wikipedia.org/wiki/Rainforest_Alliance** (accessed May 29, 2009); **www.rainforest-alliance.org** (accessed May 28, 2009).

27. "Corporate America vs. Workers: Companies Do More with Fewer Employees," *NY Daily News,* November 5, 2009, **http://www.nydailynews.com/money/2009/11/05/2009-11-05_corporate_america_vs_workers_companies_do_more_with_fewer_employees.html** (accessed March 4, 2010).

28. Kim Komando, "Why You Need a Company Policy on Internet Use," **http://www.microsoft.com/smallbusiness/resources/management/employee-relations/why-you-need-a-company-policy-on-internet-use.aspx#Whyyouneedacompanypolicyoninternetuse** (accessed February 12, 2010).

29. Michael D. Maginn, *Effective Teamwork,* 1994, p. 10. © 1994 Richard D. Irwin, a Times Mirror Higher Education Group, Inc., company.

30. video; Jennifer Ludden, "The End of 9-To-5: When Work Time Is Anytime," npr, March 16, 2010, **www.npr.org/templates/story/story.php?storyId=124705801** (accessed April 29, 2010); Patrick J. Kiger, "Throwing Out the Rules of Work," Workforce Management, **www.workforce.com/section/09/feature/24/54/28** (accessed April 28, 2010); "Smashing the Clock," *BusinessWeek,* December 11, 2006, **http://www.businessweek.com/magazine/content/06_50/b4013001.htm** (accessed May 1, 2010).

Chapter 8

1. "What the World's Biggest Carmaker Can Learn from Other Corporate Turnarounds," *The Economist,* December 12, 2009, p. 11; Phil LeBeau, "Toyota Issues a 2nd Recall," *The New York Times,* January 21, 2010, **http://www.nytimes.com/2010/01/22/business/22toyota.html** (accessed February 24, 2010); "Toyota Motor Corporation," *The New York Times,* February 3, 2010, **http://topics.nytimes.com/top/news/business/companies/toyota_motor_corporation/index.html** (accessed February 24, 2010); Hiroko Tabuchi and Nick Bunkley, "Toyota Announces Steps to Restore Confidence

on Safety," February 17, 2010, **http://www.nytimes.com/2010/02/18/business/global/18recall.html** (accessed February 24, 2010); "Toyota May Recall Corolla After U.S. Investigation (Update 3)", February 18, 2010, **http://www.businessweek.com/news/2010-02-18/toyota-may-recall-corolla-after-u-s-investigation-update2-.html** (accessed February 24, 2010); Daisuke Wakabayashi, "Adherents Defend the Toyota 'Way,'" February 24, 2010, **http://online.wsj.com/article/SB10001424052748703510204575084840073648572.html?mod=WSJ_latestheadlines** (accessed February 24, 2010).

2. Adam Kuban, "Domino's Online Ordering Show You Your Pizza as You Build It," *Serious Eats,* December 11, 2008, **http://slice.seriouseats.com/archives/2008/12/dominos-online-ordering-shows-you-your-pizza-as-you-build-it.html** (accessed March 5, 2010); Julie Jargon, "Domino's IT Staff Delivers Slick Site, Ordering System," *The Wall Street Journal,* November 24, 2009, **http://online.wsj.com/article/SB10001424052748704779704574552080042033284.html** (accessed March 5, 2010).

3. Rina Rapuano, "Check Please!," *The Washingtonian Blog,* February 18, 2010, **http://www.washingtonian.com/blogarticles/restaurants/bestbites/15008.html** (accessed February 23, 2010).

4. Leonard L. Berry, *Discovering the Soul of Service* (New York: The Free Press, 1999), pp. 86–96.

5. Valerie A. Zeithaml and Mary Jo Bitner, *Services Marketing,* 3rd ed. (Boston: McGraw-Hill Irwin, 2003), pp. 3, 22.

6. Bernard Wysocki Jr., "To Fix Health Care, Hospitals Take Tips from the Factory Floor," *The Wall Street Journal,* April 9, 2004, via **http://www.chcanys.org/clientuploads/downloads/Clinical_resources/Leadership%20Articles/LeanThinking_ACF28EB.pdf** (accessed March 5, 2010).

7. "Success Story," Google AdWords, **https://www.google.com/intl/en_us/adwords/select/success/cordarounds.html** (accessed February 23, 2010).

8. Faith Keenan, "Opening the Spigot," *BusinessWeek* e.biz, June 4, 2001, **www.businessweek.com/magazine/content/01_23/b3735616.htm** (accessed March 5, 2010).

9. David Kaplan, "The Right Place at the Table," *Houston Chronicle,* June 21, 2009, pp. D1; **http://investing.businessweek.com/research/stocks/private/snapshot.asp?priveapId=29487238** (accessed February 23, 2010); **www.igniterestaurantgroup.com** (accessed February 23, 2010).

10. Ryan Underwood, "Dear Customer . . . Managing E-mail Campaigns," *Inc.,* March 2008, p. 59.

11. "Fun Facts," Hershey (n.d.), **http://www.hersheys.com/kisses/about/index.asp?contentid=3** (accessed February 16, 2010).

12. "Environmental Stewardship," PNM, **http://www.pnm.com/environment/home.htm** (accessed February 23, 2010); "Climate Change: PNM's Position," PNM, **http://www.pnm.com/climate/position.htm** (accessed February 23, 2010).

13. "Top 10 Solar Friendly States," *Cooler Planet,* **http://solar.coolerplanet.com/Articles/top-10-solar-friendly-states.aspx** (accessed February 23, 2010).

14. "Shopping for Subsidies: How Wal-Mart Uses Taxpayer Money to Finance its Never-Ending Growth," *Good Jobs First,* May 2004, **http://www.goodjobsfirst.org/pdf/wmtstudy.pdf** (accessed March 5, 2010).

15. "North American Robot Orders Fall 25% in 2009 But Positive Signs Emerge in Fourth Quarter," *Robotics News,* February 8, 2010, **http://www.robotics.org/content-detail.cfm/Industrial-Robotics-News/North-American-Robot-Orders-Fall-25-in-2009-But-Positive-Signs-Emerge-in-Fourth-Quarter/content_id/1990** (accessed February 23, 2010).

16. Gina Kolata, "Results Unproven, Robotic Surgery Wins Converts," *The New York Times,* February 13, 2010, **http://www.nytimes.com/2010/02/14/health/14robot.html?pagewanted=1** (accessed February 16, 2010).

17. "Sustainability," Walmart, **http://walmartstores.com/sustainability** (accessed February 16, 2010).

18. Bryan Walsh, "Why Green Is the New Red, White and Blue," *Time,* April 28, 2008, p. 53.

19. "Introducing Chevrolet Volt," Chevrolet, **http://www.chevrolet.com/pages/open/default/future/volt.do** (accessed February 16, 2010).

20. Megan Kamerick, "How To Go Green," *New Mexico Business Weekly,* May 23–29, 2008, p. 3.

21. O. C. Ferrell and Michael D. Hartline, *Marketing Strategy* (Mason, OH: South-Western, 2011), p. 215.

22. John Edwards, "Orange Seeks Agent," *Inbound Logistics,* January 2006, pp. 239–242.

23. Ferrell and Hartline, *Marketing Strategy,* p. 215.

24. Bob Daniell, John Tracy, and Simon Kaye, "Made in China: Perspectives on the Global Manufacturing Giant," *Inbound Logistics,* March 2008, pp. 46–49.

25. Marc Gunther, "Best Buy Wants Your Junk," *Fortune,* December 7, 2009, pp. 96–99; Best Buy, **www.bestbuy.com** (accessed February 12, 2010); "Best Buy Ramps Up Recycling," "Wastes—Information Resources," Environmental Protection Agency, **http://www.epa.gov/ osw/inforesources/news/2009news/03-bestbuy.htm** (accessed February 24, 2010)

26. Susan Carey, "Airlines Play Up Improvements in On-Time Performance," *The Wall Street Journal,* February 10, 2010, p. B6.

27. "2009 Award Recipients and Keynote Speakers," **http://www.baldrige.nist.gov/ QEXXII/Award_Recipients_Keynotes. htm** (accessed February 16, 2010).

28. Christopher Lawton, "The War on Product Returns," *The Wall Street Journal,* May 8, 2008, p. D1.

29. Philip B. Crosby, *Quality Is Free: The Art of Making Quality Certain* (New York: McGraw-Hill, 1979), pp. 9–10.

30. Nigel F. Piercy, *Market-Led Strategic Change* (Newton, MA: Butterworth-Heinemann, 1992), pp. 374–385.

31. "Compuware Gomez Introduces Free Web Performance Benchmarking Tool," *CNN Money,* February 16, 2010, **http://money.cnn.com/news/newsfeeds/ articles/globenewswire/184336.htm** (accessed February 23, 2010).

32. "Employment Opportunities," Careers in Supply Chain Management, **http:// www.careersinsupplychain.org/career-outlook/empopp.asp** (accessed March 5, 2010).

33. James Wetherbe, "Principles of Cycle Time Reduction," *Cycle Time Research,* 1995, p. iv.

34. Stan Davis and Christopher Meyer, *Blur: The Speed of Change in*

the Connected Economy (Reading, MA: Addison-Wesley, 1998), p. 5.

35. video; **www.craftbeer.com** (accessed May 3, 2010); "Craft Brewer Defined," **http://www.brewersassociation.org/ pages/business-tools/craft-brewing-statistics/craft-brewer-defined** (accessed May 4, 2010); **http://www. captainlawrencebrewing.com/** (accessed May 4, 2010); **http://www.newbelgium. com/** (accessed May 5, 2010).

Chapter 9

1. Kelly K. Spors, "Top Small Workplaces 2008," *The Wall Street Journal,* February 22, 2009, **http://online.wsj.com/article/ SB122347733961315417.html** (accessed March 12, 2010); Kurt Begalka, J.A. Frate, **www.jafrate.com** (accessed March 12, 2010).

2. Dan Heath and Chip Heath, "Business Advice from Van Halen," *Fast Company,* March 1, 2010, **http://www.fastcompany. com/magazine/143/made-to-stick-the-telltale-brown-mampm.html,** accessed March 11, 2010.

3. "100 Best Companies to Work For 2010," *Fortune,* **http://money.cnn.com/ magazines/fortune/bestcompanies/2010/ snapshots/4.html** (accessed February 18, 2010); "Benefits," Google Jobs, **http:// www.google.com/support/jobs/bin/ static.py?page=benefits.html** (accessed February 18, 2010).

4. "How Much Does Absenteeism Cost Your Business," Success Performance Solutions, December 10, 2008, **http://www.super-solutions.com/ CostofAbsenteeism.asp,** accessed march 11, 2010.

5. "Careers," Nikebiz.com, **http://www. nikebiz.com/careers/benefits/other/ whq_campus.html** (accessed February 9, 2010).

6. Spors, "Top Small Workplaces 2008"; "Organic Pioneers to Receive Organic Trade Association's Highest Honor, the Organic Leadership Award," Organic Trade Association, May 11, 2009, **http:// www.lundberg.com/_documents/ releases/Organic%20Pioneers%20to%20 Receive%20OTA2009%20Organic%20 Leadership%20Award%20%20-%20 final.pdf** (accessed June 15, 2009); **www.lundberg.com** (accessed May 28, 2009); Steve Lawrence, "Growing Number of Calif. Ag Businesses Go Solar," SFGate.com, December 5, 2008,

http://sfgate.com/cgi-bin/article.cgi?f=/ n/a/2008/12/05/financial/f164526S76. DTL (accessed May 28, 2009).

7. "Top 10 Highest Paid Execs," **http:// money.cnn.com/galleries/2009/ news/0910/gallery.highest_paid_ceos/ index.html** (accessed February 9, 2010).

8. "L.L. Bean Named #1 in NRF Foundation Customer Service Survey," L.L. Bean News, February 21, 2008, **http:// www.llbean.com/customerService/ aboutLLBean/newsroom/ stories/02212008_LLBean_News.html,** accessed March 12, 2010.

9. Douglas McGregor, *The Human Side of Enterprise* (New York: McGraw-Hill, 1960), pp. 33–34.

10. Richard Siklos, "Sony: Lost in Transformation," *Fortune,* July 6, 2009, pp. 69-74; Yuri Kageyama, "Sony Struggling as Walkman Hits 30th Anniversary," *ABC News,* July 1, 2009, **http://abcnews.go.com/Technology/ GadgetGuide/wireStory?id=7974904** (accessed February 23, 2010); Hiroko Tabuchi, "Sony Chief Takes Over Company's Presidency," *The New York Times,* February 27, 2009, **www. nytimes.com/2009/02/28/technology/ companies/28sony.html?_r=1** (accessed February 23, 2010).

11. McGregor, *The Human Side of Enterprise.*

12. Jon L. Pierce, Tatiana Kostova, and Kurt T. Kirks, "Toward a Theory of Psychological Ownership in Organizations, *Academy of Management Review* 26, no. 2 (2001), p. 298.

13. "2009 National Business Ethics Survey: Ethics in the Recession," Ethics Resource Center, p. 33.

14. Archie Carroll, "Carroll: Do We Live in a Cheating Culture?" *Athens Banner-Herald,* February 21, 2004, **www. onlineathens.com/stories/022204/ bus_20040222028.shtml,** accessed March 12, 2010.

15. Geoff Colvin, "How Top Companies Breed Stars," September 20, 2007, **http:// money.cnn.com/magazines/fortune/ fortune_archive/2007/10/01/100351829/ index.htm** (accessed March 12, 2010).

16. My Guides USA.com, "Which Jobs Offer Flexible Work Schedules?" **http:// jobs.myguidesusa.com/answers-to-my-questions/which-jobs-offer-flexible-work-schedules?/** (accessed March 12, 2010).

17. Robert Preidt, "Workplace Flexibility Can Boost Healthy Behaviors," Wake Forest University Baptist Medical Center, news release, December 10, 2007, via **http://yourtotalhealth.ivillage.com/workplace-flexibility-can-boost-healthy-behaviors.html** (accessed March 12, 2010).

18. My Guides USA.com, "Which Jobs Offer Flexible Work Schedules?"

19. "Telework Revs Up as More Employers Offer Work Flexibility," *WorldatWork,* February 17, 2009, **http://www.workingfromanywhere.org/news/pr021609.html** (accessed February 9, 2010).

20. "Telecommuting Benefits," **www.telecommutect.com/content/benefits.htm** (accessed March 12, 2010).

21. "HR Executives Split on Telecommuting," *USA Today,* March 1, 2006, p. B1.

22. Hudson Valley Fresh, **http://www.hudsonvalleyfresh.com/,** accessed March 12, 2010; Peter APplebome, "To Survive, Dairy Farmers Go Coop," *The New York Times,* February 8, 2010, **http://www.nytimes.com/2010/02/08/nyregion/08towns.html?ref=smallbusiness** (accessed March 12, 2010).

23. "Best Places For Business and Careers," *Forbes,* March 25, 2009, **http://www.forbes.com/lists/2009/1/bizplaces09_Best-Places-For-Business-And-Careers_Rank.html** (accessed February 23, 2010).

24. video; "Microsoft Corporate Citizenship," "Employee Programs," **http://www.microsoft.com/about/corporatecitizenship/en-us/our-actions/in-the-community/employee-programs.aspx** (accessed May 1, 2010); "VoluntEARS Efforts Around the World," **http://disney.go.com/disneyhand/voluntears/details.html** (accessed May 1, 2010); Eve Lopez, "How to Implement a Corporate Volunteer Program," suite101, April 5, 2010, **http://social-corporate-responsibility.suite101.com/article.cfm/how-to-implement-a-corporate-volunteer-program** (accessed May 2, 2010); **www.pointsoflight.org** (accessed May 2, 2010); **www.newyorkcares.org** (accessed May 2, 2010).

Chapter 10

1. Douglas MacMillan, "How Four Rookie CEOs Handled the Great Recession," and "Yammering is Good,"

BusinessWeek, March 1, 2010, pp. 37–38; Molson Coors, **http://www.molsoncoors.com** (accessed February 25, 2010).

2. Phil Izzo, "Economists Expecting Shifting Work Force," *The Wall Street Journal,* February 11, 2010, **http://online.wsj.com/article/SB10001424052748703382904575059424289353714.html?KEYWORDS=companies+hiring** (accessed March 16, 2010).

3. Procter & Gamble Recruiting Process, **http://www.pg.com/jobs/recruitblue/recprocess.shtml** (accessed March 13, 2010).

4. Burgerville, **http://www.burgerville.com** (accessed October 28, 2009); Sarah E. Needleman, "Burger Chain's Health-Care Recipe," *The Wall Street Journal,* August 31, 2009, **http://online.wsj.com/article/SB125149100886467705.html** (accessed September 1, 2009).

5. "Job Opportunities," *Borders,* **https://wss6a.unicru.com/hirepro/C406/applicant.jsp?Eurl=4%2Fhirepro%2FC406%2Fapplicant.jsp%3FSite%3D-3%26C%3D406%26k%3Dno%26content%3Dsearch%26Lang%3Den&Site=100585&C=406&k=no&content=start&Lang=en** (accessed March 9, 2010).

6. "What Does Employee Alcohol & Drug Use Cost Your Business," DWI Resource Center, **http://www.dwiresourcecenter.org/bizcenter/workplace/cost.shtml** (accessed March 16, 2010).

7. Associated Press, "Food Network Chef Fired After Resume Fraud," *USA Today,* March 3, 2008 **http://www.usatoday.com/news/nation/2008-03-03-chef-fired_N.htm** (accessed March 16, 2010).

8. Christopher T. Marquet and Lisa J.B. Peterson, "Résumé Fraud: The Top Ten Lies," Marquet International, Ltd., **http://www.marquetinternational.com/pdf/Resume%20Fraud-Top%20Ten%20Lies.pdf** (accessed March 9, 2010).

9. "Job Bias Charges Approach Record High in Fiscal Year 2009, EEOC Reports," U.S. Equal Employment Opportunity Commission, January 6, 2010, **http://www.eeoc.gov/eeoc/newsroom/release/1-6-10.cfm** (accessed March 9, 2010).

10. Joseph Daniel McCool, "Diversity Picture Rings Hollow," *BusinessWeek,* February 5, 2008, **http://www.businessweek.com/managing/content/feb2008/ca2008025_080192.htm?chan=search** (accessed March 16, 2010).

11. "America's Changing Workforce: Recession Turns a Graying Office Grayer," Pew Research Center: A Social and Demographic Trends Report, September 3, 2009, **http://pewsocialtrends.org/assets/pdf/americas-changing-workforce.pdf** (accessed March 8, 2010).

12. Stephen Bastien, "12 Benefits of Hiring Older Workers," *Entrepreneur.com,* September 20, 2006, **http://www.entrepreneur.com/humanresources/hiring/article167500.html** (accessed March 17, 2010).

13. Catherine Rampell, "The Gender Wage Gap, Around the World," March 9, 2010, **http://economix.blogs.nytimes.com/2010/03/09/the-gender-wage-gap-around-the-world** (accessed March 13, 2010).

14. Sue Shellenbarger, "New Workplace Equalizer: Ambition," *The Wall Street Journal,* March 25, 2009, **http://online.wsj.com/article/SB123801512551141207.html** (accessed March 8, 2010).

15. "Our Curriculum," Hamburger University, **http://www.aboutmcdonalds.com/mcd/careers/hamburger_university/our_curriculum.html** (accessed March 9, 2010).

16. Doug Stewart, "Employee-Appraisal Software," *Inc.,* **http://www.inc.com/magazine/19940615/3288_pagen_2.html** (accessed March 10, 2010).

17. Maury A. Peiperl, "Getting 360-Degree Feedback Right," *Harvard Business Review,* January 2001, pp. 142–48.

18. Chris Musselwhite, "Self Awareness and the Effective Leader," *Inc.com,* **http://www.inc.com/resources/leadership/articles/20071001/musselwhite.html** (accessed March 16, 2010).

19. Laura Lorber, "A Corporate Culture Makeover," *The Wall Street Journal,* April 15, 2008, **http://online.wsj.com/article/SB120827656392416609.html** (accessed March 16, 2010).

20. Marcia Zidle, "Employee Turnover: Seven Reasons Why People Quit Their Jobs," **http://ezinearticles.com/?Employee-Turnover:-Seven-Reasons-Why-People-Quit-Their-Jobs&id=42531** (accessed March 16, 2010).

21. "GM, Chrysler to Cut 50,000 Jobs," *CBC News,* February 17, 2009, **http://www.cbc.ca/money/story/2009/02/17/**

carbailout.html (accessed March 10, 2010); "2009 Chrysler Will Shed 789 Dealers," **http://www.carpictures. com/vehicle/09EDD063625060.html** (accessed March 10, 2010).

22. Kelly K. Spors, "Top Small Workplaces 2008," *The Wall Street Journal,* February 22, 2009, **http://online.wsj.com/ article/SB122347733961315417.html** (accessed March 16, 2010); **http://www. kingarthurflour.com** (accessed March 16, 2010); "King Arthur Flour Leads the Way with B-Corp Logo," CSRwire, February 15, 2008, **http://www.csrwire.com/press/ press_release/14672-King-Arthur-Flour-Leads-the-Way-with-B-Corp-Logo** (accessed March 16, 2010); "2009 Best Places to Work in Vermont," **http:// bestplacestoworkinvt.com/ index.php?option=com_content&task= view&id=39** (accessed March 16, 2010); "George Washington," About the White House: Presidents, **http://www. whitehouse.gov/about/presidents/ georgewashington** (accessed June 24, 2009).

23. "Wage and Hour Division (WHD)," U.S. Department of Labor, **http://www. dol.gov/whd/flsa/index.htm** (accessed March 10, 2010).

24. Associated Press, "Santa Fe Not Likely to Raise Minimum Wage," kvia. com, December 22, 2009, **http://www. kvia.com/global/story.asp?s=11716158** (accessed March 10, 2010).

25. "Kele & Co: First Innovative Jewelry Company in Direct Sales," May 5, 2008, **http://www.pressreleasepoint.com/ kele-amp-co-first-innovative-jewelry-company-direct-sales** (accessed March 16, 2010).

26. Corey Rosen, "Five of Fifteen Top Small Workplaces in 2009 Are Employee Ownership Companies," The National Center for Employee Ownership, October 1, 2009, **http:// www.nceo.org/main/column.php/ id/341** (accessed March 10, 2010); Chris Casacchia, "Employee-Owned Stock Outperforms Wall Street," *Phoenix Business Journal,* July 31, 2009, **http:// phoenix.bizjournals.com/phoenix/ stories/2009/08/03/story2.html** (accessed March 10, 2010).

27. "Employer Costs for Employee Compensation," U.S. Bureau of Labor Statistics, March 10, 2010, **http://www.bls. gov/news.release/ecec.nr0.htm** (accessed March 16, 2010).

28. Jamie Page, "Pensacola City Employees' Benefits Cut," *Pensacola News Journal,* March 17, 2010, **http:// www.pnj.com/article/20100317/ NEWS01/3170329/1006/news01/ Pensacola-city-employees--benefits-cut** (accessed March 17, 2010).

29. John Schmitt, "The Unions of the States, Center for Economic and Policy Research," February 2010, **http://www. cepr.net/documents/publications/ unions-states-2010-02.pdf** (accessed March 10, 2010).

30. "Royal Mail and Union Reach Deal to End Postal Strikes," *guardian.co.uk,* March 8, 2010, **http://www.guardian. co.uk/uk/2010/mar/08/royal-mail-postal-strikes-deal** (accessed March 10, 2010); Stephen Bates, "Postal Strikes Drive Customers to Royal Mail's Rivals," **guardian.co.uk**, September 18, 2009, **http://www.guardian.co.uk/uk/2009/ sep/18/postal-strikes-royal-mail-rivals** (accessed March 10, 2010).

31. "Work Stoppages Summary," Bureau of Labor Statistics, February 10, 2010, **http://www.bls.gov/news.release/wkstp. nr0.htm** (accessed March 10, 2010).

32. Colin Barr, "Will Bonus Backlash Pay for Investors?" *CNNMoney.com,* January 15, 2010, **http://money.cnn. com/2010/01/15/news/companies/ bonuses.fortune/index.htm** (accessed March 5, 2010); Joe Bel Bruno and Jessica Papini, "Morgan Stanley's Gorman: No Bonus, but $9 Million Package," *The Wall Street Journal,* January 23, 2010, **http://online.wsj.com/ article/SB1000142405274870382404 575019650173532966.html** (accessed March 5, 2010); V.G. Narayanan, "Getting Executive Compensation Right," *BusinessWeek.com,* January 22, 2009, **http://www.businessweek.com/ print/managing/content/jun2009/ ca20090623_810874.htm** (accessed March 5, 2010).

33. National Population Projections 2010-2050, U.S. Census Bureau, released 2009, **http://www.census.gov/population/ www/projections/2009cnmsSumTabs. html** (accessed March 17, 2010).

34. Pamela Babcock, "Diversity Accountability Requires More Than Numbers," Society for Human Resource Management, April 13, 2009, **http:// www.shrm.org/hrdisciplines/Diversity/ Articles/Pages/MoreThanNumbers.aspx** (accessed March 10, 2010).

35. Taylor H. Cox Jr., "The Multicultural Organization," *Academy of Management Executives* 5 (May 1991), pp. 34–47; Marilyn Loden and Judy B. Rosener, *Workforce America! Managing Employee Diversity as a Vital Resource* (Homewood, IL: Business One Irwin, 1991).

36. video; "Best Places to Work 2009," crain's, **http://www.crainsnewyork.com/ apps/pbcs.dll/gallery?Site=CN&Date= 20091207&Category=GALLERIES&Art No4=120209998&Ref=PH&Params= Itemnr=31** (accessed May 2, 2010); John Tozzi, "The Case Against Vacation Policy," *BusinessWeek,* July 2, 2008, **http://www. businessweek.com/smallbiz/content/ jul2008/sb2008072_456680.htm** (accessed May 2, 2010).

Chapter II

1. Michelle Conlin, "Look Who's Stalking Wal-Mart," *BusinessWeek,* December 7, 2009, pp. 30–33; Ann Zimmerman, "Target Cooks Up Rebound Recipe in Grocery Aisles," *The Wall Street Journal,* May 12, 2009, p. B1; Andrew Ross Sorkin, "As It Battles Ackman and Wal-Mart, Target Pushes Basics," *The New York Times,* May 27, 2009, **http://dealbook. blogs.nytimes.com/2009/05/27/ as-it-battles-ackman-and-wal-mart-target-pushes-basics** (accessed March 25, 2010); Anthony Zumpano, "Target Changes Strategy, And Possibly Future of Supermarkets," *brandchannel,* January 22, 2010, **www.brandchannel.com/ home/post/2010/01/22/Target-Changes-Strategy-And-Possibly-Future-of-Supermarkets.aspx** (accessed March 25, 2010); Pallari Gogoi, "How Walmart Turned the Tide Against Archrival Target," *Daily Finance,* February 17, 2010, **http://www.dailyfinance.com/story/ in-epic-battle-of-discounters-wal-mart-is-winning-ad-war-with-t/19361004** (accessed March 25, 2010); Nicole Maestri, "Wal-Mart, Target Seek Big Returns in Small Store," *Reuters,* February 4, 2010, **http://www.reuters.com/article/ idUSTRE6134ZR20100204?type=small BusinessNews** (accessed March 25, 2010).

2. Adapted from Pride and O.C. Ferrell, "Value-Driven Marketing," *Foundations of Marketing,* 4th ed. (Mason, OH: South-Western Cengage Learning), pp. 13–14.

3. Jason Daley, "If It's Broke, Decorate It," *Entrepreneur,* July 2009, **www. entrepreneur.com/magazine/ entrepreneur/2009/july/202202.html**

(accessed March 25, 2010); **www.casttoos. com** (accessed March 25, 2010); Gladys Edmunds, "Tightrope: Look to life's daily details for great business ideas," *USA Today,* June 23, 2009, **www.usatoday. com/money/smallbusiness/columnist/ edmunds/2009-06-23-opportunity-is- all-around-you_N.htm** (accessed March 25, 2010).

4. Jaime Holguin, "McDonald's Scrapping 'Supersize,'" March 3, 2004, *CBSNews. com,* **http://www.cbsnews.com/ stories/2004/03/03/health/main603735. shtml** (accessed March 30, 2010).

5. Marguerite Higgins, "McDonald's Labels Nutrition," *The Washington Times,* October 26, 2005, **http://www. washingtontimes.com/news/2005/ oct/25/20051025-102731-2213r** (accessed March 30, 2010).

6. "McDonald's Fries Switched to Trans-Fat-Free Oil," *Associated Press,* May 22, 2008, **http://www.msnbc.msn.com/ id/24777284** (accessed March 30, 2010).

7. "Beauty Queen," *People,* May 10, 2004, p. 187.

8. Michael Treacy and Fred Wiersema, *The Discipline of Market Leaders* (Reading, MA: Addison Wesley, 1995), p. 176.

9. "2009 Form 10-K/A filed January 25, 2010," Apple Investor Relations, **http://phx.corporate-ir.net/phoenix. zhtml?c=107357&p=irol-index** (accessed March 25, 2010).

10. Venky Shankar, "Multiple Touch Point Marketing," American Marketing Association, Faculty Consortium on Electronic Commerce, Texas A&M University, July 14–17, 2001.

11. "Dell Targets Students with New Netbook," *Business Mirror,* June 29, 2009, **http://businessmirror. com.ph/index.php?option=com_ content&view=article&id=12418: dell-targets-students-with-new- netbook&catid=52: technology&Itemid=1** (accessed April 6, 2010).

12. "Key Facts about Women-Owned Businesses," Center for Women's Business Research, **http://www. womensbusinessresearchcenter.org/ research/keyfacts** (accessed March 30, 2010).

13. Laurel Wentz, "Olive Garden and Don Francisco Go to Tuscany," *Advertising Age,* March 25, 2010, **http://adage.com/ hispanic/article?article_id=142977** (accessed March 30, 2010).

14. Les Christie, "Census: U.S. Becoming More Diverse," *CNNMoney.com,* May 14, 2009, **http://money.cnn.com/2009/05/14/ real_estate/rising_minorities/index.htm** (accessed March 30, 2010).

15. Moon Ihlwan, "Samsung's Plan to Widen its Range," *BusinessWeek,* August 24 and 31, 2009, p. 30.

16. Charisse Jones, "Airlines Get Ready for Return of Elite Fliers," *USA Today,* March 16, 2010, p. 6B.

17. Sarah Kabourek & Kim Thai, "Barbie Gets a Makeover," *Fortune,* **http://money.cnn.com/galleries/2009/ fortune/0907/gallery.barbie_makeover. fortune.html** (accessed March 25, 2010); Aarthi Sivaraman, "Barbie at 50: Is Mattel's Star Still in Fashion?" *Reuters,* March 6, 2009, **http://www. reuters.com/article/lifestyleMolt/ idUSTRE52603B20090307** (accessed March 25, 2010); Jessica Michault, "Looking Half Her Age: Barbie at 50," *The New York Times,* January 5, 2009, **http://www.nytimes.com/2009/01/06/ style/06iht-fbarbie.1.19084850.html** (accessed March 25, 2010); Louisa Lim, "Mattel Hopes Shanghai is a Barbie World," *NPR,* March 6, 2009, **http:// www.npr.org/templates/story/story. php?storyId=101479810** (accessed March 25, 2010).

18. "The Coca-Cola Company Fact Sheet," **http://www.thecoca-cola company.com/ourcompany/pdf/ Company_Fact_Sheet.pdf** (accessed March 30, 2010).

19. Hannah Elliott, "Most Fuel-Efficient Cars For The Buck," *Forbes,* March 30, 2009, **http://www.forbes. com/2009/03/30/fuel-efficient-cars- lifestyle-vehicles-efficient-cars.html** (accessed March 30, 2010).

20. Valerie Bauerlein, "U.S. Soda Sales Fell at Slower Rate Last Year," *The Wall Street Journal,* March 25, 2010, **http:// online.wsj.com/article/SB100014240527 48704266504575141710213338560.html** (accessed April 8, 2010).

21. "MSPA North America," Mystery Shopping Providers Association, **http:// www.mysteryshop.org/index-na.php** (accessed April 1, 2010).

22. Mya Frazier, "CrowdSourcing" *Delta Sky Mag,* February 2010, via **http://msp. imirus.com/Mpowered/imirus.jsp? volume=ds10&issue=2&page=72** (accessed February 18, 2010), p. 73.

23. Ibid., p. 70.

24. Jack Neff, "P&G Embraces Facebook as Big Part of Its Marketing Plan," *Advertising Age,* January 25, 2010, **http:// adage.com/digital/article?article_ id=141733** (accessed February 18, 2010).

25. "A Special Report on Social Networking," *The Economist,* January 30, 2010, p. 13.

26. "The Seven Sins of Greenwashing," *Terrachoice,* **http://sinsofgreenwashing. org/findings/the-seven-sins** (accessed March 25, 2010); Matthew Knight, "It's Not Easy Being Green," *CNN,* July 23, 2008, **http://edition.cnn.com/2008/ TECH/science/07/16/greenwash/index. html** (accessed March 25, 2010); Melissa Singer, "LG Fridges: Life's Not So Good," *The Sydney Morning Herald,* March 17, 2010, **http://www.smh.com.au/ technology/lg-fridges-lifes-not-so-good- 20100317-qcu8.html** (accessed March 25, 2010).

27. "Shopping Behavior to Change as a Result of New Marketplace Realities, According to PricewaterhouseCoopers and Kantar Retail," *PR Newswire,* March 9, 2010, **http://www. prnewswire.com/news-releases/ shopping-behavior-to-change-as-a- result-of-new-marketplace-realities- according-to-pricewaterhousecoopers- and-kantar-retail-87104307.html** (accessed March 30, 2010).

28. B. Powell, "Toxic Shock," *Fortune,* October 12, 2009, p. 12.

29. Bryan Walsh, "Why Green Is the New Red, White and Blue," *Time,* April 28, 2008, pp. 45–58; Denis Ryan, "Taking the Green Change," *The Vancouver Sun,* May 31, 2008, pp. 136–37.

30. "Harvesting the Air," *The Economist,* April 3, 2010, p. 32.

31. New Belgium Brewing, **www. newbelgium.com** (accessed May 10 1, 2010).

Chapter 12

1. Ronald Grover, "I Can Make Your Product a Star," *BusinessWeek,* July 13 & 20, 2009, pp. 68–69; **www. propagandagem.com** (accessed April 8, 2010); Noah Joseph, "REPORT: BMW Using Money Saved from F1 Pullout for More Product Placement,"

autoblog.com, November 24, 2009, **www. autoblog.com/2009/11/24/report-bmw-using-money-saved-from-f1-pullout-for-more-product-p** (accessed April 8, 2010).

2. Narendra Rao, "The Keys to New Product success (Part 1)—Collecting Unarticulated & Invisible Customer-Needs," *Product Management & Strategy,* June 19, 2007, **http://productstrategy. wordpress.com/2007/06/19/the-keys-to-new-product-succeess-part-1-collecting-unarticulated-invisible-customer-needs/** (accessed April 1, 2010).

3. Gwendolyn Cuizon, "SWOT Analysis of Dell Computers," Suite101.com, March 5, 2009, **http://strategic-business-planning.suite101.com/article.cfm/ swot_analysis_of_dell_computers** (accessed March 31, 2010).

4. "Coke Blak Goes Black," *BevNet,* August 31, 2007, **http://www.bevnet.com/ news/2007/08-31-2007-Blak_coca-cola. asp** (accessed April 1, 2010).

5. Green Car Journal Editors, "Innovative Chevy Volt Wins 2009 Green Car Vision Award," GreenCar.com, February 4, 2009, **http://www.greencar.com/articles/ innovative-chevy-volt-wins-2009-green-car-vision-award.php** (accessed April 1, 2010).

6. "Vision and Innovation: The Shuffle Master Story," ShuffleMaster Incorporated, **http://www.shufflemaster. com/01_company/history/index.asp** (accessed April 1, 2010).

7. Faith Keenan, "Friendly Spies on the Net," *BusinessWeek e.biz,* July 9, 2001, p. EB27.

8. Dan Sewell, "P&G Testing Cheaper Tide," *AP Newswire,* July 1, 2009, via **http://abcnews.go.com/Business/ wireStory?id=7980911** (accessed March 8, 2010); Jessica Noll, "Have Tide of Economy Affected P&G?", *WCPO.com,* July 16, 2009, **http://www. wcpo.com/news/local/story/Have-Tides-Of-Economy-Affected-P-G/ Lv-KS4cBT0ihwO1lUz8hHQ.cspx** (accessed April 8, 2010).

9. "McDonald's Opens First McCafe in U.S.," *Entrepreneur,* May 14, 2001, **http:// www.entrepreneur.com/franchises/ franchisezone/thisjustin/article40494. html** (accessed April 2, 2010); "McDonald's Poised to Rival Starbucks Nationwide Starting Today," *QSR,* May 5, 2009, **http://www.qsrmagazine.com/**

articles/news/story.phtml?id=8625 (accessed April 2, 2010).

10. "Electric Cars for 2010," *Clean Fleet Report,* December 14, 2009, **http://www. cleanfleetreport.com/electric-vehicles/ electric-car-for-2010/** (accessed April 8, 2010).

11. Jo Piazza, "It's Pancakes. In a Can. It's Made $15 Million," *CNNMoney. com,* January 1, 2010, **http://money.cnn. com/2009/12/23/smallbusiness/batter_ blaster.fsb/index.htm** (accessed January 6, 2010).

12. James "Dela" Delahunty, "iPod Market Share at 73.8 Percent, 225 Million iPods Sold, More Games for Touch than PSP & NDS: Apple," *After Dawn News,* September 9, 2009, **http://www.afterdawn.com/ news/article.cfm/2009/09/09/ ipod_market_share_at_73_8_ percent_225_million_ipods_sold_more_ games_for_touch_than_psp_nds_apple** (accessed April 2, 2010).

13. Bruce Horovitz, "Snacks: Does This Bag Make Me Look Fat?" *USA Today,* February 20, 2008, p B1.

14. "Product Life Cycle," Answers.com, **http://www.answers.com/topic/product-life-cycle** (accessed March 31, 2010).

15. Ann Zimmerman, "Are Mattel's New Dolls Black Enough?" *The Wall Street Journal,* December 3, 2009, pp. B11, B14; Ann Zimmerman, "Mattel Hopes Barbie Facelift Will Show Up Younger Rivals," *The Wall Street Journal,* December 21, 2009, pp. A1, A20.

16. "Private Label Gets Personal," *Shopper Culture,* **http://www.shopperculture. com/shopper_culture/2009/10/private-label-gets-personal.html** (accessed April 2, 2010).

17. Mona Doyle, "What Packaging Will Consumers Pay More For?" *Food & Beverage Packaging,* August 1, 2001, **http://www.foodandbeveragepackaging. com/Articles/Article_Rotation/ BNP_GUID_9-5-2006_A_1000000000 0000401665** (accessed April 2, 2010).

18. Mike Barris, "20-Ounce Sales Lose Fizz, Sinking Coke Enterprises," *The Wall Street Journal,* May 28, 2008, **http://online.wsj.com/article/ SB121197848027325835.html** (accessed April 8, 2010).

19. "Cable & Satellite TV," ACSI Scores and Commentary, **http://www.theacsi.**

org/index.php?option=com_content& task=view&id=147&Itemid=155&i= Cable+%26+Satellite+TV (accessed April 2, 2010); "Wireless Telephone Service," ACSI Scores and Commentary, **http://www.theacsi.org/index. php?option=com_content&task=vie w&id=147&Itemid=155&i=Wireless+ Telephone+Service** (accessed April 2, 2010); "National Quarterly Scores," ACSI Scores and Commentary, **http://www. theacsi.org/index.php?option=com_con tent&task=view&id=31&Itemid=35** (accessed April 2, 2010); "About ACSI," ACSI, **http://www.theacsi.org/index. php?option=com_content&task=view &id=49&Itemid=28** (accessed April 5, 2010).

20. "Airline Performance Improves for First Time in Five Years, According to Airline Quality Rating," *Airline Quality Rating,* April 6, 2009, **http://www.aqr. aero/pressreleases/AQR2008.pdf** (accessed April 2, 2010).

21. "American Demographics 2006 Consumer Perception Survey," *Advertising Age,* January 2, 2006, p. 9. Data by Synovate.

22. Rajneesh Suri and Kent B. Monroe, "The Effects of Time Constraints on Consumers' Judgments of Prices and Products," *Journal of Consumer Research* 30 (June 2003), pp. 92.

23. "Talisman," De Beers, **http://www. debeerseu.com/Collections/Talisman/ icat/maintalisman** (accessed April 5, 2010); Andy Stone, "Drill Bits Are Forever," *Forbes,* December 10, 2007, p. 200.

24. Kevin J. Laverty, "Cascadian Farm a.k.a. General Mills," September 2004, **http://bschool.washington.edu/ciber/ PDF_WORD/Cascadian_Farm_case_ Laverty.pdf** (accessed June 15, 2009); **www.cascadianfarm.com** (accessed June 11, 2009); Bill Virgin, "General Mills Buys Out a Major Organic Food Company," purefood.org, December 16, 1999, **www. purefood.org/Organic/genmillsorg. cfm** (accessed June 11, 2009); "Organic/ natural," General Mills, **http://www. generalmills.com/corporate/brands/ category.aspx?catID=19433&grou pID=19433** (accessed March 30, 2010).

25. Rags Srinivasan, "Instant Coffee Price Is About Skimming," *Iterative Path,* September 30, 2009, **http://iterativepath. wordpress.com/2009/09/30/**

instant-coffee-price-is-about-skimming/ (accessed April 5, 2010).

26. David Luhnow and Chad Terhune, "Latin Pop: A Low-Budget Cola Shakes Up Markets South of the Border," *The Wall Street Journal,* October 27, 2003, pp. A1, A18.

27. "Internet Usage Statistics," *Internet World Stats,* **http://www. internetworldstats.com/stats.htm** (accessed April 5, 2010); Market Research. com, "Online Retail Sales Expected to Rebound in 2010," *News Blaze,* August 3, 2009, **http://newsblaze.com/ story/2009080308380100001.mwir/ topstory.html** (accessed April 5, 2010).

28. "Top Threats to Revenue," *USA Today,* February 1, 2006, p. A1.

29. Brad Howarth, "Hear This, iPods from a Vending Machine," *The Sydney Morning Herald,* November 14, 2006, **http://www.smh.com.au/news/biztech/ hear-this-ipods-from-a-vending-mac hine/2006/11/13/1163266481869.html** (accessed April 8, 2010).

30. "Welcome to the Future of Shopping," Zoom Systems, **http://www. zoomsystems.com/zoomshops/zs_index. html** (accessed April 5, 2010).

31. Jason Ankeny, "Art & Commerce," *Entrepreneur,* January 2010, pp. 19–21; **www.thebirdmahcine.com** (accessed January 5, 2010); Cassie Walker, "Screen Gem: Artist and Screen Printer Jay Ryan Draws Worldwide Acclaim from Skokie Studio," *Chicago Mag,* December 2009, **http://www.chicagomag.com/ Chicago-Magazine/December-2009/ Screen-Gem-Artist-and-screen-printer- Jay-Ryan-draws-worldwide-acclaim- from-Skokie-studio/index.php? cparticle=1&siarticle=0#artanc** (accessed January 6, 2010).

32. Abbey Klaassen, "Even Google Has to Advertise," *Advertising Age,* June 2, 2008, p. 4.

33. Brad Wilson, *Bradsdeals* homepage. **http://bradsdeals.com/** (accessed April 28, 2009); Michael S. Malone, "The Twitter Revolution," *The Wall Street Journal,* April 18, 2009, p. A11; Ann Meyer, "Facebook, Twitter, Other Social Media Help Drive Business for Small Firms," *Chicago Tribune,* April 27, 2009, **http://archives.chicagotribune. com/2009/apr/27/business/chi-mon- minding-social-media-042apr27** (accessed April 8, 2010); Bill Pride and

O.C. Ferrell, *Marketing,* 15th ed. (Boston, MA: Houghton-Mifflin, 2010), p. 35.

34. Jonathon Ramsey, "Danica Patrick's GoDaddy.com Ad Banned from Super Bowl Because of Beavers," autoblog.com, Jan 24th 2008, **http://www.autoblog. com/2008/01/24/danica-patricks- godaddy-com-ad-banned-from-super- bowl-because-o/** (accessed April 8, 2010).

35. Kenji Hall, "McDonald;s Quarter Pounder Buzz Marketing in Tokyo," *BusinessWeek,* November 19, 2008, **http:// www.businessweek.com/globalbiz/blog/ eyeonasia/archives/2008/11/mcdonalds_ quart.html** (accessed April 5, 2010).

36. Gerry Khermouch and Jeff Green, "Buzz Marketing," *BusinessWeek,* July 30, 2001, pp. 50– 56.

37. Andrew Romano, "Now 4 Restaurant 2.0," *Newsweek,* February 28, 2009, **http:// www.newsweek.com/id/187008** (accessed April 5, 2010).

38. Abigail Bassett, "Beat the Recession, One Penny at a Time," *CNNMoney. com,* April 29, 2009, **http://money.cnn. com/2009/04/28/pf/coupon_savings/ index.htm** (accessed April 5, 2010).

39. Kate MacArthur, "Sierra Mist: Cie Nicholson," *Advertising Age,* November 17, 2003, p. S-2.

40. "Kimberly Clark: Becoming the Indispensable Partner for Retailers," *Retail Solutions,* **http://www.t3ci.com/pdfs/ Retail_Solutions_Kimberly_Clark_ Case_Study_2009-01.pdf** (accessed April 5, 2010).

41. "Coca-Cola North America Announces the Launch of VAULT," February 17, 2006, **http://www.thecoca- colacompany.com/presscenter/pdfs/ VAULT_Launch_Release.doc**, accessed April 8, 2010.

42. Sources: Oberweis Dairy, **http://www. oberweis.com** (accessed May 2, 2010).

Chapter 13

1. Matthew Schwartz, "NASCAR: Driving Social Media," *Advertising Age,* November 16, 2009, pp. C3, C13; Sara Page, "NASCAR Digs Up Old Roots in a New Way," *WSLS 10,* Media General News Service, September 23, 2009, **www.2wsls. com/sls/sports/motor_sports/nextel/ article/nascar_digs_up_old_roots_ in_a_new_way/49154** (accessed January 23, 2010); "NASCAR and Vision Critical Win Award for Listening to Fans Using

Online Panel," Vision Critical, October 27, 2009, **www.visioncritical.com/2009/10/ nascar-and-vision-critical-win-award- for-listening-to-fans-using-online- panel** (accessed January 23, 2010); **www. nascar.com** (accessed February 16, 2010); Laurie Burkitt, "NASCAR Ads, Coming to a Theatre Near You," *Forbes,* October 21, 2009, **http://www.forbes. com/2009/10/21/nascar-screenvision- cmo-network-cinema-ads.html** (accessed February 17, 2010).

2. This material in this chapter is reserved for use in the authors' other textbooks and teaching materials.

3. "Fortune 500: Amazon.com," *Fortune,* 2009, **http://money.cnn.com/ magazines/fortune/fortune500/2009/ snapshots/10810.html** (accessed March 19, 2010); Josh Quitter, "How Jeff Bezos Rules the Retail Space," *Fortune,* May 5, 2008, pp. 127–132.

4. "Media Info," Hulu, **http://www.hulu. com/about** (accessed March 19, 2010).

5. G. Jeffrey MacDonald, "Education of Global Reach," *USA Today,* February 27, 2008, p. D6.

6. Bobby White, "The New Workplace Rules: No Video-Watching," *The Wall Street Journal,* March 4, 2008, p. B1.

7. "A Special Report on Social Networking," *The Economist,* January 30, 2010, p. 4.

8. "Internet Usage Statistics," Internet World Stats, **http://www. Internetworldstats.com/stats.htm** (accessed March 21, 2010).

9. Michael V. Copeland. "Tapping Tech's Beautiful Mind," *Fortune,* October 12, 2009, pp. 35–36.

10. Miguel Bustillo and Geoffrey A. Fowler, "Walmart Uses its Stores to Get an Edge Online," *The Wall Street Journal,* December 15, 2009, p. B1.

11. Care 2, **www.care2.com** (accessed April 2, 2010); Treehugger, **www. treehugger.com** (accessed April 2, 2010).

12. Aaron Back, "China's Big Brands Tackle Web Sales," *The Wall Street Journal,* December 1, 2009, p. B2.

13. "2009 Digital Handbook," *Marketing News,* April 30, 2009, p. 13.

14. Cameron Chapman, "The History and Evolution of Social Media." *WebDesigner Depot,* October 7, 2009, **http://www. webdesignerdepot.com/2009/10/**

the-history-and-evolution-of-social-media/ (accessed April 2, 2010).

15. "The history of social media in a blink," Windows Live, November 22, 2007, **http://mbresseel.spaces.live.com/Blog/cns%2133234018BF280C82%21345.entry** (accessed February 18, 2010).

16. Chapman, "The History and Evolution of Social Media."

17. Emily Schmall, "Growing Pains," *Forbes,* August 11, 2008, pp. 60–63.

18. Charlene Li and Josh Bernoff, *Groundswell* (Boston: Harvard Business Press, 2008), pp. 41–44.

19. "2009 Digital Handbook," p. 11.

20. Li and Bernoff, *Groundswell,* p. 43.

21. A.C. Neilson, "Global Faces and Networked Places: A Neilson Report on Social Networking's New Global Footprint," March 2009, **http://server-uk.imrworldwide.com/pdcimages/Global_Faces_and_Networked_Places-A_Nielsen_Report_on_Social_Networkings_New_Global_Footprint.pdf** (accessed June 3,2010).

22. "Couldn't stop the spread of the conversation in reactions from other bloggers," from Hyejin Kim's May 4, 2007, blog post "Korea: Bloggers and Donuts" on the blog Global Voices at **groundswell.forrester.com/site1-16** (accessed January 10, 2010).

23. Randy Tinseth, "Randy's Journal," Boeing, **http://boeingblogs.com/randy/** (accessed January 10, 2010).

24. Li and Bernoff, *Groundswell,* pp. 25–26.

25. "2009 Digital Handbook," p. 11.

26. Jessi Hempel, "Google (Still) Loves YouTube," *Fortune,* April 17, 2009, pp. 37–42.

27. David Meerman Scott, *The New Rules of Marketing & PR* (Hoboken, NJ: John Wiley & Sons, Inc., 2009), p. 224; "Mainframe: The Art of the Sales, Lesson One," YouTube, **http://www.youtube.com/watch?v=MSqXKp-00hM** (accessed January 10, 2010); Ryan Rhodes, "The Mainframe: It's Like a Barn," IBM Systems, March–April 2007, **http://www.ibmsystemsmag.com/mainframe/marchapril07/stoprun/11984p1.aspx** (accessed February 18, 2010).

28. "Search Giant Google to Buy YouTube for $1.65B," *FoxNews.com,* October 10, 2006, **http://www.foxnews.com/story/0,2933,218921,00.html** (accessed January 8, 2010).

29. Zeke Camusio, "Flickr Marketing—6 Awesome Tactics to Promote Your Website on Flickr," The Outsourcing Company, February 19, 2009, **http://www.theoutsourcingcompany.com/blog/social-media-marketing/flickr-marketing-6-awesome-tactics-to-promote-your-website-on-flickr/,** accessed January 11, 2010.

30. Bianca Male, "How To Promote Your Business on Flickr," *The Business Insider,* December 1, 2009, **http://www.businessinsider.com/how-to-promote-your-business-on-flickr-2009-12?utm_source=feedburner&utm_medium=feed&utm_campaign=Feed%3A+businessinsider+(The+Business+Insider),** accessed January 11, 2010.

31. "How to Market on Flickr." Small Business Search Marketing. **http://www.smallbusinesssem.com/articles/marketing-on-flickr/#ixzz0cLIpJUTW,** accessed January 11, 2010.

32. "GM blogs' Photostream," Flickr, **http://www.flickr.com/photos/gmblogs/** (accessed January 11, 2010); "About the Lab," The Lab, **http://thelab.gmblogs.com/about/** (accessed January 11, 2010).

33. "Barack Obama's Photostream," Flickr, **http://www.flickr.com/photos/barackobamadotcom** (accessed January 11, 2009).

34. Sage Lewis, "Using Flickr for Marketing," YouTube, uploaded February 13, 2007. **http://www.youtube.com/watch?v=u2Xyzkfzlug,** accessed January 11, 2010.

35. "2009 Digital Handbook," p. 14.

36. Christopher S. Penn, "About the Financial Aid Podcast," *FinancialAidNews.com,* **http://www.financialaidnews.com/about-2/** (accessed January 11, 2010).

37. "2009 Digital Handbook," p. 13.

38. Li and Bernoff, *Groundswell,* p. 22.

39. "2009 Digital Handbook," p. 13.

40. Kathy Chu and Kim Thai, "Banks Jump on the Twitter Wagon," *USA Today,* May 12, 2009, p. B1.

41. "Facebook: Largest, Fastest Growing Social Network," *Tech Tree,* August 13, 2008, **http://www.techtree.com/India/News/Facebook_Largest_Fastest_Growing_Social_Network/551-92134-643.html** (accessed January 12, 2010).

42. "2009 Digital Handbook," p. 13.

43. Nick Summers. "Heated Rivalries: #9 Facebook vs. MySpace." *Newsweek.* **http://www.2010.newsweek.com/top-10/heated-rivalries/facebook-vs-myspace.html** (accessed January 13, 2010).

44. "2009 Digital Handbook," p. 13.

45. Ibid.

46. Hansen's Cakes, **http://hansencakes.blogspot.com/; http://www.facebook.com/pages/Hansens-Cakes/171578118691** (both accessed May 6, 2010).

47. "Pepsi Refresh Project," **http://www.refresheverything.com/index** (accessed February 18, 2010); Stuart Elliot, "Pepsi Invites the Public to do Good," *The New York Times,* January 31, 2010, **http://www.nytimes.com/2010/02/01/business/media/01adco.html** (accessed February 18, 2010).

48. Jack Neff," Marketing: Prilosec Works to Become 'Sponsor of Everything,'" *Advertising Age,* February 17, 2010, **http://adage.com/digital/article?article_id=142150** (accessed February 18, 2010).

49. "2009 Digital Handbook," p. 13.

50. Alison Doyle, "LinkedIn and Your Job Search," *About.com,* **http://jobsearch.about.com/od/networking/a/linkedin.htm** (accessed January 8, 2010).

51. Personal Communication with Toni Leigh and her Web site, **www.desertblends.com** (accessed April 26, 2010).

52. Jefferson Graham, "Cake Decorator Finds Twitter a Tweet Recipe for Success," *USA Today,* April 1, 2009, p. 5B.

53. "2009 Digital Handbook," p. 11.

54. Claire Cain Miller, "Twitter Loses its Scrappy Start-Up Status," *The New York Times,* April 15, 2010, **http://www.nytimes.com/2010/04/16/technology/16twitter.html** (accessed May 10, 2010).

55. Devra J. First, " 'Tweets' on the Menu Are a Sweet Deal," *Boston.com,* June 29, 2009, **http://www.boston.com/ae/food/restaurants/articles/2009/06/29/restaurants_finding_twitter_a_cheap_effective_marketing_tool/** (accessed January 13, 2010).

56. Chu and Thai, "Banks Jump on the Twitter Wagon."

57. Josh Tyrangiel, "Bing vs. Google: The Conquest of Twitter," *Time,* October 22, 2009, **http://www.time.com/time/business/article/0,8599,1931532,00.html** (accessed January 7, 2010).

58. "Real Cars Drive into Second Life," *CNNMoney.com,* November 18, 2006, **http://money.cnn.com/2006/11/17/ autos/2nd_life_cars/index.htm** ().

59. "Sun Chief Researcher John Gage to Host Second Life's First-Ever Fortune 500 Press Conference," Sun Microsystems, October 6, 2006, **http://www.sun.com/ aboutsun/media/presskits/secondlife/** (accessed January 13, 2010).

60. Alice Truong, "Q&A: A Real Study of Virtual Worlds," *The Wall Street Journal,* May 4, 2010, **http://blogs.wsj.com/ digits/2010/05/04/qa-a-real-study-of- virtual-worlds/** (accessed May 6, 2010).

61. "CNN Enters the Virtual World of Second Life," November 12, 2007, *CNN.com,* **http://www.cnn.com/2007/ TECH/11/12/second.life.irpt/index.html** (accessed April 2, 2010).

62. Roger Yu, "Smartphones Help Make Bon Voyages," *USA Today,* March 5, 2010, p. B1.

63. Mickey Alam Khan, "Jiffy Lube Mobile Coupons Bring 50 Percent New Households," *Mobile Marketer,* January 30, 2009, **http://www.mobilemarketer. com/cms/news/commerce/2551.html** (accessed May 10, 2010).

64. Claire Cain Miller, "Mobile Phones Become Essential Tool for Holiday Shopping," *The New York Times,* December 18, 2009, **http://www.nytimes. com/2009/12/18/technology/18mobile. html?_r=1&ref=technology** (accessed January 6, 2010).

65. Li and Bernoff, *Groundswell,* p. 41.

66. Li and Bernoff, *Groundswell,* pp. 41–42.

67. Li and Bernoff, *Groundswell,* p. 44.

68. Li and Bernoff, *Groundswell,* pp. 44–45.

69. Justin Lahart, "Taking an Open-Source Approach to Hardware," *The Wall Street Journal,* November 27, 2009, p. B8; "Code: All the Code That's Fit to printf()" blog, *The New York Times***, http://open.blogs.nytimes.com/?scp=1- spot&sq=open%2520source&st=cse** (accessed February 8, 2010); Michael Zimbalist, "Imagining a World of Hardware Mashups," *The New York Times,* February 8, 2010, **http://bits. blogs.nytimes.com/2010/02/08/ imagining-a-world-of-hardware- mashups/?scp=2&sq=open%20**

source&st=cse (accessed February 8, 2010).

70. Mya Frazier, "CrowdSourcing" *Delta Sky Mag,* February 2010, p. 70, via **http:// msp.imirus.com/Mpowered/imirus. jsp?volume=ds10&issue=2&page=72** (accessed February 18, 2010).

71. "A Special Report on Social Networking," *The Economist,* January 30, 2010, p. 13.

72. Li and Bernoff, *Groundswell,* pp. 26–27.

73. Emily Steel, "Web Privacy Efforts Targeted," *The Wall Street Journal,* June 25, 2009, p. B10.

74. "About TRUSTe," TRUSTe, **http:// www.truste.com/about_TRUSTe/index. html** (accessed March 21, 2010).

75. Better Business Bureau Online (n.d.), **www.bbbonline.org/** (accessed May 10, 2010).

76. Larry Barrett, "Data Breach Costs Surge in 2009: Study," *eSecurityPlanet,* January 26, 2010, **http://www. esecurityplanet.com/features/article. php/3860811/Data-Breach-Costs-Surge- in-2009-Study.htm** (accessed January 28, 2010).

77. "Javelin Study Finds Identity Fraud Reached New High in 2009, but Consumers Are Fighting Back," *PR Newswire,* World News, February 15, 2009, **http://article.wn.com/ view/2010/02/15/Javelin_Study_Finds_ Identity_Fraud_Reached_New_High_ in_2009_/** (accessed March 21, 2010).

78. Sarah E. Needleman, "Social-Media Con Game," *The Wall Street Journal,* October 12, 2009, p. R4.

79. "Facebook Takes Strong Stance Against Haiti Fraud," *Media Street,* January 19, 2010, **http://www.media- street.co.uk/our-blog/2010/01/19/16- facebook-haiti-fraud** (accessed January 18, 2010).

80. Abigail Field, "Viacom v. YouTube/ Google: A Piracy Case in Their Own Words," *Daily Finance,* March 21, 2010, **http://www.dailyfinance.com/story/ company-news/viacom-v-youtube- google-a-piracy-case-in-their-own- words/19407896/** (accessed May 10, 2010).

81. Kevin Shanahan and Mike Hyman "Motivators and Enablers of SCOURing," *Journal of Business Research* 63 (September–October 2010), pp. 1095–1102.

82. Max Chafkin, "The Case, and the Plan, for the Virtual Company," *Inc.,* April 2010, p. 68.

83. Miral Fahmy, "Facebook, YouTube at Work Make Better Employees: Study," *Reuters,* April 2, 2009, **http://www.wired. com/techbiz/media/news/2009/04/ reuters_us_work_internet_tech_life** (accessed May 5, 2010); Sharon Gaudin, "Study: Facebook Use Cuts Productivity at Work," *Computer World,* July 22, 2009, **http://www.computerworld.com/s/ article/9135795/Study_Facebook_use_ cuts_productivity_at_work** (accessed May 5, 2010); Sharon Gaudin, "Study: 54% of Companies Ban Facebook, Twitter at Work," *Computer World,* October 6, 2009, **http://www.computerworld. com/s/article/9139020/Study_54_of_ companies_ban_Facebook_Twitter_at_ work** (accessed May 5, 2010); Anthony Balderrama, "Social Media at Work—Ban or Boon?" *CNN Living,* March 8, 2010, **http://www.cnn.com/2010/LIVING/ worklife/03/08/cb.social.media.banned/ index.html** (accessed May 11, 2010).

Chapter 14

1. O.C. Ferrell, John Fraedrich, and Linda Ferrell, *Understanding the Importance of Business Ethics in the 2008–2009 Financial Crisis;* Steven A. Holmes, "Fannie Mae Eases Credit to Aid Mortgage Lending," *The New York Times,* September 30, 1999, **http://www.nytimes.com/1999/09/30/ business/fannie-mae-eases-credit-to- aid-mortgage-lending.html** (accessed April 1, 2010); "Freddie Mac Pays Record $3.8 Million Fine," *The Associated Press,* April 18, 2006, **http://www.msnbc.msn. com/id/12373488/from/RSS** (accessed April 1, 2010); "Fannie Mae, Freddie Mac Subprime Restrictions Ease." *Reuters,* September 19, 2007, **http://www.cnbc. com/id/20869608** (accessed April 1, 2010).

2. "Break up the Big Four?" *CFO,* June 1, 2004, **http://www.cfo.com/article. cfm/3014059** (accessed April 1, 2010).

3. "Report to the Nation," Association of Certified Fraud Examiners, **http:// www.acfe.com/resources/publications. asp?copy=rttn** (accessed March 31, 2010).

4. "About the ACFE," The Association of Certified Fraud Examiners, **http://www. acfe.com/about/about.asp** (accessed April 1, 2010).

5. Mary Williams Walsh, "State Woes Grow Too Big to Camouflage," *The New*

York Times, March 29, 2010, **http://www. nytimes.com/2010/03/30/business/ economy/30states.html** (accessed March 31, 2010).

6. Karola Saekel, "Frog's Leap Wine Comes with a Bit of Whimsy," *SFGate. com,* May 3, 2009, **http://sfgate.com/ cgi-bin/article.cgi?f=/c/a/2009/05/03/ TR18171TB6.DTL** (accessed April 1, 2010); Eric Asimov, "In Napa, Some Wineries Choose the Old Route," *The New York Times,* August 20, 2008, **http://www. nytimes.com/2008/08/20/dining/20pour. html** (accessed April 1, 2010); Kathy Hovis, "Alum's Organic Frog's Leap Winery Uses 'Green' to Make Reds and Whites," *Cornell Chronicle,* May 14, 2008, **http://www.news.cornell.edu/stories/ May08/FrogsLeap.kh.html** (accessed April 1, 2010); **http://www.frogsleap.com** (accessed April 1, 2010).

7. Michael Sisk, "Paperless Possibilities in a Digital World: Go Green and Spend Less," June 25, 2009, **http:// adobe.americanbanker.com/index. php?option=com_content&vie w=article&id=19** (accessed April 1, 2010); "Motivating Consumer Adoption of Green-Paperless-Banking," *paymentsnews.com,* June 2008, **http:// www.paymentsnews.com/2008/06/ motivating-cons.html** (accessed March 31 ,2010); PayItGreen, payitgreen.org (accessed March 31, 2010).

8. Andrew Ross Sorkin, "Suspending Mark-to-Market: Bad Policy, Bad Time," *The New York Times DealBook Blog,* March 31, 2009, **http://dealbook. blogs.nytimes.com/2009/03/31/ suspending-mark-to-market-bad- policy-bad-time/?scp=1&sq=mark%20 to%20market%20accounting&st=cse** (accessed March 31, 2010); Floyd Norris, "Banks Get New Leeway in Valuing Their Assets," *The New York Times,* April 2, 2009, **http://www.nytimes. com/2009/04/03/business/03fasb. html?scp=2&sq=mark%20to%20 market%20accounting&st=cse** (accessed March 31, 2010).

9. Bureau of Labor Statistics, "Accountants and Auditors," *Occupational Outlook Handbook 2010–2011,* **http:// www.bls.gov/oco/ocos001.htm** (accessed April 1, 2010).

10. Sources: Mike Brown, "Caution is new league's strength," *Tulsa World,* September 27, 2009, **http://www.**

tulsaworld.com/news/article.aspx?subje ctid=407&articleid=20090927_223_B1_ Howcan164403** (accessed May 6, 2010); The Associated Press, "Arena Football 1 to launch in 2010," ESPN, December 10, 2009, **http://sports.espn.go.com/ extra/afl/news/story?id=4512394&ca mpaign=rss&source=ESPNHeadlines** (accessed May 6, 2010); Sheena Quinn, "Arena Football League Re-launches", AFL, February 17, 2010, **http://www. arenafootballmedia.com/omk.php?pid= 1614&sid=S201002171952389HSP3D &pr=1769** (accessed May 6, 2010); "Arena Football League: A history of playing rough indoors,"

Chapter 15

1. General Electric, **www.ge.com** (accessed April 6, 2010); General Commercial Finance, **http:// gecommercialfinance.gecapsol.com/ cms/servlet/cmsview/ComFin_Corp/ prod/en/main/index.html** (accessed April 6, 2010); GE Capital, **http:// gecapsol.com/cms/servlet/cmsview/ GE_Capital_Solutions/prod/en/index. html** (accessed April 6, 2010).

2. "How Currency Gets into Circulation," Federal Reserve Bank of New York (n.d.), **http://www.newyorkfed.org/ aboutthefed/fedpoint/fed01.html** (accessed April 2, 2010).

3. Weird and Wonderful Money Facts and Trivia," *Happy Worker,* **http://www. happyworker.com/magazine/facts/ weird-and-wonderful-money-facts** (accessed April 2, 2010).

4. Ibid.

5. "About the Redesigned Currency," The Department of the Treasury Bureau of Engraving and Printing, **http://www. newmoney.gov/newmoney/currency/ aboutnotes.htm** (accessed April 2, 2010).

6. "US Mint Cost to Produce the Penny and Nickel," *Coin Update News,* **http:// news.coinupdate.com/us-mint-cost-to- produce-the-penny-and-nickel-0137** (accessed March, 31, 2009).

7. "Credit Card Statistics, Industry Facts, Debt Statistics," *CreditCards.com,* **http:// www.creditcards.com/credit-card-news/ credit-card-industry-facts-personal- debt-statistics-1276.php** (accessed April 1, 2010).

8. Bank of America 2008 Annual Report, p. 16; "Bank of America Wins Top Environmental Leadership

Award from California Governor," *TradingMarkets.com,* November 26, 2008, **http://www.tradingmarkets.com/. site/news/Stock%20News/2051715/** (accessed April 6, 2010); Jonathan Stempel, "Bank of America Creates Environmental Banking Team," *Reuters,* February 12, 2008, **http://www.reuters. com/article/companyNewsAndPR/ idUSN1225091020080212** (accessed April 6, 2010).

9. "Deposit Insurance Simplification Fact Sheet," FDIC Web site, **http://www.fdic. gov/deposit/deposits/DIfactsheet.html** (accessed April 2, 2010).

10. Deloitte 21, **http://public.deloitte. com/media/0564/swfs/deloitte21.html** (accessed April 6, 2010).

11. "NACHA Reports More Than 18 Billion ACH Payments in 2007," NACHA: The Electronic Payments Association, May 19, 2008, **http://nacha.org/News/ news/pressreleases/2008/Volume_Final. pdf** (accessed April 2, 2010).

12. Tyler Metzger, "ATM Use in the United States," *CreditCards.com,* **http:// www.creditcards.com/credit-card-news/ atm-use-statistics-3372.php** (accessed April 2, 2010).

13. Federal Deposit Insurance Corporation Web site, **http://www.fdic. gov** (accessed April 1, 2010).

14. Nell Lake, "This Man or Some Geek Like Him Will Save the Planet & May Even Turn a Profit," *Spirit,* October 2009, pp. 70–73; **www.microwindtechnologies. com** (accessed April 6, 2010); "Alternative Energy, Tufts Entrepreneurial Leadership and Michael Easton," *Entrepreneurial Leadership News,* Tufts University School of Engineering, **http://gordon.tufts.edu/ about/news/ELP/altEnergy.asp** (accessed April 6, 2010); "MicroWind Team Makes Semis of Clean-Energy Competition," *Wicked Local Lexington,* July 17, 2009, **www.wickedlocal.com/lexington/news/ business/X135758277/MicroWind- team-makes-semis-of-clean-energy- competition** (accessed April 6, 2010).

15. Colin Barr, "Treasury's Citi sale: TARP's last hurrah?" *Fortune,* March 30, 2010, **http://money.cnn.com/2010/03/30/ news/companies/banks.tarp.fortune** (accessed April 2, 2010).

16. "CSI Pennsylvania," *CFO Magazine,* March 2008, p. 92.

17. Stacy Perman, "For Some Small Businesses, Recession is Good News,"

BusinessWeek, February 6, 2009, **http://www.businessweek.com/smallbiz/content/feb2009/sb2009025_083042.htm** (accessed May 1, 2010); Rachel Streitfeld, "Small-business owners, hit by recession, seek remedies," CNN, December 6, 2009, **http://www.cnn.com/2009/US/12/06/small.business.recession/index.html** (accessed May 1, 2010); Patrick Thibbdeau, "IBM layoffs blamed on offshoring," Computer World, March 2, 2010, **http://www.computerworld.com/s/article/9164379/IBM_layoffs_blamed_on_offshoring** (accessed May 1, 2010).

Chapter 16

1. Y Combinator, **http://ycombinator.com** (accessed April 6, 2010); Paul Graham, "A New Venture Animal," March 2008, **www.paulgraham.com/ycombinator.html** (accessed April 6, 2010); Sean Ellis, "Y Combinator Hatches Brilliant Entrepreneurs," Start Up Marketing Blog by Sean Ellis, December 2, 2008, **http://startup-marketing.com/y-combinator-hatches-brilliant-entrepreneurs/** (accessed April 6, 2010); Andy Louis-Charles, "Ignore Y Combinator at Your Own Risk," *The Motley Fool,* April 28, 2009, **www.fool.com/investing/general/2009/04/28/ignore-y-combinator-at-your-own-risk.aspx** (accessed April 6, 2010); Josh

Quittner, "The New Internet Start-Up Boom: Get Rich Slow," *Time,* April 9, 2009, **www.time.com/time/magazine/article/0,9171,1890387-1,00.html** (accessed April 6, 2010).

2. First Solar, **www.solar.com** (accessed April 6, 2010); "First Solar, Inc.," *Google Finance,* **http://www.google.com/finance?q=NASDAQ:FSLR** (accessed April 6, 2010).

3. Financial information, Apple, Inc., **http://finance.yahoo.com/q?s=AAPL** (accessed April 6, 2010).

4. "Our Company," On Deck Capital, Inc., **http://www.ondeckcapital.com/our-company/overview** (accessed April 6, 2010); Ryan McCarthy, "Loans You Pay Every Day," *Inc.,* May 2009, **www.inc.com/magazine/20090501/loans-you-pay-every-day.html** (accessed April 6, 2010); Zoran Basich, "Lending, With a Twist," *The Wall Street Journal,* October 13, 2008, p. R11.

5. "Company Research," *The Wall Street Journal,* **http://online.wsj.com** (accessed June 17, 2004); Selena Maranjian, "The Math of the Dow," *Sarasota Herald Tribune,* April 26, 2007, via **http://news.google.com/newspapers?nid=1755&dat=20070426&id=70AgAAAAIBAJ&sjid=qYQEAAAAIBAJ&pg=5677,235134** (accessed June 3, 2010).

6. Ilan Brat, "The School Hershey Built," *The Wall Street Journal,* December 2, 2009, pp. B1, B6; **www.mhs-pa.org** (accessed December 10, 2009); "Our Heritage and Milton Hershey School," **www.thehersheycompany.com/social-responsibility/heritage.asp** (accessed December 10, 2009); Sean Scully, "In Hershey's Possible Cadbury Bid, a School's Fate," *Time,* December 15, 2009, **www.time.com/time/business/article/0,8599,1947492,00.html** (accessed December 15, 2009); "Executive Summary," *Bloomberg BusinessWeek,* January 18, 2010, p. 11.

7. Vincent Ryan, "From Wall Street to Main Street," *CFO Magazine,* June 2008, pp. 85–86.

8. Morningstar , **http://corporate.morningstar.com** (accessed May 1, 2010); John Cook, "The Quiet Billionaire," ChicagoMag.com, June 2006, **http://www.chicagomag.com/Chicago-Magazine/June-2006/The-Quiet-Billionaire/** (accessed May 12, 2010); Jody Clarke, "Joe Mansueto: The simple idea that made me $1bn," *MoneyWeek,* September 4, 2009, **http://www.moneyweek.com/news-and-charts/entrepreneurs-my-first-million-joe-mansueto-moneyweek-45135.aspx** (accessed May 12, 2010).

Glossary

A

absolute advantage a monopoly that exists when a country is the only source of an item, the only producer of an item, or the most efficient producer of an item.

accessibility allows consumers to find information about competing products, prices, and reviews and become more informed about a firm and the relative value of its products.

accountability the principle that employees who accept an assignment and the authority to carry it out are answerable to a superior for the outcome.

accounting the recording, measurement, and interpretation of financial information.

accounting cycle the four-step procedure of an accounting system: examining source documents, recording transactions in an accounting journal, posting recorded transactions, and preparing financial statements.

accounting equation assets equal liabilities plus owners' equity.

accounts payable the amount a company owes to suppliers for goods and services purchased with credit.

accounts receivable money owed a company by its clients or customers who have promised to pay for the products at a later date.

accrued expenses all unpaid financial obligations incurred by an organization.

acquisition the purchase of one company by another, usually by buying its stock.

addressability the ability of a business to identify customers before they make a purchase.

administrative managers those who manage an entire business or a major segment of a business; they are not specialists but coordinate the activities of specialized managers.

advertising a paid form of nonpersonal communication transmitted through a mass medium, such as television commercials or magazine advertisements.

advertising campaign designing a series of advertisements and placing them in various media to reach a particular target market.

affirmative action programs legally mandated plans that try to increase job opportunities for minority groups by analyzing the current pool of workers, identifying areas where women and minorities are underrepresented, and establishing specific hiring and promotion goals, with target dates, for addressing the discrepancy.

agenda a calender, containing both specific and vague items, that covers short-term goals and long-term objectives.

analytical skills the ability to identify relevant issues, recognize their importance, understand the relationships between them, and perceive the underlying causes of a situation.

annual report summary of a firm's financial information, products, and growth plans for owners and potential investors.

arbitration settlement of a labor/management dispute by a third party whose solution is legally binding and enforceable.

articles of partnership legal documents that set forth the basic agreement between partners.

Asia-Pacific Economic Cooperation (APEC) an international trade alliance that promotes open trade and economic and technical cooperation among member nations.

asset utilization ratios ratios that measure how well a firm uses its assets to generate each $1 of sales.

assets a firm's economic resources, or items of value that it owns, such as cash, inventory, land, equipment, buildings, and other tangible and intangible things.

attitude knowledge and positive or negative feelings about something.

automated clearinghouses (ACHs) a system that permits payments such as deposits or withdrawals to be made to and from a bank account by magnetic computer tape.

automated teller machine (ATM) the most familiar form of electronic banking, which dispenses cash, accepts deposits, and allows balance inquiries and cash transfers from one account to another.

B

balance of payments the difference between the flow of money into and out of a country.

balance of trade the difference in value between a nation's exports and its imports.

balance sheet a "snapshot" of an organization's financial position at a given moment.

behavior modification changing behavior and encouraging appropriate actions by relating the consequences of behavior to the behavior itself.

benefits nonfinancial forms of compensation provided to employees, such as pension plans, health insurance, paid vacation and holidays, and the like.

blogs Web-based journals in which writers can editorialize and interact with other Internet users.

board of directors a group of individuals, elected by the stockholders to oversee the general operation of the corporation, who set the corporation's long-range objectives.

bonds debt instruments that larger companies sell to raise long-term funds.

bonuses monetary rewards offered by companies for exceptional performance as incentives to further increase productivity.

boycott an attempt to keep people from purchasing the products of a company.

branding the process of naming and identifying products.

bribes payments, gifts, or special favors intended to influence the outcome of a decision.

brokerage firms firms that buy and sell stocks, bonds, and other securities for their customers and provide other financial services.

budget an internal financial plan that forecasts expenses and income over a set period of time.

budget deficit the condition in which a nation spends more than it takes in from taxes.

business individuals or organizations who try to earn a profit by providing products that satisfy people's needs.

business ethics principles and standards that determine acceptable conduct in business.

business plan a precise statement of the rationale for a business and a step-by-step explanation of how it will achieve its goals.

business products products that are used directly or indirectly in the operation or manufacturing processes of businesses.

buying behavior the decision processes and actions of people who purchase and use products.

C

capacity the maximum load that an organizational unit can carry or operate.

capital budgeting the process of analyzing the needs of the business and selecting the assets that will maximize its value.

capitalism, or free enterprise an economic system in which individuals own and operate the majority of businesses that provide goods and services.

cartel a group of firms or nations that agrees to act as a monopoly and not compete with each other, in order to generate a competitive advantage in world markets.

cash flow the movement of money through an organization on a daily, weekly, monthly, or yearly basis.

centralized organization a structure in which authority is concentrated at the top, and very little decision-making authority is delegated to lower levels.

certificates of deposit (CDs) savings accounts that guarantee a depositor a set interest rate over a specified interval as long as the funds are not withdrawn before the end of the period—six months or one year, for example.

certified management accountants (CMAs) private accountants who, after rigorous examination, are certified by the National Association of Accountants and who have some managerial responsibility.

certified public accountant (CPA) an individual who has been state certified to provide accounting services ranging from the preparation of financial records and the filing of tax returns to complex audits of corporate financial records.

checking account money stored in an account at a bank or other financial institution that can be withdrawn without advance notice; also called a demand deposit.

classical theory of motivation theory suggesting that money is the sole motivator for workers.

codes of ethics formalized rules and standards that describe what a company expects of its employees.

collective bargaining the negotiation process through which management and unions reach an agreement about compensation, working hours, and working conditions for the bargaining unit.

commercial banks the largest and oldest of all financial institutions, relying mainly on checking and savings accounts as sources of funds for loans to businesses and individuals.

commercial certificates of deposit (CDs) certificates of deposit issued by commercial banks and brokerage companies, available in minimum amounts of $100,000, which may be traded prior to maturity.

commercial paper a written promise from one company to another to pay a specific amount of money.

commercialization the full introduction of a complete marketing strategy and the launch of the product for commercial success.

commission an incentive system that pays a fixed amount or a percentage of the employee's sales.

commitee a permanent, formal group that performs a specific task.

common stock stock whose owners have voting rights in the corporation, yet do not receive preferential treatment regarding dividends.

communism first described by Karl Marx as a society in which the people, without regard to class, own all the nation's resources.

comparative advantage the basis of most international trade, when a country specializes in products that it can supply more efficiently or at a lower cost than it can produce other items.

competition the rivalry among businesses for consumers' dollars.

compressed workweek a four-day (or shorter) period during which an employee works 40 hours.

computer-assisted design (CAD) the design of components, products, and processes on computers instead of on paper.

computer-assisted manufacturing (CAM) manufacturing that employs specialized computer systems to actually guide and control the transformation processes.

computer-integrated manufacturing (CIM) a complete system that designs products, manages machines and materials, and controls the operations function.

concentration approach a market segmentation approach whereby a company develops one marketing strategy for a single market segment.

conceptual skills the ability to think in abstract terms and to see how parts fit together to form the whole.

conciliation a method of outside resolution of labor and management differences in which a third party is brought in to keep the two sides talking.

connectivity the use of digital networks to provide linkages between information providers and users.

consumer products products intended for household or family use.

consumerism the activities that independent individuals, groups, and organizations undertake to protect their rights as consumers.

continuous manufacturing organizations companies that use continuously running assembly lines, creating products with many similar characteristics.

contract manufacturing the hiring of a foreign company to produce a specified volume of the initiating company's product to specification; the final product carries the domestic firm's name.

control Consumers' ability to regulate the information they receive via the Internet, and the rate and sequence of their exposure to that information.

controlling the process of evaluating and correcting activities to keep the organization on course.

cooperative or co-op an organization composed of individuals or small businesses that have banded together to reap the benefits of belonging to a larger organization.

corporate charter a legal document that the state issues to a company based on information the company provides in the articles of incorporation.

corporate citizenship the extent to which businesses meet the legal, ethical, economic, and voluntary responsibilities placed on them by their stakeholders.

corporation a legal entity, created by the state, whose assets and liabilities are separate from its owners.

cost of goods sold the amount of money a firm spent to buy or produce the products it sold during the period to which the income statement applies.

countertrade agreements foreign trade agreements that involve bartering products for other products instead of for currency.

credit cards means of access to preapproved lines of credit granted by a bank or finance company.

credit controls the authority to establish and enforce credit rules for financial institutions and some private investors.

credit union a financial institution owned and controlled by its depositors, who usually have a common employer, profession, trade group, or religion.

crisis management or contingency planning an element in planning that deals with potential disasters such as product tampering, oil spills, fire, earthquake, computer virus, or airplane crash.

culture the integrated, accepted pattern of human behavior, including thought, speech, beliefs, actions, and artifacts.

current assets assets that are used or converted into cash within the course of a calendar year.

current liabilities a firm's financial obligations to short-term creditors, which must be repaid within one year.

current ratio current assets divided by current liabilities.

customer departmentalization the arrangement of jobs around the needs of various types of customers.

customization making products to meet a particular customer's needs or wants.

D

debit card a card that looks like a credit card but works like a check; using it results in a direct, immediate, electronic payment from the cardholder's checking account to a merchant or third party.

debt to total assets ratio a ratio indicating how much of the firm is financed by debt and how much by owners' equity.

debt utilization ratios ratios that measure how much debt an organization is using relative to other sources of capital, such as owners' equity.

decentralized organization an organization in which decision-making authority is delegated as far down the chain of command as possible.

delegation of authority giving employees not only tasks, but also the power to make commitments, use resources, and take whatever actions are necessary to carry out those tasks.

demand the number of goods and services that consumers are willing to buy at different prices at a specific time.

departmentalization the grouping of jobs into working units usually called departments, units, groups, or divisions.

depreciation the process of spreading the costs of long-lived assets such as buildings and equipment over the total number of accounting periods in which they are expected to be used.

depression a condition of the economy in which unemployment is very high, consumer spending is low, and business output is sharply reduced.

development training that augments the skills and knowledge of managers and professionals.

digital marketing uses all digital media, including the Internet and mobile and interactive channels, to develop communication and exchanges with customers.

digital media electronic media that function using digital codes—when we refer to digital media, we are referring to media available via computers, cellular phones, smart phones, and other digital devices that have been released in recent years.

direct investment the ownership of overseas facilities.

directing motivating and leading employees to achieve organizational objectives.

discount rate the rate of interest the Fed charges to loan money to any banking institution to meet reserve requirements.

discounts temporary price reductions, often employed to boost sales.

distribution making products available to customers in the quantities desired.

diversity the participation of different ages, genders, races, ethnicities, nationalities, and abilities in the workplace.

dividend yield the dividend per share divided by the stock price.

dividends profits of a corporation that are distributed in the form of cash payments to stockholders.

dividends per share the actual cash received for each share owned.

double-entry bookkeeping a system of recording and classifying business transactions that maintains the balance of the accounting equation.

downsizing the elimination of a significant number of employees from an organization.

dumping the act of a country or business selling products at less than what it costs to produce them.

E

e-business carrying out the goals of business through utilization of the Internet.

earnings per share net income or profit divided by the number of stock shares outstanding.

economic contraction a slowdown of the economy characterized by a decline in spending and during which businesses cut back on production and lay off workers.

economic expansion the situation that occurs when an economy is growing and people are spending more money; their purchases stimulate the production of goods and services, which in turn stimulates employment.

economic order quantity (EOQ) model a model that identifies the optimum number of items to order to minimize the costs of managing (ordering, storing, and using) them.

economic system a description of how a particular society distributes its resources to produce goods and services.

economics the study of how resources are distributed for the production of goods and services within a social system.

electronic funds transfer (EFT) any movement of funds by means of an electronic terminal, telephone, computer, or magnetic tape.

electronic marketing refers to the strategic process of distributing, promoting, pricing products, and discovering the desires of customers using digital media and digital marketing.

embargo a prohibition on trade in a particular product.

entrepreneur an individual who risks his or her wealth, time, and effort to develop for profit an innovative product or way of doing something.

entrepreneurship the process of creating and managing a business to achieve desired objectives.

equilibrium price the price at which the number of products that businesses are willing to supply equals the amount of products that consumers are willing to buy at a specific point in time.

equity theory an assumption that how much people are willing to contribute to an organization depends on their assessment of the fairness, or equity, of the rewards they will receive in exchange.

esteem needs the need for respect—both self-respect and respect from others.

ethical issue an identifiable problem, situation, or opportunity that requires a person to choose from among several actions that may be evaluated as right or wrong, ethical or unethical.

eurodollar market a market for trading U.S. dollars in foreign countries.

European Union (EU) a union of European nations established in 1958 to promote trade among its members; one of the largest single markets today.

exchange the act of giving up one thing (money, credit, labor, goods) in return for something else (goods, services, or ideas).

exchange controls regulations that restrict the amount of currency that can be bought or sold.

exchange rate the ratio at which one nation's currency can be exchanged for another nation's currency.

exclusive distribution the awarding by a manufacturer to an intermediary of the sole right to sell a product in a defined geographic territory.

expectancy theory the assumption that motivation depends not only on how much a person wants something but also on how likely he or she is to get it.

expenses the costs incurred in the day-to-day operations of an organization.

exporting the sale of goods and services to foreign markets.

extrinsic rewards benefits and/or recognition received from someone else.

F

factor a finance company to which businesses sell their accounts receivable—usually for a percentage of the total face value.

Federal Deposit Insurance Corporation (FDIC) an insurance fund established in 1933 that insures individual bank accounts.

Federal Reserve Board an independent agency of the federal government established in 1913 to regulate the nation's banking and financial industry.

finance the study of money; how it's made, how it's lost, and how it's managed.

finance companies business that offer short term loans at substantially higher rates of interest than banks.

financial managers those who focus on obtaining needed funds for the successful operation of an organization and using those funds to further organizational goals.

financial resources the funds used to acquire the natural and human resources needed to provide products; also called capital.

first-line managers those who supervise both workers and the daily operations of an organization.

fixed-position layout a layout that brings all resources required to create the product to a central location.

flexible manufacturing the direction of machinery by computers to adapt to different versions of similar operations.

flextime a program that allows employees to choose their starting and ending times, provided that they are at work during a specified core period.

floating-rate bonds bonds with interest rates that change with current interest rates otherwise available in the economy.

franchise a license to sell another's products or to use another's name in business, or both.

franchisee the purchaser of a franchise.

franchiser the company that sells a franchise.

franchising a form of licensing in which a company—the franchiser—agrees to provide a franchisee a name, logo, methods of operation, advertising, products, and other elements associated with a franchiser's business, in return for a financial commitment and the agreement to conduct business in accordance with the franchiser's standard of operations.

free-market system pure capitalism, in which all economic decisions are made without government intervention.

functional departmentalization the grouping of jobs that perform similar functional activities, such as finance, manufacturing, marketing, and human resources.

G

General Agreement on Tariffs and Trade (GATT) a trade agreement, originally signed by 23 nations in 1947, that provided a forum for tariff negotiations and a place where international trade problems could be discussed and resolved.

general partnership a partnership that involves a complete sharing in both the management and the liability of the business.

generic products products with no brand name that often come in simple packages and carry only their generic name.

geographical departmentalization the grouping of jobs according to geographic location, such as state, region, country, or continent.

global strategy (globalization) a strategy that involves standardizing products (and, as much as possible, their promotion and distribution) for the whole world, as if it were a single entity.

goal the result that a firm wished to achieve.

grapevine an informal channel of communication, separate from management's formal, official communication channels.

gross domestic product (GDP) the sum of all goods and services produced in a country during a year.

gross income (or profit) revenues minus the cost of goods sold required to generate the revenues.

group two or more individuals who communicate with one another, share a common identity, and have a common goal.

H

human relations the study of the behavior of individuals and groups in organizational settings.

human relations skills the ability to deal with people, both inside and outside the organization.

human resources the physical and mental abilities that people use to produce goods and services; also called labor.

human resources management (HRM) all the activities involved in determining an organization's human resources needs, as well as acquiring, training, and compensating people to fill those needs.

human resources managers those who handle the staffing function and deal with employees in a formalized manner.

hygiene factors aspects of Herzberg's theory of motivation that focus on the work setting and not the content of the work; these aspects include adequate wages, comfortable and safe working conditions, fair company policies, and job security.

I

identity theft when criminals obtain personal information that allows them to impersonate someone else in order to use their credit to obtain financial accounts and make purchases.

import tariff a tax levied by a nation on goods imported into the country.

importing the purchase of goods and services from foreign sources.

income statement a financial report that shows an organization's profitability over a period of time—month, quarter, or year.

inflation a condition characterized by a continuing rise in prices.

information technology (IT) managers those who are responsible for implementing, maintaining, and controlling technology applications in business, such as computer networks.

infrastructure the physical facilities that support a country's economic activities, such as railroads, highways, ports, airfields, utilities and power plants, schools, hospitals, communication systems, and commercial distribution systems.

initial public offering (IPO) selling a corporation's stock on public markets for the first time.

inputs the resources—such as labor, money, materials, and energy—that are converted into outputs.

insurance companies businesses that protect their clients against financial losses from certain specified risks (death, accident, and theft, for example).

integrated marketing communications coordinating the promotion mix elements and synchronizing promotion as a unified effort.

intensive distribution a form of market coverage whereby a product is made available in as many outlets as possible.

interactivity allows customers to express their needs and wants directly to the firm in response to its communications.

intermittent organizations organizations that deal with products of a lesser magnitude than do project organizations; their products are not necessarily unique but possess a significant number of differences.

international business the buying, selling, and trading of goods and services across national boundaries.

International Monetary Fund (IMF) organization established in 1947 to promote trade among member nations by eliminating trade barriers and fostering financial cooperation.

intrapreneurs individuals in large firms who take responsibility for the development of innovations within the organizations.

intrinsic rewards the personal satisfaction and enjoyment felt after attaining a goal.

inventory all raw materials, components, completed or partially completed products, and pieces of equipment a firm uses.

inventory control the process of determining how many supplies and goods are needed and keeping track of quantities on hand, where each item is, and who is responsible for it.

inventory turnover sales divided by total inventory.

investment banker underwrites new issues of securities for corporations, states, and municipalities.

ISO 9000 a series of quality assurance standards designed by the International Organization for Standardization (ISO) to ensure consistent product quality under many conditions.

ISO 14000 a comprehensive set of environmental standards that encourages a cleaner and safer world by promoting a more uniform approach to environmental management and helping companies attain and measure improvements in their environmental performance.

J

job analysis the determination, through observation and study, of pertinent information about a job—including specific tasks and necessary abilities, knowledge, and skills.

job description a formal, written explanation of a specific job, usually including job title, tasks, relationship with other jobs, physical and mental skills required, duties, responsibilities, and working conditions.

job enlargement the addition of more tasks to a job instead of treating each task as separate.

job enrichment the incorporation of motivational factors, such as opportunity for achievement, recognition, responsibility, and advancement, into a job.

job rotation movement of employees from one job to another in an effort to relieve the boredom often associated with job specialization.

job sharing performance of one full-time job by two people on part-time hours.

job specification a description of the qualifications necessary for a specific job, in terms of education, experience, and personal and physical characteristics.

joint venture a partnership established for a specific project or for a limited time.

journal a time-ordered list of account transactions.

junk bonds a special type of high interest rate bond that carries higher inherent risks.

just-in-time (JIT) inventory management a technique using smaller quantities of materials that arrive "just in time" for use in the transformation process and therefore require less storage space and other inventory management expense.

L

labeling the presentation of important information on a package.

labor contract the formal, written document that spells out the relationship between the union and management for a specified period of time—usually two or three years.

labor unions employee organizations formed to deal with employers for achieving better pay, hours, and working conditions.

leadership the ability to influence employees to work toward organizational goals.

learning changes in a person's behavior based on information and experience.

ledger a book or computer file with separate sections for each account.

leveraged buyout (LBO) a purchase in which a group of investors borrows money from banks and other institutions to acquire a company (or a division of one), using the assets of the purchased company to guarantee repayment of the loan.

liabilities debts that a firm owes to others.

licensing a trade agreement in which one company—the licensor—allows another company—the licensee—to use its company name, products, patents, brands, trademarks, raw materials, and/or production processes in exchange for a fee or royalty.

limited liability company (LLC) form of ownership that provides limited liability and taxation like a partnership but places fewer restrictions on members.

limited partnership a business organization that has at least one general partner, who assumes unlimited liability, and at least one limited partner, whose liability is limited to his or her investment in the business.

line of credit an arrangement by which a bank agrees to lend a specified amount of money to an organization upon request.

line-and-staff structure a structure having a traditional line relationship between superiors and subordinates and also specialized managers—called staff managers—who are available to assist line managers.

line structure the simplest organizational structure in which direct lines of authority extend from the top manager to the lowest level of the organization.

liquidity ratios ratios that measure the speed with which a company can turn its assets into cash to meet short-term debt.

lockbox an address, usually a commercial bank, at which a company receives payments in order to speed collections from customers.

lockout management's version of a strike, wherein a work site is closed so that employees cannot go to work.

long-term (fixed) assets production facilities (plants), offices, and equipment—all of which are expected to last for many years.

long-term liabilities debts that will be repaid over a number of years, such as long-term loans and bond issues.

M

management a process designed to achieve an organization's objectives by using its resources effectively and efficiently in a changing environment.

managerial accounting the internal use of accounting statements by managers in planning and directing the organization's activities.

managers those individuals in organizations who make decisions about the use of resources and who are concerned with planning, organizing, staffing, directing, and controlling the organization's activities to reach its objectives.

manufacturer brands brands initiated and owned by the manufacturer to identify products from the point of production to the point of purchase.

manufacturing the activities and processes used in making tangible products; also called production.

market a group of people who have a need, purchasing power, and the desire and authority to spend money on goods, services, and ideas.

market orientation an approach requiring organizations to gather information about customer needs, share that information throughout the firm, and use that information to help build long-term relationships with customers.

market segment a collection of individuals, groups, or organizations who share one or more characteristics and thus have relatively similar product needs and desires.

market segmentation a strategy whereby a firm divides the total market into groups of people who have relatively similar product needs.

marketable securities temporary investment of "extra" cash by organizations for up to one year in U.S. Treasury bills, certificates of deposit, commercial paper, or Euro-dollar loans.

marketing a group of activities designed to expedite transactions by creating, distributing, pricing, and promoting goods, services, and ideas.

marketing channel a group of organizations that moves products from their producer to customers; also called a channel of distribution.

marketing concept the idea that an organization should try to satisfy customers' needs through coordinated activities that also allow it to achieve its own goals.

marketing managers those who are responsible for planning, pricing, and promoting products and making them available to customers.

marketing mix the four marketing activites—product, price, promotion, and distribution—that the firm can control to achieve specific goals within a dynamic marketing environment.

marketing research a systematic, objective process of getting information about potential customers to guide marketing decisions.

marketing strategy a plan of action for developing, pricing, distributing, and promoting products that meet the needs of specific customers.

Maslow's hierarchy a theory that arranges the five basic needs of people—physiological, security, social, esteem, and self-actualization—into the order in which people strive to satisfy them.

material-requirements planning (MRP) a planning system that schedules the precise quantity of materials needed to make the product.

materials handling the physical handling and movement of products in warehousing and transportation.

matrix structure a structure that sets up teams from different departments, thereby creating two or more intersecting lines of authority; also called a project-management structure.

mediation a method of outside resolution of labor and management differences in which the third party's role is to suggest or propose a solution to the problem.

merger the combination of two companies (usually corporations) to form a new company.

middle managers those members of an organization responsible for the tactical planning that implements the general guidelines established by top management.

mission the statement of an organization's fundamental purpose and basic philosophy.

mixed economies economies made up of elements from more than one economic system.

modular design the creation of an item in self-contained units, or modules, that can be combined or interchanged to create different products.

monetary policy means by which the Fed controls the amount of money available in the economy.

money anything generally accepted in exchange for goods and services.

money market accounts accounts that offer higher interest rates than standard bank rates but with greater restrictions.

monopolistic competition the market structure that exists when there are fewer businesses than in a pure-competition environment and the differences among the goods they sell are small.

monopoly the market structure that exists when there is only one business providing a product in a given market.

morale an employee's attitude toward his or her job, employer, and colleagues.

motivation an inner drive that directs a person's behavior toward goals.

motivational factors aspects of Herzberg's theory of motivation that focus on the content of the work itself; these aspects include achievement, recognition, involvement, responsibility, and advancement.

multidivisional structure a structure that organizes departments into larger groups called divisions.

multinational corporation (MNC) a corporation that operates on a worldwide scale, without significant ties to any one nation or region.

multinational strategy a plan, used by international companies, that involves customizing products, promotion, and distribution according to cultural, technological, regional, and national differences.

multisegment approach a market segmentation approach whereby the marketer aims its efforts at two or more segments, developing a marketing strategy for each.

mutual fund an investment company that pools individual investor dollars and invests them in large numbers of well-diversified securities.

mutual savings banks financial institutions that are similar to savings and loan associations but, like credit unions, are owned by their depositors.

N

National Credit Union Association (NCUA) an agency that regulates and charters credit unions and insures their deposits through its National Credit Union Insurance Fund.

natural resources land, forests, minerals, water, and other things that are not made by people.

net income the total profit (or loss) after all expenses, including taxes, have been deducted from revenue; also called net earnings.

networking the building of relationships and sharing of information with colleagues who can help managers achieve the items on their agendas.

nonprofit corporations corporations that focus on providing a service rather than earning a profit but are not owned by a government entity.

nonprofit organizations organizations that may provide goods or services but do not have the fundamental purpose of earning profits.

North American Free Trade Agreement (NAFTA) agreement that eliminates most tariffs and trade restrictions on agricultural and manufactured products to encourage trade among Canada, the United States, and Mexico.

O

offshoring the relocation of business processes by a company or subsidiary to another country. Offshoring is different than outsourcing because the company retains control of the offshored processes.

oligopoly the market structure that exists when there are very few businesses selling a product.

online fraud any attempt to conduct fraudulent activities online.

open market operations decisions to buy or sell U.S. Treasury bills (short-term debt issued by the U.S. government) and other investments in the open market.

operational plans very short-term plans that specify what actions individuals, work groups, or departments need to accomplish in order to achieve the tactical plan and ultimately the strategic plan.

operations the activities and processes used in making both tangible and intangible products.

operations management (OM) the development and administration of the activities involved in transforming resources into goods and services.

organizational chart a visual display of the organizational structure, lines of authority (chain of command), staff relationships, permanent committee arrangements, and lines of communication.

organizational culture a firm's shared values, beliefs, traditions, philosophies, rules, and role models for behavior.

organizational layers the levels of management in an organization.

organizing the structuring of resources and activities to accomplish objectives in an efficient and effective manner.

orientation familiarizing newly hired employees with fellow workers, company procedures, and the physical properties of the company.

outputs the goods, services, and ideas that result from the conversion of inputs.

outsourcing the transferring of manufacturing or other tasks—such as data processing—to countries where labor and supplies are less expensive.

over-the-counter (OTC) market a network of dealers all over the country linked by computers, telephones, and Teletype machines.

owners' equity equals assets minus liabilities and reflects historical values.

P

packaging the external container that holds and describes the product.

partnership a form of business organization defined by the Uniform Partnership Act as "an association of two or more persons who carry on as co-owners of a business for profit."

penetration price a low price designed to help a product enter the market and gain market share rapidly.

pension funds managed investment pools set aside by individuals, corporations, unions, and some nonprofit organizations to provide retirement income for members.

per share data data used by investors to compare the performance of one company with another on an equal, per share basis.

perception the process by which a person selects, organizes, and interprets information received from his or her senses.

personal selling direct, two-way communication with buyers and potential buyers.

personality the organization of an individual's distinguishing character traits, attitudes, or habits.

physical distribution all the activities necessary to move products from producers to customers—inventory control, transportation, warehousing, and materials handling.

physiological needs the most basic human needs to be satisfied— water, food, shelter, and clothing.

picketing a public protest against management practices that involves union members marching and carrying anti-management signs at the employer's plant.

plagiarism the act of taking someone else's work and presenting it as your own without mentioning the source.

planning the process of determining the organization's objectives and deciding how to accomplish them; the first function of management.

podcast audio or video file that can be downloaded from the Internet with a subscription that automatically delivers new content to listening devices or personal computers.

preferred stock a special type of stock whose owners, though not generally having a say in running the company, have a claim to profits before other stockholders do.

price a value placed on an object exchanged between a buyer and a seller.

price skimming charging the highest possible price that buyers who want the product will pay.

primary data marketing information that is observed, recorded, or collected directly from respondents.

primary market the market where firms raise financial capital.

prime rate the interest rate that commercial banks charge their best customers (usually large corporations) for short-term loans.

private accountants accountants employed by large corporations, government agencies, and other organizations to prepare and analyze their financial statements.

private corporation a corporation owned by just one or a few people who are closely involved in managing the business.

private distributor brands brands, which may cost less than manufacturer brands, that are owned and controlled by a wholesaler or retailer.

process layout a layout that organizes the transformation process into departments that group related processes.

product a good or service with tangible and intangible characteristics that provide satisfaction and benefits.

product departmentalization the organization of jobs in relation to the products of the firm.

product layout a layout requiring that production be broken down into relatively simple tasks assigned to workers, who are usually positioned along an assembly line.

product line a group of closely related products that are treated as a unit because of similar marketing strategy, production, or end-use considerations.

product mix all the products offered by an organization.

product-development teams a specific type of project team formed to devise, design, and implement a new product.

production the activities and processes used in making tangible products; also called manufacturing.

production and operations managers those who develop and administer the activities involved in transforming resources into goods, services, and ideas ready for the marketplace.

profit the difference between what it costs to make and sell a product and what a customer pays for it.

profit margin net income divided by sales.

profit sharing a form of compensation whereby a percentage of company profits is distributed to the employees whose work helped to generate them.

profitability ratios ratios that measure the amount of operating income or net income an organization is able to generate relative to its assets, owners' equity, and sales.

project organization a company using a fixed-position layout because it is typically involved in large, complex projects such as construction or exploration.

project teams groups similar to task forces which normally run their operation and have total control of a specific work project.

promotion an advancement to a higher-level job with increased authority, responsibility, and pay.

promotional positioning the use of promotion to create and maintain an image of a product in buyers' minds.

psychological pricing encouraging purchases based on emotional rather than rational responses to the price.

public corporation a corporation whose stock anyone may buy, sell, or trade.

publicity nonpersonal communication transmitted through the mass media but not paid for directly by the firm.

pull strategy the use of promotion to create consumer demand for a product so that consumers exert pressure on marketing channel members to make it available.

purchasing the buying of all the materials needed by the organization; also called procurement.

pure competition the market structure that exists when there are many small businesses selling one standardized product.

push strategy an attempt to motivate intermediaries to push the product down to their customers.

Q

quality the degree to which a good, service, or idea meets the demands and requirements of customers.

quality control the processes an organization uses to maintain its established quality standards.

quality-assurance teams (or quality circles) small groups of workers brought together from throughout the organization to solve specific quality, productivity, or service problems.

quasi-public corporations corporations owned and operated by the federal, state, or local government.

quick ratio (acid test) a stringent measure of liquidity that eliminates inventory.

quota a restriction on the number of units of a particular product that can be imported into a country.

R

ratio analysis calculations that measure an organization's financial health.

receivables turnover sales divided by accounts receivable.

recession a decline in production, employment, and income.

recruiting forming a pool of qualified applicants from which management can select employees.

reference groups groups with whom buyers identify and whose values or attitudes they adopt.

relationship marketing the creation of relationships that mutually benefit the marketing business and the customer.

reserve requirement the percentage of deposits that banking institutions must hold in reserve.

responsibility the obligation, placed on employees through delegation, to perform assigned tasks satisfactorily and be held accountable for the proper execution of work.

retailers intermediaries who buy products from manufacturers (or other intermediaries) and sell them to consumers for home and household use rather than for resale or for use in producing other products.

retained earnings earnings after expenses and taxes that are reinvested in the assets of the firm and belong to the owners in the form of equity.

return on assets net income divided by assets.

return on equity net income divided by owner's equity; also called return on investment (ROI).

revenue the total amount of money received from the sale of goods or services, as well as from related business activities.

routing the sequence of operations through which the product must pass.

S

S corporation corporation taxed as though it were a partnership with restrictions on shareholders.

salary a financial reward calculated on a weekly, monthly, or annual basis.

sales promotion direct inducements offering added value or some other incentive for buyers to enter into an exchange.

savings accounts accounts with funds that usually cannot be withdrawn without advance notice; also known as time deposits.

savings and loan associations (S&Ls) financial institutions that primarily offer savings accounts and make long-term loans for residential mortgages; also called "thrifts."

scheduling the assignment of required tasks to departments or even specific machines, workers, or teams.

secondary data information that is compiled inside or outside an organization for some purpose other than changing the current situation.

secondary markets stock exchanges and over-the-counter markets where investors can trade their securities with others.

secured bonds bonds that are backed by specific collateral that must be forfeited in the event that the issuing firm defaults.

secured loans loans backed by collateral that the bank can claim if the borrowers do not repay them.

securities markets the mechanism for buying and selling securities.

security needs the need to protect oneself from physical and economic harm.

selection the process of collecting information about applicants and using that information to make hiring decisions.

selective distribution a form of market coverage whereby only a small number of all available outlets are used to expose products.

self-actualization needs the need to be the best one can be; at the top of Maslow's hierarchy.

self-directed work team (SDWT) a group of employees responsible for an entire work process or segment that delivers a product to an internal or external customer.

separations employment changes involving resignation, retirement, termination, or layoff.

serial bonds a sequence of small bond issues of progressively longer maturity.

small business any independently owned and operated business that is not dominant in its competitive area and does not employ more than 500 people.

Small Business Administration (SBA) an independent agency of the federal government that offers managerial and financial assistance to small businesses.

social classes a ranking of people into higher or lower positions of respect.

social needs the need for love, companionship, and friendship—the desire for acceptance by others.

social network a Web-based meeting place for friends, family, co-workers, and peers that lets users create a profile and connect with others users for the purposes that range from getting acquainted, to keeping in touch, to building a work-related network.

social responsibility a business's obligation to maximize its positive impact and minimize its negative impact on society.

social roles a set of expectations for individuals based on some position they occupy.

socialism an economic system in which the government owns and operates basic industries but individuals own most businesses.

sole proprietorships businesses owned and operated by one individual; the most common form of business organization in the United States.

span of management the number of subordinates who report to a particular manager.

specialization the division of labor into small, specific tasks and the assignment of employees to do a single task.

staffing the hiring of people to carry out the work of the organization.

stakeholders groups that have a stake in the success and outcomes of a business.

standardization the making of identical interchangeable components or products.

statement of cash flows explains how the company's cash changed from the beginning of the accounting period to the end.

statistical process control a system in which management collects and analyzes information about the production process to pinpoint quality problems in the production system.

stock shares of a corporation that may be bought or sold.

strategic alliance a partnership formed to create competitive advantage on a worldwide basis.

strategic plans those plans that establish the long-range objectives and overall strategy or course of action by which a firm fulfills its mission.

strikebreakers people hired by management to replace striking employees; called "scabs" by striking union members.

strikes employee walkouts; one of the most effective weapons labor has.

structure the arrangement or relationship of positions within an organization.

supply the number of products—goods and services—that businesses are willing to sell at different prices at a specific time.

supply chain management connecting and integrating all parties or members of the distribution system in order to satisfy customers.

sustainability conducting activities in such as way as to provide for the long-term well-being of the natural environment, including all biological entities.

T

tactical plans short-range plans designed to implement the activities and objectives specified in the strategic plan.

target market a specific group of consumers on whose needs and wants a company focuses its marketing efforts.

task force a temporary group of employees responsible for bringing about a particular change.

team a small group whose members have complementary skills; have a common purpose, goals, and approach; and hold themselves mutually accountable.

technical expertise the specialized knowledge and training needed to perform jobs that are related to particular areas of management.

test marketing a trial minilaunch of a product in limited areas that represent the potential market.

Theory X McGregor's traditional view of management whereby it is assumed that workers generally dislike work and must be forced to do their jobs.

Theory Y McGregor's humanistic view of management whereby it is assumed that workers like to work and that under proper conditions employees will seek out responsibility in an attempt to satisfy their social, esteem, and self-actualization needs.

Theory Z a management philosophy that stresses employee participation in all aspects of company decision making.

times interest earned ratio operating income divided by interest expense.

Title VII of the Civil Rights Act prohibits discrimination in employment and created the Equal Employment Opportunity Commission.

top managers the president and other top executives of a business, such as the chief executive officer (CEO), chief financial officer (CFO), and chief operations officer (COO), who have overall responsibility for the organization.

total asset turnover sales divided by total assets.

total quality management (TQM) a philosophy that uniform commitment to quality in all areas of an organization will promote a culture that meets customers' perceptions of quality.

total-market approach an approach whereby a firm tries to appeal to everyone and assumes that all buyers have similar needs.

trade credit credit extended by suppliers for the purchase of their goods and services.

trade deficit a nation's negative balance of trade, which exists when that country imports more products than it exports.

trademark a brand that is registered with the U.S. Patent and Trademark Office and is thus legally protected from use by any other firm.

trading company a firm that buys goods in one country and sells them to buyers in another country.

training teaching employees to do specific job tasks through either classroom development or on-the-job experience.

transaction balances cash kept on hand by a firm to pay normal daily expenses, such as employee wages and bills for supplies and utilities.

transfer a move to another job within the company at essentially the same level and wage.

transportation the shipment of products to buyers.

Treasury bills (T-bills) short-term debt obligations the U.S. government sells to raise money.

turnover occurs when employees quit or are fired and must be replaced by new employees.

U

undercapitalization the lack of funds to operate a business normally.

unemployment the condition in which a percentage of the population wants to work but is unable to find jobs.

unsecured bonds debentures, or bonds that are not backed by specific collateral.

unsecured loans loans backed only by the borrowers' good reputation and previous credit rating.

V

value a customer's subjective assessment of benefits relative to costs in determining the worth of a product.

venture capitalists persons or organizations that agree to provide some funds for a new business in exchange for an ownership interest or stock.

viral marketing a marketing tool that uses a networking effect to spread a message and create brand awareness. The purpose of this marketing technique is to encourage the consumer to share the message with friends, family, co-workers, and peers.

W

wage/salary survey a study that tells a company how much compensation comparable firms are paying for specific jobs that the firms have in common.

wages financial rewards based on the number of hours the employee works or the level of output achieved.

warehousing the design and operation of facilities to receive, store, and ship products.

whistleblowing the act of an employee exposing an employer's wrongdoing to outsiders, such as the media or government regulatory agencies.

wholesalers intermediaries who buy from producers or from other wholesalers and sell to retailers.

wiki software that creates an interface that enables users to add or edit the content of some types of Web sites.

working capital management the managing of short-term assets and liabilities.

World Bank an organization established by the industrialized nations in 1946 to loan money to underdeveloped and developing countries; formally known as the International Bank for Reconstruction and Development.

World Trade Organization (WTO) international organization dealing with the rules of trade between nations.

Photo Credits

CHAPTER 1
p. 3, BONNY MAKAREWICZ/The New York Times/Redux; p. 6, © Creatas/PunchStock; p. 5, Courtesy of TerraCycle, Inc.; p. 7, © 2009 America's Milk Processors; p. 12, © Comstock Images/Jupiter Images; p. 17, Courtesy of the U.S. Department of the Treasury, Bureau of the Public Debt; p. 22, © Bloomberg via Getty Images.

CHAPTER 2
p. 35, © Getty Images; p. 38, © AP Photo/Mary Altaffer; p. 40, © Bill Greenblatt/UPI/Landov; p. 42, © CBS via Getty Images; p. 45, © Bloomberg via Getty Images; p. 51, © Getty Images; p. 54, © Getty Images; p. 56, © Ryan McVay/Getty Images; p. 57, Courtesy of Home Depot; p. 62, © Photodisc/Getty Images; p. 69, © Steve Labadessa; p. 79, © The McGraw-Hill Companies, Inc./John Flournoy, photographer.

CHAPTER 3
p. 85, Courtesy of Nokia; p. 86, Courtesy of Zurich; p. 90, Courtesy of AT&T Intellectual Property. Used with permission; p. 92, Courtesy of Action Plagiarius; p. 94 left, © Ryan McVay/Getty Images; p. 94 right, © Stockbyte; p. 98, © Stockdisc; p. 106, Courtesy of Domino's; p. 107 left, © AP Photo/Vincent Yu; p. 107 right, © Getty Images.

CHAPTER 4
p. 119, Courtesy of Kiva; p. 121, © Brand X Pictures/PunchStock; p. 126, © AP Photo/Tammie Arroyo; p. 131, © James Paul Photographers; p. 133, © AP Photo/Ben Margot; p. 134, © Digital Vision/Getty Images; p. 136, © AFP/Getty Images; p. 138, © Ryan McVay/Getty Images; p. 141, © Getty Images North America.

CHAPTER 5
p. 149, Courtesy of Ocean Farm Technologies Inc.; p. 152, Courtesy of Rush Trucking; p. 153, © AP Photo/Paul Sakuma; p. 154, © AP Photo/Marcio Jose Sanchez; p. 157, © Imagestate Media (John Foxx); p. 161, Courtesy of localnewsonly.com; p. 162, Courtesy of 1-800-GOT-JUNK?; p. 165, © Creatas/JupiterImages; p. 166, Jack Dorsey / @ jack.

CHAPTER 6
p. 177, Courtesy of Xerox Corporation. Photo by Lonnie Major; p. 178, © Bloomberg via Getty Images; p. 181, © Eric Audras/Photoalto/PictureQuest; p. 182, © Getty Images North America; p. 184, © Steve Cole/Getty Images, p. 190, © AFP/Getty Images; p. 195 top, © Courtesy of Southwest Airlines; p. 195 bottom, © Bloomberg via Getty Images; p. 200, Courtesy of LinkedIn.

CHAPTER 7
p. 207, Reproduced with permission of Yahoo! Inc. ©2010 Yahoo! Inc. YAHOO! And the YAHOO! Logo are registered trademarks of Yahoo! Inc.; p. 210, Courtesy of W.L. Gore & Associates; p. 213, Library of Congress; p. 216, © BananaStock/JupiterImages; p. 226, © Rob Kim/Landov; p. 228, © The McGraw-Hill Companies, Inc./John Flournoy, photographer.

CHAPTER 8
p. 237, © Bloomberg via Getty Images; p. 241, © TastingMenu.com; p. 242, © The McGraw-Hill Companies, Inc./John Flournoy, photographer; p. 245, Courtesy of Clayton Homes Inc.; p. 247, © AP Photo/Carolyn Kaster; p. 250, Courtesy of Autodesk, Inc.; p. 251, © Ingram Publishing/Fotosearch; p. 253, Courtesy of FAC; p. 254, © Royalty-Free/Corbis; p. 261, © Kent Knudson/PhotoLink/Getty Images.

CHAPTER 9
p. 271, Courtesy of JA Frate; p. 272, © liquidlibrary/PictureQuest; p. 275, © Getty Images; p. 277, © Sarah M. Golonka/Brand X Pictures/JupiterImages; p. 279, © Getty Images Publicity; p. 284, © Jack Hollingsworth/Corbis; p. 285, © AP Photo/Karen Tam; p. 287, © AP Photo/Chris O'Connor.

CHAPTER 10
p. 295, © AP Photo/The Canadian Press, Graham Hughes; p. 296, © Brand X Pictures/PunchStock; p. 298, Courtesy of LinkedIn; p. 299, © The McGraw-Hill Companies, Inc.; p. 301, © Comstock Photos/Fotosearch; p. 307, Courtesy of Linden Lab®; p. 317, © AFP/Getty Images.

CHAPTER 11
p. 337 left, © The McGraw-Hill Companies, Inc./John Flournoy, photographer; p. 337 right, © AP Photo/Charles Krupa; p. 339, © AP Photo/Larry Crowe; p. 344, © AP Photo/Brian Kersey; p. 347, © Scott Brauer/OnAsia Images; p. 348, Courtesy of J&D's; p. 351, Courtesy of KFC Corporation; p. 352, Courtesy of Western Wats; p. 356, Reprinted with permission from *Packaging World*; p. 357, Courtesy of Benetton USA.

CHAPTER 12
p. 365, © WireImage; p. 367, © The McGraw-Hill Companies, Inc./Jill Braaten, photographer; p. 370 top, © Ingram Publishing/Alamy; p. 370 bottom, Courtesy of W. W. Grainger, Inc.; p. 374, © Digital Vision/PunchStock; p. 379, © Getty Images; p. 385, Courtesy of Ruan; p. 386, © Getty Images; p. 389, © The McGraw-Hill Companies, Inc./Andrew Resek, photographer.

CHAPTER 13
p. 401, Courtesy of Sprint; p. 404, Courtesy of Benjamin Moore & Co.; p. 407, © Getty Images North America; p. 409, Courtesy of NASCAR. Reproduced with permission; p. 412, Courtesy of Joel Moss Levinson; p. 417, Courtesy of Yowza!!; p. 421, TRBfoto/Getty Images; p. 426, © AP Photo/Richard Vogel.

CHAPTER 14
p. 435, © AP Photo; p. 439, Courtesy of Huron Consulting Group; p. 440, © Comstock Images; p. 441, © Duncan Smith/Getty Images; p. 442, © Fancy Photography/Veer; p. 446,

Name Index

Company Index

Subject Index

Boldface entries denote glossary terms and the page numbers where they are defined.